Patchwork Nation

PATCHWORK NATION

Sectionalism and Political Change in American Politics

James G. Gimpel & Jason E. Schuknecht

The University of Michigan Press
Ann Arbor

To Graciela,
and Dad, Mom,
and Sarah

First paperback edition 2004
Copyright © by the University of Michigan 2003
All rights reserved
Published in the United States of America by
The University of Michigan Press
Manufactured in the United States of America
♾ Printed on acid-free paper

2007   2006   2005   2004   5   4   3   2

A CIP catalog record for this book is available from the British Library.

Library of Congress Cataloging-in-Publication Data

Gimpel, James G.
     Patchwork nation : sectionalism and political change in American
politics / James G. Gimpel and Jason E. Schuknecht.
        p.   cm.
     Includes bibliographical references (p.   ) and index.
     ISBN 0-472-11314-3 (cloth : alk. paper)
        1. Party affiliation—United States—States.   2. Political
parties—United States—States.   3. Elections—United States—
States.   4. Voting—United States—States.   5. Political culture—
United States—Regional disparities.   6. State governments—United
States.   I. Schuknecht, Jason E., 1973-   II. Title.

JK2261 .G564   2003
324.973'092—dc21   2002156536

ISBN 0-472-03030-2 (pbk. : alk. paper)

Contents

Preface and Acknowledgments

American politics is not just national politics. State and local governments offer us the opportunity to study political variations that cannot be understood by focusing on national political institutions. To the extent that national politics is an aggregation of interests that are locally defined, states and localities add to what we must study in order to understand Congress, the presidency, the national parties, national elections, and the courts. Of course, states and localities are also worth studying in their own right. As the eminent political scientist V. O. Key Jr. once put it, "The size of their populations and the magnitude of their operations make many of our states quite as important political units as many of the independent nations of the world" (1956, v).

The study of state and local political institutions and behavior has sometimes been hampered by the absence of relevant information and the difficulties of comparing diverse political systems. Frequently these challenges have resulted in the production of volumes in which the chapters written on individual jurisdictions do not permit comparison. In *Patchwork Nation* we try to meet that challenge by using a common outline for each of our chapters along with an analytic framework that will enhance comparability. We show that states are unique electoral battlegrounds, but we need to develop systematic methods for coping on a comparative basis with the political characteristics that make states both distinct from and similar to other states. This was the approach developed by Key, from whom we take our inspiration.

We want to thank our colleagues at the University of Maryland who discussed the ideas we present and read pieces of the work, including Irwin Morris, Karen Kaufmann, Paul Herrnson, Peter Burns, and Eric Uslaner. Colleagues at other institutions were also helpful at various stages, including Luc Anselin, Barry Burden, Tom Carsey, Wendy Tam Cho, Todd Donovan, Robert Eisinger, Robert Huckfeldt, Aubrey Jewett, Gary King, John Sprague, Christopher Stream, and Steve Voss. Our editor at the University of Michigan Press, Jeremy Shine, was efficient and professional in shepherding the manuscript through multiple reviews.

We consulted with several others about politics, history, and elections in their individual states, including Richard Juliano, Brad Stark, John Bullock, Chris Bullock, Sue Piatt, Dawn Wirth, C. J. Mucklow, Rob Bovett, and Jennifer Shank.

This book presents original data analysis and makes creative use of techniques not yet widely used in political science. But we work to keep our treatment nontechnical, and we confine finer details to appendixes. If by taking some risks with the data analysis, we have planted some seeds that will lead to more and better work in this area, we will have accomplished our main goal.

We thank our families for their support and endurance through the regular frustrations that arose during the undertaking. On balance, however, this book was a great pleasure to write, and we look forward to the next opportunity to collaborate. Finally, we want to give credit to God for granting us the opportunity to pursue our research interests in this manner. There are many talented people who never get the chance to realize such goals, and we feel blessed and fortunate to number among those who have achieved something so substantial.

INTRODUCTION

Federalism, Political Identity, and American
State Politics

This book is about electoral diversity and change within the U.S. federal system. Because the structure of the American political system carves out substantial autonomy for states to act on their own in matters of politics and policy formation, we cannot assume that states are all alike, or that they have developed in the same way. The decentralization of power inherent in federalism acts against unity, making the political system a barrier to homogeneity. Aside from the Constitutional provisions that allow states to chart their own course, history has played a role in producing this diversity. The country is vast, and states were admitted to the Union at different times and under different circumstances (Mayhew 1986, chap. 8; Elazar 1994, 44–69). While it is true that all states confront the same choices in presidential elections, their responses to these candidates are variable, and this is even more true for the large number of state and local offices that are regularly contested. The general question we ask is, What accounts for this electoral variability as we move from place to place? The Constitution only permits such diversity, it does not mandate that it develop. So we can only begin to answer this question by noting key features of founding documents and discourse. Since we could imagine a federal system where there was little electoral variation across the political landscape, we must look beyond the nation's institutional framework if we are to understand what has created a patchwork nation.

The thrust of our project is not simply to document that one state differs from another. That theme has been communicated many times before, and only a few people still need to be persuaded that California's politics and policy are different from Florida's. Rather, we want to go inside states to suggest that the obvious cross-state differences mask important variations internal to them. There is no question that we have learned from studies that explain why Democratic support in New York is generally higher than Democratic support in Colorado, or why some states are more generous welfare providers than others.

Our interest, however, is to study how the groups comprising the Democratic voting bloc differ as one moves from Colorado to New York, and how the content or meaning of the party label changes due to differing constituencies. Cataloging these differences is foundational to understanding the complexity of political attitudes and behavior, and, at a more practical level, essential to the formation of intelligent campaign strategy. Because the constituencies comprising a party's base can be quite dissimilar, a candidate will have to campaign rather differently in Oregon than in Georgia. So there is much more to understanding local politics in a federal system than knowing why one state votes Republican and another Democrat. Understandings of the same political words, such as *conservative* and *liberal, Democrat* and *Republican,* are likely to vary according to local interests, demography, and custom. At the extremes, party identifiers at one locale may have little in common with those in another locale except for their party label.

A second, related concern in this book is to explain political regionalism within states. By expressing their views and interests from a given geographic location, people create political spaces in which they are allied with like-minded citizens to fight political battles (O'Reilly and Webster 1998). We believe that we can add to our understanding of American political life by examining the geographic concentration and dispersion of voters and specific voting blocs. Federalism makes geography highly relevant because federal systems allow substantial freedom for *places* to chart their own course of policy action. More so than unitary systems where all power is centralized, the decentralization of power in federal government maximizes the relevance of local political preferences to the formation of public policy. Taking note of geographic settlement patterns of the party followers within states, we will evaluate how this background has shaped each place's electoral identity.

While our book presents a number of new and interesting facts, it is also informed by theories of political geography. Electoral geography has been investigated from two dominant perspectives suggesting rather different meanings of *regionalism*. The first is sometimes labeled "the compositional approach," the second as "the contextual approach" (Johnston, Shelley, and Taylor 1990; Reynolds 1990, 28; Huckfeldt 1986). According to the compositional view, regional patterns on maps of political behavior simply reflect the geography of economic interest, race, and other politically relevant social groupings. Geography, then, is relevant to politics because it points to the traits of populations that cause them to act differently at the polls (Johnston, Shelley, and Taylor 1990; Archer and Taylor 1981). Political regions do not influence political behavior per se, but merely reflect where particular blocs of voters live (Huckfeldt 1986, 6; Key 1964, 233; Wirt et al. 1972). From this standpoint, maps of electoral history reveal the changing spatial concentration of social and economic interests.

The contextual approach suggests that the geographic clustering of like-minded voters does not just indicate the presence of particular social groups at those locations, but adds something extra to these communities through the instrument of political socialization. Even after accounting for group traits, regional or local effects can frequently be detected because people who are proximate to one another influence each other's attitudes and behavior (Huckfeldt and Sprague 1995; MacKuen and Brown 1987; Mutz 2002). For example, if we examine two groups of blue-collar workers with similar background traits but from two different geographic settings, one group may vote 60 percent Democratic, the other group only 45 percent Democratic (Johnston 1986). Holding the relevant individual traits (e.g., income, occupation, race) constant across the two communities, the big difference between the two groups may be accounted for by "neighborhood effects"—the tendency for people to be socialized by those they live around. According to this body of work, people's political thinking is influenced by their local social interactions (Baybeck and Huckfeldt 2002a, 2002b; Huckfeldt 1986; Huckfeldt et al. 1995; Huckfeldt and Sprague 1995; Putnam 1966; Berelson, Lazarsfeld, and McPhee 1954). Even after controlling for the usual individual attributes considered relevant to vote choice, contextual effects remain significant predictors of a wide range of behavior and attitudes, including partisan loyalty, ethnic loyalty, and political participation (Huckfeldt 1986; Kuklinski, Cobb, and Gilens 1997, 336–38). An emerging body of research indicates that contextual explanations work especially well in explaining the attitudes and behavior of individuals who are socially connected and receptive to political communication (Huckfeldt et al. 1995; Johnson, Shively, and Stein 2001, 2002).

Both compositional and contextual approaches have essential roles to play in explaining the microfoundations of regionalism, and the two approaches need not be thought of as mutually exclusive. When compositional variables fail to account for cross-regional variations in political behavior, contextual effects are probably present to unify (or divide) otherwise disparate (or similar) individuals within these regions. And even when regionalism can be explained in terms . of compositional traits, contextual forces may still be at work generating local consensus and cleavage. It is not unreasonable to suggest that black neighborhoods vote Democratic for both compositional and contextual reasons. Compositional explanations may be the only ones that are directly testable, however, unless one has detailed survey data of individuals and their communication partners. For this reason it is understandable why those working with aggregate data (counties, precincts) have usually leaned on compositional explanations to account for regional political variation.

Although we will be working with aggregate data in much of this project, we will rely upon theories that are rooted in the psychology of social groups and social context, as well as theories of individual voting behavior. A person's political thinking is not *strictly* determined by her demographic and economic traits, or by those of her neighbors, but it is not controversial to assert that people gravitate toward a party, or toward a particular set of political attitudes, based on individual or group identifications captured by demographic and economic characteristics combined with communications with discussion partners in the neighborhood and workplace.

For an illustration of how both compositional and contextual accounts can play a role in explaining political behavior, we can turn to a now dated but still classic study, John H. Fenton's *Midwest Politics* (1966). Geographic proximity, in Fenton's view, is a strong mediating force between groups of voters sharing similar characteristics and the strength of their loyalty to a particular party or cause. The degree of geographic concentration helps to define the extent of group solidarity by facilitating communication among group members. In an especially brilliant chapter, Fenton explained that the reason why Ohio voted Republican in the 1950s and 1960s in spite of its large working-class population (a population that voted Democratic in other states) was due to the geographic dispersion of heavy industry in that state. Working-class voters in Ohio were not a predictable Democratic voting bloc because they were geographically isolated (150). Fenton elaborates:

> The effect of a diffusion of the working population, as opposed to their concentration, on attitudes and voting behavior was profound. In mining communities or large cities where workers tended to live in working-class ghettos, every aspect of the environment reinforced a working-class psychology and identification. People in such environments identified with the working class and judged political candidates on the basis of their support of or opposition to measures which promoted the interests of the working class. Because of the high level of cohesion in such laboring-group communities and the possession of common attitudes vis-à-vis the outer community, the residents tended to be rather well informed concerning the identity of conservative and liberal candidates. (1966, 151)

Geographic concentration is instrumental for organization and mobilization around a cause because it facilitates communication. As communication is disrupted by distance, messages are lost, and so is their mobilizing potential. Fenton goes further to note that in an era of GOP domination, Ohio's working-class voters did not interact with one another in the neighborhoods where they lived. This lack of interaction also had its source in a compositional factor—the occupational heterogeneity of the working-class population. They had less in common because they did not work in the same places. In this example, compositional variables, geographic dispersion, and communication patterns are all complementary explanations of differences in group behavior across settings. In Fenton's theory, the level of group solidarity behind a political party depends critically on the members of that group having low-cost lines of interaction and communication, which is facilitated by dense rather than sparse settlement, as well as an occupational homogeneity that ensured commonality of interest. Richard J. Johnston (1986) makes a similar argument in a fascinating article about differences in British Labour party voting among blue-collar workers in urban and rural areas. We will return to these themes throughout the book.

Our third concern in this work is to understand electoral change, in terms of both group loyalty to political parties and political regionalism. In recent scholarship, there has been increasing recognition that partisan change is not uniform across the nation (Nardulli 1995; Petrocik 1981). If federalism allows states and substate regions to vary, it also permits various mechanisms of political change, all working at the same time but in different places, to reshape local political landscapes. We intend to examine the variability of change across states and localities, with an aim to understanding how some places change more rapidly than others. Our study of electoral change is aided by a set of theories that have advanced our understanding of party change and political realignment in the national electorate (Nardulli 1995; Burnham 1970; Abramson 1976; Chubb 1978; Silbey, Bogue, and Flanigan 1978; Andersen 1979; Carmines and Stimson 1981; Petrocik 1981; Clubb, Flanigan, and Zingale 1990; Brown 1988; Gimpel 1996). In applying these theories to understand local political change, we find that they do not apply universally, or singularly, and that they are best employed in combination, to explain changes in state and local politics.

A Local Component to Politics? Boundaries and Context Formation

We have just introduced this book as a work on local variations in American political behavior—their nature and extent. Some may doubt that these variations amount to much; after all, there has been discussion in recent years about the nationalization of American politics through the watering-down of local distinctions (Agnew 1987, 1988; Lunch 1987; Petrocik 1987; Reynolds 1990, 28). Supporting this view, one can point to the nation's unprecedented geographic mobility and advanced communications and transport links. People travel across state lines on daily shopping trips. Communications technology has made it routine to view a live local Los Angeles news broadcast from Boston. It is common to find that your neighbors were born in distant places, but places that you have visited a time or two. Population mobility and technology have diluted the distinctiveness of states and localities as repositories of unique population traits and characteristics. In many respects, then, there is less difference today between Maine and California than in times past. The country (indeed, the world) is shrinking (Chapman 1979). Yet, even in modern times, jurisdictional boundaries still shape identities.

Lewiston, Idaho, and Clarkston, Washington, are neighboring cities lying on the Washington-Idaho border two hundred miles north of Boise, Idaho, and one hundred miles south of Spokane, Washington. Most of the time, the residents of the two cities hardly notice that their cities lie in different states. Regardless of which side of the state line they hail from, residents of the Lewiston-Clarkston Valley work at the same factories, shop at the same malls, read the same morning paper, watch the same local television station, and drive on the same streets. Perhaps the most striking characteristic of border-city life may be the healthy number of Washington state license plates one sees on cars puttering through Lewiston, and the equally large number of Idaho-registered cars traveling through Clarkston. In general, residents are oblivious to the fact that many of their friends and neighbors live across the river in another state.

Below the surface, however, there are some significant differences in the lives of citizens in this area that are directly attributable to the cities' separation by a state boundary. Washington has no income tax while Idaho does. Many Washingtonians bemoan that the Valley's largest industrial employer is located on the Lewiston side: thus Washingtonians are required to send a portion of their earnings to the tax collector's office in Boise. Washington State does not levy a sales tax on food items while Idaho levies its standard 5 percent tax on foodstuffs. Consequently, many Lewiston residents find it worth the effort to cross the river to buy groceries. Washington, however, imposes a sales tax on nonfood items. So Clarkston residents frequently cross the river to Idaho to make these purchases.

Differences between these two states come into play in the structure of educational opportunity. Clarkston High graduates may elect to apply for in-state admission to the University of Washington or to Washington State University, two top-tier national universities that are funded in part by the mammoth Puget Sound tax base in faraway western Washington. Lewistonians, on the other hand, have the options of attending the less well-known, less well-financed University of Idaho or Boise State University (although Idaho statute does stipulate that residents may attend state schools on a tuition-free basis).

Why do boundaries matter so much? In our case, boundaries are important because they define territory, and the laws and customs governing a territory structure human activity (Elazar 1994, chap. 1). But boundaries need not be officially established in order to have real meaning. In the field of environmental psychology, researchers sometimes study people's activity patterns—they simply watch and record what people do during an ordinary day. Such activity studies provide a picture of everyday life lived outside the home in a particular place at a particular time (Hanson and Hanson 1993; Chapin 1974). By examining such activity patterns for a large number of individuals, it becomes possible to define what a "place" actually is for people (Groat 1995; Altman and Low 1992). A variety of things have been hypothesized to affect activity patterns. Attributes of the household certainly matter: its wealth and means of transportation, for instance. But spatial context also influences people's decisions about what they do and where they go. By *spatial context,* geographers and psychologists mean a variety of things: transportation networks, land use patterns, pleasant and unpleasant social interactions, threats to personal safety, and the effort required to go one place as opposed to another.

Because cognitive boundaries limit human activity patterns, people create specific geographies that manifest themselves in politics, often independent of officially drawn boundaries. By living one's life within a certain physical space, one's political interests come to be expressed within that space (O'Reilly and Webster 1998; Ormrod and Cole 1996). In addition, it is a fact of political life in the United States that citizens are not permitted to vote any place they want, but must cast their ballots according to their residential address. When a citizen becomes active in a campaign, it is usually a local campaign, although perhaps for a national office. In this manner, politics is expressive of local populations, regardless of whether these populations are collected within or divided by an officially designated jurisdictional boundary.

Not all politically relevant boundaries are figments of one's psychology, however. Many activities will be shaped by official political boundaries because those boundaries define the area within which certain actions are regulated by law. Political jurisdictions, carved out by boundaries, affect people's activity patterns mainly by altering elements of spatial context, as in the case of shoppers who cross state boundaries in order to take advantage of certain tax laws, or high school students who decide which college to attend on the basis of tuition costs. The costs of alternative locations for college may bear little relationship to physical distance, but have much to do with the political boundaries determining where citizens send their tax dollars.

Economies are usually regional, and natural resources do not respect boundaries on a map. But many economic institutions, such as banks and corporations operating in particular areas, are influenced by state regulations peculiar to their locations. States also channel economic activity through governmental expenditures on transportation and infrastructure, education and social welfare, or by adopting probusiness or antibusiness legislation (Holmes 1998). Through the power of municipal incorporation, states can actually create and name new places within their boundaries, giving these places considerable power to regulate and organize life on a more local scale (Burns 1994; Teaford 1997).

There is little reason to expect that most social practices would be influenced by state political boundaries except insofar as these borders define who is required to respect and obey state laws. Where one lives relative to a state boundary has determined the age at which one can legally drink alcohol and whether one can legally gamble or, in Nevada, hire a prostitute without fear of prosecution. Although the American South is an increasingly heterogeneous region, numerous studies have distinguished it as a collection of states with cultural and political traditions that differ from other parts of the country. Most of what has given the South its distinctive tradition boils down to the fact that within the borders of the old Confederacy slavery was tolerated as official law and policy. The South may be less distinctive today than it was in 1950, but Southern states probably still have more in common with each other than they do with states outside the South. The myriad practices that have come to govern political, social, and economic life across states in the American federal system contribute to most of the diversity of outlook and orientation one finds when traversing state lines. State boundaries have taken on great meaning partly because of the social and economic practices that are legally permitted or prohibited within them.

Not all consequences of state and local laws on patterns of activity are intended. Through its lawmaking authority, government may inadvertently promote some behaviors, such as long-distance commuting, while discouraging others, such as residential integration (Teaford 1997). With time, activity patterns that have been structured by law and policy become entrenched. It is not just physical activity, or movement, that is influenced by state and local governing institutions. Mental activity is too. First, laws foster and create public opinion in their favor (Noelle-Neumann 1993, 130). White Southerners raised in an atmosphere of official segregation would naturally have more difficulty coming to the conclusion that segregation was unjust than if they had been raised in an atmosphere where racial discrimination was illegal. One finds more public support for gambling in Nevada, where it has been legal for decades, than in states where it is not allowed, or allowed only in certain highly regulated venues. Second, governments focus the attention of the news media on a particular place (the state capital), on the institutions that regulate many aspects of life within the state's boundaries, and on a particular set of leaders who govern. The flow of information is therefore structured by borders because territoriality determines the scope of our interests and concerns (Burbank 1995; Elazar 1994).

A person's political identification with a place is also cemented by knowledge that a particular pair of candidates is running for office here, but nowhere else. Familiar incumbent politicians represent us, but not the people across the border just a few miles away. My neighbors and I can reelect the sitting governor, but those living just outside my state's boundaries cannot. The identification of the citizenry with their states remains sufficiently strong at the beginning of the twenty-first century that people in otherwise similar adjacent states still proudly identify themselves as from one state or the other. To boast to an Iowan that "I am from Minnesota!" means not just that we call the place that I am from *Minnesota*, but that Minnesota is the name of the place that has defined many aspects of my way of life and thinking, giving me a past against which new settings can be judged (Proshansky, Fabian, and Kaminoff 1995). It may not be literally everything we mean by *home*, but the name of the state certainly labels a location that is more familiar than even similar locations a short distance away.

Our focus here has been on the theoretical considerations that provide good reasons for believing that a local electorate will have features that will distinguish it from another, even if the two groups share substantially similar social and economic traits. States, cities, and counties are discrete geographic places that structure life and activity differently. We are not so naive as to suggest that local electorates are totally dissimilar. Four decades after the official end of segregation, the Southern states still share some distinctive features. There is evidence for other regional similarities that transcend state boundaries in the Northeast, Midwest, Mountain, and Pacific states. Many aspects of life are not locally or even regionally distinctive, however, but are part of national traditions and practices. Even when comparing nonadjacent states, at opposite ends of the continent, many similar features can be found.

Some of the similarities across states are the product of constitutional mandates that specifically limit the extent to which states can act on their own. Those who supported ratification of the Constitution knew that national supremacy and uniformity in many areas of law- and policy-making were required to maintain some modicum of cohesion in an otherwise decentralized system. Hence, Congress was given exclusive power to coin money and raise armies and navies. Clauses in Article IV such as Full Faith and Credit, or Privileges and Immunities, were intended to quell parochial practices that might otherwise impede national commerce. Even the national government's guarantee of a republican form of government to every state was apparently intended to prevent undemocratic practices from taking hold in local communities.

Other similarities across states are the product of institutions that may not be the product of constitutional mandate but have been almost universally adopted anyway, such as electoral laws mandating single-member winner-take-all election districts and the adoption of preference primaries for many elected offices. Adherence to two major political parties is not constitutionally mandated, but seems to have taken hold across the nation because of the unifying nature of presidential elections and the widespread adoption of electoral laws that discourage third-party emergence. Still, differences in ballot access requirements, loyalty to the two-party system among voters, and campaign finance regulations across states have given third parties a better chance at garnering support in some places than in others.

To summarize, boundaries may have little meaning on paper. Drawn on a map, borders typically reflect longitude and latitude coordinates, the location of bodies of water, or other geophysical features. Once governing institutions are put in place by national and local elites, however, these boundaries take on significance and meaning for inhabitants and outsiders alike—as well as for subsequent generations. The existence of governments has the effect of unifying those who wind up living within the state's borders by some common experiences, particular choices, legal traditions, and understandings. This shared sense of identity, the sense of belonging to a particular political community as the result of residing in a particular location, is defined by the political practices and institutions prevailing within a given set of jurisdictional boundaries. These institutions and practices come to impute great meaning to those boundaries, defining the perception and outlook of those living within them as well as those outside of them. Finally, the boundaries within which governments function are not the only politically relevant ones. People develop cognitive boundaries that influence the extent of their activities independent of where official boundaries have been drawn. The tendency to place imaginary boundaries in certain locations explains why adjacent neighborhoods within a city can move in politically different directions, in spite of having similar populations.

Using This Book to Understand State Electorates

If a state's political history is independent of national history and the history of other states, it makes sense to spend some time investigating how local electorates have developed. The implications of federalism for state and local politics should not be glossed over simply because it is pedagogically easier to pretend that voters are unaffected by locality. Presidential, congressional, and gubernatorial candidates know that to understand Maryland is not to understand Michigan, a fact we were reminded of endlessly during the waning days of the 2000 presidential election cycle as the race tightened. While we believe that states are worth studying individually, we are equally strong in our conviction that states should be studied in comparison to one another; by setting states side-by-side we are able to determine what is unique and what is similar. To secure an appreciation of both the commonalities and differences in the contemporary electoral histories of states we make several types of useful comparisons in the coming chapters.

1. Aggregate differences in *group* support for a candidate or party (e.g., percentage of blacks or farmers for Roosevelt or Hoover in California vs. Texas)
2. Differences in group polarization within states in support for a candidate or party (e.g., percentage of blacks for Roosevelt vs. percentage of whites for Roosevelt in California vs. Texas)

3. Differences in geographic polarization within states in support for a candidate or party (e.g., regional polarization in a particular election in California vs. Texas)

The second and third types of comparison are rare in previous research, and we believe using statistical methodology to make such comparisons yields new insights. Since we are also interested in political change, comparisons over time within individual states will also be important. Did the geographic distribution of support for Democrats look the same in California in the 1930s as it did in 2000? Some states have hardly changed in seventy years, while others have experienced volatile shifts. The state chapters show that the geographic bases of party support have generally become more diffuse, but in the process, Republicans have typically become dominant in some areas, Democrats in others. The parties had less in common in terms of the territorial basis of their campaigns as the twenty-first century began than they did in the middle of the last century. This move toward rival geographic bases of support may coincide with the growing partisan intransigence in American politics.

For classroom use, this book is perhaps best utilized as a supplement in state politics, elections, and political behavior courses that seek to address the critical topic of how federalism decentralizes and diversifies the electoral system. Considerations of length have permitted us only to include twelve states in the present volume. We have chosen to study states that are electorally consequential in presidential elections (California, Texas, Florida, New York, and Illinois), as well as several states that provide some regional representation (Connecticut, Georgia, Maryland, Michigan, Minnesota, Colorado, and Oregon). Understandably, some may grumble that their favorite state has not been included, but we have chosen to include five of the largest states because they cast such a large proportion of the electoral college vote (nearly one-third). From a strategic standpoint, no serious presidential campaign can ignore these prize states. Campaign strategists target resources toward larger states with higher numbers of electoral votes, and there should be widespread interest in understanding how to win them regardless of where one is currently living (Murauskas, Archer, and Shelley 1988; Shaw 1999; Smith and Squire 1987). The smaller states have been included because it was not practical to write chapters for every state and because we consider them to share features of other states in their geographic vicinity (Connecticut for New England; Maryland for the mid-Atlantic; Georgia for the South; Colorado for the Mountain states; Oregon for the Pacific Northwest; Michigan for the industrial Midwest; and Minnesota for the rural Midwest). While our choice of states is not random, and is pointed toward larger states, this collection does present wide variation across a number of interesting phenomena, including the extent of regionalism, the extent of two-party competition and partisan change, economic diversity, population mobility, and ethnic heterogeneity.

In presenting a book that covers twelve states and runs some 400 pages, one cannot expect readers to be equally interested in all of the chapters. A sensible strategy for classroom use would be to assign the first two chapters, the final chapter, and several of the individual state chapters. We hope in the future to extend much of this analysis to other states, perhaps producing a second or even a third volume. Much depends upon the feedback we receive from making this initial attempt to fill a niche that has long been neglected in studies of American elections and political behavior.

CHAPTER 1

GOING INSIDE STATES
The Geography of Local Political Behavior

Understanding how distinct political contexts have emerged from the institution of state government requires that we learn something about the internal character of states. State boundaries are not the only lines that matter. Subdivisions within states, defining counties, towns, and districts, to say nothing of the cognitive maps that define neighborhoods and other place locations, structure information and influence political activity, creating local variation. County and city boundaries differentiate states internally by steering people toward the places they live and work (Peterson 1981; Tiebout 1956). Within every state, then, we can find locations of Republican and Democratic concentration, some liberals and some conservatives. It is the uneven geographic distribution of these salient political traits that we mean by the term *geographic sectionalism,* or *sectionalism*. Sectionalism signals that political disagreements have a geographic dimension.

We could imagine states where political characteristics were evenly dispersed across substate jurisdictions (counties, cities, precincts). At every location we would find, say, equal numbers of Republicans and Democrats, liberals and conservatives. Mapping that even distribution across geographic subunits would reveal no clustering or regional basis of support for candidates or political parties. For a state to be sectional, there must be diversity across substate units in the propensity to support (or oppose) particular candidates or parties. Sectionalism, as we define it here, requires that Republicans (or Democrats) have a strong presence in some places, but not in others. Just as important, sectionalism is a matter of degree, with some states being more uneven in the geographic distribution of partisanship than others. Sectionalism can also vary over time within the same state, with some elections creating gaping geographic cleavages while other elections submerge these differences through widespread consensus.

Sectionalism in American politics has usually been understood in straightforward partisan terms, and usually construed regionally, contrasting the states that support Democrats with states that are more evenly matched, or else support Republicans. Political scientists and historians used to conceive of sectionalism in broad North-South terms, a legacy of the Civil War and Jim Crow laws adopted throughout the South to keep racial segregation in place and sustain white political dominance (Key 1949; Bensel 1984; Sundquist 1983). Historians still speak of the nation's great "sectional conflict" as the issue of slavery that precipitated the Civil War.

Between the Civil War and the early 1970s, discussions of North-South differences as the epitome of American sectionalism made a good deal of sense. The South stood out for its monolithic support of ideologically conservative Democratic candidates, whereas the North was more politically competitive and ideologically diverse. But by the 1980s and 1990s, the Republican party had made a serious comeback throughout the South with the consequence that the Southern states are more like Northern states than ever before, particularly in their degree of political competitiveness (Lamis 1999, 1984a; Schantz 1992). The growing political homogeneity across states that has brought the North and South closer together has raised serious questions about whether North-South sectionalism remains as relevant to the study of American politics as it once was (Ayers et al. 1996; DiMaggio, Evans, and Bryson 1996, 732; Hesseltine 1960). Certainly the evidence showing the rise of a two-party South suggests that the classical form of sectionalism is not a constant. While some form of North-South sectionalism has been present throughout most of U.S. history, it is clearly not the same now as it was in 1950, much less 1860 (Hesseltine 1960). As early as 1960, Southern historians were noting that with the urbanization and industrialization of their region, centers of strain and conflict were being relocated from the older cross-state sectionalism to newer regional conflicts within states (Vance 1960, 50–51). As we generalize the notion of sectionalism beyond the traditional confines of the North-South distinction, it is the variable nature of sectionalism across and within states that makes it a "complex" fact (Bensel 1984), and one worth studying.

Sectionalism within States and the
Meaning of *Region*

Viewing the evidence for sectionalism on maps early in the new century shows that the most evident regional political conflict today is within states, rather than across them. Just as the classic North-South differences have faded, partisan geographic divisions within states have often persisted and intensified (Agnew 1987; Johnston, Shelley, and Taylor 1990; Luebke 1990; Murauskas, Archer, and Shelley 1988; Ormrod and Cole 1996; O'Reilly and Webster 1998; Shelley and Archer 1989; Wolfinger and Greenstein 1967). These substate tensions are perhaps most evident in the rival party leanings of particular locales—nearly all of which can be identified as Republican, Democratic, or competitive between the two parties.

To be sure, substate jurisdictions are not always politically monolithic. Much depends upon scale. A county that is politically competitive may have several towns and many neighborhoods that are politically similar. Where a jurisdiction is politically one-sided—and many remain so for decades—it is worth pondering how these distinct sections stand the test of time. One explanation for this durability is rooted in social psychology. Partisanship and political attitudes are widely shared and long lasting because the people living within these communities exercise social pressure on each other to enforce conformity to local tradition.

Minority views wind up being squelched because minorities have few politically compatible neighbors and so resist discussions of politics (Huckfeldt and Sprague 1995; Huckfeldt 1986). Minorities generally keep quiet, so the theory goes, because people have a sensitive "social skin" that makes them fear isolation and adopt conforming attitudes to avoid it (Noelle-Neumann 1993). One's political views and attitudes can be either weakened or strengthened depending on the extent of social support one finds for expression of one's views (Dogan and Rokkan 1969; Huckfeldt and Sprague 1995; Berelson, Lazarsfeld, and McPhee 1954). Finding little compatible social support, minorities will be less likely to express their viewpoints, and their influence within the community will be limited. The supply of political information within a particular jurisdiction, then, is determined by the political orientation of majority groups (Huckfeldt and Sprague 1995, 155; Huckfeldt, Plutzer, and Sprague 1993; Huckfeldt and Sprague 1990; Huckfeldt 1986; Berelson, Lazarsfeld, and McPhee 1954). By supplying only certain types of information and reinforcement, local populations wind up being politically homogeneous for long periods of time, and therefore they can be easily recognized on a map when we plot partisanship or candidate choice across counties, cities, or precincts. Even though counties may appear to be especially large and potentially heterogeneous aggregations, Huckfeldt et al. (1995) found that for voters with more extended social networks, even county-level political attributes have an impact on political attitudes and perceptions.

Although there may be many ways of measuring political regionalism, we evaluate political diversity (or similarity) within states in terms of support for a particular party. We prefer to found our identification of political sections in these concrete terms, rather than fall back on a multifaceted, but poorly understood concept such as "political culture" (Elazar 1984, 1994) to describe regional differences. Partisanship is a good way to recognize political sections because partisanship has a direct, demonstrable impact on election outcomes, people identify with parties indicating some public awareness of what they stand for, and candidates run under party labels. We also know, however, that political viewpoints and party affiliations are affected by group traits and memberships. If we are to understand the basis for the unevenness in support for the Democratic party within a state, we must ask what has caused the state to exhibit distinctive regional clusters in its political support.

Among the causes we could catalog, people's race, income, occupation, mobility patterns, and religion are relevant to the study of sectionalism because these characteristics have been found to be relevant to patterns of social interaction and, in turn, with the formation of people's political values (Petrocik 1996, 827). Often, then, sectionalism, as revealed by the geographic distribution of party support, signals an underlying social, economic, or religious identity that has caused it (Bensel 1984; Key 1964). A variety of identities could generate sectionalism in contemporary American politics.

1. *Racially based sectionalism:* where the uneven distribution of partisanship is traceable to race-based settlement patterns, with black areas supporting Democrats while predominantly white areas are more politically divided or support Republicans.

2. *Ethnically based sectionalism:* where geographic differences in support for a party are founded upon ethnic diversity in the underlying population and the geographic concentration of ethnic groups with distinct political identities. Areas of ethnic diversity and recent immigration are more likely to support Democrats than areas that are predominantly white and native born.

3. *Economically based sectionalism:* where the uneven distribution of partisanship is rooted in economic disparities among substate jurisdictions, with lower-income areas supporting Democrats, and wealthier areas supporting Republicans. Economically based sectionalism may have its roots in the uneven distribution of occupational groups, such as farmers, professionals, or manufacturing workers.

4. *Ideologically based sectionalism:* where the uneven distribution of partisanship is based in ideological differences on issues, so that support for candidates and parties rests on the geographic concentration of, for example, conservative or liberal voters, or traditionalists vs. progressives.

5. *Religiously based sectionalism:* where the geographic differences in party support are traceable to differences in the religious traditions and moral beliefs of the underlying population.

Some may choose to call this collection of traits and characteristics "political culture" (Axelrod 1997; Elazar 1994, 9), and we have no quarrels with that language. But if we want to be precise about what underlies the unevenness of partisan electoral strength across a state, attributing that variation to political culture may obscure more than illuminate. We would rather attempt to pinpoint a few specific economic, religious, or social characteristics that account for that variation than lump all of the explanations together into a catchall descriptor called *culture.*

Of the five explanations for political regionalism listed, economic variation, or differences in "material interests," has probably been the single most popular (Archer and Taylor 1981; Key 1964; Turner 1932). But the social and economic underpinnings of political regionalism can vary widely from state to state, and over time within the same state, for the very same reason that survey research has shown that individuals' partisan preferences can have variable foundations (Campbell et al. 1960; Miller and Shanks 1996). Studies of voters have revealed that people have different understandings of what they are doing when they identify with a political party. Partisanship varies according to short-term forces much as candidate choice does (Allsop and Weisberg 1988; Fiorina 1981; Stanley, Bianco, and Niemi 1986; Sniderman, Brody, and Tetlock 1991). If partisanship is subject to period effects, or "epochal forces" (Sniderman, Brody, and Tetlock 1991, 192), it is equally reasonable to suggest that partisanship may be subject to contextual forces—influences brought to bear on voters as a result of residing in a particular place within a decentralized system (Clarke and Stewart 1998; Niemi, Wright, and Powell 1987). The policy expectations of Republicans in Phoenix are quite dissimilar to the policy expectations of Republicans in Boston, even though both groups are likely to vote for the same presidential candidate. Political scientists have rarely investigated whether Arizona Republicans evaluate the leadership qualities of their party's officeholders in the same way that Massachusetts Republicans do. The notions that voters have of parties and candidates, and the issues that motivate them to vote for one party or the other, are important for understanding the variable meaning of the choice made in the voting booth.

Just as voters may offer different reasons for supporting particular candidates and parties, the foundations of sectionalism may vary from state to state depending on the disagreements that are salient and the way populations with distinct interests are geographically concentrated (Wolfinger and Greenstein 1967). The geographic distribution of particular population groups is not the same in every state. For example, sometimes the black population will be highly concentrated in one, two, or a few counties. In other states (or at other times) it will be more dispersed. Such differences in settlement patterns will have an obvious bearing on race-based sectionalism when issues such as civil rights and affirmative action polarize the electorate.

Often the presence of sectionalism rooted in demographic differences boils down simply to the size of particular population groups within states—again, the compositional explanation for electoral geography (Gimpel 1996; Key 1956). Racial conflict has not informed sectionalism in Oregon because the black population has been so small there. Religious conflict was not as relevant to the nineteenth-century politics of Alabama as it was in Connecticut because the Old South lacked the religious diversity one could find in the Northeast. By understanding the foundations for substate sectionalism, we can evaluate how the federal structure of American government has created contexts in which political party constituencies vary from place to place.

Critics might argue that the historic North-South sectionalism is not at all the same thing as the type of regionalism within states we have been discussing. White Southerners were often a distinct political group even after controlling for their social and economic characteristics. In the introduction, we discussed two approaches to understanding regionalism: the compositional view and the contextual one. We have just admitted here that political regionalism within states may be explained primarily by reference to the presence and geographic concentration of particular groups—the compositional explanation. An important group of scholars in geography and political science have insisted that regional differences amount to more than just population characteristics—but point to communicative interactions within those populations that add something not captured by models containing the usual compositional variables (Huckfeldt 1986; Huckfeldt and Sprague 1995; Johnston, Shelley, and Taylor 1990; Kuklinski, Cobb, and Gilens 1997; Mondak, Mutz, and Huckfeldt 1996; Prysby 1989).

In favoring compositional explanations for regionalism in this book, we are not agnostic on the subject of the independent influence of context effects on attitudes and behavior. There are excellent theoretical reasons for believing that local communication patterns add something to people's behavior and attitudes not captured by their demographics. Nevertheless, not every "region"-related variable points to a true context effect (Hauser 1974; Kelley and McAllister 1985). Hence, we believe that it is pedagogically useful to begin by taking a skeptical stance—doubting whether *political* regions are anything more than a collection of people with shared traits and opinions.

To examine whether regional designations have an impact on behavior separate from the compositional traits of the underlying population, we might evaluate whether regional distinctions in political behavior amount to anything more than differences in population characteristics such as race, class, or occupation. Take the well-rooted urban-rural distinction in behavioral research on electoral politics (Key 1949, 1956; Lipset 1981; Lockard 1959; Webster 1987). The mere condition of residing in a densely populated area, compared with a less densely populated one, appears insufficient to generate a unique brand of political thinking productive of political cleavage. There are certainly plausible theories for why population size might matter to political *participation* (Dahl and Tufte 1973; Dahl 1967; Oliver 2000). But arguments have not been developed to explain why living in areas of differing size or density would make voters oppose one another. Those who have moved beyond compositional explanations to explain urban-rural cleavages in British political behavior have suggested that the gap rests upon the institutional arrangements that organize social life, including churches, workplaces, trade unions, and political parties. Working-class voters in rural Britain, for instance, are less likely to be trade union members, which helps us to account for their greater support for Conservative party candidates (Johnston 1987). Our point is that by controlling for the underlying variables that make urban and rural regions politically distinct (e.g., occupation, race, union membership, or the presence of certain institutional arrangements), references to unhelpful explanations to account for these differences (e.g., political culture) could be pushed out of the analytical lexicon, leaving us with a more concrete sense of what is responsible for generating the differences observed between locations (Gimpel and Schuknecht 2000; Kelley and McAllister 1985; Wirt et al. 1972).

A Proper Role for Context

While the *most obvious* forms of political regionalism are traceable simply to the characteristics of the people who live within the region, does this mean that place location, or context, adds absolutely nothing to our understanding of political sections? No; while perhaps not appearing on the surface, locational effects may figure prominently at the microlevel in several ways. First, who comes to reside in a particular location, and how they wind up expressing their political preferences, may be explained by the characteristics of the place itself. Location characteristics shape distinct regional identities initially by imposing various limitations and opportunities that attract some populations and repel others (Gastil 1973, 1975; Kollmorgen 1936; Turner 1932). Among these limitations, we could count environmental resource constraints that circumscribe the range of economic activities in an area—there can be no mining where there are no minerals of value, no farming in an area with little precipitation or groundwater. Environmental limitations may also raise the salience of certain conflicts, because of the unique challenges posed by resource constraints—water availability in the Western states is a good example (Lowitt 1995). Physical and geographic barriers to social interaction (rivers, mountain ranges) may prevent some populations from mingling, which produces political differences that are absent in areas that are similarly populated but lack those barriers to interaction.

Place locations are influential on attitudes and behavior because they bind their populations to the established local laws and customs under which the people live and labor. Not only does law set certain preconditions for social life by governing, it also creates social meaning, creating opinion in its favor because legality plays a legitimating role (Noelle-Neumann 1993, chap. 15; Hunt 1993). In a federal system, institutional practices and understandings will not be uniform, and local variation in law and policy will steer even similar populations toward dissimilar political identities. In this sense, "sections are fields for experiment in the growth of different types of society, political institutions and ideals" (Turner 1932).

Finally, the manner in which a place is settled, in interaction with the people who wind up settling there, conspire to create social environments that shape the tone and texture of politics. From a social standpoint, people are selective about where they live because they want to be around others who are like them (Huckfeldt 1984, 402). Accordingly, local environments become important social units because proximity and distance structure the social interactions citizens will experience, their exposure to information, and consequently the pressures toward conformity that will come to bear on them (Huckfeldt 1986, 117–18; Huckfeldt et al. 1995). Huckfeldt (1986, chap. 10) found that the actors' own characteristics do not fully determine their behavior, but that contextual influences extend to friendship selection, party loyalty, political participation, ethnic loyalty, residential satisfaction, and migration. Prysby's (1989) study of party activists in North Carolina primaries suggested that geographic context does not directly influence the vote once attitudes are taken into account, but that attitudes are shaped by context, giving context an indirect but no less important role to play in predicting behavior. In a study showing the importance of macroenvironmental factors on perceptions of political support for candidates, Huckfeldt et al. (1995) show that a county's political climate has substantively important effects on those whose discussion partners extend beyond their family, even after controlling for the respondent's race and party identification—two of the most important compositional explanations for vote choice. Finally, there is a case to be made that many so-called individual-level (compositional) variables could also be measures of context. While taking such a position muddies the waters, it is undoubtedly true that certain objective elements of a respondent's personal history indicate context. Level of education, for example, probably signals context by pointing to who a person associates with, what she reads, the kind of clothes she wears, the music she listens to, and so forth. In these cases, individual characteristics and contextual influences are inseparable joint phenomena (Sprague 2001).

Sectionalism Changes over Time

The causes of political sectionalism may be highly variable across geographic units for both compositional and contextual reasons, but political geography can also change over time. Among voters, survey research has shown that the salience of some types of political conflict has waxed and waned across decades and generations (Abramson 1975; Carmines and Stimson 1981; Wolfinger 1965). Other studies have shown that there are geographic variations in the extent to which changes in the issue agenda influence attitudes (Marchant-Shapiro and Patterson 1995; Clarke and Stewart 1998; Galderisi et al. 1987). When studies ignore location-specific variations in attitudes and behavior, they mislead us into thinking that political change occurs at the same time and at the same pace across the nation. But it is unreasonable to assume that changes in one location mirror changes in another in a diverse nation with a system of semisovereign local units.

Various notions of political party realignment have been commonly advanced as explanations for electoral change, and they can help explain rising and falling sectionalism over time (Key 1955, 1959; Sundquist 1983; Burnham 1970; Shafer 1991). Party realignment was once understood to occur principally as the result of a critical election—an election in which the electoral outcome and subsequent electoral outcomes depart in significant and lasting ways from previous patterns of partisan politics (Key 1955). How radical this lasting departure must be to be indicative of a "critical" election is a matter of some contention. Conservative estimates suggest that the nation has undergone three or four realignments where partisan patterns have been dramatically altered by critical elections. The 1932 and 1936 presidential elections are often said to be the best examples of critical elections because they resulted in significant and lasting changes in the social groups underlying the political parties (Petrocik 1981; Shafer 1991; Axelrod 1972). Aggregate levels of party support may not change much in a realignment. Democrats and Republicans may be about as competitive (or noncompetitive) as before the critical election. But the 1932 and 1936 elections resulted in a major shift in partisan support—with groups of low socioeconomic status serving as the new foundation for the Democrats and groups of higher socioeconomic status crystallizing around Republicans (Axelrod 1972, 1986). New partisan cleavages also emerged between black and white voters, between immigrants and natives, and between farmers and industrial workers. To the extent that these groups were geographically clustered, their political realignment altered sectionalism. Maps of substate sections may be one of the best ways, in fact, of illustrating party realignment in the New Deal era.

If we are attentive to changing patterns of substate sectionalism, we can observe electoral changes that do not appear to be driven by major economic earthquakes or critical events such as the Great Depression. Such observations have taught us that partisan change is not strictly dependent upon the rare critical election. Even the most major realignments have now been discovered to be partial, occurring among some populations and in some locations, but not universally (Petrocik 1981; Carmines and Stimson 1981; Galderisi et al. 1987; Mayhew 2002; Nardulli 1995; Gimpel 1996). In related work, a number of studies have focused on how local economic conditions and issues influence voting in state elections, providing strong evidence that political behavior is conditioned by local forces, not just national ones (Atkeson and Partin 1995; Beck 1977, 1982; Campbell 1977a; Dyer, Vedlitz, and Hill 1988; Galderisi et al. 1987; Hadley and Howell 1980; Lewis-Beck and Rice 1983; Nardulli 1995; Stanley 1988; Wolfinger and Arseneau 1978). The implication of these studies is that realignment theory should be either scrapped altogether or recast to assist us in explaining local political shifts.

But to say that realignment can help us to explain changing political geography within states is not very useful unless we also examine the forces that drive realignment. Three primary mechanisms are thought to be the sources of partisan realignment, whatever its magnitude: (1) the *conversion* of existing voters from one party to another, (2) the *mobilization* of new voters into the electorate, and (3) *generational replacement,* or the aging and mortality of one group of voters and its subsequent replacement by a younger one (Abramson 1975, 1976; Carmines and Stimson 1981; Erikson and Tedin 1981; Campbell 1985; Erikson 1986; Anderson 1976, 1979; Carmines and Stimson 1981; Brown 1988; Gimpel 1996).

There is little reason to expect that any of these processes behind party change work uniformly across the nation. Given the social and political diversity of the United States, it is a long stretch of the imagination to think that conversion from one party to another occurs the same way everywhere. Voter interests are sufficiently diverse that converts to the other party will be more easily won in some locales than in others. Arguably, in some locales, there will be no converts because those areas are already strongly supportive of the party to which most voters are shifting their allegiance.

Large-scale partisan change has usually been precipitated by some expansion of the number of people who vote (Petrocik 1981; Andersen 1979). In addition to conversion, then, mobilization is a key source of electoral dynamics. Since mobilization rates vary across the nation at the beginning of any period of electoral change, the mobilization of new voters will only make a significant difference in electoral outcomes in those places where turnout is especially low and where the voters not initially mobilized are different from those who are. Mobilization's impact will not be any more uniform across states and localities than that of conversion.

Finally, with respect to generational change, the age distribution of the electorate also varies by location, with some places having a larger elderly population than others. The size of the elderly population is critical because it reflects the potential for change in the electorate due to mortality. In 1990, for example, the median age of residents across California counties ranged from a low of 28 to a high of nearly 41. And in Florida, home to many elderly retirees, the range in median age ran from a low of 28 to a high of 53! The potential for partisan change due to generational replacement is far higher in Florida's counties than California's. This is because the proportion of residents of retirement age is a good indicator of how many people will soon be exiting the electorate through death. Naturally, whether mortality contributes to realignment depends on whether there are

pronounced generational differences in partisan affiliation and attitudes (Carmines and Stimson 1981). For instance, one could easily
determine through survey research whether the population over age
65 was politically distinct from the population under age 65. Where
these differences are minimal, generational replacement of the elderly population will not result in dramatic political change. High birth
rates are not as likely to contribute to partisan change as high mortality rates. This is because most new voters are politically socialized
by their families and children adopt the same political attitudes as
their parents. They may carry some differing viewpoints into the electorate as they enter it, but those views are not likely to redefine the
politics of a place. The size of the retirement-age population, then, is
a predictor of potential political change in a way that the size of the
preadult population is not.

Population Mobility as a Neglected but Important
Force for Change

In most states the electorate has become more dispersed as residents
have fled central cities for suburbs. This outward movement has balkanized states into Republican and Democratic strongholds in a manner
not seen early in the twentieth century. Parties once fought side by
side for voters in urban areas, but have gradually moved apart, finding
that they have less intersecting turf (Gimpel and Schuknecht 2002).
This is not to say that fierce competition does not exist anywhere at
the local level. But it does mean that there are fewer jurisdictions
where the two parties are competing to mobilize the same voters.

Simultaneous with population movement away from large central
cities, many rural areas have been abandoned and farms have been
consolidated, creating a countervailing centralizing force within
many states. By the beginning of the twenty-first century, a solid plurality of the electorate could be found in just a handful of counties,
usually in one, two, or a few metropolitan areas, with vast territories
within states contributing little to the statewide vote for either party.
This reshuffling of the population has had profound implications for
the nature of substate sectionalism, to say nothing of how it has altered political campaigns. These considerations lead us to believe that
population mobility has been the most important force shaping the
political identity of regions within states.

Why has the impact of population mobility been neglected in much of the literature on electoral politics? We suppose it's mostly because questions about population mobility are absent from many surveys and partly due to the false assumption that mobility redistributes voters evenly or randomly across the nation. At most, population mobility can be said to restrict voter turnout due to burdensome regulations on voter registration that vary from place to place (Squire, Wolfinger, and Glass 1987; Timpone 1998). Mobility is commonly thought to be a net wash in terms of its impact on partisan and ideological change. And if movers are a random subset of the population, we would have little reason to suppose that their migration would contribute to political change or a redistribution of party strength. If Democrats and Republicans, liberals and conservatives, are equally likely to move and settle in a new locale, then there probably are no political consequences stemming from this reshuffling of the demographic deck.

But the assumption that migrants are a random and representative subset of the total population is almost always incorrect. Moving imposes heavy financial and psychological costs on migrants, and particularly on those who move long distances, such as across state lines. Because of the costs associated with migration, there is likely to be an economic bias in who moves and who does not, with wealthier people exhibiting much more mobility than poorer people. Demographers and economists have established that this bias exists. Internal migrants (as opposed to immigrants) are most likely to be better educated, young, white, and upwardly mobile (Gimpel 1999; Gabriel and Schmitz 1995; Borjas, Bronars, and Trejo 1992). The poor and unskilled are the least likely to move (Clark and Whiteman 1983). The social characteristics of movers were highly associated with Republican party identification in the final decades of the twentieth century. Hence, those locations with more residents born in the United States, but outside their current state of residence, exhibited strong Republican leanings (Gimpel 1999). By contrast, areas of low population mobility were often composed of poor and minority residents with entrenched Democratic loyalties.

To the three main explanations for partisan change (conversion, mobilization, and generational replacement) we add a fourth, population mobility. These four explanations will serve as a platform to help us to understand how the sectionalism rooted in a particular type of political conflict is either reinforced or replaced by something new. Given the nature of our data, we will not be able to draw definitive conclusions about the sources of political change in all circumstances, but we can indicate where some explanations of political change are more probable than others. It takes little sophistication to hypothesize that fast-growing states (Florida, California) are more likely to be subject to partisan changes brought about by population mobility than slower-growing states (North Dakota, Iowa). The slow-growth states are likely to see partisan change only through the gradual process of generational replacement.

Anticipating where political mobilization is likely to produce electoral change is a bit more difficult, but we can advance some hunches. Mobilization's potential to effect change will be greatest in areas where there are large disenfranchised populations whose activism could potentially alter political outcomes. In states with large African-American populations, such as Georgia, Michigan, or Illinois, we would expect greater political changes to follow on the heels of the civil rights movement than in states such as Oregon, Connecticut, or Colorado, with their much smaller black populations.

Conversion's impact is hard to anticipate as most studies suggest that mass conversions are rare. To the extent that conversion is thought to be contingent upon the emergence of new issues and cleavages, one could say that a converting electorate must meet some minimum standard of attentiveness or education. But although converts must display some modicum of attention, these voters do not adhere to the prevailing or majoritarian views within their party, because partisans who are happiest with the substance of national party platforms are least likely to convert. From these considerations, we hypothesize that the potential for partisan change attributable to conversion is likely to be greater in states with high levels of migration coupled with voters who wind up alienated from their party's most significant platform positions. Electoral change stemming from conversion, then, is more likely to be found in regions and states that are peripheral to party support than those that are considered the core of support. White Democratic voters in Southern states have held views on racial issues that became peripheral to the national party following because they came to constitute a minority within their party on civil rights matters by the mid-1960s. As such, these white voters were good candidates for conversion, and many have changed parties in the years since. Western states are the next best candidates to look for conversion during the twentieth century as they are home to the most migratory populations and have been home to minority interests that are uneasy with mainstream party stands on matters such as land use regulation and environmental protection. The support for Ralph Nader's 2000 presidential bid among voters in the Pacific Northwest was one sign that this restless bloc is of considerable size. Finally, with the twenty-first century beginning, the Northeastern states have grown increasingly peripheral to Republican party support as that party's base has shifted toward the West and South—pulling these once peripheral regions toward the core of party support. As the Northeast has lost its influence within GOP ranks, we might expect the conversion of many Republicans in this area who no longer find their views embodied in presidential and congressional agendas.

Plan for the Book

No event more clearly demonstrated the importance of states as distinct fields of play than the 2000 presidential election. George W. Bush plainly admitted in a postelection interview on CBS News' *60 Minutes II* that his campaign strategy had been dictated by a focus on winning electoral college votes rather than by the popular vote, which he lost by 340,000 votes. In the end, Bush won thirty states, to Gore's twenty-one (counting the District of Columbia), dividing the electoral college 271 to 267. Evidence from studies of previous campaign efforts show how sensitive campaigns are to the political geography of state politics (Shaw 1999). Because so many campaign activities, from voter mobilization programs to advertising, center on states as particular fields of play, we take up individual states in chapters 3 through 14. This state-by-state approach can exploit variations in political behavior across both time and space, within states. We present a comprehensive analysis of substate sectionalism, pausing to analyze maps of candidate choice within states from 1928 through 2000. Using electoral geography, we explore the states' different patterns and nuances rather than gloss over them in an aggregate or pooled analysis. The last chapter, however, reaches across the myriad electoral settings to draw some general conclusions about political development and partisan change.

For each state we will describe how the economic and social trends of the last century have influenced political geography. Maps of the state's political sections illustrate the important changes across the period since the New Deal realignment. For some states, the geographic foundation for political conflict changed dramatically. Places that were Democratic strongholds moved into the Republican column, and vice versa. For other states, broad sectional patterns remain much the same as in the 1930s, sometimes in spite of significant social and economic changes. Displaying these patterns on thematic maps, then explaining them in terms of the main theories of partisan and political change from the literature on party realignment will be a major goal of each chapter.

Some political conflicts are highly salient in some states, irrelevant in others. To highlight these differences, each chapter will include an analysis of ecological (county level) data from the 1928 to the 2000 presidential elections. The dependent variable will be Democratic vote choice in presidential elections. The independent variables will be demographic indicators of the race, occupation, education, and migration patterns of residents. We lean on the county-level data to make inferences about individual-level behavior because state-level polls are scarce prior to the 1980s. In the past, the use of aggregate data, at the county or precinct level, for this purpose resulted in misleading or nonsensical conclusions (e.g., 130 percent of blacks vote Democratic or −30 percent of voters over age 65 vote Republican). This is because the previous techniques for inferring individual behavior from aggregate data do not allow for the fact that many quantities of interest are proportions (percentages) and therefore cannot exceed 100 or drop below 0. Recent methodological resources, in particular Gary King's 1997 *A Solution to the Ecological Inference Problem,* have allowed us to make more accurate inferences about individual attributes based on aggregate data (see appendix A). King's method is a significant advance because it overcomes many of the problems of older techniques, including those estimates that are above 100 percent or below 0 for quantities that we have just described. The method does not guarantee perfection. Not every estimate will be faithful to reality and the method has some prominent detractors (Tam Cho 1998; Anselin and Tam Cho 2002). But compared to alternative methods, King's approach has been advanced as a major improvement.

Each state chapter presents tables of results generated via ecological inference estimation to describe the political leanings of a variety of demographic groups in the state electorate and to reason about political change. To reduce the sheer quantity of information to be presented and to improve the quality of the estimates, presidential elections are combined in groups of two or three from 1928 to 2000. Precise estimates for every state and every politically relevant group are not always attainable: data limitations, including the number and size of geographic units and their heterogeneity, affect the precision of the estimates. For purposes of drawing inferences about political change within a state, however, we believe our results approximate reality. For more recent elections, we are able to examine the plausibility of the ecological inference estimation with polling data. For those elections where polling data are not available, it is probably best to compare the ecological inference estimates over time, examining the figures for given elections in light of estimates from later and earlier elections within individual states. Otherwise, cross-state comparisons of these figures can shed light on the extent of political differences between rival groups as one moves from state to state.

The final chapter will highlight comparisons and contrasts across states while reminding readers of why the similarities and differences exist. On the one hand, the dominance of two national party labels ensures some measure of uniformity in the way people think about candidates and issues. On the other hand, federalism ensures that within the basic framework set by the U.S. Constitution and the historical development of our two major parties, there is amazing leeway to develop autonomous and distinctive political orientations. The seemingly interminable saga of the 2000 election campaign in Florida demonstrated that there is demand by journalists, academic researchers, political consultants, and politicians to understand the local nuances and subtleties that make states unique political environments. This book will have succeeded if it meets even some of that demand.

CHAPTER 2

STATE POLITICS
AND PRESIDENTIAL
VOTING, 1988–2000

We started with the noncontroversial idea that states differ from one another in their political identities and that these differences are the result of the federal structure of American government (chap. 1). Presidential elections and the domination of two national parties have gone a long way toward watering down the effects of federal structure on political diversity across states and localities. The political institutions that force everyone to live with the same two major parties impose order on what might otherwise be political chaos. The focus of campaign media coverage through nightly network news shows is not customized to individual locales. But serious presidential candidates realize that a one-size-fits-all strategy does not work, preferring to tailor their message according to the prevailing winds at local campaign stops (Shaw 1999).

Accounting for the myriad ways in which states and localities differ is a more complicated task. Local political orientations will vary mainly for compositional but also for contextual reasons (as discussed in chap. 1). Composition refers to the fact that constituencies are simply different from one locale to the next: in one state African Americans are a consequential voting bloc, in another they are not. Contextual explanations can vary according to the aspects of place location that are emphasized, but in recent years scholars have understood context mainly in terms of local communication and socialization patterns that disrupt or otherwise alter the usually smooth linkage between compositional traits and political attitudes and behavior.

For example, two blue-collar workers in the same industry—one from suburban Pittsburgh, the other from suburban Nashville—may

wind up voting differently. The Pennsylvania worker's economic interest guides his vote, and the psychological connection between occupation and vote is upheld by a social setting that never questions
this long-standing identification—the vote choice may never be open
to discussion, and it is certainly never challenged. The Tennessee
worker, though, traffics among those who think differently about politics and confronts regular challenges to the notion that workers in
his industry should vote the way they do in Pennsylvania (see Fenton
1966, chap. 5). The result: in Tennessee, occupation (the compositional trait) fails to account for much of a voter's political attitudes or
behavior, while in Pennsylvania it does. In Tennessee, we need an additional variable to explain voting that may not be necessary in Pennsylvania, namely, some measure of the voter's social setting (the context). In Pennsylvania, though, the voter's composition and setting
are identical, and the context variable explains no more than what we
captured by including the voter's occupation. This does not mean that
context effects are absent in the Pennsylvania voter's neighborhood,
but that they play a silent and congruent role (a collinear one, in statistics parlance), rather than an incongruent and vocal one.

In this and subsequent chapters, we present information showing
that states share some important similarities but are also remarkably
variable in the way their electorates divide when presented with the
same candidates. While regions within states are sometimes easily
identifiable, in many cases the political distinctiveness of substate sections disappears once we control for the compositional characteristics
that make these regions unique. Not every region has a discernible impact on political attitudes independent of its basic population composition (Huckfeldt and Sprague 1995, 61). In addition, the foundations
for political regionalism differ from state to state. What makes
Chicago stand out from the rest of Illinois is not necessarily the same
thing that makes Houston a unique political setting within Texas.
What this means is that regionalism within states is not easily re-
ducible to one or two population characteristics that are common to
all states—a fact that greatly complicates the task of electioneering.

In the next few pages, we set several states side by side in an examination of presidential voting between 1988 and 2000. Comparing
states' presidential votes makes sense because each state is con-
fronting the same candidate choices, whereas in congressional and
gubernatorial elections, different alternatives are present in each

state. If state electorates choose differently when confronted by candidates running for national office, then they are likely to differ even more when they turn to consider their local candidates. By *choose differently* we mean that electorates are dissimilar in the extent to which basic political traits and characteristics of populations cue the vote. These political variables typically include items pollsters care a lot about and political scientists have identified as influences on decision making. Various theories of voting have suggested that among the predictors of candidate support are party identification and political ideology, along with traits that are associated with group identities, such as race, income, sex, age, and religious affiliation (Campbell et al. 1960; Nie, Verba, and Petrocik 1976; Page and Jones 1979; Markus and Converse 1979; Conover and Feldman 1981; Niemi and Weisberg 1984; Miller and Shanks 1996).

Although we do not have comparable survey data on all twelve of the states we cover in chapters 3 through 14, we do present models of presidential vote choice for seven of them in the 1988–96 elections and all twelve in the 2000 presidential race. The appendix at the end of this chapter presents complete results for these models. Our data source is the Voter Research and Surveys and Voter News Service network-sponsored exit polls conducted on election day of each year. These polls are conducted only among voters as they leave the polling booth at randomly selected locations within each state. Because the VRS/VNS surveys are very short polls, containing few questions, we are unable to use them to estimate the impact of every theoretically relevant influence on presidential voting, but we have made our model as complex as the data allow.

Another drawback of these exit polls is that measures are not as elaborate as in university-sponsored surveys such as the *American National Election Studies*. Partisan identification, for instance, is measured on a simple 3-point scale that exaggerates the presence of independent voters in the electorate and does not capture the variable strength of voters' partisan commitments. A more complex 7-point scale would more accurately gauge the extent to which partisanship predicts vote choice (Green and Schickler 1993). Still, the 3-point scale is not far off the mark. In comparing its performance to the more reliable 7-point scale, Green and Schickler found that the simpler scale was a slightly weaker predictor of vote choice ($r = .653$, compared with $r = .670$ for the 7-point scale) (524). Researchers inevitably make compromises in empirical inquiries based on data availability. The main advantage of the exit polls is that they represent states, whereas national polls do not. We traded a survey that drew on a sample representing state electorates, but had slightly more error-prone instrumentation, for alternatives that had optimal instrumentation but could say nothing about state electorates.

Our model of vote choice is summarized in figure 2.1. We estimate the influence of a number of key variables on the presidential vote to determine whether differences across states are real or trivial. Generally speaking we draw the following hypotheses from the extensive voting behavior literature: Democratic support will be (1) higher among self-identified Democrats than among self-identified Republicans; (2) higher among liberals than among moderates and conservatives; (3) higher among blacks and Latinos than among non-Hispanic white voters; (4) higher among women than men; and (5) higher among low-income voters than among the wealthy. From previous research, we would also have good reasons for suspecting that (6) elderly voters will be more likely to support Democrats than younger voters and (7) Democratic support will be greater among Jewish voters than among Catholics and Protestants.

Voting in the 1988–1996 Presidential Elections

We have insisted that we are likely to find important differences across states in the extent to which the preceding hypotheses hold. What are these? The most obvious prediction would be about the generally conservative tone of the electorate in states such as Texas, Florida, and Georgia. In these states, we expect to find less Democratic support among self-identified conservatives and Republican voters than we might in other states. Consistent with the findings of national polls, it is also reasonable to expect less Democratic support among women, lower-income voters, and Jews. In states such as New York and Maryland, with strong politically liberal traditions, we might find the least support for Republicans among women, Jews, the poor, blacks, and Latinos, groups typically given to Democratic voting according to national election studies. In states with moderate political traditions, such as Illinois and Michigan, we might expect the traditional hypotheses based on national polls to hold up well.

Results from our tests of these long-standing hypotheses about

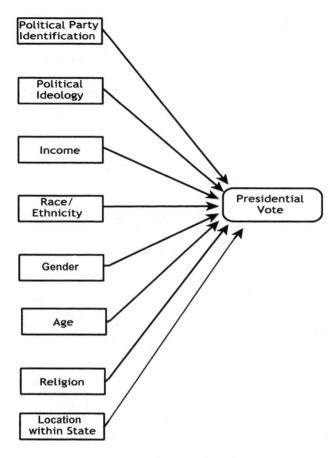

Fig. 2.1.   A model of the presidential vote

voting behavior appear in table 2.1. The cell entries in this table show the percentage of each group listed on the far left column that supported the Democratic candidate in the 1988–96 presidential elections controlling for all of the other variables listed in the table. The difference in support between each group listed (e.g., Republican

TABLE 2.1. Estimated Percentage of Each Group Voting Democratic, 1988–96, by State

Variable and State	CA	FL	GA	IL	MI	NY	TX
Non-Democrat	46	38	35	43	37	45	33
Democrat	71	60	60	68	72	70	64
Difference	25	22	25	25	35	25	31
Non-Republican	65	55	52	61	58	61	52
Republican	41	31	29	32	33	41	30
Difference	24	24	23	29	25	20	22
Liberal	71	64	58	67	62	70	59
Conservative	43	35	36	40	40	41	37
Difference	28	29	22	27	22	29	22
Poor	59	53	47	54	53	55	50
Wealthy	55	40	43	51	46	55	41
Difference	4	13	4	3	7	0	9
Nonblack	55	44	39	50	49	53	43
Black	72	71	71	75	64	74	66
Difference	17	27	32	25	15	21	23
Non-Hispanic	56	47	45	52	50	55	45
Hispanic	61	49	60	69	47	65	54
Difference	5	2	15	17	3	10	9
Men	55	44	45	50	46	49	42
Women	58	49	45	53	52	57	47
Difference	3	5	0	3	6	8	5
Age 18–29	56	41	43	51	48	50	44
Over age 60	58	51	47	53	52	58	47
Difference	2	10	4	2	4	8	3
Non-Catholic	58	48	45	53	51	58	46
Catholic	55	46	42	52	49	51	46
Difference	3	2	3	1	2	7	0
Non-Jewish	57	46	45	52	50	54	46
Jewish	65	62	57	66	63	60	52
Difference	9	16	12	14	13	6	6
Non-Protestant	58	49	46	53	50	56	47
Protestant	53	45	44	52	51	50	44
Difference	5	4	2	1	1	6	3
Outside region A[a]	58	47	45	52	49	53	46
Inside region A	54	51	47	53	64	58	47
Difference	4	4	2	1	15	5	1
Outside region B[a]	57	47	44	53	48	53	46
Inside region B	58	47	48	52	55	68	47
Difference	1	0	4	1	7	5	1

TABLE 2.1.—*Continued*

Variable and State	CA	FL	GA	IL	MI	NY	TX
Outside region C[a]	56	48	44	52	49	54	45
Inside region C	61	46	47	53	54	60	50
Difference	5	2	3	1	5	6	5
Outside region D[a]	57	47	—	—	49	55	45
Inside region D	56	48			55	53	47
Difference	1	1			6	2	2
Election year 1988	59	48	45	53	52	55	48
Election year 1992	50	46	45	52	47	54	42
Difference	9	2	0	1	5	1	6
Election year 1988	57	46	44	52	50	54	45
Election year 1996	57	52	47	53	51	57	48
Difference	0	6	3	1	1	3	3

Source: ICPSR, Voter Research and Surveys and Voter News Service, *Election Day Exit Polls* 1988, 1992, 1996.

Note: Cell entries show the estimated percentage of each group voting Democratic in the pooled 1988–96 presidential elections and the difference in Democratic support between the groups listed in each row computed from multivariate probit models (table A2.1) with the remaining independent variables held constant at their sample means. Differences reported are absolute values.

[a]Regions are coded as follows:

CA: A = Southern California; B = Los Angeles city; C = Bay Area; D = Central CA.
FL: A = Miami; B = South Florida; C = North Florida; D = Tampa.
GA: A = Central; B = Atlanta; C = North.
IL: A = Chicago; B = Chicago suburbs; C = South.
MI: A = Detroit; B = Oakland County and Detroit suburbs; C = University Belt; D = Southwest MI.
NY: A = Long Island; B = New York City; C = Upstate Urban; D = Rural NY.
TX: A = East TX; B = Dallas; C = Houston; D = South.

identifiers vs. Other identifiers) is also presented to gauge the total effect each indicator had on increasing the percentage of support for the Democrat. For example, we can see from the table that in California, about 46 percent of non-Democrats voted for Democratic presidential candidates, and 71 percent of Democrats voted for Democratic presidential candidates. The difference is 25 points, indicating the magnitude by which Democrats favor Democratic presidential candidates compared with non-Democrats. The percentage of Democratic identifiers declaring that they voted for Democratic presidential candidates does vary, ranging from a high of 72 percent in Michigan to a low of 60 percent in Georgia and Florida. In fact, Democratic loyalty to Democratic candidates is lowest in the three Southern states shown: Georgia, Texas, and Florida (table 2.1).

Republican support for Democratic presidential candidates also varies widely from state to state. The results in table 2.1 show that over 40 percent of New York and California Republicans voted for the Democratic candidate, compared with only 29 percent of Georgia Republicans. Ideological polarization—the difference between liberal and conservative support for Democratic candidates—ranged from a high of 29 points (Florida) to a low of 22 (Texas, Georgia, and Michigan). Those identifying themselves as conservatives were most likely to vote for Democrats in New York and California and least likely to vote for Democrats in the three Southern states.

Testing for differences in the political preferences of rich and poor people is important because it shows where economic cleavages may exist independent of political party identification, ideology, and related variables such as race. Our results show that class cleavages are present in some states and absent in others. The biggest difference between wealthy and poor voters was in Florida. The difference between wealthy and poor voters in New York and Illinois, on the other hand, was negligible. Wealthy and poor voters both gave majorities of their support to Democratic candidates in California, New York, and Illinois.

Race-based voting is evaluated by examining the differences between black and nonblack voters, and Hispanic and non-Hispanic voters (table 2.1). Extremely high percentages of black voters support Democratic candidates, but there was surprising variation too. Black voters were least supportive of Bill Clinton and Michael Dukakis in Texas and most supportive of these Democrats in Illinois and New York. Hispanic voters were least supportive of the Democrats in Florida and Michigan and most supportive of Democrats in California, Illinois, and New York. Democratic support among Illinois Hispanics (at 69 percent) was much higher than among Florida Hispanics (at 49 percent).

The gender gap refers to the difference in support for a candidate or policy position that exists between men and women. When we consider the gap in support for Democratic presidential candidates in 1988 through 1996, we see that the differences are not vast—ranging from 0 to 8 points. The gap was widest in New York, but there was no gender gap in Georgia, and it was negligible in Illinois, once we controlled for other variables that influenced vote choice.

Age differences are important because they signal intergenerational change. In the table we compare the oldest age cohort (those over age 60) to the youngest (those between 18 and 29). Ten points separated the oldest from the youngest age cohorts in Florida, with the elderly being far more supportive of Democratic candidates. A similar generation gap existed in New York. In none of these states did we find the older voters to be more Republican than the younger voters, although in several states, such as California, Illinois, Texas, and Michigan, the difference between the two was too small to be statistically different from zero.

In the past, religion has been an influential predictor of political behavior. The importance of religious cleavages in the American electorate has faded. Catholics were once far more Democratic than they are now, at the beginning of the new century, and Protestants far more Republican. The generalization that Jews have been found to be more liberal and Democratic than non-Jews probably still held through the 2000 election. In fact we found that Jews are more Democratic than non-Jews, but there was considerable geographic variation in the extent to which Jews were loyal to Democratic candidates. The Jewish vote was solidly Democratic in California, Illinois, Michigan, and New York, as compared to only an estimated 52 percent in Texas and 57 percent in Georgia. Moreover, in New York, the gap between Jewish and non-Jewish support for Democrats was only 6 points, suggesting weaker cleavage along this dimension than exists in many other states.

By the 1980s, Catholics were no longer to be counted among the Democratic faithful in every state. Catholics were slightly less likely than non-Catholics to vote Democratic in all of the states but Texas (table 2.1). The gap in support between Catholics and non-Catholics was highest in New York. Those declaring themselves to be generic Protestants were somewhat less likely to vote Democratic than non-Protestants, but the difference was not great given the heterogeneity of Protestant denominations and belief systems. The widest gap was in New York, where Protestants were 6 points less likely to vote Democratic than those not so affiliated.

As a final addition to our models, we included the impact of substate regions on citizens' vote choices. The substate regions defined in the VRS/VNS exit polls do not always correspond to the true economic and political regions within each state, nor do they correspond to our coming discussions of political geography in chapters 3 through

14. It is likely that context is most relevant at a more precise level of aggregation than the expansive regions given to us in these polls (Erikson, Wright, and McIver 1993). But we can examine whether any of these regions made a difference to vote choice, once the main individual-level ingredients of voting models have been included. Is it possible that there are contextual effects once partisanship, ideology, race, income, gender, and age have been addressed?

For the most part, table 2.1 reveals that these regional effects on Democratic voting in the 1988–96 elections are small, but for a very important reason relating to the compositional explanation for geographic differences. Regions, counties, and neighborhoods take on their character largely because of the social, economic, and political characteristics of the people that reside within them. Often there is no distinctive source of regionalism that can be isolated as a source of conflict apart from other attributes of voters (Hahn 1971, 15; Kelley and McAllister 1985; King 1996; Wirt et al. 1972). In our regression model, we have taken account of the survey respondents' most important political characteristics explicitly. In other words, the region of residence describes very little about the voter's politically relevant identity that is not already captured by their race, partisanship, political ideology, income, and religion. The inclusion of these other variables left very little for region or context to explain (King 1996).

Nevertheless, there are exceptions in several states, including Michigan, California, and New York, where there are apparent contextual effects associated with living in Detroit, the San Francisco Bay area, and New York City. A few other broad geographic areas appeared to impose a distinct contextual imprint, including Long Island, the Detroit suburbs, southwestern Michigan, Atlanta, Houston, and southern California. Places with no distinct regional identity in these presidential elections included south and east Texas, all of Florida except Miami, southern Illinois, the Chicago suburbs, and New York's upstate urban and rural areas. Clearly these places may be politically unique from other substate regions, but the reason for this was captured by other traits. Once these variables were accounted for, the distinctiveness of the region faded. Interestingly, Chicago also did not stand out from the rest of Illinois in its support for Democratic presidential candidates, once race, partisanship, and related variables were included in the model. Apparently, Los Angeles's politically unique character was captured by other political variables, as it did not stand out in relief against the rest of California in our multivariate analysis.

Voting in the 2000 Presidential Election

The Voter News Service election day exit polls in the 2000 election used different regional categories in Illinois, Georgia, and Michigan than were used in the previous three elections. Table 2.2 presents results similar to those of table 2.1, only for Democratic voting in the 2000 election for all twelve states. Region codes for several other states not included in table 2.1 were also altered for the 2000 poll. Across these states, there are about a dozen regions that stand out as having an independent impact on vote choice even after the most obvious individual-level causes of voting have been taken into account. We find, for example, that several large cities voted decisively for Albert Gore for reasons other than just the partisanship, ideology, race, income, and related traits of their constituents (see table 2.2). These included Denver, Chicago, Detroit, Minneapolis, and Portland. Houston area voters were about 10 percent more likely to vote for George W. Bush than those from other parts of Texas. And south Texas, north Florida, and central California all stand out as political regions where contextual effects may be creating a distinctive politics. As in table 2.1, the effects of region are not usually very large, but some are as big as 9 or 10 percent, typically exceeding the effects of age and gender, and equaling the effect of income.

There are two ways of looking at these intriguing results. First, if we were to insist on the compositional route to explanation, it is possible that if we specified additional individual attributes, the uniqueness of the regions we have just mentioned would disappear. Perhaps if we were to control for the respondents' occupation or employment status (variables that were not included on the VNS survey), region would have no separate impact. But a second possibility is that at least some of these broadly defined regions do exhibit a real context effect on political behavior, independent of voter characteristics. Perhaps this is where we must develop explanations rooted in unique local institutional arrangements (church, school, labor unions, kinship ties) that disrupt lines of communication that would otherwise bring the region into conformity with other places. Or these local arrangements may create unusual networks of communication that make the

TABLE 2.2. Estimated Percentage of Each Group Voting Democratic, November 2000, by State

Variable and State	CA	CO	CT	FL	GA	IL	MD	MI	MN	NY	OR	TX
Non-Democrat	40	35	47	43	42	46	47	45	37	47	35	40
Democrat	73	65	70	67	64	74	73	71	60	76	66	60
Difference	33	30	23	24	22	28	26	26	23	29	31	20
Non-Republican	62	57	63	62	60	63	65	63	57	65	56	55
Republican	37	19	31	33	34	37	44	35	17	44	26	32
Difference	25	38	32	29	26	26	21	28	60	21	30	23
Liberal	65	54	70	63	64	69	72	69	60	69	58	58
Conservative	44	39	37	43	42	41	47	41	31	47	36	43
Difference	21	15	33	20	22	25	25	28	29	22	22	15
Poor	56	45	60	55	52	51	58	52	46	56	44	54
Wealthy	53	50	52	50	52	61	61	56	48	61	49	45
Difference	3	5	8	5	0	10	3	4	2	5	5	9
Nonblack	53	47	54	49	44	55	53	53	46	57	46	39
Black	67	57	73	76	71	73	78	67	57	74	66	78
Difference	14	10	19	27	67	18	25	14	11	17	20	39
Non-Hispanic	53	46	54	53	52	52	60	54	47	58	60	57
Hispanic	59	51	64	51	50	57	67	53	45	68	46	48
Difference	6	5	10	2	2	5	7	1	2	10	14	9
Men	52	45	51	52	52	54	58	52	47	56	43	48
Women	57	49	58	53	52	59	61	57	47	61	49	52
Difference	5	4	7	1	0	5	3	5	0	5	6	4
Age 18–29	51	47	56	53	52	56	56	55	45	57	44	49
Over age 60	57	46	54	52	52	57	64	53	49	60	8	52
Difference	6	1	2	1	0	1	8	2	4	3	4	3
Non-Catholic	54	45	53	53	52	57	59	54	48	58	47	50
Catholic	56	52	57	52	54	56	61	54	45	59	45	50
Difference	2	7	4	1	2	1	2	0	3	1	2	0

	CA	CO	CT	FL	GA	IL	MD	MI	MN	NY	OR	TX
Non-Jewish	54	47	54	52	52	56	59	54	46	57	46	50
Jewish	66	40	68	75	70	70	72	75	64	71	59	56
Difference	12	7	14	23	18	14	13	21	18	14	13	6
Non-Protestant	55	47	54	53	52	58	59	54	46	59	47	51
Protestant	53	49	57	51	53	53	62	55	47	57	46	49
Difference	2	2	3	2	1	5	3	1	1	2	1	2
Outside region A[a]	56	43	54	52	52	55	59	53	44	58	44	50
Inside region A	52	54	57	53	53	64	69	63	51	60	54	52
Difference	4	11	3	1	1	9	10	10	7	2	10	2
Outside region B[a]	54	44	52	53	52	55	59	54	46	58	46	50
Inside region B	56	54	59	50	54	61	61	57	48	62	46	53
Difference	2	10	7	3	2	6	2	3	2	4	0	3
Outside region C[a]	54	47	53	55	53	58	59	52	46	59	47	49
Inside region C	56	47	60	47	49	51	62	60	49	58	44	59
Difference	2	0	7	8	4	7	3	8	3	1	3	10
Outside region D[a]	56	—	—	53	—	58	—	54	—	59	—	47
Inside region D	49	—	—	51	—	52	—	56	—	56	—	55
Difference	7	—	—	2	—	6	—	2	—	3	—	8

Source: ICPSR, Voter News Service, *Election Day Exit Polls 2000*.

Note: Cell entries show the estimated percentage of each group voting Democratic in the 2000 presidential election and the difference in Democratic support between the groups listed in each row computed from multivariate probit models (table A2.2) with the remaining independent variables held constant at their sample means.

[a]Regions are coded as follows:

CA: A = Southern California; B = Los Angeles city; C = Bay Area; D = Central CA.

CO: A = Denver/Boulder; B = Jefferson and Arapahoe County Suburbs; C = Mountains.

CT: A = Large Cities; B = CT Valley; C = NY Suburbs.

FL: A = Miami; B = South Florida; C = North Florida; D = Tampa.

GA: A = Central; B = Atlanta; C = North.

IL: A = Chicago; B = Cook County; C = Collar; D = South.

MD: A = Baltimore city; B = Baltimore suburbs; C = Washington suburbs.

MI: A = Detroit; B = Oakland County and Detroit suburbs; C = University Belt; D = Southwest MI.

MN: A = Minneapolis; B = Metro area; C = Rural Democrats.

NY: A = Long Island; B = New York City; C = Upstate Urban; D = Rural NY.

OR: A = Portland; B = Coast; C = Southern OR.

TX: A = East TX; B = Dallas; C = Houston; D = South.

area distinct. Alternatively, this may be the place where "political culture" explanations come into play. To us, though, the superior alternative to political culture explanations is to investigate the collection of socialization experiences unique to individual locales, examining why certain places create political biases that are not explained simply by compositional characteristics.

Similarities and Differences across States

As we compare the data in tables 2.1 and 2.2 across states, we find that not all of the differences were statistically significant, but the larger ones are. Let us now take note of some of the more obvious differences across settings for some of the same population subgroups. Florida and Georgia are very similar in their political behavior, but Michigan and Florida are worlds apart. Illinois and Texas differ considerably, while California and New York share some electoral characteristics.

Hispanics in Texas and Florida were far less likely to vote for Democrats than Hispanics in Illinois, New York, or California. Why is this the case? The answer probably relates to the ancestry and nationality of the Latino population—that is, an unspecified compositional variable. Cubans are drawn to the Republican party in Florida, and so too are many of the native-born Hispanics in Texas. Illinois and New York, by contrast, have a larger Puerto Rican population, and these voters have long-standing ties to the Democratic party. In California, the Hispanic population is predominantly Mexican and more supportive of issue positions consonant with the Democratic party platform, such as college admissions quotas and spending on public assistance (Alvarez and Garcia Bedolla 2001; de la Garza et al. 1992, 90, 110). Alternatively, Hispanics in Texas may not think of themselves as a cohesive group sharing a collective sense of political grievance, whereas Latinos in California and Illinois do (Skerry 1993). From the contextual standpoint, some of these political and policy differences may be traceable to the fact that Latinos in California and Illinois are an overwhelmingly urban constituency, principally concentrated in each state's largest cities in highly segregated neighborhoods, whereas the Hispanic population in Texas is more evenly dispersed in smaller cities and rural areas where it comes into more regular contact with Anglo Texans.

In the 2000 presidential race, ideological polarization between liberals and conservatives was greater in Connecticut, Illinois, Michigan, and Minnesota than it was in Georgia, Colorado, or Texas (see table 2.2). This variability suggests that ideology does not do the same work in all states. Contextual and compositional explanations may account for these differences. Ideological polarization reflects the diversity of the populations in these states (Hero 1998). The extent of ideological extremism is caused by the mobilization of competing biases within communities. Bias is mobilized, in part, by interest groups, and interest group activity is more intense in more diverse states than in more homogeneous ones (Gray and Lowery 1996). Among the states where interest groups are the most prevalent are California and Florida.

Rival and competing interests will also be highly mobilized in states that are key political battlegrounds in presidential elections. California, Florida, and Illinois are among the most populous, and together they cast over 100 electoral votes. Campaign politics is carried out with unusual intensity in these states given their status as prizes in the presidential sweepstakes. The intensity of campaign politics contributes directly to the ideological polarization of their electorates on election day. Georgia is an important state casting 13 electoral votes, but it isn't nearly as important as these others. The presidential contenders cannot ignore it entirely, but it is usually not a major target, either.

Race and ideology differed considerably across states in the manner in which they acted to cue votes on election day, but partisanship did as well. Morris Fiorina has pointed out that partisanship changes over time, according to conditions such as international tension, the domestic economic situation, and personal unemployment, as well as in response to the candidates who are running (1981). It is equally plausible that partisanship will vary from place to place, and across groups that claim to be affiliated with each party (Clarke and Stewart 1998). In Georgia, an estimated 29 percent of Republicans voted for Democratic candidates in the 1988–96 presidential elections, compared with an estimated 41 percent in California and New York (see table 2.1). (A closer inspection reveals that it was Bill Clinton who won so many GOP votes in California, not Michael Dukakis.) These differences are too large to be written off as random errors of survey research. That so many California Republicans voted for Bill Clinton, but many fewer Georgians did, speaks to the way in which the Republican identifiers in these two states evaluated the choices before them. Partisans of the California GOP obviously saw far more in Bill Clinton than those so identifying in Georgia.

Findings like these lead inexorably to the important but often neglected question of what determines one's partisanship and whether the content of the party labels is different in one location than in another. Partisanship may be stable over time, but variable across space. Discussions of what determines partisanship have focused on affect—voters' likes and dislikes about parties and party candidates, as well as their issue positions and responses to major events (Campbell et al. 1960; Fiorina 1981; Sniderman, Brody, and Tetlock 1991). The source of many of these affective preferences is preadult socialization—what voters learn about political party positions as children at home and in school. What people like and dislike about the parties will almost certainly vary with the social context in which they are raised. Georgians may be attracted to the Republicans because they have learned to be attentive to where the parties stand on issues such as gun control, abortion, and school prayer. Californians who call themselves Republicans might do so chiefly because they have learned to be attentive to partisan positions on free trade and national defense, and to appreciate where the typical GOP candidate stands on these matters. Partisans' loyalty to their party on election day will depend on the issue positions that candidates make central to their campaigns and how those positions square with what the voters have learned to care about.

The Electoral Foundations of the Two Major Parties

We do not have the detailed polling data necessary to exhaustively evaluate these propositions about the variable meaning of party identification across settings, but previous work has shown that the constituency groups underlying each party vary in size and influence across states (Gimpel 1996; Brown 1995). These differences help us to understand how Democrats like Bill Clinton and Albert Gore might be more attractive to Republicans in California than in Georgia.

If the coalitions underlying support for a candidate vary across states, then it is probably reasonable to hypothesize that the electoral coalitions underlying the local parties also vary to a nontrivial degree. States known for being one-party Democratic strongholds are

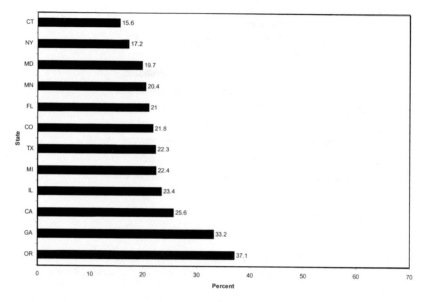

Fig. 2.2.   Proportion of Republicans identifying themselves as conservative Protestants, November 2000, by state. (Data from Voter News Service, *Election Day Exit Polls.*)

probably that way because they have larger proportions of traditional Democratic constituencies than states that are more competitive or Republican.

To highlight some compositional differences of momentous importance, we have identified the proportion of Republicans identifying themselves as ideologically conservative Protestants in each of the twelve states in the 2000 elections (see fig. 2.2). While it is surely true that the Republican party has become the political home of Christian traditionalists and the Democratic party the home of religious liberals and secularists (Layman and Carmines 1997), our evidence suggests that this generalization holds for some states far better than for others. In Georgia and Oregon, for instance, more than one-third of all self-identified Republicans also classified themselves as Protestant and conservative. In Connecticut and New York, these voters are a much smaller share of the GOP pie (fig. 2.2). A Republican candidate campaigning for nomination in Oregon will be required to appease a larger bloc of traditionalist Christian voters than the candidate in Connecticut.

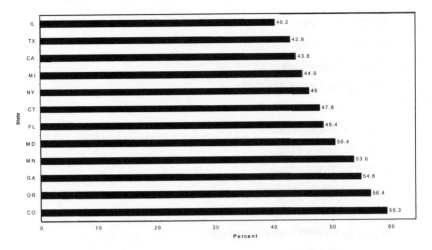

Fig. 2.3.   Proportion of Democrats in middle-income brackets (between $30,000 and $75,000), November 2000, by state. (Data from Voter News Service, *Election Day Exit Polls.*)

We also examined the size of the middle-class population identifying with the Democratic party on the supposition that Democratic politics is more likely to be informed by the economic values of middle-class voters in some states, and less so in others (see fig. 2.3). The comparisons are striking. In Colorado, 59.3 percent of self-identified Democrats were earning between $30,000 and $75,000 in 2000, compared with only 40.2 percent of Illinois Democrats (fig. 2.3). In Georgia, Oregon, and Colorado, the Democratic party is firmly anchored in the middle class. In Illinois, Texas, California, and Michigan, a much larger percentage of the Democratic electorate sits on the lower rungs of the economic ladder. These comparisons are of consequence because Democratic candidates are far more likely to support Republican-sponsored tax cuts valued by middle-income voters in the places where their base is predominantly middle class than in areas where a sizable plurality of their constituency is dependent upon social welfare assistance.

In racial terms, the parties had starkly contrasting electoral bases at the beginning of the new century. For more than forty years Republicans have not had a racially diverse electoral base in any of these states, but especially not in Minnesota where they were 97 percent white (Democrats in Minnesota are almost equally white). The

Texas Democratic party was the most racially diverse. Maryland and Georgia Democrats were close behind. In the final two decades of the twentieth century, black voters were a significant constituency within the Maryland, Texas, Illinois, and Florida Democratic parties, but were a relatively small proportion of the Democratic rank and file in Minnesota and Colorado. Hispanic voters were a significant Democratic bloc in Texas, Colorado, Florida, and California, but had almost no presence in Georgia, Maryland, Michigan, or Minnesota.

These contrasting electoral bases *within* each party clearly indicate the need for careful scrutiny of individual states as a precursor to the formation of a comprehensive campaign plan. A campaign designed to appeal to Minnesota's predominantly white Democrats would almost certainly go awry in Maryland, where 40 percent of Democratic identifiers are black. These polls are only suggestive of what more detailed studies might reveal about differences in the social, economic, religious, and ideological bases of the two major parties as one moves from state to state. In examining other differences, we found that in some states, the most wealthy voters constituted about the same proportion of the electoral base for both parties, suggesting an absence of economic biases in the local political system. According to recent polls from New York state, about one out of every seven Democrats earned more than $100,000 per year, compared with only one out of every nine Republicans. The notion that the Republicans are the party of the rich and the Democrats are not is simply wrong in some states and in some elections.

Republican and Democratic Issue Priorities:
The 2000 Election

We have suggested that parties may look very different from one state to another simply because of the size of particular constituencies—the compositional explanation carries a lot of weight. Both compositional and contextual influences play a role in defining the issues that are salient in particular locales. Republicans in California spent a great deal of time through the 1990s addressing the immigration issue. Not a word could be heard about immigration matters from the Maryland Republican party. The peculiar issue sensitivities of local party electorates place a premium on detailed studies of individual states. No candidate can afford to campaign nationwide without having some information about the receptivity of voters to alternative messages.

We sought for ways of testing just how different local issue agendas can be through use of the VNS exit polls from November 2000. These polls asked respondents about the issue that was most important for them in the presidential election. The voters surveyed were given seven choices reflecting major campaign issues that year: (1) world affairs; (2) medicare and prescription drug coverage; (3) health care more generally; (4) the economy and jobs; (5) taxes; (6) education; and (7) the social security system. Given the generality of these themes, and the truncated choice presented to respondents, we may not find as much variation as we would if the question were open-ended, but examining the variation within parties across states may still be instructive.

The tabulations are presented for each state in table 2.3. Taxes ranked highest among Republicans across all states in 1996, but was clearly not the most important theme in 2000. The theme ranked *consistently* highest across all states was "the economy and jobs," although "world affairs" was also ranked highly. Even so, these items were more of a concern among the GOP voters in some states than in others. Oregon and Texas Republicans were more concerned about education than those in the other ten states. In Maryland and New York, Republicans highlighted world affairs above all other priorities. The differences were great enough that, armed with this information, a GOP candidate would be well advised to spend more time talking about foreign policy in certain states, but not others.

Democrats clearly had different issue priorities than Republicans, judging from table 2.3, with a consistently higher percentage ranking the economy and jobs their number one issue. Predictably, for Democrats in Florida, social security ranked quite high. In Minnesota, Democrats gave the nod to education as their second priority behind the economy. Education was not as important to Democrats in Maryland (13.9 percent) and Texas (15.0 percent) as it was in Colorado (21.2 percent) and Oregon (28.7 percent).

One may be led to ask whether the differences shown in table 2.3 are sufficiently important that a presidential candidate would be led to change his message and approach as he traveled from state to state. Our answer is that although a few major issues consistently dominate the voters' minds across most states, variations in the intensity

TABLE 2.3. Issues That Mattered Most, November 2000, by State

Issue	CA	CO	CT	FL	GA	IL	MD	MI	MN	NY	OR	TX
						Republicans						
World affairs	20.4	18.5	19.2	15.9	15.8	16.0	28.6	18.5	13.7	22.5	13.3	13.8
Medicare/prescriptions	4.5	6.5	11.1	6.3	5.0	10.9	5.0	13.2	7.2	6.1	6.0	6.9
Health care	8.4	4.8	13.8	12.6	5.8	9.3	6.7	7.0	9.6	10.0	12.0	5.2
Economy and jobs	21.7	26.8	23.0	20.9	29.5	24.5	20.2	21.6	22.1	20.3	15.7	17.2
Taxes	16.2	15.5	11.5	16.3	23.0	12.5	13.4	16.0	19.3	11.3	12.0	22.4
Education	17.2	19.6	13.4	17.2	8.6	16.0	18.5	14.6	17.7	16.4	28.9	22.4
Social security	11.7	8.3	8.0	10.9	12.2	10.9	7.6	9.1	10.4	13.5	12.0	12.1
						Democrats						
World affairs	11.6	11.0	12.9	12.2	12.4	10.5	10.5	12.2	12.5	15.9	6.9	11.4
Medicare/prescriptions	8.5	5.5	10.8	12.8	12.4	11.5	11.5	7.5	9.4	10.2	14.4	14.3
Health care	10.2	12.3	13.6	8.2	8.9	14.9	14.9	10.1	13.1	10.0	8.6	8.6
Economy and jobs	25.2	31.4	27.1	28.9	33.3	28.9	28.9	36.8	24.0	26.4	23.6	17.1
Taxes	5.5	6.4	5.8	5.0	6.2	7.1	7.1	3.4	6.4	4.3	3.4	9.3
Education	18.7	21.2	16.9	16.2	14.0	13.9	13.9	16.3	20.7	20.8	28.7	15.0
Social security	20.3	12.3	12.9	16.6	12.9	13.2	13.2	13.7	14.0	12.4	14.4	24.3

Source: Voter News Service, *Election Day Exit Polls,* 2000, weighted data.

Note: Cell entries in the first section of the table reflect the percentage of all Republican respondents who mentioned this item as the issue that mattered most for them. Cell entries in the second section of the table reflect the percentage of all Democratic respondents who mentioned this item as the issue that mattered most for them.

of feeling about these issues will be hard to ignore. Florida voters will be more concerned about a candidate's position on medicare, the cost of prescription drugs, and the solvency of social security than those elsewhere. Going into Florida without a well-considered message on aging-related issues would be a mistake. If a Democratic candidate has a strong record on education, the places to discuss that record are Colorado, Minnesota, New York, and Oregon, states where Democratic voters perceived education to be an important issue.

A candidate who ignores key issues in a place where voters care greatly about them is risking the loss of those voters to an opponent. Hence, Bill Clinton and Al Gore won Republican and Independent voters in California, New York, and Florida by having a more convincing message than their opponents on social security and health care. Independent voters in Oregon and Illinois gave their votes to Gore if they were most concerned about education and the economy in 2000. It would appear that in most states, the education issue did not work to George W. Bush's advantage among those who listed it as their top concern.

Conclusions

This chapter provided a side-by-side comparison of electorates as they behaved in the 1988–96 and 2000 presidential elections. Even though there were key similarities across states, there were significant cross-state differences in the degree to which certain groups of voters supported the Democratic candidate for president. We have also emphasized that the contribution of a number of demographic groups to each party's electoral base not only differed across parties, but also across states within the same party. Because demographic groups such as blacks, Hispanics, Jews, and the poor have distinct ways of thinking about politics and view campaigns differently, the relative contribution of these groups to a party's support base guides the issue positions and policy priorities of party candidates and officeholders. We have also shown that state electorates had differing issue agendas in these presidential elections. Although national campaigns typically wind up hammering on just a few simple themes, the degree to which voters respond to these themes does vary from place to place. The message candidates get out will determine the loyalty of their own partisans, as well as the extent to which they can attract crossover voters.

Finally, we have seen that regionalism within many states, as defined in the VNS exit polls, disappears when you control for important compositional elements of the electorate: party identification, race, political ideology, religion, and other demographic variables. Notably, the voting locales where regionalism persisted are often those in or adjacent to large central cities such as Minneapolis, Detroit, Baltimore, Portland, and Denver. Although these regional effects in urban areas are small, they are potentially quite significant, adding between 5 and 8 percentage points to a presidential candidate's margin in most cases. In admitting that these regional effects may point to patterns of communication that have distinguished these areas from others sharing the same population characteristics, we open ourselves to the criticism that not all of the compositional variables have been included that could account for the apparent uniqueness of the places that stand out. Perhaps our measures of party identification and ideology, for example, are too crude in that they do not measure the multiple meanings or dimensions of the concepts they represent. We know, for example, that to be an economic liberal is not the same thing as being a social liberal. What may make large cities distinct from other areas is that they are especially high in social liberalism, but are highly similar on a scale of economic liberalism (Gimpel and Schuknecht 2000). Our simplistic measure of ideology does not distinguish these two.

It is also the case that sectionalism can either persist or disappear if the substate regions are defined differently than they were in the VNS exit polls. In the end, however, we would argue that it does no harm to the study of political geography to suggest that regional effects are often traceable to the collection of political and demographic traits of populations clustered in certain places. In this spirit, Gary King (1996) argues that the goal of political geographic research should be to make regional effects disappear—presumably by specifying the appropriate compositional variables. If anything, our findings take the mystery out of the study of electoral geography and regionalism, clearing a place for geographic research within political science and other disciplines without relying upon hazy notions such as "political culture."

Appendix   *(following page)*

TABLE A2.1. Complete Probit Results: Influences on the Democratic Presidential Vote 1988–96, by State

Variable	CA	FL	GA	IL	MI	NY	TX
Democrat	.91***	.82***	.96***	.91***	1.19***	.80***	1.08***
	(.06)	(.06)	(.08)	(.06)	(.06)	(.05)	(.05)
Republican	-.85***	-.91***	-.94***	-1.01***	-.90***	-.67***	-.86***
	(.06)	(.07)	(.09)	(.06)	(.06)	(.06)	(.06)
Ideology	-.55***	-.60***	-.46***	-.52***	-.43***	-.51***	-.47***
	(.04)	(.04)	(.05)	(.04)	(.04)	(.03)	(.03)
Income	-.04***	-.12***	-.04	-.03	-.07***	.001	-.08***
	(.02)	(.02)	(.03)	(.02)	(.02)	(.017)	(.02)
Black	.75***	1.14***	1.29***	1.04***	.66***	.80***	.97***
	(.09)	(.09)	(.10)	(.10)	(.11)	(.09)	(.08)
Hispanic	.21***	.05	.70	.75***	-.15	.40***	.40***
	(.08)	(.10)	(.43)	(.19)	(.20)	(.11)	(.08)
Women	.12***	.12***	-.001	.07	.12**	.14***	.12***
	(.04)	(.05)	(.069)	(.05)	(.05)	(.05)	(.05)
Age	.02	.12***	.04	.02	.03	.08***	.04
	(.02)	(.03)	(.04)	(.03)	(.03)	(.02)	(.03)
Catholic	-.10*	-.12*	-.18	-.03	-.09	-.26***	.01
	(.06)	(.07)	(.12)	(.05)	(.07)	(.07)	(.07)
Jews	.39***	.71***	.56***	.61***	.57**	.23***	.28
	(.12)	(.12)	(.24)	(.14)	(.24)	(.09)	(.18)
Protestants	-.22***	-.16**	-.07	-.02	.03	-.23***	-.17***
	(.06)	(.07)	(.08)	(.07)	(.07)	(.07)	(.06)
Region A[a]	-.17**	-.17**	.10	.04	.62***	.16**	.06
	(.07)	(.08)	(.11)	(.08)	(.13)	(.08)	(.08)

Region B[a]	.06	.02	.20**	-.05	.30***	.23***	.04
	(.09)	(.07)	(.10)	(.07)	(.08)	(.09)	(.08)
Region C[a]	.22**	-.07	.12	.03	.23***	-.01	.25***
	(.08)	(.08)	(.10)	(.08)	(.08)	(.08)	(.09)
Region D[a]	-.09	.03	—	—	.27***	-.10	.08
	(.07)	(.09)			(.09)	(.10)	(.07)
1992	-.39***	-.10	.02	-.06	-.25***	-.05	-.28***
	(.06)	(.06)	(.15)	(.06)	(.06)	(.06)	(.06)
1996	.01	.28***	.13	.05	.08	.11	.11**
	(.05)	(.06)	(.15)	(.06)	(.06)	(.07)	(.06)
Constant	1.17	.81	.36	.89	.41	.59	.53
N	5,129	4,238	2,359	4,168	3,970	4,402	5,061
% correct	83	82	83	81	82	79	83
Null model	60	52	55	53	50	55	54
llX^2	2,938.9	2,546.3	1,484.3	2,268.3	2,303.5	1,958.1	3,119.6
df	16	16	16	16	16	16	16
Significance	$p \leq .0001$	$p \leq .0001$	$p \leq .0001$	$p \leq .0001$	$p \leq .0001$	$p \leq .0001$	$p \leq .0001$

Note: Multivariate probit regression; maximum likelihood estimation; regression coefficients with standard errors in parentheses. Dependent variable: 0 = vote for non-Democrat; 1 = vote for Democrat.

[a]Regions are coded as follows:

CA: A = Southern California; B = Los Angeles city; C = Bay Area; D = Central CA.

FL: A = Miami; B = South Florida; C = North Florida; D = Tampa.

GA: A = Central; B = Atlanta; C = North.

IL: A = Chicago; B = Chicago Suburbs; C = South.

MI: A = Detroit; B = Oakland County and Detroit Suburbs; C = University Belt; D = Southwest MI.

NY: A = Long Island; B = NY City; C = Upstate Urban; D = Rural NY.

TX: A = East TX; B = Dallas; C = Houston; D = South.

*p < .05; **p < .01; p < .001.

TABLE A2.2. Complete Probit Results: Influences on the Democratic Presidential Vote, November 2000, by State

Variable	CA	CO	CT	FL	GA	IL	MD	MI	MN	NY	OR	TX
Democrat	1.16**	1.09**	.77**	.95**	.98**	1.09**	1.09**	.96**	.84**	.97**	1.06**	1.02**
	(.09)	(.14)	(.12)	(.11)	(.14)	(.12)	(.16)	(.11)	(.11)	(.09)	(.17)	(.18)
Republican	-.92**	-1.39**	-1.07**	-1.11**	-1.17**	-1.04**	-.97**	-1.03**	-1.44**	-.73**	-1.06**	-1.22**
	(.09)	(.18)	(.13)	(.12)	(.16)	(.14)	(.20)	(.11)	(.15)	(.10)	(.19)	(.28)
Ideology	-.44**	-.31**	-.57**	-.45**	-.57**	-.52**	-.62**	-.56**	-.55**	-.41**	-.43**	-.47**
	(.06)	(.09)	(.08)	(.07)	(.09)	(.08)	(.11)	(.07)	(.08)	(.06)	(.11)	(.12)
Income	-.02	.05	-.06	-.06	.00	.09*	.03	.04	.02	.04	.05	-.12*
	(.02)	(.04)	(.04)	(.03)	(.05)	(.04)	(.05)	(.03)	(.04)	(.03)	(.05)	(.06)
Black	.62**	.55	.78**	1.26**	1.28**	.85**	1.26**	.65**	.48	.72**	.90	1.93**
	(.16)	(.38)	(.26)	(.17)	(.15)	(.21)	(.21)	(.18)	(.34)	(.16)	(.67)	(.29)
Hispanic	.28**	.23	.38	-.11	-.10	.22	.41	-.07	-.06	.41**	-.61	-.56*
	(.10)	(.17)	(.36)	(.16)	(.52)	(.24)	(.42)	(.27)	(.56)	(.16)	(.55)	(.23)
Women	.23**	.19	.25*	.06	.03	.26**	.18	.20*	.01	.18*	.28*	.21
	(.07)	(.12)	(.10)	(.09)	(.12)	(.10)	(.14)	(.09)	(.10)	(.08)	(.15)	(.17)
Age	.10**	-.01	-.02	-.02	-.02	.01	.16*	-.04	.05	.04	.07	.08
	(.04)	(.07)	(.04)	(.05)	(.07)	(.05)	(.08)	(.05)	(.06)	(.04)	(.08)	(.10)
Catholic	.11	.31**	.15	-.01	.12	-.01	.11	.12	-.13	.04	-.07	-.01
	(.09)	(.15)	(.14)	(.12)	(.20)	(.13)	(.18)	(.13)	(.13)	(.10)	(.23)	(.24)
Jew	.59**	-.34	.56*	1.19**	1.11*	.68*	.74*	1.02**	.81	.57**	.59	.38
	(.18)	(.42)	(.26)	(.30)	(.58)	(.28)	(.33)	(.35)	(.50)	(.15)	(.71)	(1.30)
Protestant	-.09	.12	.12	-.09	.05	-.24	.20	.08	.03	-.08	-.02	-.08
	(.10)	(.15)	(.15)	(.12)	(.14)	(.14)	(.19)	(.12)	(.13)	(.11)	(.17)	(.22)
Region A[a]	-.18*	.50**	.14	.02	.08	.42*	.58	.47**	.30*	.06	.42*	.16
	(.11)	(.17)	(.16)	(.14)	(.17)	(.20)	(.30)	(.17)	(.14)	(.13)	(.20)	(.31)

	MD	MI	MN	NY	OR	TX	CA	CO	CT	FL	GA	IL
Region B[a]	.10	.45**	.26	-.16	.11	.26	.08	.13	.10	.18	-.03	.24
	(.16)	(.17)	(.14)	(.16)	(.16)	(.15)	(.21)	(.15)	(.16)	(.13)	(.20)	(.32)
Region C[a]	.13	.12	.27	-.39**	-.22	-.33*	.17	.37**	.15	-.04	-.12	.70*
	(.12)	(.20)	(.16)	(.14)	(.16)	(.16)	(.23)	(.14)	(.16)	(.12)	(.20)	(.32)
Region D[a]	-.34**			-.12		-.28		.10		-.12		.56*
	(.12)			(.16)		(.16)		(.14)		(.12)		(.27)
Constant	.27	-.42	.86	1.11	.76	-.16	-.18	.53	.68	.15	1.11	.90
N	2,098	737	880	1,332	980	1,077	691	1,263	961	1,666	482	582
% correct	83	81	79	84	86	83	87	82	80	80	83	89
Null model	62	56	58	60	75	59	62	61	53	63	66	54
llX²	1,287.6	439.8	413.1	885.11	770.8	669.3	499.1	750.5	531.1	804.8	278.8	501.0
df	16	15	15	16	15	16	15	16	15	16	15	16
Significance	$p \leq .0001$	$p \leq .0001$	$p \leq .0001$	$p \leq .0001$	$p \leq .0001$	$p \leq .0001$	$p \leq .0001$	$p \leq .0001$	$p \leq .0001$	$p \leq .0001$	$p \leq .0001$	$p \leq .0001$

Note: Multivariate probit regression; maximum likelihood estimation; regression coefficients with standard errors in parentheses. Dependent variable: 0 = vote for non-Democrat; 1 = vote for Democrat.

[a] Regions are coded as follows:

MD: A = Baltimore City; B = Baltimore Suburbs; C = Washington Suburbs.

MI: A = Detroit; B = Oakland County and Detroit Suburbs; C = University Belt; D = Southwest MI.

MN: A = Minneapolis; B = Metro Area; C = Rural Area.

NY: A = Long Island; B = New York City; C = Upstate Urban; D = Rural NY.

OR: A = Portland; B = Coast; C = Southern OR.

TX: A = East TX; B = Dallas; C = Houston; D = South.

CA: A = Southern California; B = Los Angeles city; C = Bay Area; D = Central CA.

CO: A = Denver/Boulder; B = Denver Suburbs; C = Mountains.

CT: A = Large Cities; B = CT Valley; C = NY Suburbs.

FL: A = Miami; B = South Florida; C = North Florida; D = Tampa.

GA: A = Central; B = Atlanta; C = North.

IL: A = Chicago; B = Cook County; C = Collar; D = South.

*p < .05; **p < .01.

CHAPTER 3

CALIFORNIA

Major Forces for Electoral Change in California
- Immigration from Asia and Latin America
- Domestic (Internal) Migration from Other States
- Suburbanization of the Population
- Mobilization of Blacks, Latinos, and New Immigrants
- The Rise of High-Tech Professionals

California's identity is tied closely to its coastline and warm climate. Non-Californians most commonly associate it with beaches, citrus, and sunshine—reflections of how the state was marketed to the nation by corporations and institutions promoting growth in the nineteenth century (Spooner 1997). Those willing to go beyond such simple impressions also link the Golden State with social experimentation, a relaxed, casual attitude toward life, New Age religion, Silicon Valley, and the entertainment industry that defines so much of American popular culture. The politically astute will be aware of California's regular and highly divisive initiatives and referenda, and may also be aware of the state's reputation for political extremism—the opposing ideologies had sectional foundations for most of the twentieth century—left-wing radical politics in the Bay Area, right-wing conservative politics in southern California (Wolfinger and Greenstein 1967).

No other state has as many travel and tour guides written about it—testimony to the widespread interest in going there. From its very beginnings prior to statehood in 1850, California's social geography has been shaped and reshaped by vast waves of migration. Settlement patterns for the state's earliest arriving Anglo migrants were dictated by where they thought they could strike gold: the mountains and valleys of northern and central California (Baldassare 2000, chap. 5). Sacramento and San Francisco were large cities when Los Angeles was little more than a tiny port. Subsequent mass migrations in the 1930s and 1940s brought entirely new population groups into the state, mainly from the politically conservative plains and Southern states, permanently altering the politics of the Central Valley. For these migrants, the lure was not gold, but the state's excellent agricultural climate that promised a better future than the arid southern plains (Gregory 1989; Morgan 1992).

In the closing decades of the twentieth century, the economic lure of California waned in importance as a motive for relocation. From 1960 onward, the state's culture was increasingly transformed by a new kind of migrant—the life-style migrant who sought anonymity. California was seen as a place to free oneself of restrictive moral codes (Spooner 1997). These new residents fled from small towns in the Midwest where they were not free to express their individuality. The values expressed by these newcomers had a libertarian tinge that added texture to the state's freewheeling politics. In the 1980s and 1990s, hippies, homosexuals, and high-tech entrepreneurs forged a distinct ideology of technology and freedom found nowhere else (Barbrook and Cameron 1996). Most of California's "knowledge class" are well-educated professionals who constitute an oppositional intelligentsia with social values different from those of the traditional business class (Brint 1985, 392).

The migration of natives to California slowed in the early 1990s with the vast majority of new residents arriving from other countries. As the new century begins, immigration is the major force behind social change, with most of the newcomers arriving from Latin American and Asian nations (Baldassare 2000; Culver 1991; Gimpel 1999). The influx of immigrants in the 1980s and 1990s depressed wages in low-skill economic sectors, making it difficult to make ends meet in places where modest two-bedroom homes cost $300,000 (Frey 1995). The unbearable economic competition for employment drove out some natives in lower-skill, blue-collar occupations. Demographers also observed that upper-income residents were leaving because the places that once attracted them had been despoiled by growth. Population mobility promises to be a major source of political change in California for decades into the new century as the Anglo population is expected to be a minority by 2020.

The effects of population mobility have not been uniform across the state. The Asian population has concentrated most heavily in the counties surrounding the San Francisco Bay: San Francisco, Marin, Alameda, Contra Costa, San Mateo, Santa Clara. San Jose marks the location of Silicon Valley—if not the birthplace of the microcomputer industry, certainly the nursery that promoted its development. In 1960, San Jose was simply another fast-growing medium-sized California city. No one would have predicted that it would become the state's third largest city by the mid-1990s, behind Los Angeles and San Diego.

The growth in the high-tech sector was fueled by Stanford University's decision to lease university property to businesses that would be beneficial to the university. The dean of Stanford's engineering school, Frederick Terman, persuaded the university to lease only to high-tech companies, and in 1953 the first company (Varian Associates, a leading supplier of scientific instruments) moved into the Stanford Industrial Park. Varian was soon followed by Eastman Kodak, General Electric, Admiral Corporation, Shockley Transistor Laboratory of Beckman Instruments, Lockheed, Hewlett-Packard, and others (Tajnai 1995). Although Stanford is located north of San Jose in San Mateo County, growth quickly spilled out of Palo Alto into neighboring areas. The first personal computer was produced by Apple Computers in 1976. Spread of their use fueled growth in the demand for workers to produce them. By the mid-1980s most of the Silicon Valley labor force lived in San Jose, particularly workers in lower-skill assembly jobs (Rogers and Larsen 1984). This population was highly diverse by the dawn of the new century: less than 50 percent of the city's population was Anglo, and over half were of Asian or Latino ancestry.

Los Angeles is the most populous city in the state and has long been considered the hub of southern California. About 40 percent of county residents lived in Los Angeles proper by 2000, a fraction that had not changed since 1960. With one million more residents moving in between 1960 and 1995, Los Angeles hardly followed the example of abandonment set by Detroit, Cleveland, and Chicago. Through most of its history, Los Angeles has been a majority white city, remarkable for being governed by a black mayor, Tom Bradley, from 1973 to 1993. To be sure, the white population in the city did shrink to less than half of the total by the mid-1980s, but those who left were quickly replaced by a rapid flow of Asian and Latin American (mainly Mexican) immigrants. The increasing diversity of Los Angeles has elevated the potential for racial divisiveness such that economic hardship can quickly result in racial recriminations and hostility toward the foreign-born. The Los Angeles riots of April 1992, triggered by a controversial jury verdict exonerating police officers who had severely beaten black motorist Rodney King, resulted in over 16,000 arrests, 52 fatalities, and nearly a billion dollars in property damage (Kaufmann 1998; Sears 1994). Ironically, just as the white population has declined, Los Angeles elected a white mayor, Richard Riordan, in 1993, largely on his pledges to bring crime under control. Riordan's two-term mayoralty was followed by the 2001 election of a white liberal Democrat, James K. Hahn.

Suburban Los Angeles extends eastward toward San Bernardino and Riverside Counties and northward into Ventura County (see map 3.1). Ventura County includes the suburbs of Simi Valley and Oxnard—places heavily populated by former residents of the city of Los Angeles and their children. They have escaped the big city. They have fought for growth controls because they are upset by the over-crowding, heavy traffic, and racial diversity they have come to associate with blight, welfare, and crime. The Los Angeles of their youth—a predominantly white, middle-class, Ozzie-and-Harriet world—was different than it is today. When they look toward the city, they see a place they no longer want to go, even for a brief visit. Much of the hostility to immigration comes from this region (Baldassare 2000).

The Los Angeles County suburbs to the east have had more difficulty resisting diversity because they are situated adjacent to the city's lowest-income neighborhoods. The Asian and Hispanic populations have been migrating out of Los Angeles along the I-10 corridor toward San Bernardino. The suburbs closest to Los Angeles are home to various proportions of black, Asian, and Latino residents, with few whites. As far out as Pomona, on the border with San Bernardino County, half of the population is Latino. White residents have greeted the growth and diversity pressures with a variety of measures designed to limit residential and commercial construction. These measures have driven up the cost of housing, putting home ownership out of the reach of most people in lower-income brackets, segregating them into areas where rental housing can be found.

San Diego, well known as a navy town, was home to 1.2 million people by 2000, ranking it sixth in the nation. Locations throughout San Diego County served as staging areas for the Pacific theater of World War II, and the navy has maintained a considerable presence since then, establishing its major marine corps training center there.

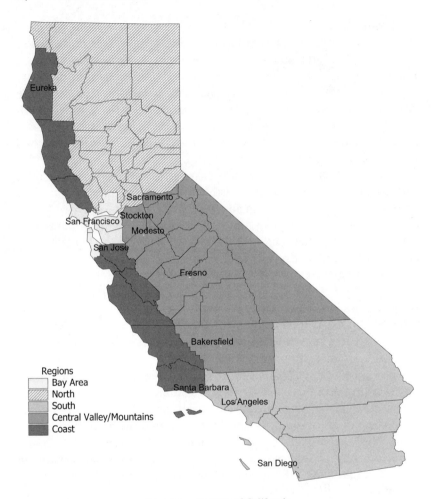

Map 3.1.   Regions of California

Following the war, the city's growth was fueled by returning troops who chose to settle there following discharge or retirement. Beginning in the 1970s, San Diego began to develop a high-tech industrial base rooted in biomedical technology, telecommunications, and software. As large cities go, San Diego is affluent, and in spite of its position on the nation's southern border with Mexico, it was home to a rather small proportion of Hispanics—only 25 percent in 2000. Illegal immigration is highly visible to the residents of San Diego, but most illegal immigrants crossing in the 1980s and 1990s were destined for Los Angeles and other parts of California. Even so, county residents have been described as exceedingly hostile to illegal immigration and give strong support to candidates who pledge to tighten border enforcement.

Orange County, like many other affluent suburban counties, is the product of freeways. Once covered with citrus and dairy farms, the major highways constructed following World War II contributed to the rapid development of the county. As in San Diego, soldiers who had trained at one of several military bases in the Los Angeles area decided to settle down following the war. The farms are now gone, and the county has a diverse economy that includes banking and financial services, oil production, and aerospace defense including Hughes Aircraft, Rockwell, and Northrop. With military downsizing at the end of the cold war, a large share of these defense jobs disappeared resulting in a severe recession in the early 1990s.

Having reached the limits of its growth in the early 1980s, Orange County began to show signs of economic and social stratification as residents closer to Los Angeles abandoned older neighborhoods to move to Riverside County further east. A major force driving social and political change is the growing Latino and Asian population that has transformed these neighborhoods. Anaheim and Santa Ana are the county's largest cities and the most ethnically diverse. Santa Ana tripled in size between 1950 and 1990, and both cities experienced a surge in their Hispanic populations after 1970. At the start of the twenty-first century, one out of three residents in the eastern part of the county is Latino, a demographic trend that is recasting southern California's conservative politics (Kling, Olin, and Poster 1991).

California's San Joaquin Valley extends from Kern County's oil fields in the south to the city of Stockton in the north (see map 3.1). Rich soil is deposited on the Valley's east side by rivers flowing down from the Sierra Nevada. Wheat was a staple crop until settlers learned that the water table was close to the surface and it would take little effort to dig wells and irrigate crops. With irrigation, farmers could make an excellent living on a small acreage, and for an agricultural region, the Valley has come to support a surprisingly large population. At the close of the century, agriculture remains the major economic activity, including spin-off operations in food processing, packaging, and distribution.

This area was socially and politically transformed by the great southwestern migration of the 1930s and 1940s (Morgan 1992; Gregory 1989). Between 1930 and 1960, Kern County's population grew from 83,000 to 290,000, mostly from migration. As late as 1990, the bulk of the cross-state migrants to Fresno and Bakersfield were from Southern states. The impact of this migration was to create a strong Southern subculture in central California that was rooted in fundamentalist Protestantism, racial segregation, and a culture of toughness (Gregory 1989, chap. 5). For several generations, this subculture would present a challenge to the liberal sentiments of Californians in other parts of the state. Reliance on an immigrant workforce comprised mainly of Mexican migrants has contributed to ethnic diversity. By early in the new century, Hispanics comprised 40 percent of Fresno County's population, 35 percent of Kern's, and 28 percent in San Joaquin's.

Northern California includes the city of Sacramento and the rural counties above it between the Pacific coast and the Nevada border (see map 3.1). Aside from Sacramento, a city that recorded just over 400,000 residents by 2000, this area remains the most sparsely populated part of the state, and a region to which residents from the more urban areas still flee to escape the rat race. With affordable housing prices, the rural north is one of the few remaining places in California one can retire on a fixed income. The counties between Sacramento and San Francisco are known as the heartland for California wine production. The counties further north are heavily forested. Aside from local school systems, retail trade and services related to tourism and recreation were the dominant employment sectors in the closing decades of the century, replacing the forest products industry that once offered high wages (Cross 2000). With few prospects for large-scale economic development, northern California has not attracted the waves of migration that can be found further south or along the coast. One could find many "amenity migrants"—tourists who have bought second homes or decided to retire part of the year in the foothills of the Sierra Nevada (Cross 2000). The 2000 Census revealed that 90 percent of Nevada County's new residents had come from other counties in California. Even so, California's ethnic diversity had still not touched this part of the state as the twentieth century wound down.

Lacking any familiarity with the state's history, one might think that California's political regionalism is fixed: Democratic and liberal in the Bay Area and along the Pacific coast, conservative in the San Joaquin Valley and the rural north, Republican in the south (Wolfinger and Greenstein 1967; Gimpel and Schuknecht 2002). In fact, these political tendencies are undergoing rapid change. The influx of immigrants into southern California has changed Orange County from a single-party Republican stronghold to one where the parties are highly competitive. The Bay Area, including Oakland and San Jose, was still the most Democratic part of the state by 2000, but it was once Republican, and the San Jose area could tip that way again depending on the direction its libertarian politics takes. Throughout the second half of the twentieth century, the Central Valley was the most ideologically conservative part of the state, and it is likely to stay that way. Both Democrats and Republicans could still win elections in this agricultural region, but the Democrats have to sound like Republicans. The most politically reliable part of the state between 1970 and 2000 was rural northern California, from Sacramento to the Oregon border. The relative political stability of this region is due to the smaller number of people that have moved to these counties. Here, partisan change has been driven by the slow process of generational replacement.

For the first half of the twentieth century, California was a one-party Republican state, with progressive sympathies. By *progressive* we mean that Californians were sympathetic to the appeals of the progressive reformers who favored measures to weaken the influence of political machines and powerful corporations in state and local politics. These measures included nonpartisan elections, reforms to professionalize the civil service system and eliminate political patronage, and direct primaries to democratize the party nomination process. California progressives went further than in most other states with party-weakening reforms. One peculiar institution, cross-filing, allowed candidates to run for both party nominations at the same time. This allowed some candidates, usually incumbents, to capture both party nominations so that they faced no opposition in the general election. Cross-filing heavily advantaged the majority Republicans at the expense of the underdog Democrats. In a number of statewide races, Republican candidates won both party endorsements and went on to win in November without general election competition. In fact, between 1900 and 1950, Democrats won only a single gubernatorial election, in 1938.

The 1932 and 1936 landslide elections of Franklin Roosevelt did have the impact of helping California's Democrats, but the impact was not uniform across the state's counties. Examining the political sectionalism of the state during this period in map 3.2, we see some striking patterns that are different from those visible just a few decades later. In this map, we have averaged the 1928, 1932, and 1936 presidential votes to display one measure of the state's prevailing regionalism. The lightly shaded counties are those in the lowest quartile in terms of Democratic strength—these are the strong Republican counties. Among them are most of the then sparsely populated southernmost counties such as Orange, San Diego, and Riverside, as well as several in the San Francisco Bay area, including Alameda, Santa Clara, and Santa Cruz. The Republican leaning of Alameda County (Oakland, Berkeley, Hayward) is particularly striking given its overwhelming Democratic loyalty by the 1980s and 1990s. The darkly shaded counties include several in the Central Valley, including Madera and Fresno. In the short term, these counties became even more Democratic with the influx of migrants from Texas, Arkansas, and Oklahoma throughout the 1930s and 1940s. In the long term, these counties would become thick Republican turf, particularly in statewide elections.

Support for Democratic presidential candidates dropped in the 1950s with the Republican nominations of Eisenhower and Nixon, but some new bastions of Democratic strength emerged following the New Deal realignment. These included Oakland and vicinity (Alameda County), which had been one of the least Democratic counties in the 1928–36 period. San Jose had resisted the New Deal tide, but its support for the GOP was weakening as its population grew more diverse. Los Angeles County remained politically competitive, and Eisenhower and Nixon did not rack up the big victory margins there that they did elsewhere. With the steady influx of Southerners, Democrats enlarged upon their majorities in Fresno, Madera, Merced, Stanislaus, and other counties in the San Joaquin Valley. California easily went to Lyndon Johnson in 1964, but the conservative appeal of Barry Goldwater weakened the Democratic loyalty of the agricultural counties where Southern transplants now outnumbered California natives. Orange County and San Diego remained reliable GOP turf through the turbulent 1960s, although San Diego chose Johnson over Goldwater in 1964.

By the final decade of the twentieth century, California's electoral

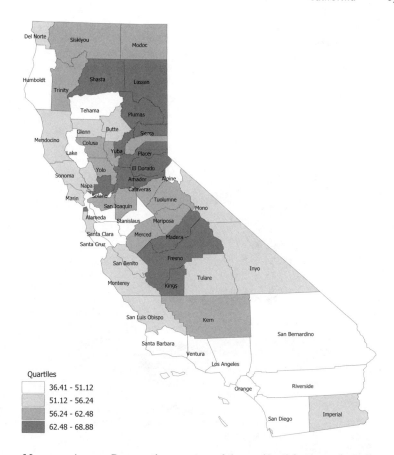

Quartiles

	36.41 - 51.12
	51.12 - 56.24
	56.24 - 62.48
	62.48 - 68.88

Map 3.2.   Average Democratic percentage of the presidential vote, 1928–1936

geography looked entirely different from that of the 1950s and 1960s. The average Democratic share of the county vote for the presidential elections of 1988, 1992, 1996, and 2000, grouped by quartile, is displayed on map 3.3. The coastal counties running from Monterey to Del Norte are remarkable for their propensity to support Democratic presidential candidates. The San Francisco Bay area counties have turned overwhelmingly against the Republicans by this time, as has Los Angeles County. Suburban flight from Los Angeles pushed Ventura County toward the GOP, and ideologically conservative Kern County turned predictably Republican after 1970. Several of the rural northern counties (Shasta, Placer, Lassen, Yuba, El Dorado) totally realigned in the last half of the century, going from the highest

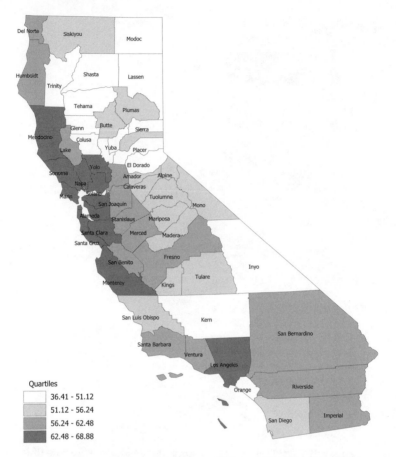

Map 3.3.   Average Democratic percentage of the presidential vote, 1988–2000

Democratic quartile in the 1930s to the highest Republican quartile by the late 1990s. In fact, very few of the Golden State's counties exhibit the same voting tendencies in both maps. Given the magnitude of population change in the state, we could hardly expect otherwise.

Where Are the Votes in California? Republican and Democratic Mobilization Targets

California is the most populous state in the nation, but as in other states, the population is not evenly distributed throughout the state's fifty-eight counties. Geographers have long known that one should not read simple choropleth maps such as maps 3.2 and 3.3 as if all counties were of equal importance. Yet these tend to be the dominant types of maps presented in press coverage and analysis. Given that election victories depend upon winning majorities in voter-rich areas, though, it follows that parties and candidates must direct their resources accordingly. Some counties are sufficiently large that neither party can afford to ignore them. Other counties are important for one party but not for the other. Some counties may cast such trivial vote shares that neither party should bother to expend much effort there. When mapping electoral behavior, we should keep population distribution clearly in mind so as to not be misled about the true nodes of partisan concentration.

To pinpoint the areas of Republican and Democratic strength, we recorded the average Democratic (or Republican) vote in each county and assigned a weight to that value by multiplying it by the proportion that each county contributed to the total Democratic (or Republican) vote in the 1988–2000 presidential elections. For example, if a given county awarded an average of 45 percent of its vote to the Democratic candidate, and it constituted about 3 percent of the Democratic party's total base of support, the index would be calculated as $.45 \times .03 = .0135$. Calculating this figure for each county, and for Republicans as well, gives us a set of values we can then rank from highest to lowest (see table 3.1). Evaluating the counties in this manner avoids attributing too much influence to areas of sparse population.

TABLE 3.1.   California's Top Ten Strongest Counties for Republicans and Democrats in the 1988–2000 Presidential Contests

Rank	Democratic	Republican
1	Los Angeles (Los Angeles)	Los Angeles (Los Angeles)
2	Alameda (Oakland)	Orange (Anaheim)
3	San Francisco (San Francisco)	San Diego (San Diego)
4	Santa Clara (San Jose)	San Bernardino (San Bernardino)
5	San Diego (San Diego)	Riverside (Riverside)
6	Orange (Anaheim)	Sacramento (Sacramento)
7	Contra Costa (Walnut Creek)	Santa Clara (San Jose)
8	Sacramento (Sacramento)	Ventura (Oxnard)
9	San Mateo (San Mateo)	Contra Costa (Walnut Creek)
10	San Bernardino (San Bernardino)	Kern (Bakersfield)
% of total vote	72.3	70.2

The rankings for the parties show that one county stands out above all others in importance: Los Angeles. While the parties draw on separate parts of this county and it is internally balkanized by race and class, the county contributed about 28 percent of the statewide Democratic vote and 22 percent of the statewide GOP vote in the four presidential elections between 1988 and 2000. Below these counties in rank are several others that are of importance to both parties, including San Diego, Orange, Contra Costa, Santa Clara, and Sacramento (table 3.1). Notably, though, the importance of these counties differs. Orange County, for example, ranks sixth for Democrats, casting 6 percent of Democratic votes, but second for Republicans, casting 12 percent of all GOP votes. Santa Clara, which encompasses the city of San Jose, ranks fourth for Democrats, but seventh in importance for Republicans.

Alameda (Oakland) and San Francisco are crucial for Democrats, but not nearly as important for Republican campaign efforts (see map 3.4). Conversely, Republicans draw strength from the suburban counties in southern California, especially San Bernardino, Riverside, and Ventura—these GOP strongholds are much less important mobilization targets for the Democrats. We learn from this that both Republicans and Democrats must compete to win in the state's most urbanized counties, but that each party also has separate suburban strongholds. For Democrats, the Bay Area suburbs are critical. For Republicans, it is the southern California suburbs that are an important foundation stone for victory.

The tendency for Republicans and Democrats to be pulled toward separate geographical bases, rather than gravitating toward the same turf, is a post–New Deal phenomenon that has come with growth, suburbanization, and migration-driven partisan change. In the 1930s, both parties found Los Angeles, Alameda, and San Francisco at the top of their lists as the key mobilization targets. Democrats also counted among their critical turf several counties in the Central Valley, including Fresno, Kern, and San Joaquin. By early in the new century, however, Alameda had dropped from second to twelfth on the GOP target list, and San Francisco had dropped precipitously from third to twenty-sixth! The Central Valley cities that had once been the locus of Democratic registration growth had become much more valuable to Republicans than to Democrats.

We have found in many states that the Republican vote is more

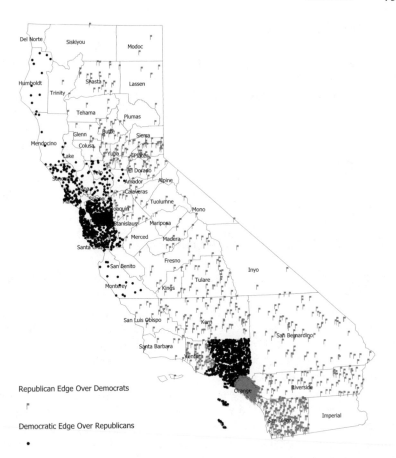

Map 3.4.   Areas of Republican and Democratic dominance, 1988–2000

widely dispersed than that of the Democrats. To mobilize their base, Republicans must go to more places and do more sifting to get out the vote. Democrats have an advantage because their vote is more concentrated and therefore less costly to activate. This may explain why in many locations Republicans tend to raise and spend more money than Democrats, but do not consistently win more elections. Republican votes may well cost more due in part to their geographic dispersion.

In California, we found that the parties were more evenly matched territorially than in other states. The Republican support concentrated in Orange, Riverside, San Bernardino, and San Diego Counties counterbalanced the locus of Democratic support in Los Angeles, San Francisco, and Alameda Counties (map 3.4). In the end, the ten most populous counties cast 72.3 percent of the total statewide vote for Democrats and 70.2 percent for Republicans. There isn't much of a difference in the rural areas either—in the thirty-eight most rural counties the GOP found 12.2 percent of its base, compared with 10.8 percent for the Democrats. Candidates of both parties know to focus their attention on the urban and suburban locales, but given that almost even proportions of the vote come from the most rural counties, Democrats are forced to consider out-of-the-way areas that they can often ignore in other states.

California's Changing Electoral Foundations

We have suggested that electoral change is the product of several forces: population mobility, the mobilization of new voters, the conversion of existing voters, and generational replacement of the elderly by the young (chap. 1). We cannot convert this suggestion into an argument, though, without some evidence showing that key components of California's population did change politically over the course of several decades.

To make our case, polling data would be the best source of information. We could then show how political trends among the state's major population groups changed with time. We could examine the voting tendencies of the elderly population relative to the nonelderly to see how generational replacement was changing the state's electorate. We could examine the voting tendencies of the migrant and native California population to determine what political impact newcomers were having. Our major obstacle is that polling data are largely absent prior to the 1980s. A second-best source would be to go to data collected at some aggregate level for certain jurisdictions in the state, such as precincts or census tracts. But finding precinct returns that are matched to social and economic characteristics is not easy even for local areas, much less the entire state. Census tracts have the social and economic information, but not the political data. County-level data have the advantage of both, though, and are available back to the last century. Counties are gross levels of aggregation in California, but for historical purposes they are about the best thing going.

Aggregate data, whether at the precinct, tract, or county level, are highly imperfect sources of information about the habits and inclinations of voters. This is because statistics based on counties, cities, or some similar jurisdiction represent an aggregation of individuals that may contain considerable internal diversity not captured by particular statistics. Take two California counties. One county is home to a population that is 19 percent black and voted 65 percent Republican in the most recent election. Another county is home to a population that is only 3 percent black but voted only 48 percent Republican. We cannot conclude from this information, or from similar additional observations we subsequently add to our investigation, that blacks are responsible for Republican voting. Indeed, blacks may not be turning out to vote in the counties where they are a larger presence. And if this is true, inferences based on the county-level data can be highly misleading (King 1997; Achen and Shively 1995; Goodman 1953; Robinson 1950). When researchers naively draw conclusions about individuals from aggregate-level statistics, they commit the *ecological fallacy*. The observations at the county level based on aggregations of everyone in the county really tell us nothing certain about the tendencies of specific groups of voters. This tendency for aggregate-level data to obscure individual-level tendencies is called the *ecological inference problem*. The desire to extract information about individuals from observations of aggregate units is the challenge of making accurate ecological inferences.

In spite of the challenges inherent in making ecological inferences from county-level observations, sometimes this is the best we can do. Since state-level polling data are unavailable for many of the years that interest us most, we must look for information about electorates and electoral change where we can find it. To improve upon the accuracy of our inferences about individual behavior from these aggregate units, we have utilized Gary King's (1997) ecological inference technique to estimate the Democratic leaning of each of several groups of voters from 1930 to the 2000 election. Our estimates are based on county-level data describing the Democratic percentage of the presidential vote combined with census data on the percentage of the county comprised of the electoral groups that are of most interest. Since the census data are not highly detailed at the county level for the 1930s, 1940s, and 1950s, we have less information on which to draw for these elections than for later ones. For elections after 1982, we are also in the advantageous position of being able to check some of the ecological inference estimates with available surveys.

To economize on the sheer amount of information available in the electoral data we collected, we have found it convenient to bloc or pool the information by groups of elections. For example, in the results presented in table 3.2, in the following subsection, we have estimated the proportion of each of several electoral groups that voted Democratic in the 1928 and 1932 presidential elections combined. We next estimate the proportion voting Democratic in the 1936, 1940, and 1944 elections combined. Then we estimated the proportion voting Democratic for the 1948 and 1952 presidential elections, and so on through the 2000 election. It is useful to think of the results, then, as an average Democratic vote across two or more elections. This scheme of combining several adjacent elections for purposes of analysis has the additional advantage of neutralizing or reducing the influence of election-specific factors on a particular group's vote for president. Since we use the same scheme of combining elections in each of our chapters, it is also possible to compare the results across states, as well as over time within a single state. Some of our estimates in these tables are more reliable than others (those marked with an asterisk indicate estimates that are generally more precise). Consistent with the ecological inference model, we present estimates for both the percentage of each group that vote Democratic, as well as the percentage of those not in the group that vote Democratic. Complete results are presented in the appendixes B and C.

Population Mobility

Population growth and mobility account for a significant portion of the state's political change, as we have seen in the analysis of substate sectionalism. Massive waves of new voters streamed into California from 1930 onward, remaking the electorate in many counties. Migration internal to the state resulted in suburbanization of formerly big-city populations in places like Orange and Ventura Counties. In more recent times, Placer County's once agricultural character has been transformed by a flood of residents leaving Sacramento and the bigger coastal cities. Riverside County was once empty and deserted, but now numbers among the most highly populated places in the state (see table 3.1). Growth from out-of-state also contributed to the growth of suburbs as wealthier white in-migrants chose to settle in pricey new developments in outlying towns, while lower-income blacks and Hispanics remained stuck in inner-city areas (Gimpel 1999). These patterns of mobility and immobility helped to turn Los Angeles and Alameda Counties into Democratic strongholds.

California voters fall into three categories of birthplace and migration status seldom examined by pollsters and pundits. They are either natives to the state, immigrants, or internal "domestic" migrants—the latter born in some other state but relocated to California. They are not immigrants, but they are not native to California either. Some of the most interesting results in table 3.2 are those estimating the Democratic support among native Californians and these internal

TABLE 3.2. Estimates of the Democratic Percentage of the Presidential Vote for Various Electoral Groups in California, 1928–2000 (ecological inference maximum likelihood)

Pooled Presidential Election Years	Blacks/ Nonblacks		Elderly/ Nonelderly		Immigrants/ Nonimmigrants		Farmers/ Nonfarmers		Whites/ Nonwhites	
1928, 1932	55.3	46.5*	38.7	47.1*	49.3	46.1*	56.4*	45.5*	46.7*	45.6*
1936, 1940, 1944	82.3	59.9*	51.7*	61.0*	56.9	60.8*	56.7*	60.6*	62.0*	23.9
1948, 1952	99.2	43.0*	10.9	48.5*	37.7	46.1*	40.2*	45.6*	45.0*	51.0*
1956, 1960, 1964	83.3	48.9*	44.2	55.6*	59.8	50.0*	51.3	50.9*	50.8*	52.7*
1968, 1972	74.4	40.7*	29.1	44.4*	72.6	40.2*	19.0	43.2*	39.4*	71.9
1976, 1980, 1984	87.9	37.8*	56.3	40.8*	64.1	37.7*	48.5	41.8*	36.7*	58.8*
1988, 1992	85.6	43.6	27.9	48.9*	70.5	40.7*	56.3	46.7*	39.6*	62.5*
1996, 2000	90.2	49.5*	30.5	55.1*	99.4	39.6*	48.1	52.5*	36.4*	85.3*

	Mfg. Workers/ Non Mfg. Workers		College Educated/ Non College Educated		Native to State/ Nonnatives		Internal Migrants/ Nonmigrants		Hispanics/ Non- Hispanics	
1928, 1932	—	—	—	—	—	—	—	—	—	—
1936, 1940, 1994	—	—	—	—	—	—	—	—	—	—
1948, 1952	65.7	41.0*	12.4	48.1*	—	—	—	—	—	—
1956, 1960, 1964	64.0	47.1*	42.7	51.8*	59.1*	44.5*	43.8*	57.4*	—	—
1968, 1972	57.9	39.0*	68.8	39.0*	45.5*	41.1*	27.1*	57.7*	—	—
1976, 1980, 1984	50.9	39.6*	52.7	39.9*	37.0*	46.0*	32.9*	47.5*	43.9*	41.2*
1988, 1992	64.1	43.3*	82.5	35.9*	39.7*	52.8*	30.1*	54.3*	45.7*	47.1*
1996, 2000	55.5	52.0*	66.2	49.5*	18.3*	82.7*	36.9*	59.7*	60.2*	49.1*

Note: Cell entries show the estimated percentage voting Democratic in the listed presidential elections. Complete variable definitions and results from the ecological inference estimation appear in appendix B, with standard errors and bounds.

*Reflect estimates with lower and upper bounds narrower than 0,1.

migrants. We do not have data for internal migrants or native Californians prior to the 1960 census, but what we did have suggests that native Californians are more Democratic than nonnatives (including immigrants) until the 1970s and 1980s. Specifically, about 59 percent of native Californians supported Democrats in the 1956–64 presidential elections, compared with only 45 percent of those not born in California. By the 1990s, though, those born in California are substantially less Democratic than those who have moved in from elsewhere. These results make sense if we realize that by the latter years, more of the nonnatives are immigrants of predominantly Hispanic and Asian ancestry who have come to identify with the Democratic party.

To examine more precisely the political leanings of the nonnative population who are internal migrants, excluding the immigrants, we estimated the Democratic voting tendency of this population (see table 3.2). Here we see some very interesting and consistent patterns since the 1960s. Internal migrants—those born elsewhere in the United States but now living in California—are far more Republican than those who are not internal migrants. Only 27 percent of internal migrants cast Democratic ballots in the combined 1968–72 presidential elections, compared with 58 percent for the rest of the California electorate (including the natives and immigrants). In the later elections, the difference in support for the Democratic party between internal migrants and others is still substantial—supporting the idea that population in-migration from other states has greatly benefited the GOP. We can infer from these figures that population growth from domestic sources outside of California has contributed to the Republican party's base, but has been of limited value to the Democrats.

Generational Replacement

Fifty years is nearly two generations, so generational replacement has to figure prominently in the list of explanations for partisan change. From 1930 to 1950, older Republicans were dying off to be replaced by younger, New Deal–era Democrats. This helps to explain why the California Democrats began to win elections in the late 1950s after a prolonged drought. By the 1980s, voters who were young adults during the New Deal were beginning to retire and die, to be replaced by younger cohorts that leaned more Republican. As the second post–New Deal generation entered the electorate in the 1970s and 1980s, it appears that the Republicans surged back to recover some of the ground they lost in the era between 1930 and 1960.

The estimates in table 3.2 for the Democratic allegiance of the elderly population help to bolster our case that generational replacement initially helped swing California toward the Democrats. In our analysis presented in table 3.2 we separated the population over age 65 from those younger than retirement age and evaluated the Democratic voting tendency for each group. If the political orientation of those of retirement age is significantly different from those under age 65, the potential for partisan change due to mortality will be high. Through the 1970s, it is clear that the oldest voters are substantially less Democratic than the younger population. Our most reliable estimate is for the pooled 1936–44 elections, where there was a 10-point gap in Democratic support between the elderly and nonelderly. We are less confident of our results after this, but the estimates we present indicate that the tendency for the young to be more Democratic than the aged also holds up from 1988 to 2000. Exit polling data from the 2000 election showed that elderly Californians favored George W. Bush with 49 percent of their vote, compared to the 41 percent he received among those younger than 65.

That the elderly in California are consistently more likely to vote Republican than the young across the early part of this period suggests that Republican presidential candidates were most likely to suffer at the polls from the effects of mortality and generational replacement. If only about one-third of the elderly are Democrats, then only one out of three voters who leave the electorate due to death are Democrats and the other two are Republicans. These voters are then replaced by younger voters who are more evenly divided between the parties. With time, this pattern of generational replacement, if untempered by other forces, such as population migration, would generate considerable Democratic strength in the electorate, as it appears to be doing in the first decade of the twenty-first century.

Political Conversion

A lesser, but probably not negligible, source of political change has been the conversion of some voters from Democratic to Republican party affiliation, and vice versa. The New Deal is most closely associated with party realignment, and some have argued that conversion was at work to turn many Republicans into Democrats. New issues also emerged on the agenda in the 1960s and 1970s that may have changed the party loyalties of some Californians. Among these were civil rights, women's rights, the antiwar movement, the expansion of the welfare state, environmental protection, and increasing crime rates. Some of these issues, such as crime control and the environment, became salient purely because of local conditions and circumstances. Others, such as the civil rights and antiwar movements, were national political issues that resonated with Californians.

To learn whether conversion played a role in changing California politics we estimate a simple "voter transition model" where we examine the relationship between the vote for a party in one presidential year and the vote for that party in the following presidential year (Achen and Shively 1995; Irwin and Meeter 1969). The goal of such an undertaking is to examine whether voters remain loyal to a party from one election to the next. The data we use are aggregated at the county level and do not give us an exact measure of the degree of loyalty, but given the absence of polls for individual states, estimates based on county-level data are a suitable second-best option.

Our results are presented in table 3.3 for the relationship between Democratic and Republican presidential voting in two eras: the early 1930s and the late 1960s. The table entries display our best guess as to the percentage of Democratic voters in 1928 who also voted Democratic in 1932, and the percentage of Democratic voters in 1932 who voted Democratic in 1936. Similar results are shown for Republicans and for the later period.[1] What we see is that Democrats remained highly loyal to their party from 1928 to 1932, and from 1932 to 1936. Republicans, though, bolted in large numbers from 1928 to 1932. Only an estimated 57.8 percent of Republican voters in 1928 cast GOP ballots in 1932, the remainder deserting the party for Roosevelt. Republican defections were not as great from 1932 to 1936, but only 77.7 percent of the remaining Republican voters from the 1932 election supported Landon in the 1936 race. Not all of these voters who abandoned the GOP turned out to be long-term converts, but certainly some of them were, and their conversion helps to explain Democratic resurgence in California in subsequent years.

Another time where we might look for possible voter conversion was the 1960s, and particularly the 1964 and 1968 elections when many conservative Democrats of Southern extraction lost faith in their

TABLE 3.3. Estimates of Party Loyalty and Conversion across Presidential Elections in California (ecological inference maximum likelihood)

Presidential Election Years	Voted Democratic 1928/Non-Democratic 1928	Voted Democratic 1932/Non-Democratic 1932	Presidential Election Years	Voted Republican 1928/Non-Republican 1928	Voted Republican 1932/Non-Republican 1932
Voted Democratic 1932	92.0* 41.3*		Voted Republican 1932	57.8* 1.0*	
Voted Democratic 1936		94.4* 28.3*	Voted Republican 1936		77.7* 4.6*

Presidential Election Years	Voted Democratic 1960/Non-Democratic 1960	Voted Democratic 1964/Non-Democratic 1964	Presidential Election Years	Voted Republican 1960/Non-Republican 1960	Voted Republican 1964/Non-Republican 1964
Voted Democratic 1964	91.8* 27.5*		Voted Republican 1964	52.0* 29.1*	
Voted Democratic 1968		59.7* 24.1*	Voted Republican 1968		95.7* 14.3*
Voted Wallace 1968		6.7* 6.9*	Voted Wallace 1968		9.5* 4.9*

Note: Cell entries show the estimated percentage voting Democratic, Republican, or for George Wallace in the presidential elections listed on each row who voted Democratic (or Republican) in the previous election. Complete variable definitions and results from the ecological inference estimation appear in appendix C, with standard errors and bounds.

*Reflect estimates with lower and upper bounds narrower than 0,1.

party as it moved to the left across a wide spectrum of issues. While we see in the bottom half of table 3.3 that 91.8 percent of Kennedy supporters (1960) voted for Johnson (1964), only an estimated 60 percent of Johnson supporters wound up supporting Hubert Humphrey in 1968. About 6.7 percent of California's Johnson supporters voted for George Wallace. On the GOP side of the ledger, we learn that only 52 percent of the Californians who had supported Richard Nixon (1960) also supported Barry Goldwater four years later. But 95.7 percent of the Goldwater voters went on to vote for Richard Nixon in 1968. About 9.5 percent of Goldwater supporters cast votes for George Wallace. Wallace voters were unhappy with both the GOP and Democratic nominees in 1968, and a majority went on to vote for Nixon over McGovern in 1972, indicating that Wallace may have been a stopover on the way to conversion from Democratic to Republican party identification.

Other evidence from table 3.2 may point to the conversion of certain electoral blocs across the six decades between the 1930s and the 2000 contest. Manufacturing workers and the college educated exhibit changing patterns of partisan support. It is not surprising that blue-collar workers employed in manufacturing would be allied with Democrats in the 1940s, but their support for Democratic candidates wanes to the point where they awarded Bill Clinton and Al Gore only 56 percent of their votes in the 1996–2000 elections. Education is associated with higher socioeconomic status and upward mobility, usually traits accompanying Republican party affiliation. Yet clearly our estimates show that since the late 1960s, the college educated in California are more likely to support Democratic presidential candidates than are those lacking a four-year degree. Polling data indicate that these ecological results are not far from the truth: the college educated were more likely to support Dukakis, Clinton, and Gore than they were their GOP opponents.

Activism and Partisanship of New Voting Blocs

Mobilization of voters has made a contribution to California's changing politics, moving the state toward the Democrats with each new decade. One of the most remarkable developments of the 2000 election was how early the Bush campaign wound up writing-off California as a Gore victory—a major concession given its 54 electoral votes.

Fifty years earlier, California was considered a "likely Republican" state in presidential elections, and local Democrats had trouble contesting elections for statewide office. Blacks and Hispanics have played the most consequential roles in changing the state's destiny, and legions of newly naturalized immigrants have bolstered Democratic strength. In the 1928 and 1932 elections, our results for whites and nonwhites, and for blacks and nonblacks, indicate rather small racial differences in support for Smith and for Roosevelt. Whatever edge the Democrats had among the minority population during the Great Depression, it was not a huge one. The Democratic allegiance of black voters increased dramatically in the wake of the New Deal realignment. After 1960, white voters were generally far less Democratic than nonwhite voters, suggesting that mobilization created a significant race gap in support for the parties.

Our earlier results suggest that California's sectionalism has been the result of an increasing nonwhite population that has contributed to the political balkanization of the state into Democratic and Republican areas. The results in table 3.2 also indicate that the foreign born are much more heavily Democratic than those born in the United States beginning in the late 1950s. Although our data for the 1988 and subsequent elections probably overstate the percentage of immigrants casting Democratic ballots, there is little question that the Democratic party has benefited far more from the naturalization of new immigrants than the Republicans.[2] The perception of the GOP as an anti-immigrant party in the wake of Governor Pete Wilson's 1994 gubernatorial reelection, in which he vigorously campaigned for passage of Proposition 187, contributed mightily to this development. The estimates in table 3.2 indicate that the Hispanic population moved sharply toward the Democratic party in the 1996–2000 elections; polls from this period show that Latinos are registered Democrats by at least a two-to-one margin, and they supported Bill Clinton and Al Gore over Bob Dole and George W. Bush by even more lopsided margins than our ecological results indicate.

Conclusions

Until the mid-1990s, California was considered a competitive state in presidential elections, but one that often leaned Republican. For statewide offices, Democrats have been competitive with Republicans on a steady basis only since the late 1950s. But as the 2000 election results showed, the Democrats have surpassed Republicans, with Al Gore winning the state by a comfortable margin. Conversion and generational replacement stirred the Democratic party back to life from 1930 to 1960. Even as old Republicans continued to be replaced by younger Democrats who had come of age during the New Deal, mobilization of new voters helped make the Democrats competitive through the 1960s and 1970s. California's post-1960s history would have been one of complete Democratic dominance had it not been for the countervalent force of internal migration. The flood of newcomers to the state was the single greatest force behind GOP growth, and it helped the Republicans beat back some determined Democratic assaults in the last three decades of the century, creating a politics that was well worth watching. California's elections have attracted such great interest not simply because it is the largest state in the union, but because so many contests have gone down to the wire. It remains to be seen whether record high levels of immigration at the end of the twentieth century will translate into a consistent Democratic majority in the new one.

Sectionalism in California was greater in the early 2000s than it had been at any time since 1928. The geographic balkanization of the California electorate is attributable to the state's population growth and the increasing racial diversity that has come with it. Anglos, Latinos, Asians, and blacks have not mixed easily. Because Anglo voters are, on average, more affluent than the others, they are more mobile and can afford to be more choosy in where they want to live. Their choices most often lead them away from communities of mixed race and ethnicity. Geographic separation of these groups limits contact among them, and contact is a prerequisite for reconciliation of political and other differences. With the prospects for residential integration seeming remote in the short term, the future of sectionalism in California hinges on whether the Republicans can improve their vote-getting prospects among Latinos, Asians, blacks, and white liberals who live on the coast. Sectionalism would also subside if Democrats could gain ground among conservative suburban and rural white voters in southern and central California. Given the ideological polarization in the California party system over issues such as immigration and affirmative action, it is unlikely that Republicans will gain much ground among minority voters, although they may manage to maintain their current level of support from these groups. For the same reason, Democrats are not likely to gain much ground among the most conservative rural and suburban Republicans. This leaves the affluent whites along California's coast open to the appeals of GOP libertarians. Everyone is waiting to see whether the entrepreneurial knowledge workers of the South Bay and other high-tech enclaves are moved more by their conservative business instincts or their socially liberal instincts. The path they choose is likely to tip the electoral balance in the twenty-first century.

Notes

1. Ordinarily we would not have to present results for both parties separately since the ecological inference technique displays results for Democrats and non-Democrats (Republicans and third partisans) who voted Democratic in the next election. We ran separate models for two reasons: (1) not all non-Democrats voted Republican or call themselves Republican and (2) as a double check of the estimates for each model. Democratic support among non-Democrats and Republicans should closely match, as should the percentage support for Democrats and non-Republicans.

2. We used a couple of variables to measure the voting tendencies of the foreign-born population, one for the percentage foreign born (naturalized or nonnaturalized) and another that measured only the foreign born that had naturalized. The results for our ecological inference estimates were highly similar for all states and elections.

CHAPTER 4

FLORIDA

Major Forces for Electoral Change in Florida

- Immigration from South and Central America and from Cuba
- Domestic (Internal) Migration from Other States
- Retirement Migration from Northeast and Midwest
- Demise of Old South Culture in North Florida
- The Growing Importance of Tourism and Defense-Related Employment

Ask someone on the street what comes to mind when the state of Florida is mentioned and an amazing variety of places and things will come up: Disney World, the Everglades, Miami, Cape Canaveral, Cubans, warm weather, elderly retirees, hurricanes, palm trees, beaches, oranges, tourists, crime, and those troublesome punch card ballots that injected so much controversy into the 2000 presidential election. Florida is all of that, and more. But the state wasn't always as diverse as one finds it at the beginning of the twenty-first century. In 1949, V. O. Key Jr. wrote of a Florida that was sparsely populated below the Panhandle. The hot weather, the beaches, and the fruit could be found, but there was none of the development then that would eventually be responsible for the identification of Florida with Disney, Miami, Cubans, the elderly, or highly publicized violent crime.

Dade County is home to Miami—Florida's best-known city—as well as some very large suburbs, including Miami Beach, Hialeah, and Coral Gables. Dade has undergone amazing social transformation since mid-century. In 1950, Dade County was growing modestly, with a predominantly Anglo population of about 935,000—only one in ten were foreign born. The elderly population was already a presence, drawn primarily to Miami Beach and smaller settlements along the shore rather than the city of Miami. Still, the elderly had discovered south Florida long before anyone else had, and they were busy turning it into a retirement colony. From the beginning, the colonizers were Northeasterners from New York, New Jersey, and Connecticut. Early in the twenty-first century, the population of the Atlantic Coast side of the Florida peninsula was still drawing heavily from Northeastern states.

Dade County's growth explosion took place after 1959 when thousands of Cuban exiles fled Fidel Castro's communist revolution. The exiles came in three waves: 1959–62 (the largest influx), 1965–73 (a smaller, more sporadic flow), and 1980 (the Mariel Boatlift) (Grenier and Stepick 1992; Garcia 1996). More than half of the Cuban population settled in Dade County, mainly because south Florida was close to Cuba (eighty miles) and the exiles hoped to return. By 2000, Miami was a plurality Cuban city—about 39 percent of the population reported that they were ethnic Cubans, with Nicaraguans and Puerto Ricans taking up distant second and third places. Cubans were slightly more dilute in Dade County, constituting about 30 percent of the population in 2000, but people of Hispanic origin were a slight but growing majority of the population.

The majority status of Latinos in Dade County is likely to be cemented by the out-migration of Anglo (non-Hispanic white) residents to Broward County (Fort Lauderdale, Hollywood) directly north (see map 4.1). Broward is both more affluent and more white than Dade, and a comparably scant percentage of its population was of Hispanic origin in 2000, although it was moving upward. Between 1985 and 1990, 86,000 people moved from other parts of Florida into Broward, with most of these coming from Dade County. Broward has become the preferred Atlantic Coast destination for retirees many of whom initially settled in Dade County. Word is out to the rest of the country that Dade County is overcrowded and has been taken over by "foreign elements." As a consequence, the Northeastern states sent more elderly migrants to live in Broward than in Dade County through the final decades of the twentieth century.

From St. Petersburg to Naples, the Gulf Coast is home to some of the wealthiest and most exclusive retirement and resort communities in the nation. The Gulf Coast has been the preferred destination for elderly migrants from Midwestern states and the more affluent among East Coast retirees. The population is not nearly as diverse in these counties as one finds in the Miami–Fort Lauderdale area, but it has grown at nearly the same rate. St. Petersburg was the first major

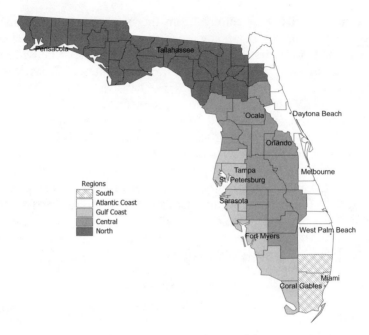

Map 4.1.   Regions of Florida

city in the region to attract large numbers of retirees in the 1940s and
1950s. Tampa and the towns further south (Bradenton, Sarasota, Port
Charlotte, Fort Myers, and Naples) developed later. With development has come a rising tide of affluence. In the 1960s, most of the
Gulf Coast communities were slightly above the state mean on most
indicators of wealth but lagged well behind Dade and Broward. By
2000, the income gap between the coasts had closed. Migrants who
had been attracted initially to the Atlantic side of the peninsula began to relocate to the less crowded Gulf Coast side. In the new century, the state's growth is likely to come mainly along the Gulf, not
along the Atlantic, but it will have to overcome significant opposition
from growth control advocates in Gulf Coast towns.

Central Florida is located north of Tampa but below Gainesville.
Orlando, Kissimmee, Daytona Beach, and Melbourne are the major
cities in this region. The area is known best for tourism and the aerospace industry. Having attracted young professionals and their families from other states, the population of central Florida is younger
than further south. In the 1990s, the birth rate rather than in-migration

was the major source of growth. Brevard County is home to Cape Canaveral and Patrick Air Force Base and attendant high-tech industries thriving off defense contracts. The elderly have a presence here, but Brevard's main constituency is the young, professional family, usually imported by the military or an aerospace company to work in a NASA spin-off operation.

Orlando owes much of its postwar growth to the military training outposts that were located here during World War II. After the war, two large airbases were converted to civilian use, and aerospace giant Martin-Marietta (now Lockheed-Martin) set up shop, creating 10,000 jobs and sparking new housing development. For the next twenty years, Orlando would be a mixed economy of citrus farms and engineers working to refine armaments technology. Orlando's development was further aided by the construction of two north-south interstate highways, I-75 and I-95, in the 1950s. In turn, these thoroughfares were connected by two interstate highways, I-4 and the Florida Turnpike, that intersect at a hub within city limits. In the late 1960s, when Walt Disney was searching for a site to build Disney World, he flew over this intersection in a helicopter. Plans had already been made to build on a site near Ocala to the north, but seeing the striking convergence of these two freeways from the air, he instead declared Orlando to be the location for the mammoth new theme park. Disney bought up thousands of acres of property, and to prevent inflation Orlando officials cooperated with Disney in keeping the purchaser's identity secret. Disney World opened in 1971, and Sea World, Universal Studios, numerous smaller attractions, and hundreds of hotels and restaurants soon followed. Long-term residents remember orange groves and open space prior to 1970: before the Disney era, 60 percent of Orange County property was occupied by farms. Cold weather in the 1980s helped to finish off citrus in central Florida. Freezes ruined orange crops and encouraged farmers to sell to developers. By the late 1980s Orlando had become a major city with residents worrying about big city problems: traffic, crime, growth, and schools. At the dawn of the new century, central Florida is uneasy with its growing ethnic diversity and the new populations that are finding their way here to work in the plentiful but low-paying service sector jobs associated with tourism. As the area runs short of affordable housing, wages will not keep pace with living costs, producing greater social and economic stratification.

North Florida, from Jacksonville to Pensacola, is home to the most significant concentrations of black residents in Florida (see map 4.1). When V. O. Key Jr. wrote at mid-century, this area most resembled the Old South in its social and political culture. Close proximity to Georgia, Alabama, and Mississippi meant that the population was substantially similar to those states. Except for Jacksonville, which has taken its own course of rapid development, this was probably still true in the early 2000s. The north Florida counties have a stronger sense of history than those of the peninsula—probably because they have an established population that can trace its roots to the antebellum period. Growth pressures began to overtake the Panhandle in the 1980s, fueled by expansion of naval facilities in Pensacola and a steady stream of business into Tallahassee brought there by the availability of cheap land and low taxes—incentives that have disappeared in the overgrown parts of the state.

The state's changing political sectionalism can be understood largely by reference to the contemporary developments that have brought legions of newcomers. Internal migration and immigration have reshaped the politics of south Florida, the Gulf Coast, and central Florida by increasing the proportion of foreign-born voters, voters from other states, and ethnic minorities. The growing military presence around Pensacola (Escambia County) and Melbourne (Brevard County) have made these areas conservative Republican strongholds.

Elderly migration to sunny coastal settlements has generally boosted GOP prospects along the Atlantic and Gulf shores, but Democrats who framed their campaigns around social security and health care could still be elected. The Gulf Coast counties from Hillsborough to Collier are the most reliably Republican at the start of the twenty-first century primarily because the Northern influx there has been more likely to originate from conservative Midwestern states than liberal Northeastern states. For years, Cuban exile politics in Dade County heavily advantaged Republicans, but the GOP hold has weakened with new arrivals from Central and South America and the Caribbean in the 1990s and early 2000s. Broward and Palm Beach, directly north of Miami, have usually leaned toward the GOP, but Bill Clinton and Al Gore closely contested these areas in 1992, 1996, and 2000.

North Florida's politics has also taken a turn toward the GOP, but the trend has not been a function of population growth, except in Pensacola and Jacksonville. Explanations for the partisan changes in north Florida must be grounded in generational replacement and the conversion of white Florida natives. The area has gone more Republican because older Democratic loyalists have died off and been replaced by younger Republicans. Conversion of Southern whites from the Democratic to the Republican party is also a component of partisan change in this region as it is in nearby Georgia and Alabama.

Early in the twentieth century, the population of the state was concentrated in north Florida, partly because that's where the only arable agricultural land could be found, but also because the summer weather became so much more unpleasant further south in the days before air conditioning. Still, Miami was a city of about 200,000 in the late 1940s with its economy relying largely on tourism even then. Along the Atlantic and Gulf Coasts, there was little more than a few small fishing villages and some resorts that attracted Northerners in the winter (Huckshorn 1998). In those days, the balance of political power rested firmly in the north around cities and small towns. Reflecting the influence of the Old South, the party preference was overwhelmingly Democratic.

The exceptionally one-sided nature of electoral politics in the northern counties can be seen in map 4.2 showing the average Democratic vote for president in the 1928–36 elections. Most of the panhandle counties are in the highest quartile (dark shading). While most of the peninsular counties are also in the Democratic camp, it is noteworthy that the counties along the Atlantic Coast in south Florida (Dade, Broward, Palm Beach) have the strongest Republican loyalties. Central Florida, around Orlando (Orange County), is also in the lowest Democratic quartile. These parts of Florida along the Atlantic Coast were least like the Old South, and they were among those least likely to have been influenced by the proximity of Georgia and Alabama.

Beginning in the 1950s, the population center of the state moved steadily southward as Miami, Fort Lauderdale, Tampa, and St. Petersburg quickly outgrew the northern cities. The source of the population growth was migration from the North. The new population was far more Republican than the natives were, and Florida was one of the first Southern states to defect to the GOP, giving a slight edge to

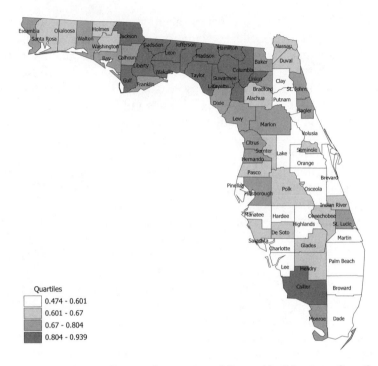

Map 4.2.   Average Democratic percentage of the presidential vote, 1928–1936

Nixon over Kennedy in 1960 even as Alabama and Georgia went solidly for the Democrat.

By 1964, Florida was uniformly less Democratic than in the 1930s and 1940s, but particularly so in the peninsular counties. It is notable that Florida still voted for Lyndon Johnson in 1964—Florida's new Republicanism did not necessarily translate into sympathy for Goldwater's anti–civil rights platform. Several of the southern and central counties that are darkly shaded in map 4.2, including Collier (Naples) and St. Lucie (Fort Pierce), were developed later than those closer to Miami, Fort Lauderdale, and Tampa. Consequently, in-migration did not overwhelm the Democratic inclination of the native population in these locales until the late 1950s and early 1960s.

By the late 1980s, Florida had become a two-party competitive state with a slight tilt toward the GOP. Even the Democratically inclined rural northern counties were far less Democratic than in previous decades (see map 4.3). The generally strong Republican gains statewide did not always translate into GOP victories in the areas of

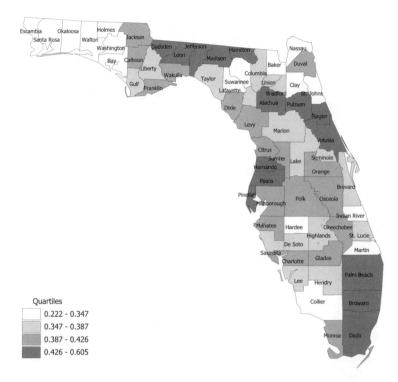

Map 4.3.   Average Democratic percentage of the presidential vote, 1988–2000

previous Republican strength though. Some areas have obviously undergone political realignment, swapping political allegiances, as
shown in map 4.3. In the 1988–2000 presidential elections, Democrats
excelled in Dade, Broward, and Palm Beach Counties, all of which
are in the highest Democratic quartile (see the dark shading in map
4.3). Recall that in map 4.2, these counties were in the lowest Democratic quartile. Similarly, the most solidly Republican area of the state
is the western Panhandle, around Pensacola. These counties were
among the most Democratic in the earlier period.

Where Are the Votes in Florida? Republican and
Democratic Mobilization Targets

No event reminded us more clearly of the importance of political geography than the fiercely contested results from the 2000 election

campaign in Florida. Still, maps 4.2 and 4.3 show only the partisan inclination of each county but do not show the number of Democratic (or Republican) voters. For strategic purposes in a statewide race, a campaign manager or candidate needs to direct resources toward the areas of greatest partisan strength. The goal of maximizing turnout among the party faithful requires knowledge not only of the partisan orientation of each county, but also of the number of voters there. It makes little sense to commit substantial resources to a place where there are friendly voters, but few of them. At the same time, one may choose to allocate some resources in rather unfriendly areas, simply because these places contain so many voters that turnout among the small proportion of favorables will be vital to the overall effort.

Each party's most important counties can be determined by combining the partisan leaning of the county with the total population of partisan voters there and then ranking the lists from highest to lowest.[1] The results for the top ten counties for each party appear in table 4.1 for the 1988–2000 presidential elections. Note that several counties appear on both lists. Dade (Miami) and Broward (Fort Lauderdale) have such large populations that neither party can afford to ignore them. Nevertheless, in presidential elections, Dade is slightly more important for Republicans (ranks first) than for Democrats (ranks second). Broward is more important for Democrats (ranks first) than for Republicans (ranks fifth). Palm Beach County, locus of

TABLE 4.1.   Florida's Top Ten Strongest Counties for Republicans and Democrats in the 1988–2000 Presidential Contests

Rank	Democratic	Republican
1	Broward (Fort Lauderdale)	Dade (Miami)
2	Dade (Miami)	Pinellas (St. Petersburg)
3	Palm Beach (West Palm Beach)	Hillsborough (Tampa)
4	Pinellas (St. Petersburg)	Duval (Jacksonville)
5	Hillsborough (Tampa)	Broward (Fort Lauderdale)
6	Orange (Orlando)	Orange (Orlando)
7	Duval (Jacksonville)	Palm Beach (West Palm Beach)
8	Volusia (Daytona Beach)	Brevard (Melbourne)
9	Pasco (North Tampa Suburbs)	Lee (Fort Myers)
10	Brevard (Melbourne)	Polk (Winter Haven)
% of total vote	67.1	56.8

Map 4.4.   Areas of Republican and Democratic dominance, 1988–2000

the well-known legal challenges of the 2000 presidential election, is more important to Democrats (ranks third) than for Republicans (ranks seventh). Several counties are listed in one or the other column, but not both. An example is Lee County (Fort Myers), which ranks in the top ten for Republicans, but not for Democrats. Volusia County, another site where ballots were recounted in the 2000 presidential election, ranks eighth for Democrats, but is not in the top ten for the GOP. Orange County (Orlando) is about equally important in presidential elections for both parties, ranking sixth on both top ten lists (see table 4.1, map 4.4).

The political geography of election campaign targets looked very different in the 1930s, and this is not simply due to the rise of two-party competition. Population growth and suburbanization have moved the state's center of political gravity further south. Early in the twentieth century, Jacksonville (Duval County) and Pensacola (Escambia

County) were at least as important as Miami, and Broward County was scarcely on the radar screen. Northern in-migration changed the state's political landscape after World War II, elevating Broward County's importance and submerging the influence of the northern counties. Remarkably, the GOP's strongest counties in the 1930s were Dade, Pinellas, and Duval, two of which contributed most to the Republican vote seventy years later. Republican prospects for victory in Florida steadily improved over the course of the century, and the growth in the GOP's share of the vote was most noteworthy along the Gulf Coast in retirement communities between Tampa and Fort Myers.

Although the GOP's vote share has become larger, it has also grown more geographically diffuse, while the Democratic base has become more geographically concentrated. Florida is one of those states where Democrats have had an advantage over Republicans because a highly concentrated electorate reduces organization costs by making it easier to find and mobilize friendly voters. In the 1988–2000 presidential elections, about 25 percent of the statewide Democratic vote was to be found in Dade and Broward Counties. Republicans found just 17 percent of their vote there. In the ten most populous counties, Democrats gathered 67 percent of their votes, compared with just 57 percent for Republicans. The GOP must continue to develop and utilize mobilization strategies that work in less densely populated terrain and in locations where Democratic and Republican households are often found side by side. Democrats can still depend upon areas where their votes are not only concentrated, but monolithic in their support for Democratic candidates. Little wonder that George W. Bush vigorously fought vote recounts in Broward, Dade, and Palm Beach Counties, all increasingly dependable Democratic strongholds. Al Gore's insistence on recounts would have looked far more credible if his campaign had challenged the vote totals in a few of the Republican-leaning counties. But the Bush campaign calculated that it would probably not have won a statewide recount given that the Democratic counties provided far more support to Gore than the Republican-leaning counties did for Bush. A recount may well have added to Gore's totals in the heavily Democratic counties, while the recount in the more evenly divided and smaller GOP counties would have been a wash. With hindsight, we now know that recounts did not change the election results, but in

December 2000, the campaigns could only guess what the result of a recount might be.

Florida's Changing Electoral Foundations

The political geography of party support has changed in Florida, and the maps presented earlier show that pretty decisively. Major counties such as Dade and Broward that were positioned in the lowest quartile of Democratic support in the 1930s were in the highest support quartile by the 1990s. Counties in the panhandle that were once Democratic strongholds had moved just as strongly into the GOP camp by the year 2000. What accounts for the changes? Is it population mobility? The mobilization of voters who had been inactive? The conversion of native Floridians from one party to another? Or is it the gradual generational replacement of older voters with younger ones?

Our survey of previous research on the subject strongly suggests that each explanation of partisan change has a role to play in accounting for Florida's changing electorate. We are not convinced, however, that all of the explanations are of equal importance. Obtaining a clear picture of the sources of partisan change across a seventy-year period is not easy given the lack of survey data on Florida voters before the 1980s. Consistent with our approach in other chapters, we have tried to make good use of county-level data to draw reasonable ecological inferences about the political inclinations of key groups. Results from our estimates are reported for presidential elections in table 4.2 for blacks, whites, the elderly, immigrants, internal migrants, those native to Florida, and the college educated. This table shows the estimated percentage of each group voting Democratic compared with the Democratic support of those not in that group. In table 4.3 we examine the role of conversion during the New Deal period and the late 1960s, following the example we followed for California in chapter 3.

Population Mobility

First, population mobility across state lines has produced major attitudinal and partisan shifts (Parker 1988). Many of the new Florida residents on the Atlantic side of the peninsula hail from the Northeast, including states with politically liberal traditions: New York, New Jersey, and Connecticut. In the 1940s and 1950s, these Northerners introduced liberal political values, particularly on civil rights issues, into a strongly conservative state. With time, they also began to tip the state away from Democratic domination, as a sizable share of these voters imported Republican party identification. And, as mentioned previously, this migration also began to build the political strength of the peninsular cities and counties at the expense of the entrenched power base in the panhandle.

Accelerating this historical shift in political power from north to south Florida has been the arrival of immigrants in Dade and Broward Counties. Beginning in 1960, the influx of Cuban refugees brought a fierce cold war–dominated style of political thinking to Miami. For twenty years, the anticommunism of the Cuban population favored Republicans, as it was the GOP that generally took the more confrontational posture of the two parties in cold war politics. Beginning in the early 1980s, however, Democrats began to make inroads into Dade County as the older generation's influence on the political life of the community began to weaken. Second-generation Cuban-Americans expressed little interest in returning to the island and do not necessarily identify Republicans as the pro-Cuban, anti-Castro party in the way that their parents often did. In addition, new immigrant populations from Haiti, the Dominican Republic, and South and Central America are not naturally drawn to either party. Consequently, Democrats and Republicans must compete to win the allegiance of this largely unattached and unaffiliated population. Dade and Broward Counties have become a battleground at the dawn of the twenty-first century that they were not in 1970.

For many years scholars have wondered about the origins of the South's growing Republicanism. Some have been reluctant to credit this realignment to the coming of migrants from outside Florida, instead resting the explanation on the conversion of native Southern whites from the Democratic to the Republican party. The estimates in table 4.2 show, though, that migrants from outside of Florida are considerably more Republican than other residents (either immigrants or natives). In the 1956–64 pooled elections, an estimated 35 percent of internal migrants voted Democratic, compared to 69 percent of nonmigrants. This difference disappears in 1968 through 1972, due to the unpopularity of Hubert Humphrey, the 1968 Democratic nominee, among native Floridians. But in elections after 1976, internal migrants have generally been less Democratic than Florida natives.

The results for natives vs. nonnatives in table 4.2 reflect very similar results. The estimates for 1968 and 1972 are somewhat anomalous because of the low levels of support for Hubert Humphrey in 1968. Generally, however, Florida natives are much more Democratic in the 1950s, 1960s, and 1970s than are nonnatives. This makes sense given that many native Floridians were socialized into the traditional politics of the Old South prior to the 1970s. In more recent years, the political predispositions of Florida natives have changed. Through 1992, they were still more Democratically inclined than the state's nonnative population, but the gap between the groups has narrowed and appears to have been reversed in the 1996–2000 elections due to the growing Democratic allegiance of the foreign born.

Immigration to Florida by the first wave of Cuban refugees arriving

TABLE 4.2. **Estimates of the Democratic Percentage of the Presidential Vote for Various Electoral Groups in Florida, 1928–2000 (ecological inference maximum likelihood)**

Pooled Presidential Election Years	Blacks/ Nonblacks		Elderly/ Nonelderly		Immigrants/ Nonimmigrants		Farmers/ Nonfarmers		Whites/ Nonwhites	
1928, 1932	85.2*	52.8*	50.0*	63.0*	76.0*	61.8*	74.9*	59.5*	52.6*	85.8*
1936, 1940, 1944	91.5*	68.5*	13.9*	79.2*	16.3*	77.2*	92.8*	71.3*	68.8*	90.5*
1948, 1952	46.8*	48.4*	1.6	52.4*	10.5	47.4*	86.9*	44.5*	48.9*	45.1*
1956, 1960, 1964	66.3*	46.0*	31.5	51.9*	10.9	51.8*	74.1*	49.1*	46.4*	64.1*
1968, 1972	37.1*	23.6*	33.1*	24.4*	37.9*	37.6*	20.1*	25.7*	23.6*	36.6*
1976, 1980, 1984	79.9*	36.4*	31.5	51.9*	34.2	43.4*	59.3*	42.3*	46.4*	64.1*
1988, 1992	52.4	34.0*	40.7	35.5*	47.2	34.9*	40.5	36.5*	33.6*	50.5*
1996, 2000	73.9	44.8*	63.0	45.7*	78.4	44.6*	50.3	48.9*	43.2*	75.7*

	Mfg. Workers/ Non Mfg. Workers		College Educated/ Non College Educated		Native to State/ Nonnatives		Internal Migrants/ Nonmigrants		Hispanics/ Non- Hispanics	
1928, 1932	—	—	—	—	—	—	—	—	—	—
1936, 1940, 1944	—	—	—	—	—	—	—	—	—	—
1948, 1952	73.7*	45.1*	1.7	51.1*	—	—	—	—	—	—
1956, 1960, 1964	70.1*	46.7*	3.3	53.5*	67.3*	38.8*	35.1*	68.6*	—	—
1968, 1972	17.0*	27.0*	53.1*	22.5*	20.9*	27.9*	26.6*	24.4*	—	—
1976, 1980, 1984	77.7	37.6*	22.7	44.9*	60.0*	34.4*	28.1*	62.0*	38.2*	42.8*
1988, 1992	27.3	37.5*	36.8	36.4*	40.1*	34.9*	32.7*	41.4*	47.9*	34.9*
1996, 2000	29.1	50.9*	67.9	45.6*	41.5*	52.2*	48.8*	49.1*	62.1*	46.6*

Note: Cell entries show the estimated percentage voting Democratic in the listed presidential elections. Complete variable definitions and results from the ecological inference estimation appear in appendix B, with standard errors and bounds.

*Reflect estimates with lower and upper bounds narrower than 0,1.

in the 1960s produced a surge in GOP strength. This strength has waned, however, as the immigrant population has produced a new generation of native-born Floridians with different political preferences than the earlier arrivals. As late as 1992, the ecological estimates show a small gap between immigrant and nonimmigrant voters, although the loyalties have been reversed with immigrants showing strong support for the Democrats in 1996–2000. These results correspond to the resurgence of Democratic party building efforts in Dade and Broward Counties and attendant successes in electing Democrats to prominent local, state, and federal offices. Polls from the last two presidential elections confirm that Florida's foreign-born population became less presidentially Republican in the closing decade of the twentieth century.

Generational Replacement

Generational replacement of elderly voters with young voters has also played a role in realigning parts of the state, as it has in California. It is no secret that retirees have become an increasingly important political force in Florida. The results of the ecological inference estimation suggest that their voting was less Democratic than that of voters under age 65 until the 1970s, when they became slightly more Democratic. In the Roosevelt period, the gap between the two was especially wide. In the 1936, 1940, and 1944 elections combined, an estimated 14 percent of those over age 65 voted Democratic, compared to 80 percent of those younger than 65. These results are generally consistent with those of California (chap. 3). As in California, the voting allegiance of older and younger cohorts in Florida eventually reverses itself. In the elections since 1988, for example, elderly voters appear more likely to vote for Democrats than younger voters (see table 4.3). Confirming that our estimates are not so far off, exit polling data from the 1996 and 2000 elections indicate that the elderly population is more Democratic than the rest of Florida with several points separating the political preferences of retirees and younger voters.

The force behind generational replacement has been high birth rates among the state's booming population of family-age migrants. Much of the state's growth has been the result of an economic boom with many new employers crossing state lines to set up shop. It is not the elderly that wind up taking these jobs, and it hasn't always been native Floridians either. Young, family-age voters have flooded into Florida with their military and private sector employers, fueling population growth in formerly placid locations such as Orange County (Orlando), Hillsborough County (Tampa), and Brevard County's Space Coast.

Because of the youth and family characteristics of this migration, it brought with it increased birth rates. Natural increase, then, has fueled political change as these new migrants bore children who then laid claim to Florida as their native turf—displacing the older Florida natives steeped in the politics of the Old South. This pattern of migration-stimulated generational replacement has resulted in a more rapid transition to two-party politics than one finds elsewhere in the South where the forces of generational change were much slower to replace old Democrats with younger Republicans. Florida elected a Republican governor as early as 1966, whereas Georgia did not elect one until 2002 and Alabama only did so in the 1980s.

Political Conversion

Much has been written about the conversion of the Southern white male to the Republican party in the wake of the civil rights revolution. And we are inclined to ask what has stimulated partisan change in those areas of Florida that have not been inundated by Northern migration. Looking to the Panhandle counties in the north, we can see that even in those counties that rank in the highest Democratic quartile in map 4.2, Democratic strength has waned considerably since the 1930s (compare maps 4.2 and 4.3). Even the counties that are darkly shaded in both maps show less support for the Democrats in the most recent contests than in the 1930s. One must seek an explanation for this in causes other than migration since these areas have attracted far less development than one finds in the peninsula. Generational replacement of older voters with younger ones may account for some of the difference. Nearly three generations come between 1930 and 2000. Across the nation, those coming of age in the post–New Deal period are much less Democratic than those who entered the electorate to vote for Roosevelt (Abramson 1975). But conversion of white Democrats to the Republican party has also been influential in north Florida, as it has been just across the state line in Georgia and Alabama.

To evaluate evidence for the conversion hypothesis, we looked at two periods where we would be most likely to find voters switching from one side to the other: the 1930s and the 1960s. Specifically, we sought to determine what proportion of Democrats (Republicans) in 1928 supported the same party in the 1932 presidential election, and so on for 1932–36, 1960–64, and 1964–68. We find that Democrats remained loyal to their party through the New Deal period. The results also indicate that Republicans were less loyal to their party in Florida than in California during the New Deal era (compare table 4.3 to table 3.3 for California). Only 33.7 percent of Florida Republicans in 1928 also voted Republican in 1932, compared with 57.8 percent of Republicans who had remained loyal in California. From 1932 to 1936, 69.7 percent of Florida Republicans remained steadfast, while 77.7 percent of Californians did.

In the 1960s, the Florida electorate was highly unstable, due to the changing politics of the national Democratic party and because of the candidacies of Barry Goldwater and George Wallace whose conservative views on civil rights were attractive to many native white Floridians desiring either slow or no movement toward racial justice. According to our results, an estimated 57.7 percent of Kennedy supporters in 1960 voted Democratic in 1964. Of the Democrats who voted for Lyndon B. Johnson in 1964, only about 57 percent went on to support Humphrey in 1968. An estimated 25 percent of the Johnson supporters cast votes for George Wallace in 1968. Support for Wallace among Johnson voters was a much lower 6.7 percent in California (see table 3.4 for comparison).

On the Republican side, we found that only 54.6 percent of Nixon supporters in 1960 voted for Goldwater four years later. So while Democrats were unhappy with their nominee in 1964, so too were many Republicans. Those who supported Goldwater, in turn, were not especially pleased with Nixon in 1968—only an estimated 59 percent of Goldwater supporters voted for him. Fully 36.6 percent of Goldwater voters cast ballots for George Wallace. In California, only 9.5 percent of Goldwater supporters voted for Wallace four years later.

We can see from these figures that conversion to the Democrats was a stronger force for political change in Florida than in California in the 1930s. In the short term, the New Deal solidified the already

TABLE 4.3. Estimates of Party Loyalty and Conversion across Presidential Elections in Florida (ecological inference maximum likelihood)

Presidential Election Years	Voted Democratic 1928/Non-Democratic 1928	Voted Democratic 1932/Non-Democratic 1932	Presidential Election Years	Voted Republican 1928/Non-Republican 1928	Voted Republican 1932/Non-Republican 1932
Voted Democratic 1932	92.2* 64.3*		Voted Republican 1932	33.7* 12.2*	
Voted Democratic 1936		95.6* 20.8*	Voted Republican 1936		69.7* 7.4*

Presidential Election Years	Voted Democratic 1960/Non-Democratic 1960	Voted Democratic 1964/Non-Democratic 1964	Presidential Election Years	Voted Republican 1960/Non-Republican 1960	Voted Republican 1964/Non-Republican 1964
Voted Democratic 1964	57.7* 45.1*		Voted Republican 1964	54.6* 42.6*	
Voted Democratic 1968		57.3* 4.1*	Voted Republican 1968		59.0* 19.7*
Voted Wallace 1968		25.1* 34.9*	Voted Wallace 1968		36.6* 23.4*

Note: Cell entries show the estimated percentage voting Democratic, Republican, or for George Wallace in the presidential elections listed on each row who voted Democratic (or Republican) in the previous election. Complete variable definitions and results from the ecological inference estimation appear in appendix C, with standard errors and bounds.

*Reflect estimates with lower and upper bounds narrower than 0,1.

overwhelming Democratic majority in Florida. In the 1960s, though, we see Democrats in Florida moving toward the GOP, particularly in their strong support for Goldwater in 1964. Florida Democrats were also far more likely to abandon Humphrey in 1968 to vote for Wallace than were Democrats in California. Florida Republicans, on the other hand, were not always loyal either. Goldwater lost nearly half of the Nixon vote of four years earlier, and Nixon also lost GOP votes to George Wallace in 1968.

Through time, certain subgroups of the voting population have undergone political transformation akin to conversion. In the 1950s and 1960s, a college education strongly predicted wealth. Compared to late in the century, relatively few people possessed a college education in that period, and those who did made much higher incomes than those who did not. Because of the link between education and wealth, and because of the social-class differences in support for the parties since the 1930s, we expected that our estimates for the Democratic inclination of college educated voters would be very low in the early elections, but would later rise. Our results mainly confirm this expectation (see table 4.2). More than half of the non–college educated voted Democratic in the earlier presidential elections, while the proportion of Democratic voters among the college educated is much lower. Our estimates for how much lower are not precise given the limitations of our model and the unavailability of additional information, but they are indicative of the social-class cleavage underlying partisan preference. The narrowing of this gap in the 1968–72 presidential elections indicates that the college educated were more supportive of the Democratic candidate than the less educated because of George Wallace's popularity among lower-status whites. The gap between the educated and less educated diminishes by the 1970s and 1980s as more voters become well educated. The conversion of native white Southerners with less than a college education to the GOP is reflected in the subsequent results indicating that less educated voters were drawn more to Republican candidates than to Dukakis, Clinton, and Gore. Exit polls from the 2000 election indicated that George W. Bush led Al Gore among those with less than a college education by a considerable margin of 55 percent to 41 percent, a dramatic turnabout from earlier in the century.

Historically, Florida has not been a leading manufacturing state, and this has been reflected in the state's hostility to labor unions and the general weakness of the union movement (Dauer 1972). More industry moved to the South after 1970 to take advantage of low input costs, and much of it has found its way to Florida. The size of the blue-collar labor force grew from about 10 percent of the state's labor force in 1950 to 21 percent in 1990. About 1.3 million Floridians were employed in the manufacturing sector by 2000. The estimates for the proportion of manufacturing workers who vote Democratic are predictably high in the 1950s and 1960s (see table 4.2). Those in blue-collar occupations cast Democratic ballots over 70 percent of the time, compared with only about 45 to 47 percent for those in nonmanufacturing jobs. The difference was wiped out in the 1968–72 period largely because of the support for George Wallace among working-class voters in 1968 and for Richard Nixon in 1972. By the late 1980s and 1990s, the county-level data indicate that areas of manufacturing activity are not nearly as Democratic as they were previously. While our estimates for the behavior of manufacturing workers are not highly reliable for the pooled presidential elections after 1988, available polling data indicate that these working-class white voters had lost much of their ardor for the Democratic party by this time—again suggesting that this bloc had dealigned, as it has elsewhere.

Mobilization and Its Impact on Conversion

The civil rights movement of the 1960s activated many black voters who had never voted before (Button 1989; Timpone 1995). During most of the New Deal period, Southern blacks remained unmobilized—voting in small numbers and dividing their votes between Republicans and Democrats (Abramson 1975). After 1950, two significant developments took place that would forever change Florida politics: (1) blacks registered as never before, and (2) they allied themselves with the Democratic party. The impact of this new electorate was to steer the Democratic party to the left on many social and civil rights issues, alienating a large segment of the white electorate. Black mobilization drove more white voters away from the Democratic party than it drew in blacks, eroding the electoral prospects for Democrats in predominantly white districts throughout the South (Black 1998; Giles and Hertz 1994). In our estimates for Florida, we see that the black vote was solidly behind the Roosevelt revolution of the 1930s. In the 1948 and 1952 elections, the gap between black and white support for the Democratic candidate was pretty narrow, reflecting the significant number of blacks who still identified with the GOP (Price 1955). In elections after 1950, though, black support for Democratic presidential candidates ran substantially higher than does the support by nonblacks, and of course it is during this period that black turnout is rising.

Related findings support the conclusion that blacks voted for Democrats in far higher proportions than whites did in most presidential elections. Examining the results for whites vs. nonwhites in table 4.2 shows that the white support for Democrats across these elections ranges from a low of 23.6 percent to a high of 68.8 percent. The low in 1968–72 was undoubtedly due to the Wallace candidacy in 1968 that drew the support of many would-be Democratic voters, followed by the unpopular McGovern nomination four years later. Among nonwhites, support for the Democratic presidential candidate never drops below 36.6 percent and ranges as high as 90.5 percent. Our rough estimates for Democratic support among blacks are lower than one might expect them to be, and lower than polling data indicate. We found that once we controlled for the rural population, estimates for black voting in 1996–2000 moved sharply upward from 80 to 93 percent, consistent with exit polls. This suggests one of two possibilities about our original estimate in table 4.2: that rural blacks are more likely to vote Republican than urban blacks, or that rural African Americans remain strong Democratic identifiers, but are much less likely to participate than their urban brethren.

Mobilization's main influence on the Florida electorate in the second half of the century was to change the tone of Democratic party politics across the South, making the party less appealing to native-born whites who had been politically socialized to accept officially sanctioned racial discrimination (Giles and Hertz 1994). In this sense, one cause of party change acted to effectuate another, in that mobilization of blacks contributed to the conversion of Southern whites. Ironically, black mobilization did more to bolster Republican prospects in Florida than any other force except migration from the North.

Conclusions

Florida reminds us that the forces for partisan change often work in combination, rather than singly, to transform a state electorate. Electoral coalitions underlying the parties were changed by new membership resulting from migration and mobilization. Mobilization of black voters was followed by the conversion of white voters who resented the new liberal drift of the national Democratic party. The arrival of Cubans in south Florida has generated something of a political backlash by Anglo voters in Dade and Broward Counties, leading to a reshuffling of local electoral support (Moreno and Rae 1992). The large number of elderly voters migrating into the state has mitigated the impact of generational replacement on political change by creating a larger and more politically heterogeneous cohort of older citizens than would live there otherwise. Because both the elderly and the young divided their vote between the parties after 1976, the role of generational replacement in changing the politics of Florida has been smaller than it would have been had the elderly consisted mainly of long-term Florida natives. We are led to conclude that migration has been a greater force behind political change in Florida than any of the other causes, although conversion comes in as a not-too-distant second, with mobilization of new voting blocs placing somewhere behind conversion.

Florida's political future hangs in a delicate balance that could be determined by the economic fortunes of new migrants and immigrants. Not everyone in Florida will prosper, and some will use their political voice to express economic grievances. Much of Florida's future hinges upon the politics of the ethnic minority population in south Florida. The new generation of Cubans does not relate to the cold war politics responsible for the GOP allegiance of their parents. For them, partisanship is defined by issues that could steer them toward either party. The sizable share of voters from Central America and Haiti have no natural alliance with the Republicans and are more likely to cast their lot with the Democratic party given their relatively low socioeconomic status.

Florida's old north-south sectionalism is giving way to a regionalism that may increasingly divide the peninsula along east-west terms— with the Atlantic Coast of south Florida moving toward the Democrats, and the Gulf Coast toward the Republicans. Military and high-tech industries have created a new kind of balkanization, with central Florida and the Space Coast (Brevard, Orange, Seminole, Lake Counties) joining Pensacola and the western Panhandle (Escambia and neighbors) as islands of GOP strength. Isolated pockets of the old

Florida remain along the upper Gulf Coast and along the Georgia border, but migration will continue to erode the Democratic loyalty of these smaller counties.

Democrats have sensed that a reliance on elderly Democratic transplants and old-time Floridians does not make an electoral majority. Their strategic task in the new century will be to enlarge upon their gains among south Florida's Latinos while holding their own among central Florida's professional and service class. With the cold war over, and Fidel Castro's demise on the horizon, Republicans need to find new issues that will attract and hold the loyalty of younger Cubans and newer, non-Cuban Latinos, while maintaining their current share of the elderly vote and the support of less educated whites. Tailoring a winning message for such a diverse constituency will not come easily for candidates in the new century.

Note

1. The formula for creating the index is simply the proportion of each county's voters voting Republican (Democratic) multiplied by the proportion of the total statewide population of Republican (Democratic) voters in each county. For example:

	Republican 1988–2002		Statewide Republican Vote		Index Score
County X	.45	×	.005	=	.0023
County Y	.41	×	.153	=	.0627
County Z	.72	×	.019	=	.0137

So even though County Z has a stronger GOP leaning given that 72 percent of the voters there voted Republican, it has smaller share of the total statewide Republican vote than County Y — the difference of 1.9 percent compared with 15.3 percent. Hence, in the rankings, County Z would rank well below County Y in overall strategic importance.

CHAPTER 5

TEXAS

Major Forces for Electoral Change in Texas

- Immigration from Latin America, Mainly Mexico
- Domestic (Internal) Migration from Other States
- Conversion of White Democrats to the Republican Party
- Mobilization of Black and Latino Voters
- Booms and Busts in the Petroleum and Energy Sector

Texas is among the fastest-growing and most diverse states in the nation, and yet one of the most simply stereotyped. Ask people what they think of when the Lone Star state is mentioned, and a handful of mental images are conjured up: cattle, cowboys, guns, oil, desert heat, and the border. The most common political descriptor is conservative, even redneck. The state's size is often mentioned. To be Texas is to be big. Outsiders have little appreciation for the complexity that is contemporary Texas.

Curiously, Texas's public image has not changed with the times and circumstances of its development. Partly this is because Texas natives have worked so hard at preserving the state's historical image as an independent frontier outpost. By the late 1970s, the frontier had largely closed as the state became home to three of the nation's ten largest cities: Houston, Dallas, and San Antonio. In 1960, only Houston ranked in the top ten. El Paso and Austin ranked in the top twenty-five by 1990, soaring upward from forty-sixth and sixty-seventh place thirty years before. As in Florida, the growth in the state's population has been the result of both internal migration and immigration.

The growth from domestic sources, coupled with the conversion of Southern whites to the Republican party, has contributed to a political shift toward the GOP. In the 1930s and 1940s, there was hardly a single county in Texas that voted Republican—certainly none could be counted on to do so. By the beginning of the new millennium, the state's counties were evenly divided in presidential elections, and Republicans were routinely capable of contesting all major statewide offices. Texas is less Democratic at the turn of the twenty-first century than it has ever been.

In the early 2000s, Texas could be divided into a number of socioeconomic regions set apart by a combination of economic activity, population characteristics, and physical geography. Southwest Texas—from Corpus Christi running along the Rio Grande to El Paso—could be classified as a distinct region in ethnic and economic terms. The remoteness of this region from the rest of Texas and the nation makes transportation an unusually large sector of employment. In some of these counties as many as one worker in five was involved in some aspect of getting people and goods from place to place. Economically, southwest Texas is a mix of cattle ranches and farms that specialize in vegetables and citrus, sparsely populated by towns like Laredo, Del Rio, and McAllen that serve as regional trade, health-care, and transport centers. Much of the population is Latino, of Mexican ancestry. The area's ranches and farms are owned predominantly by Anglos. Most of the agricultural labor force is Mexican American or supplied through Mexican temporary guest-worker programs and through employment of illegal immigrants. The North American Free Trade Agreement (NAFTA), signed by President Clinton in 1993, has accelerated economic and population growth along the border, particularly in El Paso, a city of nearly 600,000 at the dawn of the new century. The Democratic allegiance of the population in the 1980s and 1990s could be explained by reference to the high concentration of Latino residents of Mexican descent. Ninety-four percent of Laredo's population was Hispanic, as was 77 percent of El Paso's. Their ethnicity is not what aligns them with the Democratic party, however. Relatively low socioeconomic standing coupled with seldom reconsidered voting habits incline them to vote for the party that favors government intervention, investment, and relief. The border towns of Brownsville and McAllen contain some of the poorest people in the nation. Immigration from Mexico and Central America since 1970 has increased the population of southwest Texas, but has not had a pronounced electoral impact given that many of these immigrants do not naturalize, while those who do behave in the same way as the local citizen population. Anti-immigrant sentiment among the minority Anglo population of south Texas facilitated the conversion of native whites to the Republican party as the twentieth century ended.

The Texas Panhandle (see map 5.1), including the large cities of Lubbock and Amarillo, has an economy anchored in cattle ranching, cotton, and wheat production. Because it was known for droughts and billowing windstorms, people were slow to populate the region and quick to leave for California during the dust bowl years of the Great Depression (Gregory 1989). The original settlers of this region were land speculators from Iowa and Illinois. Railroads came to Lubbock and Amarillo in the 1910s and made these cities the regional hubs for the warehousing and shipment of agricultural produce. Settlers from Kansas and the upper plains arrived to populate the towns, importing their Republican party loyalties. Through much of the twentieth century, the Panhandle would remain the most Republican part of the state, and the part that least resembled the Old South. These counties have small black populations, although the Latino population has steadily increased. Even so, when compared to other areas of Texas, population growth in this area has been unnoticeable and the politics slow to change.

East Texas consists of about forty eastern counties bordered by Louisiana on the east, the Dallas–Fort Worth metropolitan area to the west, and the Houston metropolitan area to the south (see map 5.1). This is the most racially diverse part of the state, containing the highest proportion of African Americans, many of whom are the descendants of slaves brought to the region to work cotton farms in the early nineteenth century. Because of its population composition, history, geography, and climate, it is the part of Texas that most resembles the Old South, with particularly high levels of racial segregation both across and within communities (Maxwell and Crain 1998, 2; Key 1949). Oil and natural gas wells fueled booms in many east Texas towns early in the twentieth century and continue to sustain the economic life of the region. Cotton, rice, and poultry production remain leading agricultural commodities. After 1970, the economically strategic location of this region, proximate to Houston, Dallas, and Shreveport, Louisiana, became obvious to many employers who relocated or expanded their businesses in east Texas towns such as Tyler and Longview with the added incentives of low prevailing wages, cheap land, and low taxes. Politically, the counties of east Texas were competitive between the two political parties through the 1990s

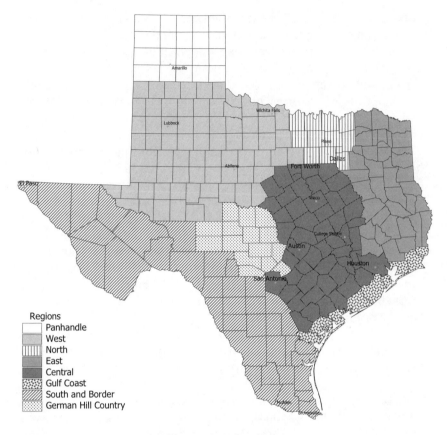

Map 5.1.   Regions of Texas

and early 2000s, although the counties with the largest black populations along the Louisiana border have strongly favored Democrats in
presidential elections.

North Texas consists of the Dallas and Fort Worth metropolitan
areas, along with outlying cities such as Denton and Sherman (see
map 5.1). Known for having a hard-core probusiness mentality, this
area has grown rapidly since mid-century, drawing in both rural Texans as well as many cross-state migrants from the Midwest and Northeast who have followed plant relocations or found opportunities in locally grown operations. North Texas is a classic example of a place
whose prosperity has been constructed on postindustrial enterprise—
manufacturing remained a small proportion of overall employment as
the twentieth century came to a close (about 13 percent). The energy
business, financial and health services, and transportation were the

staple employment sectors. Interstate migration to Dallas–Fort Worth
has served to dilute the traditional Democratic leaning of north Texas,
steering it sharply away from any mooring it once had to the Old
South. We can be sure that migration has had this impact because
nearby counties that have not experienced the same degree of inun-
dation remain Democratic strongholds. While this region supported
Republicans in presidential elections since Richard Nixon, north
Texas is not as Republican as the Panhandle.

West Texas lies northwest of San Antonio and Austin, running as
far westward as Odessa and Midland. Near Midland, the economy
rests mostly on petroleum with one worker in six employed on the oil
rigs. Further north as one moves toward the Panhandle, the economy
shifts toward agriculture, especially sheep and cattle ranching, with
small towns serving as local retail and wholesale trade centers. The
eastern part of west Texas is bounded by San Angelo, location of a
major air force training center, but otherwise serving as a trade and
commerce center for Tom Green County and its more rural neighbors. West Texas has been among the slower-growing areas of the
state, drifting toward the GOP in presidential elections since the
1960s and likely to stay there well into the new century.

Central Texas includes Austin (Travis County), suburbs of Houston,
southern suburbs of San Antonio and Dallas–Fort Worth, and several
smaller cities (Temple, Waco, Huntsville, Bryan). The Houston suburbs of central Texas lie in Montgomery County, a locale whose population has grown tenfold between 1960 and 2000 based largely on interstate migration. Two established and well-financed universities,
Texas A&M and the University of Texas, have attracted high-tech industries to the region, including the spectacularly successful Dell
Computer Corporation in Round Rock (Williamson County north of
Austin). The demand for workers in information-age industries has
outstripped the local supply, generating a steady stream of migrants
from other states. This migration has not been without political consequences as new populations eventually become active and change
the electoral composition of the faster-growing counties. Politically,
central Texas was a patchwork of Republican and Democratic strength
in the 1990s and early 2000s. Austin itself was a liberal Democratic
stronghold for most of the twentieth century, as were several neighboring counties. But population growth has contributed to the political realignment of some of the mid-sized counties, contributing to the
success of Republican candidates.

The Texas Gulf Coast—running from Beaumont and Port Arthur,

through Galveston to Corpus Christi—is sometimes considered a distinct region because of its economic base (see map 5.1). Rapid growth in these counties has been fueled by the petroleum and chemical industries. In the 1970s and 1980s, the Gulf Coast attracted many migrants from the depressed industrial Midwest, particularly Michigan, Ohio, and Illinois. This migration has not had a dramatic impact on the partisan orientation of the Port Arthur and Galveston areas because the new arrivals have often been blue-collar, semiskilled workers with Democratic loyalties and have been slow to get involved in local politics. Compared to the rest of Texas, the Gulf Coast has voted more Democratic in presidential elections during the final decades of the twentieth century.

One other small area of the state is worth mentioning because of its historical and political distinctiveness—the German Hill Country lying between San Antonio and Austin and extending nearly as far westward as San Angelo. This region was originally settled by Germans, Czechs, and Poles in the late nineteenth and early twentieth centuries. The area's economic base has been and remains cattle ranching and fruit and vegetable farms, but the growth of San Antonio and Austin has spread into this region to dilute its unique character. Outside the Texas Panhandle, the Hill Country has the most long-standing GOP tradition. These counties heavily favored Herbert Hoover over Al Smith in the 1928 presidential election. They went for Franklin D. Roosevelt in the 1932 and 1936 presidential elections but not by the wide margins that were typical in other locations. In gubernatorial elections, residents of the Hill Country considered Republican candidates when few other Texans would.

Because of their size, Houston (Harris County) and San Antonio (Bexar County) are worth discussing as separate entities, distinct from other regions. Through aggressive annexation they managed to escape the fate of cities in the Northeast and Midwest that were hemmed in by affluent suburbs that sapped the central city of its tax base (Rusk 1995). Houston's economic growth has been based in oil and gas exploration, which led to key spin-offs in chemical manufacturing. But Houston's future (like Dallas's) would not be pegged only to petroleum and heavy industry. The energy sector remains Houston's most important moneymaker, but by the 1990s, the bulk of the city's employment was in transportation (e.g., Sysco Systems, Continental Airlines), high-tech services (e.g., Hewlett Packard's Compaq division), and particularly in engineering and consulting related to energy production. Since oil and gas exploration has always relied upon a sizable semiskilled, blue-collar labor force, Houston has attracted a less educated, less professional workforce than Dallas. The Houston area has become more ethnically diverse than north Texas as it has drawn in a growing black population from rural parts of east Texas and Louisiana and a large Hispanic population from south Texas. Politically, the area's growing ethnic diversity has converted the black and Latino neighborhoods into Democratic bastions that serve as the foundation for Texas-style liberalism (Davidson 1990). Houston's outlying neighborhoods populated by more affluent Anglo populations send some of the most conservative Republicans to Congress and the state legislature. Turnout determines whether Democrats or Republicans carry Harris County in close elections (Davidson 1990).

San Antonio's economy was built around two large air force installations that serve as major training centers: Lackland and Kelly Air Force Bases. At the turn of the new century, the government remained the area's largest single employer. Unlike Orange County, California, or Orlando, Florida, the presence of major military installations did not serve as a magnet for the aerospace industry, although several companies maintained a nominal presence. San Antonio did become home to USAA Insurance, a company employing 13,800 people (in the home office, as of March 2000) that specialized in providing insurance and financial services to military families. While not on the scale of Houston, oil and mineral extraction was an important component of the local economy through the last two decades of the twentieth century, as were retail trade and services related to the brisk tourist flow drawn to the city's famous historic sites (the Alamo). By the early 2000s, slightly more than one-third of the city's population was of Latino origin, and they constituted a loyal Democratic voting bloc in most elections. The Anglo population in the city and the suburbs was more affluent and better educated than the Latino population, and these neighborhoods could be counted upon to go Republican. The black population in San Antonio constituted just 7 percent of the city's one million people and has proven to be a political force only in coalition with the Latino population.

Texas is a huge land mass, larger than France and many other countries, but at the dawn of the new century, much of it remains sparsely settled. The areas that have been untouched by population

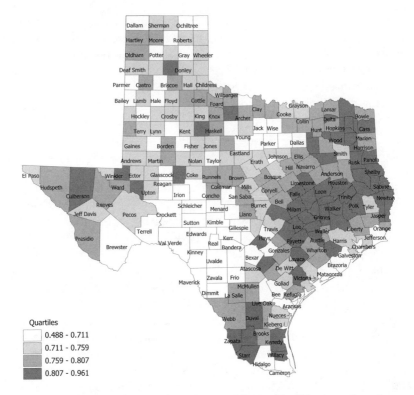

Map 5.2.   Average Democratic percentage of the presidential vote, 1928–1936

growth have seen very little political change since the 1930s. Map 5.2 illustrates the average Democratic percentage of the presidential vote from 1928 to 1936 for each of the state's counties, grouped by quartile. While almost none of the state's counties voted Republican in this period, differences in Democratic strength are worth noting. The darkly shaded areas are those in the most Democratic quartile, and the white ones are the most Republican. There is a pronounced regional split in the state, with the counties of east Texas being the most heavily Democratic, while those of west Texas were less swayed by the Roosevelt revolution. Notably, Dallas (Dallas), Tarrant (Fort Worth), and Bexar (San Antonio) Counties are in the lowest quartile of Democratic support.

The 1950s found Texas moving toward a two-party politics, but it was still about twenty years away from electing a Republican governor. With the increased mobilization of black and Hispanic voters into the Democratic party in the 1960s, factionalism erupted as the state's Democratic base grew increasingly heterogeneous (Davidson 1990). In the state legislature, Democrats divided along urban and rural–small town bases of support. This factionalism continued through the 1980s and 1990s, with rural and small town Democrats drawing on a mostly Anglo population with conservative values, while urban Democrats attracted ethnic minority populations that shared a liberal ideology.

With minority mobilization and Democratic factionalism has come Republican resurgence. Like Florida, Texas is uniformly less Democratic now than it was in the 1930s (see maps 5.2 and 5.3). Areas of sectional continuity include east Texas, especially along the Louisiana border, where the mobilization of significant black populations turned back the rising Republican tide among Anglo voters. Elsewhere in Texas, slow growth from sources outside the state has been a predictor of continuity. Many counties, though, have undergone a complete realignment. Consistent with other Southern states, Republicans have picked up many voters from the ranks of disaffected whites unhappy with the liberal drift of the national Democratic party on issues ranging from civil rights to abortion to gun control. Casualties have been particularly heavy among rural and small town Democrats in the Panhandle and in west Texas. These regions were more politically cohesive as geographic sections in the early 2000s than they were in the 1930s.

In terms of sheer numbers, though, the biggest GOP gains have been in the counties that have experienced an influx of residents from outside Texas. Take the counties in the Houston metropolitan area, for instance. At mid-century, most of Houston's neighboring counties (Montgomery, Fort Bend) were easy pickings for Democratic candidates at all levels of elective office. By the 2000s, this was far less true because population and income growth irreversibly altered their rural character. Montgomery County, north of Houston, is probably the best example. Montgomery had emerged as one of the state's leading GOP strongholds as early as 1980. Collin, Denton, Ellis, and Rockwall Counties, bordering Dallas, underwent a similar transformation.

Map 5.3 reveals that the state's sectionalism has undergone substantial change. For example, south and southwest Texas stand out as a

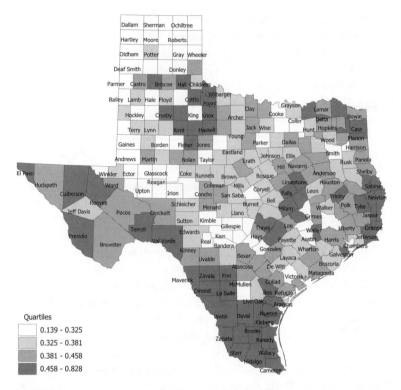

Map 5.3. Average Democratic percentage of the presidential vote, 1988–2000

politically uniform region of Democratic dominance. The mobilization of Mexican Americans into the Democratic party in the last decades of the century produced political change in many south Texas counties once dominated by Anglo voters. The state's largest cities have become Democratic strongholds with the flight of Republicans to the suburbs. El Paso stood in the second lowest quartile in Democratic strength in map 5.2, but had moved into the highest quartile by the 1990s (compare to map 5.3). Austin is more Democratic relative to the rest of the state than it was at mid-century, as are San Antonio (Bexar County), Corpus Christi (Nueces County), Brownsville (Cameron County), and McAllen (Hidalgo County). Sectionalism has not disappeared in Texas politics with the rise of two-party competition, but new sections have emerged and others have been reshaped by the forces of demographic change.

Where Are the Votes in Texas? Republican and Democratic Mobilization Targets

Since most elections for statewide office in Texas were competitive by the late 1960s, and because the state's population is distributed over such a vast area, Republicans and Democrats must target their resources carefully. Texas political campaigns rank among the most costly in the nation. It makes little sense to spend time and money in sparsely populated areas of the state where there are few voters. But even after eliminating the 100 or so most sparsely populated counties, that still leaves a vast territory and a far-flung population to analyze and capture on election day.

To provide some indication of where the geographic bases of party support lie, we have ranked the top ten counties for both political parties in table 5.1 based on the results from the 1988–2000 presidential elections.[1] Harris County ranked first for Republicans, meaning that their mobilization resources should be targeted at the Houston area above all others. About 15.1 percent of the statewide Republican vote for president came from Harris County in the pooled 1988–2000 elections. For Democrats, it contributed about 15.4 percent of the statewide Democratic base. Given its size, Harris County is still the most important voter-rich area, for both parties, so it ranks first in table 5.1 for Democrats also. Similarly, Dallas County (Dallas) ranks second in importance for both parties.

Below the top two counties, however, the targeted areas diverge in their relative importance to each party's statewide mobilization effort, suggesting that the bases for political support are geographically distinct. Tarrant County (Fort Worth), for instance, ranks third in importance for Republicans, but fifth for Democrats. Travis County (Austin) is slightly more important for Democrats (ranks fourth) than for Republicans (ranks sixth). In their top ten list, Republicans have three major suburban counties (Collin, Montgomery, and Fort Bend) that do not appear in the Democrats' top ten. Democrats have two working-class areas along the Gulf Coast among their top mobilization targets: Jefferson (Beaumont-Port Arthur) and Galveston (Galveston). These counties rank much lower—twenty-second and nineteenth, respectively—on the GOP target list. Notably, the Democrats rank among their top ten counties two heavily Mexican-American counties: Nueces (Corpus Christi) and Hidalgo (McAllen-

Edinburg), and these ranked far lower in importance to GOP campaign efforts. As in other states, the Democratic vote is highly concentrated in the major urban centers but is also dispersed throughout south and east Texas.

Comparisons of the mobilization targets in the most recent elections with those of the 1930s reveal some dramatic changes in Texas politics corresponding to population growth from suburbanization and from outside the state (see map 5.4). For Democrats, south Texas has surged in its importance, with Corpus Christi and McAllen-Edinburg providing far more votes in recent elections than they had earlier in the century. Until the 1960s, the Republican party—not a competitive force—found most of its scanty vote dispersed throughout medium-sized and small cities, including those in south Texas. The Houston and Dallas suburban counties emerged in the 1960s and 1970s as the most significant centers of GOP growth, even as the Republicans lost significant vote shares with growing Hispanic mobilization along the border. As in California, the Republicans and Democrats have increasingly had to gravitate toward different territorial sections in mobilizing their bases.

We conclude from these geographic comparisons of partisan strength that parties and candidates at the dawn of the new century must compete on some of the same turf in the five most heavily populated areas, particularly Houston and Dallas. But outside of these locations, the parties' geographic bases are more contrasting than alike.

TABLE 5.1   Texas's Top Ten Strongest Counties for Republicans and Democrats in the 1988–2000 Presidential Contests

Rank	Democratic	Republican
1	Harris (Houston)	Harris (Houston)
2	Dallas (Dallas)	Dallas (Dallas)
3	Bexar (San Antonio)	Tarrant (Fort Worth)
4	Travis (Austin)	Bexar (San Antonio)
5	Tarrant (Fort Worth)	Collin (Suburban Dallas)
6	El Paso (El Paso)	Travis (Austin)
7	Hidalgo (McAllen)	Denton (Denton)
8	Jefferson (Beaumont)	Montgomery (Suburban Houston)
9	Nueces (Corpus Christi)	Lubbock (Lubbock)
10	Galveston (Galveston)	Fort Bend (Suburban Houston)
% of total vote	57.3	52.4

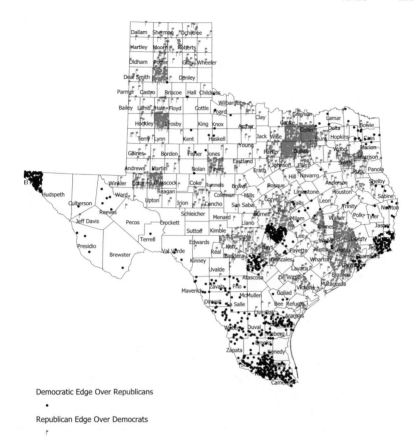

Democratic Edge Over Republicans

•

Republican Edge Over Democrats

ʳ

Map 5.4.   Areas of Republican and Democratic dominance, 1988–2000

What is unique about Texas compared to other states we have examined is that the Republican base has actually grown more concentrated, while the Democratic base has grown more dispersed since the New Deal era (Gimpel and Schuknecht 2002). Democrats have expanded their vote-getting ability in rural areas of south and east Texas, where blacks and Latinos are concentrated most heavily, whereas Republicans have gained significantly in the Houston and Dallas suburbs as a function of Northern migration. Campaigning in Texas requires a special effort to understand the concerns and issues pertaining to rural and small town minorities, a bloc that is considerably different from the blacks and Latinos that populate large central cities.

Texas's Changing Electoral Foundations

In the late 1940s, V. O. Key Jr. predicted Texas would soon have a two-party competitive politics, and he was right. Key recognized that the domination of Texas politics by east Texas was coming to an end. Population growth to the north, west, and south shifted the state's center of gravity to central Texas. In the era when east Texas was the population center of the state, the Old Southern character of this region defined the state's politics. With in-migration from outside the state, and from regions other than the South, a two-party Texas was inevitable.

To trace developments in the voting allegiance of Texans since the New Deal era, we have relied upon Gary King's ecological inference technique (1997) (for information on this method see appendix A). Table 5.2 estimates the Democratic proportion of the presidential vote in the state from 1928 to 2000 for several politically relevant demographic groups.

Population Mobility

Maps of Texas electoral patterns show that the state looks very different at the turn of the twenty-first century than it did in the 1930s (compare maps 5.2 and 5.3). The most significant political changes have been driven by the growth of suburban Texas. Political realignment has been most pronounced in the fast-growing counties around Dallas, such as Denton, Collin, and Rockwall, as well as in the Houston metropolitan area. The instrument of partisan change in these places has been interstate migration fueled by economic growth (Frendreis 1989; Gimpel and Schuknecht 2001). Population in-migration from domestic sources has also accelerated the transforming process of generational replacement because new births follow from the influx of young, working-age families. With no historic ties to the traditional Democratic leanings of Texas, these families raise their children in accord with their own political traditions, which have often enough been Republican.

South Texas has moved in the opposite direction politically from north Texas. These counties have seen growth from immigration as well as increased mobilization of Mexican Americans native to the country. Democrats have gained considerable ground along the entire border region, or at least have lost less of their base than in the rest of Texas. In some notable cases, strong Republican gains among native whites have been more than offset by the mobilization of Mexican Americans and other minorities into the Democratic party.

Whether population in-migration from outside a state will alter the partisan composition of a local electorate depends upon the political orientations of both natives and newcomers. If large numbers of new residents import Republican party affiliation to a Democratic area, partisan change will be the likely result. Texas is replete with counties that have been inundated with Republican migrants from elsewhere. Data on the number of migrants from outside of Texas has been available since the 1960 Census. Estimates of the Democratic inclination of this population show that it is considerably less Democratic than the population of nonmigrants. In the 1956–64 elections, for example, an estimated 25 percent of internal migrants voted Democratic, compared to 60 percent for other Texas residents (natives and immigrants combined) (see table 5.2).

While partisan change in Texas has been driven by in-migration to the state's major metropolitan areas, places that have not experienced this type of growth have also undergone change. These changes among native Texans are reflected in our estimates that show the allegiance of native Texans to the Democratic party has waned since the 1950s and 1960s, dropping from above 60 percent to just above 50 percent (see table 5.2). Still, natives have remained more Democratic than cross-state migrants. Comparing the results for natives and internal migrants in more recent elections reveals that narrow majorities of native Texans support Democratic candidates, but newcomers are solidly in the GOP camp. Conversion and generational replacement have contributed to the changing partisanship of native-born Texans. But a much faster force for local political change has been the movement of non-Texans into the state (Frendreis 1989).

We expected the estimates for immigrants to show this population to be much more Democratic than the population of nonimmigrants since the counties with the largest foreign-born populations were very Democratic in the 1980s and 1990s. In fact, however, the results from ecological inference estimation are mixed. The immigrant population is far more Democratic than the nonimmigrant population in the presidential elections between 1956 and 1972, probably because so many natives abandoned the Democratic party. From 1976 to 1992 there appears to be a much narrower gap between immigrant and nonimmigrant voting, as the foreign-born population appears to favor Reagan and George H. W. Bush over their Democratic counterparts. The estimates for the 1996–2000 elections appeared to be a close approximation of a renewed Democratic commitment among the immigrant population and corresponded to press reports about how newly naturalized citizens (mainly of Mexican ancestry) voted. The figures for Hispanics in Texas may be more accurate than those for immigrants. From 1976 to 2000, the estimates in table 5.2 show that solid majorities of Hispanics voted Democratic. The difference in support for the Democratic party between Hispanics and non-Hispanics is typically 15 to 16 points. Survey data indicate that this is an

TABLE 5.2.   Estimates of the Democratic Percentage of the Presidential Vote for Various Electoral Groups in Texas, 1928–2000 (ecological inference maximum likelihood)

Pooled Presidential Election Years	Blacks/ Nonblacks		Elderly/ Nonelderly		Immigrants/ Nonimmigrants		Farmers/ Nonfarmers		Whites/ Nonwhites	
1928, 1932	94.7*	64.4*	62.8*	69.1*	99.3*	68.4*	70.9*	67.5*	64.9*	80.0*
1936, 1940, 1944	87.1*	78.7*	35.0*	82.5*	43.3*	81.3*	84.9*	77.5*	78.8*	86.6*
1948, 1952	60.7*	55.3*	26.2*	58.1*	31.9*	56.9*	63.7*	54.4*	55.3*	60.5*
1956, 1960, 1964	60.3*	51.7*	74.1*	51.0*	67.1*	52.3*	72.2*	51.3*	51.7*	60.3*
1968, 1972	44.3*	41.4*	72.3*	38.8*	99.3	40.4*	65.4*	36.4*	41.4*	43.9*
1976, 1980, 1984	78.2*	38.5*	49.2	42.8*	46.4*	43.0*	43.7*	43.2*	36.5*	69.0*
1988, 1992	80.7	35.3*	70.1	37.3*	32.6*	41.4*	22.6	40.9*	31.3*	69.3*
1996, 2000	78.1	37.2*	40.2	42.4*	79.3*	38.5*	2.0	42.6*	28.7*	81.8*

	Mfg. Workers/ Non Mfg. Workers		College Educated/ Non College Educated		Native to State/ Nonnatives		Internal Migrants/ Nonmigrants		Hispanics/ Non-Hispanics	
1928, 1932	—	—	—	—	—	—	—	—	—	—
1936, 1940, 1944	—	—	—	—	—	—	—	—	—	—
1948, 1952	61.1*	55.3*	30.0	57.3*	—	—	—	—	—	—
1956, 1960, 1964	49.0*	53.5*	38.5*	54.4*	61.7*	25.1*	25.1*	60.3*	—	—
1968, 1972	31.6*	44.0*	52.1*	40.5*	49.2*	25.3*	21.1*	50.1*	—	—
1976, 1980, 1984	62.7*	39.3*	4.9*	48.3*	53.0*	22.7*	9.9*	55.0*	56.2*	39.8*
1988, 1992	53.8	38.5*	3.8*	50.1*	50.8*	22.1*	2.9*	54.2*	53.5*	36.3*
1996, 2000	71.3	38.1*	46.1	41.4*	48.3*	30.8*	15.4*	51.7*	58.8*	35.0*

Note: Cell entries show the estimated percentage voting Democratic in the listed presidential elections. Complete variable definitions and results from the ecological inference estimation appear in appendix B, with standard errors and bounds.

*Reflect estimates with lower and upper bounds narrower than 0,1.

accurate estimate of the difference between the two populations, and according to exit polling data, even Texas governor George W. Bush was only able to close the gap to 11 points in the 2000 presidential election (54 percent of Hispanics voted for Gore, 43 percent for Bush), and this result was facilitated by low turnout in the areas of Latino concentration.

Generational Replacement

Generational replacement has been the driving force for long-term political change in some of the sparsely populated towns of west Texas and the Panhandle, and medium-sized towns in east Texas. We know that the force for change in these places has been the replacement of elderly Democrats with younger Republicans because population growth has not been especially strong, and conversion to the Republican party has not been a sudden, overnight phenomenon.

Generational change can produce political realignment over a long enough period (Abramson 1975). The older generation of Democrats who contributed to the sweeping Democratic success of Roosevelt and Truman had died by the turn of the new century, and two younger generations entered the electorate during the time of Republican domination in presidential elections between 1952 and 1992. These changes occurred coincident with the historical shift of the Texas Democratic party away from its once–small town base toward larger cities with more ethnically diverse populations. Seeing that the Democrats had less to offer rural white Texas after 1970 than at any time in the state's history, these voters were far more likely to back GOP candidates in subsequent years.

Evaluating the political inclinations of those over age 65 is important because they indicate whether the replacement of this population by younger cohorts in coming years will contribute to partisan change. With an average life expectancy of about 75 years of age, many of those who are over 65 today will no longer be in the electorate ten years from now. If their partisanship is significantly different from that of younger age groups, the mortality of this population stands to contribute to political change.

Elderly support for Democrats in the 1928 and 1932 elections appears to have been a rather fleeting phenomenon (based on the estimates in table 5.2). From 1936 to 1952, the vote of those of retirement age was much more Republican than that of younger voters. This would make sense if Roosevelt's popularity was only temporary among a group of elderly Texans who returned to their GOP anchorage after 1932. Younger Texans, on the other hand, held fast to their Democratic allegiance made only stronger by Roosevelt's progressive politics. In the pooled 1948–52 elections, an estimated 26 percent of those over age 65 voted Democratic, compared to 58 percent of the nonelderly. Of course, in the short term, the GOP support among the elderly would mean increasing Democratic dominance as mortality weakened Republican ranks, replacing older Republicans with younger Democrats.

The aging process began to alter the loyalties of the elderly in Texas by the 1960s. Older Republicans had died out by then, and the new retirement-age voters had previously moved into the Democratic camp during the Great Depression. Now habituated to nearly a lifetime of Democratic affiliation born out of economic hard times, these Texans would wind up more resistant to GOP appeals than younger voters. In the pooled 1968–72 presidential elections, an estimated 72 percent of elderly voters cast Democratic ballots, compared with just 39 percent of those in younger age cohorts, many of whom voted for George Wallace (1968) and Richard Nixon (1972). Until the 1996–2000 presidential elections, the estimates show that older Texans have been decisively more Democratic than younger ones.[2] Exit polling data from the 2000 election verify this age gap, with 48 percent of those over age 65 voting for Gore, compared with 37 percent of voters age 64 and younger—an 11 point difference.

Conversion

Generational replacement has been responsible for the long-term political change in the state's less populated areas, but there may also be evidence of dramatic short-term changes such as one would find if legions of voters decided suddenly to jump ship. We get a sense for where this may have happened when we look at electoral periods such as the 1930s and 1960s where new issues surfaced to divide the electorate in unfamiliar ways. In table 5.3 we present estimates of the proportion of Democrats who remained loyal to their party from one election to the next during these two eras of electoral upheaval. From 1928 to 1932, 95.6 percent of Democrats remained loyal to their party, and from 1932 to 1936, 94.9 percent remained with the Democrats. On the Republican side, however, we see massive defections, with only 17.7 percent of Hoover voters in 1928 voting for him again in 1932. Texas Republicans were more disloyal than those in either Florida (chap. 4) or California (chap. 3). Most of the large-scale switching was over by 1932, though, because about 70 percent of the die-hard Hoover supporters in 1932 remained supportive of their party's nominee in 1936, figures comparable to those of Florida and California (see tables 3.3 and 4.3 for comparison). Texas had been a solidly Democratic state since the Civil War, and the New Deal realignment wiped out most remnants of Republican strength.

In the 1960s, Southern Democrats were wary of the leftward drift of their party, but Lyndon B. Johnson was a favorite son, so there are far fewer Democratic defections to Barry Goldwater in Texas than in Florida. About 93 percent of Kennedy supporters remained loyal to Johnson in 1964, compared with only 58 percent in Florida. Johnson's home-state supporters were not as enthusiastic about Hubert Humphrey—about 65 percent of Johnson supporters voted for Humphrey, with 11 percent supporting Wallace and the remainder supporting Nixon. Wallace support among Texas Democrats (11 percent) was not as high as it was among Florida Democrats (25 percent). Republicans were not altogether happy with Goldwater, and only 64 percent of Nixon supporters (from 1960) remained with their standard-bearer in 1964, although this was more loyalty than was exhibited in either California or Florida. About one in three Goldwater supporters voted for Wallace in 1968, similar to the support Wallace received from Goldwater supporters in Florida (see table 4.3 for comparison).

There are several areas where the vote for Wallace in 1968 was followed by new and strong Republican showings in subsequent years—suggesting that long-term conversions occurred. Since Wallace was a conservative Democrat who attracted many white Southerners, we can infer that areas in which he did well were ripe for conversion. Hence, places where Wallace did well that went Republican shortly thereafter fit the criteria for conversion, particularly if they were not experiencing much population growth or decline, and turnout remained stable. Many desolate rural counties fit this pattern, particularly in west Texas in and around Midland. Notably, though, several larger counties in east Texas do too, particularly Smith, Rusk, and

TABLE 5.3. Estimates of Party Loyalty and Conversion across Presidential Elections in Texas (ecological inference maximum likelihood)

Presidential Election Years	Voted Democratic 1928/Non-Democratic 1928	Voted Democratic 1932/Non-Democratic 1932	Presidential Election Years	Voted Republican 1928/Non-Republican 1928	Voted Republican 1932/Non-Republican 1932
Voted Democratic 1932	95.6* 81.3*		Voted Republican 1932	17.7* 4.3*	
Voted Democratic 1936		94.9* 29.8*	Voted Republican 1936		69.9* 4.9*

Presidential Election Years	Voted Democratic 1960/Non-Democratic 1960	Voted Democratic 1964/Non-Democratic 1964	Presidential Election Years	Voted Republican 1960/Non-Republican 1960	Voted Republican 1964/Non-Republican 1964
Voted Democratic 1964	93.1* 33.3*		Voted Republican 1964	64.0* 10.1*	
Voted Democratic 1968		65.4* 1.0*	Voted Republican 1968		75.7* 10.2*
Voted Wallace 1968		10.9* 32.0*	Voted Wallace 1968		33.0* 10.3*

Note: Cell entries show the estimated percentage voting Democratic, Republican, or for George Wallace in the presidential elections listed on each row who voted Democratic (or Republican) in the previous election. Complete variable definitions and results from the ecological inference estimation appear in appendix C, with standard errors and bounds.

*Reflect estimates with lower and upper bounds narrower than 0,1.

Panola (cities of Tyler, Henderson, and Carthage). These cities are situated in the part of Texas that most resembles the Old South. We should not be surprised, therefore, to have found an easy transition in these places from Wallace Democrats to Reagan Republicans.

Clearly, combinations of factors have been at work to propel partisan change in Texas, the most prominent ones being conversion, population mobility, and generational change. Key discussed political cleavages in Texas as being a function of class. Data on the voting tendencies of educated and less educated voters confirm Key's generalization. In the 1930s and 1940s, college graduates were far more Republican than those with less than a four-year degree. If there have been conversions since that time they have come mainly among voters with less than a college education. In the 1956, 1960, and 1964 elections, an estimated 39 percent of college-educated voters cast Democratic ballots, compared with 54 percent of remaining voters. By the 1996–2000 elections, as Democratic allegiance among the non–college educated fell, an estimated 41 percent of those lacking a four-year degree voted Democratic. Survey data indicate that these estimates may understate the precipitous loss of support by presidential Democrats of those with less educational attainment. Exit polls from the 2000 presidential election indicated that only 28 percent of those lacking a college education voted for Al Gore, compared to his 41 percent among those with a four-year degree.

Texas became much more urbanized in the twentieth century, and this development raises questions about how rural and nonrural voting blocs have behaved. Our general expectation is that rural Texas became more Republican and urban Texas more Democratic. The results in table 5.2 comparing Democratic support among farmers and nonfarmers generally bear out the idea that farmers have become less Democratic. But only in elections after 1972 do farmers come to support Republicans to a greater extent than do nonagriculture workers. Texas's rural Hispanic population in the Southwest and rural black population in east Texas account for sustained Democratic voting among the population employed in agriculture. Unlike states in the Midwest and West where the farm population is mainly Anglo, Texas has a large Latino farm population that has remained loyally Democratic. Perhaps if a distinction was made between farm proprietors and farm workers, with our data reflecting the former, our results might show that the rural population was Republican, as it is in the Panhandle and in west Texas. Our data do not make this distinction, however, and therefore show little of the rural Republicanism that came so early to Illinois, California, and other non-Southern states.

Voters in manufacturing, because of their union affiliations, were associated with the Democratic party for years following the New Deal realignment. Unions have never been strong in Texas, though, and white union members have been cross-pressured by issues of race, translating first into support for George Wallace and more recently into support for Ronald Reagan. While we do not have data with which to estimate the Democratic inclination of blue-collar workers in the 1930s and 1940s, the data for the pooled 1948–52 elections show that those employed in this sector were only slightly more likely to vote Democratic than those in other sectors. Democrats do poorly among manufacturing workers in the 1968–72 contests mainly due to the popularity of George Wallace and the contempt shown for George McGovern. Since the mid-1970s, though, our estimates show that blue-collar workers have voted much more Democratic than those employed in other sectors. We believe that our estimates may overstate the distance between the two groups, but that the general trends are still accurate. Partly, the difference between those in manufacturing and those not in manufacturing is a function of the growing number of people who have surged into the state to swell the ranks of the white-collar labor force. Nonmanufacturing workers have become more Republican, while manufacturing workers have remained loyal to the Democratic coalition, particularly as more of these blue-collar jobs have been filled by Latinos and blacks. The gap between manufacturing and nonmanufacturing workers is one that separates skilled from semiskilled employment, as well as Anglos from minorities.

Mobilization and Its Impact on Conversion

When blacks voted in small numbers, whites were content to vote Democratic. Regardless of how blacks voted, they were not an important coalition member in a generally one-party state and could therefore have little influence on the politics of the Democratic party. As in Florida, though, black mobilization after 1950 encouraged many white voters to reconsider their allegiance to the Democratic party (Giles and Hertz 1994). In this manner, the mobilization of blacks led to the conversion of whites and the rise of steady two-party competition in Texas. Our data show that white support for Democratic presidential candidates drops drastically from the mid-1940s to the early 1950s, and drops steadily through the 1996–2000 set of elections (see table 5.2).

The low estimates of support for Democrats by blacks in the 1968–72 elections are the result of the divided Democratic vote in the 1968 race. By the 1988–92 elections, an estimated 81 percent of blacks supported the Democratic candidate, compared to just 35 percent of nonblacks (see table 5.2). Since 1976, racial polarization has been far greater than in previous times. By the early 1990s, only about 31 percent of whites supported the Democratic candidate for president, compared to 69 percent of nonwhites (see table 5.2). These figures slightly understate Bill Clinton's support among whites, but the historical trend showing Texas whites abandoning the Democratic party is still valid and worth noting. Al Gore had little appeal to the white population in the 2000 election, winning an astonishingly scant 24 percent of their votes. As the black voting bloc has become an essential part of the Texas Democratic coalition, economic cleavages between the parties have been submerged by racial and ethnic ones (Davidson 1990).

Latinos in Texas have also become part of the Democratic coalition, but they divide their vote much more evenly than blacks. Our results indicate that just over half of Hispanics voted Democratic in the presidential elections after 1976. The increasing numbers of Hispanics, and their mobilization, have helped to keep the Democratic party competitive as other forces such as the conversion of Anglos and domestic migration threaten to overwhelm it. But to a greater extent than the black population, Latinos in Texas are a potential swing vote, particularly in north and west Texas, far from the politically homogeneous borderlands.

Conclusions

For all the changes that have come to Texas, it is remarkable that the state's regionalism has been so stable. Unlike in Florida, population growth has not redefined political regionalism. This is not to say, however, that Texas's political geography is the same as it was in the 1930s.

Support for Democratic candidates has dropped since mid-century nearly everywhere, but one can find clear regional pockets of Democratic support along the Mexican border, along the Louisiana border, in big city neighborhoods, and in pockets of central Texas. GOP support is to be found in the Panhandle, west Texas, north Texas, and the German Hill area outside of San Antonio. Texas has exhibited more sectional continuity than Florida because it drew in migrants who placed a higher premium on relocating to areas where job opportunities would be best. This meant that areas of high income and better education at mid-century attracted migrants with high incomes and college degrees. Working-class areas with Democratic loyalties along the Gulf Coast attracted working-class populations from outside the state to fill semiskilled jobs in the petroleum industry. In few places in Texas do we find elderly migrants moving in to gentrify areas occupied by long-term natives, as we do in Florida.

Big political changes did come to counties adjacent to Texas cities. In-migration from outside the state fueled suburbanization in Houston, San Antonio, Austin, and Dallas–Fort Worth. These suburbs full of Northern transplants and Anglo natives became solid Republican turf, while the city's populations become more racially diverse. The mobilization of the black and Latino populations in the most urban counties, and growing GOP strength in the suburbs, served to diminish the internal political cohesion of east and central Texas. Yet the loss of intraregional cohesion in these regions was counterbalanced by the addition of intraregional homogeneity in other areas such as southwest Texas, west Texas, the Panhandle, and the Dallas–Fort Worth area. The net result of these regional transformations was a gradual increase in the extent of sectional tension in presidential elections between 1928 and 2000.

For students of political change, Texas is a bonanza because the state is so large, and local conditions so diverse, that every source of partisan transformation can be found at work. The arrival of new voters, the conversion of long-term natives, the mobilization of minorities, and the slow replacement of younger voters with older voters has produced a new geography without washing away substate sectionalism. In the new century, two areas of the state bear watching because of their large populations and because they have already undergone significant political change: central Texas and east Texas. Forces for change in these regions will include the geographic dispersion and eventual mobilization of the Latino population as well as continued influx from other parts of Texas and from outside the state. Immigration will eventually add new voters to the central city and suburban counties, probably making them more Democratic. Republicans will be hard pressed to become something more than an Anglo-only party, and their narrow path toward diversity points in the direction of the Mexican-American household—not in hopelessly Democratic south Texas, but in locations in central and east Texas, Houston, Dallas, and Austin, where the Latino population has exhibited rapid upward mobility.

Notes

1. The listed counties have the largest Republican (or Democratic) populations and also have the strongest Republican (or Democratic) support calculated as a percentage of the total county vote. As in previous chapters, the rankings were obtained simply by multiplying the percentage of all statewide Republican (or Democratic) votes cast in each county by the percent support the county gave to the Republican (or Democratic) candidate for president, averaged across four presidential elections (1988–2000). For example, Harris County (Houston) provided about 15.6 percent of all statewide Republican votes in the three elections and cast an average of 49.8 percent of its votes for the GOP candidate. Multiplying these two figures together, one obtains an index of Republican voter strength ($.156 \times .498 = .078$). After this index is calculated for each county and for each party, the counties are then ranked from highest to lowest.

2. We added a control variable (zb) for the percentage of the population in rural areas to the ecological inference model predicting the vote for those over age 65 in the 1996–2000 elections. The results were dramatic: the elderly vote moved from 40 percent to 59 percent Democratic once we separated the rural elderly population from the rest of the retirement-age electorate. These figures suggest that support for Bob Dole and George W. Bush was strongest among the elderly living outside the most urban and suburban counties in the state.

CHAPTER 6

COLORADO

Major Forces for Electoral Change in Colorado

- Domestic (Internal) Migration from Other States
- Suburbanization of the Population
- Rise of the Tourism and Recreation Industry
- Decline of the Manufacturing and Mining Economy
- Decline of the Agricultural Economy
- Mobilization of the Latino Population

The chances are good that someone asked to list images they associate with the American West will base their responses in part on their perceptions of Colorado. The popular image of Colorado cultivated by television shows, movies, and the state tourism board is to many American minds a comprehensive encapsulation of the West's character. Colorado's image is defined as much by long, dusty cattle drives across open rangeland as by skiers and snowboarders plowing through powdery snow. Ghost towns are nestled deep in Colorado's Rocky Mountains, visible monuments to the prominence that mineral wealth played in the state's early economic development. Latinos compose the state's largest minority population and contribute to the tapestry of cultures present in modern Colorado. Several counties in southern Colorado have Hispanic majority populations.

Americans not native to the West often have a difficult time identifying and understanding the differences that exist among the eleven continental Western states. For many people living east of the Mississippi River, all points west comprise an amorphous tract of land that is home to a homogeneous population and a uniform culture. After all, what *are* the differences between, say, Colorado and Oregon, or Arizona and Montana? But questions such as these arise primarily from unfamiliarity: they are akin to asking about the differences between New York and Pennsylvania or North Carolina and South Carolina, which, as residents of these states will not hesitate to point out, are numerous. The West is a region of contrasts, where in-migration has mixed populations of different origins, preventing these states from being easily characterized as a cohesive political region in the manner in which we sometimes describe the American South.

Comparing Colorado and Oregon (chap. 11) is expedient here because these two Western states share several physical similarities. Both states are bisected by mountains, Oregon by the Cascades and Colorado by the Rockies. Recent population growth in both states has been concentrated within one region. One side of the mountains is more heavily populated than the other. Both states were overwhelmingly Republican at the time of the New Deal but have since undergone considerable political transformation. The social, political, and economic characteristics of each state's regions differ largely on the basis of physical geography and the uneven distribution of natural resources. Despite these important similarities, however, Colorado and Oregon have taken different political paths since the middle of the twentieth century. Why?

Water is plentiful in western Oregon, and its abundance is part of the driving force behind the state's economy. But water is far more precious a resource in Colorado, often compared to blood. The heavy winter snowfalls that blanket the Rockies are the state's primary source of fresh water, and demand for snowmelt arises in the arid plains of eastern Colorado and in the burgeoning cities along the Front Range (Simmons 1984). Denver, Boulder, and Colorado Springs are rapidly expanding, and with growth comes demand for public works and the construction of water delivery projects (Davis 1995; Wrinkle 1971). But not all or even most of the demand for the Colorado Rockies' runoff is made by in-state residents: the Rockies are the headwaters of the Colorado River, a water lifeline vital to much of the Southwest and southern California (Hundley 1975). Contentious disputes concerning water allocation have arisen in the past between Colorado, Arizona, and Nevada, and continued growth throughout the West and its attendant demands promise to keep water rights a front-burner issue well into the future.

National social issues are often part of Colorado's political scene, sometimes brought up via direct legislation as ballot initiatives (McVeigh 1995; Ormrod and Cole 1996). In 1984, the state's voters banned the use of public funding for abortion services and permitted casino gambling in Pueblo. In 1988, they made English the state's official language. In 1990, Colorado voters extended gambling to two historic mining towns. Perhaps most controversial of all, in 1992, Colorado's citizens approved by a 53 to 46 percent majority an initiative that amended the state constitution to:

> (1) repeal any existing law or policy that protected a person with a "homosexual, lesbian, or bisexual orientation" from discrimination in Colorado and any of its cities, towns, counties, and school boards and (2) prohibit future adoption or enforcement of "any [such] law or policy." (Keen and Goldberg 1998)

The battle over the initiative was framed as one of the elimination of special rights for gays by its proponents versus the enactment of an antigay amendment by opponents, and the outcome captured national interest. Finally, in April 1999, a horrific high school shooting incident at Columbine High School in Littleton, an affluent Denver suburb, in which fifteen people were killed, resulted in widespread calls for tougher federal gun control laws and sparked national debates over the easy availability of weaponry, the glorification of violence in the media, and the misuse of the Internet. Perhaps by accident, then, Colorado has had a role in shaping debate over the nation's social issues disproportionate to its size.

Colorado's Popularity Breeds Prosperity

A 1970 study of the capacity of metropolitan Denver's local governments to provide services to increasing populations begins with an assessment of predictions concerning the area's growth by the year 2000.

> The first of these, appearing in a 1958 issue of *U.S. News and World Report,* foresaw the present Denver area as the fulcrum of a strip city along the foothills of the Rockies [often called the "Front Range"]. This concept envisions future growth in the Denver-Boulder, Colorado Springs, and Pueblo SMSAs as resulting in one metropolitan area extending from Boulder—and perhaps from the Fort Collins–Greeley area—to an area south of Pueblo. (*U.S. News and World Report,* cited in Bernard 1970, 3)

More than forty years after this prediction was offered, we see that this was a prescient guess. In fact both Fort Collins and Greeley now compose their own metropolitan statistical areas, and the spaces between Front Range cities are continually shrinking. Douglas County, which separates Denver and Colorado Springs, has exploded with new development: Douglas's population increased from 60,391 to 176,000 between 1990 and 2000, an increase of 191 percent, winning the title as the fastest-growing county in the nation (Gimpel 1999, chap. 3). Pueblo continues to mark the southern terminus of Front Range growth.

The second forecast proclaimed that "Colorado's Front Range will become the nation's 11th largest urban area with a population of 3.2 million by the year 2000" (Jerome P. Pickard, quoted in Bernard 1970, 3). Again, this prediction has come close to its mark. Using 2000 U.S. Census estimates, summing together the populations of all Front Range metropolitan statistical areas (Denver-Boulder-Greeley, Fort Collins–Loveland, Colorado Springs, and Pueblo) yields a combined population of 3.2 million, a population numerous enough that the Front Range would be the nation's fourteenth largest metropolitan area.

Although it may still be too soon to classify Denver as an economic power equal to the likes of New York or Chicago, certainly the potential exists for Denver (with the entire Front Range region) to join the upper echelon of America's major cities. Denver's robust local economy has been predicated in part on its serving as a major national communications and transportation hub. Several companies maintain headquarters or regional operations at Denver, including Verizon, Telecommunications, Inc. (TCI), and Primestar, Inc. (telecommunications), Sun Microsystems (computer technology), and Ryder-TRS (moving supplies). Denver's coming-of-age as a high-tech center is quite a change from its hastily constructed, boomtown beginning.

Denver sprang into being in the late 1850s, its formation and growth spurred by the discovery of gold in the nearby Rocky Mountains. The city quickly grew to be the region's primary commercial center as prospectors often purchased provisions at Denver before ascending the mountains in search of a quick fortune. Despite occasional streaks of luck where miners happened across a valuable vein, prospectors and investors were usually disappointed. As instant wealth appeared increasingly unlikely, Denver's economy stalled, and the city teetered on the brink of extinction. Technological advances in the mining industry played a major role in the city's resurgence (Brundage 1994, 11). With the completion of branch lines to the primary east-west intracontinental railroad route in the 1880s (which had been laid one hundred miles north through Cheyenne, Wyoming), Denver was finally connected to the technological superhighway of its time. "Between 1880 and 1900, the number of manufacturing establishments in the city climbed from 259 to 1,474, and the value of their product leapt from $9.4 to $41.4 million" (Brundage 1994, 14). By the 1950s, Denver had become a headquarters city for the regional oil and mineral extraction industries and a favored location for subsidiary operations of national and international corporations (Whitson and Judd 1991).

In spite of being landlocked by suburbs, Denver, like Portland, has apparently skirted the phenomenon of central city decay. Between 1960 and 1980 Denver's population shrank by only 1,200 residents, a 0.25 percent loss. The population diminished more rapidly during the 1980s, as Denver lost 5.1 percent of its citizenry between 1980 and 1990, mainly to the suburban counties. But Denver's rebound throughout the 1990s was strong—by 2000, Denver's population was estimated at 554,636, an impressive 19 percent increase over the 1990 census.

Denver has attracted a diverse citizenry by virtue of its establishment as the Rocky Mountain region's primary economic center and by its proximity to areas of Latino concentration. In 1960, just 6.1 percent of Denver's citizenry was of African-American descent. By 1980 that proportion had doubled to 12 percent, with an additional 19 percent of all city residents reporting Hispanic ancestry (Hispanics can be of any race). By 2000 Denver was more diverse than ever before: the black population remained steady at 12 percent, but the Hispanic share of the total had jumped to one-third.

For decades, political power had been inaccessible to the city's minority residents, not according to law but in practice (Kaufmann 1998; Muñoz and Henry 1990; Peirce 1972a, 38–39). The city's minorities were unable to coalesce so as to form an electoral bloc for the purpose of electing minorities to the Denver city council or mayor's office. The conspicuous absence of minorities in local elected positions was initially rather puzzling given Denver's relatively large and geographically concentrated Latino population, but class-based cleavages within the Hispanic community prevented the presentation of a united front since Hispanics were "deeply split between a wealthy minority of those who try to, and often succeed at, 'passing' in the Anglo world, and the more militant, separatist segments" (Peirce 1972a, 38). In the 1970s, two "Hispanic" city council districts were created, but both elected white legislators (Muñoz and Henry 1990, 183). A subsequent study identified two possible reasons for Hispanics' failure to elect members of their own community to what were supposedly their seats: Hispanics had lower voter registration rates than other groups, and Denver's Hispanics did not unite behind the banner of ethnicity in support of either Mexican-American candidate (Lovrich and Marenin 1976; Muñoz and Henry 1990, 183). While Hispanics may not vote predictably for Hispanic candidates, non-Hispanic whites are not wedded to candidates of their background either. Federico Peña became the city's first Mexican-American mayor in 1983 on the basis of a broad cross-racial coalition in which non-Hispanic whites were the majority bloc (Kaufmann 1998; Hero 1987, 1989). The future of minority group success in Denver politics appears bright. Wellington Webb followed Peña as the city's first African-American mayor in 1991.

While not as racially segregated as other metropolitan areas (James 1995), the Denver suburbs were not as diverse as the city: of Adams County's population, 75.0 percent were non-Hispanic whites, as were 85.4 percent of Arapahoe's, 89.5 percent of Boulder's, 95.0 percent of Douglas's, and 90.1 percent of Jefferson's. In recent years, an emerging economic and political gulf has developed between the northern Front Range and the southern Front Range. Denver's suburbs to the south are more affluent and less ethnically diverse than the suburbs lying to the north. Consequently, Arapahoe, Douglas, and Elbert Counties generally voted more Republican than the northern counties lying along I-25, and the difference is only likely to grow as population gains result in greater social and economic stratification.

Outside of the Denver metropolitan area, agriculture and mining once figured heavily in the state's gross domestic product. Those industries declined in significance through the twentieth century, though they still remain important occupations in some parts of the state. Colorado has a strong manufacturing base that is rooted primarily in food processing operations and, more recently, in the production of high-tech equipment. The U.S. military has also subsidized the state's economic well-being. In 1997 the Department of Defense employed approximately 65,000 workers statewide (3 percent of Colorado's labor force) with a majority of those stationed in El Paso County (Colorado Springs). The military annually pumps billions of dollars into Colorado Springs's local economy through its maintenance of several primary installations, including the U.S. Air Force Academy, the North American Aerospace Defense Command Center at Cheyenne Mountain (NORAD), Peterson and Schreiver Air Force Bases, and Fort Carson. Despite the closure in 1994 of Lowry Air Force Base and the forthcoming redesignation of the Rocky Mountain Arsenal as a national wildlife refuge pending completion of environmental cleanup projects, the Denver metropolitan area receives the majority of federal expenditures in Colorado. Defense contractor Lockheed-Martin's Denver-area operations alone received over $973 million in 1997 from the federal government for its production of high-tech missile defense and space exploration systems.

Colorado is divisible into five regions, which would be encountered in roughly the following order when crossing Colorado from east to west: eastern plains, Front Range, eastern mountains, the San Luis Valley, and the Western Slope (see map 6.1). The landscape of the eastern plains is probably more properly thought of as midwestern plains rather than Western. The dry prairie landscape is comprised of large acreage plots amid wide-open spaces: wheat farming and cattle ranching are mainstays of the eastern counties' economies. Although the region contains only 4 percent of Colorado's population, that proportion is great enough to distinguish the eastern plains as the state's third most populous region behind the Front Range and the Western Slope. The number of people living on farms in eastern Colorado has decreased since the 1960s, although the acreage farmed has not changed much and production has increased. This is a sign that farming operations are more concentrated and efficient than before, requiring fewer people to do the work. Consequently, the children of farmers often arrive at adulthood unable to enter the family business and therefore migrate to the Front Range cities to find work. Between 1960 and 2000, Logan County (Sterling) experienced a 12 percent drop in population while Otero County's (La Junta) population declined by 14 percent.

Colorado's Front Range is the place where it can be said that the American West truly begins. The Front Range is the easternmost

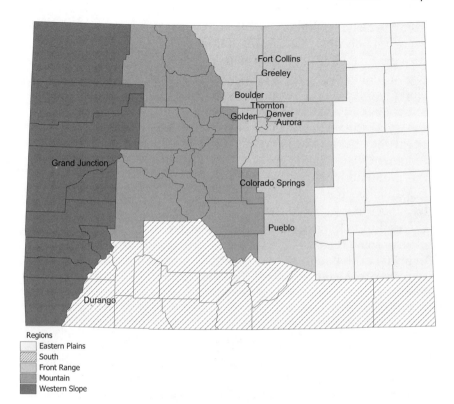

Map 6.1.   Regions of Colorado

ridgeline of the Rocky Mountains and presents an impressive contrast to the flat plains of eastern Colorado. Pike's Peak at Colorado
Springs rises 14,110 feet above the plains; locals note with pride that
the breathtaking view from the summit inspired Katherine Lee Bates
to author the lines of her famous poem "America the Beautiful." The
range runs north-south, and the counties straddling it are home to
Colorado's most populous cities, including (from north to south) Fort
Collins (Larimer County), Greeley (Weld County), Boulder (Boulder County), Denver (Denver County), and Colorado Springs (El
Paso County). Eighty-one percent of Coloradans live along the Front
Range, and the state's current migration patterns indicate that this
percentage should grow.

Southern Colorado's history and current conditions distinguish it from the rest of Colorado, and its uniqueness is manifested in a lower per capita income and its reputation as a perennial Democratic stronghold. Pueblo (Pueblo County) is foremost among cities in this region, and though it is also classified as a Front Range city, it consistently had the highest unemployment rate of all metropolitan areas in the state throughout the second half of the twentieth century: in 1991, Pueblo's unemployment rate stood at 7.0 percent and peaked at 7.8 in 1993 before declining to 4.7 in 1997. Pueblo's location on the Arkansas River and its proximity to the coal and iron ore rich eastern mountain counties (sometimes called the Headwaters region) helped it become the West's premier steel-producing town during the late 1800s and well into the twentieth century. John D. Rockefeller's Colorado Fuel and Iron was the primary employer in Pueblo, employing some 10,000 people as late as 1950 (Peirce 1972a, 46). Subject to brutal exploitation, miners eventually organized labor unions that came to play an important role in local politics, but the elimination of union jobs in Pueblo with the economic globalization since the 1970s has tempered labor's influence.

Though lightly populated, the San Luis Valley is home to Colorado's highest concentration of Latino citizens. Through the 1990s, Hispanics composed 77 percent of Costilla County's population, 60 percent of Conejos's, and over 40 percent of both Rio Grande's and Saguache's populations. The residents of these areas are among Colorado's poorest. Census Bureau estimates show that nearly one-quarter of the Valley's population in 1995 lived in poverty, ranging from 22.3 percent in Alamosa County to a high of 32.1 percent in Costilla. Local economies tend to be based on traditional occupations. Agriculture, forestry, and retail trade are primary sources of employment in Alamosa County (Alamosa). Tourism also is a prominent industry: Alamosa is located near both San Luis Lake and the headwaters of the Rio Grande making fishing and water recreation popular attractions. Trinidad (Las Animas County) was once a large coal mining town, but the city depopulated when Colorado Fuel and Iron began scaling back its operations. Since the late 1980s, the town's past has been a major factor in Trinidad's modern economy. Visitors stop to peruse antique shops, tour the Corazon de Trinidad (Heart of Trinidad) National Historic District, and stay at one of several guest ranches located in the area.

The rugged eastern mountains are picturesque tourist destinations, but they are best thought of as Colorado's "working mountains." This is the area where Colorado's mining ghost towns are clustered, including Cripple Creek (Teller County), Salida (Chaffee County), and Leadville (Lake County). Leadville was home to the nation's richest supply of silver: "In the early 1880s, the annual output of silver from this single camp surpassed that of every nation except Mexico" (Brundage 1994, 13). Park County enjoyed a fair amount of notoriety from its association with *South Park,* a randy cartoon running on late night television in the late 1990s and early 2000s that played on the county's reputation as a haven for extraterrestrial visitors. Though tourism is a growing part of the region's economy, the ski industry has not played so large a role here as it has in the mountainous counties of the Western Slope.

Colorado's Western Slope begins high and ends low, at least in terms of altitude. Colorado's world-famous ski slopes are located throughout the backcountry, many within a short drive of Interstate 70, which connects Denver to Grand Junction (Mesa County). The ski industry developed in the aftermath of World War II when members of the U.S. Army's Tenth Mountain Division, trained originally near Leadville, founded the industry after the war. Mom-and-pop ski operations eventually gave way to big business, and by the end of the twentieth century, all of the major slopes were controlled by national corporations (Rogers and Horman 2000). Aspen (Pitkin County), Breckenridge (Summit County), and Vail (Eagle County) are among the state's best-known resort towns. The amount of money these towns contribute to Colorado's economy is sizable, as Colorado recently ranked sixth among states in the amount of revenue generated by tourism.

Traveling westward toward the Utah border brings one out of the mountains to the flat land below. This portion of the Western Slope is ecologically akin to the eastern plains. Grand Junction is Colorado's most populous city west of the Front Range, its population having grown by 40 percent between 1990 and 2000. Services industries and retail trade figure prominently in Grand Junction's local economy, but manufacturing, construction, communications, and harvesting of tree fruits are important sources of employment. Grand Junction also benefits from tourism as a consequence of its central location near several major vacation destinations, including the Grand Mesa, Little Bookcliffs Wild Horse Area, and the Dinosaur National Monument.

Durango (La Plata County), also part of the Western Slope, is south-western Colorado's largest city. Given its proximity to Mesa Verde National Park, Durango's local economy is based primarily upon tourism. Government, health care, and education are also major employers, but trade from visitors to the area provides the bulk of employment for residents.

Map 6.2 shows Colorado's political geography at the time of the Great Depression and subsequent New Deal. Though the entire state reflected a Democratic disposition, the map distinguishes between counties where Democratic support was merely strong and other counties where it was very strong. Democratic bastions, where the average Democratic percentage of the presidential vote ranged between 56 and 70 percent of ballots cast, were located in southern Colorado and in the eastern mountains. Democratic ascendancy was assured by the weighty role played by labor unions. Democrats could readily count on the votes of steelworkers in the Pueblo area and unionized miners in the eastern mountain counties. Republicans did best in the ranching and agriculturally oriented areas of the state on the eastern plains and in the numerous small towns that served as regional trade centers. The counties along the Front Range did not monolithically favor either party, though Denver and its suburbs tended toward Democrats while Colorado Springs stood fast against the Roosevelt landslide.

Although Democratic dominance had subsided by the 1950s, the geographic divisions separating Republicans from Democrats remained largely unaltered. The New Deal had driven a pronounced ideological cleavage through the state's politics, separating those who clung to values of self-sufficiency and limited government from those who believed the government had a positive role to play in regulating economic life and protecting the little guy. Metropolitan Denver, Pueblo, and impoverished southern Colorado continued to supply Democrats with the bulk of their votes. The emerging Denver suburbs became two-party battlegrounds. Republicans' votes were dispersed throughout the rest of the state with the greatest concentration in El Paso County (Colorado Springs). Colorado Springs was not as staunchly Republican as it had been thirty years earlier, but it still cast only about one-third of its votes for Democratic presidential candidates. Although Eisenhower and Nixon won the state in the presidential elections between 1952 and 1960, Democrats remained competitive in statewide elections, winning the governorship in 1954, 1956, and 1958.

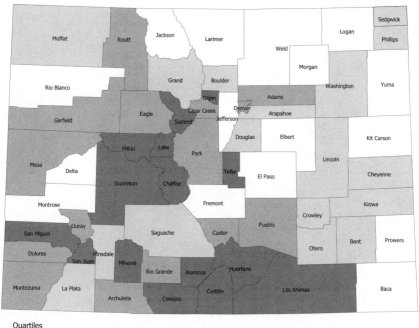

Quartiles
- 0.363 - 0.458
- 0.458 - 0.504
- 0.504 - 0.564
- 0.564 - 0.702

Map 6.2.   Average Democratic percentage of the presidential vote, 1928–1936

The political landscape had changed in some significant ways by 2000 (map 6.3). Democratic dominance in the mountains of the Western Slope was tempered by the declining importance of the mining industry. Concurrent with the declining influence of labor statewide has been the development of Colorado's gunbelt economy. The Department of Defense contributed significantly to the state's prosperity through the cold war, particularly along the Front Range. Military installations and defense contractors remain mainstays of modern Colorado's economy. As in other areas of the nation, localities and counties dependent upon federal military dollars have usually thrown their support to the defense-friendly Republican party. Denver, Boulder, and southern Colorado continued to favor Democratic presidential candidates. The rise of a more ideologically polarized politics from 1970 onward has widened the gulf between areas where liberals reside

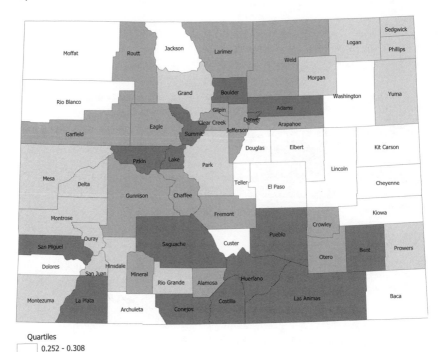

Quartiles

☐ 0.252 - 0.308
▨ 0.308 - 0.374
▧ 0.374 - 0.443
▨ 0.443 - 0.679

Map 6.3. Average Democratic percentage of the presidential vote, 1988–2000

(such as Boulder) and areas of prevailing conservatism (Colorado Springs). A small cluster of Republican counties emerged in the southwestern corner of the state on the basis of a declining union presence due to the closure of small mining and manufacturing operations. Republicans continued to run up their biggest margins of victory on the depopulating, but politically conservative eastern plains.

Where Are the Votes in Colorado? Republican and Democratic Mobilization Targets

As with Oregon, the heavy political influence exerted by Colorado's major metropolitan area is illuminated by examining the relative importance of each county to the political parties' statewide campaign

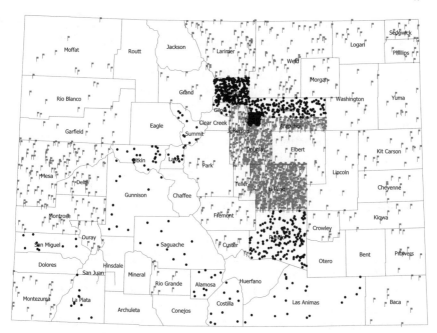

Democratic Edge Over Republicans
•
Republican Edge Over Democrats
ꞵ

Map 6.4. Areas of Republican and Democratic dominance, 1988–2000

efforts. The rank ordering of each party's primary mobilization targets reflects the fact that the majority of Colorado's population lives along the Front Range (see table 6.1 and map 6.4). Seven of the Democrats' ten most important counties in the 1988–2000 presidential elections were located in this region: only Mesa (Grand Junction), Pueblo (Pueblo), and Weld (Greeley) did not lie along the base of the Rockies. And eight of the Republicans' ten most important counties were situated in the shadow of the Rockies, excepting only Mesa and Weld. The ten counties listed in the respective columns of table 6.1 provided about 83 percent of the total Democratic vote and 75 percent of the total Republican vote in the 1988–2000 presidential elections.

   The four most important jurisdictions for Democrats included Denver and its suburbs (Denver, Jefferson, Arapahoe, and Adams Counties), which together contributed 50 percent of the Democrats' statewide vote in the combined 1988–2000 presidential elections. These same counties were less important to the efforts of George H. W. Bush, Bob Dole, and George W. Bush, contributing only 38 percent of the GOP's statewide vote. Combining Denver with its suburbs, though, makes the state's principal metropolitan area appear to be more politically balanced than it actually is, masking the fact that Denver is much more Democratic than all of its surrounding suburban counties. In the four presidential elections between 1988 and 2000, Denver gave Democratic presidential candidates 19 percent of their total statewide vote, but contributed only 8 percent to the statewide GOP base.

Colorado Springs's reputation as a Republican stronghold is borne out by its rank at the top of the GOP list as it contributes over 14 percent of the GOP's statewide vote compared to only 8 percent of Democrats'. The military and high-tech orientation of Colorado Springs's economy, bolstered by long tradition, made this predictably Republican turf through the early elections of the new century.

When we compare the changing political landscape of Colorado across the post–New Deal period, taking into account the political importance of each county, several major changes stand out since the early 1930s. First, Denver was once of nearly equal importance for both parties, with Republican and Democratic neighborhoods to be found within city limits in nearly equal proportions. With the rapid growth of suburbs after 1960, Denver's centrality to state elections diminished for both parties, but far more so for the GOP. As Republicans lost much of their base in Denver, they gained significantly along

TABLE 6.1. Colorado's Top Ten Strongest Counties for Republicans and Democrats in the 1988–2000 Presidential Contests

Rank	Democratic	Republican
1	Denver (Denver)	El Paso (Colorado Springs)
2	Jefferson (Golden)	Jefferson (Golden)
3	Boulder (Boulder)	Arapahoe (Littleton)
4	Arapahoe (Littleton)	Denver (Denver)
5	Adams (Brighton)	Larimer (Fort Collins)
6	Pueblo (Pueblo)	Boulder (Boulder)
7	Larimer (Fort Collins)	Adams (Brighton)
8	El Paso (Colorado Springs)	Douglas (Castle Rock)
9	Weld (Greeley)	Weld (Greeley)
10	Mesa (Grand Junction)	Mesa (Grand Junction)
% of total vote	83.0	74.5

the Front Range, while maintaining an edge in a majority of the rural counties to remain competitive statewide. For Democrats, the heavily industrial Pueblo was a major prize at mid-century, but its centrality dropped considerably with deindustrialization and an increasing Latino population made up of many nonvoters. Democrats have remained competitive in Denver's suburbs, and they dominate in many of the older ones.

For both parties, the urban and suburban development of Colorado has meant a movement toward more geographically centralized campaigns. Still, the Democrats have a geographic advantage when it comes to mobilizing voters because their electorate is highly concentrated in a more compact geographic area. In some states, the Republicans' lopsided advantage in the suburbs helps them to pull even with the Democrats' urban advantage in the largest cities. But in Colorado, the suburban counties provide about as much of the Democratic vote as they do the Republican. Republicans remained competitive in recent decades because they were able to rely on the stable support of so many of the state's small towns. In the 1988–2000 presidential elections, the least populous forty counties contributed about 10 percent of the Republican vote, compared with just 5 percent for Democrats. With a shrinking number of voters in these outlying locations, Republicans must pick up more suburban votes. Democratic gains in the Denver suburbs seriously threaten to consign the Republican party to minority status.

Colorado's Changing Electoral Foundations

We have suggested that Colorado and Oregon, though different in many respects, share several political similarities common to growing Western states. The influx of new residents into Colorado over the course of the past ten years will certainly have an effect on the state's politics. But in what ways? Should we expect Colorado to continue to plod along a staid political path, or will newcomers import political attitudes and orientations dissimilar to those held by natives and long-time residents? These questions are difficult to answer without detailed polls. Despite the limitation of our not having state-level voter survey data available to us back to 1930, we can produce reasonable estimates of the Democratic (or Republican) support provided by each of several relevant demographic groups. The rest of this chapter's

analysis is based on county-level data using Gary King's (1997) ecological inference technique (see appendix A).

One of the most fascinating aspects about America's political landscape is that it does change: crisis events, salient issues, and key political actors occupy the limelight for a period, then new events, issues,
and actors take their places. Most often such change is incremental
and thus imperceptible, merely reflecting the passage of time; occasionally, change occurs rapidly, having been precipitated by some momentous event or series of circumstances. But national political
change is an aggregation of changes occurring at the local level. The
American electorate, the sine qua non of American politics, is con-
stantly being reshaped and reconstituted.

Of course, the "American electorate" is in actuality a collective of
smaller electorates. As a result of our having a federal system of government, we speak of the *national* electorate as well as of various *state*
and *local* electorates. Every day, individuals are both added to and re-
moved from the country's electorates by a variety of forces. When
young Americans turn eighteen, they become (perhaps unwittingly in
many cases) members of the electorate. When someone moves from
one jurisdiction to another, whether from one city to another city ten
miles away or from one state to another, that person leaves one electorate and joins another. Moving to another place implies that one
electorate has grown while another has shrunk. Electorates also lose
members through natural means as people age and eventually pass
away. The key point is that the composition of electorates determines
what issues will be important, who among several candidates will be
selected to provide leadership, and which political party is generally
most favored in a jurisdiction. Each new voter brings a unique set of
attitudes, values, and experiences to the public arena.

Population Mobility

Broadly speaking, Colorado's political geography has been remarkably unchanged over the course of the past seventy years. Republican
or Democratic strength across counties in the 1930s still predicted Republican or Democratic strength in 2000 and 2004. Still, partisan
change across Colorado has resulted from generational replacement,
electoral mobilization, and conversion, but most of all from population
mobility. As we have seen, the story of Colorado since the end of

World War II has been one of steady growth, with the Front Range receiving the overwhelming majority of the state's new residents. In the 1920s and 1930s, the Front Range was not an especially Democratic region. Though Denver and Adams County weakly favored the Democratic party, the remainder of the metropolitan area was competitive territory, and Colorado Springs was ardent in its Republican support.

The results of growth are not limited merely to increasingly congested traffic arteries, lengthened commute times, and declining air quality. In Colorado, it appears that growth from outside Colorado has reinforced the Republican party. Internal migrants were much less likely to vote Democratic than nonmigrants, according to our estimates in table 6.2, by a considerable margin until the most recent

TABLE 6.2.   Estimates of the Democratic Percentage of the Presidential Vote for Various Electoral Groups in Colorado, 1928–2000 (ecological inference maximum likelihood)

Pooled Presidential Election Years	Blacks/ Nonblacks		Elderly/ Nonelderly		Immigrants/ Nonimmigrants		Farmers/ Nonfarmers		Whites/ Nonwhites	
1928, 1932	47.2	44.2*	40.7*	44.5*	82.3	40.8*	38.7*	46.3*	43.1*	58.8*
1936, 1940, 1944	99.1	50.9*	42.6	52.2*	63.9	50.6*	29.8*	57.7*	51.5*	45.9
1948, 1952	58.6	45.1*	21.1	49.6*	61.9	50.8*	29.2*	48.1*	45.2*	52.2
1956, 1960, 1964	54.9	48.5*	31.5	50.4*	56.7	48.7*	29.9*	50.1*	48.6*	51.5
1968, 1972	61.4	36.9*	27.0	38.7*	88.8	36.2*	12.5*	38.7*	36.6*	62.0
1976, 1980, 1984	61.7	35.2*	75.5	34.1*	76.1*	35.3*	21.2*	36.5*	34.3*	52.5*
1988, 1992	58.5	41.6*	36.1	43.0*	65.9	41.2*	5.9	42.8*	39.3*	64.6
1996, 2000	70.2	42.7*	31.9	45.2*	97.2	41.5*	3.3	44.4*	38.1*	84.3*

	Mfg. Workers/ Non Mfg. Workers		College Educated/ Non College Educated		Native to State/ Nonnatives		Internal Migrants/ Nonmigrants		Hispanics/ Non-Hispanics	
1928, 1932	—	—	—	—	—	—	—	—	—	—
1936, 1940, 1944	—	—	—	—	—	—	—	—	—	—
1948, 1952	68.4	42.3*	42.4	45.5*	—	—	—	—	—	—
1956, 1960, 1964	58.7*	46.9*	31.5	50.6*	64.4*	33.7*	32.0*	63.9*	—	—
1968, 1972	46.9	36.1*	43.5	36.6*	49.7*	27.8*	26.4*	50.0*	—	—
1976, 1980, 1984	71.0	30.8*	19.6*	39.6*	56.3*	21.8*	17.8*	58.1*	74.2*	31.1*
1988, 1992	52.4	40.8*	50.1	39.4*	51.0*	35.9*	31.5*	54.2*	77.6*	37.1*
1996, 2000	60.9	41.7*	75.0	35.5*	42.6*	44.8*	42.0*	46.0*	68.8*	39.4*

Note: Cell entries show the estimated percentage voting Democratic in the presidential elections listed on each row. Complete variable definitions and results from the ecological inference estimation appear in appendix B, with standard errors and bounds.

*Reflect estimates with lower and upper bounds narrower than 0,1.

elections. In the 1996–2000 races, voters who had moved to Colorado from some other state collectively cast 42 percent of their ballots for Democrats compared with 46 percent for those native to the state. When we add a control for college education, the Republican bias among new residents drops considerably, indicating that it is the large number of well-educated professionals moving to Front Range cities that has contributed to the GOP's strength. Estimates of native Coloradans' propensities to vote Democratic lend support to these data: 51 percent of natives voted Democratic compared with only 36 percent of nonnatives in the pooled 1988–92 elections. The dawn of the new century saw a shrinking gap between natives and migrants in support for Democratic candidates (Gimpel 1999). In another recent work, one of the present authors found that influx from outside Colorado did not always increase GOP party registration. But one should not necessarily conclude that the Democrats benefited by arrivals from outside Colorado (Gimpel 1999, chap. 3). Independent and unaffiliated registration increased during the 1980s and 1990s, particularly in those counties with the most out-of-state migrants. The idea that independents would gain from population migration is consistent with the notion that mobility weakens the party attachments of movers (Brown 1988).

Generational Change

Partisan change occurs through the slow process of population replacement in locales where there is low net in-migration, stable voter turnout, and no precipitous events to stimulate voters to reconsider their standing political commitments. Much of the time, a surprisingly large number of jurisdictions around the United States fit this description, particularly in rural areas where the population is aging and fertility and in-migration rates are low. Except for the Hispanic counties of southern Colorado, most of the state's rural and small town residents were registered as Republicans at mid-century. Places with the largest proportion of elderly residents in the 1950s and 1960s became friendlier to Democrats in the early 2000s, including some locations along the northern Front Range such as Larimer (Fort Collins) and Boulder (Boulder) Counties. At least some of this partisan change could be attributed to the dying of older Republicans and their replacement with younger Democrats. Along the northern Front Range, in-migration interacted with generational replacement to accelerate political change in rapidly growing towns. Even if a migration stream is predominantly Republican, it may still be less Republican than the population of aging natives. Hence if eight out of ten natives who die are Republican, but only six of ten newcomers are, in-migration combined with population replacement will gradually water down the GOP's electoral strength.

The estimates in table 6.2 suggest that there may be some concrete evidence that population replacement has benefited Democratic presidential candidates. In the 1930s and 1940s, there was little difference between the voting of the elderly and that of the nonelderly. The generation gap grew wider after 1948 when those of retirement age voted decidedly more Republican than those under age 65. After 1964, our data show no statistically reliable trend.[1] Checking the recent estimates against available polling data indicates that the generation gap has closed in recent years, but that the elderly were more likely to be Republican party identifiers than the nonelderly by the late 1990s. In the 2000 presidential election, exit polls indicated that Colorado's elderly favored George W. Bush over Al Gore by a margin of 56 to 43 percent and were more likely to vote Republican than younger voters by a margin of 56 to 50 percent.

Conversion

Where might we find partisan converts in Colorado? Examining the county-level data suggests that one population may have been converted to the Democratic party by Roosevelt in the 1930s: much of the farm population on the dry eastern plains who badly needed the relief of price supports for their wheat crop. Massive overproduction in 1931 and 1932 depressed prices for wheat and other crops to nearly historic lows (Schlesinger 1957). Colorado farmers, like farmers elsewhere, struggled under debt burdens because they could not make enough money to cover their production costs. Between 1929 and 1932, farmers had grown increasingly restless at the increasing number of farm foreclosures—some of them were verging on radicalism and violence. Roosevelt's plan was to offer farmers a price subsidy in return for promising to limit output. Through production controls, farm prices would increase, and farmers would be able to recoup their production costs, perhaps even operate at a profit.

Those in small towns, but not on farms, apparently were less impressed by what the New Deal had to offer. We found little evidence of conversion among small town Coloradans. Democrats improved their vote share in Denver, Pueblo, and mining and manufacturing towns in the mountains, but these gains may not have been the result of conversion as much as mobilization of new voters (Anderson 1979). In the areas where the electorate expanded between 1928 and 1932, without the benefit of general population growth, Roosevelt's electoral performance improved greatly on Smith's 1928 totals. These were Colorado's less prosperous, slower-growing counties, often in rugged mining areas west of Denver where the newly mobilized helped bring about the New Deal realignment.

In the 1960s, Colorado opposed Barry Goldwater's candidacy in spite of the candidate's Western roots. Republicans who voted for Johnson had no problem returning to vote for Nixon in 1968, though. George Wallace's independent candidacy had little appeal in 1968, winning less than 8 percent of the state's vote, suggesting that there was no groundswell of dissatisfaction with the liberal drift of the Democratic party as there was throughout the South. These facts suggest that there is only a slight prospect that partisan change between 1928 and 2000 resulted from the conversion of Colorado voters. To examine the magnitude of the changes due to conversion we used a voter transition model (Achen and Shively 1995; Irwin and Meeter 1969) to estimate the percentage of Democratic (or Republican) voters in one presidential election who voted for the same party in the following election. Our estimates are for elections in the 1930s and the 1960s—eras in which we would most likely find support for the conversion theory (see table 6.3).

Roosevelt's electoral strategy in the 1932 elections partly entailed winning Republican votes on the arid plains and rural West, separating this region from the Northeast where stalwart GOP voters were less likely to buy into the New Deal plan for economic recovery. The strategy worked in Oregon (chap. 11) and California (chap. 3), where sizable chunks of Hoover's support in 1928 went to Roosevelt in 1932. According to our estimates, Roosevelt was also successful in Colorado where only 56 percent of Hoover's supporters in 1928 returned to vote for him in 1932 (table 6.3). Roosevelt built on his Colorado majority in the next election, as Landon lost nearly one-fourth of the Hoover voters from 1932. Did the Republicans pick up any

TABLE 6.3. **Estimates of Party Loyalty and Conversion across Presidential Elections in Colorado (ecological inference maximum likelihood)**

Presidential Election Years	Voted Democratic 1928/Non-Democratic 1928	Voted Democratic 1932/Non-Democratic 1932	Presidential Election Years	Voted Republican 1928/Non-Republican 1928	Voted Republican 1932/Non-Republican 1932
Voted Democratic 1932	84.8* 40.0*		Voted Republican 1932	56.0* 13.4*	
Voted Democratic 1936		89.1* 24.4*	Voted Republican 1936		76.2* 10.2*

Presidential Election Years	Voted Democratic 1960/Non-Democratic 1960	Voted Democratic 1964/Non-Democratic 1964	Presidential Election Years	Voted Republican 1960/Non-Republican 1960	Voted Republican 1964/Non-Republican 1964
Voted Democratic 1964	90.9* 37.5*		Voted Republican 1964	57.4* 14.6*	
Voted Democratic 1968		60.6* 12.4*	Voted Republican 1968		90.8* 24.7*
Voted Wallace 1968		3.2* 14.5*	Voted Wallace 1968		14.5* 3.3*

Note: Cell entries show the estimated percentage voting Democratic, Republican, or for George Wallace in the presidential elections listed on each row who voted Democratic (or Republican) in the previous election. Complete variable definitions and results from the ecological inference estimation appear in appendix C, with standard errors and bounds.

*Reflect estimates with lower and upper bounds narrower than 0.1.

votes from the Democrats? Not many. Perhaps as many as 12 to 13 percent switched from Smith (1928) to Hoover in 1932 and another 10 percent from Roosevelt (1932) to Landon in 1936. As in other states, the New Deal realignment was highly imbalanced because Democrats gained far more voters than they lost.

As for the 1960s, our estimates show considerable continuity in support between Kennedy in 1960 and Johnson in 1964. Johnson voters, though, were not enthusiastic about Humphrey in 1968—undoubtedly because so many of the Texan's voters were Republicans who would not vote for Goldwater but would support Nixon. Goldwater did poorly among Nixon's (1960) supporters. Only 57 percent of those who had voted for Nixon remained loyal to the conservative Arizona senator (table 6.3). Wallace performed poorly in Colorado in 1968, but most of his support came not from disaffected Democrats, but from Republicans. An estimated 14.5 percent of Goldwater's voters supported Wallace, compared with only 3 percent of Johnson voters. Nearly all of these Wallace voters then supported Nixon's reelection against George McGovern in 1972. Clearly, few Colorado Democrats came out of the 1960s as Republicans. Republican support for the Democrats appeared to be fleeting as Humphrey lost about the same proportion of Johnson voters as Johnson had won from the GOP four years before.

Other evidence for conversion can sometimes be adduced by examining the political behavior of key voting blocs over time. Most of the industries that employed the great bulk of Colorado's working-class laborers in 1900 became less important to the local economies where they were located. The populations of several mining towns were decimated when mines were closed in the 1960s. Pueblo never fully recovered from the downsizing of the Colorado Fuel and Iron Corporation. Although blue-collar manufacturing jobs were not an integral part of Colorado's growth equation in the 1980s and 1990s, we have observed in other states that those employed in manufacturing grew unhappy with the liberal reorientation of the Democratic party following the civil rights era.

When we examined support for Democratic presidential candidates among blue-collar workers in the Centennial State, we found that this group was consistently more likely to vote Democratic than workers employed in other labor sectors. In the combined 1956, 1960, and 1964 elections, the Democratic vote among blue-collar workers was approximately 12 percentage points higher than the percentage of Democratic votes cast by those in other occupational sectors. The recession in the mining and manufacturing sector that hit energy-producing states in the early 1980s took away any hope Republicans had of a realignment among working-class voters. Our estimates indicate that manufacturing workers were far more likely to vote Democratic than Republican in the 1976, 1980, and 1984 elections. Democratic support among manufacturing workers who remained employed during this period was considerably lower, however, suggesting that there were "Reagan Democrats" in Colorado but they did not number among the poor and jobless.[2] Evidence from the 1990s also indicated that the vote among the shrinking number of manufacturing workers had become less Democratic than in the past, but it remained more Democratic than the vote among non–blue-collar workers.

With little evidence of conversion to be found among the state's blue-collar workers after 1950, we turned toward rural Colorado to examine Democratic support among the farm population. Given that the Roosevelt strategy was to attract farm voters in the Midwest and West to his candidacy by promises of agricultural adjustment and recovery, we would expect him to have succeeded in winning a significant share of the state's farm vote. Our estimates show that there was very little difference between the farm and nonfarm vote for Democrats in the 1928–32 elections—suggesting that farmers may have been persuaded by economic crisis to support the Democrats (table 6.2).

But there were aspects of local politics that militated against consolidating these gains into a permanent conversion. Colorado has a history of urban-rural conflict. Years before the U.S. Supreme Court announced its "one man, one vote" principle in *Reynolds v. Sims* (1964), the Colorado General Assembly was dominated by antiurban (that is, anti-Denver) elements from the state's rural backwaters (Simmons 1984). For farmers in Colorado and other states who had long conceptualized politics in this way, the Democrats could not, at the same time, be for both industry and agriculture, city and countryside. Our estimates show that urban-rural political conflict grew more intense after 1932 as farmers voted increasingly Republican in presidential elections. Urban-rural conflict became highly ideological following reapportionment in the 1960s when the Democrats more clearly became the party of big cities, and the Republicans the party of rural America. After 1964, both farm and nonfarm support for Democrats diminished, but support among farmers for Humphrey and McGovern virtually dropped through the floor. In more recent elections, farm support for Republicans has been as much as 20 points higher than nonfarm support. Agricultural Colorado, then, does appear to have converted over the course of the twentieth century; but with fewer farmers in the voting population than ever before, this rural realignment has had limited influence on statewide politics.

Activism and Partisanship of New Voters

The proportion of Colorado's population of African-American descent in 2000 was still small (about 4 percent) in comparison to their nationwide proportion of the population (12.3 percent). The overwhelming majority of Colorado's black population lived in Denver and in the Adams County suburbs. Like in Connecticut (chap. 9), this population was not sufficiently large for progress on civil rights to be threatening to the majority white population in the way that it was in the South, or in states such as Illinois or New York. For example, we looked for but did not find much evidence of a white backlash to black mobilization in the 1950s and 1960s. George Wallace, a candidate well known for his conservative stands on civil rights issues, won less than 10 percent of the vote in Colorado, most of it among Republicans, very little among Democrats. As in Oregon (chap. 11), then, we expected the gulf between black and white voting to increase only because of the growing loyalty of African Americans to the Democratic party following Lyndon Johnson's Great Society and his signing of the Voting Rights Act, not because the Democratic party was being abandoned by whites on a large scale.

The estimates for black voters' behavior are prone to error due to the small size of the black electorate and so are not as reliable as our estimates for other states. Nevertheless, the figures in table 6.2 point to an increasing tendency for Colorado's blacks to vote for Democratic presidential candidates. The estimates for Colorado's white voting population are more trustworthy, showing that whites moved in a more Republican direction after 1972. We doubt that this shift in white support toward the Republicans was the result of a white reaction to black activism since racial conflict was not a prominent feature of Colorado's state and local scene during the 1970s. A more likely explanation is that the white vote moved more Republican as the result of population growth. Black support for Democrats appears to have peaked in the 1996–2000 election with our estimates showing that more than 70 percent of African Americans supported Bill Clinton and Al Gore.

Hispanics are Colorado's largest minority group, and as such we expect them to exert a measure of influence on politics in areas where they are most heavily concentrated, in southern Colorado and along the Front Range. Turnout among the Hispanic population is quite low, but appears to have improved with time, redounding to the benefit of Democrats. Our estimates show that after 1976, when data on the Latino population became available, about three out of four Hispanics voted Democratic, compared with only one in three non-Hispanics. Colorado's Hispanic population is very different from Oregon's in this respect: in Oregon, less than half of the Hispanic population voted Democratic, and there was little difference between Hispanic and non-Hispanic support. In Colorado, however, the Hispanic population was poorer than in Oregon—giving the Hispanic population in Colorado a class interest in voting for Democrats. The Latino population in the Centennial State is also more concentrated, and the Democratic traditions of the Hispanic counties go back at least as far as the 1930s, making the socialization pressures more intense than they would be if Hispanics were residentially integrated with non-Hispanic whites.

Conclusions

Colorado's politics reminds us that highly sectional elections can often benefit one party at the polls. Because so much of the Democratic vote is concentrated in Denver and its suburbs, it is of great benefit to Democrats when the metro area behaves cohesively—it means that the vast majority of voters are supporting Democrats. With a much more dispersed base of support, Republicans typically gain ground in Colorado when the state's sectionalism subsides. With a declining rural base of support, Republicans will only avoid minority status in the new century if they can make successful appeals to the state's fast-growing suburbs. A new sectional pattern arose at the turn of the twenty-first century on the heels of demographic change along the Front Range. The suburbs and cities straddling I-25 north of Denver are more ethnically and economically diverse than those to the south. Consequently, Democrats are more competitive in Adams, Boulder, Larimer, and Weld Counties than they are in Arapahoe, Douglas, Elbert, and El Paso Counties. With a growing Hispanic population in the northern suburbs, and a growing black population in Adams, Colorado Republicans have a powerful incentive to become a more diverse party than they were in the 1990s when some 93.3 percent of all GOP identifiers in the state were white (see chap. 2).

Labor unions in manufacturing and mining towns such as Pueblo were once the most reliable base of the Democratic party, but this is no longer true in the new economy. Between 2000 and 2020, Democrats will find more of their support in the suburbs than they did in the last century. Numbering among this suburban population are middle-income blacks, Hispanics, and Asians, as well as ideologically liberal whites.

The future of the Republicans' safest jurisdiction, Colorado Springs, looks secure in the short term. But the El Paso County economy has been heavily subsidized by the Pentagon for years. The area's economic and political future could be in doubt if defense allocations to the region shrink. The end of the cold war brought little change to El Paso County in the 1990s, as the state's representation in Congress has been very competitive in the fight for funding. But coming presidential administrations promise regular review of defense spending priorities that could diminish the share of federal expenditures flowing to Colorado.

Continued population growth from outside Colorado will probably help the Republicans more than the Democrats because most of this migration is in response to corporate relocations and promises of professional and managerial career growth. Pressures to limit new development along the Front Range are likely to bid up the cost of moving to the state, slowing growth and making migration even more highly selective than it is now. If this occurs, Colorado will be destined for greater political balkanization across Denver area jurisdictions.

Finally, the controversial series of ballot initiatives stirred up since the late 1980s has polarized the state's electorate along ideological lines. Because Denver's suburbs are not as Democratic as Portland's are, ideology does not have the same clear geographic foundation in Colorado that it does in Oregon where eastern conservatives are pitted against western liberals. But the Denver suburbs are not as conservative or as Republican as either Colorado Springs or the state's eastern plains. In short, Republicans badly need to find a formula to convert independent, dealigned, and nonaligned voters into party stalwarts. If the state's population outgrows its capacity to provide jobs, something that has happened before in Colorado's old mining and manufacturing economy, then the classic cleavage between haves and have-nots will widen, helping the GOP recover its ascendancy on taxing and spending issues—something that it lost with the economic prosperity accompanying the Clinton years.

Notes

1. The unusually high figure for Democratic support among the elderly in the 1976, 1980, and 1984 elections (76 percent) dropped to just 41 percent when we added a control variable (zb) for income, although the estimate still had a large error. We can infer from this that the vote of the elderly population during this time was heavily influenced by economic standing; the elderly living in low-income areas were far more likely to vote Democratic than those in higher-income locations. The estimate for the Democratic vote among the elderly was also highly sensitive to the size of the rural population and the size of the Hispanic population, as the counties with the highest proportions of elderly residents were in rural southern Colorado.

2. A control variable (zb) for median income added to the ecological inference model resulted in a considerable drop in Democratic support among those employed in manufacturing for the pooled 1976, 1980, and 1984 elections. Without the control Democratic support was estimated at about 71 percent of the manufacturing workforce (see table 6.2). After controlling for income, Democratic support dropped to 52.1 percent, suggesting that it is the poorer of the manufacturing workers who are most Democratic.

CHAPTER 7

MINNESOTA

Major Forces for Electoral Change in Minnesota

- Decline of the Mining and Manufacturing Economy
- Decline of the Agricultural Economy
- Suburbanization of the Population
- The Declining Significance of White Ethnicity and Religion
- Rise of the Tourism and Recreation Industry

For outsiders, Minnesota is associated most clearly with its cold climate and a distinctly Scandinavian dialect of American English. The accent, often exaggerated in well-known movies such as *Fargo,* is most noticeable on the vowel *o,* as in, "I'm from Minnesōta." Lakes are perhaps the next most common thing associated with the state: license plates proudly proclaim Minnesota the "Land of 10,000 Lakes" (though there are actually more than 10,000), and pro basketball's Los Angeles Lakers were originally the Minneapolis Lakers. Among non-Minnesotans, the state is not often thought of in terms of its largest city as are Illinois, New York, and Georgia. Minneapolis does not conjure up the well-known mental images that the state's name does, and its relative obscurity is partially a function of size. With only 383,000 people at the start of the twenty-first century, Minneapolis did not stand out to those beyond the Midwest the way Chicago does. Minneapolis seems determined to avoid appearances of the parochial pride that sometimes pits large cities against the rest of the state, preferring instead to emphasize itself as a hub city for all Minnesotans. The professional football, baseball, hockey, and basketball sports franchises, all based in Minneapolis, are called the Minnesota Vikings, Minnesota Twins, Minnesota Wild, and the Minnesota Timberwolves.

Minneapolis is the state's trade and finance center. The city originally served as an agricultural center and was once called the Mill

City—in fact, the major league baseball team was once called the Minneapolis Millers. Several large food and grain interests still make their headquarters there, including Pillsbury, Cargill, and General Mills. Service sector companies also play a major role in the local economy. Corporate offices for the Target and Best Buy chain stores are located in Minneapolis, together employing about 75,000 people. Northwest Airlines is also headquartered here, providing an additional 53,000 jobs. Minneapolis is a serious business town with a heavy flow of commuter traffic running in from the suburbs on weekday mornings. There are some unique costs to doing business in Minneapolis: more than sixty city blocks are connected through an elaborate skyway system to protect downtown workers and shoppers from weeks of subzero temperatures during winter.

Minneapolis has a reputation for progressive government and a politically liberal citizenry, but this progressive spirit has not kept people from moving to the suburbs (Orfield 1997). The city was 31 percent smaller in 2000 than it was in 1950 when it hit its historic high-water mark of 521,700. In spite of out-migration to the suburbs, Minneapolis has maintained a majority white population—minorities comprised only 22 percent of the population in 2000. Although running in an overwhelmingly white city, Sharon Sayles-Belton won the distinction of becoming Minneapolis's first black and first woman mayor in 1993. She won reelection in 1997 but was then soundly defeated in 2001 by a political neophyte, R. T. Rybak.

Even if it wished to, Minneapolis probably could not pretend to be the sole axis around which the state turns because it has a natural rival in its neighbor, St. Paul. Home to 297,000 people in 2000, it is Minnesota's second largest city and its capital. St. Paul is the state's major industrial center—the more blue collar of the two cities. Together, Minneapolis and St. Paul are known as the Twin Cities. However, these twins are hardly identical: Separated by the Mississippi River, the Twin Cities' different social histories have led them down different political and economic paths. Minneapolis was settled primarily by Scandinavians, whereas St. Paul was settled predominantly by Irish and Germans. Minneapolis was dominated by Lutherans, St. Paul by Catholics (Federal Writers' Project 1938, 154). Minneapolis's predominantly Scandinavian stock inclined them toward a policy progressivism unheard of in St. Paul. In the early 1990s, St. Paul elected a Republican mayor, an outcome that would be anathema in Minneapolis.

But because the residents of St. Paul have not been as upwardly mobile as those in Minneapolis, the city has lost far less of its population to competition with the suburbs. St. Paul is only 13 percent smaller in the early 2000s than it was in the 1950s. The city is home to a Ford Motor Company assembly plant and the gargantuan 3M corporation (Minnesota Mining and Manufacturing), which started by manufacturing sandpaper and other abrasives in 1902, evolved to the manufacture of masking tape in the 1920s, and branched out into a dizzying variety of products from computer and office equipment to synthetic materials production.

Beyond a recognition that Minneapolis is in Minnesota and that St. Paul is the state capital, non-Minnesotans know very little about the rest of the state. If pressed, some might mention the farms that cover the landscape of the southern and plains counties along the border with the Dakotas. Minnesota's rural areas are still populated by descendants of some of its original settlers: Swedish, Norwegian, Finnish, and German immigrants who arrived in the latter half of the nineteenth century. The population of the state's small towns and farms has been shrinking since the 1950s. The story behind this development has been farm consolidation. The number of farms has been cut in half since mid-century in many of these jurisdictions even though the total acreage farmed has dropped only slightly.

Once-busy rail lines that carried freight between Minneapolis and points further south and west are now nearly abandoned, and the small town depots have been torn down or have disintegrated under the extreme weather conditions. On the state's western plains, some towns are almost abandoned, and looking at them now it is hard to believe they once thrived. Plant closings in southwestern Minnesota, primarily in food processing, have also fueled the out-migration. In the late 1990s, both Campbell's Soup and Iowa Beef Packers (IBP) closed major operations in towns along Interstate 90. The unemployed have to move to find work—many will join the legions of former residents of southwestern Minnesota who have moved to Minneapolis–St. Paul or into nearby Sioux Falls, South Dakota (see map 7.1).

Northern Minnesota is known for its proud history of iron ore mining and lumber production. The high-grade ore that was once shipped out of busy ports on Lake Superior had been used up by the end of World War II, leaving a smaller workforce to dig for the lower-grade taconite ore still used in steel production. With American steel

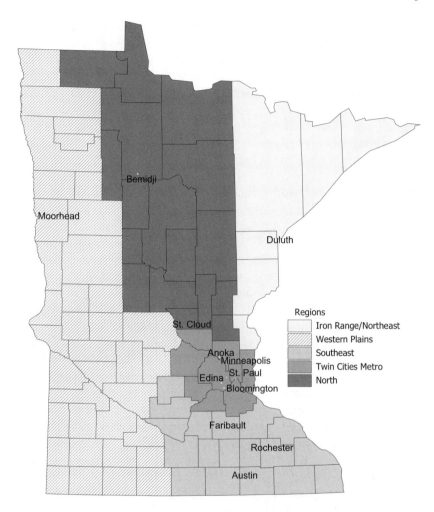

Map 7.1.   Regions of Minnesota

production reaching historic lows in the early 2000s, the mining workforce had shrunk to just a tiny fraction of what it once was. Northern
Minnesota did not stand still in the face of unemployment in the mining and forest products sectors. This region has fared better than the
farmlands in the southwest because it has built a thriving tourist and
recreation trade. The booming service and retail trade sectors in
small towns such as Bemidji, International Falls, and Grand Rapids

have kept these towns afloat. They attract snowmobilers in the winter and spring, and fisherman, trekkers, and hunters in the summer and fall. The smaller towns out on the northwestern plains near the North Dakota border have not fared as well. The population of these towns is aging, and where there has been employment growth, it has resulted from the expansion of health-care services designed to care for an elderly and declining population. The prospect for these towns appears bleak.

Some would also know that Minnesota is a Great Lakes state, forming much of the northern shore of Lake Superior. The city of Duluth was once a bustling mining and industrial port on the western tip of this cold, immense lake and remained the state's third largest city until the 1990s. Ships linked up with railways at the city's port to carry bulky loads of iron ore, coal, and grain to all parts of the world. Duluth was also the center of much labor radicalism in the 1920s and 1930s, and the birthplace of the American Communist Party. The city's economic position declined with the closing of many of the iron ore mines in the 1950s and 1960s. Shipping traffic has dropped off, and railroad operations have been sharply curtailed. The number of jobs available in the transportation and mining sectors has declined by half from 1960 to 2000. Duluth's citizens have sought economic recovery through development of a brisk tourist trade similar to that of Michigan's Upper Peninsula.

Fortunately for Minnesota, the economic decline and corresponding population losses in Duluth have been more than offset by the growth of suburbs outside Minneapolis and St. Paul since mid-century. By the early 1990s, Bloomington was the state's third largest city, capturing that distinction from Duluth. Situated directly south of Minneapolis, Bloomington was a small town long before it was a suburb. In 1950, at the dawn of suburban development, it was home to just 10,000 people. Ten years later it had jumped to 50,000. By 2000, it had leveled off at a historic high of 85,000. No longer a mere residential suburb, Bloomington found itself home to many clean industries, including companies producing computers and pharmaceuticals. A major event in Bloomington's history was the 1992 opening of the Mall of America, the nation's largest indoor shopping center employing about 13,000 people.

As an older suburb, Bloomington has offered affordable housing attractive to families of moderate income who have moved into the area from rural Minnesota or have fled the Twin Cities. Even so, median housing prices are roughly one-third higher in Bloomington than in Minneapolis proper, and few racial minority families have settled there. To the north of Bloomington, the western suburbs of Minneapolis are even more exclusive and racially homogeneous. Edina is home to the state's wealthy establishment. In the early 2000s, the median housing value in Edina was more than double that of the city of Minneapolis. Eden Prairie, Minnetonka, and Wayzata are full of upscale new housing built to attract young professionals and upper-middle-class families. Large homes on expansive wooded lots are settled on golf courses around lakes and across from parks. These suburbs profited heavily from the population losses experienced by Minneapolis and St. Paul, more than doubling in population between 1960 and 2000. Having reached the limits of their growth, the western suburbs are increasingly concerned about protecting and maintaining their quality of life. Once they were primarily residential suburbs, but through the 1990s they led the metro area in job growth. The frontier of residential development is now further out from the Twin Cities. Upscale development has moved northeastward into Washington County, gobbling up farmland around White Bear Lake, Stillwater, and Mahtomedi. To the west, an exclusive elite has settled in Orono, a tiny village with more million-dollar homes than exist within the entire city of Minneapolis.

Just beyond the Minneapolis suburbs, southeastern Minnesota has been one of the more prosperous parts of the state. The cities of Rochester and Winona have grown since mid-century. Rochester's famous Mayo Clinic is a series of hospitals that formed around the world's first multispecialty group practice. Because the clinic draws from an international patient/client base, its prosperity and future do not depend on the demography of the local population. A full-blown economy has emerged around the health sector, with manufacturing and high-tech businesses tied closely to medical specialties, and services to support the city's population of medical professionals and their patients. Since 1960, the population of Olmsted County has nearly doubled, moving from 65,000 to 125,000 by 2000. Southeastern Minnesota is also the hub of the state's dairy farming and market gardening. As in other areas of the state, the number of farms has dropped by nearly 40 percent since 1960, but the ex-farmers and their children have been able to find work in other industries without having to leave Minnesota.

Minnesota's economic path has been similar to that of other states in the final decades of the twentieth century. The farm population has declined, although at no expense to actual farm production. Towns that manage to serve as trade centers for their regions have maintained a stable share of the population and in some cases have benefited from the migration off the farm. Smaller towns that have lost in the competition for customers to these regional trade centers are struggling to maintain a dignified presence on the prairie. While the most rural areas of the state have suffered economic and population losses, so have the largest cities. Duluth and the towns of the iron and lumbering counties of northern Minnesota have shrewdly tried to replace these heavy industries with tourism and services. Many have prospered in this new economy, but it has not been a dollar-for-dollar trade. As in other states, the transition from good-paying, union-protected jobs to the more chaotic service sector has meant a declining standard of living. Facing either long-term unemployment or serious wage cuts, many ex-industrial workers left northern Minnesota to move to the more centrally located Minneapolis and St. Paul, fueling the growth of these cities' working-class suburbs.

The Farmer-Labor Party and the Democrats

Like its Midwestern neighbors, Minnesota was settled in the nineteenth century as a farm state, with outposts of lumbering and mining in the north. Agriculture was king, and farmers were the most politically important force in the state's electorate. Initially, these farmers were predominantly Lutheran Scandinavians who affiliated themselves with the antislavery, prohibitionist, anti-Catholic, and nativist Republicans further east (Fenton 1966, 76). Minnesota was fiercely prounion during the Civil War, and disdain for the proslavery Democratic party extended well into the beginning of the twentieth century. Late nineteenth century immigration brought diversity to Minnesota, an unwelcome development as far as the Scandinavians were concerned. Splits in the Minnesota electorate emerged along Protestant vs. Catholic lines over the issues of prohibition and immigration. Scandinavians were Protestant, dry, and against the newer waves of foreigners that included Germans, Catholics, beer drinkers, and likely Democrats (Fenton 1966).

Between 1916 and 1918, North Dakota's radical socialist political party, the Nonpartisan League, spread its gospel to Minnesota, gaining a receptive foothold in two disparate communities: farmers on the western plains who resented profiteering by the railroads that shipped their grain and laborers who chafed under the poor wages and working conditions of the mines and industries in northern Minnesota (Valelly 1989; Haynes 1984; Gieske 1979). This electoral coalition became the basis for the Farmer-Labor party that met with considerable success at the state level, but never achieved a national following.

Republicans managed to maintain control over state government through the 1920s, in spite of mass desertions of their party by reform-minded farmers, including many Scandinavians, who enlisted with the Farmer-Labor party. Democrats had been almost equally afflicted by desertions to the Farmer-Labor camp by German farmers, miners, and industrial workers. The 1930s, then, saw the Minnesota electorate splintered into three factions. The Farmer-Labor ticket won four gubernatorial elections in 1930, 1932, 1934, and 1936. Republicans managed to regain power in 1938 and maintain it uninterrupted through 1954. Following the New Deal, and GOP victories in the 1938, 1940, and 1942 gubernatorial elections, it became clear to both Democrats and Farmer-Labor adherents that their differences were making for easy Republican victories (Haynes 1984). Following considerable internal debate, the Farmer-Labor party fused with the Democratic party, creating what became known as the DFL—the Democratic-Farmer-Labor party. Success for the DFL was not immediate upon its formation in 1944, but by 1954 it had won its first gubernatorial election, and it ran competitive races afterward, winning the governorship eight out of fourteen times in the remaining years of the twentieth century. Even with the decline of farming and labor, the party maintains the DFL moniker.

In presidential elections most Farmer-Labor voters cast Democratic ballots for Franklin D. Roosevelt in the 1932–44 elections. The farmers in the coalition were especially amenable to Democratic pleas. But in northeastern Minnesota, generic New Deal Democrats were much too moderate. Prolabor radicals on the Iron Range pushed support for socialist party candidates and won the support of a large cross-section of union members in the mining community. The lukewarm support for Roosevelt in northeastern Minnesota is shown clearly in map 7.1. Carlton, St. Louis, Aitkin, Lake, and Cook Counties are in his *lowest* quartiles of support when the Democratic presidential vote is averaged across the three elections starting with 1928 (see

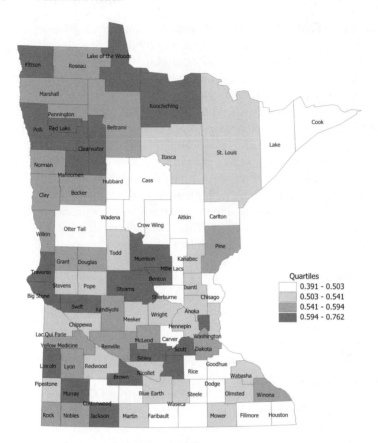

Map 7.2.   Average Democratic percentage of the presidential vote, 1928–1936

map 7.2). The darkly shaded agricultural regions far out on the northern plains were much more supportive of Roosevelt. Industrial Ramsey County (St. Paul) was Roosevelt territory, but Hennepin County (Minneapolis) remained competitive between the parties through the New Deal era. The GOP areas of the state included the agricultural southern and especially the southeastern counties (see map 7.2).

By the early 1950s, iron ore mining had already been seriously depleted, and the socialist ardor on the Iron Range had died down. Most of the labor radicals found their way into the Democratic party, and the Farmer-Labor party had fused with the Democrats. St. Louis County (Duluth) became a predictable Democratic stronghold. Bene-

fiting from realignment and the mobilization of new voters, Democrats had solidified their gains in the state's larger cities, including
Minneapolis. Voters on the remote western plains that had become so
dependent on railways for transportation of agricultural produce favored Roosevelt's progressive regulatory regime that promised close
scrutiny of shipping rates. More prosperous farmers closer to the Twin
Cities were not as inclined to participate in federal production control
programs, and they continued to support the GOP. Republicans remained highly competitive in presidential elections, even though
Democrats managed to break the GOP stranglehold on the governorship. In 1952, 1956, and 1960, Eisenhower and Nixon did particularly well among farmers across southern Minnesota, on the western
plains, and in Minneapolis. Republican presidential candidates made
no inroads among labor union members on the Iron Range and in
working-class St. Paul.

By the end of the twentieth century, much of rural Minnesota had
realigned, and the suburbs had become a critical political variable in
the formula for electoral victory. While the GOP picked up support in
many of the rural counties that had been part of the Farmer-Labor
coalition, there were fewer voters in these places than in the past. On
the northwestern plains, in particular, Republican gains were dramatic,
but because of sparse populations these gains made little difference to
statewide totals. Depressed and deindustrialized, northeastern Minnesota remained as Democratic as it had been in the 1950s (see map
7.3). Bill Clinton won 61 percent of the vote in St. Louis County (Duluth) in 1996, and Al Gore won with 60 percent in 2000. In areas where
the recreation industry brought in new populations from other parts of
the state, the newcomers have often imported Republican attachments.

The Minneapolis and St. Paul suburbs have become political
battlegrounds that divide along class or economic lines. Thousands of
residents from the Iron Range region moved from Duluth to the
Twin Cities. These voters settled in working-class suburbs north of
Minneapolis and transported their Democratic party affiliation with
them. White-collar suburbs west of Minneapolis and extending eastward into Washington County have more Republican traditions.
Rural Minnesotans who have deserted the farm and moved to the
suburbs have brought along both Republican and Democratic loyalties, turning older suburbs such as Bloomington and Roseville into
political swing areas that both parties must sift for votes. Statewide,

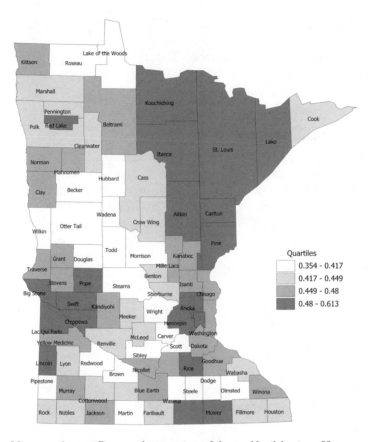

Map 7.3.   Average Democratic percentage of the presidential vote, 1988–2000

though, Minnesota typically went Democratic in presidential elections. Often, the margin was not even close, with the Democrats winning several hundred thousand more votes than the Republicans
(350,000 in 1996). No one would ask for a recount in this state in the
2000 presidential election: Al Gore won by 59,000 votes.

Where Are the Votes in Minnesota? Republican and
Democratic Mobilization Targets

By examining the contribution each county makes to each party's political base, one can obtain some understanding of the state's political

geography from the perspective of candidates who must find their supporters and turn them out on election day. Counties are not of equal importance in a statewide election. By studying the geographic distribution of votes for each party, we can also obtain some sense of how politically balkanized a state has become. In most states, Republicans and Democrats have come to draw from distinct regional pockets, although there are some locations where the balance of party strength is even and political sectionalism is less pronounced.

With the growth of the suburbs and the decline of outlying areas, we should not be surprised to find that the suburban counties surrounding Minneapolis and St. Paul have become critical turf for both parties. We have ranked the top ten Minnesota counties by their contribution to each party's presidential election effort in the 1988–2000 elections in table 7.1. The principal suburban counties are Dakota, Anoka, Washington, and Carver. The first three of these appear in both lists, suggesting that candidates had to wage serious neighborhood-by-neighborhood combat in these locales. A few places ranked high for one party, but low for the other. Carver County, on the outer rim of the Twin Cities metro area, ranked tenth for Republicans, but much lower for Democrats (ranked twenty-fifth). Democrats had substantial support in Rice County (ranked tenth), home to the liberal college town of Northfield, but for Republicans, Rice ranked twenty-third.

In the 1930s, Minnesota's political campaigns were different in that

TABLE 7.1.   Minnesota's Top Ten Strongest Counties for Republicans and Democrats in the 1988–2000 Presidential Contests

Rank	Democratic	Republican
1	Hennepin (Minneapolis)	Hennepin (Minneapolis)
2	Ramsey (St. Paul)	Dakota (Eagan)
3	Saint Louis (Duluth)	Ramsey (St. Paul)
4	Dakota (Eagan)	Anoka (Anoka)
5	Anoka (Anoka)	Washington (Stillwater)
6	Washington (Lake Elmo)	Olmsted (Rochester)
7	Stearns (St. Cloud)	Stearns (St. Cloud)
8	Olmsted (Rochester)	Saint Louis (Duluth)
9	Rice (Northfield)	Wright (Buffalo)
10	Wright (Buffalo)	Carver (Chaska)
% of total vote	66.7	60.6

both parties looked further afield for their votes. To be sure, Minneapolis, St. Paul, and Duluth cast sizable proportions of the statewide vote even then, but the suburban counties were undeveloped. Candidates would find themselves spending much more time visiting towns such as Winona, East Grand Forks, Fergus Falls, and Mankato than they would seventy years later. With the rise of the suburbs, the state's center of political gravity moved much closer to the Twin Cities metropolitan area. In other states, Republicans would come to rack up lopsided gains in the suburbs, but not in Minnesota where the Democrats could still win many of them by convincing margins well into the twenty-first century.

In summary, our analysis of the electoral foundation of Minnesota politics shows that neither party can afford to ignore the most populous cities and suburbs in Hennepin (Minneapolis) and Ramsey (St. Paul) Counties. Beyond these, however, parties and candidates have developed different priorities. Democrats must move northward to Duluth, while Republicans focus on the suburban counties. Outside of the metro area, Republicans still find some support in Duluth, but Rochester (Olmsted County) is much more important, followed by the St. Cloud area (Stearns County) (see table 7.1). The numerous mid-sized counties containing small towns and farm populations are split between the parties, with Republicans capturing many votes in the southern counties and scattered counties on the western plains, while Democrats dominate in the northeast.

Although Hennepin and Ramsey Counties ranked first and second in importance for both parties (table 7.1), the Democrats had more voters than the Republicans in both. About 39 percent of the Democrats' total statewide votes were cast in the Twin Cities, compared with 32 percent for the Republicans. With another 16 percent of the statewide Democratic vote coming from the suburban counties, it is clear that well over half of Democratic voters have been concentrated in the state's major metropolitan area. Republicans, on the other hand, had a more widely dispersed base of support (see map 7.4). Democratic campaign efforts aimed at mobilization and turnout could be highly focused on just a few areas, while Republican campaign efforts had to go further afield. Minnesota is an example of a state where the geographic centralization of the population has benefited the Democratic party and not even the middle-income suburbs could be counted on for the GOP.

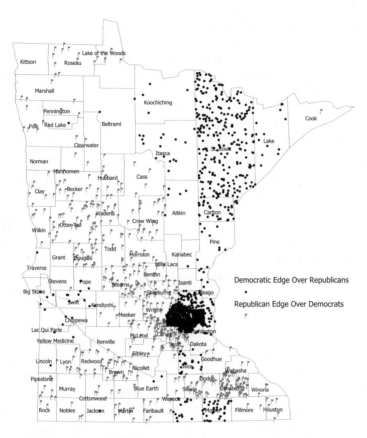

Map 7.4.   Areas of Republican and Democratic dominance, 1988–2000

Minnesota's Changing Electoral Foundations

Political scientists have several preferred approaches for studying electoral change. Perhaps the best method is to compare voters at different points in time, either the same voters (as in a panel design) or perhaps random samples of different voters (repeated cross-sections). Both methods are based on survey research, and the best-known studies have used these approaches to build our knowledge base (Miller and Shanks 1996; Page and Shapiro 1992; Campbell et al. 1960; Berelson, Lazarsfeld, and McPhee 1954). In this project, our goal is to learn about political change across a long period of time and within individual states, and these aims have limited our ability to use polls. Surveys of Minnesota voters are difficult to find prior to 1982. Bearing this limitation in mind, we turned to ecological inference estimation as a means of studying changes in the political support patterns of several demographic groups.

Across Minnesota, partisan change is evident when we compare maps 7.2 and 7.3. Many rural areas on the state's western plains that were Democratic strongholds in the 1930s had become predictably Republican areas by the turn of the century. Other areas, such as northeastern Minnesota, have gone in the reverse direction, with Democrats gaining ground on the GOP and third parties since mid-century. What explains these changes?

Several forces behind political change may come into play to help account for such developments. These forces include conversion, generational replacement, population migration, and the mobilization of new voters. Briefly, conversion produces partisan change when individuals change their party identification (Sundquist 1983). Mobilization produces partisan change when new voters become activated for the first time, surging into the electorate to sway political contests in one direction or the other (Andersen 1979). Similarly, demobilization could also have an influence on the political complexion of an area, if large groups of voters suddenly become inactive. Generational replacement has an impact when partisans die and are replaced by voters of a different party, altering the political leaning of a place through the natural processes of birth and mortality (Abramson 1975). Population migration, if it is of sufficient volume, can alter the politics at both the site that is left behind as well as the destination (Brown 1988; Gimpel 1999; Gimpel and Schuknecht 2001).

Generational Replacement

The surge in Republican strength on the state's western plains has been mainly a function of generational replacement. One important clue is that the political change in these counties has been so gradual. Between 1930 and 1960, the drift toward the Republicans in the farming counties was slow but steady. After 1960, as the older farmers who identified with the Farmer-Labor faction began to die off, we observed a steady current begin to carry these areas toward the GOP. By 1980, the older farmers had been replaced by younger voters, fewer of whom were employed in agriculture. Even the younger farmers were unfamiliar with the issues that originally attracted the farm population to reformist ranks. Generational replacement has had the effect of watering down the old ethnic lines of cleavage that once divided Republicans from Democrats. German Catholics and Scandinavian Protestants were once drawn to opposing parties because of issues such as prohibition and immigration. These issues are no longer relevant in most Minnesota communities and were not the basis of people's party identification at the beginning of the new century as they had been at the beginning of the previous one.

The political loyalties of the elderly are worth studying because they often exhibit a voting allegiance significantly different from younger cohorts'. In such cases, we can anticipate electoral change through the process of generational replacement. Our estimates indicate that the proportion of elderly voters casting Democratic ballots was quite small during the New Deal but rose sharply thereafter (table 7.2). While the elderly population became significantly more Democratic by the 1940s, younger Minnesotans were still more likely to vote for Roosevelt than the older generation. This began to change, however, as the cohorts that most strongly supported the New Deal began to retire in the 1960s. By the 1968–72 elections, our estimates suggest that about one out of three of those over age 65 were casting Democratic ballots, and this rose steadily through the rest of the century. Available exit polling data confirm that in 1996 and 2000, support among elderly Minnesotans for Bill Clinton and Al Gore was higher than among younger age groups, figures that are bolstered by the results reported in table 7.2.

Our estimates for Democratic support among those under age 65 are more reliable across the entire period, and they show a gradual weakening of support for Democrats between 1928 and the end of the century. By the time we reach the 1996–2000 contests, an estimated 49 percent of those under age 65 supported Democratic candidates, compared with 53 percent in the 1928–32 elections. The figures for the 1980s and 1990s shown in table 7.2 match available exit polling data quite closely. In sum, generational replacement of elderly Republicans with young, New Deal Democrats helped the latter party gain ascendancy for most of the century and only in very recent elections does there appear to be a reversal. If the recent propensity for the elderly to vote more Democratic than those aged 18 through 64 will hold through the next several elections, Republicans could make up lost ground through the deaths of aging baby boomers between 2005 and 2025. Presidential elections in Minnesota may be more competitive in the new century than they have been in many years.

Population Mobility

Out-migration has benefited the GOP in agricultural areas because the farmers that ran smaller, less successful operations were more likely to vote Democratic than those that ran the larger farms that were the product of corporate consolidation. As the smaller farmers and their adult children have left the farms to find other lines of work,

TABLE 7.2.   Estimates of the Democratic Percentage of the Presidential Vote for Various Electoral Groups in Minnesota, 1928–2000 (ecological inference maximum likelihood)

Pooled Presidential Election Years	Blacks/ Nonblacks		Elderly/ Nonelderly		Immigrants/ Nonimmigrants		Farmers/ Nonfarmers		Whites/ Nonwhites	
1928, 1932	51.4	50.4*	13.8	52.9*	18.2*	56.2*	55.5*	47.7*	50.4*	58.5*
1936, 1940, 1944	36.7	55.2*	38.1	56.6*	81.2	52.1*	48.2*	58.3*	54.8*	87.9
1948, 1952	52.9	50.4*	18.0	55.3*	85.2	47.8*	40.8*	53.6*	50.4*	56.6
1956, 1960, 1964	54.6	53.4*	26.0	56.6*	68.0	54.8*	46.9*	54.8*	53.4*	54.7
1968, 1972	52.7	49.0*	29.9	51.3*	49.1	50.1*	44.2*	49.7*	48.8*	61.1
1976, 1980, 1984	87.8	49.9*	39.2	51.2*	62.6	51.5*	31.0*	52.0*	50.1*	58.7
1988, 1992	94.9	46.6*	48.6	47.5*	68.2	47.4*	37.2	48.2*	46.5*	67.6
1996, 2000	58.9	49.2*	52.9	48.9*	76.4	48.9*	35.9	50.3*	48.1*	68.3

	Mfg. Workers/ Non Mfg. Workers		College Educated/ Non College Educated		Native to State/ Nonnatives		Internal Migrants/ Nonmigrants		Hispanics/ Non-Hispanics	
1928, 1932	—	—	—	—	—	—	—	—	—	—
1936, 1940, 1944	—	—	—	—	—	—	—	—	—	—
1948, 1952	80.0*	45.1*	44.6	50.8*	—	—	—	—	—	—
1956, 1960, 1964	52.5*	53.3*	41.5	54.4*	53.6*	52.7*	38.5*	56.5*	—	—
1968, 1972	61.7*	45.7*	37.5	50.5*	49.2*	48.5*	42.4	51.0*	—	—
1976, 1980, 1984	40.7	52.6*	41.0	51.7*	48.6*	55.5*	43.6	52.3*	43.5	50.4*
1988, 1992	35.6	50.3*	50.7	46.8*	47.9*	47.0*	50.8*	46.7*	50.1	47.6*
1996, 2000	34.4	52.3*	71.9	44.4*	47.9	54.4*	48.9*	49.8*	67.3	49.1*

Note: Cell entries show the estimated percentage voting Democratic in the presidential elections listed on each row. Complete variable definitions and results from the ecological inference estimation appear in appendix B, with standard errors and bounds.

*Reflect estimates with lower and upper bounds narrower than 0,1.

the larger, more successful operations have remained behind. These surviving farmers had always possessed a modern, businesslike view of farming and had generally aligned themselves with Republican agricultural interests, including the large Minneapolis mill companies. In addition, the movement off farms has strengthened rural Republicanism because there is evidence that the strongest basis of GOP support in rural America since the 1950s has been in small towns, on Main Street, rather than on the farm (Gimpel and Schuknecht 2000). As the farm sector has shrunk relative to the other mainstays of the rural economy (services, retail and wholesale trade), the Republican share of the vote in the most sparsely populated counties has steadily risen.

The Minneapolis suburbs have benefited from population migration from three sources: flight from Minneapolis and St. Paul, flight from agricultural consolidation on the plains, and flight from the collapse of the mining economy in northeastern Minnesota. Overall, the effect of these migration streams on the suburbs has been to make the metropolitan area more Democratic, particularly in the northern suburbs, but also in the middle-income suburbs of Hennepin County. The suburbs to the south, particularly in Dakota and Scott Counties, have trended more Republican.

Minneapolis and St. Paul remained Democratic strongholds in most elections. Flight from these cities in the 1960s and 1970s took many affluent Republicans with it, leaving a poorer and older population behind. The minority population in these cities is not large, but it has grown more influential with increased mobilization and the departure of white voters to the suburbs. Since mid-century, Minneapolis has expressed more liberal political values in its politics than the conservative working-class voters in St. Paul. In presidential elections, St. Paul could be counted on to turn in a Democratic majority through the 1980s, but in the 1990s it became more competitive. In the early 1990s, Minneapolis elected a black mayor on the basis of a lopsided white majority population at the same time that St. Paul turned to elect a Republican mayor. The evolved political scene has brought fresh hope for Republican party-building efforts in the state capital, although Minneapolis has followed other large central cities in going increasingly Democratic.

Throughout this book we have been very interested in elucidating the way in which population movement can change the politics of a place. In most states, we have found that population migration from within the country but from outside a state's borders strengthens the Republican party at the expense of Democrats and independents (Gimpel 1999). Exceptions include Maryland, where out-of-state migrants were often drawn to the state to work for the federal government, and Michigan, where a significant migration stream in the mid-twentieth century consisted of industrial workers. For Minnesota, however, our generalization holds up—internal migrants were less supportive of Democrats than other voters (the combined population of immigrants and natives) in most presidential elections after 1956, although the distinction between the two groups faded in the late 1980s. By the 1996–2000 elections, the political distinction between internal migrants and international migrants was largely erased, and native Minnesotans appeared to be slightly more Republican than nonnatives (nonnatives equal the combined population of internal migrants and immigrants). But if internal migrants have been moving toward the GOP, it must be the foreign born who have contributed to the Democratic bent of the nonnative group. Our estimates for the Democratic inclination of the immigrant population are not highly reliable due to severe aggregation bias in our data, but they do indicate that Minnesota's immigrant population resides in the most Democratic areas of the state and probably contributes to the Democratic majority, as our estimates for the Hispanic population in 1996–2000 corroborate. Still, immigrants constituted only 2.6 percent of the state's population by 1990, and less than half of those were naturalized. This population's Democratic loyalty made a difference only in the very closest races.

Finally, we should remember that Minnesota has not attracted large numbers of cross-state migrants compared with Southern or Western states. A more important aspect of population migration has been movement internal to the state, off the farms and away from mining towns and into the Minneapolis–St. Paul metro area. The political consequences of this internal redistribution are mainly felt in local elections; they are probably a wash in the major statewide contests.

Conversion

Conversion from one party to another played a role in moving labor radicals in northeastern Minnesota into Democratic party ranks after

1940. The fusion of the Democratic party with the Farmer-Labor party improved Democratic prospects across the state, but particularly around Duluth and anywhere there were large concentrations of union laborers and new immigrants. The political impact of the fusion was almost immediate, first making the Democratic party a competitive force, then making them a dominant force in state politics beginning in the mid-1950s. Had the Farmer-Labor loyalists not found a new home in the Democratic party, the Democrats would not have been capable of winning statewide offices as frequently. It is fair to say that the uniting of these two political forces at mid-century created a Democratic majority in Minnesota that will continue well into the twenty-first century.

To examine the extent of conversion in Minnesota politics we estimated voter transition models for presidential elections in the 1930s and the 1960s. The point of such a model is to estimate the extent of Republican (or Democratic) support that carries over from one election to the next. If 50 percent of the voters who cast Republican ballots in the last election defect to another party in the current election, we have an approximate measure of partisan conversion. Granted, some of these converts may only be temporary, but the model does give us a figure that we can then compare to other states to gauge the relative magnitude of party disloyalty and movement.

We infer from table 7.3 that voters who had supported Al Smith's Democratic candidacy in 1928 were highly loyal to Roosevelt in 1932, with 88.2 percent casting ballots for the New Dealer. They were joined by 40.8 percent of those who had voted for someone other than Smith—presumably these are mainly Republican crossovers, although their number may include some third-party voters as well. Only an estimated 58.6 percent of Hoover voters in 1928 returned to vote for him in 1932, and Hoover only picked up a handful of voters who had cast their ballots for other candidates in the previous election—once again showing how lopsided the realignment was. Nor was the party switching over in 1932. In 1936, only 66.5 percent of those who had backed Hoover in 1932 returned to vote for Landon. Minnesota is highly comparable to Michigan (chap. 12). Republicans were more resistant to the New Deal tide in Minnesota than in Oregon and Maryland, but less resistant than in Connecticut, New York, or Illinois (chaps. 11, 10, 9, 13, 14).

The 1960s gave some voters good reason to switch parties. The

Democrats took aggressively liberal positions on civil rights, alienating Southern white voters and working-class whites in Northern cities who often found themselves in competition for jobs and housing with similarly situated blacks (Cummings 1977, 1980). In 1964, Republican candidate Barry Goldwater championed a go-slow, states rights approach on civil rights, while trumpeting fierce anticommunist themes and the traditional GOP message of smaller, less intrusive government. Goldwater lost by a landslide but his campaign left a lasting imprint on the American political scene (Phillips 1970). In subsequent elections, the conservative wing of the Republican party would be substantially strengthened, culminating in the election of Ronald Reagan in 1980.

Minnesota Democrats had little reason to bolt from their party from 1960 to 1964 as the transition from a Kennedy vote to a Johnson vote was an easy one—94.2 percent of Kennedy's supporters backed Johnson. They were joined by about 32 percent of Nixon's (1960) supporters as Johnson won a lopsided majority in the state (table 7.3). Just over half of Nixon's (1960) supporters remained faithful to Goldwater four years later, the others either defecting to support Johnson, or perhaps not voting at all. In 1968, Minnesota's native son, Hubert Humphrey, led the Democratic ticket and carried the state with 54 percent of the vote. Richard Nixon won back the loyalty of many "Johnson Republicans" with roughly one-third of Johnson backers choosing him over Humphrey or George Wallace. About 7 percent of Goldwater's supporters voted for American Independent candidate George Wallace in 1968, compared with only 3 percent of Johnson supporters. The Wallace vote is a good indicator of the magnitude of dealignment and subsequent conversion as most Wallace voters eventually became Republicans, but it is clear that Wallace had little support in this Northern, liberal state. In few other states did Wallace do as poorly as he did in Minnesota, winning less than 100,000 votes.

For further evidence of political conversion we might review the changing Democratic support figures from table 7.2. We have learned from many other sources that farmers in Minnesota have a political history distinct from that of many other states. While their loyalties were split by ethnicity and class, a large proportion of farmers joined with labor union members in the years leading up the Great Depression to form the radical Farmer-Labor party. Wealthier dairy farmers

TABLE 7.3. Estimates of Party Loyalty and Conversion across Presidential Elections in Minnesota (ecological inference maximum likelihood)

Presidential Election Years	Voted Democratic 1928/Non-Democratic 1928		Voted Democratic 1932/Non-Democratic 1932		Presidential Election Years	Voted Republican 1928/Non-Republican 1928		Voted Republican 1932/Non-Republican 1932	
Voted Democratic 1932	88.2*	40.8*			Voted Republican 1932	58.6*	5.4*		
Voted Democratic 1936			69.8*	49.5*	Voted Republican 1936			66.5*	11.1*

Presidential Election Years	Voted Democratic 1960/Non-Democratic 1960		Voted Democratic 1964/Non-Democratic 1964		Presidential Election Years	Voted Republican 1960/Non-Republican 1960		Voted Republican 1964/Non-Republican 1964	
Voted Democratic 1964	94.2*	32.5*			Voted Republican 1964	54.5*	48.2*		
Voted Democratic 1968			80.8*	6.7*	Voted Republican 1968			59.2*	31.5*
Voted Wallace 1968			3.1*	6.5*	Voted Wallace 1968			7.4*	2.6*

Note: Cell entries show the estimated percentage voting Democratic, Republican, or for George Wallace in the presidential elections listed on each row who voted Democratic (or Republican) in the previous election. Complete variable definitions and results from the ecological inference estimation appear in appendix C, with standard errors and bounds.

*Reflect estimates with lower and upper bounds narrower than 0,1.

in southern Minnesota remained staunchly Republican during this period. A few German Catholics clung stubbornly to the Democratic party. The splintered political loyalties of farmers meant that there was little urban vs. rural cleavage in most Minnesota elections (Fenton 1966, 110). Since the middle of the twentieth century, though, farm radicalism has dropped from sight. Farm consolidation has meant fewer farmers and larger operations. It has also meant that farmers have become increasingly Republican, a fact that is borne out in the data we present (table 7.2).

In the 1928–32 elections, farmers were more likely than nonfarmers to support Roosevelt. Urban-rural cleavages are not very pronounced, as only a few points separate the Democratic support of farmers from that of nonfarmers. The farm sector's ardor for the Democratic party weakened considerably at the end of the Roosevelt era, and by the late 1970s only about 31 percent of the farm population voted Democratic, compared with 52 percent of the nonfarm population, a considerable gap. The gap closes slightly in the 1980s and 1990s, but Minnesota farmers remained less likely to support Democrats than at any previous time since the late 1920s. Comparing these results to those of other states shows that Minnesota still has more Democratic farmers than one finds in other Northern states — the waning legacy of the rural radicalism of earlier in the century.

Industrial labor has a famous and colorful past in Minnesota politics. Like farmers, though, this group became more politically conservative over the course of the twentieth century. In the 1990s, the city of St. Paul, known for its laboring population, elected a Republican mayor, Norm Coleman. We would expect our estimates to indicate that manufacturing workers were overwhelmingly Democratic at mid-century, but less so as time went on. The results in table 7.2 clearly bear this out. In the 1948–52 presidential elections an estimated 80 percent of manufacturing workers supported Truman-Stevenson, compared with just 45 percent of those in nonindustrial jobs. By the late 1970s, our estimates show that blue-collar labor had shifted toward the GOP camp — an indication of the Reagan Republicanism that had taken hold. Our estimates for the combined 1996–2000 elections show that the support for Democrats among blue-collar laborers remained quite low, 34 percent as compared to 52 percent among those in nonmanufacturing jobs. These figures suggest a trend and indicate that the working-class labor force has changed. It may not consider itself to be loyally in the GOP column, but it has become less reliably Democratic than it once was.

We have seen some evidence, then, of conversion among farmers and manufacturing workers—once the fodder for socialist radicalism on the upper plains. What about the well educated? If Republicans have gained among working-class voters, have they lost ground among professional and managerial elites? Throughout the twentieth century, college-educated voters generally earned more money than those lacking a college degree. Education, then, was an indicator of class standing, especially early in the century when fewer people sought education beyond high school. At the same time, Minnesota also has a reputation for liberal intellectualism and a history of issue-oriented campaigns. Our best guess is that the college educated will vote less Democratic than those lacking a college degree but that class cleavages may not be as pronounced as they are in other states. The data in table 7.2 bear this out quite well. In the 1948–52 elections, an estimated 45 percent of those with a college degree cast Democratic ballots, compared with 51 percent of those lacking higher education, a rather small gap compared to states such as California and Illinois. In more recent elections, our estimates show that the well educated are more likely to vote Democratic than the less well educated—a finding consistent with the results for manufacturing workers described previously. When we checked these results against available polling data we discovered that they were not far off. Polls in 1996 and 2000 indicated that support for Bill Clinton and Al Gore dropped almost imperceptibly as one moved up in years of formal education. Minnesota is still not as cleaved by class and education as many other states—a fact that points up the importance of a place's unique political history and social context to the nature of local political allegiances.

Activism and Partisanship of New Voters

The minority population in Minnesota is very small, although St. Paul residents proudly claim Dred Scott as one of their own. Since the civil rights era, the black population has been closely allied with the Democratic party, and we would not expect that to be any different in Minnesota given the state's proud liberal tradition. Unfortunately, the tiny proportion of black voters in the state and their concentration in just a few areas made it difficult to obtain accurate estimates of their voting inclination from county-level data. Still, some interesting tendencies are revealed in table 7.2 exhibiting the increasing Democratic loyalty of the areas of black concentration. In the 1928–32 elections, according to our estimates, blacks are not much more likely to vote Democratic than whites. By the 1970s, however, the results follow much of the anecdotal and survey evidence in suggesting that black voters supported Democrats overwhelmingly, while only about half the white voters did.

The estimates for white support in table 7.2 are more reliable and show that it remained mostly unchanged over the seventy-year period. In the 1928–32 elections, about half of white voters supported Democratic candidates, and the same was true in the 1976–2000 elections. Democratic support among nonwhites (blacks, American Indians, others) generally ran well ahead of that for whites across this era. The general stability of the white vote suggests that there was no massive reaction to black mobilization in the 1960s. As in Connecticut and Colorado, the black population in Minnesota was not large enough to constitute much of a threat to working-class whites. Mobilization's impact on the state's electoral balance was to tip it further toward Democratic domination. While the black population is small, it is highly concentrated in Minneapolis and St. Paul and is sufficiently influential that it could steer the metropolitan area toward Democrats in high turnout elections, countering the GOP vote in the western suburbs. The challenge for Democrats is to mobilize this highly reliable vote in gubernatorial elections where Republicans, and more recently third parties, have launched more competitive bids.

Conclusions

The most important development in the seventy years of Minnesota politics following the Great Depression was the creation of a Democratic majority in the state through the fusion of Democrats with the radical Farmer-Labor party. From the late 1940s onward, sectionalism in the state was characterized by a northeast vs. southeast split with the western plains dividing between the parties. The changing political geography of Minnesota is worth studying because it is a result of underlying forces that have transformed the state's economy. The state's western plains were once Democratic or Farmer-Labor strongholds but have become more Republican since mid-century. The force behind this change has been generational replacement and out-migration. The older generation of farmers has been replaced by a younger one with no memory of Farmer-Labor radicalism or the hardships of the 1930s. Forces that have transformed the farm economy also undergird the political changes. Farm operations are larger, and there are fewer marginal operators who would be attracted to Democratic farm policy.

While farm radicalism is a fading memory, so is industrial radicalism. Duluth and northeastern Minnesota vote loyally Democratic, but it is not clear that they are pushing an aggressive program—the area is depressed and dependent on government investment and relief, something Democrats are good at providing. Manufacturing workers in St. Paul and other areas were more likely to vote Democratic at the beginning of the new century than they were earlier. But unlike other cities, it is not clear that this dealignment among working-class white voters is the result of black activism and mobilization into the local Democratic party. Republican voting by blue-collar whites is not simply a function of GOP or Democratic policy views on civil rights and affirmative action.

We have noted elsewhere that high turnout diminishes sectionalism because in elections where more people participate, weaker partisans and political moderates come to the polls, whereas in low turnout contests, only the most partisan and ideologically extreme voters show up. Sectionalism has diminished in Minnesota's vote for president, but it has increased in the gubernatorial contests. The gulf between the two offices is probably reflective of the generally higher turnout in presidential elections compared with the lower turnout gubernatorial contests. The 1998 gubernatorial race saw sectionalism reach a peak that it had not reached since the 1940s. This contest brought out the older north-south line of cleavage in the state, with the Democratic candidate taking much of the north, the Republican winning most of southern Minnesota, and Reform Party candidate Jesse Ventura winning in the heavily populated Minneapolis–St. Paul metropolitan area (Lacy and Monson 2002).

While Duluth and the northeastern counties are still in Democratic hands, and Rochester and the southeast safely in the GOP camp, the rest of the state is more volatile and could go either direction depending on who shows up to vote. The 1998 election taught both Republicans and Democrats that the Twin Cities are home to a highly volatile electorate where both parties must now spend even more money and effort on voter identification and mobilization. The competition for the Reform party's voters—many of whom were previously unmobilized young white males with little interest in politics—began the day after Jesse Ventura's surprising upset in the 1998 gubernatorial election and will continue well into the first decade of the new millennium.

CHAPTER 8

GEORGIA

Major Forces for Electoral Change in Georgia

- Migration of Black Voters from Rural to Urban Areas
- Migration from the North and from Other Southern States to Atlanta Metro Area
- Decline of the Agricultural Economy
- Mobilization of the Black Population
- Conversion of Southern Whites from the Democratic to the Republican Party

As the most prosperous of the Deep South states, Georgia stood as one of the nation's brightest economic lights as the new century began. Outsiders associate Georgia with its largest city, Atlanta—best known for Coca-Cola, the Braves baseball team, communications mogul Ted Turner, and the 1996 Olympic Games. Suburban Atlanta conjures up the image of the controversial Newt Gingrich, former Speaker of the U.S. House of Representatives. Many rural Southerners have come to reject Atlanta and its suburbs as a Yankee haven, a transplanted piece of the North—a place for Southerners to move only after they have rejected their friendly, small town roots. All of the headaches rural Georgians have associated with the North can be found in Atlanta and its suburbs: high taxes, unfriendly people, aggressive drivers, and urban sprawl.

Outside of Atlanta, the most widely recognized city in Georgia is Savannah (Chatham County), associated with traditional Old South culture and architecture, including the ubiquitous veranda porches. Rural Georgia reminds us of the crops that made Georgia famous: peaches, peanuts, and cotton, along with plantation estates, the most famous of which is the highly clichéd Tara from *Gone with the Wind*. Where agriculture is not dominant, Georgia's small towns are often dependent upon a single major plant or industry that dominates the local economy. Paper, textiles, and food processing plants dot the landscape, along with several major military installations.

To say that Georgia is a model of Sun Belt prosperity is not to say that all of its constituent parts have prospered. The city of Atlanta has declined in population since 1950, although not as much as Chicago, Cleveland, Detroit, and other Midwestern cities. Atlanta's middle- and upper-income population has been drawn out of the city by the suburbs of Fulton County and the adjacent counties: Cobb, Gwinnett, DeKalb, and Clayton. In 1960, when Atlantans numbered 487,000, the city was larger than all of the suburbs combined. Desegregation of the city's schools in the 1960s frightened many white residents, and they packed up and left for the suburbs. By the dawn of the new century, the suburbs were home to two million people, compared with about 416,000 for the city itself. Since Atlanta's population losses have included such high proportions of whites, the city was 61 percent African American by 2000, up from 38 percent in 1960. Black control of city government dates to 1973 with the election of the city's first black mayor, Maynard Jackson.

In spite of its regional image as Yankeeville, most of suburban Atlanta's residents are rural Georgians and other transplanted Southerners (and their offspring) who found that their upward mobility was limited in their small hometowns. Migration from the Northeast and Midwest has been an important component of growth, but more people have moved in from rural Georgia and from other Southern states than from regions outside the South. Between 1985 and 1990, for example, DeKalb County (Decatur–Stone Mountain) gained 86,531 residents from outside Georgia, but 56 percent of those were from other Southern states, 17 percent from the Midwest, 17 percent from the Northeast, and 9 percent from the West. Cobb County's (Marietta-Smyrna) proportions were similar: 58 percent of migrants moving in were from the South, 19 percent from the Midwest, 13 percent from the Northeast, and 9 percent from the West. In the 1970s, the migration stream was similar, with a solid majority of the Atlanta metro area's new residents coming from the South.

With out-migration from Atlanta has come the suburbanization of a large middle-class black population that has moved principally into DeKalb County, the largest of the four suburban counties. Following the same path taken by suburban areas elsewhere, blacks have become majority populations in the older suburbs inside Atlanta's belt-

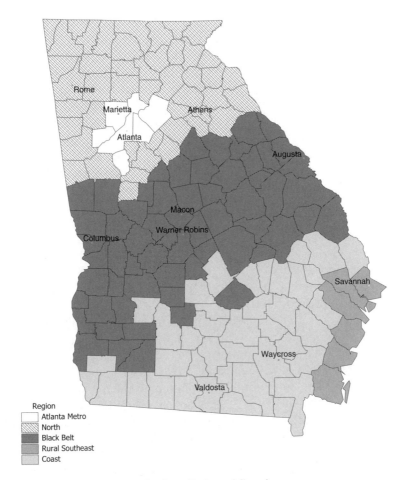

Map 8.1.   Regions of Georgia

way (I-285) such as East Point and College Park (Fulton County) and Gresham Park (DeKalb County). By 2000, an estimated 54 percent of the DeKalb County population was African American, and this percentage was headed upward. In wealthier Cobb County, about 19 percent of the population was black, and while at a trickle compared with DeKalb, this proportion was also inching upward.

Outside of Atlanta, there are four geographic regions worth considering separately (see map 8.1): Savannah (Chatham County) and the Georgia coast; southeast Georgia—from the city of Columbus

(Muscogee County) eastward to Macon (Bibb County) then south to the Florida border; rural southwest Georgia inland from Savannah; and north Georgia—an area outside the Atlanta suburbs north and east to the South Carolina, North Carolina, and Tennessee borders.

Savannah (Chatham County) was the first settlement in the state, and the onetime state capital. Old Savannah is known for its physical layout—not a grid, but a series of public squares around which about forty residential lots were placed, along with public buildings. By the time the city had expanded to fill its borders, in 1856, there were about twenty-four such squares. Several have since been demolished as part of urban renewal or to make way for public works projects. The city was once a major port, thriving on cotton exports. As the United States lost market share in cotton and textiles, the city fell on hard times, attracting only a couple of large industries early in the twentieth century. Following World War II, the city's population steadily dropped as its suburbs grew. In the 1960s, historic preservation forces stepped up their efforts to salvage the city's most historic homes and neighborhoods. The restoration of Old Savannah produced a major tourist industry (Peirce 1974). By the early 2000s, Savannah was home to about 131,000 people, down from 150,000 at mid-century. South of Savannah, along the coast, are several smaller rural counties that have seen rapid growth from tourism and resort development. The most notable demographic change in these counties has been the shrinking proportion of black residents with the influx of white migrants. In 1960, Camden County was 40 percent black; by 2000, only 16 percent of the population was black. The black population has grown since 1960 (in numbers), but much more slowly than the white population—a majority of which has arrived from outside Georgia.

Southeast Georgia, inland from the coast, is known principally for its small towns, an agricultural economy, and white, conservative population. Valdosta, Waycross, and the other small towns are regional trade centers and trans-shipment points for surrounding agricultural produce, including cotton, soybeans, pecans, and peaches. Parts of south Georgia are heavily forested with pine trees, so lumber and paper mills abound. Where agriculture does not dominate, residents characterize the settlements here as "company towns"—in the sense that usually a single industry or plant employs most of the people in the town. The majority of white residents are religious conservatives belonging to large Protestant evangelical churches. Political attitudes can be described as socially conservative but protectionist and populist on economic matters.

Southwest Georgia, including the cities of Columbus, Macon, and Albany, contains the historic "black belt" counties described by V. O. Key Jr. (1949)—rural counties with high proportions of African Americans (see map 8.1). Towns and neighborhoods are highly segregated—either predominantly black or predominantly white. The economy is rooted in agriculture, mainly cotton. Columbus and Macon are regional trade centers for the entire region, and Macon is known for textile and paper production. Government employment in the military is important in Columbus, where Fort Benning is a major employer, and south of Macon at Robins Air Force Base. The white populations of the towns in southwest Georgia are usually registered as Democrats, but have conservative attitudes on such issues as flagburning, civil rights, abortion, and gun control. Consequently, in most national elections they find it easy to vote Republican. The rural black populations are overwhelmingly Democratic and have had increasing power since they began voting in large numbers in the 1960s. The most rural counties in the black belt were depopulated with the increasing mechanization and concentration of agriculture (Wright 1986). In most cases, the out-migration left them even more Democratic than before. In some towns, white politicians are still the power holders, as described by Key (1949), but this older political arrangement has given way with black mobilization. Several biracial counties were under black political control by the turn of the twenty-first century.

North Georgia contains a few of the most historically Republican counties in the Old South—places that had prounion sympathies during the Civil War. Ironically, the mountain counties contain some of the poorest populations in the state, but some of the most loyal GOP voters. The mainly white "mountain people" have a reputation for being independent-minded, salt-of-the-earth, hillbillies—blue-collar workers often looked down upon by the white establishment further south. The economy of north Georgia was historically founded on copper mining, paper, and textiles. Agriculture (aside from forestry) is a minor economic activity in the northern counties, but there are some small-acreage farms. Traditional Georgia politicians running mostly on proagriculture platforms had less appeal to the mountaineers (Key 1949). There was little slaveholding in north Georgia, and even in recent decades these counties have very small black populations. There is still more manufacturing in north Georgia than in the rest of the state, but it is no longer distinctive for being the lone bastion of GOP support.

Map 8.2 illustrates the political geography of Georgia at the time of the New Deal realignment. Darkly shaded counties are those in the highest quartile of Democratic support for the combined 1928–32 elections. Georgia, like Texas (chap. 5), was overwhelmingly Democratic in the 1930s, with only three counties going Republican: Towns, Pickens, and Fannin, all in north Georgia.

Notably, suburban Atlanta is not distinct from the rest of north Georgia in map 8.2. Aside from north Georgia, only three regions stand out: southwest Georgia, where the black belt counties are concentrated, is the most Democratic region; southeast Georgia, inland from the coast, is a mix, but appears less enthusiastic about the New Deal than the black belt counties along the Alabama border; and finally, Savannah and the coastal counties join north Georgia as being the least supportive of Smith and Roosevelt.

The dominant cleavage across the state through mid-century, as shown in map 8.2, was black vs. white and urban vs. rural (Key 1949). The black belt counties are the most Democratic not because blacks voted—most did not—but because the plantation agriculture interests of rural Georgia were so loyal to Democrats as the party of the status quo on race relations (Key 1949). The up-country whites of north Georgia were less committed to Jim Crow not because they had more enlightened views about civil rights, but because there were few blacks there to threaten their political position.

In the 1950s and 1960s, politics in Georgia were turbulent. Atlanta was the headquarters of Martin Luther King Jr.'s civil rights movement. Desegregation was countered with the politics of massive resistance and ensuing white flight from areas with substantial black populations. Black mobilization and activism within Democratic party ranks sent Georgia's small town white population into the ranks of the Republican party. Barry Goldwater's candidacy in 1964, with his victory in Georgia and three other Southern states, is often touted as the critical election that proved the turning point for white Southerners. But even in previous elections, the Democratic party was losing ground among white voters in Atlanta and its growing suburbs, as well as throughout north Georgia in areas of population growth.

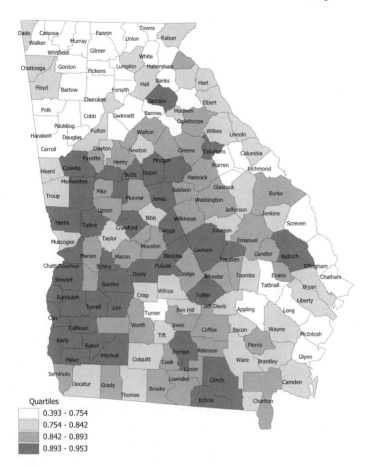

Map 8.2.   Average Democratic percentage of the presidential vote, 1928–1936

Democrats gained ground in Georgia after the New Deal wherever the white population was in decline and in locations where the influx of non-Georgia natives was insignificant. From 1930 to 1960, the Atlanta suburbs and northwest Georgia saw tremendous population gains from migrants from the state's rural counties. Most of these migrants to north Georgia were white, and the white proportion of the population in the northern counties increased dramatically during the post–World War II years. Blacks had fewer opportunities to gain from north Georgia's boom because official segregation still prevailed. Blacks either stayed put hoping that the departure of whites from black belt areas would improve their economic prospects, or they fled the state to take low-skill industrial jobs in Northern cities. The growth of the white population in north Georgia helped to reinforce and strengthen its GOP proclivities through the 1960s, while the depopulated black belt areas became more Democratic on the basis of traditional partisan ties and increasing black mobilization.

The one area where the population remained stable and agriculture remained prosperous was in southeastern Georgia, where there had been much less tenant farming than in the black belt. With agricultural consolidation, the tenant farmers had been pushed out, contributing to the depopulation of the black belt. The counties in and around Waycross and Valdosta saw some population decline, but because they had fewer marginal farms, that area remained more stable. Politically, the southeast was a mixed bag. Savannah's politics remained stable and Democratic, but the counties immediately around it voted heavily Republican in the 1952–60 elections. How fast an area went Republican depended on how fast the population grew and who moved in (Campbell 1977b; Converse 1966). The faster the population growth in the postwar era, the more partisan change is evident in maps of the state's political geography.

The 1964 and 1968 presidential elections did mark a turning point in the South's political history, so it is worth pausing to consider the impact these elections had on regional political alignments. Both Goldwater and Wallace ran campaigns that were hostile to civil rights and desegregation precisely to win white Democratic votes in Southern states. The strategy worked, and both drew sufficient support for them to run highly competitive races. Goldwater won Georgia and three other Southern states while being blown out everywhere else except Arizona, his home state. Wallace won five states, including Georgia.

Within the state, both Wallace and Goldwater ran weakly in Atlanta proper—no surprise given that city's growing black population. In the suburbs, though, Goldwater was highly competitive with Johnson. In 1968, Wallace did better than Humphrey in Atlanta's suburbs, but was not as popular as Nixon—signaling just how far the Republicans had come in just four years. Neither Wallace nor Goldwater had especially strong support in the traditional Republican areas of rural north Georgia, although Goldwater fared better than Wallace did in those counties. Both Wallace and Goldwater did best in areas of population stability or decline—one of Wallace's poorest counties was fast-growing DeKalb (Decatur–Stone Mountain). What is most interesting about the support for Wallace and Goldwater is that it did not rest as much on white newcomers to the state as it did white natives.

By the early 1980s, this once solidly Democratic state was decidedly less loyal to the Democrats. Fierce two-party competition emerged in presidential elections with Bill Clinton barely winning the state in 1992 (43.5 percent), and Bob Dole and George W. Bush taking it in 1996 and 2000, respectively. By the beginning of the new century, the realignment of white voters in small town Georgia was nearly complete, as they were now regularly voting Republican not only for president but for lower offices as well. Georgia's black voters had their Democratic loyalties cemented by the civil rights movement, the Goldwater-Johnson campaign, and the ensuing flight of whites to the GOP. The smaller number of blacks who voted regularly, though, would prove an inadequate basis for Democratic victories except in local elections. Democratic candidates found themselves reaching out to white liberals, elderly voters, and lower-income whites.

Geographically, the first few years of the twenty-first century saw Republicans racking up big victory margins in north Georgia where they had always been strong. In these years, Republicans made especially strong gains near the South Carolina border along the I-85 corridor between Atlanta and Greenville, South Carolina. In suburban Atlanta, Cobb and Gwinnett Counties, with their large affluent white populations, including many Georgia newcomers, saw Democratic support shrivel after 1960. Fulton and DeKalb Counties, though, went in the opposite direction. These two counties most fiercely resisted the rising Republican tide because they became home to large black populations that remained loyally Democratic (see map 8.3).

While Democratic margins have dropped almost everywhere since mid-century, some of the Democrats' best counties remained in the southeast, near Columbus, the heart of the black belt. Democrats can still find support among elderly low-income Georgians, in small towns and rural areas, that refuse to give up their partisan past. Democrats continued to do well in Bibb County (Macon) and throughout central Georgia. They didn't lose much ground along the coast, compared to elsewhere. Chatham County (Savannah) remained one of Bill Clinton's highlights, although suburban Bryan County, next door, went

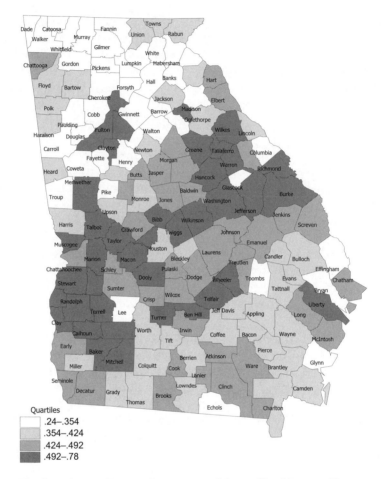

Map 8.3.   Average Democratic percentage of the presidential vote, 1988–2000

GOP. Consistent with the period between 1930 and 1960, Democrats lost ground after 1960 in areas with the highest concentrations of native white small town Georgians, particularly in the southeast.

Where Are the Votes in Georgia? Republican and Democratic Mobilization Targets

Before the courts forced Georgia to reapportion on a strict population basis in the early 1960s, elections for state office operated on the basis of a county unit system. Democratic candidates were chosen in primaries on the basis of county unit votes—similar to the electoral college in presidential elections. Each county had a certain number of unit votes, independent of its population. The candidate that received a popular plurality in a county received all of that county's unit votes. Unit votes were then tallied in determining the winner. Under a 1917 act that allocated the units according to legislative apportionment, the eight most populous counties received six unit votes, the next 30 received four unit votes and the remaining counties two unit votes (Key 1949, 119). This system grossly underrepresented the most urban counties and cleaved state politics along urban-rural lines.

While the Supreme Court's rulings on malapportionment put rural counties in their proper place in the mid-1960s, it is important to recognize that rural and urban areas are on a much more even plane in Georgia than in many other states. At the turn of the new century, the lion's share of votes came from metropolitan Atlanta, but candidates had to campaign outside Atlanta too. The need to gather votes outside of Atlanta was even more true in earlier times—something often overlooked in the earlier literature in its preoccupation with the injustices of the county unit system. But even in the post-reapportionment era, Georgia voters are a scattered lot.

On the other hand, Georgia is one of the largest states in terms of land area, and many counties are sparsely populated. While votes are more widely dispersed than in many other states, no candidate for statewide office can afford the time and money to go everywhere. Campaign efforts and resources must be targeted carefully at the most voter-rich locations. As in other states, though, Democrats and Republicans do not always find their voters in the same places. Table 8.1 lists the top ten counties for each party in the 1988–2000 presidential elections. The rankings are determined by the number of party voters in the county, as a percentage of the total statewide vote for each party, and how supportive the county is of each party, measured as the percentage of votes in the county that go to the Republican or Democratic candidates. The rankings show that the state's center of gravity is metropolitan Atlanta. Fulton (Atlanta), Cobb (Marietta-Smyrna), and DeKalb (Decatur) Counties are important for both parties (see map 8.4).

Georgia's political life did not always revolve around the Atlanta metro area. Fulton County contained just 9 percent of the state's

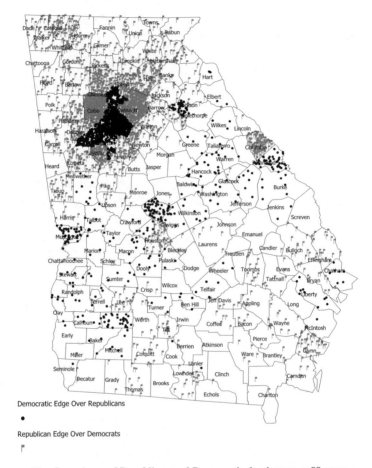

Democratic Edge Over Republicans

•

Republican Edge Over Democrats

⌐

Map 8.4.   Areas of Republican and Democratic dominance, 1988–2000

Democratic electorate in the combined 1928–1936 elections. In the years since, suburban Cobb County moved from seventeenth to third in its centrality to Democratic campaign efforts, while mid-sized towns such as Rome and Carrollton have dropped. Republicans were not much of a force in the 1930s, but outside of Atlanta, their strength could be found mainly in tiny towns in north Georgia, places that are of little consequence to campaigns in more recent years.

Our analysis shows that even though the GOP has become a competitive party in the Peach State, the Democrats and Republicans have different geographic bases of electoral support (see map 8.4; table 8.1). The Republicans were a much more thoroughly suburban party at the beginning of the new millennium. The geographic distribution of votes is similar to other states in that Democrats benefit from having more voters in fewer places. The concentration of Democratic votes in the state's largest cities lowers the cost of mobilization because the return on the expenditure of campaign resources can be maximized more easily when people live closer together than when they live further apart. This shift in the Democratic base from rural to urban represents a significant change from mid-century. The hallmark of the Democratic party in the 1950s was its strength in Georgia's rural areas, not only because of county unit voting, but because of the actual population distribution. Fifty years later, the Democratic party had a mainly urban base, having developed a constituency resembling many Northern states. The loss of Southern distinctiveness in Georgia is more than a story about white realignment to the Republicans, it's also a story about the voters the Democrats have retained and the new ones they have mobilized.

Georgia's Changing Electoral Foundations

Population mobility, generational replacement, mobilization, and the conversion of Democrats to the Republican party have played major

TABLE 8.1. Georgia's Top Ten Strongest Counties for Republicans and Democrats in the 1988–2000 Presidential Contests

Rank	Democratic	Republican
1	Fulton (Atlanta)	Cobb (Marietta-Smyrna)
2	DeKalb (Decatur)	Gwinnett (Lawrenceville)
3	Cobb (Marietta-Smyrna)	Fulton (Atlanta)
4	Chatham (Savannah)	DeKalb (Decatur)
5	Richmond (Augusta)	Chatham (Savannah)
6	Clayton (Forest Park)	Cherokee (Lebanon-Canton)
7	Gwinnett (Lawrenceville)	Columbia (Martinez)
8	Bibb (Macon)	Fayette (Fayetteville)
9	Muscogee (Columbus)	Hall (Gainesville)
10	Dougherty (Albany)	Richmond (Augusta)
% of total vote	54.7	44.9

roles in the last four decades of Georgia politics (Lamis 1999; Stanley 1988; Campbell 1977a, 1977b; Schreiber 1971). In this section, we are searching for clues that will explain how these forces have shaped the state's recent electoral history. To that end, we must understand the changing behavior of the state's voters.

For most states, it is very difficult to infer the political behavior of individuals from looking only at behavior aggregated to the county level. Ideally, we would learn about the voting behavior of manufacturing workers by directly asking a random sample of them how they voted and why. This is what pollsters do, and surveys of voters, providing they are conducted properly, are the best way of learning about people's political preferences. But surveys that represent states are not widely available prior to the 1980s. In order to learn about the voting behavior of people in local areas, before pollsters began scrutinizing individual states, we must rely on aggregate data, by county or precinct. The results for the ecological inference estimates are presented in table 8.2. Its entries show an estimate of the percentage of each demographic group that voted Democratic in the indicated presidential elections.

Conversion

The conversion of Southern whites from the Democratic to the Republican party has received considerable scholarly attention in academic journals. The New Deal realignment is considered the classic period of political conversion—where many lower- and middle-income voters switched their allegiance from the Republican to the Democratic party in response to economic crisis. In other chapters, we have observed that the magnitude of this conversion varied widely across states. In New York and Illinois, where the Republican party was well developed and voters' partisanship was well anchored, there was less defection by GOP voters between 1928 and 1932 than in Texas, Florida, or California, although the sheer number of voters in these two states still made conversions there weigh heavily on the political outcome.

Our estimates for Georgia show that conversion among Republicans was as massive as it was in Texas, with only 21 percent of Hoover's original (1928) supporters staying with him in 1932. Democrats, on the other hand, remained highly loyal across the realignment period. It is clear that the Roosevelt elections simply enlarged upon the Democratic party's sizable majority in Georgia, as it did in Texas and Florida.

In many studies of Southern politics, considerable attention is given to the 1964 Johnson-Goldwater contest, followed by the Wallace independent candidacy four years later. These elections are considered watershed contests in the history of Southern politics because they were characterized by massive defections from Democratic party identification among Southern white voters. Throughout the South, the politics of massive resistance found its electoral expression in the votes for Goldwater and Wallace. During the civil rights era, roughly between 1955 and 1970, conversion worked in tandem with

TABLE 8.2.   Estimates of the Democratic Percentage of the Presidential Vote for Various Electoral Groups in Georgia, 1928–2000 (ecological inference maximum likelihood)

Pooled Presidential Election Years	Blacks/ Nonblacks		Elderly/ Nonelderly		Immigrants/ Nonimmigrants		Farmers/ Nonfarmers		Whites/ Nonwhites	
1928, 1932	84.5*	71.2*	86.3*	75.7*	64.6*	76.1*	79.3*	73.1*	70.1*	86.4*
1936, 1940, 1944	92.2*	78.6*	43.3*	85.7*	81.7*	83.3*	87.1*	80.4*	78.3*	92.8*
1948, 1952	68.0*	64.3*	18.8*	68.6*	50.3	65.5*	80.1*	59.7*	63.9*	68.8*
1956, 1960, 1964	62.0*	58.1*	43.7*	60.5*	43.1	59.3*	64.3*	58.6*	57.4*	63.9*
1968, 1972	46.2*	18.2*	69.1*	21.7*	32.0*	25.4*	5.4*	26.3*	18.1*	46.4*
1976, 1980, 1984	73.1*	48.0*	48.0	55.1*	45.9	54.9*	92.1	53.9*	48.7*	69.8*
1988, 1992	55.5*	34.7*	51.5	39.1*	42.6	40.3	53.8	40.1*	34.6*	54.4*
1996, 2000	83.2*	30.5*	68.3	43.1*	31.7	45.3*	66.4	44.6*	28.7*	83.4*

	Mfg. Workers/ Non Mfg. Workers		College Educated/ Non College Educated		Native to State/ Nonnatives		Internal Migrants/ Nonmigrants		Hispanics/ Non- Hispanics	
1928, 1932	—	—	—	—	—	—	—	—	—	—
1936, 1940, 1944	—	—	—	—	—	—	—	—	—	—
1948, 1952	62.0*	66.4*	16.7	67.5*	—	—	—	—	—	—
1956, 1960, 1964	51.1*	61.9*	29.4*	61.0*	64.1*	38.1*	37.1*	64.1*	—	—
1968, 1972	15.6*	29.2*	88.8	19.0*	21.4*	19.9*	22.2*	26.5*	—	—
1976, 1980, 1984	56.6*	54.2*	14.8	59.3*	62.1*	36.6*	35.0*	62.1*	48.8	54.8*
1988, 1992	39.8*	40.4*	22.1*	44.6*	46.9*	28.3*	27.3*	46.7*	40.9	40.3*
1996, 2000	38.2*	46.2*	32.0	47.3*	51.3*	33.4*	31.5*	51.5*	49.6	44.8*

Note: Cell entries show the estimated percentage voting Democratic in the listed presidential elections. Complete variable definitions and results from the ecological inference estimation appear in appendix B, with standard errors and bounds.

*Reflect estimates with lower and upper bounds narrower than 0,1.

black mobilization to alter the social profile of the parties and bring about two-party competition in many Southern states.

In table 8.3, we can see evidence that the events of the 1960s threw the Georgia electorate into considerable turmoil. Thousands of Democrats who had supported Kennedy in 1960 abandoned Lyndon Johnson to vote for Barry Goldwater in 1964, adding Georgia to Goldwater's tally of five states. While Georgia's few Nixon (1960) supporters were not thrilled with Goldwater—only an estimated 55 percent of GOP voters in 1960 voted for the Arizona conservative four years later—they remained more loyal than the Democrats. In 1968, Democrats and Republicans would prove highly independent once again. Only 37 percent of Johnson's (1964) supporters voted for Humphrey, with solid majorities of white Democrats voting for George Wallace or Richard Nixon. An even smaller proportion of Republicans who had supported Goldwater voted for Nixon in 1968—about 23 percent. A majority of Goldwater supporters joined with about 26 percent of the Johnson supporters to help Wallace win the state. Clearly this shows that the pathway to Wallace in 1968 ran through a vote for Barry Goldwater rather than through support for President Johnson. Democrats were even less enthusiastic about McGovern in 1972 than they were about Humphrey (1968), and the Wallace supporters overwhelmingly turned to Nixon that year. Georgia's movement to presidential Republicanism was sudden and conservative, but it was not followed by an immediate surge of Republican strength at the state level (although congressional seats regularly began going to Republicans). In gubernatorial elections, Democrats would cling to steadily decreasing majorities through the end of the century.

In other states, we have seen that blue-collar workers are among those who converted to the Republican party after 1970. Can we find any evidence for conversion among this voting bloc in Georgia? Our estimates for Democratic support among manufacturing workers begin with the 1948–52 elections, when data on manufacturing employment became available. Manufacturing workers in Georgia's many smaller towns were apparently part of the group that first left the Democratic party. We see support for Democratic presidential candidates drop from 1948–52 to the 1956, 1960, and 1964 series of elections. In 1968–72, their support for Humphrey and McGovern was much lower than among voters in other occupations. In more recent

TABLE 8.3. Estimates of Party Loyalty and Conversion across Presidential Elections in Georgia (ecological inference maximum likelihood)

Presidential Election Years	Voted Democratic 1928/Non-Democratic 1928	Voted Democratic 1932/Non-Democratic 1932	Presidential Election Years	Voted Republican 1928/Non-Republican 1928	Voted Republican 1932/Non-Republican 1932
Voted Democratic 1932	98.6* 84.5*		Voted Republican 1932	21.4* 1.7*	
Voted Democratic 1936		90.8* 61.2*	Voted Republican 1936		69.6* 6.9*

Presidential Election Years	Voted Democratic 1960/Non-Democratic 1960	Voted Democratic 1964/Non-Democratic 1964	Presidential Election Years	Voted Republican 1960/Non-Republican 1960	Voted Republican 1964/Non-Republican 1964
Voted Democratic 1964	45.9* 44.5*		Voted Republican 1964	55.1* 54.3*	
Voted Democratic 1968		36.9* 18.7*	Voted Republican 1968		23.3* 37.8*
Voted Wallace 1968		26.4* 57.0*	Voted Wallace 1968		56.9* 26.5*

Note: Cell entries show the estimated percentage voting Democratic, Republican, or for George Wallace in the presidential elections listed on each row who voted Democratic (or Republican) in the previous election. Complete variable definitions and results from the ecological inference estimation appear in appendix C, with standard errors and bounds.

*Reflect estimates with lower and upper bounds narrower than 0,1.

contests, manufacturing workers are estimated to be slightly more Democratic than those in other employment niches (see table 8.2). Blue-collar workers do not appear to be a key to Republican presidential victory in Georgia as they have been in other states.

Population Mobility

Population mobility has been as consequential to the state's political development as conversion. In Georgia, four separate migration streams have remade the electoral map: rural to urban migration, urban to suburban migration, in-migration from outside of Georgia, and out-migration from Georgia to other states. Rural to urban migration occurred in the postwar period as the most agricultural counties lost population. White and black voters moved to Atlanta and its suburbs—re-centering the state's center of gravity on the state's major metro area. Rural to urban migration probably did not have much of an impact on partisan change in the short term. Rural Democrats became urban Democrats. But in the 1960s, when blacks who had moved to Atlanta and its suburbs from rural areas mobilized in mass within Democratic party ranks, the full political impact of this migration stream was realized. The impact of out-migration on rural areas was equally dramatic. The shrinking African-American population in black belt counties has meant that Republicans have been able to run competitive races on the basis of their support among white voters who have remained.

Urban to suburban migration fueled the growth of suburbs around Atlanta and the smaller cities (Savannah, Columbus, Augusta) as it did in many other states. The initial suburbanites were white, young, and upwardly mobile, but in the 1960s and 1970s this began to change as family age, middle-income African Americans found their way into certain suburbs where blacks were not screened out by unscrupulous realtors and mortgage lenders. The subsequent settlement pattern in suburban Atlanta has been a patchwork of black suburbs (mainly in Fulton and DeKalb Counties) and white suburbs (Outer DeKalb and Cobb Counties). Few places are truly integrated. Black out-migration from Atlanta has kept the Democratic party competitive in DeKalb County. White out-migration from Atlanta has contributed to Cobb and Gwinnett Counties' Republican predictability.

Philip Converse first noted that the in-migration of Northerners in the 1950s greatly improved the Republicans' political standing in the

South (1966). Nowhere outside of Florida was Northern migration more significant in this regard than in Atlanta. Employment growth in the 1950s attracted newcomers who were white, well-educated, managers and professionals. They settled predominantly in the suburbs of Atlanta and Savannah, helping to speed the journey these counties were already taking toward Republican predominance. From 1960 onward, the influx of Northerners continued to benefit Republicans. Northern migration to the South was distinct, however, from migration within the South. The majority of out-of-state migrants after 1950 still came from other Southern states, and these voters were not necessarily a boon for Republicans. Whereas Northerners imported GOP attachments immediately, Southern migrants to Georgia's fastest-growing towns were more likely to sign up as Democrats than as Republicans. Many of the better-off and white among this population would eventually convert to the GOP, but this did not happen overnight. For Southern migrants, mobility had to be followed by conversion for partisan realignment to be realized.

Since an important part of Georgia's development has been its population growth from outside the state, we were interested in estimating the voting inclinations of this consequential and growing population. What we found helps to establish the fact that migration contributed to the demise of one-party rule. From 1956 onward, our figures indicate that the population of interstate migrants was considerably more Republican than the population of Georgia natives (or the foreign born). The difference in Democratic support between the two groups diminishes in the 1968–72 elections only because Humphrey and McGovern won about equal support from both groups given that natives found George Wallace so appealing and interstate migrants voted Republican.

The immigrant population comprised 7 percent of the population in 2000, and it has never been larger. Two-thirds of those immigrants were recent arrivals, having set foot in Georgia only in the previous ten years. More than half of them lived in Atlanta and its suburbs. Due to the small size of the immigrant population in most counties, we were unable to use King's (1997) ecological inference model to generate precise estimates of its voting behavior. Our best guess is that most recent immigrants are nonvoters, but among the few who did vote, there was a more even division of support between the parties than we find in most states.[1]

Georgia is not a port-of-entry state for the immigrant population, although some Mexican and Haitian workers do agricultural labor. Beginning in the mid-1990s, Mexican and Southeast Asian immigrants were also being recruited to work on construction sites and in poultry processing plants in north Georgia. But in prior decades, many immigrants arrived in Georgia because they are well-educated, white-collar workers with professional and technical training. They moved to Georgia because their companies relocated them there. They may have subsequently petitioned for the entry of their elderly parents and other relatives, but they live in middle-class neighborhoods in Fulton, DeKalb, and Cobb Counties. The same issues that have generated support for Republicans among the suburban white population (education, crime, and infrastructure) have led these immigrants to support GOP candidates too. The immigrant population may be changing in Georgia with the growing reliance on Mexican workers in food processing and agriculture, but until this population naturalizes and votes, it will remain politically inert.

Urban-rural differences were said to be crucial to understanding support for rival candidates in the Democratic primary in Georgia's period of one-party rule (Key 1949). A theory of partisan change emphasizing the importance of population mobility would predict that a gap would emerge between urban and rural voting once Georgia became more competitive. Our expectation is that the low-mobility rural areas would remain more Democratic than the urban areas, distinguishing Georgia from Northern states with rural Republican traditions. We evaluated differences between urban and rural voting by estimating the level of Democratic support among farmers compared with those in other occupations. Until the 1950s, there isn't much of a difference between the two groups because Democrats were the only game in town. Support for Democrats among farmers dropped in the 1948–52 elections and dropped further still in the 1956, 1960, and 1964 series. Still, they were more loyal to the Democrats than nonfarmers were. In the 1968–72 elections, farmers turned to George Wallace or, to a lesser extent, to Richard Nixon, deserting the Humphrey and McGovern candidacies. But after 1976, farmers remained more Democratic, on average, than those in nonagricultural occupations. These results make sense if we understand that the Republican progress in Georgia has been driven by suburban and small town voters, not farmers. In addition, many farmers in Georgia are black and live in the heavily Democratic black belt counties. Their

Democratic allegiance may help explain why our estimates for farmers are so much more Democratic in Georgia than in the other states we have studied.[2]

Population mobility has brought many well-educated voters into the new Southern economy centered in Atlanta. Perhaps it is among the well educated that we can find evidence for political realignment rooted in population migration. The ecological inference model failed to generate reliable estimates of the voting tendencies of the college educated except in the 1956, 1960, and 1964 series and in the elections after 1988. In these instances, the college educated were much more Republican than those lacking college degrees. When we checked the latter of the two estimates against available survey data, the polls showed that such a gap between the voting of the better educated and less educated does exist, although support for Dukakis and Clinton (1988–92) among the college educated is 10 to 15 points higher than the low estimate reported in table 8.2.

Socioeconomic cleavages were not important to Georgia politics in the era of one-party rule, but have emerged as the Republican party has moved into a competitive position. One stimulant behind the Republican momentum is education. Still, even less educated voters are more likely to vote Republican in recent elections than in earlier times. Predictably, less educated voters in Georgia started in the Democratic camp in the 1948–52 elections (see table 8.2). But by the 1980s and 1990s, this support had diminished considerably, from about 68 percent in 1948–52 to about 47 percent in the most recent presidential elections. A college education no longer separated Republican from Democratic voters as it once did.

Generational Replacement

On top of migration and conversion, we might expect population replacement to have accelerated the restoration of two-party politics. As the elderly population loyal to the Democrats gradually died, younger Republican voters took their place, resulting in a secular realignment. The most obvious locations where generational replacement has made a difference are in the rural black belt counties of central Georgia located in the geographic triangle between Atlanta, Augusta, and Macon. In counties such as Jasper, Butts, Morgan, Baldwin, and Pike, the retirement-age population was at a peak in the early 1960s. These counties attracted almost no newcomers from out of state, and out-migration of younger Georgians, both black and white, to nearby cities, left behind an aging population. These older voters were strong Democrats, but by the mid-1970s they had been replaced by a smaller population of voters new to the electorate. These younger voters, combined with older white voters who had lost their ardor for the Democratic party in the 1970s and 1980s, helped the Republicans run competitive races even when black turnout was high.

Do we find trends consistent with generational replacement in our analysis? Aged voters in Georgia show some expected patterns in their presidential voting between 1928 and 2000, according to the data in table 8.2. Initially, in the 1928–32 elections, there was little difference in political support between those of retirement age and younger voters because everyone was voting Democratic in those early elections. This changes in the late 1930s, and elderly voters are much less supportive of Democrats for the next two decades. This diminished enthusiasm for presidential Democrats may be explained by the fact that many elderly voters arriving in Georgia after 1940 were Northern migrants who imported Republican sympathies.

Our estimates for the voting inclination of those under age 65 show that the nonelderly are becoming consistently less Democratic in their preferences between the 1930s and the 2000 election (table 8.2). Young voters are more Democratic than the elderly until the late 1950s, when a reversal begins to take place. At this point, voters moving into retirement age were more comfortable with the post–New Deal Democratic liberalism than their predecessors. Support for Humphrey (1968) and McGovern (1972) was especially low among younger Georgians, whereas the elderly were more comfortable staying with the Democratic ticket.

Our estimates for the elderly vote after 1976 are not highly reliable due to severe aggregation bias in the data (extremely small values for the percentage over age 65). Older voters appeared to split their vote evenly in the 1976–84 elections and were slightly less Democratic than younger voters. Interestingly, though, younger voters have increasingly GOP sympathies opening up a significant and growing generation gap between the mid-1980s and the end of the century. Exit polls from the 1996 and 2000 presidential elections indicated that among voters over age 65 there were still more Democratic party identifiers than Republicans, while the reverse was true among younger cohorts. We conclude from this that generational replacement is likely to improve Republican party prospects for the first two decades of the twenty-first century.

Activism and Partisanship of New Voters

In studies of the entire Southern electorate, political scientists have found that blacks mobilized into the Democratic party in 1964 and thereafter, deserting the GOP almost entirely. As black mobilization bolstered Democratic prospects, support for Republicans among Southern white voters increased too, although the shift occurred gradually over twenty years. Mobilization of one group resulted in the conversion of another (Giles and Hertz 1994).

Georgia's black citizens were not in the habit of voting in large numbers prior to the civil rights era. Following black mobilization in the 1950s and 1960s, we should begin to see a gap emerge between black and nonblack voters in their support for the Democratic party. So it should come as no surprise that there is not much racial polarization in the initial estimates of black and nonblack voting in table 8.2. In the 1928–32 elections, for instance, an estimated 85 percent of blacks voted Democratic, compared with 71 percent of whites. In the late 1930s and 1940s, black support for Roosevelt increased, and so too did white support—as our figures in table 8.2 suggested. Republicans simply had no appeal in the wake of the New Deal, and lacking a second option, whites and blacks voted for the same candidates even though turnout was pathetically low (Key 1949).

By the 1950s, African-American support for Democratic candidates diminished somewhat (see table 8.2). One possibility is that black turnout increased during this era, and with that increase in black turnout came some black support for Republicans. But there is even less racial polarization in voting during this period than in the 1930s and 1940s. Democratic candidates were popular with both blacks and whites, and white flight from the Democratic party had not yet begun. The 1968–72 elections present somewhat anomalous results because of George Wallace's independent candidacy. In table 8.2, the 1968–72 estimates are for Humphrey and McGovern support. The results make sense because they show a wide gap between blacks and whites in their support of these unpopular liberal Northern Democrats. An estimated 46 percent of black voters supported Humphrey and McGovern, compared with only 18 percent of whites. In the late 1990s, racial polarization widened, with Democrats taking an estimated 83 percent of the black vote in the 1996–2000 elections, while winning less than half of the white vote. Exit polls placed the figure for black support of Al Gore at 92 percent. Race clearly remained a key predictor of the Georgia vote in the 2000 presidential election. But in spite of the increasing racial polarization, race is probably not the foundation for substate sectionalism that it once was, given the deconcentration of blacks from the black belt to metropolitan Atlanta.

Conclusions

The story to be told about the twentieth-century history of Georgia politics is one of how it became a two-party competitive state. The major components of this transformation were population mobility, black mobilization, and conversion. Northerners have transformed the Atlanta metro area by importing Republican party identification. Conversions of Southern whites following on the heels of the civil rights movement spread the GOP gospel into areas where migration from outside Georgia has not been a force. The electoral map has been transformed as Republicans have broken out of their tiny traditional pocket in the mountains of north Georgia to locate support throughout the state. In those elections where we observe the most widespread Republican support, we also see declining sectionalism.

Much of the politically consequential migration has been North to South, but migration internal to the state has shifted the political balance of many counties. Migration off the farm has followed from greater economic opportunity elsewhere (Gimpel 1999; Wright 1986). The migration of blacks and whites away from the farms and small towns and into the larger cities had the effect of creating a heterogeneous suburban middle class with a greater awareness of politics than that of their parents who came of age in a one-party era dominated by personalities. As Georgians have been lured to Atlanta, Savannah, Columbus, and their suburbs by new and relocating businesses, the movement of the population from rural to suburban areas has been associated with rising income and education levels. These developments have led to higher participation rates and greater political competition.

Democratic margins have dropped since mid-century across the entire state, but that does not mean that the state's older regional cleavages have disappeared. Georgia, like Texas, shows us that the rise of a more competitive party system does not necessarily change a state's fundamental political character. In gubernatorial elections, party competition and population growth have made the state more highly sectional at the end of the century than it was in V. O. Key Jr.'s day (1949). Perhaps if Northern migrants had been drawn to the black belt counties, we would have seen some erosion of substate sectionalism. But migrants were drawn mainly to north Georgia—the part of the state where there were Republican patches even in the one-party era.

For the foreseeable future, Democrats are likely to maintain strong support from the black belt counties, even though these counties contain a smaller proportion of the electorate than in years past. Republicans will build upon their existing strength in north Georgia, although Democrats must focus attention on Atlanta and its suburbs, too. Democrats will run well in Fulton and DeKalb Counties, and Republicans will take Cobb and Gwinnett. Savannah, Macon, and Augusta are likely to remain Democratic targets of opportunity, but the rest of Georgia (outside the black belt) will be competitive contingent upon the turnout of black voters in rural areas and small towns. Finally, the forces of generational replacement and migration are likely to help the Republicans pick up the governorship and state legislative seats. The dual partisans who have been content to vote for Republican presidents and Democratic governors are dying off and will be replaced by lifelong Republicans. It is a safe bet that the first GOP governor since Reconstruction will take office early in the new century.

Notes

1. We estimated Democratic voting among the immigrant population controlling for education (percentage with four-year college degree) for the 1996–2000 presidential elections and found that support for Democratic candidates moved upward from 31.7 percent to 46 percent—suggesting that Democratic support is strongest among immigrants with lower levels of education.

2. We tested this notion explicitly by including a control variable (zb) for the percentage of the population that was black. Our expectation was that the support of farmers for Democrats would be reduced by controlling for

race (percentage black)—a control that would separate the black farming population from the white farming population. Our results confirmed the expectation for the pooled 1996–2000 elections, reducing estimated support for the Democratic candidate (Clinton and Gore) from 66 to 50 percent. The upper and lower bounds remained wide, however, undermining our confidence in the estimate's precision.

CHAPTER 9

CONNECTICUT

Major Forces for Electoral Change in Connecticut

- Migration from New York to Fairfield County
- Suburbanization of the Population
- Decline of the Manufacturing Economy
- Defense Downsizing
- Growing Economic Inequality across Connecticut's Towns and Cities

Every square inch of territory in Connecticut lies within one of the state's 169 incorporated towns. There is no county governing authority, except for the sheriff—counties are little more than lines on a map. Citizens have unbreakable attachments to their towns, reinforced by strong home rule authority. With local power to tax and regulate land use, and with no unincorporated areas in which any town can expand, local government has resulted in the social and economic balkanization of the state (Burns 1994; Janick 1975; McKee and Petterson 1997; Peterson 1981).

Using strict land use regulations, some towns have protected themselves from the encroachment of industrial and commercial land uses, establishing themselves as exclusive residential enclaves. Other locales with a long history of mixed industrial, commercial, and residential land use patterns have seen their industrial base wither and are now stuck with ugly abandoned industrial sites and a decaying housing stock. Given the state's small size, these starkly contrasting scenes are found in close proximity to one another. In less than a thirty-minute drive, one can go from the unimaginably wealthy neighborhoods of Greenwich to the most pathetic slum in Bridgeport or New Haven. For being such a small state, it is remarkably diverse, with quaint towns and small farms in the northeast, rising poverty in the state's largest cities, steadily growing middle-class suburbs just outside those cities, and the sprawling lots and accompanying mansions in Fairfield County's richest towns.

To outsiders, the most visible part of Connecticut is Fairfield County (see map 9.1)—the exclusive and wealthy suburbs closest to New York City, home to famous celebrities and television personalities. In social and economic terms, Fairfield has become the most distinctive part of the state, characterized by its wealth, fiscal conservatism, and social liberalism. Outside of Fairfield, regionalism in the state can be defined mainly by its large cities: Hartford, Waterbury, New Haven, Bridgeport, and Stamford. All of these towns were heavily industrialized at mid-century, each with a specialized niche in the labor market. For Waterbury, it was brass, machine parts, and tool and die making. For Bridgeport, the so-called arsenal of democracy, it was submarine and helicopter parts, the Remington Arms company, and companies that made army trucks and shell casings. New Haven was known as a transportation, communications, and trade center, headquarters of the New Haven Railroad and Southern New England Telephone Company. Hartford was home to defense industries such as Colt Arms and Pratt & Whitney, in addition to insurance giants such as Aetna, Travelers, The Hartford, and others. Stamford was once an industrial town, but growth pressures from New York City led municipal leaders to recognize that there was more economic potential in turning the town's nonresidential areas into a corporate business center. As early as the 1940s, the foresighted city fathers of Stamford attracted federal financing to clear out aging industrial sites from the central city and completely redevelop downtown. By early in the new century, the city was home to headquarters offices of several Fortune 500 companies, including Conoco (oil and gas), Xerox (business machines, copiers), and Champion International (paper and printing).

For years, Connecticut's heavy industries escaped the economic doom suffered in New York and Pennsylvania because of heavy government subsidies from Pentagon defense contracts. Pratt & Whitney aircraft engines, Winchester Arms, Remington-Rand, Sikorsky helicopters, Groton's General Dynamics submarine works, and numerous spin-off companies that manufactured machine parts for planes, tanks, ships, and other military vehicles made the state's economy nearly recession proof. With the end of the cold war in the late 1980s, however, defense downsizing set in. Pentagon contracts shrank in size or disappeared altogether. The early 1990s found Connecticut suffer-

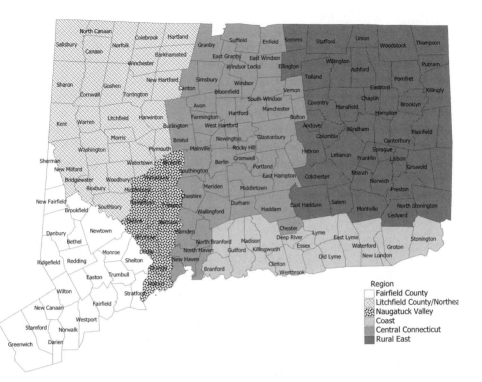

Map 9.1.   Regions of Connecticut

ing an economic malaise that had been unknown in the state to that point.

As people have sought to escape aging central city neighborhoods, Connecticut has experienced an unusual degree of stratification associated with the growth of suburban and rural areas. Because Connecticut is small, but is dotted with several cities of substantial size, the flight to the suburbs had a statewide impact. As a result of highly selective mobility patterns, some towns have become residential enclaves where people live, but with little industrial or commercial development. To live in these towns is to work somewhere else. Many of the wealthy communities of Fairfield County, such as New Canaan, Greenwich, and Westport, are exclusive commuter shed areas for professionals who work in New York City or locations within the state. Upper-income residents do not want to live in towns that are heavily commercial or industrial—even if it means they must commute longer distances to work. Consequently, jobs and homes have grown further apart with the rise of suburban Connecticut (Janick 1975).

The older towns are known to be places to work, some with more than three hundred years of commercial and industrial development behind them, but they have not attracted much new residential development. In these towns, there is less available land for new development. In New Britain and Waterbury, for example, old industrial districts are clogged with battered, decaying buildings on brownfield sites overgrown with weeds and tainted with chemical waste. The housing stock has aged; the population has declined and become older and poorer. Those who can afford to leave to the residential suburban towns for better schools and more open space made their exit in the 1970s or before.

Hartford and Bridgeport are examples of cities that have suffered the worst of industrial decline (see map 9.1). In spite of its reputation as a finance and insurance center, Hartford has not attracted the kind of postindustrial enterprise that could forestall stagnation. Hartford lost 25 percent of its population between 1960 and 2000, and Bridgeport lost 11 percent. New Haven was 19 percent smaller in 2000 than it was in 1960, but it had not reached the economic depths of Hartford and Bridgeport mainly because Yale University pumps millions of dollars into the local economy every year. Waterbury's growth since mid-century has been slow, and the city was less prosperous in the early 2000s than it was when the Brass City was still center of the nation's metal refining industry, but its economic decline has not been as precipitous as that of Bridgeport and Hartford. Within its boundaries, Waterbury has accommodated the development of new industrial parks and some new housing away from the oldest sections of town.

Some of the more prosperous towns such as Stamford and Shelton have managed a balance of commercial and residential growth. These cities have done well because they attracted an upper-income, white-collar workforce that has been unwavering in its demand for low-density development and clean industry. Other prosperous towns have attracted high-income residents from Connecticut's older towns because they were late in developing. Only a few years ago, farming was the dominant enterprise in places such as Trumbull and Farmington. Their existing land had not been pocked with ugly industrial sites during Connecticut's manufacturing buildup in the nineteenth and early twentieth centuries. As these late-blooming towns have developed on the fringes of Connecticut's older cities, they have succeeded in becoming affluent residential enclaves while attracting unobtrusive postindustrial enterprises.

White ethnicity in Connecticut provided a stronger sense of identity at the turn of the twenty-first century than it did in many other states. Ethnic identity was reinforced by historical conflicts between natives and immigrants that pitted native-born Yankee Protestants against Irish and German Catholics (McKee 1983; Lockard 1959). These conflicts resulted in residential segregation of the native and foreign-born populations. Outside of Fairfield County, the geographic mobility of the population has been low with few people moving in from outside the state to dilute the long-standing attachments of people to their neighborhoods. As a result, white ethnic neighborhoods from this earlier era of immigration have been slow to disappear. White ethnic clubs can still be found in Waterbury, Bridgeport, and New Haven. There are distinct Italian, German, Irish, Eastern European, and Jewish neighborhoods in many smaller and larger towns.

Connecticut remained a predominantly white state through its first two centuries, and its racial complexion has only recently begun to change. Black migration from the South began in the 1940s, but by 1960 the U.S. census reported that only 4.4 percent of the state's total population was nonwhite. During the 1980s, the most dramatic development in the state's demography was the rapid increase in the Hispanic population to about 6 percent while the black population hovered at 8 percent. Fairfield and Hartford Counties drew in the largest Latino populations, predominantly from Puerto Rico. This population is highly concentrated in just a few cities, principally Hartford, Bridgeport, and New Britain. The Asian population remained small according to 2000 census figures, at about 2.4 percent. The Hispanic population displaced the black population as the largest minority in Connecticut by 2000, as the Latino population stood at 9.4 percent of the total, compared with 8.7 percent for blacks.

Politically, the state divided along urban-rural and immigrant-native lines in the 1930s, as shown in map 9.2. The darkly shaded areas of the map include the major cities such as Bridgeport, New Haven, Stamford, Hartford, Danbury, and Waterbury, and the lightly shaded areas include the most rural areas of the northeast and northwest.

Notably, however, there are some heavily Democratic rural areas, particularly along the Rhode Island border and in central Connecticut. These were places where Roosevelt's prolabor agenda appealed to a working-class Catholic population with fresh immigrant roots (White 1983; Lockard 1959). The Republicans had a long-standing reputation at the time as New England's nativist party. Republicans in Massachusetts, including U.S. senator Henry Cabot Lodge, had led the charge to restrict immigration in the 1920s (White 1983). Catholic immigrants also found themselves opposing Yankee Republicans on prohibition. By 1928, the combination of the prohibition and immigration issues had largely defined the differences between the Republican and Democratic parties throughout lower New England.

Urban and industrial Connecticut was hard hit by the Great Depression, but the locations of the major layoffs were Democratic strongholds to begin with. It is not obvious that there were many working-class converts to Roosevelt during the 1930s since the vast majority of these voters were already Democrats. The Roosevelt years did widen the class cleavage in the Connecticut electorate, adding economic division to ethnic division. Immigration policy and alcohol became nonissues with the repeal of prohibition and the high unemployment of the early 1930s, but ethnic voting divisions would remain important for decades after they had disappeared at many other locations. White ethnicity remained salient largely because there was such a small black population in the state. In a recent work, historian Noel Ignatiev argues that white ethnic divisions lost much of their salience in the nineteenth century wherever there was a significant local black population that all whites could band together to exclude (1995). But in Connecticut, the black population remained so small that white ethnic divisions persisted well into the twentieth century (Lockard 1959; Dahl 1961).

By the 1950s, the class dimension of the New Deal had become solidified in the difference between strong labor union areas and nonunion areas across Connecticut. Dwight Eisenhower did well across the state in 1952 and 1956, but the strong labor towns with a heavy manufacturing presence, such as Waterbury and New Haven, voted for Stevenson. Beginning in the late 1940s, lower Fairfield County became attractive to wealthy New Yorkers, as Greenwich, Stamford, Darien, and nearby towns began to fall into the orbit of New York City. The affluence of this suburbanizing county turned it even more

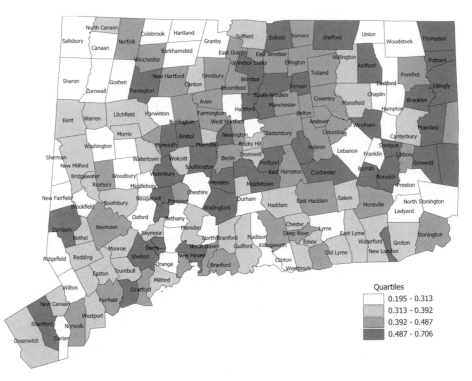

Map 9.2.   Democratic percentage of the presidential vote, 1928–1936

toward the GOP in state and national elections. Northwest Connecticut (Litchfield County), home to Connecticut's Yankee farmers,
remained firmly tethered to the Republican party because the area
defined its politics in opposition to urban Connecticut (Key 1956,
236–39).

Lacking a large black population, the civil rights movement of the
1960s had less influence on statewide elections than in other states,
but did create Democratic factionalism in some local elections between conservative forces resistant to black incorporation and liberal
forces favoring it. As New Haven, Hartford, and Bridgeport experienced population decline due to white flight to suburbs such as Ham-
den, Bloomfield, and Trumbull, the influence of African-American
voters in the central cities correspondingly increased (Janick 1975).
White control of urban politics would persist into the new century

partly because blacks had not reached majority status in most cities, but also because black grievances were often met by progressive policy action. New Haven was ahead of most other cities in addressing urban poverty, and school desegregation plans were met with less hostility in Bridgeport, New Haven, and Hartford than in many other places. Even the Catholic school system in Hartford bused black students to suburban Catholic schools to help achieve the goals of integration (Janick 1975, 93). Connecticut cities faced race rioting and protest in the summer of 1967, but not on the scale that provoked massive political conversion among white voters. Connecticut remained on its liberal political trajectory because progress toward racial justice just wasn't as threatening to the status quo as it was in other states with a larger minority presence.

Between 1970 and the early 2000s, the two most noteworthy developments in Connecticut electoral politics were the partisan dealignment of blue-collar working-class voters who found it easier to vote Republican after 1980 and the increasing social liberalism of wealthy Republicans in Fairfield County. Both developments had a regional foundation within the state. In the politically conservative Naugatuck Valley, just west of New Haven in a north-south corridor running from Bridgeport in the south to Waterbury and Bristol in the north, there was a decisive shift of political allegiance from Democratic to Republican across the thirty-year period. The small town of Ansonia was once a Democratic stronghold, but was visited by George Bush in his 1992 campaign because it was known to be thick with Reagan Democrats. In rural eastern Connecticut, along the Rhode Island border, generational replacement was at work as older Democrats found themselves being replaced by younger GOP voters.

At the same time, many wealthy towns in Fairfield and Litchfield County found themselves warming up to Bill Clinton even though they would have never considered voting for Adlai Stevenson in the 1950s and choked while voting for Lyndon Johnson in 1964. By the end of the twentieth century, Fairfield was still the most solidly Republican area of the state, as map 9.3 shows, but there were noteworthy areas of Democratic support in these elections, including Stamford and Westport. The changes in Fairfield were not only the result of generational replacement and in-migration of liberals from New York, but also the result of changing party orientations toward issues

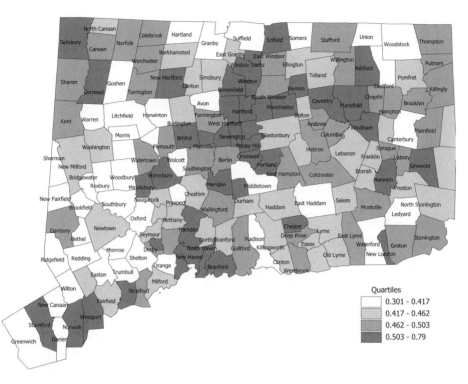

Map 9.3.   Democratic percentage of the presidential vote, 1988–2000

at the national level. Connecticut's wealthy voters began to stand out in the 1970s and 1980s, as the national GOP moved in an ideologically conservative direction. Consistent with a New England tradition rooted in class conflict, Fairfield's Republicans were usually against taxes and suspicious of government involvement and intervention, but in favor of liberal or libertarian positions on social issues such as abortion rights, equal rights for women, and gun control (White 1983). By the late 1970s, the national party leadership positions were increasingly occupied by conservatives from the South and West, who took highly public stands opposite to these. During the 1990s, a Democrat such as Bill Clinton who took moderate positions on taxing and spending issues, and liberal positions on most social issues, was well poised to pick up votes in Fairfield in numbers that would have been unthinkable in 1956.

Where Are the Votes in Connecticut? Republican and Democratic Mobilization Targets

Democrats have a geographic advantage over Republicans in that the Democratic base is more geographically concentrated in urban areas, while Republicans must mobilize a more dispersed suburban and rural population, as we have seen in previous chapters. Connecticut is a small and highly urbanized state, and one wonders if the same advantage accrues to Democrats in such a setting. Results from our analysis of where the votes come from appear in table 9.1. This table ranks the top ten Democratic and Republican locations according to each town's contribution to the statewide Democratic and Republican vote in the 1988–2000 presidential elections multiplied by each town's Democratic or Republican percentage of the vote in those elections.

The rankings in table 9.1 show that when we divide a state up into towns, the parties still share the same geographic base in a few of the population centers such as Stamford and Waterbury, but there is not as much common turf as there was in previous decades. By the beginning of the new century, the Democrats were doing far better than the Republicans in the state's largest cities: New Haven, Hartford, and Bridgeport. The Republican vote is also more dispersed than the Democratic vote. The top ten cities for the GOP cast about 22 per-

TABLE 9.1.   Connecticut's Top Ten Strongest *Towns* for Republicans and Democrats in the 1988–2000 Presidential Contests

Rank	Democratic	Republican
1	Hartford	Greenwich
2	New Haven	Stamford
3	Bridgeport	Fairfield
4	Stamford	Waterbury
5	Waterbury	Norwalk
6	Norwalk	Trumbull
7	West Hartford	Stratford
8	Hamden	Shelton
9	West Haven	Milford
10	Bristol	Danbury
% of total vote	25.7	21.7

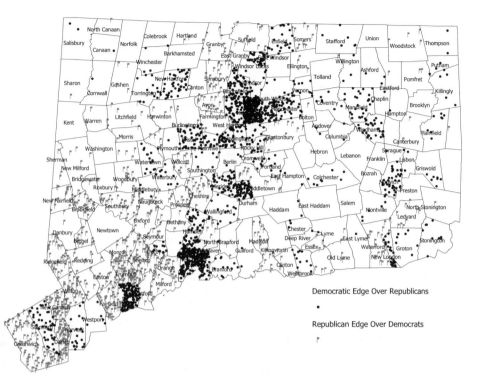

Map 9.4.   Areas of Republican and Democratic dominance, 1988–2000

cent of the total Republican presidential vote in the state, with the top ten Democratic cities casting about 26 percent of that party's statewide presidential vote. Similarly, the smallest towns in the state contribute slightly more Republican votes than Democratic votes in presidential elections (map 9.4).

As for the specific towns that are targets of opportunity, the data show that Republicans benefit most from the turnout of three towns in Fairfield County: Greenwich, Stamford, and Fairfield. Stamford also ranks high for Democrats, but Greenwich and Fairfield are not even among the Democrats' top twenty. Hartford and West Hartford are Democratic bastions, ranking first and seventh respectively for Democrats, but much lower for Republicans. Shelton, a fast-growing Fairfield County town, climbed into the Republicans' top ten rather suddenly at the close of the twentieth century, but did not appear among the Democrats' top twenty. These findings suggest that the state is politically balkanized, and this geographic polarization has increased with the social and economic stratification of the state.

In the 1930s, both Republicans and Democrats could be found contesting Bridgeport, Hartford, and New Haven, although Democrats usually won all three. Democrats and Republicans were also closely matched in Stamford, Danbury, and Norwalk. As the suburbs drew the affluent population out of the declining industrial cities after World War II, Democratic margins grew more lopsided in central Connecticut, while Fairfield County became the locus of wealth-induced Republicanism. At the beginning of the new century, the difference between the Democratic towns and the Republicans' is affluence. The Fairfield County towns contribute mightily to Republican efforts because their interests are in low taxes and less government spending. Democrats pick up votes in the state's older cities of heavy industry, poverty, a growing elderly population, and high unemployment. Connecticut is likely to remain politically competitive in statewide elections, but the foundations of that competition are in a more sectional geography than in the past.

Connecticut's Changing Electoral Foundations

Connecticut is more geographically balkanized today than it was in the 1930s, and we have learned that this is mostly due to changes occurring in Fairfield County and central Connecticut's Rust Belt cities (Gimpel and Schuknecht 2001). But the patterns we have examined across towns and counties have their roots in the behavior of individual voters. Understanding the behavior of individuals is difficult without polling data, and polls of Connecticut voters are scarce before the 1980s. Using ecological inference methodology (King 1997), we can derive the best possible estimates of individual-level behavior using aggregate data. For most of Connecticut's history, detailed census data for each of the 169 towns is unavailable. But we can use a mix of available town-level and county-level data to make approximate inferences about the behavior of voters. In this section we present estimates of the Democratic percentage of the vote for each of several demographic groups for pooled presidential elections between 1928 and 2000.

Population Mobility

We have seen that in many states the most important source of partisan change is the in-migration of new populations from elsewhere, and the out-migration of old ones. Newly arriving voters import political attitudes and thought patterns different from that of the local natives. If these in-migrants are of sufficient number, they may not be socialized into prevailing ways, but instead alter the political composition of the neighborhoods and towns where they settle (Gimpel 1999; Huckfeldt and Sprague 1995). Whether they turn these localities in a Republican or Democratic direction naturally depends on where they are coming from. Cross-state migrants are often moving long distances, and these distances impose costs that not everyone can afford to pay. The costs involved with such a move make migration highly selective, and migrants in the latter half of the twentieth century have been more likely to have a Republican social profile than a Democratic one (Gimpel 1999).

Our generalization that in-migration from outside the state is more likely to benefit the Republican than the Democratic party appears to hold true for Connecticut too, although it should also be noted that Connecticut was not an especially attractive destination for migrants in the last three decades of the twentieth century. On balance, more people have left the state than have moved in. If in-migration has had any impact on Connecticut, that impact could be most easily observed in Fairfield County. By the 2000s, the towns that had the largest populations of out-of-state residents, such as Wilton, Weston, Darien, and New Canaan, were all in Fairfield, and they numbered among the most Republican in the state. The migration northward out of New York City and New York's Westchester County has not dampened enthusiasm for the GOP, although it has contributed to the growing social liberalism of this part of Connecticut.

We have observed that Connecticut has become a more sectional state because of the growing Republicanism across Fairfield County's more affluent towns. It should come as no surprise, then, that we see internal migrants voting far more Republican than nonmigrants (see table 9.2). In the pooled 1956, 1960, and 1964 elections, we see that only 31.7 percent of migrants from outside Connecticut cast Democratic ballots, compared with 57 percent of the rest of the population. The gap shrinks some in 1968 and 1972 because the Democratic candidates in those years were unpopular even among those native to the state. But by the 1980s and 1990s, the difference is again quite stark, accounting for much of the partisan change that has come to separate growing Fairfield County from the rest of Connecticut. Natives were more Democratic in the 1950s than either out-of-state migrants or immigrants. Beginning in the late 1960s, though, natives were estimated to be slightly less Democratic than other Connecticut residents, particularly the foreign born. The gap in Democratic support between natives and nonnatives reemerged in the late 1980s. In the pooled 1996–2000 presidential elections, an estimated 65 percent of Connecticut natives voted Democratic, compared with 53 percent

TABLE 9.2.   Estimates of the Democratic Percentage of the Presidential Vote for Various Electoral Groups in Connecticut, 1928–2000 (ecological inference maximum likelihood)[†]

Pooled Presidential Election Years	Blacks/ Nonblacks		Elderly/ Nonelderly		Immigrants/ Nonimmigrants		Farmers/ Nonfarmers		Whites/ Nonwhites	
1928, 1932	50.7	43.8*	48.4	43.7*	46.5	42.3*	36.7	43.1*	42.6*	56.3
1936, 1940, 1944	62.4	49.6*	41.8	50.5*	45.2	51.7*	22.5	50.8*	49.8*	50.6
1948, 1952	51.3	42.1*	50.1	41.6*	45.7	41.7*	40.3	42.4*	41.2*	77.3
1956, 1960, 1964	46.5	52.5*	49.9	49.8*	49.9	49.9*	—	—	49.7*	52.3
1968, 1972	69.3	40.9*	57.4	41.5*	99.6	37.2*	—	—	40.7*	70.8
1976, 1980, 1984	85.0*†	38.5*†	49.5	38.9*	60.1	38.1*	—	—	37.9*†	76.9†
1988, 1992	91.6*	48.4*	62.9	50.4*	51.3	52.1*	56.6	52.0*	46.3*	90.7*
1996, 2000	99.3*	56.4*	66.6	58.9*	79.4	58.2*	1.0	60.1*	55.3*	79.7*

	Mfg. Workers/ Non Mfg. Workers		College Educated/ Non College Educated		Native to State/ Nonnative		Internal Migrants/ Nonmigrants		Hispanics/ Non-Hispanics	
1928, 1932	—	—	—	—	—	—	—	—	—	—
1936, 1940, 1944	—	—	—	—	—	—	—	—	—	—
1948, 1952	66.7*	27.1*	24.1	43.6*	—	—	—	—	—	—
1956, 1960, 1964	57.5*	45.1*	39.3	50.9*	52.6*	45.9*	31.7*	57.4*	—	—
1968, 1972	32.6	48.4*	36.8	44.0*	40.7*	46.1*	39.6*	44.8*	—	—
1976, 1980, 1984	20.2*	48.7*	54.7	36.8*	37.9*	43.4*	31.8*	44.2*	89.9†	39.8*†
1988, 1992	41.0	54.6*	31.5*	59.6*	54.2*	48.4*	42.3*	56.1*	63.9*	51.2*
1996, 2000	66.9	58.3*	34.7*	69.3*	64.5*	52.5*	53.6*	62.6*	97.4*	56.7*

Note: Cell entries show the estimated percentage voting Democratic in the presidential elections listed on each row. For previous elections, data are based on a combination of available town and county level data. Complete variable definitions and results from the ecological inference estimation appear in appendix B, with standard error and bounds.

*Reflect estimates with lower and upper bounds narrower than 0,1.

†Estimates for all 1988–2000 models, and marked 1976-1980-1984 models, are based on data for all 169 towns.

of the combined population of out-of-state migrants and immigrants (see table 9.2).

The foreign-born population in Connecticut is small but has grown quickly in the 1990s and 2000s. Due to aggregation bias, our estimates of the voting inclination of this population are not highly reliable, but the figures indicate that the places that immigrants were settling were far more likely to be Democratic bastions than Republican ones. This finding corresponds to what we know about how immigrants have been drawn to settle in the state's largest and most industrialized cities, where they are socialized into Democratic party politics. By the late 1970s, our estimates indicate that 60 percent of the foreign-born population was voting Democratic, compared with only 38 percent of the rest of Connecticut (combined natives and out-of-state migrants). The estimates for the pooled 1996–2000 presidential elections indicate that the gap between the foreign born and native born has remained wide, although both groups supported Democratic candidates. Current estimates of the voting inclination of the growing Latino population in Connecticut show that sizable majorities have voted Democratic in the elections since 1976 (see table 9.2).

Conversion

The electoral geography of Connecticut has changed noticeably over time (see maps 9.2 and 9.3). Fairfield County has become more Republican since the Roosevelt era, although it has also become more liberal on social issues. The state's most urban areas have become more Democratic. Some eastern Connecticut towns have moved from Republican to Democratic, and others have moved in the opposite direction. Partisan change has several causes that have been identified by political scientists. People can convert from one party to another, shedding their Republican affiliation, for example, and deciding to vote Democratic, or Independent. Mobilization, generational replacement, and population mobility can also change the politics of places by shifting the local balance of party loyalists.

Conversion is a relatively rare form of partisan change most often associated with periods of serious political turmoil. The 1930s and 1960s were just such eras—the sluggish Republican response to the Great Depression moved many to reconsider their party affiliation and previous patterns of political support, with resultant mass conversions to the Democratic party. In the 1960s, the civil rights movement was the source of massive dealignment and eventual conversion of conservative white voters who moved from the Democratic to the Republican party. In other chapters, we have seen that the magnitude of these conversions, as revealed by voter transition models, varied widely from state to state. The New Deal virtually wiped out the already minuscule GOP presence in the South. But in Illinois and New York, a large majority of Hoover's 1928 supporters remained faithful to him again in 1932. In the 1960s, conversion from Goldwater (1964) to Wallace (1968) to Nixon (1972) was a smooth path of political conversion for many Southern Democrats, but in the Northern states, Democrats did not see much to like in Barry Goldwater or George Wallace. Democrats may not have gained many permanent converts from the GOP side because of Goldwater's unpopular candidacy, but the rise of conservatism within Republican ranks caused significant splits within the party that Democrats were able to exploit to their advantage throughout the following decades.

To examine the magnitude of party conversion in Connecticut, we followed the pattern of previous chapters by considering the relationship between Democratic (and Republican) support in the 1928 presidential election and Democratic (and Republican) support four years later. We were especially interested in knowing whether Republicans in the state were converts to Roosevelt's New Deal. We also examine the relationship between Democratic and Republican voting in the 1932 and 1936 elections, and then turn to the elections of the 1960s.

Connecticut was one of only six states, all in the Northeast, that Roosevelt did not win in 1932, although he kept Hoover to slightly less than a majority. That the contest was this tight leads us to expect rather little party switching among Yankee New Englanders. When we estimated the interelection loyalty of voters between 1928 and 1932, we found rock solid stability—an estimated 96 percent of Smith (1928) voters voted for Roosevelt in 1932 compared with 89.4 percent of Republican voters who supported Hoover in both elections (table 9.3). Connecticut's loyalty to Hoover stands in striking contrast to the defection of Republicans in Oregon (chap. 11), where only 41 percent remained with the incumbent president, and Maryland (chap. 10), where only 38 percent were steadfast. The promises

TABLE 9.3. Estimates of Party Loyalty and Conversion across Presidential Elections in Connecticut (ecological inference maximum likelihood)

Presidential Election Years	Voted Democratic 1928/Non-Democratic 1928	Voted Democratic 1932/Non-Democratic 1932	Presidential Election Years	Voted Republican 1928/Non-Republican 1928	Voted Republican 1932/Non-Republican 1932
Voted Democratic 1932	95.7*	11.2*	Voted Republican 1932	89.4*	4.6*
Voted Democratic 1936	95.9*	21.2*	Voted Republican 1936	78.9*	4.1*

Presidential Election Years	Voted Democratic 1960/Non-Democratic 1960	Voted Democratic 1964/Non-Democratic 1964	Presidential Election Years	Voted Republican 1960/Non-Republican 1960	Voted Republican 1964/Non-Republican 1964
Voted Democratic 1964	96.9*	35.0*	Voted Republican	65.4*	2.7*
Voted Democratic 1968	72.4*	2.4*	Voted Republican 1968	97.3*	18.7*
Voted Wallace 1968	4.7*	8.9*	Voted Wallace 1968	9.7*	4.3*

Note: Cell entries show the estimated percentage voting Democratic, Republican, or for George Wallace in the presidential elections listed on each row who voted Democratic (or Republican) in the previous election. Complete variable definitions and results from the ecological inference estimation appear in appendix C, with standard errors and bounds.

*Reflect estimates with lower and upper bounds narrower than 0,1.

of the New Deal made almost no dent in Connecticut. Nor did the unprecedented legislative successes of Roosevelt's first term yield much crossover support in 1936. Our estimates indicate that about 78.9 percent of Hoover voters in 1932 returned to vote for Landon in 1936. If anything, Connecticut Republicans were galvanized with their New England brethren to slow down the Roosevelt juggernaut.

With a small black population, we would not expect Connecticut to exhibit the kind of political instability during the 1960s that we observed in Southern states such as Florida, Georgia, and Texas. The politics of the civil rights movement was largely lost on this state except in a few of the largest cities. The rise of conservative candidates within Republican ranks was likely to stir up some GOP defections from the Goldwater ticket in 1964, however, as his conservative platform charted a new course for national party leadership. Connecticut's white ethnic Catholics adored John F. Kennedy in 1960, and the vast majority of them returned to vote for Johnson in 1964. But Barry Goldwater was not so adept at winning the loyalty of Nixon's 1960 supporters, losing more than one-third of them to Johnson (see table 9.3). In 1968, the Republicans that had supported Johnson returned to Nixon, and they were joined by the vast majority of Goldwater voters. Apparently Connecticut Republicans who had voted for Goldwater did not do so out of much depth of conviction because conservatives were not able to steer the local party apparatus to the right as they did in other states.

Given the dearth of evidence for conversion in Connecticut during two periods where we would most likely expect it, one might reasonably ask if there is other evidence that might indicate that significant blocs of voters changed their loyalties. We have already observed that some conversion took place in the 1980s as conservative blue-collar Democrats in Connecticut's Naugatuck Valley region found themselves attracted to Ronald Reagan and George H. W. Bush. Their conversion may not have been total, or complete, but they were jarred loose from their traditional moorings.

Connecticut has long been considered a manufacturing state, and skilled blue-collar laborers remain a powerful presence in the workforce. We have excellent data on manufacturing employment beginning with the 1950 census, and the estimates that our data produce indicate that manufacturing workers are initially much more Democratic than those in nonmanufacturing jobs. These loyalties undergo change, though, in the 1970s. In the pooled 1968–72 elections, we see that an estimated 32.6 percent of manufacturing workers supported Humphrey and McGovern, compared with 48.4 percent of those outside of manufacturing. During the Reagan years, the proportion of manufacturing workers supporting Democrats dropped to 20 percent, giving some credence to the idea that Reagan Democrats were a volatile influence in Connecticut politics during this time. By the late 1980s and early 1990s, though, the difference between manufacturing workers and others had diminished to 15 points, with manufacturing workers heading back toward the Democratic fold, where they found themselves encamped in the 1996–2000 contests. Connecticut's working-class voters have not realigned, but apparently they have dealigned—meaning that they are not highly loyal to either party.

While Republicans may sporadically gain the support of dealigned working-class whites unhappy with the liberal drift of the national Democratic party, Democrats may benefit from dealigned upper-income whites alarmed at the GOP's social conservatism. One of the most politically important developments in Connecticut electoral history has been the rise of the well-educated professional in Fairfield County and in the suburban towns outside of New Haven, Hartford, and Waterbury. Differences in voting by level of education were a clear sign of class cleavage in the early years following the Depression. But later in the century, the class division in the Connecticut electorate faded, as some wealthy but liberal Republicans supported Democratic presidential candidates while working-class voters supported GOP nominees. Our expectation is that the well educated voted far less Democratic than the rest of Connecticut for most of the century, but then began to move toward the Democrats with the rise of the Republicans' conservative social agenda. The results from our estimates in table 9.2 are consistent with the idea that these two groups are swapping allegiances. In the 1948–52 presidential elections, an estimated 24 percent of those with a four-year degree voted Democratic, compared with 45.2 percent of those with less than a college education. Democratic support among the college educated increases in successive elections, through the 1976, 1980, and 1984 series. But we also see a change in the loyalties of those with less than a college degree. The waning Democratic support among those with less than a college education reflects the rise of the working-class Republicans—manufacturing workers and former manufacturing workers now employed in the service sector who supported Ronald Reagan. The less educated seemed easily able to go back to their Democratic moorings after 1988. The figures for the pooled 1988–92 elections show that an estimated 32 percent of the college educated voted Democratic, compared with 60 percent of those with less than a college degree. The results for 1996–2000 also show a surge in support for the Democratic ticket among the less educated. Polls indicate that the gap in Democratic support shown in table 9.2 is probably not this stark except at the extremes—between those with less than a high school diploma and those with a four-year college degree.

Generational Replacement

In the small towns of eastern and northwestern Connecticut, the major force for partisan change has been generational replacement. The populations of the state's tinier villages have remained the same or are shrinking, leaving an older population behind. The aging and mortality process has sometimes helped Republicans and at other times Democrats. Rural Litchfield County, in the northwest, was the most predictable Republican turf in the 1950s. It has become a better place for Democrats than it was in the past due mainly to the passing of older Republicans. Waterbury, on the other hand, has moved toward the Republicans as the result of the dying-off of the generation of voters that came of age during the New Deal. Generational replacement has changed the politics in Fairfield County, although not as much as population migration has. Older Fairfield residents who lacked college degrees have been replaced by professionally trained, upward-climbing residents who hold more liberal values on issues such as abortion, gun control, and environmental protection (White 1983, 38).

The extent of generational replacement can be examined by comparing political support among the elderly to that of younger age groups. If there is a wide generation gap, then it is an indication that mortality will change the electoral balance of a place. Our analysis suggests that the elderly often vote differently than younger voters, but no obvious trends emerge in our estimates until late in the twentieth century when the elderly appear to be shifting into the Democratic column. Apparently, the New Deal made few immediate converts among Connecticut's oldest voters. But by the mid-1950s, most of the people entering retirement had been on the Roosevelt band-wagon. The most recent estimates for the pooled 1996–2000 presidential elections show that those over age 65 are as much as 8 percent more Democratic than younger voters, 67 percent to 59 percent. Checking these results against exit polls from these elections suggests that they accurately capture the generation gap in presidential support, but overstate Democratic voting among the elderly. Inasmuch as the elderly *are* more Democratic than younger voters, the forces of mortality and generational change would appear to benefit the GOP cause in the early decades of the new millennium.

Activism and Partisanship of New Voters

When substantial populations that have been inactive suddenly become active, the partisan balance of the electorate can shift decisively (Andersen 1979). Dramatic partisan change is usually not precipitated by minor movements in participation levels. Change resulting from mass mobilization is the product of sudden shocks, such as economic crises, that precipitate mass mobilization on a scale that alters the proportion of Republicans or Democrats in the electorate. The economic crisis of the 1930s is credited with creating a Democratic majority in many states through the addition of new voters to the electorate (Andersen 1979). In Connecticut, though, it appears that the areas that saw the biggest gains in the size of the electorate from 1928 to 1932 were precisely the areas most likely to vote Republican in subsequent elections. The towns of Stratford, Stamford, and much of the rest of Fairfield County experienced at least a 10 percent gain in the number of total voters casting ballots from 1928 and 1932, and these areas put up the most resistance to Roosevelt in 1932, 1936, and subsequent elections. It was in the larger cities of Waterbury and Hartford where there was no gain in the size of the electorate that Roosevelt won his most lopsided victories. Following the 1930s, we see little significant partisan change in Connecticut occurring on the basis of mobilization and turnout alone.

We mentioned that Connecticut has never had an especially large black population. But this has not kept the areas of black population concentration from behaving differently from those with no minorities. The figures in table 9.2 indicate that the gap in Democratic support between blacks and nonblacks has been as wide as 50 percent and that the gap opens up after 1968. The estimates comparing whites and nonwhites also show that the difference in Democratic support is wider after 1968 than before. Exit polls indicated that about 86 percent of the black population voted for Al Gore in 2000, compared with only 54 percent of whites.

Did some white Democrats convert to the Republican party as a direct result of black mobilization into Democratic ranks? We have noted the appearance of Reagan Democrats in the 1980s, and this support follows consistently from the drop in white support for Humphrey and McGovern in the 1968–72 elections. But given the small black population in Connecticut, it is doubtful that the local mobilization of this population produced white conversion, and where it did it was certainly not of the magnitude found in Southern states. Rather, the white conversions were the result of other issues on which the Democrats began to take liberal views, including the war in Vietnam, equal rights for women, and later abortion and homosexual rights. The Reagan Democrats were not necessarily among these converts. They voted for Reagan mainly because of the bad economic times that had accompanied the Carter presidency. They almost as easily abandoned Bush for Clinton in 1992 when the economy soured again.

Conclusions

Scholars writing on Connecticut history have described it as a state of "steady habits" (Lockard 1959; McKee and Petterson 1997; Peirce 1976). Our review of the state's political behavior suggests that this reputation is well deserved. The most striking thing about the state's politics during the last century was its resistance to Roosevelt in the 1930s. The state's steadiness has been assaulted in more recent decades by new issues and the increasing ideological polarization of contemporary American politics. Connecticut and New England have lost political power to the more conservative regions of the country. The rightward movement of the national Republican party on social issues has made it important for local Republicans to convince the state's voters that the more moderate tradition of the Connecticut GOP still prevails locally.

Economic developments underlie the state's sectional politics. Fairfield has long been a Republican area, but its partisanship has been reinforced by steady flow of in-migrants drawn there by expanding postindustrial enterprise. Hartford, New Britain, New Haven, and northeastern Connecticut, on the other hand, have suffered from population losses, industrial decline, and rising poverty. Voters who remain behind include the elderly, low income, blacks, Hispanics, and other groups generally aligned with the Democratic party. In the rural northeast, Democratic realignment has occurred with both out-migration of those prepared to seek opportunity elsewhere and the death of an older generation of Republicans. These separate demographic and economic trajectories have led to greater regionalism based on political party support.

Connecticut is a fiercely competitive state where Republicans and Democrats have alternated in most major offices, but it may not always be so evenly divided. In the new century, Republicans will continue to struggle to accommodate both their conservative, moralistic faction and their more business-oriented, libertarian faction, within the same party. In Connecticut, the probusiness, socially liberal wing of the GOP is likely to sustain the upper hand, but may find itself with shrinking electoral support. Fairfield County contained only one-fourth of the state's population by the early 2000s, not a sufficiently large electorate to control statewide elections even if everyone there voted Republican. Outside of Fairfield County, all signs point to continued economic struggle as an industrial state tries to find ways to prosper in a postindustrial age without the huge subsidies of Reagan-era defense budgets. Democrats have less factionalism to worry about in the short term. With their electoral roots firmly anchored in the soil of the state's largest cities, and with a racial minority population that didn't quite reach 20 percent of the state's total population in the 2000 census, Democrats are relatively free of the factional divisions that have hindered them elsewhere. They will remain a white, ethnic, urban, and ideologically liberal party that will likely capitalize on the state's economic woes and growing low-income population to build a safe electoral majority.

CHAPTER 10

MARYLAND

Major Forces for Electoral Change in Maryland

- Growth of Federal Government Employment in Washington, D.C.
- Migration of Black Voters from the South and Border States, and from Washington, D.C.
- Suburbanization of the Population
- Mobilization of the Black Population
- Decline of the Manufacturing Economy

Maryland's identity is hazy and unclear to most residents west of the Appalachian Mountains. Americans everywhere know that Baltimore is the state's largest city,[1] but this declining industrial port does not conjure up the clear associations that Chicago and New York do. Some may know a few geographic facts from a school project—that the state is on the Chesapeake Bay, or is home to the U.S. Naval Academy in Annapolis—but they probably don't have mental maps to associate with those facts. Maryland does not stand out to the rest of the country as a major center of industry, agriculture, or much of anything else. Those living closer to the state will know more colorful details—picturing the heraldic design of the state flag with its black and gold bars and red and white crosses, or perhaps remembering that Maryland natives are fond of eating blue crabs doused in Old Bay seafood spice. They will have some inkling of an idea that a majority of the state's residents reside within twenty miles of Washington, D.C., and that the federal government is the state's largest employer. They will know that the Chesapeake Bay is not the fishing ground that it once was, but that it is still an inviting place for recreation. Few will know much about the state's distinctive regions.

Maryland's diverse character has been lost on the rest of the country. The state's lack of identity to outsiders is due to its small size and its proximity to better-known places such as New York, Philadelphia, and Virginia. As a border slave state, Maryland was sympathetic to the South on the eve of the Civil War, and only the threat of federal military intervention by President Lincoln kept it from seceding. The state song, written during the Civil War, rejoices that Maryland "spurns the Northern scum." While it does lie south of the Mason-Dixon line, Maryland lacks the rich Southern agricultural heritage that characterizes Virginia or North Carolina, or even border states such as Kentucky or Tennessee. Maryland is too North to be South, and too South to be North. Even with the passage of time since the Civil War and the in-migration of people from other states, Maryland's ambiguous identity has not been resolved. From 1960 to 2000, the state's population grew by a brisk 71 percent to 5.3 million. Most of the growth is directly attributable to the expansion of federal government employment and government-related contracting (Schuknecht 2001).

Maryland's state tourism board once promoted the idea that Maryland is "America in Miniature," touting the range of environments located in a compact tract of land. While the state is small, there are several unique regions, and these were historically defined by a diverse geography. The Chesapeake Bay juts up through the state nearly to the Pennsylvania border severing the Eastern Shore from the main body of terrain on the western side of the Bay. The Eastern Shore, including several islands, was once home to some large fishing fleets. There are still a few people who make their living this way, but they are a tiny group compared to decades past. Inland, the Eastern Shore is mostly agricultural, with a few small towns such as Easton, Cambridge, and Salisbury serving as trade centers. Chicken processing is the state's major agricultural enterprise, and the headquarters of Frank Perdue's poultry empire is in Salisbury (Wicomico County). The Eastern Shore does have a short stretch of coastline along the Atlantic, and the summer resort town of Ocean City, sitting on a barrier island just offshore, is the coast's major landmark.

The rest of Maryland can be divided into five regions: Baltimore city, the Baltimore suburbs (including Baltimore County), the Washington suburbs, southern Maryland, and rural western Maryland (see map 10.1). Baltimore is a typical declining Rust Belt city that has endured a rocky and difficult transition to the postindustrial age. In 1960, there were 939,000 people in Maryland's largest city. By 2000, the population had dropped to 651,154—a decline of 31 percent. The population losses have followed on the heels of deindustrialization, with the city losing 62,000 manufacturing jobs between 1960 and the late-1990s. Major investments in infrastructure and new construction during the 1980s and 1990s reinvigorated tourist traffic and retail trade along the waterfront, and the city's core running along Charles Street remained an attractive place to live and work. The costly construction of two new sports stadiums in the 1990s stood as a prominent symbol of Baltimore's commitment to downtown renewal and development. But one doesn't have to travel much beyond Charles Street to the east or west to find abandoned industrial districts, high crime rates, and deteriorating renter-occupied housing.

Baltimore city did not experience the same level of urban unrest and violence in the 1960s that characterized Detroit and Los Angeles, but that didn't keep the white population from moving to the suburbs. Approximately 64 percent of Baltimore city's population was black by 2000, up from 35 percent in 1960. Because the Chesapeake Bay blocks development to the east—only two working-class suburbs lie east of Baltimore city, Essex and Dundalk—suburban Baltimore extends to the north, west, and south (see map 10.1). The most affluent suburbs are on the city's northern border with Baltimore County (Towson, Timonium, Lutherville) and at the fringes of development extending as far west as Carroll County (Westminster), as far south as Howard County (Ellicott City, Columbia), and as far north as Harford County (Bel Air).

The blue-collar suburbs lie on the city's south side, closest to its industrial districts, warehouses, and docks. Highway signs through these areas warn that "THIS AREA IS SUBJECT TO DENSE SMOKE," although deindustrialization has meant that the smoke was not nearly as thick in the 2000s as it was in earlier decades. Bethlehem Steel continues to operate a mill at Sparrow's Point, but employs only a small fraction of the number it did during its heyday. The populations of Dundalk, Essex, and Glen Burnie could be accurately described as working-class white, and none of these industrial suburbs could be described as racially diverse—as employment opportunities have declined, blacks have been greeted with open hostility by entrenched white residents. The more affluent and established suburbs between Baltimore city and Washington along Interstate 95 have become home to a growing population of middle-class blacks, but blacks have been

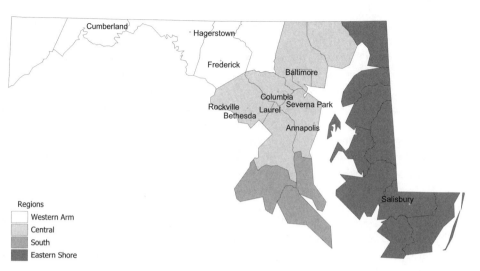

Map 10.1.   Regions of Maryland

slower to migrate to the north and west where the rural and small town white population has been less receptive to their presence.

The Washington suburbs in Montgomery and Prince George's Counties (see map 10.1) have emerged as the dominant population growth centers since mid-century and contained one-third of the state's five million people by 2000. Much of the state's population growth has occurred in these two counties, and their increasing importance in statewide elections and in the state legislature has corresponded directly with Baltimore city's decline. The expansion of federal government employment has fueled the population growth of both suburban counties, drawing out the upwardly mobile population of Washington, D.C., and attracting residents from other states, principally in the Northeast and South. Montgomery is the more affluent of the two and has attracted the bulk of white upwardly mobile residents and higher-level civil servants, along with a growing Asian immigrant population. Places within Montgomery such as Potomac, Bethesda, and Chevy Chase have a deserved reputation for affluence, but pockets of poverty emerged near the end of the twentieth century, mostly in the county's north-central and eastern tracts.

For Washington's black population, discrimination in the private sector means that upward advancement has come mostly through public sector employment. Prince George's County was home to only 30,000 blacks in 1960, then less than 10 percent of the county's population. It became a majority black jurisdiction in the late 1970s based on the attraction of a large number of blacks migrating from Southern states to find secure, good-paying government jobs. Federal government workers who had been making income gains through steady advancement in the civil service system also moved from Washington, D.C., into the suburbs in search of better housing, schools, and safer neighborhoods. The movement of blacks into Prince George's County propelled many whites to the county's outer tracts and into neighboring jurisdictions. Figures from the 1990 census revealed that Prince George's had doubled in population since 1960; the white population had dropped by about 10,000, while the black population was eleven times larger. By 2000, the scope of suburban Washington had extended into areas not long ago considered by Washingtonians to be rural backwaters, including Charles, St. Mary's, Anne Arundel, and Calvert Counties and northward into Howard and the edge of Frederick near West Virginia. In exchange for less dense and less costly residential development, workers in these far-flung locations in Washington's outer ring were willing to commute upward of two hours each way to get to their jobs downtown.

Southern Maryland, consisting of Charles, Calvert, and St. Mary's Counties (see map 10.1), is sometimes regarded as a distinct region, and the latter two jurisdictions are home to some of the most scenic vistas on the Chesapeake Bay. Maryland was founded as a Catholic colony, and these counties are home to several of the state's oldest settlements dating to the seventeenth century, including the state's original capital. Given that southern Maryland has been more resistant to population growth than Prince George's or Montgomery Counties, much of its Catholic heritage remains visible three hundred years later. Along roadsides, it is still common to see shrines to the Virgin Mary. Before the encroachment of the Washington metro area, these counties were also at the heart of Maryland tobacco farming. Even now, one can still see tobacco barns for drying the leafy crop and can visit annual tobacco auctions when farmers sell to the highest bidders. But with tobacco under attack from the state and federal governments, and the entire area under assault by developers through the last two decades, tobacco farmers found themselves pressured to sell out or, less frequently, to switch to other crops. Charles County, immediately south of Prince George's, struggled the most with the pressures of suburban growth, and local governments were often bitterly divided between growth and antigrowth factions. St. Mary's, home to the Patuxent Naval Test Flight Center, found itself the destination for a growing number of defense contractors that had relocated because they found no room to build or expand their operations closer to the Pentagon. In the coming years, these three counties are likely to be pulled more completely into the Washington orbit as the metro area reaches outward.

Western Maryland lies west of Baltimore city, extending from Carroll County through Frederick County to the border with West Virginia. This area is still dotted with small towns and farmland, but the small towns are becoming cities, and the farms are becoming subdivisions. The principal source of growth is in-migration from more densely populated areas closer to Washington and Baltimore city. Carroll County (Westminster) has become the outer fringe of suburban Baltimore, more than tripling in population between 1960 and 2000. Housing prices skyrocketed during the 1990s, as the population boomed in towns such as Eldersburg and Sykesville close to Interstate 70. Further west, Frederick (Frederick) doubled in population between 1960 and 2000 by drawing government employees out from Montgomery County and Washington. Much of the growth occurred in the 1990s, as locations closer to the state's urban labor markets filled up.

Away from the coast, the remote mountainous thin arm of Maryland is sandwiched between West Virginia and Pennsylvania (see map 10.1). People here are more likely to identify with Pittsburgh than with either Baltimore or Washington—but are quick to dissociate themselves from West Virginians, whom they look down upon as an inferior caste. Several state parks take up large tracts of forest land, and service jobs have grown up around a burgeoning recreation and tourism industry (hiking, skiing, camping, canoeing). Part-time residences of wealthy Washingtonians can be found around Garrett County's Deep Creek Lake. Not only has the development of western Maryland's recreation industry saved the region from going under, Garrett County managed to grow 40 percent between 1960 and 2000, to about 30,000. A substantial number of in-migrants have come from West Virginia in search of jobs and better schools for their children.

Cumberland (Allegany County) is still western Maryland's largest city and serves as a major regional trade center, but it has steadily lost population since mid-century. Young people realize that there is little future in the area, and they leave upon graduation. This out-migration has meant that the population is aging. Cumberland once had an employment base in mining and manufacturing, including coal, man-made textiles, automobile tires, and glass. The coal industry collapsed in the 1920s after years of gradual decline. It was revived during World War II, but eventually surface mining replaced shaft mining, and modern mining techniques required only a fraction of the workers. The Great Depression wrecked much of the county's manufacturing base closing all but a few glass plants (Stegmaier, Dean, Kershaw, and Wiseman 1976, 396). By the 1960s, even those plants that had survived the Depression had closed. Most of the mining and manufacturing jobs have been replaced by lower-paying service sector jobs, culminating in the closure of the Kelly-Springfield automobile tire plant in 1998 after a buyout from Ohio-based Goodyear Tire and Rubber.

Map 10.2 illustrates the political geography of Maryland counties at the time of the New Deal realignment by averaging the Democratic percentage of the vote from 1928 to 1936. Western Maryland stands out as the most Republican part of the state, and central Maryland, from Baltimore city to the Washington suburbs, is the most Democratic. The Eastern Shore was a patchwork of Republican and Democratic territory. Hoover's 1928 candidacy was especially popular in Maryland with only two of the most rural counties voting for Smith. Some scholars have dated the beginning of the New Deal realignment to Al Smith's candidacy in 1928 (Sundquist 1983), and it may have started that early in Maryland. Baltimore city had been a Republican stronghold, but with Smith's candidacy, the GOP's margin of victory in the Charm City narrowed to just 3.5 percent (Willis 1984). The urban areas of the state would move overwhelmingly into the Roosevelt camp in 1932 and 1936. The most loyal Democratic constituencies in Maryland were laborers and blacks—the latter bearing the brunt of the economic hardship brought on by the Great Depression (Willis 1984).

Maryland's rural areas and smaller towns, though, had less to gain from an enduring alliance with Roosevelt. State and federal legislation to prevent the foreclosure of banks helped larger banking inter-

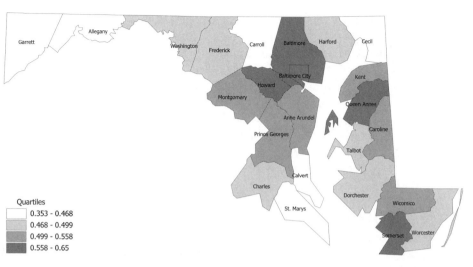

Map 10.2.   Average Democratic percentage of the presidential vote, 1928–1936

ests, but not smaller ones. Work relief projects benefited the unemployed in rural Maryland, but were often opposed by conservative
leaders for putting inflationary pressure on local wage scales. Small
town Republicans also blamed organized labor for their inability to
attract new business, and Cumberland officials even adopted ordi-
nances to restrict picketing, although these were later declared un-
constitutional. Conservative forces resistant to Democratic liberalism
were also present in much of rural Maryland where there had been
sympathy for the Ku Klux Klan in the 1920s. This resistance appears
in the state's political geography as Allegany, Garrett, and Calvert
Counties were the least enthusiastic about Roosevelt's candidacy
(see map 10.2).

The most significant political development in Maryland electoral
history was the growth of government employment in the Washington suburbs following the New Deal. The expansion of the federal
bureaucracy resulted in a demand for labor that Maryland alone
could not fulfill. As a result, migrants from other states flooded into
Prince George's and Montgomery Counties to meet the need. The
bulk of these new government workers were employed in the alpha-
betocracy of domestic agencies created by Roosevelt to ameliorate
the nation's economic problems. Naturally, these workers became

committed to the party that created and generously supported these programs. Military employment also expanded after World War II, in conjunction with the cold war threat, but the vast majority of military jobs were located in northern Virginia. A majority of these defense workers would eventually become loyal Republicans, helping to restore two-party competition in the Old Dominion.

By 1960, then, the growth of government employment had made Prince George's and Montgomery Counties much more Democratic than they would have been had they been located on the fringe of any other large city. In most states, the suburbs within Prince George's and Montgomery would have become easy Republican pickings during the 1950s, and predictable GOP turf for decades afterward. But because of the Democratic loyalties of Maryland's civil service class, Democrats could regularly compete in both counties, usually winning easily in Prince George's while keeping Washington's northern suburbs highly competitive. Montgomery became known after 1960 as a pocket of affluent liberalism.

The flood of new residents into the Washington suburbs in search of government work stood as a stark contrast to the sluggish growth of rural Maryland after World War II. The western counties had settled back into their comfortable Republican ways by the 1950s precisely because the population there had changed so little. Because of its rural black population, the Eastern Shore's political loyalties remained mixed in presidential elections, although Republicans won easy victories in statewide contests when blacks failed to turn out. Civil rights legislation resulted in more rural unrest than urban violence because whites did little to resist in Baltimore city or the Washington suburbs. The Maryland General Assembly passed antidiscrimination laws that were regional in nature, initially exempting the Eastern Shore from state statutes prohibiting restaurants and hotels from denying service on the basis of race, creed, color, or national origin (Burdette 1983). This led civil rights forces to protest in the Eastern Shore town of Cambridge in 1963, prompting rioting and vandalism in June of that year. The antidiscrimination law was soon extended to the Eastern Shore counties in the 1964 legislative session (Burdette 1983).

The New Deal had converted Baltimore city's working-class white and poor black populations into the most predictable Democratic blocs in the state. Whether at the docks or in the city's manufacturing plants, union labor emerged as an influential political voice. Interracial violence did not damage race relations in Baltimore city to the same extent that it did in Detroit and Los Angeles. First, whites did not feel trapped in the city. They moved out into adjacent suburban areas that were relatively open and free of development. Second, Baltimore city's white politicians were progressive on civil rights and were not as resistant to the policy demands of black leaders as those in other cities. White Democrats worked in coalition with black members of the city council and neighborhood leaders through the 1960s, and rank-and-file blacks were slow to reject the leadership of white liberals in the mayor's office. Baltimore city did not elect a black mayor until 1987, turning back to a white mayor, Martin O'Malley, in 1999.

To be sure, the white population did move out of many Baltimore city neighborhoods, although they managed to preserve for themselves several neighborhoods with the collusion of real estate brokers who refused to sell to blacks. While blacks were screened out of some neighborhoods, at the other extreme, the practice of blockbusting was perfected to a science in others. Blockbusting was the unscrupulous real estate practice "of introducing an African American household into a formerly white residential area for the purposes of provoking panic-driven racial turnover" (Orser 1994, 87). Typically, blockbusters would make exploitative profits because whites would be panicked into selling their homes at below market rates and brokers would re-sell them to African Americans at above market value. Desertion of these neighborhoods by whites was facilitated by the fact that the Baltimore County suburbs were relatively undeveloped. This meant that flight from the city imposed lower moving costs on white Baltimoreans than it did on those fleeing from larger cities hemmed in by suburbs. The flight of the white population and the political activation of blacks within Democratic party ranks rapidly eroded GOP prospects in the city. By the mid-1960s, the Republican party had ceased to be a serious political force in local elections.

After 1970, the Democratic hold on statewide political offices only grew stronger as the Washington suburbs filled up. After Spiro Agnew's victory in 1966, Republicans did not win the governorship again until 2002. In fact, only one of the contests between 1966 and 2000 was even closely competitive, in 1994, but Democrat Parris Glendening still won by 6,000 votes. Map 10.3 illustrates average Democratic presidential election voting in the 1988–96 elections. The

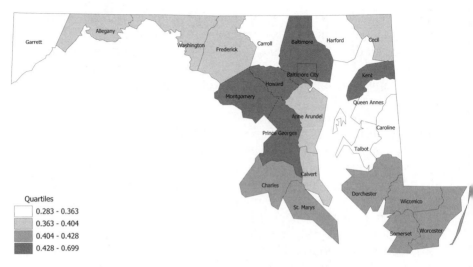

Quartiles
- 0.283 - 0.363
- 0.363 - 0.404
- 0.404 - 0.428
- 0.428 - 0.699

Map 10.3.   Average Democratic percentage of the presidential vote, 1988–2000

regional patterns show that voter-rich Baltimore city and Prince George's and Montgomery Counties were among the most Democratic jurisdictions—unchanged in their positions relative to the rest of the state since the 1960s. From 1960 through the 2000s, government spending fueled a rapid expansion of the suburban population. Because of their size, Prince George's and Montgomery Counties came to control the fate of candidates for statewide offices. The combination of loyally Democratic black voters in Prince George's and Baltimore city, combined with the Democratic voting of federal civil servants in Prince George's and Montgomery Counties, proved to be a sufficiently large bloc that the GOP found it difficult to compete. Local Republicans were hampered by their national party's insistence on a small government message, particularly with respect to domestic policy-making—not likely to play well in suburbs crowded with people who made their living in the federal bureaucracy.

Western Maryland, with the exception of Allegany County (Cumberland), remained supportive of Republicans (see map 10.3). Allegany's more Democratic inclination was due to the sustained economic malaise of Cumberland, a city once identified with heavy industry, that struggled to make a smooth transition into the postindustrial age. With population stagnation, younger, more Republican-inclined voters left the county, leaving a population of aging Democratic identifiers and less skilled workers behind. Outside of Cumberland, allegiance to the party of Roosevelt, never anything to write home about in the first place, was strained under the weight of the Democratic party's ideologically liberal drift. Voters in Hagerstown, Frostburg, and Oakland were conservative on matters such as gun control, civil rights, abortion rights, and the use of welfare. Republican party identification came ever more easily to Maryland's small town and rural voters coming of age after 1964.

Republicans made some notable gains in Baltimore County and the suburban fringe counties, Carroll and Harford. These were more typical suburban jurisdictions than one could find near Washington—lacking in government employees, and defining themselves in contrast to the Democratic politics of Baltimore city. Through the Reagan era, businesses continued to leave Baltimore city to locate in new attractive suburban office parks in towns such as Towson, Timonium, Owings Mills, and Lutherville. Clean industries and businesses opened at these sites, employing professionals, managers, and engineers. Transportation infrastructure accommodated this growth, enabling commuters to live further out from the central city, fueling housing booms in Harford and Carroll Counties. By the early 2000s, the Baltimore "suburbs" included towns that were as far away as the Delaware and Pennsylvania borders to the northeast, and as far as Frederick County to the west.

In spite of their growth, migration was sufficiently selective that Harford and Carroll remained two of the most Republican counties in the state by 2000. A new kind of GOP voter had moved in, however, importing values different from the farmer and retail merchant who had dominated these counties during the previous decades. The older suburbs closer to Baltimore became more Democratic after 1980 as white, affluent professionals moved further out, and African Americans from Baltimore city succeeded them. Baltimore County, once a reliable GOP stronghold, had become evenly competitive between the parties by the late 1980s.

The Eastern Shore experienced growth from an expanding recreation and tourism sector in the 1990s and 2000s. Luxurious residential developments sprang up along the bay shore and near Ocean City. Often they were occupied only part of the year, but those residents who were permanent usually imported a Republican aversion to high taxes and generally conservative views on other issues. Parts of the Eastern Shore are remote and lie off primary thoroughfares running to the Maryland and Delaware shores. These isolated counties remained relatively untouched by new residential development, and their consequent politics remained much the same as it had been in 1960, changing only gradually with the mortality of the population.

Where Are the Votes in Maryland? Republican and Democratic Mobilization Targets

Maryland is different from other states because Republicans do not have the advantage in the affluent suburbs that they do elsewhere. More precisely, the Baltimore suburbs have usually favored the GOP in presidential elections, but the Washington suburbs are a mix of friendly and enemy territory. For the last third of the twentieth century, Democrats had a decisive electoral edge in party registration. Maryland Republicans have had little success attracting government employees or blacks to their candidacies and have succeeded in doing so only by being disloyal to their national party leadership. Democrats not only benefit from a much larger number of sympathetic voters, they have a second advantage in that their base is concentrated in the most urban areas of the state. Republicans must cover a much wider, sparsely settled territory, which imposes burdensome costs on candidates and political party organizations. At the same time, Maryland is a geographically small state with a highly concentrated population. The state's geography, then, suggests that the two parties will be competing side by side for votes in the Washington and Baltimore suburbs.

The rank ordering of counties in table 10.1 shows that Montgomery and Baltimore Counties are critical for both parties. Montgomery ranks as the most important county for Republicans and the second most important for Democrats. Democrats found about one out of every five of their presidential voters in Montgomery County in the 1988–2000 elections, while Republicans took 17 percent of their base from these suburbs. Baltimore County was about of equal importance to both parties, providing about 14.3 percent of the Democrats' statewide electoral base and 14.1 percent of the total statewide vote for the GOP.

Not surprisingly, Baltimore city is a Democratic stronghold (ranks third), casting about 16 percent of the statewide Democratic vote in the 1988–2000 presidential elections, but is much less important for Republican efforts (ranks ninth), providing 8 percent of their total statewide vote. Conversely, Carroll County, the fast-growing suburban county west of Baltimore, is noteworthy for ranking fifth on the GOP top ten list, while ranking twelfth for Democrats (see table 10.1 and map 10.4).

Since the 1930s, the most dramatic development in the geographic redistribution of political influence has been the decline of Baltimore city and the rise of the Washington, D.C., suburbs. In the 1928–36 series of elections, Montgomery County provided a scant 2 percent of the statewide Democratic vote, with Prince George's providing just slightly more. Howard and Carroll Counties were considered rural backwaters, and the mid-sized towns in western Maryland were relatively more influential. Both parties centered their campaigns on the city of Baltimore. With industrial decline and rapid population losses to suburban Baltimore County, Baltimore city steadily lost influence after 1960. Coincident with Baltimore's declining population was the government-stimulated growth of Prince George's and Montgomery Counties. For decades, candidates from Baltimore were considered shoo-in victors in major elections due to their familiarity to the state's largest bloc of voters. By 1994, however, the Washington suburbs had managed to elect one of their own, Prince George's County executive Parris Glendening, as governor. Sustained growth has placed politicians from Prince George's and Montgomery Counties on a steeply upward trajectory of influence.

TABLE 10.1 Maryland's Top Ten Strongest Counties for Republicans and Democrats in the 1988–2000 Presidential Contests

Rank	Democratic	Republican
1	Prince George's (Upper Marlboro)	Montgomery (Rockville)
2	Montgomery (Rockville)	Anne Arundel (Annapolis)
3	Baltimore city	Baltimore (Towson)
4	Baltimore (Towson)	Harford (Bel Air)
5	Anne Arundel (Annapolis)	Carroll (Westminster)
6	Howard (Columbia)	Frederick (Frederick)
7	Harford (Bel Air)	Howard (Columbia)
8	Frederick (Frederick)	Prince George's (Upper Marlboro)
9	Charles (St. Charles)	Baltimore city
10	Washington (Hagerstown)	Washington (Hagerstown)
% of total vote	89.5	82.6

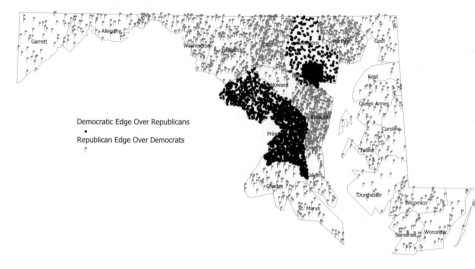

Map 10.4.   Areas of Republican and Democratic dominance, 1988–2000

In spite of the diminishing importance of Baltimore city, the
Democrats still benefited from a highly concentrated bloc of voters.
Nearly 70 percent of all Democratic votes come from the Democrats' four top counties listed in table 10.1. Republicans must go to
seven counties to find a comparable share of their total vote. As in
other states, the most rural counties on the Eastern Shore and in
western Maryland are often ignored in statewide political campaigns, but are more important to the Republicans than to the Democrats. About 5 percent of the GOP base resided in the state's five
smallest counties in 2000, compared with less than 2 percent of the
Democratic base. Republicans, then, are doubly disadvantaged in
Maryland both by being a minority party and by having to comb
more territory in search of votes. The GOP's best hope is to attract
crossover voters with unconventional issues or extraordinarily attractive candidates, such as their 2002 gubernatorial nominee, Bob
Ehrlich.

Maryland's Changing Electoral Foundations

Much of the data we analyzed for this book consists of election returns aggregated to the county level. Using this data has enabled us to

focus on the changing political geography within states. Students of politics realize, however, that what is true at the aggregate level is not necessarily reflective of individual voters. A county with a majority black population can vote Republican even though very few of the black voters vote that way. Polls of individual voters reveal verities that county- or precinct-level data will obscure. At the same time, the scarcity of surveys of Maryland voters has proved to be an obstacle to obtaining a precise picture of the voting tendencies of specific groups, especially prior to the 1980s.

Following the precedent set in previous chapters, we have utilized Gary King's (1997) ecological inference maximum likelihood technique to obtain estimates of the percentage of Maryland voters in each of several demographic groups who supported the Democratic party in presidential elections between 1928 and 2000. The application of this method does not always generate precise estimates of such quantities, but they are usually closer to reality than older, alternative methods. Estimates of Democratic presidential support by various demographic groups are presented in table 10.2 based on county-level data.

Partisan change is driven by several forces, all, some, or none of which can be in play at any given time. Generational replacement is operating if an older generation of partisans is being replaced by a younger generation that is aligned either with the other party or with no party at all. Often it is in the most rural areas of the country where generational replacement is the primary force behind electoral change. The other forces for partisan change include population mobility, conversion, and mobilization. Population mobility is often a source of electoral change in rapidly growing areas or areas that are being abandoned because of economic decline. In the former case, outsiders bring in new ideas and attitudes from elsewhere, altering the balance of partisanship in a place. In the latter case, a place is changed because those who can afford to leave do so, usually leaving the poor and elderly behind (Gimpel 1999). Conversion from one party to another is a rare phenomenon, but it happens in exceptional cases when partisans are so upset with their party that they abandon it for another. Mobilization can be a source of party change in an area if new voters suddenly flood into the electorate, registering and voting for the first time. Providing they remain active, mass mobilization can be the source of realignment (Andersen 1979).

Population Mobility

The New Deal's impact was felt more through the expansion of government employment than through short-term party change. It was
the new populations that moved in that had the most lasting impact
on Maryland politics following Roosevelt. Most important of these
new populations were the government employees that moved into
Washington's suburbs. During the 1950s, Maryland strongly supported Eisenhower, but the places with the largest populations from
out of state supported Stevenson. A large number of these new civil
servants were blacks who had migrated from Southern states and
who proved to be lasting Democratic loyalists. They settled mostly in
Washington, D.C., and in Prince George's County. The state's support
for Republicans was sufficiently strong during the 1950s that only the
forces of rising government employment and black mobilization
were capable of steering the state leftward toward the Democrats.

Population growth fueled by government employment was clearly
responsible for the dismal fate of the GOP after 1960. Where the
population was growing fastest, in the Washington suburbs, the progovernment liberalism of the Great Society would become the bread
and butter of the citizenry. The Baltimore suburbs, lacking government employment and with fewer middle-class blacks, followed a
more conventional political path. They defined their politics partly in
opposition to Baltimore city—reflexively casting Republican votes
simply because the city was doing the opposite and that couldn't be
right. In areas of population decline, such as Baltimore's older industrial suburbs, we often saw the GOP beginning to run competitive
elections. Working-class voters were sensitive to job losses in area
manufacturing plants due to foreign competition, and politics took
on a populist and conservative flavor that benefited the Republicans.

In the more affluent suburbs on Baltimore's fringes (Harford, Carroll, and Frederick Counties), growth was as likely to come from inside the state (from older suburbs and Baltimore city) as from outside,
and the politics was decidedly Republican, favoring low taxes, less
government spending, and traditional family values. These values did
not represent a major departure from the past because these places
had often expressed such views. But the fact that these counties could
maintain their traditional political moorings under the pressure of
tremendous growth indicated how selective the in-migration was.

Only certain populations found their way into the sparkling subdivisions of Carroll and Harford Counties in the early 2000s. And yet this exclusive population was not small in number. Thousands relocated from older, more crowded suburbs, even if it meant commuting over an hour to work.

In most states, we would expect internal migrants arriving from outside the state to exhibit Republican sympathies. But in Maryland, the lure has been government employment in the civil service system—a haven for Democrats. In table 10.2, we see that internal migrants are more Democratic than nonmigrants. In the late 1950s, an estimated 61 percent of migrants supported the Democratic candidate, compared with only 49 percent of nonmigrants (natives and immigrants combined). When we added a control variable to separate the newcomers who were employed by government from those who had settled in the state to pursue other occupations, we found that only 43.7 percent of the nongovernment migrants voted Democratic in the combined 1956, 1960, and 1964 elections, compared with 48.8 percent of nonmigrants. This bolsters our conclusion that it was migrants specifically coming to work for the federal government who helped to make Maryland a lopsided Democratic state. By the time of the 1988–92 elections, the gap between migrants and nonmigrants grew wider, with 60 percent of migrants voting Democratic, compared with about 42 percent of nonmigrants. Once again, when we controlled for the percentage employed in government, we found that the share of out-of-state migrants voting Democratic dropped to 52 percent, compared with 45 percent of nonmigrants. Our data analysis, combined with the evidence from previous research (Schuknecht 2001), establishes firmly that population growth from elsewhere has helped to build a substantial Democratic edge in party registration.

Maryland is not known for being an immigrant receiving state, but the immigrant population is growing rapidly in two counties: Prince George's and Montgomery. Because of its still small size, however, we have not been able to reliably estimate the political support among this population with the ecological inference model. The county-level data show that the places with large immigrant concentrations voted decisively more Democratic in the 1996–2000 elections than they did in the 1988–92 contests, but of course this may have had nothing to do with the behavior of immigrants. Interestingly, the ecological inference estimates for immigrant voting show exactly the opposite in table 10.2 and suggest that Democratic voting was sharply up in 1996–2000 among non-immigrant voters, and down among immigrants. Anecdotal information suggested that immigrant voting patterns in the Washington suburbs were heavily class dependent, but in a one-party state the immigrant population was still more likely to throw its support toward the Democratic party than toward the minority Republicans. Bolstering this conclusion, our rough estimates for the voting tendency of the steadily growing Latino population (4.3 percent of the total by 2000) suggest that it is considerably more Democratic than the reminder of the population (table 10.2).

Generational Replacement

After 1960, the playing field tipped decidedly against the GOP in the state's major population centers. In western Maryland and on the Eastern Shore, generational replacement of older Democrats with younger Republicans kept the GOP running competitive races. But in the more populated areas, older GOP supporters were being replaced through mortality by younger Democrats and Democrats arriving from outside the state. In analyzing the election data, our thought was that if elderly voters exhibited voting tendencies distinct from those in younger age cohorts, it is a sure sign that generational change in partisanship would follow. The mortality of an older generation, and its replacement with a younger one, will alter the political prospects for one of the two parties. In Maryland, we found considerable differences in Democratic support between those over age 65 and younger voters, as evidenced by the results in table 10.2. While our estimates lack statistical significance due to aggregation bias (the percentage of elderly voters in most counties is very small), they suggest that elderly voters began to drift more Republican than younger voters beginning in the 1950s. If our estimates approximate the truth, then, Republicans have been badly hurt by generational replacement throughout the latter half of the twentieth century as these older Republicans have exited the electorate through death. Between the 1968 and 1984 elections, the estimates suggest that for every one hundred people over age 65, between sixty and seventy were Republican voters. Younger cohorts, however, were more evenly divided in their political views. These figures suggest one line of explanation for the decline in GOP electoral fortunes after Spiro Agnew left the governorship to become Richard Nixon's vice president. Republicans were aging and dying at a higher rate than Democrats, and they were not being replaced on a one-to-one basis. Our estimates show that this generation gap closed by the end of the century. Even so, election-day exit polls from the 1996 and 2000 presidential elections showed that older Maryland voters remained less enthusiastic about Bill Clinton and Al Gore than younger voters. Survey data indicate that the gap in Democratic support between those under age 65 and those older ran between 4 and 8 points, consistent with our figure in table 10.2.

Conversion

Mobilization of new voting blocs and the expansion in the size of the electorate contributed to the realignment of the 1930s in Baltimore

TABLE 10.2.   Estimates of the Democratic Percentage of the Presidential Vote for Various Electoral Groups in Maryland, 1928–2000 (ecological inference maximum likelihood)

Pooled Presidential Election Years	Blacks/ Nonblacks		Elderly/ Nonelderly		Immigrants/ Nonimmigrants		Farmers/ Nonfarmers		Whites/ Nonwhites	
1928, 1932	64.9*	50.3*	60.6	52.3*	95.0	50.2*	51.9*	52.9*	50.7*	63.0*
1936, 1940, 1944	48.3*	60.4*	29.3	60.5*	94.3	56.7*	37.2*	61.6*	66.6*	17.0*
1948, 1952	56.4	45.1*	54.7	46.3*	51.3	46.8*	35.0*	47.9*	48.7*	38.2
1956, 1960, 1964	69.3*	49.9*	44.2	53.8*	71.8	52.6*	39.7	53.7*	50.2*	67.7*
1968, 1972	65.0*	35.2*	29.4	41.5*	47.3	40.3*	15.2	41.0*	35.0*	65.1*
1976, 1980, 1984	86.1*	38.8*	33.6	50.5*	60.6	48.9*	37.3	49.6*	39.3*	79.2*
1988, 1992	88.2*	37.2*	49.4	49.9*	99.5	46.4*	1.0	50.2*	34.6*	87.3*
1996, 2000	94.6*	43.8*	49.3	57.5*	48.5	57.2*	1.0	57.7*	45.3*	83.2*

	Mfg. Workers/ Non Mfg. Workers		College Educated/ Non College Educated		Native to State/ Nonnatives		Internal Migrants/ Nonmigrants		Hispanics/ Non-Hispanics	
1928, 1932	—	—	—	—	—	—	—	—	—	—
1936, 1940, 1944	—	—	—	—	—	—	—	—	—	—
1948, 1952	52.1	45.4*	24.5	48.6*	—	—	—	—	—	—
1956, 1960, 1964	33.1*	59.2*	70.6	51.4*	48.3*	60.4*	61.0*	48.6*	—	—
1968, 1972	35.5*	41.8*	73.0	34.3*	36.4*	45.3*	45.1*	37.1*	—	—
1976, 1980, 1984	25.6	53.3*	54.0	48.7*	43.3*	56.7*	59.9*	42.1*	88.6	48.9*
1988, 1992	56.5	49.1*	63.3*	45.1*	33.8*	65.9*	60.1*	42.0*	88.1	48.9*
1996, 2000	33.9	58.9*	52.1*	57.6*	39.0*	75.6*	80.0*	39.9*	62.4	56.4*

Note: Cell entries show the estimated percentage voting Democratic in the presidential elections listed on each row. Complete variable definitions and results from the ecological inference estimation appear in appendix B, with standard errors and bounds.
*Reflect estimates with lower and upper bounds narrower than 0,1.

city and Montgomery County. Conversion of voters from one party to the other was evident through the 1930s in rural Maryland where there was very little expansion in the size of the electorate, but Roosevelt won major victories anyway. But the New Deal did not immediately turn Maryland into a Democratic stronghold. Republicans battled back to win significant victories beginning in 1948 when Dewey defeated Truman locally. The rural counties in the western arm moved back into the GOP camp by the late 1940s, and even Baltimore city remained competitive between the parties in presidential elections through the 1950s. In spite of the GOP resistance, multiple forces of partisan change were conspiring to swell the Democratic tide. A major source was in Franklin D. Roosevelt's Maryland converts—blacks and workers throughout the state who had clear memories of the economic hardships of the Great Depression. If these converts turned out in large numbers, joined by the legions of government employees in the Washington suburbs, the Republicans would surely wind up in the minority.

Republicans had some potential converts in those voters alienated by the liberal drift of the Democratic party in the 1960s. Some dealignment and realignment with a basis in conversion also took place in the 1960s. George Wallace made inroads with disaffected conservative Democrats in 1968 and 1972 on Maryland's Eastern Shore, and several of these counties, including Dorchester (Cambridge), site of the earlier race riots, subsequently moved into the Republican column. Nevertheless, the Democrats got the better of any swap in support because far more voters came their way than abandoned them to vote Republican.

For evidence of conversion in these two eras of electoral instability, we constructed voter transition models to gauge the extent to which Democrats and Republicans remained loyal to their party's nominee in elections where they may have faced a strong temptation to defect. Our results in table 10.3 show the percentage of Democrats (and Republicans) in 1928 who voted Democratic (or Republican) in 1932. We also present results showing the loyalty of voters from 1932 to 1936, and for elections during the 1960s (see table 10.3).

Estimates for party loyalty during the 1930s reveal that 85.5 percent of Smith voters in 1928 voted for Roosevelt in 1932. Of Roosevelt's 1932 supporters, 77.4 percent went on to vote for him in 1936. Maryland's Democratic voters do not exhibit the same level of loyalty

TABLE 10.3. Estimates of Party Loyalty and Conversion across Presidential Elections in Maryland (ecological inference maximum likelihood)

Presidential Election Years	Voted Democratic 1928/Non-Democratic 1928	Voted Democratic 1932/Non-Democratic 1932	Presidential Election Years	Voted Republican 1928/Non-Republican 1928	Voted Republican 1932/Non-Republican 1932
Voted Democratic 1932	85.5* 40.8*		Voted Republican 1932	37.7* 42.7*	
Voted Democratic 1936		77.4* 27.2*	Voted Republican 1936		77.5* 19.0*

	Voted Democratic 1960/Non-Democratic 1960	Voted Democratic 1964/Non-Democratic 1964	Presidential Election Years	Voted Republican 1960/Non-Republican 1960	Voted Republican 1964/Non-Republican 1964
Voted Democratic 1964	73.1* 56.8*		Voted Republican 1964	59.7* 12.7*	
Voted Democratic 1968		61.8* 11.7*	Voted Republican 1968		76.4* 22.1*
Voted Wallace 1968		10.2* 23.1*	Voted Wallace 1968		23.3* 10.1*

Note: Cell entries show the estimated percentage voting Democratic, Republican, or for George Wallace in the presidential elections listed on each row who voted Democratic (or Republican) in the previous election. Complete variable definitions and results from the ecological inference estimation appear in appendix C, with standard errors and bounds.

*Reflect estimates with lower and upper bounds narrower than 0.1.

that voters in California, New York, Georgia, and Texas do. In these states there were few defections, and the New Deal realignment was quite one-sided. Maryland resembles Michigan and Illinois, where Democrats may have exchanged some support with Republicans. Still, our analysis indicates that Republicans lost far more ground in Maryland than they won. Only an estimated 37.7 percent of GOP voters in 1928 stayed with Hoover four years later. Maryland Republicans were much less loyal to Hoover than their counterparts in California, New York, or Illinois. In these devastating GOP defections, Maryland had more in common with Texas, Georgia, and Florida than it did with Northern states.

By the 1960s, Maryland was poised on the threshold of becoming a one-party Democratic state. President Johnson's Great Society agenda spurred major growth in human services programming in Washington. Workers who signed on with these agencies were naturally sympathetic to the party that had pressed for their creation. Government had made the state's economy so dependent upon federal paychecks that Maryland was not likely to warm to the major GOP themes of less government and lower taxes. Conservative Republicans were especially at risk. Only an estimated 59.7 percent of Nixon's supporters (in 1960) cast votes for Goldwater in the next election. By contrast, 73 percent of Kennedy's supporters remained loyal to Johnson (see table 10.3). Wallace had solid support in 1968 — he received a better reception than he did in states such as California, New York, or Illinois, although not as strong as in the South. More Republicans voted for Wallace than Democrats. The Wallace independents would go on to vote overwhelmingly for Richard Nixon in 1972.

The upshot of our analysis of the electoral volatility of the late 1960s is that consonant with its ambivalent, border-state character, Maryland occupied a midpoint on the continuum of states that contributed to partisan change through political conversion. At one end stood Georgia, with its strong support for Goldwater and Wallace. At the other end one could place New York, where Goldwater had tepid support and Wallace performed poorly. Squarely in the middle was Maryland. No wonder Wallace found sufficient reason to return to the state to campaign in 1972 where he would meet his fate at the hand of a gunman whose bullet put the governor in a wheelchair for the remainder of his life. The ranks of conservative Democrats and

Republicans attracted to the likes of Goldwater and Wallace would be overwhelmed by the sustained flow of new residents into the Washington suburbs in the 1970s and 1980s. By the 2000s, candidates who had conservative views could be found, but they rarely ran competitive races in statewide elections.

In other states, we have found additional evidence of conversion in the changing partisanship of blue-collar workers. Ordinarily, we would expect that Maryland's working-class population employed in manufacturing would be more supportive of Democratic presidential candidates than those in other occupations. But given the large number of government employees with strong Democratic leanings, this may not be as true in Maryland as it is in other states. Whether manufacturing workers are more or less Democratic than "others" depends on what occupational groups "others" contains. Our estimates indicate that in Maryland manufacturing workers are actually more Republican than those in nonmanufacturing employment. In the pooled 1956, 1960, and 1964 contests, for example, an estimated 33 percent of manufacturing workers cast Democratic ballots, compared with 59 percent in other fields of endeavor. Estimates for the 1996–2000 elections suggest that those employed in manufacturing remained less Democratic than those working in other occupations. Similar estimates for the Democratic voting of government employees indicated that as much as 75 percent of this population supported Bill Clinton and Al Gore in 1996 and 2000.

Activism and Partisanship of New Voters

In Maryland, the 1930s saw short-term party change resulting from mass mobilization. Roosevelt's candidacy definitely won converts, but for this realignment to be real, these converts had to vote. Mobilization made the most dramatic difference in Baltimore city and the Washington suburbs. In Baltimore city and Montgomery County, for instance, the expansion of the electorate clearly contributed to Roosevelt's overwhelming victories in 1932 and 1936. In Baltimore city, the conversion of blacks from the Republican to the Democratic party, and their mobilization, helped erode the Republican edge the Charm City had customarily exhibited on election day.

Differences in the voting behavior of blacks and whites were so significant at the start of the new century that racial polarization seems like a constant and we assume that it has always been with us. In fact, the gap between white and black voting has widened with time, as we can see in table 10.2. In our estimates of Democratic support for the pooled 1936, 1940, and 1944 elections, blacks are more Republican in their voting than whites. But black conversion to the Democratic party progresses through the 1940s, and by 1948–52 a reversal occurred—blacks were now more supportive of Truman and Stevenson than whites (table 10.2). The difference between blacks and nonblacks in support for the Democratic candidate widened in the pooled 1968–72 contests because of the lack of enthusiasm among whites for Humphrey and the popularity of the Wallace candidacy throughout rural Maryland. In the 2000 presidential election, exit polling indicated that 92 percent of black voters supported Bill Clinton, compared with only 46 percent of whites. The story of the Democrats' rise to majority status is one of both conversion and mobilization. It took black voters several elections between 1932 and 1948 to become convinced that the Democratic party stood for racial justice as well as economic recovery. But once convinced, they had to go to the polls. When they did show up, the Republicans were consigned to long-term minority status.

Sectionalism in Maryland is partly an urban vs. rural phenomenon, and we would expect the mobilization of the state's African-American voters to have enhanced the cleavage between larger cities and small towns. Our analysis does show that the more urbanized areas of central Maryland exhibit consistently higher support for Democrats than the rural west or Eastern Shore. One way of evaluating the extent of urban vs. rural cleavage to Maryland is to examine the voting of the farm population, comparing them to those in nonfarming occupations. The results from our estimates indicate that farmers have been much less Democratic than those in other fields, beginning in the late 1930s, with the gap widening considerably with the rise of black power in urban areas (see table 10.2).

Conclusions

Examined in reference to its counties, sectionalism in presidential elections is consistently lower in Maryland than in any other state we have examined. This is mainly an artifact of the state's physical geography and the scale (size) of its counties relative to its compact borders. We do observe that sectionalism in Maryland presidential elections has increased with population growth. Whether the addition of new voters to the state will continue to increase the level of political balkanization depends upon how politically homogeneous the fast-growing counties in the Baltimore-Washington corridor become. With the out-migration of blacks from Washington, D.C., into the Maryland suburbs, and the out-migration of whites from Baltimore city, two bastions of monolithic Democratic loyalty emerged after 1960. While some speculated that blacks would change their party identification as they moved up the economic ladder, this had not happened in Prince George's County by the early 2000s. Montgomery County was less politically predictable than Prince George's, but only slightly, usually giving strong support to Democrats in presidential and gubernatorial elections, but permitting liberal, progovernment Republicans to serve in the state legislature and in the area's one congressional seat. Baltimore city has been majority black and heavily Democratic since the 1960s. Howard County is increasingly diverse. The demographic developments across central Maryland have created more safe Democratic jurisdictions than existed in previous decades.

Republicans in the state will not stand idly by waiting for all of this territory to go Democratic. The new century found them desperately in search of ambitious and attractive leadership that could lead to a brighter future for the party. But the emphasis of the national GOP on small government and less spending on a wide range of government programs Marylanders value—from social services to environmental protection—made it difficult for local Republicans to air a credible message.

In 2002, Republicans proved that it was possible to run a competitive statewide race under the right circumstances. The Washington suburbs are the key to their success in the new century. To win, GOP candidates must contest Montgomery and Howard Counties, while maintaining their usual margins in the rest of the state. Given that central Maryland is such a critical political battleground, Republicans must seek to minimize sectionalism in order to win elections, essentially bringing central Maryland into line with their impressive vote tallies in western Maryland and the Eastern Shore. Democrats, on the other hand, with little hope of making gains in conservative regions of the state, must hope that sectionalism increases, moving central Maryland out of line with the GOP-leaning counties on either side.

Note

1. Throughout this chapter we refer to Baltimore as *Baltimore city*. We use this convention only to distinguish the city of Baltimore from Baltimore County, a separate jurisdiction surrounding Baltimore that contains most of Baltimore's suburban population.

CHAPTER 11

OREGON

Major Forces for Electoral Change in Oregon
- Domestic (Internal) Migration from Other States
- Decline of the Agricultural and Forest Products Economy
- Growth of Portland and Willamette Valley Region
- Rise of Environmental Protection Movement

As we have suggested in introductions to other chapters, most states can be associated with one or two distinctive symbols: Georgia with peaches, Michigan with automobiles, and Texas with cowboys and oil derricks. Oregon is perhaps the only state that is primarily associated with a color: green. By virtue of its location in the Pacific Northwest, Oregon has long been envisioned as an American promised land consisting of lush green farmlands, deep green rivers, and dense green forests. This perception is accurate, for within Oregon's boundaries lie some of America's most fertile agricultural lands and scenic rivers, while nearly half of Oregon's total land area is forested. However, this impression is, quite literally, only half-right: Oregon is cleaved by the north-south running Cascade Mountain range, and while western Oregon is characteristically wet and verdant, eastern Oregon lacks both the rainfall and vegetation typical of the westernmost counties. Arid eastern Oregon more resembles neighboring Idaho and Nevada than the part of Oregon west of the Cascades.

Another popular perception of Oregon stems from its role in the history of the settlement of the American West. Natives note with pride that Oregon has the most famous intracontinental passageway named after it. Ironically, Oregon was not the intended destination of the majority of pioneers who traversed the Oregon Trail. Most westbound migrants dreamed of finding their fortunes in the gold-rich mountains and riverbeds of California. While the Golden

State lured hundreds of thousands of American migrants with its siren song of seemingly unlimited, abundantly available mineral wealth, the Beaver State was considered a paradise destination for less pecuniary reasons. Those who settled in Oregon were attracted by the pristine and calm life offered in one of America's most fertile environments.

Oregon has earned a national reputation for its citizens' remarkable degree of involvement in politics, in spite of the high rates of migration that are usually associated with low turnout. The state's voters have long played a primary role in determining public policy, and historical participation figures suggest that they have taken that role seriously. Late-nineteenth-century Populistic appeals resonated strongly with Oregon's predominantly rural, agricultural population, which in turn disposed Oregonians to favorably view Progressive calls for government reform. The state was the first to institute initiative, referendum, and recall elections as mechanisms by which to increase direct participation in political decision making. Beginning in 1996, Oregon experimented with mail-in ballots as a substitute for traditional in-person voting. In 2000, Oregon conducted the nation's first presidential primary and general elections in which all voting was done by mail. The experiment appears to have succeeded: a whopping 79.8 percent of Oregon's registered voters cast votes for president. Overall, 60.6 percent of the voting-age population participated.

Oregon continues to entice businesses, residents, and vacationers on the basis of its attractive and productive settings. The state's natural environment is the key to its economy. Agriculture, timber, and fishing have historically played major roles in the state's economy, though they are less dominant now than in the past. In 1950, 12.7 percent of Oregon's workforce was employed in agriculture, forestry, or fishery operations. By 1970, that percentage had dropped to 5.2 percent and remained at nearly the same level through the early 2000s. The state has expanded its economic bases by taking advantage of its natural resources. Its northern border with Washington State is the Columbia River, the Pacific Northwest's principal waterway, while a portion of the eastern border with Idaho is the Snake River. The rivers allow Oregon to profit from a wide variety of business pursuits, including manufacturing, shipping, and hydroelectricity production. Finally, tourism has become an increasingly important factor in the Oregon economy as the state is favored with some of the most spectacular scenery in the West.

Despite the Oregon economy's declining reliance on forest products, the timber industry continued to provide jobs and substantial tax revenues through the end of the twentieth century. The strength of the timber industry continues to be cyclical in nature: among the most relevant measures of the condition of Oregon's economy is the state of the national housing market. When housing starts nationwide decrease, timber industry layoffs usually follow. In more recent times, the vitality of the timber industry has been increasingly tied to trade with Pacific Rim markets. Though fishing remains an important industry for many coastal towns, it is less important to the cities along the Columbia, especially as salmon runs have declined in recent years due to both overfishing and the dangers posed to fish by dams and hydroelectric plants. The importance of agriculture to the economy is also less than it was fifty years ago, as attested to by the state's diminishing farm population. Numbering about 65,000 in 2000, Oregon only had half the population on the farm that it had in 1960. At century's end, the Oregon economy was less dependent on farming and timber due mostly to the diversified business growth of Portland (Multnomah County) and the surrounding metropolitan area (see map 11.1). Major companies headquartered in the Portland area include Nike (athletic shoes and apparel), Hyundai (automobiles), Fred Meyer (retail food stores and pharmacies), and Tektronix (high technology) as well as regional operations for other high-tech firms such as Hewlett-Packard, Intel, and Sony.

Though Portland is an important commercial center in the Pacific Northwest, it is viewed as the region's second city behind Seattle, Washington. Seattle receives nationwide attention and acclaim for its success in both attracting and retaining major businesses and for providing a high quality of life to residents. Portland is less visible to people in other parts of the country, perhaps because it is often overlooked by business trade journals and popular magazines trumpeting the virtues of setting up shop and living in the Northwest. But data on Portland's population growth provide ample evidence of its popularity as a place of residence and location for businesses.

One cannot understand Portland's present vitality with the same paradigm used to study declining Rust Belt locations such as Chicago, Cleveland, Buffalo, or Detroit. In 1970, Portland was home to 382,000 people. By 2000, the population had grown to 529,100 people, an increase of about 39 percent. Migration figures suggest that about

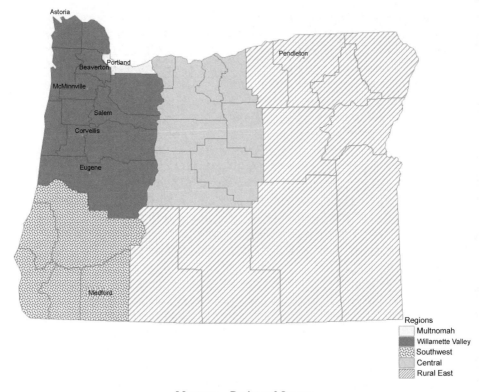

Map 11.1.   Regions of Oregon

10 percent of Portland's 1990 population had moved to the city from other Oregon counties between 1985 and 1990. Why has Portland attracted so many locals? A 1975 survey sought to determine Oregon residents' perceptions of the quality of life in their state (Mason, Faulkenberry, and Seidler 1975). These researchers concluded that in-migration from other parts of the state would continue because the Portland area provided better educational and economic opportunities (7). For many Oregonians, the road to Portland has become the path to upward mobility.

The desire for better life opportunities also motivates many non-Oregonians to leave their roots behind and incur the emotional and financial costs of migration. Twelve percent of Portland's residents had emigrated to the city from other states in the five years prior to the 1990 census. The vast majority of interstate migrants (67.7 percent) moved to Portland from other Western states. The South contributed the next largest proportion (13.6 percent) of new residents. Certainly, the prospect of greater prosperity Portland offered has played a primary role in both intra- and interstate migrants' decisions to move there, but the city's appeal cannot be couched solely in economic terms. Simply put, Portland is a city that many people are happy to call home.

Though a diversified local economy has undoubtedly been important to Portland's population growth, at least two other factors have also contributed to the city's good fortune. Farsighted city planners addressed growth concerns long before environmentally conscious urban planning was commonplace, and, because Portland's black population has remained so small, it never experienced the racial tension that cities in the Midwest and Northeast confronted. Large-scale flight to the suburbs by whites seeking to avoid integrated neighborhoods and schools never took place.

In 1973, the Oregon Legislature passed a law requiring cities and counties to plan and zone in accordance with uniform, statewide standards (Rohse 1987, 1–10). Portland, however, had been concerned with the direction of its future growth for many years prior to the enactment of the law (MacColl 1979; Abbott 1983). Though the city was haphazardly developed during the first half of the century, especially during a period of growth when several wartime industries located there, planners in the late 1960s and 1970s sought to revitalize the downtown business district, making it accessible to residents in other parts of the city and remaking it into an area that "recaptured the vitality of the streetcar era" (Abbott 1983, 227–28). Portland's successful planning was due in part to its management by city leaders who could "weave disparate ideas into a coherent strategy that mobilized a variety of constituencies. Environmental activists, good government reformers, neighborhood organizations, and the downtown establishment could support at least some parts of [the mayor's] planning package" (273). The city's attractive downtown district, numerous greenbelts and parks, and sense of community spirit serve it well as it competes with the suburbs for residents.

Reflecting the racial homogeneity of Oregon as a whole, Portland has historically been home to few minorities. If there is strength in numbers, then there is probably vulnerability in scantiness. The black population is not a major political bloc in Portland as in many other large cities and thus has endured the kinds of hardships generally suffered by powerless minorities: "With the lowest percentage (2.1) of any West Coast city, Portland's [black population] rarely entered the consciousness of Portland's business and political leaders except when problems arose that related to public accommodations and residential districts" (MacColl 1979, 268; see Abbott 1983, 165). The Ku Klux Klan played a strong role in city and state politics in the 1920s, though in Oregon most of the group's venom was reserved for Catholics rather than blacks who composed an insignificant portion (less than one-third of 1 percent) of the state's population (MacColl 1979, 162–72). By 1950, over half of the city's black population was concentrated in just two census tracts, and several schools had become predominantly black (659–60). Following the Supreme Court's school desegregation order, Portland schools were integrated, but the black population was still insufficiently large to stimulate panic among white residents. Census figures from the early 1980s showed that blacks were still largely concentrated in the same neighborhoods they had occupied for decades, but also indicated that black families had slowly started moving into middle-class neighborhoods in both Portland and its suburbs (Abbott 1983, 26).

Although blacks constituted only 7 percent of Portland's population in 2000, it is inaccurate to conclude that Portland is not attracting a diverse citizenry. Large numbers of Asian immigrants are moving to the area. In 1980, residents of Asian descent composed 2.9 percent of the city's population. The proportion of Asians living in Portland more than doubled by 2000, reaching 6.5 percent. The real population growth and influence of Asian immigrants is seen in the greater metropolitan area, where they comprise a steadily rising percentage of local county populations: 2.4 percent in Clackamas, 5.7 percent in Multnomah, and 6.7 percent in Washington.

In many Western states, a single city has been the sole beneficiary of growth, and sectional jealousies emerge between natives in outlying regions and newcomers in the state's major metropolitan area. However, Portland has neither been the sole beneficiary of growth in Oregon nor has it incurred the virulent sectional jealousies that often accompany one area's rapid growth and heightened prosperity. Suburban cities Beaverton (Clackamas County) and Lake Oswego (Washington County) have also grown, both economically and in population.

Washington was the state's fastest-growing county in the 1990s, its population increasing by one-third.

Local economies of areas south of the Portland metropolitan area continue to depend upon forest products and agriculture, although steps are being taken to diversify these counties' economic bases. The Willamette Valley includes the land that lies between the Pacific coast and the western front of the Cascades. The Valley contains the state's second largest city, Eugene (Lane County), and the state capital, Salem (Marion County). About 70 percent of the state's population lives in the Willamette Valley (including Portland). This region was the destination of many farmers who traveled the Oregon Trail and is now where the vast majority of Oregon's productive farms are located: vegetables, berries, hops, and Christmas trees are major cash crops. Education and government employment are especially important to cities in this region: 9.8 percent of Marion County's labor force worked in public administration in 1990, compared to 4.1 percent for the state; the University of Oregon's influence in Lane County is evidenced by the fact that one worker in ten is employed in education, compared to 8 percent for the rest of Oregon. High technology and manufacturing are gaining prominence: both Hyundai and Sony have recently located regional plants in Lane County.

The Coast relies upon fishing, agricultural, timber, and tourism-based economies. Newport (Lincoln County), Coos Bay (Coos County), and Astoria (Clatsop County) remain especially dependant upon tourism (map 11.1). Tillamook County is renowned for its cheeses and dairy products. Astoria's rugged coastal backdrop has made it the setting for a number of major film productions including *The Goonies* and *Kindergarten Cop*. Although overshadowed by the major shipping terminals at Portland, Astoria is an important port town in its own right by virtue of its location where the Columbia River meets the Pacific Ocean. Timber was still important in the early 2000s but attracted fewer workers than in the past because of the industry's cyclical nature and declining wages. Oregon was never known as a haven for any one particular white ethnic population. Astoria, however, is home to a large concentration of ethnic Finns, their ancestors having been "drawn to the town because of the fishing and sailing, the shipbuilding and lumbering, pursuits to which they were accustomed in the old country" (Federal Writers' Project 1940, 78).

Finnish immigrants at Astoria were well-known for their radical political views. Their pre-immigration experiences with cooperative associations in Finland, combined with the fact that they were more readily accepted and assimilated into American society than immigrants from southern and eastern Europe, emboldened them to complain against perceived social ills and "predisposed Finnish-Americans to accept socialist thought" (Hummasti 1979, 27; see chap. 1). This radical heritage left a lasting imprint. Through the final decades of the twentieth century, the northwestern counties remained the most liberal and Democratic part of the state.

Oregon's southern coastal counties suffer severely depressed economies: unemployment rates are often double or triple the national average, and the majority of young people must leave to find work. Medford-Ashland (Jackson County) and Klamath Falls-Altamont (Klamath County) round out the list of the state's most populous cities (see map 11.1). Here, too, lumber and agriculture are mainstays of local economies, but health care, manufacturing, and tourism are important as well. Southern Oregon enjoys a booming tourist industry generated in large part by the area's proximity to California: the distances separating Medford and Portland (272 miles) and Medford and Sacramento (310 miles) are similar. Natives resentfully perceive southern Oregon as having become a vacation haven for Californians who find that campgrounds and natural spaces in their home state have become too congested (Peirce 1972b, 189, 195). Crater Lake National Park is a major regional tourist destination, drawing approximately 500,000 visitors each year.

Central Oregon lies to the east of the Cascades, but the region's counties are distinguishable from those that make up eastern Oregon. Agriculture is the primary component of local economies in the north-central counties lining the Columbia River. Hood River (Hood River County) and The Dalles (Wasco County) are home to numerous cherry, apple, and pear orchards, and wheat farming and livestock ranching are common. The heart of Oregon includes Jefferson, Wheeler, and Crook Counties, where farmers grow peppermint, cereal grains, and hay.

Like Portland, The Dalles has benefited from its location on the Columbia. It is home to one of four U.S. Army Corps of Engineers dams that convert this river's water into hydroelectricity vital to the Northwest and California. Because of the availability of water and cheap electricity, a large aluminum plant operates in the city. Bend (Deschutes County) also relies on agriculture and lumber, but is growing increasingly dependent upon tourism. Its location near Mount Bachelor Ski Area and the Three Sisters Wilderness Area makes it a popular tourist destination.

The rest of the state is summarily lumped together as eastern Oregon (see map 11.1). Lightly populated, even desolate, this portion of the state has more in common with adjacent areas in neighboring states than with western Oregon, and it often is derided or simply dismissed as empty and unimportant by western Oregonians. Pendleton (Umatilla County), a major agricultural trade center, is the largest city in the northeastern counties and is well-known throughout the West for its annual rodeo, the Pendleton Roundup. Many tourists stop to visit a large Native American–operated casino that is located near town, and hunters stock up on supplies before heading out to the remote wilderness in search of their prizes. Ontario (Malheur County) serves as the agricultural hub and trade center for the southeastern counties. All of Oregon, with the exception of Malheur County, lies within the Pacific Time Zone: most of Malheur is located in the Mountain Time Zone, evidence of the county's economic and cultural ties to nearby Boise, Idaho. Livestock ranching and agriculture are mainstays of eastern Oregon's economy. Ninety-four percent of Malheur County was rangeland in the early 2000s, which makes cattle and sheep ranching profitable. Basques from the Pyrenees mountain region along the French-Spanish border immigrated to Idaho, Nevada, and southeastern Oregon in the late 1800s. Many Basques had been shepherds in their homeland, so they were ideally suited to oversee and care for the local sheep owners' flocks that grazed in the mountains and on the range. Though Basques were a minuscule immigrant group nationally, they remain a visible part of the population in southeastern Oregon and southwestern Idaho even now. Modern Basque Americans strive to protect and promote their culture, often appearing in costume and performing traditional dances at public events throughout the West. Eastern Oregon has not experienced the growth characteristic of the westernmost counties. This dry ranch land is stable and homogeneous: few people move in, but relatively few leave either. This stability has influenced the area's politics.

Map 11.2 illustrates Oregon's political sections at the time of the New Deal realignment. Oregon had a long-standing reputation as a

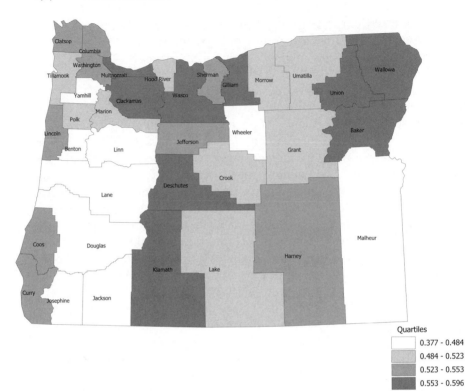

Map 11.2.   Average Democratic percentage of the presidential vote, 1928–1936

Republican stronghold, at one time saddled with the nickname "the Vermont of the West," which was supposedly reflective of the state's heavy settlement by Republican New England migrants (Peirce 1972b, 198; Seligman 1959; Swarthout and Gervais 1969, 301). The most staunchly Republican territory lay where agriculture was king: the counties south of Portland in the Willamette Valley and Malheur and Wheeler Counties east of the Cascades. Democrats ran strongest in and around Portland, in central Oregon, and in the rural northeast. The common thread among the Democratic counties was their lesser reliance upon agriculture, the influence of labor unions, and the counties' potential to benefit from federal spending on the construction of dams and other public works.

Oregon's political geography had changed only slightly by the

1950s. Oregon Democrats, wracked by the internal division between New Deal progressives and hard-line conservatives, had been unable to seize the opportunity to expand their political base presented by the Great Depression (Burton 1970, 61–89; Seligman 1959). Roosevelt victories had helped build Democratic party registration, but this registration did not automatically translate into Democratic success in local elections until the late 1950s when the New Deal generation of candidates took control of Democratic party machinery (Seligman 1959; Burton 1970; Gimpel 1996; Sundquist 1983). Republicanism maintained a foothold in the upper Willamette Valley, outside Portland, while the lower Valley, particularly around Eugene (Lane County), drifted toward the Democrats. Democrats continued to fare best in Portland, the northwestern and northeastern counties, along with Coos County in the south and Crook County in central Oregon. Despite their proximity to Portland, suburban Washington and Clackamas Counties supported Eisenhower and Nixon (in 1960). Republican presidential candidates regularly won the state, but not always by overwhelming margins. Eisenhower won 60.5 percent of the vote in 1952 and 55.2 percent in 1956, and Nixon took 52.6 percent in 1960. In spite of this string of GOP victories, the Republicans' hold on the Oregon electorate was eroding. Democrats began to win state offices in 1956 and made steady gains in subsequent elections.

Oregon's turn toward the Democratic party was preceded by an influx of blue-collar migrants from other states who had come to work in the timber industry (Swarthout 1957, 145). The suburbanization of the nation (discussed in other chapters) fueled a continual demand for lumber between 1945 and 1970. Oregon would come to supply much of the wood that found its way into houses from Long Island, New York, to Orange County, California. At the same time, Oregon natives began to lose enthusiasm for the GOP during the 1950s and 1960s. The Eisenhower administration was not as enthusiastic about federal spending on public works as the previous Democratic administrations had been. When the Eisenhower administration scaled back some planned projects on the Snake River (Idaho-Oregon border), residents of Wallowa County, one of the most Republican counties in the state, voted against the entire GOP slate in 1956 (Swarthout 1957, 146).

Between 1965 and 2000, Oregon's politics changed dramatically. The timber industry declined after the suburban housing boom slowed down in the mid-1970s. Grassroots environmental protection movements alerted Oregonians to the potential hazards of deforestation, overdevelopment, and the misuse of water resources. Legions of new residents to the state imported political views and identities that accelerated political change in Portland and the Willamette Valley. By the 1990s, Oregon politics was characterized by an east-west cleavage. Democratic support was clearly concentrated in western Oregon along the Coast, in the upper Willamette Valley, and in the Portland area. Republican support was strongest in central, eastern, and southern Oregon. Democratic strength was greatest in areas where rapid population growth had occurred, while Republicans fared best where population growth was stagnant or declining.

Notably, the suburban Portland counties were not significantly less Democratic than Multnomah County in the 1988–2000 presidential elections, averaged in map 11.3. Throughout this book, we have observed that Democratic central cities are usually surrounded by Republican counties, which is generally indicative of white flight to the suburbs. This pattern is not characteristic of Portland: in 2000, whites still composed 77 percent of the city's population. It is also surprising that none of the metropolitan counties had a Republican political bent. Given the area's diversified economic base, we might expect that in the Portland area, the decision to live in the suburbs was class-based rather than race-based. To be sure, there are several affluent enclaves in Clackamas and Washington Counties that are home to loyal Republicans: as we shall see, the Oregon GOP depends upon the Portland metropolitan area for a large percentage of its statewide vote. Even so, by the 1980s, the Portland suburbs could not be relied upon to give Republicans regular majorities.

Where Are the Votes in Oregon? Republican and Democratic Mobilization Targets

Oregon's disposition toward citizen governance through use of both the initiative and the referendum, as well as its penchant for third-party support, make the state's voters rather enigmatic to observers accustomed to the mundane regularity of Eastern and Midwestern states (Gimpel 1996; Barnett 1915; LaPalombara 1950; Mason 1994, 24–49). Though large numbers of Oregonians are registered under one of the major party labels, party loyalty means less in Oregon than in other states. Oregonians pride themselves on their ability and will-

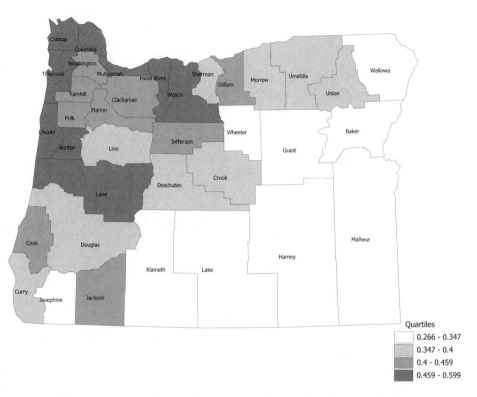

Quartiles
	0.266 - 0.347
	0.347 - 0.4
	0.4 - 0.459
	0.459 - 0.599

Map 11.3.   Average Democratic percentage of the presidential vote, 1988–2000

ingness to weigh issues carefully and to elect candidates they believe are likely to steer the state along a steady course (see Peirce 1972b, 197–202). Even in the 1960s, before ticket splitting was commonplace, Oregon voters were singled out for their willingness to ignore their party identification, electing candidates with contrary views to the highest state and federal offices (Gimpel 1996; Swarthout and Gervais 1969, 323). An inclination to discount party identification explains why Republicans Mark Hatfield and Robert Packwood enjoyed long tenure as Oregon's U.S. senators (Hatfield from 1967 to 1997, and Packwood from 1969 to 1995) despite a statewide majority of Democratic-registered voters.

The challenge for Oregon's Democrats is not only to mobilize potential voters but to retain party-registered voters. Interest in elections is high in Oregon partly as a result of that state's relatively frequent use of the referendum, and voter turnout is consistently among the highest in the nation. We have already noted that in recent elections the most heavily Democratic counties are located in western Oregon both along the coast and in the Willamette Valley. Since nearly three-fourths of the state's population resides in this area, Oregon's Democratic party has a vested interest in exploiting its ability to reach a majority of its voter base in just a few media markets. Republicans do not enjoy the benefits of such voter concentration: Republicans do well in the sparsely populated eastern counties, and reaching voters there requires more time, effort, and money.

The rank ordering of counties by their importance to the two major political parties reveals no surprises. Democrats receive over a quarter of their statewide presidential vote from Multnomah County alone, and when including adjacent Clackamas and Washington Counties, nearly half the votes cast for Democrats in the combined 1988–2000 presidential elections came from the Portland metropolitan area (see map 11.4). The full import of voter concentration is realized when we summed the percentage of the vote contributed by the top five Democratic counties: along with the 47 percent of statewide votes cast from the metropolitan Portland area, Lane County (Eugene) contributed 11 percent of the statewide Democratic vote, and Marion County (Salem) bestowed another 7 percent. In sum, just five counties provided almost two-thirds (65 percent) of the Democratic vote.

TABLE 11.1.   Oregon's Top Ten Strongest Counties for Republicans and Democrats in the 1988–2000 Presidential Contests

Rank	Democratic	Republican
1	Multnomah (Portland)	Washington (Hillsboro)
2	Lane (Eugene)	Clackamas (Oregon City)
3	Washington (Hillsboro)	Multnomah (Portland)
4	Clackamas (Oregon City)	Marion (Salem)
5	Marion (Salem)	Lane (Eugene)
6	Jackson (Medford)	Jackson (Medford)
7	Benton (Corvallis)	Douglas (Roseburg)
8	Deschutes (Bend)	Deschutes (Bend)
9	Linn (Albany)	Linn (Albany)
10	Coos (Coquille)	Josephine (Grants Pass)
% of total vote	82.2	76.9

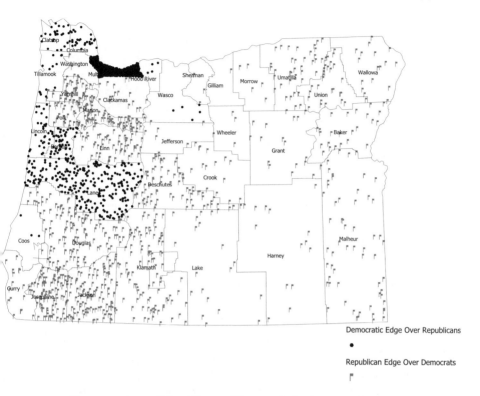

Democratic Edge Over Republicans

•

Republican Edge Over Democrats

Map 11.4.   Areas of Republican and Democratic dominance, 1988–2000

Although Oregon's electorate was more geographically dispersed at the end of the twentieth century than it was at the beginning, the Democrats have been able to count on Multnomah County for a long time. In the 1930s, Portland cast 40 percent of the state's Democratic votes. Even so, Portland was once a city that was equally divided between the parties, where Republicans could count on mobilizing one out of three of their own voters. With suburban growth, however, many of the GOP voters abandoned the city to the Democrats. On the strength of their calls for environmental protection, Democrats successfully contested elections in the Portland suburbs throughout the second half of the century. Nevertheless, we do see a trend toward greater political balkanization in Oregon, as the parties have developed separate geographical bases. Democrats have seen rapid growth in the I-5 corridor between Portland and Eugene. The Republicans' once-firm grip on this territory has been weakening, and in the decades since 1970 their most impressive gains (in percentage terms) have come in the rural reaches of southern and eastern Oregon.

The upshot of our analysis is that Republicans have had an increasingly uphill mobilization battle. The counties where GOP candidates ran strongest in the 1988–2000 presidential elections contained only 7 percent of Oregon's population (see map 11.4). Thus, the party necessarily must focus its attention on areas other than in eastern Oregon. The Republicans' five most important counties are the same as the Democrats', differing only in order of significance. For Republicans to achieve maximum reward for their mobilization efforts and maximum return on their media advertising dollars, they must dredge enemy waters. The new reality of Oregon electoral politics is that the major battleground is in the Willamette Valley. Democrats remain heavily advantaged, however, because they can focus all of their efforts in the Valley, while Republicans must seek support in the rest of the state.

Oregon's Changing Electoral Foundations

Several forces may work to induce change in the party predominantly favored by a state's voters. Partisan changes may occur as a result of the conversion or mobilization of voters during a time of national turmoil, as occurred in the years following the Great Depression. Blame for hardship conditions resulting from the 1929 national economic crisis was placed at the feet of the Republican party, who at the time controlled Congress and the White House. The nation's dire straits activated countless numbers of citizens who had never voted prior to the Depression, and they overwhelmingly supported the Democratic party (Andersen 1979). At the same time, many Republicans turned a cold shoulder to their party, investing their confidence in Roosevelt's promises of economic renewal instead (Sundquist 1983; Ladd and Hadley 1975).

Though the mobilization and conversion brought about by the Depression were quite important, enduring electoral realignments are not always precipitated by cataclysmic political events. The most common sources of partisan change work subtly over time. Mortality plays a quiet but certain role in producing partisan change: each age cohort is politically socialized in a context different from previous cohorts, and its members draw from different experiences to form their political values. As cohort members age and eventually pass away, their contributions to the electorate's marketplace of ideas are lost; in their places come younger voters who possess dissimilar issue concerns and party loyalties. Studying population mobility is also increasingly important to an informed understanding of modern American politics: this society is more mobile than any other in the world, and many people undertake several different jobs in several different locations over the course of their lifetimes rather than settling into a long-term career in a single place. Partisan change in Oregon has been fueled by all of these factors.

Conversion

Both conversion and mobilization of the electorate played roles in effecting partisan change in Oregon. Even during the early years of the Great Depression, Oregon voters were registered with the Republican party at a ratio of almost two to one. As in other states, Franklin D. Roosevelt's 1932 bid for the presidency spurred many previously inactive members of the electorate to vote and induced many active Republicans to switch their party affiliations. The election year 1936 was a watershed for Oregon Democrats: their proportion of the state's registered voters jumped 13.5 percentage points between the 1932 and 1936 presidential election years, accompanied by a corresponding 12.9 point decrease in Republican registration. Republicans maintained a slight edge in registration until 1956; by 1960, 53 percent of Oregon's voters were registered Democratic, enough to give the party an 8 percentage point registration advantage over the GOP.

The 1960s brought considerable electoral upheaval to the nation, as Republicans moved to the right on civil rights matters, and black voters fully mobilized within the ranks of the Democratic party (Sundquist 1983, 408). Goldwater's conservatism won over many Southern Democrats, while liberal Republicans felt left behind by their party's shift to the right. It is not clear to what extent these events touched the Oregon electorate (see table 11.2 for Democrats' voting blocs). Robert F. Kennedy claimed that he lost the Oregon Democratic primary to Hubert Humphrey in 1968 because there were not enough poor and black people in the state. At only 1 percent of the population at the time Kennedy was running, African Americans were hardly an important voting bloc. And if it was their mobilization and subsequent influence on the Democratic party that fueled many whites to leave, perhaps their small numbers in Oregon made the Goldwater and Wallace candidacies inconsequential.

To find the extent to which conversion was an Oregon phenomenon in the 1930s and 1960s, we estimated voter transition models to evaluate voter loyalty from election to election. In table 11.3, we estimated the percentage of Republican (Democratic) voters in 1928 that voted Republican (Democratic) in 1932. We follow those estimates up with comparisons of voter loyalty across other pairs of elections in the 1930s and 1960s.

In the 1930s, our results indicate that Republicans were major defectors between 1928 and 1932. Only an estimated 41 percent of

TABLE 11.2.   **Estimates of the Democratic Percentage of the Presidential Vote for Various Electoral Groups in Oregon, 1928–2000 (ecological inference maximum likelihood)**

Pooled Presidential Election Years	Blacks/ Nonblacks		Elderly/ Nonelderly		Immigrants/ Nonimmigrants		Farmers/ Nonfarmers		Whites/ Nonwhites	
1928, 1932	68.8	46.1*	49.7	45.9*	48.5	45.9*	44.3*	46.7*	46.0*	57.5
1936, 1940, 1944	57.3	56.4*	2.8	61.4*	56.7	56.4*	45.3*	59.8*	56.5*	49.6
1948, 1952	50.1	42.4*	53.8	41.2*	81.9	40.0*	34.1*	43.8*	42.2*	47.0
1956, 1960, 1964	52.8	51.8*	35.7	53.7*	41.0	52.3*	41.7*	52.7*	52.1*	36.8
1968, 1972	86.1	42.2*	57.5	41.0*	91.8	41.2*	35.4*	43.2*	42.9*	39.1
1976, 1980, 1984	85.1	42.7*	53.0	42.7*	82.4	41.7*	16.6	44.2*	44.0*	31.5
1988, 1992	64.6	46.3*	56.9	45.0*	68.5	45.7*	43.7	46.8*	46.8*	48.2
1996, 2000	54.0	46.9*	51.3	46.3*	50.0	46.8*	15.8	48.0*	45.3*	66.5

	Mfg. Workers/ Non Mfg. Workers		College Educated/ Non College Educated		Native to State/ Nonnative		Internal Migrants/ Nonmigrants		Hispanics/ Non- Hispanics	
1928, 1932	—	—	—	—	—	—	—	—	—	—
1936, 1940, 1944	—	—	—	—	—	—	—	—	—	—
1948, 1952	50.0*	40.2*	24.9	45.5*	—	—	—	—	—	—
1956, 1960, 1964	63.7*	48.5*	28.1	54.2*	67.1*	37.9*	35.6*	66.9*	—	—
1968, 1972	64.9*	36.7*	37.2	43.5*	40.2*	44.9*	38.2*	47.6*	—	—
1976, 1980, 1984	70.7	37.4*	53.1	42.0*	41.6*	44.7*	44.0*	42.6*	7.0	44.2*
1988, 1992	49.0	46.2*	56.6	44.1*	37.4*	54.8*	48.0*	45.5*	45.8	46.7*
1996, 2000	44.4	47.5*	46.6	47.1*	58.3*	37.4*	39.8*	54.0*	34.7	47.6*

Note: Cell entries show the estimated percentage voting Democratic in the presidential elections listed on each row. Complete variable definitions and results from the ecological inference estimation appear in appendix B, with standard errors and bounds.

*Reflect estimates with lower and upper bounds narrower than 0,1.

TABLE 11.3. Estimates of Party Loyalty and Conversion across Presidential Elections in Oregon (ecological inference maximum likelihood)

Presidential Election Years	Voted Democratic 1928/Non-Democratic 1928	Voted Democratic 1932/Non-Democratic 1932	Presidential Election Years	Voted Republican 1928/Non-Republican 1928	Voted Republican 1932/Non-Republican 1932
Voted Democratic 1932	91.6* 40.9*		Voted Republican 1932	41.4* 28.3*	
Voted Democratic 1936		72.9* 52.8*	Voted Republican 1936		65.9* 8.5*

Presidential Election Years	Voted Democratic 1960/Non-Democratic 1960	Voted Democratic 1964/Non-Democratic 1964	Presidential Election Years	Voted Republican 1960/Non-Republican 1960	Voted Republican 1964/Non-Republican 1964
Voted Democratic 1964	89.2* 40.8*		Voted Republican 1964	59.1* 10.3*	
Voted Democratic 1968		60.1* 14.9*	Voted Republican 1968		48.9* 50.5*
Voted Wallace 1968		4.0* 10.1*	Voted Wallace 1968		4.9* 6.9*

Note: Cell entries show the estimated percentage voting Democratic, Republican, or for George Wallace in the presidential elections listed on each row who voted Democratic (or Republican) in the previous election. Complete variable definitions and results from the ecological inference estimation appear in appendix C, with standard errors and bounds.

*Reflect estimates with lower and upper bounds narrower than 0,1.

Hoover's supporters in 1928 voted for him again in 1932—comparable to our estimates for Maryland (chap. 10). By contrast, Democrats were as loyal across this period as they were in many other states. From 1932 to 1936, however, Roosevelt lost considerable support. Only an estimated 73 percent of Roosevelt's initial supporters returned to him in the second election—a much lower percentage than in California, New York, or Illinois. This is somewhat surprising given that Roosevelt won more decisively in Oregon in 1936 than he had in 1932. Apparently, though, Roosevelt's losses between 1932 and 1936 were much smaller than his gains. On the Republican side, Alf Landon lost many Hoover voters while making few converts among Democrats (table 11.3). Given that there were far more Republican registrants than Democrats in Oregon at the time, Landon's GOP defectors were a much larger bloc than the few that Roosevelt lost.

In the 1960s, Oregon and California exhibited similar patterns of political support from 1960 to 1964. In Oregon, about 89 percent of Kennedy voters supported Johnson but only 60 percent of Nixon's (1960) supporters remained loyal to Barry Goldwater. Nelson Rockefeller had won the 1964 primary in Oregon, while Goldwater came in third. In the general elections, the Goldwater campaign stirred up considerable controversy among Oregon Republicans, causing key defections among GOP business leaders in Portland who went on to support the Johnson campaign (Balmer 1965).

In both California and Oregon, Johnson voters were troubled by Hubert Humphrey in 1968—only about 60 percent remained loyal. On the GOP side, however, Oregonians who had voted for Goldwater had a much more difficult time supporting Nixon in 1968 than Californians did. Nixon's victory in Oregon came from about equal shares of both Goldwater and Johnson supporters. Wallace's support in 1968 was slightly more likely to come from Goldwater than Johnson supporters, although the Alabama governor was not widely popular. Oregon's Wallace voters went on to cast most of their ballots for Nixon in 1972. The difficulty Goldwater voters had in throwing their support to Nixon in 1968 foretold the coming of factionalism within the Republican party as the conservative wing arose to challenge the established liberal tradition of the party. Moderates such as Bob Packwood and Mark Hatfield would continue to serve in the Senate until the 1990s, but they were eventually replaced by a conservative Republican, Gordon Smith, and a liberal Democrat, Ron Wyden.

We looked for other signs of conversion among the voting blocs we examined in table 11.2. At the beginning of the twentieth century, many Oregon farmers felt as though the state legislature was turning a deaf ear to agricultural concerns. In response, farmers collectively formed the Oregon Grange, a political and social organization that soon came to possess considerable political clout and was influential in bringing about the passage of laws favorable to agricultural interests (Woodell 1936). The Grange worked to ensure that farmers' interests in matters of taxation, liquor control, road building, and public utilities were represented at the state capital, and the organization played an important role in the institutionalization of the initiative, referendum, and recall powers (Woodell 1936, 57). In the 1930s, the Grange teamed up with organized labor to form part of the Democratic electoral coalition that helped Roosevelt win majorities through 1944 (Seligman 1959).

Farmers turned away from the Democrats, however, in the 1960s, when agrarians perceived the party to be moving away from its agriculturally inclusive base to a more urban-oriented platform. Our estimates in table 11.2 pinpoint the switch to have taken place in the 1968–72 elections, where an estimated 35.4 percent of farmers supported Humphrey and McGovern, compared with 43.2 percent of those in other occupations. Of course these figures also reflect the urbanization of the state and the Democrats who were moving in to make Portland the big city that it is today. In subsequent elections, the gulf between the farm and nonfarm population has widened, consistent with the state's increasing sectionalism. The loss of the farm vote has hardly hurt the Democratic party; moving from a rural and small town base of support to the larger cities and suburbs helped the Democrats shake off their minority status.

In some states we have found some inferential support for conversion by examining the changing loyalties of blue-collar workers. Oregon's working-class population makes up a sizable proportion of the state's labor force. This is reflected in the prominence of the timber industry–related manufactures. Estimates show that blue-collar laborers have supported Democrats much more strongly than those employed in other fields. We see little evidence of conversion among this group. At the height of the national recession that severely affected the Oregon timber industry in the early 1980s, an estimated 71 percent of blue-collar workers voted for Democrats, compared with

37 percent of all other workers. Our estimates suggest that this disparity in support had disappeared by the late 1990s and that blue-collar workers were slightly more likely to vote Republican than those in other occupations.

More dramatic evidence of conversion is evident in the figures for Democratic support among the college educated. In the 1950s and 1960s, it is clear that the well educated are much more Republican than those with less than a four-year degree. But as a college education ceases to be an indicator of wealth, the GOP leaning of this population erodes. By the late 1970s, our estimates indicate that the college educated have moved toward the Democratic camp, almost equally dividing their vote between the candidates in the 1996–2000 presidential elections.

Republicans have apparently been squeezed from two ends. At one end, they have lost support among the well educated. At the same time, they have won only limited and fickle support among blue-collar laborers—a dwindling number of whom are working in timber-related industries. Their only convincing gains since mid-century have come among the state's farmers and ranchers, another shrinking sector of the labor force.

Population Mobility

The influx of new residents to Oregon altered established patterns of party support. The majority of the state's population growth occurred in western Oregon, which we believe to be chiefly responsible for turning Portland and the Willamette Valley into a Democratic stronghold. When we estimated the Democratic support among the migrant population, we discovered that migrants did not begin to contribute decisively to Democratic electoral strength until the 1970s. Table 11.2 shows that in the pooled 1956, 1960, and 1964 elections, an estimated 35.6 percent of new residents supported the Democratic candidate, compared with 66.7 percent of natives. Of course there were fewer natives than newcomers, so this explains why Republicans remained highly competitive in spite of the Democratic bias among natives. By the late 1980s, we see a reversal in party support, with 44 percent of internal migrants voting Democratic, compared with 42.6 percent of natives. In the 1996–2000 presidential races, the gap between natives and new residents moves in the other direction, with an estimated 54 percent of Oregon natives supporting Clinton and Gore, while 40 percent of new residents did. It is difficult to tease a trend from these data, but they do suggest that out-of-state migrants to Oregon have not always helped the GOP, as they have in other states.

Looking to the estimates for natives and nonnatives in table 11.2, we encounter similar results. In 1960, the difference between natives and internal migrants was highly significant, with natives casting a higher proportion of Democratic votes than newcomers. But by the late 1960s, a reversal had occurred, with natives moving toward the Republicans while migrants edged up the Democratic vote. This pattern continues until the 1996–2000 elections when we observe another stunning reversal, with an estimated 58 percent of natives voting Democratic, compared with 37 percent of newcomers, perhaps an artifact of Ralph Nader's strong showing among young, liberal transplants as the Green party's candidate in the 2000 contest. The upshot of these figures is that the internal migrant population did contribute to the rise of the Democratic party in the state between 1968 and the mid-1990s, but it is less certain how internal migration will reshape the electorate in the twenty-first century.

In 1960, about 48 percent of the state's population had moved in from somewhere else. According to our figures, slightly more than one out of three of these new arrivals was a Democratic voter. These family-age in-migrants, in turn, fueled generational change by having offspring who would enter the electorate voting Democratic. The in-migration stream also shifted between the 1950s and the 1980s. In the early years, a majority of Oregon newcomers had come from Midwestern states. By the late 1980s, most had moved in from somewhere else in the West—particularly California. The 1990 census revealed that 49 percent of the state's population had arrived from somewhere else, only this time about one in two of the newcomers supported Democratic presidential candidates. At the same time, natives—the other half of the state's population—were losing their ardor for Republicans, through the processes of generational replacement and conversion. The rise of Democratic dominance in recent presidential elections appears to be a function of both in-migration and generational political change among native Oregonians born as the offspring of previous waves of migrants. In this connection, it is noteworthy that the estimates for the 1996–2000 elections show that for the first time since the 1960s native Oregonians voted more Democratic than those born outside the state (see table 11.2).

The immigrant population in Oregon is small, and we were unable to estimate its voting behavior with any degree of confidence using county-level data. The concentration of this population in Oregon's northwestern counties has done nothing to erode the Democratic bias there, and it is likely that immigrants are socialized into the Democratic fold at these locations.

Generational Replacement

Generational replacement has been most prominent in eastern Oregon where the largely rural, agriculturally oriented population has remained relatively insulated from the growth experienced by the western portion of the state. Between the 1950s and the early twenty-first century, the extreme northeastern counties (Baker, Union, and Wallowa) were transformed from Democratic bastions to Republican strongholds, but population growth was minimal. During the same time, Democrats gained influence in the counties of the Willamette Valley south of Portland. The changes in countywide political support were facilitated by the generational replacement of two groups with distinct political interests: in the northeastern counties, the older voters were timber-industry union members that had benefited from the federal government's New Deal social spending programs and thus tended to be Democratic, while in the Willamette, the older members of the electorate were farmers who generally harbored Republican sympathies.

In estimating Democratic support among the state's elderly voters, we found that we could not generate reliable figures for this population because of severe aggregation bias in the data. We surmise that the GOP bias in the electorate was eroded in the postwar years partly through the death of older Republicans and their replacement with Democrats who had come of age during the Roosevelt years. Polls from the 1980s and 1990s, however, suggest that the benefits of generational replacement were working to the narrow advantage of Republicans. Exit polls from the 1996 presidential election indicated that 47 percent of those over age 65 identified as Democrats, compared with 37 percent of those aged 18–64. Al Gore won 52 percent of the vote among the aged population in 2000, compared with his 46 percent among those younger.

Activism and Partisanship of New Voters

Between 1930 and 1940, Oregon's population increased about 14 percent; between 1932 and 1942 (the New Deal presidential years), the total number of registered voters increased approximately 10 percent. Although it is possible that migrants settling in Oregon immediately (or soon after arriving) registered to vote, most research suggests that migrants are slow to become active (Squire, Wolfinger, and Glass 1987; Brown 1988, 26–27; Rosenstone and Wolfinger 1978). Because it is unlikely that the state's population increase alone accounted for the expansion of its electorate, we suspect that a mobilization of previously inactive Oregonians occurred (Andersen 1979). Data for the 1950s and 1960s, when the Depression was a fading memory, support this idea: between 1950 and 1960, Oregon's population swelled by about 16 percent, but between 1952 and 1962, the electorate grew by less than 4 percent. In other states, we know that much of the mobilization of the 1930s occurred among lower income groups, including ethnic minorities. In the 1950s and 1960s, the civil rights movement successfully mobilized black voters, mainly into the ranks of the Democratic party. Although the black population in Oregon is quite small, it is likely that the number of blacks voting increased during this era even though their influence remained minimal. Because the black population is negligible, we would not expect racial polarization to be as great in Oregon as it was in states with much larger black populations. The size of a population greatly enhances the perception of threat among outsiders, escalating ethnic conflict and tension (Olzak 1992; Blalock 1956). Reapportionment of the state legislature, for example, was not a controversial issue in Oregon as it was in states with sizable urban black populations—voters approved a constitutional amendment to reapportion as early as 1952.

It is difficult to examine racial polarization with county-level data in a state that has been as racially homogeneous as Oregon. In 1990, African Americans constituted just 1.6 percent of the state's population, and the vast majority of them (72.9 percent) resided in Portland. Because of severe aggregation bias in the county-level observations, we were unable to generate statistically significant estimates for

Democratic support among black voters.[1] Our estimates do indicate that, from the New Deal to the mid-1960s, black voters were more likely to vote Democratic than white voters. The gap in support widens with the 1968–72 elections, with black support for Democrats surging to 86 percent. By the late 1960s, Oregon blacks had followed the national movement toward the Democratic party. However, the 1968–72 elections did not see white Oregonians' support for Democrats drop precipitously, as had occurred in the South. White voters were apparently not alienated from the Democratic party as a result of black mobilization. White support for Democrats moved up again after 1972.

Conclusions

Previously, one of the present authors argued that Oregon's electoral volatility made it difficult to organize strong political party organizations—where candidates of the same party could work together to advance party goals (Gimpel 1996). But Oregon's electorate has become more predictable. Much of what made it difficult for candidates to locate reliable pockets of electoral support was that partisanship did not have a clear foundation in issues or ideology. Local matters, such as public power and government spending to promote public works, were of critical importance in many areas; the local electorate divided differently than the national electorate on such issues. In 1950, Republicans' attitudes on government and policy spanned a wide spectrum of liberal and conservative views. Democrats too were hobbled by internal strife between New Deal progressives and an old guard. By the early 1990s, however, the parties had largely resolved these conflicts and were highly polarized by ideology. Aided by the in-migration of eco-sensitive populations from California and other states, Democrats had taken over the liberal ground that Republicans had once occupied. Republicans moved in the conservative direction of their national party. Of course this cost Republicans their majority status and threatened to make Oregon a bastion of Democratic one-partyism at the dawn of the new century.

One might ask whether Oregon, in gaining ideological clarity, now has a foundation for cohesive, strong political parties (see Gimpel's 1996 argument in *National Elections and the Autonomy of American State Party Systems*). The answer is, Probably not. The state is dangerously close to tipping away from serious two-party competition, another prerequisite for strong organizations (Key 1949, 1956). Its highly migratory population—half of the state has moved in from elsewhere—hinders a candidate's efforts to predict what impact a voter registration drive will have on the partisan balance of a neighborhood or town, so candidates are not likely to engage in such traditional party functions.

While population mobility may continue to alter the political geography west of the Cascades, ideological polarization has produced a more stable geographic basis of party support than in the past. Democrats dominate in the Portland metropolitan area and in much of the Willamette Valley. The Republicans' most reliable foundation is in eastern Oregon. If Republicans are to have a chance of recapturing the governorship, they must make gains west of the Cascades, among new voters and natives. Given the prevailing liberalism of most of the Portland area counties, it is to the GOP's advantage to suppress the national party's ideological conservatism, taking a page out of the Hatfield handbook. Democrats, for their part, are pretty secure in their majority. Lacking a large ethnic minority population, racial and ethnic cleavages do not divide the Oregon Democrats as Democrats are often divided elsewhere. With a dwindling number of timber workers and union members each year, environmental activists dominate the agenda to an extent that they could not in 1960. The state's political future hinges, as it has for the last 150 years, on whether the almost constant stream of migrants to the Willamette Valley will register with the Republicans or the Democrats. Growth often outstrips economic opportunity, creating class stratification. With growth, new issues can emerge to divide electoral coalitions in unexpected ways. Vigilant Republicans may be able to take advantage of such crosscutting issues, but they will need to recover a local sensibility that is largely independent of national party alignment and movement.

Note

1. The reader may note the implausible estimate in table 11.2 for percentage of blacks voting Democratic in the 1996–2000 election. Because of severe aggregation bias in the Oregon data for this variable, this estimate cannot be trusted. However, we were able to derive a more plausible estimate after controlling for the percentage of the population with a college education (zb). With this control in place, Democratic voting among blacks jumped to 76 percent, compared with 46 percent for nonblacks.

CHAPTER 12

MICHIGAN

Major Forces for Electoral Change in Michigan
- Migration of Black Voters from the South and Border States
- Suburbanization of the Population
- Rise and Decline of Union Labor
- Decline of the Manufacturing Economy; Decentralization and Restructuring of Manufacturing
- Mobilization of the Black Population

Perhaps no state is more closely associated with Rust Belt decline than Michigan. This is because the state is known for heavy industry—most commonly the automobile industry, but also steel, lumber, and mining—none of which have escaped the pressures of economic globalization. Outsiders often discount it as a place to avoid if you are serious about finding work. Michigan's reputation as a postindustrial failure has been seriously overblown, however, as it possesses the most diverse economic base in the Midwest. The most significant economic development since the end of World War II has been the diffusion of industry from eastern Michigan into other parts of the state. By 2000, small, specialized manufacturing plants could be found in rural areas that were once tied only to farming and logging. The strategic decentralization of business enterprise served to undermine the growth and political cohesion of labor unions, much as it had in Ohio (Fenton 1966).

Michigan's reputation as a sinkhole for welfare payments and unemployment compensation dates to the mid-1970s when the energy crisis sent the American auto industry into a deep slump. The successful comeback in the 1980s put people permanently out of work because increased efficiency came at the cost of corporate consolidation, plant closings, and layoffs. While the auto industry now has facilities and spin-off companies in nearly every corner of the state, eastern Michigan, home to the major assembly plants, took these changes especially hard. In its industrial heyday, around 1960, Wayne County (Detroit and western suburbs) boasted nearly 400,000 manufacturing employees among its 2.7 million people. By the early 2000s, the number employed in manufacturing had dropped to 192,000 and the population to 2 million. Genesee County (Flint) is perhaps the most famous depressed location, and for good reason: employment in manufacturing has dropped by one-third since 1960, but the population has increased, meaning that more people depend on fewer and lower-paying jobs in the postindustrial economy.

Detroit's wealthier suburbs in Oakland and Macomb Counties (Royal Oak, Pontiac, Warren; see map 12.1) have doubled in size since midcentury, drawing the white, middle-income population out of Detroit and older suburbs such as Dearborn, while attracting upwardly mobile migrants from elsewhere. Detroit's northern suburbs are more than residential enclaves. Dearborn's population has become increasingly diverse as a large Arab-origin (Lebanese, Syrian, Palestinian, Egyptian) population emigrated to settle there in several waves, beginning just before World War I. Oakland County has become a huge employer with earnings that are comparable to those of the much larger Wayne County. The key to prosperity in the postindustrial economy is to attract the higher skill, better paying, service sector jobs, along with newer industries in technologically advanced fields. As in the Chicago area, Detroit's northern suburbs are attracting the lion's share of these jobs, and they have made a smoother transition to the new economy than the rest of eastern Michigan.

Western Michigan includes the state's second largest city, Grand Rapids (Kent County) as well as the smaller towns of Kalamazoo (Kalamazoo County), Battle Creek (Calhoun County), Holland (Ottawa County), and Muskegon (Muskegon County) (see map 12.1). Several of western Michigan's cities have established black populations dating from the Civil War era when they served as termini on the Underground Railroad. How well these towns have fared in the postindustrial age depends on how dependent they were on heavy industry at midcentury, how willing their residents were to move elsewhere when their jobs disappeared, and how well positioned they were in the state's transportation grid. Battle Creek, situated on Interstate 94, has fared well, gaining population from nearby rural areas

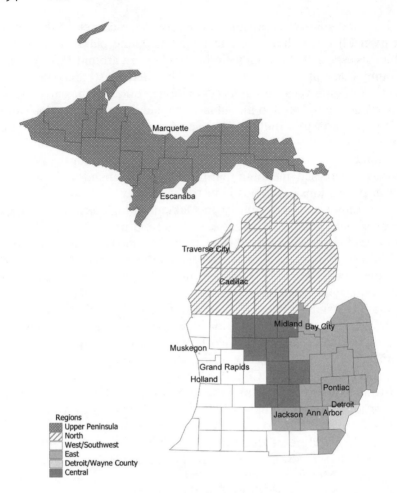

Map 12.1.   Regions of Michigan

and from ex-Detroiters looking for a better life. Food products companies such as Kellogg and Ralston-Purina have prospered even as manufacturing has declined and new companies have moved in because of Battle Creek's centrality to the Chicago and Detroit metropolitan areas. Muskegon, situated on Lake Michigan well to the north of the Chicago-to-Detroit thoroughfare, once employed 43 percent of its workforce in manufacturing, especially lumber and paper, but by the early 2000s only half that proportion was still in manufacturing jobs. After layoffs in the 1970s and 1980s, the city has made a comeback on the basis of tourism and the development of lakefront property. The city could be faring better, but few people wanted to leave when economic times went sour. By 2000, the city was only 12 percent smaller than it was in 1960, and it had one of the highest unemployment rates in the entire state.

Grand Rapids and Holland are best known for their large ethnic Dutch populations. The settlement of Holland by Dutch immigrants fleeing religious persecution dates to the 1840s. Holland became a virtual Dutch colony, and even today Dutch culture is obvious everywhere. The abundant waterways and forests made logging the major economic activity of the nineteenth century, and its natural extension was a thriving furniture and woodcraft industry. Furniture makers are fewer in number now, and only the smaller ones have remained in wood—the larger manufacturers have moved into metal and plastic modular office components. The settlements closer to Lake Michigan have benefited from a steady tourist and recreation business. Situated close to Lake Michigan, Holland has become a playground for the wealthy from Chicago and Grand Rapids. Summer cottages surround Lake Macatawa and dot the Lake Michigan shoreline.

With a black population of about 20 percent, Grand Rapids is more ethnically diverse than it has ever been, but its past is also influenced by Dutch immigration. Originally a lumber town conveniently located on the Grand River, new populations were drawn to the city after World War II with the growth of automobile manufacturing—Kent County was home to three General Motors plants still in operation by 2000. In spite of some population loss to the suburbs, Grand Rapids grew about 8 percent between 1960 and 2000, although its population is poorer and older than in the past. The schools have been integrated through busing since the late 1960s, but there is still a substantial middle-class population and a sophisticated parochial school system associated with the Christian Reformed Church operating within city limits. At the beginning of the new millennium locals can still accurately characterize Grand Rapids as a provincial, stable, conservative, Dick-and-Jane type community.

Northern Michigan can be divided into three parts: the Tri-cities area proximate to the Saginaw Bay (Saginaw, Bay City, and Midland), the rural north, and the Upper Peninsula—separated from the rest of Michigan by Lake Huron and Lake Michigan (see map 12.1). Bay City, overly dependent upon trade in lumber and shipbuilding, has been one of the most economically depressed cities in the state. Fortunately, out-migration has kept pace with the closing of sawmills as the city's population dropped from 53,000 in 1960 to 37,000 by 2000. Predictably, flight from Bay City has left an older and poorer population behind. Midland is home to the Dow Chemical Company, one of the state's largest employers, and is the most prosperous of the Tri-cities. Saginaw is the largest of the Tri-cities with an economic base in transportation, food processing, trade, metal foundries, and automobile manufacturing. Saginaw has lost population since the 1960s mainly due to General Motors downsizing.

Rural northern Michigan is not the usual combination of farms, treeless fields, and small agricultural trade centers one finds in other Midwestern states. Farm fields are mixed with forests, sawmills, resort areas, and abandoned mines. Due to the historical ties to lumber and mining, the towns support a much higher concentration of small manufacturing plants here than in other states. The rural economy also benefits from tourism along the lake shores. People come to northern Michigan for hunting, canoeing, and skiing. Whether the counties in northern Michigan have grown or declined in population is highly dependent upon how reliant they were on agriculture, mining, and lumber. Agriculture and forest products have fallen victim to corporate consolidation. Mining has declined due to international competition from places that are advantaged by lower production costs. Tourism and recreation have been the salvation of many of northern Michigan's small towns. Rising incomes in Grand Rapids, Lansing, and the Detroit suburbs have produced a demand for weekend recreation getaways and resorts. Where places have responded to this market, such as Traverse City, the population has more than doubled since midcentury.

Natives of the Upper Peninsula are affectionately known as Yoopers and are often the butt of jokes told by those from the lower peninsula. The UP has been economically depressed for decades, and its population is both shrinking and aging as younger people migrate elsewhere to find work, leaving an older and less skilled population behind. A number of large iron and copper mines attracted a diverse mix of Eastern European immigrants in the early 1900s. A low-grade iron ore called taconite was still being mined and shipped from Lake

Superior's ports in the early 2000s, but large-scale mining operations closed in the 1930s and 1940s. A few small sawmills and at least one large paper mill remain from a time when timber cutting was a major industry. Government employment and tourism were the growing economic sectors in the new century. Although the closure of Sawyer Air Force Base near Marquette (Marquette County) led to the departure of 5,500 military personnel, two of the major employers are the state prisons in Kinross (Chippewa County) and Marquette.

Map 12.2 illustrates Michigan's political regionalism at the time of the New Deal realignment. Michigan was known as a strongly Republican state during the first half of the twentieth century (Fenton 1966, 11; Pollock and Eldersveld 1942). In no county did Roosevelt muster more than 64 percent of the vote in 1932, indicating that Hoover remained far more competitive here than in many other states. Even so, the Depression led to a major collapse of the economy in Michigan's mining and manufacturing areas. Between 1929 and 1933, about 2,000 factories closed, leaving 34 percent fewer wage earners (Pollock and Eldersveld 1942, 48–49). The Upper Peninsula and eastern Michigan were the hardest hit. Relief rolls in the mining counties of the western part of the UP swelled to 43 percent in 1934. Where agriculture was strongest, the welfare burden was much lower—helping to explain why western Michigan was much less enthusiastic about the New Deal. The darkly shaded, strong Democratic counties in the 1930s included Genesee (Flint) and Wayne (Detroit) in eastern Michigan, the Tri-cities area (Bay, Saginaw Counties), and nearly the entire Upper Peninsula (see map 12.2).

The areas with manufacturing and mining jobs were most supportive of Roosevelt not primarily for his support of relief programs, but because he had a committed prolabor agenda. Without Roosevelt's National Labor Relations Act, the state's industrial workforce may have never won the right to organize and collectively bargain. Unfortunately, not long after the unionized miners in the UP won significant wage concessions through New Deal legislation, World War II ended and the profitability of mining declined sharply, leaving thousands out of work. Some of these workers found their way into the rapidly growing postwar boom in automobile manufacturing. Union labor, as represented by the United Auto Workers (UAW), was sufficiently strong by the late 1940s that it had taken over the state's Democratic party leadership.

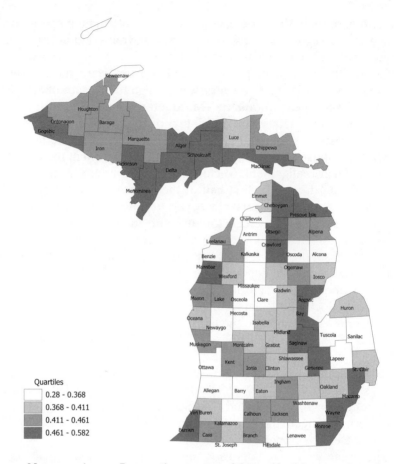

Map 12.2.   Average Democratic percentage of the presidential vote, 1928–1936

The more populous counties in western Michigan were tempted by Depression-induced economic conditions to vote for Roosevelt, but resisted more ably than the heavily industrialized east (Pollock and Eldersveld 1942). The most Republican counties were those with the most agricultural employment and those that had attracted the fewest recent immigrants. It was during the 1930s and 1940s that residents of these counties came to reflexively define their politics in opposition to eastern Michigan: if Detroiters favored it, it must be suspect. Notably, the political distance between eastern and western Michigan was more than just urban vs. rural, because many rural mining counties in northern Michigan voted the same way Wayne County did. Instead, the difference boiled down to agriculture vs. manufacturing, public assistance vs. relative self-sufficiency, and immigrant vs. native.

The New Deal resulted in a huge expansion of the Michigan electorate. Pollock and Eldersveld (1942) indicate that by 1940, participation had jumped by 41 percent over 1928 levels. A majority of these new participants were Democrats. With the growth of the UAW's membership in the 1930s and 1940s, eastern Michigan became the state's Democratic anchor. Wherever union labor was a significant presence, Democratic victories were secure. On the basis of the labor vote in eastern Michigan, Democrats were able to control the state's governorship from 1949 to 1963. After the state legislature was forced to reapportion, it too went into Democratic hands after many years of GOP domination. Blacks, ethnic whites, and union members, mainly in eastern Michigan, were finally represented in proportion to their actual numbers.

With suburban growth in the 1950s, one might have expected the emergence of a strong Republican presence in eastern Michigan. But this did not happen overnight. Oakland County leaned Republican, as it had in the 1930s, but did not become more Republican than it had been previously. These northern suburbs contained significant pockets of Democratic support, particularly in Pontiac, a blue-collar town where Pontiac automobiles were manufactured. Certainly Oakland County's support for the GOP paled in comparison to the lopsided margins Republicans ran up in the most agricultural counties. East of Oakland, Macomb County was known as one of the six most Democratic counties in the state (Pollock and Eldersveld 1942). It remained competitive between the parties until the late 1960s.

Detroit's black population came to political life in the 1960s in the midst of rising awareness of the city's deteriorating social conditions. Racial unrest had a bloodier history in Detroit than in other Midwestern cities. The boom in industrial employment that had occurred during World War II had lured many Southerners, both black and white, to Cleveland, Detroit, and Chicago, on the promise of steady work and good pay (Browne and VerBurg 1995). The city's supply of housing could not keep pace with the inflow of workers, leading to ethnic competition and conflict. Blacks were frequently the losers in these contests, winding up in the most substandard housing and in the lowest paying, dead-end jobs. Black protest of worsening living conditions culminated in the 1943 race riots, where thirty-four people were killed, twenty-five of them black (Baulch and Zacharias 1999).

In most places, riots of this scale would have been a major catalyst for social reform. But in Detroit, tension between the black and white communities only worsened once blacks found a political voice to express their grievances. In 1967, violence erupted again, in Detroit, Los Angeles, and other cities. The Detroit riots were precipitated by what lower-income blacks considered arbitrary police action in their neighborhoods (Locke 1969). Forty-three people were killed and seven thousand people were arrested. Army and national guard troops were called in to restore order. The 1967 riots were both preceded and followed by white out-migration, but the exodus was greatly accelerated in the aftermath. In 1960, 63 percent of Wayne County's population lived in Detroit. Following the riots, entire neighborhoods were depopulated. In the twenty years following the riots, Detroit had lost 700,000 people mainly to the suburbs with some leaving the area altogether. Less than half of the Wayne County population lived in the Motor City by the early 2000s, down from the 7 in 10 who had lived there in 1960. In recent years, parts of the inner city's vacant core could be seen overgrown by weeds—places where a dog could flush a pheasant. The population that remains is 77 percent black—in 1960 it had been less than 30 percent black. The majority black population has made Detroit the most predictably Democratic piece of real estate in Michigan.

Consistent with its pre–New Deal inclination, northern and western Michigan shifted toward the Republicans in the 1940s and 1950s. Grand Rapids was represented by Gerald R. Ford in the U.S. House beginning in 1949 and continuing through his appointment to the vice presidency in 1973. The reasons for western Michigan's GOP leanings are threefold. First, these towns did not have the manufacturing employment that eastern Michigan had, so there was less union labor support behind Democratic candidacies. Second, the population in western Michigan had its roots in Holland and western European immigration, not the more recent immigration from eastern and southern Europe. The newer immigrant groups were widely considered by established Michigan natives of Northern European ancestry to be of inferior stock, lazy, and less capable of making it without handouts. As the residents of western Michigan looked eastward, they saw that

an alien invasion had taken over eastern Michigan and the Democratic party earlier in the century (Eldersveld 1957)—a good reason
to remain in the GOP camp. Finally, western Michigan remained a
Republican stronghold because it was virtually untouched by the increased mobilization accompanying the civil rights revolution. There
were so few blacks living in Grand Rapids or the region's smaller
cities that Democratic candidates could not count on this constituency to make much of a difference in local elections.

By the end of the century, the state's political geography had
changed considerably since the 1960s (see map 12.3). Parts of rural
northern Michigan had become more Democratic, including once
mainly agricultural counties inland from the lakeshores where economic growth was sluggish and the population was aging. In some
rural counties, however, new factories were responsible for the
growth of a blue-collar constituency with Democratic sympathies.
Coupling slow agricultural decline with emerging small town industries, one had a recipe for Democratic gains.

In the Upper Peninsula, a similar reversal was under way. Many of
the UP's New Deal Democrats had begun to die off in the 1980s, the
economy was no longer centered on mining and manufacturing, and
the new population was voting more equivocally in presidential elections. After many years of economic blight, voters in the UP no longer
looked to Washington for the solutions to their economic problems as
they had when conditions had first gone sour decades before. Once recession becomes a constant in people's lives, through changing administrations, governors, representatives, and state legislators, they
often abandon economic cues when voting, preferring to decide on
the basis of other issues. Given that residents of the UP had socially
conservative views congruent with Republican party platforms, it is no
great surprise that some of these counties underwent a political transformation between 1960 and 2000.

Suburban Detroit continued its drift toward the Republicans,
driven by rapid in-migration to the more affluent townships in Oakland and Macomb Counties. Detroit's black population sought to
leave the city for adjacent towns, but often found the suburbs to be
impossible to crack (Hermalin and Farley 1973; Sommers 1984). Pontiac, in Oakland County, was an important exception because it already had a significant black population dating to 1960. Three Wayne
County suburbs had large black populations: Inkster, Highland Park,

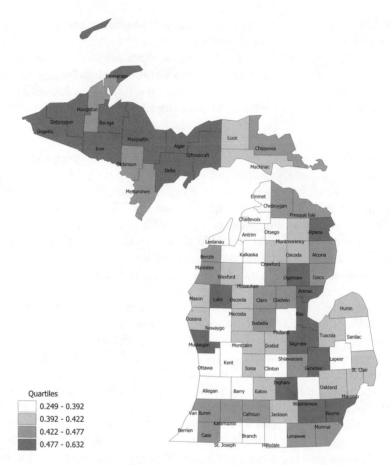

Quartiles
☐ 0.249 - 0.392
▒ 0.392 - 0.422
▓ 0.422 - 0.477
■ 0.477 - 0.632

Map 12.3.   Average Democratic percentage of the presidential vote, 1988–2000

and Hamtramck. The remaining Wayne County suburbs, where housing was often affordable for working-class blacks, were the most hostile to the prospect of residential integration. The city of Dearborn reported only 1,248 blacks living within its borders, out of a total population of 98,000 in 2000 (about 1.2 percent). Livonia reported only 951 black residents, of a population of 100,500 (0.94 percent). Detroit itself remained a depopulating Democratic fortress. Given the racial opposition to any form of integration in towns proximate to Detroit, blacks seeking to leave the Motor City often jumped the suburbs and moved to towns in western Michigan where low-skill and semiskilled jobs were available and white hostility less pronounced.

The 1996 and 2000 elections saw western Michigan, including Kent (Grand Rapids), Ottawa (Holland), and Muskegon (Muskegon) Counties, move into the GOP fold even more than they had been already (see map 12.3). A mix of generational replacement and affluent in-migration from elsewhere were responsible. The other towns in western and central Michigan were a patchwork depending on prevailing economic conditions and who moved in and out. Economic uncertainty in the early 1990s and rising black populations made Battle Creek (Calhoun County) and Jackson (Jackson County) two of Bill Clinton's best. Lansing and its suburbs (Ingham County), largely free of recession, favored George Bush and Bob Dole.

Where Are the Votes in Michigan? Republican and Democratic Mobilization Targets

In our studies of the political geography of states, we have sought to determine where the Republicans and Democrats obtain their votes. We have discovered in most cases that the Democrats have an advantage in that their supporters are more concentrated in a smaller geographic area than the Republicans'. Spatial dispersion imposes high costs, because populations that are spread out are more difficult to organize. Democrats can concentrate their campaign resources, but Republicans must spread them more thinly. What is true of other states is also true of Michigan. The rankings in table 12.1 reflect the importance of the top ten counties to each party's statewide effort.[1]

The Democrats depended on Wayne County for better than one in four of their statewide votes in the 1988–2000 presidential elections. The GOP's best county was Oakland, where 15 percent of their statewide vote was concentrated. Similar to Oregon and Illinois, then, Michigan Democrats do have the advantage of a concentrated urban vote. Republicans have the greater mobilization challenge since they must cover more ground. But unlike Illinois, Democratic and Republican votes in Michigan are more widely scattered. Much more of the state electorate is concentrated in the Chicago metro area compared to around Detroit. Democrats could win overwhelming majorities in Wayne County and still not win any statewide elections.

Some counties are indispensable to both parties, including three in the Detroit area: Wayne, Oakland, and Macomb (see table 12.1). The rank ordering of these locations varies by party in that Republicans must go first to the suburbs whereas Democrats start with Detroit. Hence, Wayne County ranks as the top priority for the Democrats, but fourth for Republicans. Kent County (Grand Rapids) contributes more to the Republicans (ranks second) than to the Democrats (ranks seventh). Washtenaw County, home of the University of Michigan's main campus in Ann Arbor, is an important Democratic stronghold, ranking fifth for Democrats, but tenth for Republicans.

In other states we have observed an increasing balkanization of the electorate throughout the twentieth century as Republican and Democratic territorial bases of support have come to diverge. Certainly the same is true of Michigan (map 12.4). In the 1930s, Wayne County provided a solid plurality of total statewide votes to both parties (28 percent of Republican base; 38 percent of Democratic base). But with the abandonment of Detroit by so many white voters, the city became a one-party stronghold and contributed only 13 percent of all statewide votes for the GOP in the 1988–2000 presidential elections. Grand Rapids has become less important to Democratic campaign efforts over the seventy-year period, while Republicans gave gained substantial vote shares there. Similarly, by the end of the century, the heavy industrial towns of Saginaw and Muskegon ranked among the top ten mobilization priorities for Democrats, but were far less important for the GOP. The parties are not competing side by side for support to the extent that they did in previous decades.

TABLE 12.1. **Michigan's Top Ten Strongest Counties for Republicans and Democrats in the 1988–2000 Presidential Contests**

Rank	Democratic	Republican
1	Wayne (Detroit)	Oakland (Royal Oak–Pontiac)
2	Oakland (Royal Oak–Pontiac)	Kent (Grand Rapids)
3	Genesee (Flint)	Macomb (Warren)
4	Macomb (Warren)	Wayne (Detroit)
5	Washtenaw (Ann Arbor)	Ottawa (Holland)
6	Ingham (Lansing)	Kalamazoo (Kalamazoo)
7	Kent (Grand Rapids)	Ingham (Lansing)
8	Saginaw (Saginaw)	Livingston (Howell)
9	Kalamazoo (Kalamazoo)	Genesee (Flint)
10	Muskegon (Muskegon)	Washtenaw (Ann Arbor)
% of total vote	68.6	61.2

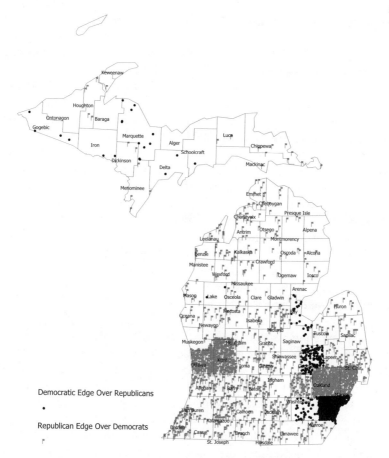

Democratic Edge Over Republicans

•

Republican Edge Over Democrats

ℾ

Map 12.4.   Areas of Republican and Democratic dominance, 1988–2000

The geographic distribution of party support early in the twenty-first century demonstrates that the Republicans had become a party of the state's suburbs. Throughout this book, the critical importance of the emergence of suburbs to Republican party growth has been a common finding. Whether we are discussing Illinois, Texas, California, Georgia, or Michigan, it is clear that Republicans must frame campaign efforts with an increasingly complex suburban electorate in mind. Michigan Democrats, on the other hand, have a highly dependable but shrinking central-city constituency in Wayne County. As Detroit has depopulated, the Democrats have had to go outside

of Wayne County in search of votes that they once could easily ignore. At the turn of the twenty-first century, there are more smaller
counties and cities that contain consequential Democratic vote
shares than in times past. In Illinois, half of the Democratic vote came
from Cook County alone (see chap. 14). But to secure half of their
vote in Michigan in recent years, Democrats had to go to three additional counties: Oakland, Macomb, and Genesee (Flint). The depopulation of Detroit has been a bad development for Democrats and a
boon for Republicans. Wayne County was once home to more than
half of the state's Democrats. With the help of strong union organizations, these voters were easily mobilized. In more recent times,
though, the Democrats have had to face the same challenge that Republicans have confronted for decades: casting a wider and more expensive net, in more remote corners of the state. The Republicans
have more experience at this and have won significant statewide victories, while the Democrats are working to adjust to this new reality.

Michigan's Changing Electoral Foundations

The partisan changes that we have observed in Michigan's political
geography beg for deeper analysis. Ordinarily, explanations for partisan change have been fourfold: (1) the conversion of voters from one
party to the other; (2) the mobilization of new voters that may help
one party or the other; (3) the influx of new population groups, or the
departure of others, from certain locales; and (4) the replacement of
the older generation with younger voters that have different political
inclinations. We have repeatedly found that these forces work in combination to generate political change. Migration is often accompanied
by conversion, for example, or mobilization of one group sometimes
results in the conversion of another. Migration may work in tandem
with generational replacement inasmuch as an influx of young, family-
age voters to an area can heighten the fertility to mortality ratio. We
now turn to an examination of change in the Michigan electorate to
determine what is at work there.

Understanding the voting behavior of a *state* electorate is a surprisingly new enterprise in political science. National polls for purposes of studying the national electorate have been available since
the 1940s, but only in the last two decades have state-representing
surveys become available. Still, there are many questions we would

like to ask about the voting of state electorates in earlier times. For instance, if we are interested in the impact of generational change on the Michigan electorate, we would like to know whether the party preference of Michigan's older voters was different from that of the state's younger voters.

Lacking surveys from this era, we must fall back on the use of ecological data (by county) to make inferences about these populations. In table 12.2, we present estimates of the Democratic support awarded by each of several important demographic groups in presidential elections. The estimates are derived from Gary King's (1997) ecological inference technique developed to improve our ability to make generalizations about the behavior of individuals from aggregate data (see appendix A).

Generational Replacement

Generational replacement is at work in two areas of the state in very different ways. The suburbs north of Detroit had high fertility to mortality ratios (birth rates higher than death rates) in the early 1960s and a preponderance of young, family-age residents. From 1960 to the 2000s, Oakland and Macomb County became less Democratic because more Republican than Democratic voters moved into the local electorate. These Republican voters reproduced rapidly, and their offspring moved into the electorate at age 18 to tip it toward the GOP. At the other end of the spectrum were the counties of the UP with an aging population and low fertility to mortality ratios. Here the opposite demographic force was at work but Republicans also benefited. Fertility rates were extremely low relative to mortality rates but the high mortality rates were killing older Democrats. The population of the UP was shrinking but these counties were nevertheless moving in a Republican direction. Generational replacement was occurring in the UP as well as in the Detroit suburbs, but it was working to benefit Republicans in completely opposite ways. To be sure, most of these UP counties were still inclined to vote Democratic by 2000, but they were far less Democratic than they were in 1950.

Whether the elderly vote differently from those under age 65 is important because the difference bears on the potential for political change in the electorate in the near term. If those nearing death are much more supportive of the Democratic party than those that have longer to live, then the impact of mortality, all other things remaining equal, will benefit the Republicans. What we find in our data is that the New Deal initially erased any generation gap in the Michigan electorate. About 42 percent of elderly voters supported the Democratic presidential candidate in the 1928–32 elections, compared with 41 percent of those under age 65. A greater gap emerged as the weight of the Depression sank in. Younger, working-age voters moved into Democratic ranks, while the older voters withstood the Roosevelt tide. Given Michigan's Republican moorings during this period, these results should come as no shock. Michigan's oldest residents remained less Democratic than the rest of the population until the late 1970s, when many of the manufacturing workers that had been Democratic

TABLE 12.2.   **Estimates of the Democratic Percentage of the Presidential Vote for Various Electoral Groups in Michigan, 1928–2000 (ecological inference maximum likelihood)**

Pooled Presidential Election Years	Blacks/ Nonblacks		Elderly/ Nonelderly		Immigrants/ Nonimmigrants		Farmers/ Nonfarmers		Whites/ Nonwhites	
1928, 1932	47.5	41.1*	42.4*	41.3*	76.2*	34.0*	37.3*	42.1*	40.9*	50.5
1936, 1940, 1944	65.9	51.8*	23.6*	54.3*	54.4	52.0*	18.8*	58.9*	51.7*	67.8
1948, 1952	67.8	43.9*	5.4	48.7*	79.3	42.0*	10.1*	49.9*	44.2*	63.0
1956, 1960, 1964	59.6	53.0*	41.7	54.7*	76.5	52.0*	11.4*	56.1*	52.8*	61.8
1968, 1972	83.8	40.2*	41.6	45.4*	99.6	42.3*	15.3*	46.0*	40.9*	76.3
1976, 1980, 1984	87.8	36.9*	64.8	41.2*	93.4	41.1*	5.5	44.2*	35.7*	88.1
1988, 1992	90.1	38.0*	77.6	40.9*	61.3	44.6*	17.0	45.6*	37.7*	83.4*
1996, 2000	95.7	44.9*	54.5	51.7*	99.5	50.6*	42.9	52.6*	44.1	90.6*

	Mfg. Workers/ Non Mfg. Workers		College Educated/ Non College Educated		Native to State/ Nonnatives		Internal Migrants/ Nonmigrants		Hispanics/ Non- Hispanics	
1928, 1932	—	—	—	—	—	—	—	—	—	—
1936, 1940, 1944	—	—	—	—	—	—	—	—	—	—
1948, 1952	68.4*	31.5*	40.5	45.8*	—	—	—	—	—	—
1956, 1960, 1964	57.4*	51.6*	41.5	54.5*	48.5*	66.9*	59.8*	52.0*	—	—
1968, 1972	40.3*	47.7*	55.5	43.9*	37.1*	62.5*	55.6*	41.3*	—	—
1976, 1980, 1984	31.1*	48.0*	26.3	45.4*	36.4*	61.8*	58.2*	39.0*	35.2	43.6*
1988, 1992	29.2*	50.5*	38.1	46.8*	41.3*	57.0*	57.8*	41.9*	42.9	45.3*
1996, 2000	36.4*	56.3*	45.8	53.0*	47.0*	68.9*	67.1*	48.5*	64.3	51.7*

Note: Cell entries show the estimated percentage voting Democratic in the presidential elections listed on each row. Complete variable definitions and results from the ecological inference estimation appear in appendix B, with standard errors and bounds.

*Reflect estimates with lower and upper bounds narrower than 0,1.

stalwarts during the period of labor union ascendancy in the 1950s and 1960s were moving into retirement. The Democratic party in Michigan has aged to the point where an ever larger share of the party's support has come from the elderly, a development that should greatly facilitate Republican efforts to control state government as this Democratic base of support dies off in coming decades. Our estimates in table 12.2 overstate the magnitude of the realignment of the elderly vote, but recent polls do indicate that Dukakis, Clinton, and Gore did better than their Republican opponents among older voters in the four elections beginning in 1988.

Population Mobility

Migration is a source of political change when new populations import attitudes and behaviors that are different from established populations. We have repeatedly argued that interstate migrants should be considerably more Republican than natives because the distance involved in their move imposes costs that only some can afford to pay. The ability to move across state lines to find work or follow an employer, then, is a sign of upward mobility. Such migrants are also usually young, white, and well educated (Gimpel 1999).

Population migration in Michigan comes in several varieties that are politically important. Migration within the state, from south to north, has followed the development of new manufacturing plants in low-cost rural counties inland from the lake shores. The diffusion of industry has brought Democratic populations to northern Michigan's rural counties. This migration stream has regenerated the Democratic party in several once Republican-dominant counties. Migration from eastern to western Michigan, particularly by blacks seeking to leave Detroit to take skilled and semiskilled jobs in Battle Creek, Jackson, and Grand Rapids, has brought new Democratic voters to these counties, making them more politically competitive.

Earlier in the century, migration brought large numbers of less educated, low-skill and semiskilled workers to eastern Michigan to work in the auto industry. These workers, many of whom were black, eventually found their way into Democratic party ranks through their labor unions. With deindustrialization in the 1980s and 1990s, the importance of semiskilled and low skilled migration has waned in volume. Migration from outside Michigan continued to bring white-collar business executives and professionals into the suburbs of Detroit and to western Michigan. Wealthy retirees have moved in from other states to settle in Holland (Ottawa County), Traverse City (Grand Traverse County), and on the lakeshore near Muskegon (Muskegon County). These transplants take less interest in state and local politics, but they vote Republican in presidential elections because of their high socioeconomic status.

In estimating our models for Democratic support among the population of internal migrants from other states, we were surprised to see that there is a consistent Democratic bias in this population (see table 12.2). From 1956 to 2000, we see that internal migrants become more Democratic than others (natives and immigrants combined) with time. By the early 1990s, as much as 15 points separates the two groups. Similar results obtain when we look specifically at the population of Michigan natives vs. nonnatives. Our estimates for the political behavior of immigrants are not highly reliable, but the results suggest that the immigrant population is much more Democratic than the population of combined natives and domestic migrants.

The Democratic inclination of internal migrants makes sense if this population in Michigan is somewhat uncharacteristic. The migrant stream to Michigan may be comprised of different populations than the ones that are most typical (Gimpel 1999, chap. 1). If many of these outsiders are blacks and whites from Southern states and have come to find work in low skill or semiskilled industrial jobs, it is easy to understand how they have strengthened the Democratic party rather than the Republican.[2] While they may not have registered to vote immediately upon arrival, eventually most did find themselves becoming politically active, at least in national elections. It is also important to consider the pronounced GOP bias of Michigan natives for much of the twentieth century. At midcentury, with migration just under way, the state was considered a Republican stronghold on the basis of its native-born population. It was only through growth in manufacturing and the recruitment of workers from other states that Democrats were able to become a competitive force. In comparison to the extremely Republican natives, then, internal migrants were more likely to be Democratic loyalists.

The immigrant population has gravitated toward Detroit and its suburbs. Because the most significant growth in the immigrant population has been in Oakland and Macomb Counties, it is often associated with declining Democratic prospects, but that pattern in the aggregate data tells us nothing about the actual voting tendencies of the foreign born. The Detroit area has an especially large population of immigrants from Middle Eastern nations, but available information suggests that they divide their vote equally between the parties, casting their ballots along class lines. Because of their still small numbers, we were unable to generate trustworthy estimates of their presidential preferences in table 12.2.

Conversion

Conversion of voters from one party to the other has been an important component of change in certain elections, but there is little evidence that such conversion has seriously undermined either party for any length of time. One could say that the allegiance of white blue-collar workers to the Democratic party weakened over the course of the century, but Democrats have mobilized new voting blocs and the GOP has lost voters too. Perhaps the realignment of blue-collar workers in the 1970s and 1980s has been overstated anyway. Places that supported Wallace did not become the predictable GOP strongholds in Michigan that they did in the South, although they were generally supportive of Ronald Reagan in 1980. What do we find when we examine the extent of political conversion in Michigan?

For our analysis of political conversion we have conducted a voter transition analysis to evaluate the extent to which Democrats and Republicans remained loyal to their parties during two eras of political upheaval: the 1930s and the 1960s. We first examined the extent to which Hoover's 1928 supporters voted for him again in 1932. Then we looked at the proportion of Hoover supporters in 1932 that went on to vote for Landon in 1936. The point of these comparisons was to estimate the magnitude of Republican defection to Roosevelt in 1932 and 1936. We present similar results in table 12.3 for the 1960, 1964, and 1968 elections. Upon obtaining these estimates for Michigan, we could then compare them to the estimates derived for other states, enabling us to judge whether the state's political system was more or less influenced by political conversion than other states.

Michigan Democrats remained loyal to Roosevelt through the New Deal realignment, but perhaps not as loyal as Democrats in other states. An estimated 84.5 percent of Smith (1928) voters supported

Roosevelt (1932), compared with 92 percent in California, 90 percent in Illinois, and 98 percent in New York. This realigning period is often described as an exchange of support, but in most states we have seen that the movement was mostly from the Republican to the Democratic side, with few voters moving in the other direction. In Michigan, however, there is some evidence to suggest that 13 to 15 percent of Smith voters may have voted for Hoover in 1932. On the GOP side, a majority of Republican voters in 1928 supported Hoover in 1932, but at 57.3 percent this was hardly impressive loyalty. Republicans in Michigan were more likely to defect than those in Illinois or New York, but less likely to defect than Republicans in Southern states. Of the Republicans who were left in 1932, 70 percent went on to support Landon in 1936—indicating that nearly a third defected. After 1936, most of the realigning was over, and the remaining GOP voters exhibited solid loyalty in subsequent elections. The effect of the New Deal conversions was to make a Republican state far more competitive than it had been previously.

In the 1960s, we have found that Kennedy Democrats (1960) remained loyal to Lyndon Johnson (1964) except in Southern states. In Michigan, however, only 75 percent of Kennedy supporters voted for Johnson, proving that the 1964 election was not characterized by a one-sided movement of votes away from the Republican candidate. What we see in Michigan during this period, then, is that the parties swap support. Still, Republicans were less enthusiastic about Goldwater than Democrats were about Johnson, perhaps because their own governor, George Romney, had lost in the presidential primaries to the GOP nominee. Our estimates indicate that only 64.4 percent of the Nixon (1960) voters cast ballots for Goldwater, compared with 81 percent in nearby Illinois. Goldwater voters were not that enthusiastic about Nixon's candidacy four years later (in 1968), but Johnson supporters also had a difficult time backing Humphrey in 1968. Again, the image we have is of two parties who are swapping blocs of supporters. In 1968, George Wallace had little appeal to Michiganders—he won 9 percent of the vote, but most of his support came from voters who had previously backed Goldwater rather than Johnson. The voters who did support Wallace wound up being overwhelming backers of Richard Nixon in 1972—a minuscule 1 percent of them were estimated to have voted for McGovern.

These findings demonstrate why Michigan's political system has

TABLE 12.3. Estimates of Party Loyalty and Conversion across Presidential Elections in Michigan (ecological inference maximum likelihood)

Presidential Election Years	Voted Democratic 1928/Non-Democratic 1928	Voted Democratic 1932/Non-Democratic 1932	Presidential Election Years	Voted Republican 1928/Non-Republican 1928	Voted Republican 1932/Non-Republican 1932
Voted Democratic 1932	84.5* 39.5*		Voted Republican 1932	57.3* 13.3*	
Voted Democratic 1936		79.1* 32.3*	Voted Republican 1936		70.1* 12.9*

Presidential Election Years	Voted Democratic 1960/Non-Democratic 1960	Voted Democratic 1964/Non-Democratic 1964	Presidential Election Years	Voted Republican 1960/Non-Republican 1960	Voted Republican 1964/Non-Republican 1964
Voted Democratic 1964	75.2* 58.0*		Voted Republican 1964	64.4* 3.0*	
Voted Democratic 1968		72.6* 1.0*	Voted Republican 1968		72.0* 25.7*
Voted Wallace 1968		6.4* 15.2*	Voted Wallace 1968		15.8* 6.2*

Note: Cell entries show the estimated percentage voting Democratic, Republican, or for George Wallace in the presidential election listed on each row who voted Democratic (or Republican) in the previous election. Complete variable definitions and results from the ecological inference estimation appear in appendix C, with standard errors and bounds.

*Reflect estimates with lower and upper bounds narrower than 0,1.

remained so competitive between the parties through periods of political turmoil. To a greater extent than in other states, the parties in Michigan swapped bases of support in the 1930s, preventing the Republican party from being completely decimated by the New Deal realignment. Similarly, in the 1960s, nearly equal proportions of Kennedy and Nixon supporters swapped sides in the 1964 election, giving each party a slightly different electoral foundation than it had before. Wallace won some Democratic votes in 1968, but most of his support was from the GOP side, and Wallace's 300,000 votes prevented Nixon from winning the state. The Democrats did not wind up losing electoral shares in Michigan in nearly the same numbers that they did in Georgia (chap. 8) or Texas (chap. 5), but Republicans were still net beneficiaries of the liberal movement of the Democratic party.

To further probe for the basis of party switching, we turn back to table 12.2 where we have estimated the Democratic percentage of the vote among key demographic groups across sets of elections between 1928 and 2000. First, we look to the support of farmers for the Democratic party and see that it has dropped drastically since the 1940s. It is abundantly clear that Michigan's farmers are far more Republican (less Democratic) than those not on the farm. And as the agricultural sector has shrunk, the gap has widened as farmers have become even more supportive of GOP presidential candidates. Our estimates exaggerate the contempt for Democrats among the rural population, but the trend is surely consistent with other available information about this loyal GOP constituency. Farmers in the central and western part of the state have typically defined their interests in direct opposition to the urban liberal tradition of eastern Michigan.

We have just observed that large numbers of farmers apparently converted from the Democratic to the Republican party in the wake of the New Deal. For additional evidence for conversion we might look to the antithesis of farming in Michigan: manufacturing. While the geographic distance between the two sectors has shrunk with rural industrialization, we would still expect manufacturing workers to be among the most Democratic voters in the state at midcentury, and that's exactly what we found. In the 1948–52 elections, an estimated 68 percent of manufacturing workers cast Democratic ballots, compared with only 32 percent of those in other occupational groups. Clearly the New Deal won the committed support of union members. But by the late 1960s, the Democrats' image became tarnished among white working-class voters by the leftward drift of the party. The elections of 1968 and 1972 were critical because they show that support for Humphrey (1968) and McGovern (1972) among manufacturing workers had dropped to 40 percent compared with 48 percent among workers in other employment sectors. In the 1976, 1980, and 1984 series of elections, only an estimated 31 percent of manufacturing workers voted Democratic, compared with 48 percent of all others. The estimates for the 1996–2000 series of elections show much the same pattern of disaffection. Half the proportion of manufacturing workers voted for the Democratic candidate in the 1990s as did in the 1950s—some of this movement must be accounted for by conversion.

In some states, we have seen Democratic support rise steadily among the ranks of the college educated. If the GOP did swap support with Democrats, we might look for the new Democrats among better educated, socially liberal voters. We could imagine such a swap occurring coincident with the declining significance of a college education to people's earnings. As more people have obtained a four-year degree, education has become less unique to the wealthy and more Democratic identifiers now hold four-year degrees. Of course certain pockets of well-educated voters have been Democratic for years. We know, for example, that Washtenaw County, home of the University of Michigan, usually threw its support to liberal Democrats. But in general, better-educated voters have high incomes and professional or managerial jobs—positions associated with Republican party identification. Our results in table 12.2 show that the college educated are less Democratic than those lacking a college degree. The exception to this occurs in 1968 and 1972, when support for Humphrey and McGovern among the well educated was particularly high. Otherwise, there seems to be the usual class cleavage between well educated and poorly educated voters that we find in many other states, and there is little evidence to suggest that the college educated have moved toward the Democrats to any decisive extent.

Activism and Partisanship of New Voters

We have seen that a sizable minority of the state's manufacturing workers turned toward the Republican party after 1960. But Democrats must have managed to counter these losses or they would have been reduced to minority status, losing every subsequent election. Instead they have remained competitive, especially in statewide elections. We have speculated that at least some Republicans have moved into the Democratic party, but it was not clear from our rough estimates that they numbered among the college educated. Internal migration has benefited the Democrats in Michigan, but the volume of new voters was probably not sufficient to maintain the party's competitive position. Democrats must have picked up the support of some GOP liberals, but we believe their competitive position has been maintained largely through the mobilization of black support in Detroit and other cities. Judging from our results in table 12.2, Michigan's black voters have been more supportive of Democratic presidential candidates than white voters since early in the century. In the 1928–32 elections, the gap in support between black and nonblack voters is quite narrow, but black voters are more Democratic. John Fenton (1966) indicated that this early Democratic support among blacks was understandable given that their industrial employment made them fast converts to the New Deal. Even so, the black population was not the political force then that it would become later. The 1930 census indicated that blacks comprised only 10 percent of the voting-age population in Michigan. Given that many of these were recent arrivals, and still others were not likely to vote, the black electorate was probably half this size. Apparently, blacks were inclined to divide their vote between the parties in the 1928–32 elections. In those early years, an estimated 41 percent of whites cast Democratic ballots, compared with 48 percent for blacks. Black allegiance to the Democratic party climbed sharply in the subsequent elections, while among whites the popularity of the Democrats remained stable (see table 12.2).

A wide chasm opened up between white and black support for Democrats in the 1968–72 presidential elections. The civil rights movement not only aroused the awareness of blacks to the importance of voting, it also aligned the African-American vote behind the Democrats. The widening of the racial gap during the years after 1968 was a function of the racial unrest of the 1960s that was so locally manifest in the Detroit riots. Republicans gained at least part-time support from thousands of white working-class ethnic voters who came to associate Detroit's black population with poverty and lawlessness. Democrats could draw on a more reliable base of black support through the end of the century even though their support among the labor union rank and file had been seriously shaken. The most recent polls indicated that blacks and whites were separated by nearly 40 points—close to what the estimates in table 12.2 show.

Conclusions

The last century of Michigan politics is principally a story about the rise and fall of organized labor. Michigan's political history has followed its economic history. With the rise of heavy industry in the state between 1920 and 1960, the Democratic party built a solid foundation of support among working-class voters in eastern Michigan and the Upper Peninsula. The appeal of the New Deal to the state's growing blue-collar workforce brought the Democratic party into a politically competitive position with the GOP after 1932. The political power of organized labor steadily increased through this period as the automobile industry thrived and the manufacturing workforce grew.

The 1960s forced both parties to address new issues that did not divide the state's electorate in the same way that the New Deal had: civil rights, the war in Vietnam, urban poverty, and the sexual revolution. Economic issues were submerged by issues of race, crime, the position of women, and patriotism—matters that led to the defection of working-class Democrats to George Wallace and Richard Nixon. The 1970s brought the energy crises that forced automakers to rethink their entire approach to business. The 1980s brought deindustrialization, global competition, and the eventual streamlining and decentralization of manufacturing operations. Labor unions did not adjust well to these new developments that halved their rank and file and extracted huge wage concessions from remaining workers. The smaller plants that sprang up around the state were more difficult for unions to organize than the centralized behemoths of old. With many small auto parts and assembly plants scattered across northern and western Michigan, factory workers now lived among wholesale and retail shopkeepers, farmers, and small town professionals and managers. This kind of economic and social integration of the industrial workforce has undermined enthusiasm for the kind of radical union politics often practiced when factory workers were the only group in the neighborhood. And the enduring liberal stance of the national Democratic party on issues such as homosexual rights, gun control, abortion, and affirmative action has sustained local suspicions of national party candidates and leaders.

With the dawning of the postindustrial age has come the decline of eastern Michigan and the Upper Peninsula as Democratic monoliths in presidential elections. Democrats have lost ground in Oakland, Macomb, and Monroe Counties since the 1960s, and Oakland and Macomb Counties now regularly vote Republican. Wayne and Washtenaw (Ann Arbor) Counties remain the only predictable strongholds for liberal Democrats. Further north, Bay City, Flint, and Saginaw remained safe Democratic areas unless liberal extremists were running. The diffusion of industry throughout the state has moved Democratic constituents into Republican counties, weakening the GOP's stranglehold on some of the smaller counties of the lower peninsula. Western Michigan (Kent and Ottawa Counties) is likely to remain solid GOP turf, although Muskegon went for Bill Clinton and Al Gore in 1996 and 2000. The outlook for GOP presidential candidates in Michigan looks very bright as long as they are matched against liberal Democrats. More moderate Democrats in the mold of Clinton and Gore are likely to reduce sectional conflict, winning Republican votes in western and central Michigan while holding on to the southeastern counties.

Republicans will continue to struggle to mobilize suburban dwellers new to the state who have a steep upward learning curve in the process of exercising the responsibilities of citizenship. With few new workers arriving to take jobs in downsized industries, Democrats are less likely to benefit from population in-migration than they did in the past. Their task will be to hold their base of support among liberals and minorities, while trying to regain the trust of working-class whites. Making inroads among well educated suburban voters is difficult in a state where the labor-business cleavage has had such a long history, but if the GOP can solidify its working-class support around positions such as gun rights, restrictions on abortion, and traditional family values, the Democrats can make gains among social liberals who hold alternative views on such matters. The politics of economics that has dominated Michigan for so long may finally be on its way out.

Notes

1. To get the rankings, the percentage of total statewide votes each county contributes to each party is multiplied by the actual performance of each party. For instance, Wayne County provided 25.6 percent of the total statewide Democratic vote for president and cast 64 percent of its votes for the Democratic candidate in the 1988–2000 elections. Multiplying these scores together yields: .256 × .64 = .166. This figure of .166 serves as an index of voter strength. Once it is calculated for each county, for both parties, the results are then ranked from highest to lowest, or from most important to least important.

2. We estimated the percentage of internal migrants who voted Democratic in the 1988–92 and 1996–2000 elections and added a control for income (*zb*) to the standard ecological inference model. The results indicated that after controlling for income, about 46.8 percent of internal migrants voted Democratic, compared with 47.9 percent of nonmigrants (natives and the foreign born combined). That the income variable would reduce estimates of the Democratic inclination of the migratory population by a significant margin strongly suggests that there is more than one migrant stream into Michigan — the traditional professional-managerial high-income stream, and a lower-skilled, lower-income stream.

CHAPTER 13

NEW YORK

Major Forces for Electoral Change in New York
- Migration of Black Voters from Southern and Border States
- Industrial Restructuring and Population Loss Upstate
- Suburbanization of the Population
- Immigration to New York City
- Mobilization of Blacks, Latinos, Asians, and New Immigrants

New York City so dominates New York that it's often the only thing outsiders think of when the state is mentioned. If the city doesn't come to mind, usually its famous landmarks do: the Statue of Liberty, Broadway, Rockefeller Center, the recently destroyed World Trade Center, and the Yankees. Rarely does anything come off the top of one's head about the 47,000 square miles that make up the rest of the state. City residents sometimes wonder if there is *anything* outside of the boroughs. But in almost any other state, cities the size of Buffalo, Rochester, and Syracuse would be major population centers that no one could overlook.

New York is the classic example of the state dominated by a single huge city. The concentration of so many people in one place has produced political cleavages within the state legislature that run largely along a city vs. anti-city pole, particularly on appropriations and budget matters. For much of the twentieth century, the legislature was about equally divided between the New York City delegation and the rest of the state because nearly one out of every two New Yorkers lived in one of the five borough counties: Richmond (Staten Island), Queens (Queens), New York (Manhattan), Kings (Brooklyn), and Bronx (The Bronx). For upstate New Yorkers, downstate literally meant New York City—a place that was associated with political corruption, greed, immigrants, Catholics, and, in more recent decades,

320

blacks and Latinos. The New York City delegation in Albany voted as a cohesive bloc, and this unity served to divide "the City" from everywhere else in people's mental maps of the state's political system.

Surprisingly enough, little has changed about the foundations of New York's politics since the middle of the last century. As we begin the new millennium, New York City is still a dominant force in state politics because it is proportionally about the same size as it was in 1950. Migration to the suburbs from the boroughs has increased the size of the suburban population, but unlike other central cities, the people who have left New York City have usually been replaced by newcomers, including a steady stream of immigrants. By 2000, about 42 percent of the state's population still lived in the five boroughs, down slightly from 46 percent in 1960.

The suburbs surrounding New York (see map 13.1) have a slightly larger share of the state's total population in 2000 than they did in 1960, and about a million more people live in the four suburban counties (Westchester, Nassau, Suffolk, and Rockland). The rise of suburbs after World War II altered the state's political landscape, to the benefit of Republicans, but probably not as much as in other states. More than fifty years after the construction of Levittown on a Long Island potato field, the suburbs are still not a controlling force in state politics, and increasing socioeconomic heterogeneity among the cities of Nassau and Westchester Counties has undermined their political cohesion. Older Long Island suburbs, such as Hempstead and Freeport, have growing black and Latino populations that turned these towns toward the Democrats in the 1990s.

Compared to California, Florida, and Texas, New York's population growth has certainly been nothing to write home about. Steadily expanding suburbs have been balanced by a more mixed picture upstate. Parts of upstate New York, including some of the medium-sized cities, have been the very epitome of Rust Belt decline. Syracuse, Rochester, and Buffalo have suffered from industrial flight and the demise of traditional manufacturing. Their aging and dilapidated skylines are matched in their dreariness only by the grayness of the cold winter sky. At the same time, these places have served as regional magnets attracting populations from even more depressed outlying areas. As industrial decline has hit smaller cities such as Elmira, Rome, and Utica, these populations have sought work in Syracuse or Rochester. This limited local migration has only added to the economic pressure on

Map 13.1.   Regions of New York

the upstate economy. The cities upstate would have been far better off if some of these displaced workers had left the state altogether. But instead we observe that the populations of the more rural counties have declined even as Monroe (Rochester) and Onondaga (Syracuse) Counties have grown. Buffalo and Erie County have declined, as has Niagara County, but not by nearly enough to bring the labor supply into line with the supply of jobs. All too often, the populations displaced by flagging industrial sectors have remained in the depressed area, contributing to higher unemployment and a declining standard of living throughout western New York.

In electoral politics, it has probably always been too simplistic to characterize the state's politics by virtue of the upstate-downstate dichotomy (Key 1964, 296–97). The cities upstate have had rich political histories distinct from their rural hinterlands, suggesting that urban-rural differences go beyond taking sides on public expenditures for New York City. Syracuse and Onondaga County have been GOP strongholds, but Rochester, Albany, and Buffalo have been much

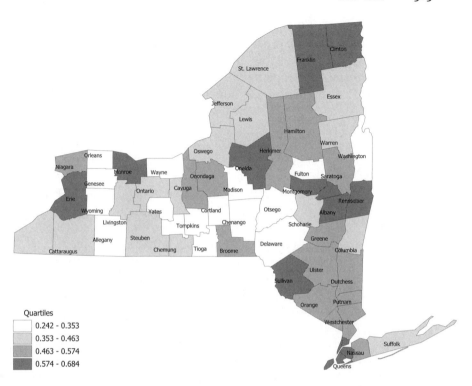

Quartiles

☐ 0.242 - 0.353
▨ 0.353 - 0.463
▦ 0.463 - 0.574
■ 0.574 - 0.684

Map 13.2.   Average Democratic percentage of the presidential vote, 1928–1936

more friendly toward Democrats. The political heterogeneity of upstate New York is clearly illustrated in map 13.2, showing the average
Democratic vote for president for the 1928–36 elections, by quartiles.
Albany (Albany), Erie (Buffalo), Monroe (Rochester), and Oneida
(Rome-Utica) Counties stand out in their support for Smith and Roosevelt. Syracuse (Onondaga) and Chemung (Elmira) resisted the appeal of the New Deal program, as did most of the rural counties. Even
in Franklin D. Roosevelt's backyard, the Hudson Valley (Orange, Putnam, Dutchess, and Ulster Counties), he failed to win a majority of the
vote in either 1932 or 1936.

   The difference between the upstate urban and rural areas in their
support for Roosevelt lies in the characteristics of the two constituencies. The upstate cities were industrial and naturally attracted to the
prolabor elements of the Roosevelt program. Vulnerable to recession

and resulting unemployment, these voters needed the social programs and public works projects that the New Deal could provide. Syracuse was exceptional mainly for economic reasons. It had a higher proportion of residents in white-collar occupations and the professions. The population was better educated than in either Erie (Buffalo) or Monroe (Rochester). It was also among the wealthier of the upstate counties.

The rural counties moved opposite New York City because they had politically conservative traditions historically rooted in religious tradition. At the beginning of the century, the electoral basis of the parties was confessional, with Protestants gravitating to the GOP and Catholics and Jews supporting Democrats (Ladd and Hadley 1975; Sundquist 1983). Most rural New Yorkers were opposed to Democratic liberalism on prohibition, and the antialcohol temperance movement had derived much of its grassroots support and organization from western New York.

By the 1940s and 1950s, though, differences between the electoral parties and party officeholders could not be characterized as religious or "ideological" as ideology might be defined in the South or Midwest in mainly moral terms. The differences dividing Republicans and Democrats usually concerned spending and government finance. And often the issue was not whether to spend, but where and on what. Thomas Dewey and Nelson Rockefeller, both Republican governors with ties to New York City, were liberal spenders who played a major role in expanding the scope and operations of state government in the 1940s and 1950s (Ahlberg and Moynihan 1960). The difference came down to Democrats typically favoring spending projects for New York City, particularly on schools, transportation, and social programs, while Republicans favored spending on their own pork barrel projects upstate. To win statewide office, however, politicians from both parties had to focus attention on the interests of the large population in the New York metropolitan area. This was particularly true of Republicans, and the need to compete for downstate voters won them a moderate reputation that Republicans elsewhere lacked (Key 1964, 297; Caro 1975). At times, the regional resentment of upstate voters cut across party lines. When Nelson Rockefeller nearly sent the state into bankruptcy on public works projects directed mainly toward New York City and its suburbs, upstate Democrats launched successful campaigns by running against his big spending (Gimpel 1996, 42).

Just as upstate has never been completely homogeneous, neither is downstate if that includes not just the boroughs but the four suburban counties (Nassau, Suffolk, Rockland, and Westchester). The suburban counties were GOP strongholds for most of the twentieth century. The two Long Island counties (Suffolk and Nassau) and Westchester became consequential political power bases in the 1950s and 1960s with accelerated out-migration from New York City. Long Island's growth was fueled by the postwar demand for housing and the federal government's creation of the Federal Housing Administration to give developers a source of up-front, government-guaranteed financing. Housing development was accompanied by massive spending on transportation projects by successive governors and legislatures (Caro 1975) and by the growth of the defense industry, and in particular Grumman Aircraft, which opened at Bethpage in 1936 and rapidly expanded during the cold war years. Rockland County, at the lower end of the Hudson Valley, emerged later, in the 1980s and 1990s, on the basis of secondary suburban migration — New Yorkers who had moved further out from older suburbs.

In the 1990s, Nassau and Westchester became two-party battlegrounds, due largely to the browning of the population. For fifty years, Nassau, Suffolk, and Westchester Counties had drawn white residents out from the boroughs with the promise of lower crime, less traffic, ethnically homogeneous neighborhoods, and better schools. The selective out-migration of white, young, upwardly mobile residents resulted in the creation of a suburban politics that defined its agenda in reaction to everything the new residents had experienced in the city (Teaford 1997). By the late 1990s and early 2000s, though, the flight to Nassau County was sustained not by whites but by minorities looking for their way out of Brooklyn and Queens. North of the City, Westchester's new populations included minorities who had migrated from The Bronx. These voters exported their Democratic party affiliation to the suburbs but were less inclined to switch parties than earlier arrivals had been, leading to a resurgence of Democratic strength in once one-party Republican towns.

While the boroughs have been overwhelmingly Democratic in presidential and gubernatorial elections, Staten Island's traditional Republicanism also stands out as an exception to the characterization of downstate as a political monolith. The predominantly white and ethnic Italian residents of Staten Island do not consider themselves

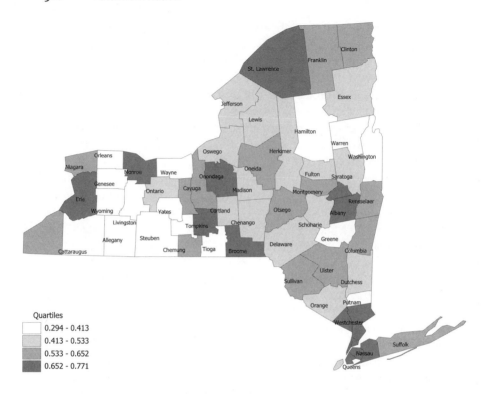

Map 13.3.   Average Democratic percentage of the presidential vote, 1988–2000

part of New York City, and the place has more in common with the Nassau and Westchester suburbs than it does with the other boroughs. Fiscally conservative politics plays well on Staten Island, and in particular hostility to higher taxes. Residents commonly believe that the New York City government mistreats them and ignores their concerns. Several attempts have been made to separate it from New York City, or to allow it to secede.

Because of its slow growth, political changes have come very slowly to New York. Upstate, the same places that were voting Democratic in the 1930s were voting that way in the 1950s. Areas of GOP strength during the New Deal remained supportive of Republican candidates for years afterward. Consequential political changes do not appear on the map until the 1980s and 1990s, two generations after the New Deal realignment. Map 13.3 illustrates the Democratic percentage of the presidential vote for the 1988–2000 presidential elections.

When we compare maps 13.2 and 13.3, we see that the boroughs and three of the suburban counties, Nassau, Westchester, and Rockland, are shaded in the highest Democratic quartile in the latter map. Among downstate jurisdictions, only Suffolk and Richmond (Staten Island) stand out as lukewarm areas for Democrats. Many parts of upstate New York have become more Democratic, particularly in central New York (cities of Ithaca, Elmira, Binghamton). Onondaga County (Syracuse) provided more support for Clinton and Dukakis than it did for Roosevelt. The Hudson Valley, above Westchester County, has been steadfast in its support for Republicans, and the greater Albany area has become more Republican with the growth of that city's suburbs. Overall trends indicate that the counties upstate have become more competitive in presidential elections than they were at mid-century. New York City has become more Democratic, in spite of the popularity of Republican mayor Rudolph Giuliani, who served two full terms. The older suburbs have become more Democratic, particularly in presidential and congressional elections. What this adds up to is potential major gains for Democrats in statewide elections in the new century. Al Gore's easy victory in this state in the 2000 election is indicative of the fact that Republicans have every reason to worry about their prospects in the coming century.

Where Are the Votes in New York? Republican and Democratic Mobilization Targets

Democrats have a geographic advantage in waging statewide political campaigns in New York. The vast bulk of Democratic voters are concentrated in just one location, New York City and the more established suburbs adjacent to Queens and The Bronx. Republicans, by contrast, must study the entire state to determine how to allocate their resources for mobilization purposes. Understanding the political geography of New York requires a knowledge of both the political proclivity of an area and also its relative population size. Obviously not all places are of equal importance. The Republican electorate has been sufficiently diffuse throughout the twentieth century that money and manpower must be targeted at those places likely to pay the greatest political dividends on election day. This means that the thirty or so smallest counties are virtually ignored (see map 13.4).

Table 13.1 lists the top ten counties comprising the political base of each party in the 1988–2000 presidential elections. The ranking is

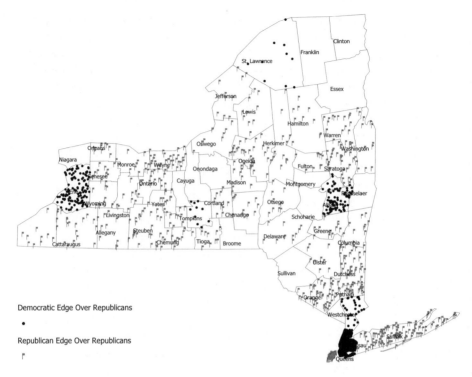

Map 13.4.   Areas of Republican and Democratic dominance, 1988–2000

calculated on the basis of each county's support for the party weighted by the proportion of the total statewide vote they award to the party. For the Democrats, the four big boroughs sit atop the list, with Manhattan (New York County) leading all other places in its value to Democratic campaign efforts. New York City, absent Staten Island, provided 39 percent of all statewide Democratic votes for president in the 1988–2000 elections. Below these in importance are two suburban counties, Nassau (ranked fifth) and Suffolk (ranked seventh), with Erie (Buffalo) sandwiched in between. The concentration of votes in New York City and its suburbs reinforces the popular impression that the Democrats draw the lion's share of their vote from downstate.

The upstate-downstate dichotomy often used to characterize two-party competition is a dangerous fallacy when it comes to political mobilization. This is because Republicans must begin their vote-getting efforts downstate—in the suburbs of Long Island. Nassau and Suffolk

Counties top the GOP list of most important mobilization targets. About 18 percent of all statewide Republican votes for president came from Long Island in the presidential elections from 1988 to 2000. Below these in importance, one must move north to Westchester, and only then does one move upstate to Rochester, Buffalo, and Syracuse. Moreover, three boroughs appear in the top-ten list for Republicans: Queens (Queens), Kings (Brooklyn), and Richmond (Staten Island). One county on the metropolitan fringe, Orange (Newburgh), emerged as an increasingly important GOP power base in the 1990s.

While the parties share some turf in New York City and the suburbs, upstate we find more political balkanization and divergence in the geographic base of support. Although we have noted that Onondaga (Syracuse) became more Democratic as the century ended, it still ranks as the seventh most important county for Republicans but the eleventh for Democrats. Monroe (Rochester) remains the fourth most important county for Republicans, but only the ninth for Democrats. Richmond (Staten Island) and Orange (Newburgh) are of greater importance to the GOP than to the Democrats. The twenty most rural counties, while often ignored in campaign politics, contribute twice as many votes to the Republicans as to the Democrats.

In the 1930s, New York City was even more central to statewide campaigns than it was at the turn of the twenty-first century, casting 56 percent of all statewide Democratic votes. Sizable blocs of Republican voters could be found in Brooklyn, Queens, and Manhattan. The rush

TABLE 13.1.   New York's Top Ten Strongest Counties for Republicans and Democrats in the 1988–2000 Presidential Contests

Rank	Democratic	Republican
1	New York (Manhattan)	Nassau (Hempstead)
2	Kings (Brooklyn)	Suffolk (Brentwood)
3	Queens (Queens)	Westchester (White Plains)
4	Bronx (Bronx)	Monroe (Rochester)
5	Nassau (Hempstead)	Erie (Buffalo)
6	Erie (Buffalo)	Queens (Queens)
7	Suffolk (Brentwood)	Onondaga (Syracuse)
8	Westchester (White Plains)	Richmond (Staten Island)
9	Monroe (Rochester)	Kings (Brooklyn)
10	Albany (Albany)	Orange (Newburgh)
% of total vote	72.1	57.9

to the suburbs with the post–World War II boom permanently redrew the state's electoral map. New York City became less important to both parties, and the suburban counties more so. Between the 1930s and 2000, Nassau County moved from tenth to fifth in importance for the Democrats, and from seventh to first in importance for the GOP. The Republicans, however, lost more ground in New York City than the Democrats, as Brooklyn (Kings County) moved from third to ninth in its contribution to Republican statewide totals, while moving from first to second for Democrats. As in other states, then, we see that the geographic bases of party support have moved to differing places on the map, with the parties sharing less common territory than in decades past.

The conclusion we draw from this comparison of the geographic basis of electoral strength is that the demographic forces of the twentieth century have made the GOP a party of the suburbs, not upstate. Even when we look upstate, we find that it is the suburban areas within the urban counties that provide the GOP's cornerstone support. The Republicans find friendly territory in the most rural counties, but the smallest twenty counties combined do not add up to as much voting power as Nassau or Suffolk singly (see map 13.4). Republicans cannot afford to ignore Queens (Queens), Kings (Brooklyn), and Richmond (Staten Island), but the first two are predictably Democratic in presidential contests. Democrats could write off much of upstate New York, and they have done so for decades. Only Erie, Monroe, and Albany Counties are of consequence, mainly as bench players in cases of low turnout in the boroughs and New York City suburbs.

New York's Changing Electoral Foundations

To study political behavior in New York as far back as 1928 requires that we make inferences about individuals based on county-level demographic and election statistics. Polling data generally did not become available on the state level until late in the century. To obtain estimates of individual-level voting tendencies from the county-level observations, we used Gary King's (1997) ecological inference method (described in appendix A). We use this method to provide estimates of the fraction of particular groups (blacks, the elderly, interstate migrants, etc.) that voted Democratic in presidential elections between 1928 and 2000.

Population Mobility

Compared to the fast-growing states of the South and West, we see very little partisan change in New York between 1930 and 2000. Hit hard by industrial restructuring and oppressed by a tax structure unfavorable to business until the Pataki administration pressed for reform in the late 1990s, New York has seen more of an exodus of its longtime residents than an attraction of newcomers. One 1994 ranking rated New York forty-eighth out of fifty states in its attractiveness to migrants from other states. Only Louisiana and Pennsylvania ranked lower (Thomas 1994). Between 1990 and 1995, New York ranked second to last in gains due to net migration because in that five-year period alone, slightly over one million people left the state. Immigration continues to fuel population growth in the New York City metropolitan area, and the lion's share of the naturalized foreign born have become loyal Democrats, but population growth from elsewhere in the nation has played a minor role. Aside from immigration, the major push behind population growth has been natural increase — fertility rates that have outstripped mortality rates in suburbs.

One of our key concerns throughout this book has been to assess the political contributions of new and native populations. Accordingly, we estimated the Democratic support among immigrants, migrants, and native New Yorkers (see table 13.2). Generally, our prediction has been that immigrants will find their way into the politics of the Democratic party. Most immigrants since the late 1960s have been ethnic minorities who chose to settle in New York City and the older suburbs where the Democratic party is traditionally well positioned to attract their loyalty. Internal or interstate migrants, on the other hand, were hypothesized to be mainly Republican in their orientation. We expected natives to be more Democratic than interstate migrants, but less Democratic than immigrants.

What we found in New York runs counter to these expectations. Native New Yorkers were the most Republican of the three groups. Between 1956 and 2000, native support for Democrats in presidential elections ranged from a low of 21 to a high of 49 percent. The Democratic support among nonnatives, most of whom were immigrants rather than interstate migrants, was much higher. Similar estimates comparing the vote of immigrants to non-immigrants indicate overwhelming Democratic support among immigrants, with Democratic support among non-immigrants lagging some 50 to 60 points behind. With the exception of the 1988–92 elections, estimates for the internal migrant population show that it is *more* Democratic than the nonmigrant population (table 13.2).

These results indicate that New York is different from other states in that its natives are more Republican than its cross-state migrants. Unfortunately, most extant polls lack questions about the birthplace and mobility patterns of New York voters. But we can at least speculate about the plausibility of the results we have obtained from examining the aggregate data. We are led to conclude that these results showing that natives are more Republican than interstate migrants may be valid as a description of the difference between migrants and

TABLE 13.2.   Estimates of the Democratic Percentage of the Presidential Vote for Various Electoral Groups in New York, 1928–2000 (ecological inference maximum likelihood)

Pooled Presidential Election Years	Blacks/ Nonblacks		Elderly/ Nonelderly		Immigrants/ Nonimmigrants		Farmers/ Nonfarmers		Whites/ Nonwhites	
1928, 1932	65.0	52.7*	22.0	54.8*	90.0*	40.5*	7.1*	55.8*	52.4*	71.7
1936, 1940, 1944	79.9	45.3*	10.0	49.5*	82.3*	36.9*	3.0*	49.2*	44.4*	96.7
1948, 1952	99.3	36.1*	12.2	42.7*	83.2*	36.7*	21.0	40.8*	35.9*	99.5
1956, 1960, 1964	99.3	36.1*	74.0	46.1*	66.9	46.1*	28.3	40.6*	35.9*	99.5
1968, 1972	99.6	34.4*	43.4	42.0*	88.7	36.1*	14.0	42.5*	34.6*	91.8
1976, 1980, 1984	94.5	39.9*	57.4	47.3*	94.3	39.9*	17.0	47.6*	37.8*	84.9*
1988, 1992	87.0	45.6*	45.0	53.3*	94.1	44.3*	27.1	52.3*	37.2*	95.8*
1996, 2000	96.2*	55.6*	35.3	66.2*	95.3	55.9*	34.7	62.3*	51.0*	93.7*

	Mfg. Workers/ Non Mfg. Workers		College Educated/ Non College Educated		Native to State/ Nonnatives		Internal Migrants/ Nonmigrants		Hispanics/ Non-Hispanics	
1928, 1932	—	—	—	—	—	—	—	—	—	—
1936, 1940, 1944	—	—	—	—	—	—	—	—	—	—
1948, 1952	54.9*	34.2*	—	—	—	—	—	—	—	—
1956, 1960, 1964	55.0*	34.2*	90.0*	44.9*	41.7*	72.9*	57.1*	48.0*	—	—
1968, 1972	33.9*	44.8*	66.4	38.9*	21.1*	87.1*	61.0*	37.4*	—	—
1976, 1980, 1984	21.6*	53.6*	76.5	42.9*	31.7*	82.7*	53.8*	46.0*	97.3	42.1*
1988, 1992	19.5*	57.8*	85.7	42.3*	35.7*	87.0*	46.8*	53.3*	95.0*	46.2*
1996, 2000	31.6	66.5*	92.4	56.5*	49.2*	89.2*	71.1*	60.4*	77.7*	59.4*

Note: Cell entries show the estimated percentage voting Democratic in the listed presidential elections. Complete variable definitions and results from the ecological inference estimation appear in appendix B, with standard errors and bounds.

*Reflect estimates with lower and upper bounds narrower than 0,1.

natives in the counties of upstate New York. In these locales, we have observed that Republican loyalties have weakened, but it is plausible that this weakening has been the result of migration from other states, particularly Massachusetts, Connecticut, and other parts of New England.

Downstate, in New York City and the suburbs, we have more doubts about the estimates presented in table 13.2. Here it seems likely that internal migration has bolstered Republican prospects, partly because the natives in these areas have such strong Democratic loyalties and also because the costs of resettlement in the New York City metro area are so high compared to alternative destinations. New York attracts high-income domestic migrants from beyond its borders, and a large number of immigrants, but it is not an attractive destination for the migrant poor from other states. While some of these interstate migrants may be attracted to expensive Manhattan apartments precisely because they can find compatible liberal views among their neighbors, most have moved to the New York suburbs into neighborhoods where their policy views on taxes, education, and police protection are shared. Finally, we should remember that interstate migration has not been a major force for population growth in New York. New Yorkers have left to become voters in other states, but relatively few other states have sent residents to become citizens of New York. Whatever the political proclivities of this interstate migrant population, it has not been a major force for political change statewide. Far more attention should be paid to differences between the politics of immigrants and native New Yorkers because the foreign-born population will be driving electoral change for decades into the twenty-first century.

The greatest impact of population mobility internal to the state can be observed in the suburban counties. Aging suburbs that were once the destination for white family-age migrants found themselves undergoing a kind of population succession fueled by local migration that benefited Democrats in the decades that closed the century. Minorities, including African Americans, Latinos, and Asians, moved to the suburbs in unprecedented numbers. Inasmuch as the neighborhoods into which they move are often racially and ethnically segregated, they do not face the same local political pressure to convert to GOP politics that the earlier Anglo migrants faced when they had moved out from Queens and Brooklyn thirty years earlier. The established Republican regulars have not always welcomed the newer immigrant and minority populations, and these feelings of exclusion have been the foundation for Democratic party renewal in Nassau County.

Generational Replacement

With natural increase and out-migration being the major forces behind population change, partisanship has shifted mainly with the slow death of old partisans and their replacement with younger voters. In a few cases, this process has benefited the Democrats, but in most cases it has helped the Republicans. The GOP has gained ground in the areas with the highest fertility rates because typically these have been suburbs where older Democratic populations have been inundated by Republicans who are in their prime childbearing years. This process of generational change first transformed the suburbs closest to New York City. One could observe it happening in the 1940s and 1950s in Nassau County but also in Staten Island and in suburban Rochester, Buffalo, and Syracuse. The close-in suburbs eventually aged, and by the 1980s and 1990s, the suburbs attracting the family-age populations were further out on the metropolitan fringe. Partisan change induced by rapid generational replacement is now moving the towns further out on Long Island and in the far-flung suburbs northwest of New York City into safer Republican hands than they have ever been.

Notably, many of the rural counties with a relatively higher mortality to fertility ratio have moved in the opposite direction—toward the Democrats. Upwardly mobile, GOP-inclined voters have avoided these areas or left them behind, resulting in an increasing concentration of elderly and poor people who either cannot afford to leave or refuse to leave. The farm population was once the most reliable Republican vote upstate. This population has declined with the economic changes that have led to the concentration of agricultural production in fewer hands. The rural elderly and poor that remain the core population of New York's small Rust Belt towns are attracted to the Democratic positions on issues such as income security, health care, and reform of the social security system. Many towns along the New York–Pennsylvania border fit this description of places that are drifting in a Democratic direction as their populations age.

Studying the voting tendencies of various age cohorts is important because it signals how the electorate may change as the result of generational replacement. In table 13.2, we see that the elderly were initially much less Democratic than those under age 65. This has been a consistent finding throughout many of the states we have examined. Older voters were slower to move into the Democratic column than younger voters because they had become habituated to voting for Republicans in previous decades. While it is true that most of the elderly that did convert were in lower income brackets, it is also true that the elderly in general were less inclined to support Roosevelt than younger voters (Abramson 1975). Hence, we see that an estimated 22 percent of retirement-age voters cast Democratic ballots in the combined 1928–36 presidential elections, compared with 54.8 percent among those younger than age 65.

The generation gap that was widened by the New Deal realignment holds up until the late 1950s and 1960s, when those of retirement age during the 1930s had died and been replaced by cohorts that had been converted by Roosevelt's progressive program. So in the pooled 1956–64 elections, we see that an estimated 74 percent of retirement-age New Yorkers voted Democratic, compared to only 46 percent of those younger than 65. The force for generational replacement that had once replaced elderly Republicans with New Deal Democrats then began replacing elderly Roosevelt Democrats with younger Republicans. By the 1990s, generational forces had reversed themselves once again, with the elderly becoming more Republican than younger voters. Recent exit polling data lend some credence to this finding from our ecological data analysis. Although Al Gore handily won New York, Gore's support was weakest among those over age 65 and strongest among those under age 30.

Conversion

Conversion takes place when people change their patterns of party support. Given that citizens usually do not pay a lot of attention to politics, conversion is rare. But there are times of social and economic upheaval that contribute to partisan change, and throughout the nation we saw such changes in the 1930s and the 1960s. In the 1930s, Republicans abandoned Herbert Hoover to vote for Franklin D. Roosevelt, contributing to a Democratic majority that would last for years afterward. In the 1960s, the civil rights movement and the expansion of the welfare state led to an abandonment of the Democratic party by conservative whites, particularly in the South. Republicans were not entirely happy with the conservative drift of their party, either. In California, many Republicans abandoned the Goldwater candidacy in 1964 (chap. 3). What happened to party loyalty in New York during these turbulent years?

The figures in table 13.3 indicate that during the New Deal period, the potential for conversion was considerably lower in New York than in, say, California. Our estimates for interelection party support show that a larger proportion of New York's Hoover voters in 1928 remained loyal to Hoover in 1932 than in California (compare tables 13.3 and 3.3). In New York, about 70 percent of Hoover's original supporters remained with him in the second election, compared with 57.8 percent that had remained loyal in California. Realignment induced by conversion was apparently much less prevalent in New York than it was in other states. Between 1932 and 1936, there was considerably less switching in New York than in Texas, Florida, or California. Only 12 percent of New York's 1932 Republicans switched to the Roosevelt side by 1936, compared with solid majorities of Hoover supporters in these other three populous states.

In the 1960s, the 1964 election saw partisans switching sides as New Yorkers found Barry Goldwater almost too much to take. About 88.6 percent of Kennedy supporters voted for Johnson in 1964, similar to California. On the GOP side, though, only half of Nixon (1960) supporters voted for Goldwater. In 1968, however, less than half of Lyndon Johnson's 1964 supporters cast votes for Hubert Humphrey, whereas in California, Johnson supporters were more loyal to Humphrey. New York Democrats appear to have been more supportive of Richard Nixon's 1968 presidential bid than California Democrats were. Both California and New York stand in sharp contrast to Southern states in their lukewarm support for the Wallace candidacy in 1968, although Wallace received more support from Goldwater Republicans than from Johnson Democrats in both states.

The process of party conversion that accompanies migration from city to suburbs is worth some attention because it is a significant force for partisan change. Population mobility is not the only force altering the politics of suburbia. Conversion must have taken place; otherwise, the sheer volume of migration from New York City to Nassau and

TABLE 13.3. Estimates of Party Loyalty and Conversion across Presidential Elections in New York (ecological inference maximum likelihood)

Presidential Election Years	Voted Democratic 1928/Non-Democratic 1928	Voted Democratic 1932/Non-Democratic 1932	Presidential Election Years	Voted Republican 1928/Non-Republican 1928	Voted Republican 1932/Non-Republican 1932
Voted Democratic 1932	97.8*	14.0*	Voted Republican 1932	70.1*	11.4*
Voted Democratic 1936	91.3*	9.2*	Voted Republican 1936	88.3*	4.6*

Presidential Election Years	Voted Democratic 1960/Non-Democratic 1960	Voted Democratic 1964/Non-Democratic 1964	Presidential Election Years	Voted Republican 1960/Non-Republican 1960	Voted Republican 1964/Non-Republican 1964
Voted Democratic 1964	88.6*	42.3*	Voted Republican 1964	51.6*	12.6*
Voted Democratic 1968	45.4*	16.6*	Voted Republican 1968	94.6*	19.5*
Voted Wallace 1968	3.2*	8.7*	Voted Wallace 1968	8.5*	3.6*

Note: Cell entries show the estimated percentage voting Democratic, Republican, or for George Wallace in the presidential elections listed on each row who voted Democratic (or Republican) in the previous election. Complete variable definitions and results from the ecological inference estimation appear in appendix C, with standard errors and bounds.

*Reflect estimates with lower and upper bounds narrower than 0.1.

Westchester Counties would have generated suburban Democratic strongholds in the 1950s and 1960s. Instead, these suburban towns, like their counterparts in many other states, managed to convert large numbers of these new voters, reinforcing and building on the traditional Republican partisanship that had been dominant for years.

Conversion to the GOP proved to be surprisingly easy for new voters in locales where the Democratic party had no candidates or ran so poorly it was not a serious option. We also know that conversion follows from the peer pressure newcomers face from established residents (Brown 1988). Newcomers want to conform to avoid social isolation. With time, fear of isolation leads to their political adaptation as they mingle with Republican-inclined natives and older converts.

If there is any shred of evidence that mass conversion has occurred, it would have to be found among white blue-collar workers. No economic sector in New York has struggled more than traditional heavy manufacturing. This decline has virtually knocked out industries such as steel, mining, and shoes, and it has drastically reduced employment in clothing, textiles, glass, and electrical appliances. With the dramatic decline in manufacturing employment, we also observe a steady decline in the Democratic loyalty of manufacturing workers (see table 13.2). In the 1948–52 elections, our model estimates that 55 percent of those in manufacturing supported Truman and Stevenson, compared with only 34 percent of those in all other economic sectors. By the 1980s, only an estimated 22 percent of manufacturing workers supported Democratic candidates, compared with 54 percent of all others. In the 1990s, blue-collar labor gave more of its support to Bill Clinton and Al Gore than it had to Carter (1976, 1980) and Mondale (1984), but these voters remained less Democratic than those in all other employment sectors.

Conversion may also be indicated by the changing degree of polarization between urban and rural New Yorkers (see table 13.2). While our estimates are not highly precise, the farm population was probably less attracted to the Democrats in the 1930s and 1940s than any other group, cementing the impression that the New Deal realignment brought farmers on board the Republican party in spite of Roosevelt's attempts to win them over with the Agricultural Adjustment Act (Sundquist 1983). Our estimates indicate that a mere 7 percent of New York farmers cast Democratic ballots in the 1928–32 elections, compared with 56 percent of those in nonfarming occupations. The gap narrows slightly in the 1950s and 1960s as some younger farmers converted by New Deal agricultural programs became a larger share of the rural electorate. By the late 1960s, however, farm support for Democrats dropped off again and has remained low since.

Our expectation for the relationship between education and voting is that the better educated would be more likely to support Republican candidates than Democrats, but that this "education gap" would shrink with time. Our hypothesis is based on the correspondence between education and socioeconomic status, and the commonplace finding that higher income groups generally give more support to Republicans than lower income groups. Our estimates in table 13.2 of Democratic support among those lacking a college degree are more accurate than the estimates of those who have degrees, and they show very little fluctuation across a thirty-year period. Unlike the pattern in other states, though, our estimates indicate that well-educated voters in New York are more likely to support Democrats than those who are less well educated—although the gap between those with and without college degrees has varied since midcentury. This difference in support is probably an artifact of the concentration of highly literate people in the most urban and Democratic areas of the state. When we reestimated this model controlling for urbanization, we found that Democratic support among the college educated drops to levels more consonant with the polling data.[1] In spite of New York City's affluent and well educated liberal voters, better educated New Yorkers are generally more likely to vote Republican than those with less than a college degree. Recent polls have indicated that the most significant difference across categories of education is at the extremes, between those with less than a high school education and those with college degrees. In the 2000 presidential race, exit polls indicated that 71 percent of those with less than a high school education voted for Gore, compared with 61 percent of those with four years of college or more.

Activism and Partisanship of New Voting Blocs

With a large and highly concentrated black population, we should not be surprised to find racial polarization in the electoral behavior of New Yorkers. The size of minority populations makes a difference to the behavior of majorities in that majorities are more likely to discriminate against larger minorities than against smaller ones (Blalock 1956; Beggs, Villemez, and Arnold 1997). This is because majorities perceive larger minorities to be more threatening (Giles and Hertz 1994; Giles 1977; Key 1949). In settings with large minority populations, then, we can expect more racial conflict to surface in disagreements about politics. The state's black population is highly concentrated in New York City, and it has contributed to the lopsided Democratic bias of the boroughs. African-American voters were not always the force in New York politics that they came to be in the 1980s and 1990s. At mid-century, black New Yorkers were a poorly educated migrant population, having recently relocated in large numbers from Southern and border states. Throughout the industrial North, black migrants had notoriously low political participation rates in that epoch.

Racial polarization should move sharply upward with the mobilization of the minority population after 1950. The civil rights movement of the 1950s and 1960s is thought to have raised the political consciousness of the black population nationwide, aligning them with the Democratic party after the racially divisive 1964 presidential election. The results in table 13.2 show that in New York polarization between the black and nonblack population has been particularly intense since the 1948–52 elections. Given that the black population did not immediately convert to the Democratic party with the New Deal realignment, it makes sense that racial polarization in the vote did not reach its peak until after 1948. Of course our estimates may slightly overstate the degree of polarization in subsequent years. It is highly unlikely that the black population was 99 percent in favor of Democrats, as table 13.2 suggests for 1968–72, although 95 percent would not be implausible. Our estimates for the white population are more reliable than our estimates for the black population, and these figures show steadily declining support for the Democrats since the New Deal, although Bill Clinton and Al Gore apparently reversed the downward trend in 1996 and 2000 (see table 13.2). Recent polling data do confirm that black and white voters are about 35 to 40 points apart as the results in table 13.2 indicate.

Conclusions

For the last seventy years, political regionalism in New York has had foundations rooted in voters' attitudes about the proper role of the government in the economic sphere. The conflict between conservatism and liberalism in New York is more about taxation, redistribution of wealth, and government regulation of private enterprise than about morality. Since beliefs about government's role in the economic sphere still divide urban and rural voters, politics in New York has long had a regional basis, especially when the gulf between candidates on these policy matters is wide (Stonecash 1989). New York presidential and gubernatorial elections became more politically balkanized in the closing decades of the twentieth century because Republican candidates took more conservative positions on taxing and spending than Nelson Rockefeller had. With more ideologically polarized campaigns came greater sectional distinctions between the urban and rural populations, while the suburbs became increasingly ambivalent.

The increasing proportion of minority voters moving to New York City and their rising level of political involvement had the impact of solidifying Democratic domination in gubernatorial and presidential elections across the four large boroughs. Racial balkanization has led to political balkanization. With the browning of their populations, the Long Island and Westchester suburbs are not as politically distinct from New York City as they once were. As the suburbs become more productive of Democratic victories, New York may be headed for a purer sectionalism dividing upstate from downstate because the suburban counties will come to resemble the City more closely. The challenge for Republicans in presidential contests is that they face the loss of the New York City suburbs without the prospect of making up much new ground upstate or in New York City. In presidential elections, then, New York looks like an increasingly dim prospect for GOP candidates, except in the most lopsided elections when the Democrat has proven to be an exceptionally poor contender well before Empire State voters stream to the polls.

Note

1. The ecological inference technique does permit the addition of third variables (zb) that may influence Democratic support. When we estimated Democratic support by education (percentage with a four-year college degree), controlling for urbanization (percentage residing in urban areas), our estimates for Democratic support among those with more than a college degree more closely approximated the results found in polling data. For the

pooled 1996–2000 elections, an estimated 56 percent of the college educated supported the Democratic candidate, compared with 63 percent for those lacking a four-year degree. In the 2000 presidential election, VNS exit polling placed the difference at 58 percent and 61 percent, respectively, for the two groups (with no controls added). For the pooled 1976–84 elections, after controlling for urbanization, an estimated 38.2 percent of the college educated supported the Democratic candidate, compared with 48.7 percent of those with less than a college education.

CHAPTER 14

ILLINOIS

Major Forces for Electoral Change in Illinois

- Migration of Black Voters from Southern and Border States
- Suburbanization of the Population
- Decline of the Agricultural Economy
- Industrial Restructuring and the Decline of Manufacturing
- Mobilization of Blacks and Latinos

Like New York, Illinois is associated by people from other states with one megacity, Chicago. The Windy City does not have landmarks nearly as well known as those in New York, though, so its professional sports teams (the Bulls, the Bears) and gangster past often come to mind. Beyond that, Illinois is vaguely associated with manufacturing, farming, small towns, and Abraham Lincoln. Perceptions of southern and central Illinois are pretty thin. Chicago residents would tell you that there isn't much there. They prefer to vacation in Michigan and Wisconsin. Perceptions of Chicago's booming suburbs are even less clear. Chicagoans view them as wealthy and Republican, lacking in character and diversity. Natives of rural Illinois view the suburbs as overly busy and congested, but as the best place to find a job when you have finally decided there is no future in small town trade and agriculture.

Chicago's history is quite unlike New York's in two important respects: its population has declined since mid-century, and it has become much poorer; in this sense it has followed the Rust Belt model of development and decline. By 2000, about 1.6 million more people lived in Chicago's suburbs than in the city itself, and this could not be said of New York (see chap. 13). Contrary to New York, as Chicago's population has fled to the suburbs, not as many people have moved in from elsewhere to replace the exiles. By the mid-1990s, New York's population had dropped by only 8 percent since 1950, compared with a 17 percent loss of population in Chicago over the same period. Chicago receives only a fraction of the immigrants that New York does, and the foreign-born population is more likely than in New York to move directly into lower income suburbs in DuPage and Cook County. Chicago once stood as the state's center of wealth and sophistication. By the late 1960s it had become associated with poverty, welfare, crime, and disorder — a place to be escaped (Jensen 1978).

The Chicago suburbs (outlying parts of Cook County and Lake, DuPage, Will, Kane, and McHenry Counties; see map 14.1) can be described with the same story of growth that one finds in most other states with declining central cities. The towns immediately adjacent to Chicago, including Evanston, Oak Park, Skokie, Park Ridge, and Cicero, predate World War I. Their populations swelled in the years immediately following World War II and have since declined. Secondary suburbs, further out from Chicago in the collar counties, including towns in DuPage, Will, and Lake Counties, saw their populations take off in the 1960s and 1970s, stimulated by out-migration from Chicago and from older suburbs. In the 1980s, development moved even further out to Kane and McHenry Counties, enabled by the increasing number of corporate headquarters offices and manufacturing facilities that had relocated to the suburbs. By the beginning of the twenty-first century, the metro area extended as far as Kendall and LaSalle Counties well to the west of what had been commonly considered metropolitan Chicago (Gove and Nowlan 1996, 218).

Flight from some of the older central city and suburban neighborhoods has brought about declining housing values. As rents have dropped, a poorer and more racially diverse population has moved in, as it has in New York (Taub, Taylor, and Dunham 1984, chap. 3). The Hispanic population has moved to Chicago's West Side neighborhoods, and more recently into the western suburbs, both near to Chicago and further out. Large Hispanic populations can be found in Kane County in the towns of Elgin and Aurora. In DuPage County, there are large Latino populations in Addison, West Chicago, and Hanover Park. Cook County has large Hispanic populations in Cicero, Melrose Park, and southern suburbs on the Indiana state line. In the early 2000s, this was a sufficiently recent population that most Hispanics did not work in highly skilled positions (Rey 1996, 151). They found work mainly in the suburban boom in construction, warehous-

Map 14.1.   Regions of Illinois

ing, and light manufacturing. Politically, the Hispanic population has been inert and nonparticipatory across Illinois. Estimates from the 1990 U.S. census indicated than 46 percent of the state's non–Puerto Rican Hispanics were not citizens (Rey 1996). In Chicago, Latinos numbered an impressive 754,000 by 2000 (26 percent of the city's population), and its concentration in several West Side wards made it impossible to ignore, but it was sufficiently heterogeneous to be a constant worry to Democratic party bosses. While Puerto Ricans,

Mexicans, and Central Americans were the dominant Latino populations, the groups did not mix easily, as they shared a common language
but different cultures. The diverse national origins of the Hispanic
population have made it difficult to rally these voters into a panethnic
bloc.

Illinois has had a black population since before the Civil War,
mainly in the state's northern cities. Their arrival was not greeted
warmly by white ethnics who watched angrily as willing black workers were recruited as strikebreakers in mines and industrial plants
across Illinois in the post–Civil War period (Wirt 1989). With the end
of plantation agriculture in the South in the 1920s and 1930s, more
blacks were pushed northward to find unskilled work in mining and
manufacturing (Leamann 1991; Wright 1986). The black population
of Chicago grew to half a million by 1950 and to 813,000 by 1960—
about 23 percent of the city's population.

The black population in Chicago has also increased as the white
population has moved out, standing at about 36 percent of the population by 2000. Black-white neighborhood integration in metropolitan Chicago has been painful and slow, proceeding only down a few
limited paths of least resistance (Wirt 1989; Taub, Taylor, and Dunham 1984; Jensen 1978). By the turn of the twenty-first century, the
Cook-DuPage County border still stood as an impenetrable wall to
black families seeking to move westward—DuPage's black population stood at a minuscule 3 percent of the total count. The black migration from Chicago has mainly moved southward into the suburbs
of southern Cook County, extending Chicago's South Side (Gove and
Nowlan 1996, 24). Lower-income blacks are clustered in the suburbs
closest to the city line, particularly in Calumet Park, Robbins, and
Harvey. Middle-income blacks typically moved to suburbs further
south into Will County. Reports in the early 2000s indicated that even
the middle-income black suburbs remain highly segregated, mimick-
ing the Chicago pattern of racial division.

Downstate Illinois is often characterized the same way upstate
New York is: as a politically homogeneous region opposed to the interests of Chicago. Until the courts forced states to redraw state legislative and congressional districts, rural Illinois did have disproportionate influence in state politics (Nardulli 1989). But rural Illinois
always had Democratic elements—particularly in the southern part
of the state—where mining and small manufacturing took prece-

dence over agriculture. The Chicago vs. downstate cleavage was conspicuous on many taxing and spending issues until the early 1960s, as it was in New York. After 1960, though, rural Illinois subsided in importance, and suburban Chicago became the city's primary opponent and competitor for limited resources. The locus of political conflict moved northward, between city and suburbs, with downstate Republicans usually siding with suburban interests and downstate Democrats occasionally cutting deals with Chicagoans (Nardulli 1989).

In electoral politics, downstate was a mix of Republican and Democratic turf during the twentieth century but trended steadily in a more Republican direction. Map 14.2 shows the Democratic percentage of the vote in the 1928–36 elections, by quartile. Reflecting the influence of Southern migration northward, much of southern Illinois was firmly in Democratic hands during this era. The southernmost counties had much more in common with Kentucky and southern Missouri than they did with the rest of Illinois (Fenton 1966). As in the Old South, voters in southern Illinois were not converted by the New Deal—they were Democrats already—but they were mobilized by it. In the downstate counties, participation was 24 percent higher in 1936 than it was in 1928, while the total number of voters had remained much the same.

The band of counties that is central Illinois was less enthusiastic about Roosevelt, but generally more supportive of Democrats than rural northern Illinois, which stands out as the thickest GOP turf in the state. Central Illinois is dotted with several towns that had a manufacturing base attracted to the prolabor planks of the New Deal program. Democrats did well wherever labor unions played a prominent role in socializing and mobilizing voters. East central Illinois (Livingston, Woodford, McLean, Ford Counties), where the economic mainstays were farming and trade, resisted the New Deal tide and became more Republican in subsequent years (Nardulli 1989).

Cook County, dominated by Chicago proper in the 1930s, was predictably supportive of Roosevelt, and this is no surprise given what we know about the appeal of the New Deal in urban industrial America (Sundquist 1983; Ranney 1960). Between 1928 and 1960, the Democratic party gained ground wherever one could find urban voters, Catholics, immigrants, children of recent immigrants, and African Americans (Fenton 1966; Ladd and Hadley 1975; Sundquist 1983). In previous times, Chicago had been more competitive between the

Map 14.2.   Average Democratic percentage of the presidential vote, 1928–1936

parties, regularly electing Republican mayors. Kristi Andersen concluded that much of the change in Chicago during the 1930s was the
result of the mobilization of new voters, mostly lower-income ethnics,
rather than conversion of the old (1979). The election returns for
Cook County indicate that voter participation was 30 percent higher
in 1936 than in 1928, but certainly the population had not grown that
quickly in the eight-year interval. Black voters were the one signi-

ficant group that did convert to the Democrats, beginning in 1936 and finally solidifying in 1944 (Andersen 1979; Grimshaw 1992, chap. 3).

In the 1930s, the suburbs were mostly contained within Cook County, but extended slightly west into DuPage and north into Lake. DuPage, with less than 100,000 people in 1930, consisted of small towns connected by a few roads running through farm fields and was largely indistinguishable from the rest of northern Illinois at the time. To the north, Lake County, containing slightly over 100,000 people, was well developed along the lake shore, but had little development inland. Still, even well before the suburban boom, the collar counties were whiter, wealthier, and more Protestant than Chicago, with a much smaller proportion of immigrants, almost no manufacturing jobs, and much less to gain from New Deal legislation. These characteristics help to explain their resistance to the Roosevelt tide and their position in the lowest quartile of Democratic support in map 14.2.

By 1960, the political geography of Illinois had changed very little from where it had been in the 1930s. Southern Illinois drifted further toward the Democrats in presidential elections partly because older Republicans died and were replaced by younger Democrats who had come of age during Roosevelt's reign. At the same time, this region had grown poorer and more dependent on government aid with the decline in mining and manufacturing. In two-thirds of the counties in this region, the population declined between 1930 and 1960.

Central Illinois fared better economically than the southernmost counties, and several of the mid-sized towns experienced sustained growth with Champaign and Peoria doubling in size by 1960. Some of the growth came from nearby rural counties as farmers and the adult children of farmers migrated into town to find work. The effects of these local migration streams on politics varied. In Peoria and Tazewell Counties (Peoria, Pekin) the Democratic bent weakened with prosperity because Peoria attracted rural residents from nearby counties with decidedly Republican traditions. Because of its industrial economy, though, Peoria remained more Democratic than other towns that attracted agricultural expatriates. Champaign (Champaign-Urbana) and Sangamon Counties (Springfield) went more Republican than Peoria because their growth was fueled by trade, services, and state government employment rather than industry.

Northern Illinois remained mostly Republican in the 1950s and 1960s, although Lake County's Republicanism weakened slightly, and

Winnebago (Rockford) and Rock Island (Rock Island) took a decidedly Democratic turn due to the influence of union labor. The best
news for the GOP came in the collar counties where accelerated out-
migration from Chicago meant more political clout in state politics.
With this out-migration came some disaffected Chicago Republicans
but even more Democrats who converted upon their arrival. As in
New York, this conversion was facilitated by the absence of Democratic candidates in local elections and was also a reaction against the
practices of the Democratic machine in the city.

From 1960 to 2000, the state's political geography changed even
more than it had in the thirty years prior to 1960. Map 14.3 presents
the average Democratic percentage of the vote in the 1988–2000
presidential elections. In the southern counties, the Democrats lost
ground as they continued to lose population. Although the southernmost counties remained in the highest Democratic quartile, in map
14.3, fewer voters lived in these towns than in earlier times. Southern
migration to the state's southernmost counties stopped in the nineteenth century, but one hundred years later, citizens still identified
more closely with Kentucky and Missouri than they did with northern Illinois. The dominant media market in the area is a triangular region bounded by Marion, Illinois, Paducah, Kentucky, and Cape Gi-
radeau, Missouri. For these reasons, we can expect southern Illinois
to move in the same political direction as western Kentucky and
southwestern Missouri—increasingly Republican in national elections with waning Democratic loyalty in local elections.

Southern Illinois's one metropolitan region underwent significant
change in the last two decades of the twentieth century. Monroe
County (Waterloo), southeast of St. Louis, is noteworthy for gaining
Republican voters who have recently fled outward from St. Louis and
from St. Clair County (East St. Louis–Belleville). East St. Louis, the
largest city in St. Clair County, is predominantly black. Belleville is
working class and white. In both of these locales, Democratic loyalties are deeply seated, making St. Clair the most predictable Democratic county outside of Chicago.

Central Illinois remains a mix of Democratic and Republican territory. Western Illinois, around Rock Island, lost many of its manufacturing jobs as farm implement manufacturers went out of business
or downsized. Displaced workers who remained in the area faced the
prospect of long-term unemployment or low-paying work in the ser-

Map 14.3.   Average Democratic percentage of the presidential vote, 1988–2000

vice sector. Often, hostility to these changing circumstances translated into support for the Democratic party and for populist rhetoric in particular.

As agricultural production became more concentrated in rural Illinois, more people moved away from the smaller counties. Leaving the farm has not usually meant moving a long distance. Rather, when the adult children of farmers recognized there was no future for them in agriculture, they preferred to take jobs in cities where they could be near their aging parents. This limited local migration has meant that the larger towns downstate have gained population even though the counties surrounding them have declined. In presidential elections, Springfield and Peoria became less Democratic in the years since 1960. GOP leaders in the 1980s and 1990s spoke of Springfield as a company town. Republicans monopolized the governorship between 1976 and 2002, and with this dominance has come loyalty to the GOP among state workers, particularly patronage employees. The Sangamon County Republican party organization was ranked among the most effective political forces in the state.

Champaign has become more Democratic since the 1960s. The expansion of the University of Illinois in Champaign-Urbana is responsible for this area's increasing Democratic liberalism in presidential politics. In state and local elections, when student turnout drops, Champaign County's more Republican roots prevail. In the more rural counties of central Illinois, political changes have been the product of the slow process of generational replacement and the gradual out-migration from agricultural areas.

In northern Illinois, Republicans have gained enormous ground in the Chicago suburbs since 1970. By the early 2000s, suburbia extended as far as McHenry, Kendall, and LaSalle Counties. Public transit and extensive investment in the metropolitan highway system have been responsible for this growth. Many more employers were located in the suburbs by the turn of the new century, so it was becoming less necessary to commute to downtown Chicago. Republicans lost some ground in the more rural counties of northwest Illinois as upwardly mobile residents moved to the Chicago suburbs to leave behind a poorer, more elderly population with fewer farmers. The city of Rockford (Winnebago County) usually went Democratic in presidential elections, although the surrounding turf was heavily GOP. Rockford came to resemble some of the worst of the Rust Belt locations in upstate New York. Manufacturing jobs have disappeared; skilled workers and white, upwardly mobile residents have vacated. Notably, Rockford has a substantial black population, about 17 percent in the early 2000s, and elected and reelected a black mayor.

Chicago remains the Democratic stronghold that it has been for decades. Its population has become more diverse as upwardly mobile whites have fled and blacks and Hispanics have moved in (Gove and

Nowlan 1996). The minority population in Chicago is more diverse than a century ago, but it is also poorer. The high-paying low-skill manufacturing jobs have disappeared, while unemployment and employment in the lower-paying service sector have expanded the size of Chicago's poor neighborhoods (Wilson 1987; Taub, Taylor, and Dunham 1984). Many good jobs have also fled the city altogether. Suburban employers frequently discriminate against central city populations, locking Chicago's minority community into one of the worst labor markets in the nation. The city's economic decline has wrought a different kind of Democratic politics than the one that operated in the 1950s and 1960s. African Americans and Latinos are now core Democratic constituencies, whereas in previous times they were marginal (Pinderhughes 1987). White ethnics control fewer of the city's wards, and white politicians are dependent upon the nonwhite vote to an extent never before seen in history. Immigration will not transform Chicago's politics as quickly as it has New York's, but it will be a major force for political change in the next fifty years.

**Where Are the Votes in Illinois? Democratic and
Republican Mobilization Targets**

With the decline of the rural population, it is no surprise that the voter-rich areas in Illinois are clustered mainly in the state's northeast corner. Both parties must begin any serious political campaign by focusing on this small geographic area where the vast majority of people live. Democrats have the same kind of advantage in Illinois that they have in New York. Fifty percent of the statewide Democratic vote for president typically originated from Cook County (especially Chicago) in the first decade of the new century. Another 10 percent came from Lake, DuPage, and Will Counties. While Chicago has declined in importance to the Democratic party over the last five decades, it still dwarfs all other jurisdictions in its centrality to that party's campaign efforts (Nardulli 1989; Ranney 1960) (see map 14.4).

Republicans collected only 35 percent of their statewide total from Cook County in the 1988–2000 elections, and this came evenly from both the city's northwest and southwest wards and its northwest suburbs. DuPage contributed about 10 percent and Lake about 6 percent of the Republicans' total statewide vote. As in most other states, then, the GOP was faced with the more complex and costly task of

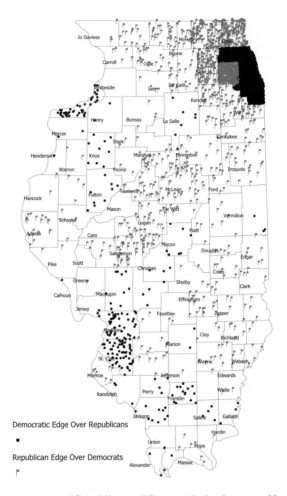

Map 14.4. Areas of Republican and Democratic dominance, 1988–2000

mobilizing voters over a larger geographic area. Getting out the vote in suburban Chicago was no easy task, particularly in state and local races. Many suburbanites had moved in from elsewhere in the state, or perhaps from outside Illinois. They were not registered in their new precincts and did not vote. Others had a suburban mind-set, that of the transient independent who had no stake in the outcome of local elections (Brown 1988; Gimpel 1999; Squire, Wolfinger, and Glass 1987).

In the 1930s, Republicans and Democrats were to be found competing on much the same turf, albeit not precisely the same wards and precincts. Republicans found 46 percent of their statewide vote in Cook County, and Democrats mobilized 53 percent of their base from there. In that era, Republicans and Democrats waged pitched battles in many other counties that would later become one-party strongholds. As in New York, the rise of the suburbs after World War II meant that Republicans could establish a separate power base outside of the central city, largely free from the threat of Democratic competition. Democrats could not allow the suburbs to remain uncontested—far too many of their voters were moving there. So the suburban counties became more important to Democratic efforts too; DuPage County contributed only a minuscule 1 percent of the total statewide vote to Democrats in the 1928–36 elections, but by the turn of the century, it provided 5 percent of the Democratic base. Still, Republicans and Democrats share less common territory today than they did a century ago, a development that has contributed to the partisan and ideological polarization of the American electorate.

Table 14.1 ranks the ten most important counties for both Democrats and Republicans in the 1988–2000 presidential elections. The rankings are based on both the percentage of the total statewide vote each county contributes to the Republican or Democratic parties, as well as the percentage of the vote each county awards to the Republican or Democratic candidates (following the example of the previous chapters). In New York, both parties depended on the most

TABLE 14.1.   Illinois's Top Ten Strongest Counties for Republican and Democrats in the 1988–2000 Presidential Contests

Rank	Democratic	Republican
1	Cook (Chicago)	Cook (Chicago)
2	DuPage (Wheaton)	DuPage (Wheaton)
3	Lake (Waukegan)	Lake (Waukegan)
4	St. Clair (East St. Louis)	Will (Joliet)
5	Madison (Granite City–Alton)	Kane (Elgin)
6	Will (Joliet)	McHenry (Crystal Lake)
7	Winnebago (Rockford)	Sangamon (Springfield)
8	Rock Island (Rock Island)	Winnebago (Rockford)
9	Peoria (Peoria)	Madison (Granite City–Alton)
10	Kane (Elgin)	McLean (Bloomington)
% of total vote	73.5	66.1

urban counties downstate. New York Republicans could not hope to win many elections by concentrating all of their efforts upstate. The same was true of Illinois at the beginning of the new millennium. The top two positions on the list were occupied by the same counties for both parties. Cook and DuPage were key battleground areas because of their size. Democrats usually took the former, and Republicans the latter, but neither party could afford to ignore either jurisdiction. Republicans competed well for Chicago's white voters along the lake shore (at least in national elections) and in the city's northwest and far southwest neighborhoods. GOP strategists hoped for low turnout in the overwhelmingly Democratic black and Latino neighborhoods.

Below the top three placeholders, the regional bases of partisan support diverge. Democrats gained a considerable share of their votes from St. Clair and Madison Counties outside of St. Louis (see map 14.4). These counties are valuable not only for their size, but because they award such a large proportion of their vote to the Democrats. Only after going to suburban St. Louis in search of high turnout did Democrats then return to suburban Chicago, to Will County (ranked sixth) and Kane County (ranked tenth). The smaller cities of Rockford, Rock Island, and Peoria rounded out the list of the most important mobilization targets for Democrats (see table 14.1).

Republican campaign efforts began upstate and pretty much remained there. Eight out of the ten most important GOP targets were in northern Illinois (see table 14.1). Only two, Sangamon (Springfield) and Madison (Granite City–Alton), were downstate. Several areas important to the Republicans were not high on the list for Democrats. And it was obvious that in spite of the concentration of GOP votes in northern Illinois, Republicans had nothing to compare to the geographical concentration of Democratic votes in Chicago. Republicans had to hope for a respectable showing in Chicago, while turning out voters in all of the collar counties along with those on the metropolitan fringe. With the geographic polarization of the Illinois electorate, political contests would remain competitive statewide, while becoming more lopsided locally.

Illinois's Changing Electoral Foundations

To understand electoral behavior in Illinois as far back as the 1930s, we have had to make inferences based on what we observe in extant county-level data. To help us make such inferences, we have relied upon Gary King's (1997) maximum likelihood ecological inference model described in appendix A. This methodology does not always generate the precise estimates of voting tendencies that a properly conducted survey would, but in the absence of polls and surveys extending back to the 1920s, it is the next best thing, and we can learn a lot from it. Results from the ecological inference analysis for sets of presidential elections in Illinois are presented in table 14.2.

Population Mobility

Illinois is similar to New York in that we do not see the dramatic partisan changes that are visible in faster-growing states in the South and

TABLE 14.2.   Estimates of the Democratic Percentage of the Presidential Vote for Various Electoral Groups in Illinois, 1928–2000 (ecological inference maximum likelihood)

Pooled Presidential Election Years	Blacks/ Nonblacks		Elderly/ Nonelderly		Immigrants/ Nonimmigrants		Farmers/ Nonfarmers		Whites/ Nonwhites	
1928, 1932	37.6	49.3*	51.2*	48.7*	49.4	48.7	51.7*	48.4*	48.9*	47.7
1936, 1940, 1944	58.6	53.1*	19.7	56.2*	51.6	53.6*	38.8*	55.4*	53.0*	61.9
1948, 1952	72.4	45.3*	47.3	47.3*	41.8	47.8*	34.6*	48.5*	44.8*	76.7
1956, 1960, 1964	79.7	46.4*	82.6	46.3*	53.4	49.6*	37.6*	50.6*	48.8*	59.0
1968, 1972	71.2	38.1*	53.9	41.0*	72.0	40.5*	28.7*	42.8*	37.3*	73.8
1976, 1980, 1984	83.9	37.4*	49.4	43.1*	38.4	44.7*	25.9*	44.8*	39.6*	59.9
1988, 1992	83.9	42.8*	51.2	48.5*	52.4	48.5*	30.1	49.1*	41.6*	75.1
1996, 2000	92.2	48.8*	49.8	56.1*	97.4	52.0*	46.5	55.9*	44.9*	91.3

	Mfg. Workers/ Non Mfg. Workers		College Educated/ Non College Educated		Native to State/ Nonnatives		Internal Migrants/ Nonmigrants		Hispanics/ Non- Hispanics	
1928, 1932	—	—	—	—	—	—	—	—	—	—
1936, 1940, 1944	—	—	—	—	—	—	—	—	—	—
1948, 1952	57.9*	42.7*	13.5	49.4*	—	—	—	—	—	—
1956, 1960, 1964	53.6*	48.2*	21.5	52.3*	47.7*	55.1*	52.9*	49.0*	—	—
1968, 1972	42.6*	42.2*	38.0	42.8*	38.7*	50.1*	50.5*	39.3*	—	—
1976, 1980, 1984	20.5*	50.7*	40.9	43.8*	40.0*	53.8*	52.7*	41.6*	35.5	43.9*
1988, 1992	15.1	57.0*	30.4	53.8*	45.9*	55.5*	53.0*	47.7*	54.5	48.4*
1996, 2000	32.7	59.9*	54.4	55.5*	48.0*	73.0*	66.3*	52.7*	86.5	52.1*

Note: Cell entries show the estimated percentage voting Democratic in the listed presidential elections. Complete variable definitions and results from the ecological inference estimation appear in appendix B, with standard errors and bounds.

*Reflect estimates with lower and upper bounds narrower than 0,1.

West. Outside of Chicago, many Illinois jurisdictions are competitive battlegrounds and have been for years (Fenton 1966; Ranney 1960). While some places lean Republican, and others Democratic, Republicans and Democrats remain on more of an equal footing across more territory than in other states. This means that we will find less drastic fluctuations in partisanship across time in Illinois than we would expect in states that had entrenched one-party traditions at midcentury.

Since Illinois has not seen a tidal wave of migration from other states, partisan change has been the result of mobility fueled by dynamics internal to the state, such as economic restructuring in agriculture and manufacturing. In some places, economic difficulties beginning in the mid-1970s have produced party converts: usually Republicans who find themselves voting Democratic. Western Illinois exemplifies how depressed agricultural and manufacturing economies have increased people's sense of grievance. Incomes and standards of living have fallen. The Democrats have usually been the party in the best position to respond to the worries of those laid off from skilled and semiskilled jobs. Western Illinois was more likely to vote Democratic in the early 2000s than at any time since the 1930s.

One of our main interests in conducting this research has been to determine whether population changes stimulated by migration have led to consequential political changes. In table 14.2 we estimated support for Democratic presidential candidates among Illinois natives and cross-state migrants. Because there is little threat of aggregation bias in the data for these two groups, our estimates are more accurate than for some of the other populations we evaluated. First we find that voters born in Illinois are slightly more Republican than those who were born elsewhere (immigrants and cross-state migrants combined). The gap between natives and those born elsewhere is particularly wide in the 1996–2000 elections, with an estimated 48 percent of natives supporting the Democratic candidate, compared with 73 percent for nonnatives (see table 14.2).

We anticipated that migrants from other states would have Republican inclinations. This is based on what we know about such migrants (Gimpel 1999; Brown 1988). They are usually white and upwardly mobile, and can afford the costs associated with moving long distances. Examining the estimates for cross-state migrants, it is clear that this group leans more Democratic than nonmigrants (natives and immigrants combined). One way of looking at these results is to suggest that however Republican the cross-state migration stream has been, it is clear that the population native to Illinois has been even more Republican. Similar results obtained for New York (chap. 13). It is noteworthy that the difference between cross-state migrants and others was a negligible 3 points in the 1948–52 elections. This gap widens in subsequent elections, indicating that cross-state migration has apparently not helped the GOP.

Because the vast majority of Illinois counties have minuscule proportions of immigrants, our estimates for Democratic support among this group are not highly reliable. Most recent immigrants choose to settle in Chicago and the western suburbs, with relatively few to be found beyond the collar counties. Other available evidence indicates that immigrants, when they do vote, have contributed far more to the Democratic party than to the Republican. Recent surveys of Hispanic voters in Illinois show that they vote Democratic by a two-to-one margin. And certainly the association of immigrants with Democrats would be consistent with the state's past (Grimshaw 1992; Pinderhughes 1987). Eastern European and Latino immigrants may eventually take their place alongside natives in the Illinois electorate, but it takes years for them to naturalize, learn about politics, and then vote, and many never make it this far.

In the new century, the foreign-born population will be the major force for political change in Illinois. While the rate of growth from immigration is much slower than in California, Texas, Florida, or New York, immigration is the main source of population influx into the city of Chicago and the older suburbs. Internal migrants, many of whom are drawn to the state because of their high-paying professional and managerial jobs, prefer to move to the suburbs—near their newly opened corporate headquarters. In some of the older suburbs, however, the same political transition is taking place that has already occurred in New York. Democratically inclined ethnic minority populations are moving in to challenge the safety of Republican officeholders. Inasmuch as these ethnic minority populations have their origins in some other country, national immigration policy holds the key to the state's political geography in 2020 and beyond.

Generational Change

There is a significant role for generational change in the differences we observe between maps 14.2 and 14.3. In other states, we see political change occurring in slow-growing rural areas as older Democrats have died off to be replaced by younger Republicans. What is different about Illinois is that this process of generational change has not always helped Republicans as it often has in other states. Much of rural central and northern Illinois, the very birthplace of the GOP, was never committed to the Roosevelt revolution (see map 14.2). Generational replacement in these rural communities in the years after 1936 meant that older Republicans were dying off. They were about as likely to be replaced by younger Democrats as Republicans—meaning that generational replacement has gradually altered the political balance of rural Illinois.

In rural southern Illinois, outside of suburban St. Louis, the process of generational change has gradually yielded better Republican prospects more in line with observations from other states. Voters in this region are socially conservative, and religious—mostly Protestant. Because the area has been economically depressed for much of the century, voters are not inclined to retaliate against either party for pervasive economic distress. People have learned to settle for economic difficulty and a lower standard of living than could be found further north. Having given up on the capacity of either party to stimulate local economic revival, voters are often cued by their attitudes on social and moral issues. Many younger voters have become dual partisans: registering and voting Democratic in local and statewide races, but voting Republican in presidential elections (Gimpel 1999; Miller and Jewell 1990). Dual partisanship is a familiar regional phenomenon that unites southern Illinois with Kentucky and states further south.

Studying the voting inclinations of older voters is important because they tell us something about the political consequences of generational transition. If the political attitudes of those nearing death are different from the attitudes of younger voters, then we can be sure that the next ten to fifteen years will bring about major changes in the partisan and political composition of a population. Our estimates in table 14.2 do show some differences between the elderly and nonelderly in Illinois—older voters are generally more Democratic than younger voters, particularly in the 1976–84 group of elections. These findings are consistent with the state's gradual drift toward the Republican party in local elections through the latter half of the twentieth century. In the short term, the death of these aging Democrats may provide the Republicans with an edge.

Generational change, rather than conversion, has probably shifted the loyalties of the college educated since mid-century. We chose to estimate Democratic support among the college educated, because education is an indicator of socioeconomic status. Our expectation was that those with college degrees would exhibit decidedly Republican loyalties compared to those with less education. We also expected that the difference between the educated and uneducated would diminish with time as more people obtained college degrees. Although our estimates for the population with less than a college education are more accurate than the ones for the well-educated, our expectations are generally borne out by our estimates in table 14.2. In the 1948–52 elections, there is a considerable gap between the two groups in their support for Truman and Stevenson with the better educated supporting Republicans. This gap diminishes in the following elections. Polling data indicate that by 1996–2000, support for Clinton and Gore was nearly as high among those with a college education (54.4 percent) as it was among those with less than a four-year degree (55.5 percent).

Conversion

Partisan conversion must also play a role in the recent political history of Illinois or else the mass movement of Democrats from Chicago to the suburbs would have produced Democratic majorities in Lake and DuPage Counties. While Chicago has always had a substantial population of Republican identifiers, it is not just Republicans who have moved from the city to the suburbs. The Lake, DuPage, and McHenry County towns are Republican strongholds in most elections because many Democrats who have moved out of Chicago have become Republicans. The conversion probably began when they first became dissatisfied with life in the city. Chicago's traffic congestion, growing minority population, and crime problems began to grate on them. They saw that municipal services were costly and unreliable. Their children were going to schools that were run down, dangerous, or undergoing racial change. They saw that one party, the Democrats, had been in control for decades. They correctly associated stories of city government corruption with the Democratic machine. But even without official corruption, a mental impression was eventually built that associated the Democratic party with all the reasons for their dissatisfaction.

Then the move occurred. It may have taken a while for these new residents of the suburbs to register and vote in their new locale. If they registered as Democrats, they probably found that the Democrats had few if any viable candidates in their new city and county. Furthermore, many of their neighbors were Republicans. While there were some aggravations in the new community, such as traffic and the distance from here to there, many of the problems of the city were not present. The schools were newer, the neighborhoods were safer, there were few people of color, and the garbage was picked up on schedule. Life was just better. Republicans held the vast majority of local offices. Through speeches and campaign rhetoric, these office-holders reinforced the belief that the Democratic party was the party of Chicago, not the suburbs. After a few elections, these new residents were voting consistently Republican. They may not have changed their party registration, but their children grew up Republican and registered with the GOP when they turned 18. Migration, conversion, and generational change conspired to produce and reproduce Republican party dominance.

Conversion from one party to another contributed something to the creation of the Democratic majority in Illinois after the 1932 elections and may have also played a role during the politically turbulent 1960s. To examine these eras, we constructed voter transition models to estimate the support Democratic and Republican voters in 1928 awarded to their party's nominees in 1932. We also examine the relationship between the 1932 and 1936 elections, as well as subsequent pairs of elections in the 1960s. What we found was that party loyalty in Illinois was unusually high from 1928 to 1932. Over 70 percent of Republican voters in 1928 supported Herbert Hoover's reelection bid. Of the Hoover voters in 1932, an estimated 73.9 percent of those went on to vote for Landon in 1936 (see table 14.3). These figures contrast sharply with estimates from California and other states that show dramatic Republican defections between 1928 and 1932. Conversion was not the force for political change in Illinois that it was elsewhere.

In the 1960s, GOP loyalty to Barry Goldwater was once again stronger than in either New York or California. An estimated 80.5 percent of Nixon (1960) voters supported Goldwater four years later, compared with only 64 percent in New York and 52 percent in California. Illinois Democrats who had voted for Lyndon Johnson were more comfortable with Hubert Humphrey than either California or New York Democrats were. Wallace was not popular in Illinois, but our estimates indicate that he won about 7.6 percent of the vote among Johnson Democrats and 10 percent of the vote among Goldwater Republicans. Surprisingly, Wallace voters in the land of Lincoln then moved back to the Democratic side for the 1972 election whereas in most states they supported Nixon. These findings underscore the conclusion that conversion was a more limited phenomenon in Illinois than it was in many other states. Illinois voters showed remarkable party loyalty in presidential elections even in turbulent times (table 14.3).

While Illinois voters may generally be more reluctant to abandon their parties than those from other states, that does not mean that all groups within the state are steadfast. We might still look for the combination of conversion and generational replacement to shift the allegiance of certain voting blocs over a decade or two. For instance, we would expect farmers to become more Republican between 1930 and 2000, and our estimates show that they do. Slightly over half of farmers cast Democratic ballots in the combined 1928–32 elections, compared with around 25 percent in 1996–2000. All of the available evidence suggests that it is the places with large farm populations that remained Republican after 1936. Rural areas where farming was not a principal economic activity, such as southern Illinois, voted Democratic. In other words, the relevant difference in Illinois after the New Deal is not rural vs. urban so much as farm vs. nonfarm.

The farm population has become more distinct in its political behavior from the nonfarm population, but ironically this has not necessarily contributed to increasing sectionalism or political balkanization within the state. Our explanation for this is simple. Sectionalism has not intensified because the number of farmers is so much smaller in Illinois in 2000 than it was in 1950. As the agricultural economy has declined in rural Illinois, differences between the rural and urban parts of the state have subsided.

We might also look for a combination of conversion and generational replacement to be at work realigning the state's working-class voters. As in most states, blue-collar workers in manufacturing supported Roosevelt's New Deal and its promise to strengthen labor

TABLE 14.3. Estimates of Party Loyalty and Conversion across Presidential Elections in Illinois (ecological inference maximum likelihood)

Presidential Election Years	Voted Democratic 1928/Non-Democratic 1928		Voted Democratic 1932/Non-Democratic 1932		Presidential Election Years	Voted Republican 1928/Non-Republican 1928		Voted Republican 1932/Non-Republican 1932	
Voted Democratic 1932	89.6*	29.9*			Voted Republican 1932	71.8*	2.9*		
Voted Democratic 1936			85.6*	23.7*	Voted Republican 1936			73.9*	14.6*

Presidential Election Years	Voted Democratic 1960/Non-Democratic 1960		Voted Democratic 1964/Non-Democratic 1964		Presidential Election Years	Voted Republican 1960/Non-Republican 1960		Voted Republican 1964/Non-Republican 1964	
Voted Democratic 1964	93.7*	25.5*			Voted Republican 1964	80.5*	1.0*		
Voted Democratic 1968			74.0*	1.0*	Voted Republican 1968			97.3*	12.2*
Voted Wallace 1968			7.6*	9.8*	Voted Wallace 1968			10.1*	7.4*

Note: Cell entries show the estimated percentage voting Democratic, Republican, or for George Wallace in the presidential elections listed on each row who voted Democratic (or Republican) in the previous election. Complete variable definitions and results from the ecological inference estimation appear in appendix C, with standard errors and bounds.

*Reflect estimates with lower and upper bounds narrower than 0.1.

unions. Our results for manufacturing workers indicate that they were more Democratic than those in other occupations in the pooled 1948–52 elections (see table 14.2). But these same voters were less inclined to vote Democratic after 1970. The ecological inference estimates pick up the tendency for these "Reagan Democrats" to act independently of their party registration. In fact, our results comparing manufacturing workers to those in other occupations may exaggerate the difference between the two groups, but the trends are clear. In the 1948–52 presidential elections, an estimated 58 percent of manufacturing workers voted Democratic, compared with only 43 percent of those who worked outside of this sector. By the 1980s and 1990s, not only had many of the manufacturing jobs disappeared, but those still working in this sector were about half as likely to vote Democratic as they were in earlier decades (see table 14.2).

Activism and Partisanship of New Voting Blocs

While Republicans gained ascendancy in state politics in the late 1970s, the state remained competitive in presidential elections due largely to the loyalty and turnout of black Democrats in Chicago, East St. Louis, and their suburbs. In the new century, Democrats probably will not win Illinois's electoral votes without this critical bloc of support. African-American voter participation was not always as high, or as Democratic, as it has been in the most recent elections. The movement of blacks into Democratic party ranks was not sudden. Comparing the voting of blacks to nonblacks, we see that black voters are far more likely than nonblack voters to support Democrats after 1948. Some scholars have placed the critical turning point at 1944, when Chicago blacks voted for Roosevelt because he spoke out against racial discrimination in a local campaign speech (Grimshaw 1992, 48). In earlier elections black support for Democrats was considerably lower, perhaps because the early converts were lower-income blacks attracted by the economic appeal of the New Deal (see table 14.2). After 1948, black realignment was complete, and subsequent mass mobilization helped make black voters a significant force. Black support for Democratic presidential candidates appears to peak in the 1970s and 1980s with acute racial polarization in the elections since 1976. The results are substantially similar for the comparison of white to nonwhite voters (table 14.2).

Conclusions

As one of the most electorally competitive states in the nation, Illinois will be a major battleground in presidential elections well into the twenty-first century. It is not an easy state for the campaign strategist to target because, outside of Chicago and East St. Louis, it is difficult to locate areas that are monolithically favorable to one party toward which all of one's mobilization resources can be directed. Presidential campaigns will be forced to study and direct resources toward many potential swing areas. In 1996 and 2000, Bill Clinton and Al Gore proved capable of winning the votes of suburban liberals in Lake County, while running up big margins in Chicago. DuPage, McHenry, and Kane Counties are more likely to go Republican, but not by an overwhelming margin. If Democratic campaigns maintain a presence in each one, they can stay close. Much of downstate is similarly up for grabs.

Illinois elections teach us that there can be strong liabilities associated with having an overly concentrated base of support. Mobilization is less costly when half of the vote is located in a single county, but Democrats also need votes outside of Chicago to win the state. Obtaining the strong commitments of liberal Chicago Democrats and more conservative downstate Democrats at the same time is not easily accomplished because of sectional differences traceable to ideology and attitudes on divisive issues.

The state's recent electoral history suggests that blue-collar workers have become a highly unreliable Democratic constituency. Republicans should take note of that and make plans to campaign hard to win converts in areas with a high proportion of workers employed in industry. College educated voters are slightly more Republican than those lacking a college degree, but the gap is not as wide as it used to be. What this means is that Democrats and Republicans are likely to compete on increasingly even ground in the collar counties—good news for Democrats who can already count on Chicago. Republicans have a significant edge in farming areas of northern and central Illinois, but Democrats can rack up even more lopsided margins among blacks, Latinos, and immigrants. Finally, the GOP will do better among those who have moved in from outside Illinois than the Democrats. Targeting neighborhoods full of newcomers for registration drives should be a key element of Republican strategy. Although the GOP has a harder time identifying specific blocs of voters they can rely upon, they will continue to win elections as long as Democrats are identified too closely with liberal and minority voters in Chicago. The key to Democratic victory will be to voice an ideologically moderate message that will cut into the softest GOP support—something the Gore campaign managed with skill and finesse in the November 2000 contest.

CHAPTER 15

SECTIONALISM AND POLITICAL CHANGE IN THE STATES

In the middle of the last century, V. O. Key Jr. received a large grant from the Rockefeller Foundation to go to the South and undertake a study of the poll tax. Fortunately for political science, the project became much larger than that, developing into his monumental work *Southern Politics*. Much of Key's research involved spending time in the region, traveling, and talking to the movers and shakers in each state. From this research, Key produced a comprehensive book about the electoral politics and party systems of eleven Southern states. While our project here cannot begin to duplicate the amount of intellectual (or financial) capital that went into the production of Key's classic, we are indebted to him for establishing a respect for states as independent and autonomous electoral entities. As much as these Old South states had in common, it is clear from Key's work that to live in Texas was not to live in South Carolina. While he frequently sought to generalize across states and regions, Key recognized that no state looked exactly like another.

Our approach in this book has been to examine a broad cross-section of states over time to understand the internal politics of each one. Given that so much political campaigning is waged on a state-to-state basis, with specific get-out-the-vote (GOTV) efforts directed at targeted locations within states, we believe that the presentation in this book has advanced our knowledge more than an approach that severs the connection between voters and the places where they cast their ballots. We chose to examine five of the most populous states because of their value in presidential elections. As we are reminded in every presidential contest, no candidate can afford to ignore California, Texas, Florida, New York, and Illinois. The inclusion of several mid-sized and smaller states has added regional variation to the study, while highlighting a range of contextual circumstances and conditions that have shaped the trajectory of state politics.

We have asked questions chiefly about the electoral behavior of each state with an aim to understanding trends and developments in electoral behavior and political geography. We have defined sectionalism within states as the uneven geographic distribution of political interests as measured at the county unit level. Although regions within states need not be understood only in partisan terms, nor studied at the county level, we have focused our attention on sectionalism of this type—highlighting contrasts between rival Republican and Democratic areas. Future work would do well to look for political sections that lie beyond (or below) the basic partisan differences we have studied.

The Geography of Voter Mobilization

In his classic *American State Politics: An Introduction,* Key called our attention to the varying geographic distribution of party support within states (1956, chap. 8). Key thought that this topic was worth studying because it set up the basic organization of a state's politics, defining where party leadership must seek votes (232). In states where rival candidates shared little intersecting turf, politics was more polarized than in states where candidates had to slug it out side by side (Gimpel and Schuknecht 2002). When they draw from distinct regions, Key argued, parties and candidates develop programs and platforms that have little statewide appeal.

Notably, Republicans and Democrats had differing mobilization priorities at the beginning of the new millennium than they did in the 1930s, or even when Key wrote in the mid-1950s. Through the centrifugal force of suburbanization, which flung only certain types of voters to the metropolitan fringe, Democrats developed a highly concentrated base of support in the largest cities. Republicans have had to go further afield in search of their voters, combing a larger geographic territory than they did early in the twentieth century. Republican campaigns must now start in the suburbs, move to larger towns outside major metropolitan areas, and then go to the more rural counties. Democrats benefit most from mobilizing central city populations, then moving to the older suburbs. The most rural counties have provided significantly more support to the GOP than to the Democrats, but farms and small towns have generally subsided in their importance to both parties. Because the Republican vote remained more geographically dispersed, however, it was more costly to reach and to mobilize. The difficulty of mobilizing voters on a door-to-door basis has forced Republicans to develop and rely upon new approaches and technologies for campaigning, including direct mail, mass media, and telephone banks. Because Democrats have benefited from the advantages of a highly concentrated electorate, they were slower to adopt new technologies and have more often maintained an old-fashioned, grassroots component to their campaigns alongside the newer innovations. All other things being equal, the Democrats have had an enormous campaign advantage in the increasing density of their electorate since the 1930s.

The concentration of the Democratic vote relative to the Republican one raises interesting questions about campaign spending that should be pursued in future research. Official observers and academic researchers have often pointed out that Republicans raise and spend more money than Democrats and have done so for more than twenty years (Federal Election Commission 2001; Herrnson 2000, 152–54). If this is so, then why don't Republicans consistently win more elections than Democrats? One answer is that they don't spend their money as wisely, that is, they are foolish or their strategy is flawed. Another answer is that Republican-inclined voters are more geographically dispersed and must be reached by costlier means than their Democratic counterparts. For reasons having to do with the costs imposed by distance, Republicans have to spend more than Democrats just to stay even.

The Variable Foundations of Substate Sectionalism

Rival political sections within states have their origin in the uneven geographic distribution of social and economic interests as well as in the differing values and priorities of voters (see chap. 1). Sectionalism reflects how people holding particular values and beliefs about politics are tied to specific locations through residence and work. As such, regionalism can usually be accounted for by examining the population composition of locations, with contextual explanations playing a secondary role. Underlying sources of substate sectionalism include:

1. Issues and ideology
2. Economic stratification
3. Ethnicity and religion
4. Race

Issues and Ideology

Issues and political ideology are a source of sectionalism when voters in a particular region or regions of a state are unified behind a particular position or view of politics not shared by voters elsewhere. The politically liberal values held by a large majority of New York City residents, or those of San Francisco's Bay Area, exemplify how a political region can be defined by widely shared political beliefs and values. The issue of water availability has unified residents in dry areas in the Western United States, creating distinct sectional interests around this issue. Public policies relating to aging, social security, and health care have produced a unique and politically cohesive constituency along Florida's Atlantic Coast. Attitudes toward individual rights, including property rights and the right to bear arms, are said to animate many voters in the Mountain West, distinguishing them from voters elsewhere (Marchant-Shapiro and Patterson 1995; Galderisi et al. 1987).

Just as issues can unify an electorate, they can also divide it. Sometimes issues emerge to divide populations that were politically homogeneous, thereby diminishing the extent of sectionalism or unifying new regions (Sundquist 1983; Nardulli 1995). Farming and agriculture interests were relatively unified across the rural counties of most states until the issue of prohibition separated farmers by ethnicity and religion, with Catholics opposing liquor controls and many Protestants favoring them. In elections where prohibition became a salient issue, we would expect customary sectional loyalties to diminish. Attitudes on busing and civil rights contributed to the widening political gap between cities and suburbs in the 1960s and after. Urban and suburban counties were dissimilar prior to the civil rights movement, but the emergence of these issues activated the black population, accelerated white flight to suburban counties, and thereby widened the differences between them, causing metropolitan areas to balkanize internally.

Economic Stratification

Economically based sectionalism often emerges on the basis of occupational interests, such as northern Minnesota's radical miners, the farmers of Minnesota's western plains, miners and steelworkers in Colorado and Pennsylvania, or eastern Michigan's autoworkers. Economic stratification and income inequality are sources of sectionalism when poverty and blight are geographically concentrated, as in rural Appalachia. Given that policy differences between the two major parties have been defined in redistributive terms since the 1930s, it is easy to understand how sectionalism could emerge on the basis of an unequal distribution of wealth. Poor voters have typically been drawn toward the Democratic party, and middle- and upper-income voters toward the Republicans. It is plausible to imagine large geographic concentrations of poverty (or wealth) that translate into a high degree of political sectionalism.

In fact, though, we rarely found income inequality lying behind sectionalism at the county level of analysis. Because income is highly variable within counties at the neighborhood and city block level, rarely does wealth or poverty unify large cross-county regions of a state. Given that income varies more by neighborhood and city than it does by county, it is more likely that economic stratification will break apart sectionalism as understood by the county-to-county linkages we have studied. Take downstate New York, for example. As a region, it consists of the five New York city boroughs as well as the two Long Island counties (Nassau and Suffolk). Economic stratification explains why the Long Island counties have become far more Republican than their urban counterparts: they are much wealthier. For sectionalism in New York to be more pronounced, Long Island and the boroughs would have to be more economically homogeneous and stand in unified contrast to poorer counties upstate.

By the 1980s and 1990s, few states proved to be highly sectional on account of income inequality. Given the pervasive economic disparity between adjacent central-city and suburban counties, we found little political regionalism because adjacent counties within metropolitan areas often supported opposing candidates rather than the same candidate. In addition, we found that economic stratification militated against sectionalism in many places: some of the lowest-income counties were in rural areas that cast overwhelmingly Republican votes. These highly GOP but rather poor counties can be found in a number of states, including Georgia, Illinois, Colorado, Maryland, Michigan, Minnesota, New York, and Texas.

Ethnicity and Religion

Ethnic differences were once prominent foundations for sectionalism in the Midwest and Northeast, although they were usually mixed in with economic and religious differences as well. European ethnic groups had differing attitudes on the issues of prohibition and immigration. Catholics were once monolithically Democratic, while the majority of Protestants were drawn toward the GOP. These religious differences have now faded and no longer serve as the foundation for substate sectionalism. The forces of assimilation, including intermarriage and geographic and socioeconomic mobility, have watered down the extent of the cleavage among European ethnic groups. Religious divisions have emerged more on the basis of doctrinal orthodoxy than on the basis of denominational adherence, with committed theological conservatives far more likely to vote Republican than those nominally identifying with a religion (Layman 1997). These politically consequential doctrinal differences do not seem to form the foundation for political regionalism, although theological conservatism is more prevalent throughout the Southern than the Northern states and is more prevalent in rural areas than in large central cities.

In the twenty-first century, ethnicity will come to play an important role in generating substate sectionalism due to sustained high levels of immigration (Gimpel 1999). The new immigrant groups from Asia and Latin America arrive on U.S. shores with little education and few skills at a time when the national economy has placed a premium on education and skills (Borjas 1999). The disparity between what immigrants can offer and what the economy demands limits the upward mobility of the immigrant population, confining them to places where they can find affordable housing and suitable employment. Low socioeconomic mobility means low geographic mobility. These immigrants may cluster in enclaves for longer periods of time than the previous waves of uneducated immigrants from Europe, who arrived to an economy that had ample jobs with minimal literacy or skill requirements. If the new waves of immigrants become politically active, their ethnic solidarity may translate into political support for a single party, leading to wider geographic cleavages rooted in ethnic identity.

Ethnic diversity can unify large areas where specific groups choose to settle, as in south Texas and southern Colorado, but can also distinguish them from adjacent areas, diminishing sectionalism as measured across counties or other large geographic units. California and Florida are perhaps the best contemporary examples of places where the influx of new populations has separated some locations from their neighbors nearby. Prior to 1960, Dade County was politically indistinguishable from much of the rest of Florida's peninsula. By the 1980s, though, it seemed to some to have become a different country altogether, with Spanish as commonly spoken as English. Similar changes are converging to distinguish Los Angeles from the rest of southern California, and Harris County (Houston, Texas) from neighboring locations.

Race

Race was a source of substate sectionalism in several states when Key wrote *Southern Politics* (1949). In most cases, black turnout was low, but sectionalism persisted on the basis of the threat that sizable black populations posed to white political dominion. More recent tests of Key's hypotheses, in the 1980s and 1990s, revealed that the most racially conservative whites were found in areas of high black concentration (Glaser 1994; Giles and Hertz 1994). We learn from this research that racial minorities do not necessarily have to vote in order for their presence to generate a distinctive politics.

In the decades following the civil rights revolution, black activism and white reaction have been the source of substate regionalism throughout the rural South and in major metropolitan areas everywhere. The immigration of new racial groups to the United States in the last three decades may reinforce sectionalism inasmuch as these groups typically do not have the means to be highly mobile. Because the vast majority of new immigrants reside in urban areas and usually come to identify with the Democratic party upon naturalization, it is easy to comprehend how partisan balkanization may result from a generous immigration policy.

We originally hypothesized that sectionalism would increase with the diversity of the population, particularly in non-Southern states. In other words, as the percentage of nonwhite residents in a state increased, we expected more political balkanization. Our expectation was based on the idea that the nonwhite population in Northern and Western states is a predominantly urban and suburban population. Given its concentration in just a few of the most populous counties, and its similarly strong tendency to support Democratic candidates, we had good reasons for believing that the growth of this population would help to distinguish these counties from those in the rest of the state — exacerbating sectionalism. But it is not quite as simple as this. First, the impact of the nonwhite vote is not nearly as great in reality as it could be because so many black, Asian, and Latino voters fail to register their preferences at the polls. Second, there are states where the growing racial minority population has contributed to diminished sectionalism because minority voters have moved into GOP-dominant areas and broken apart once homogeneous regions such as southern California and metropolitan Denver. In other places, diminishing sectionalism is the result of white flight from central cities that have become increasingly diverse. Eastern Michigan is a good example of a place that was once politically homogeneous, or at least varied its support for Democrats within a narrow range. In the early 2000s, though, the gap between Wayne County (Detroit) and the suburban counties was much wider than before due mainly to the steady out-migration of conservative white voters from Wayne to Oakland and Macomb Counties.

Where Composition Ends and Context Begins

Many of our estimates of party support varied across states for the same social groups for the same sets of elections (see chap. 2 and the separate state chapters). This suggests that composition alone cannot explain the vote, and that blacks, farmers, the elderly, manufacturing workers, cross-state migrants, the foreign born, the college educated, and other groups are subject to complicated contextual forces within states. There is no doubt that some of the differences are the result of imperfect estimation via ecological inference and do not reflect true differences — aggregation bias in the data for some groups (e.g., farmers, the foreign born) proved to be a stubborn obstacle much of the time. In searching for a role for contextual explanations of the valid differences, though, we expected to find that in states with small populations of a given group, we would have more heterogeneity in party support among members of that group. While there is some truth here, this was not a completely consistent finding. In recent elections, Latinos in Colorado were more likely to vote Democratic than those in California, in spite of their smaller numbers. Perhaps it is not the absolute size of a population that matters, but its degree of concentration or isolation from other groups within the state. Since Latinos are more geographically clustered in Colorado than they are in California, it is easier for them to maintain group cohesion and internal consensus. Their isolation reduces their interaction with dissimilar groups in the population whose influence might steer them in a different political direction (Mutz 2002; Mutz and Mondak 2002). Recall that John Fenton's (1966) account of Ohio Republicanism suggested that it was the integration of the state's blue-collar workers with those from other walks of life that attenuated their Democratic commitments.

Other findings defy the simple concentration explanation, however. The elderly in Michigan appear to be far more unified behind Democratic candidates than the elderly in Florida, despite the fact that the elderly are more geographically clustered and more numerous in the latter state. In the 1980s and 1990s, farmers in New York were much less Democratic than farmers in Georgia, but this has nothing to do with the relative density of farms. Perhaps geographic concentration matters to political cohesion only among more politicized groups whose internal communications express mostly one-sided political messages (Zaller 1992). Hence, racial and ethnic concentrations matter in keeping blacks and Latinos together, although generationally based concentrations do not seem to facilitate political unity among the elderly. Perhaps it doesn't matter if a group lives in highly concentrated settlements if their political loyalties are mixed and political conversation does not reveal the decisive majorities and minorities that trigger social psychological pressures toward conformity.

If the extent of group concentration and the variable costs of communication implied thereby do not completely explain the differences across states for many groups, what else does? With Fenton (1966, chap. 5), we suspect that the heterogeneity of occupational and economic interests within a particular group hinders the communication of political messages, but particularly one-sided messages that would promote unity. The uneven estimates of the Democratic bias among those employed in manufacturing must be attributable to the fact that this group is not only geographically decentralized, opening it up to outside influences, but is so internally heterogeneous (by race, occupation) that even when workers find themselves working and living near one another, communication about politics fails to produce a single dominant viewpoint.

The same must be true of college educated citizens. By the turn of the twenty-first century, the members of this population category can be found in such a diversity of socioeconomic circumstances and neighborhoods that there can be no bloc voting the way there might have been in 1950 when higher education was the privilege of a few. The internal heterogeneity that is so disruptive of a group's political unity might sound like a composition variable rather than a contextual one. Have we then fallen back on compositional explanations to explain cross-state differences? Not quite, because the social communication that makes context relevant and individual characteristics less relevant depends upon a very different kind of compositional variable—the unity and composition of the community with whom the individual is interacting. Departures from traditional "group positions" result when individuals regularly encounter dissimilar others, tearing down consensus within the group (Mutz 2002). In this manner, it is the interaction of the individual—including all of her compositional characteristics, with the environment—and all of its compositional characteristics—that makes contextual effects useful in explaining behavior inconsistent with the usual generalizations.

Stability and Change in Sectionalism since the New Deal

There is an important temporal dimension to understanding the politics of a place since the composition of states and substate regions is not static. Compositional explanations go further than contextual ones in accounting for most such changes. A place becomes more Democratic or more Republican primarily because the people who live there have changed—they have been generationally replaced, or their attitudes on an important issue have changed, or they are newly mobilized, or perhaps one group has moved out, to be replaced by another. Very rarely do we find a place whose politics has radically changed even though the basic compositional characteristics of the population have remained the same. Even so, we do see places with very similar demographic characteristics changing at different rates, and one must make room for contextual explanations that emphasize distinctive patterns of social interaction within these locales. These unique and changing interactions might result from disruptions of individual ties to previously established networks of influence, or the emergence of ties centered around new communication and interaction patterns. Here is where the uneven development of technology, variable patterns of land use and development, and geophysical features of the environment may be the critical contextual variables that push areas with similar compositional characteristics toward different political destinies. This line of research is empirically undeveloped, and we hope this book stimulates more work in this area.

Here we reconsider the primarily compositional forces that contribute to stability and change in the regional patterns we observed in chapters 3 through 14. These forces are:

1. Generational replacement
2. Geographic mobility
3. Partisan conversion
4. Political mobilization and party competition
5. Candidates and campaigns

Our work has shed new light on the nature of the New Deal realignment in particular locales. If white reaction to black mobilization in the 1960s varied across states, so too did resistance to national political tides in earlier times, including the New Deal earthquake that sent shock waves throughout the entire nation (see figs. 15.1 and 15.2). Clearly some states were further from the earthquake's epicenter than others. Our estimates indicated that the magnitude of GOP defection to Roosevelt in 1932 and 1936 varied widely across the twelve states we have studied. Republicans in the South, where the GOP was weak to begin with, put up little resistance to the New Dealers—our estimates show that only 17 percent of Texas's Republican voters in the 1928 election returned again to vote for Hoover in 1932. In Georgia only 21 percent of Republicans

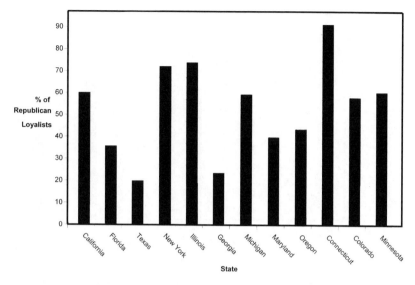

Fig. 15.1. Estimated percentage of Republican voters in 1928 who voted Republican again in 1932, by state

remained loyal, and in Florida only one in three. By contrast, in Connecticut, one of six states Roosevelt lost to Hoover in 1932, 89 percent of the GOP's 1928 voters stayed with the party four years later (fig. 15.1). New York and Illinois were also characterized by substantial party loyalty, although the large number of voters in these states made even small defections (in percentage terms) quite consequential to the national result. These results strengthen the argument that even the most sweeping party realignments are partial (Nardulli 1995; Mayhew 2002).

Our conclusion from the more detailed state findings is that all of the usual processes of partisan change can be found at work in these states, but they work in different combinations and at different rates to reshape the electorate in each. Side-by-side comparisons across states like those revealed in figures 15.1 and 15.2 show these states to be quite unique. If one were to take the results from any one of these states and try to generalize to the others, one would risk making sizable errors.

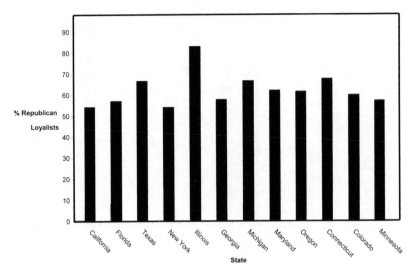

Fig. 15.2. Estimated percentage of Republican voters in 1960 who voted Republican again in 1964, by state

Generational Replacement

Substate sectionalism sometimes has its roots in the past and is not caused by any current issues or social and economic circumstances. Many aspects of a person's political outlook are passed down to them by their parents (Jennings and Niemi 1981; Huckfeldt and Sprague 1995). These traditions may be so intensely taught and reinforced that places remain the same for years, in spite of considerable change on other fronts. Partisan identification and allegiance are matters of habit among many and are seldom subject to self-scrutiny or reconsideration. This helps to explain why parts of Appalachia have remained strong Republican turf since the Civil War, while surrounding areas of the South vote reflexively Democratic. Conservatives throughout southern Illinois and Indiana voted Democratic in the 1980s and 1990s even though their conservative views would have dictated a Republican vote. Such behavior does not exhibit any clear-cut connection to economic or social concerns but instead reflects family and local traditions that remain firmly anchored to some past event or defining issue far from the consciousness of the current generation (Shelley and Archer 1989).

To say that people inherit their political values is not to say that they are a carbon copy of their parents. Generational change does occur, as a new generation comes of age in an era different from the older one (Abramson 1975; Sears and Valentino 1997). Calamitous events, such as wars and depressions, and popular social movements are responsible for disrupting the correspondence between parental and offspring attitudes (Abramson 1975). Candidates and parties change with the times, and voters will often respond to these changes by adopting views and identities different from those of their parents. Upward social mobility is a source of change, as people will adapt to the views of their peers (Huckfeldt and Sprague 1995; Huckfeldt 1986). Geographic mobility will separate children from the influence of parents and other family members (Brown 1988; Gimpel 1999). Generational change will be more evident in areas containing populations that have been geographically and economically mobile than in areas with less mobility.

We found that the effect of generational change on the partisan balance of states was highly variable depending largely on where the partisan balance stood going into the Great Depression, but also depending on fertility, mortality, and in-migration rates that influenced the sizes of the youthful and elderly population. In general, older voters were more Republican than younger voters at the dawn of the New Deal and were less likely to convert in the subsequent years. Between 1928 and 1950, generational replacement helped Democrats gain ascendancy because Republicans were dying off and being replaced by those who had come of age during powerful Democratic presidencies.

In subsequent decades, however, it is hard to gauge which party benefited from generational replacement. In Minnesota, Texas, and Georgia, it appears that the Republicans gained more ground than the Democrats, mainly through the death of the aging Democrats who entered the electorate in the 1930s and 1940s. But in many places, the elderly population is not politically distinguishable from those between ages 18 and 64, and in others it seems that the elderly remain much more Republican than younger voters—a generation gap that has contributed to Democratic ascendancy early in the new millennium.

Geographic Mobility

We have underscored the importance of population mobility as a force for political change. Established sectional patterns are generally undermined by population mobility. New populations arriving in an established locale will be unfamiliar with the issues and traditions that have defined the place's politics (Gimpel 1999; Frendreis 1989; Brown 1988). Lacking the understanding and the ties that would make such identities relevant, new residents will import and then act upon their own partisan affiliation and viewpoints. If the volume of migration is high enough, a place's political distinctiveness can be washed away rather quickly as the native population is overwhelmed and outnumbered by newcomers. For example, it is apparent that Northern migration to the South has drastically changed the political geography of Florida and Georgia, creating Republican strongholds in places that were once predictably Democratic and reconfiguring the electoral geography of these states. The southwestern migration to California from dust bowl states during the 1930s and 1940s contributed to the resurrection of the Democratic party in that state and the political transformation of central California (Gregory 1989). Still, in the long run, internal migration to California has benefited the Republicans more than the Democrats, as many of these conservative transplants came to vote for GOP candidates (Gimpel and Schuknecht 2001).

Migration is rarely of sufficient volume over the short term to unify broad cross-county regions within a state, and that's why migration will more often break apart political regions than create new ones. Migrants often have a distinctive economic and social profile that separates them from local natives. This social and economic profile is accompanied by a political worldview. In the last two decades of the twentieth century, domestic (internal) migrants in the United States have been white, upwardly mobile, and Republican. They do not move randomly about the country, but instead prefer to settle in neighborhoods and towns with a well-developed infrastructure and high-quality amenities. In choosing to live in affluent suburban and ex-urban locations, these migrants have heightened the distinctiveness of suburban politics, separating the politics of suburban counties from counties containing large central cities. By enlarging the gap between cities and suburbs, migrants have undermined regionalism within states by increasing political heterogeneity within metropolitan areas.

The results from chapters 3 through 14 showed that migration from across state lines was a key component of voter preference in Southern and Western states, and out-of-state migrants were usually much more Republican than natives (those born in their state of current residence). But there were important exceptions to this generalization. In Maryland, for instance, many out-of-state migrants arrived in the post–New Deal era to find employment in the expanding federal bureaucracy. Once we controlled for government employment, we found that Maryland fit the generalization—migrants coming to find work in non–government related occupational sectors were more Republican than natives. In Michigan we found that out-of-state migrants were more Democratic than natives. Apparently that's because the state has had two migration streams: one white collar and one blue collar. When we controlled for manufacturing employment, a draw for many blue-collar and Democratic-leaning migrants, we found that Michigan also came into line with the generalization that migrants were more Republican than natives (Gimpel and Schuknecht 2001).

Partisan Conversion

Conversion is a threat to established sectional patterns because it means that people are changing their views about parties and issues, possibly going so far as to change their party identification altogether. Conversion will alter substate sectionalism when it is significant enough to influence the attitudes and behavior of a large and geographically concentrated group of voters. Most survey research shows that conversions are rare and that conversion on a societal scale has taken place only a few times in American history. Smaller-scale local conversions are more common because groups of voters hold a wide range of political values and are therefore affected by political stimuli to different degrees (Petrocik 1981; Marchant-Shapiro and Patterson 1995).

There is substantial support for the idea that conversion has contributed to the demise of older regional patterns in Georgia, Texas, and other Southern states where white Democrats have moved into GOP ranks (Stanley 1988; Petrocik 1987; Wolfinger and Arsenau 1978). Conversion also occurs when candidates from one party emerge emphasizing new issues that are attractive to voters of the other party. Evidence from the Rocky Mountain region indicates that voters were attracted to Ronald Reagan's emphasis on individualism and moral conservatism (Marchant-Shapiro and Patterson

1995). Sustained issue leadership by GOP candidates on these matters was responsible for winning converts throughout Western states during the 1980s. When parties dissolve or fuse with other parties, voters are faced with a choice that often results in conversion, as when miners and farmers in Minnesota confronted the fusion of the Democratic party with the Farmer-Labor party in the 1940s. Most of the Farmer-Labor voters moved into the ranks of the new hybrid party, but did so only after reconciling themselves to the idea of the merger.

It is important to note that white conversion in response to black mobilization has not been uniform. Black voters clearly became more Democratic in the 1960s than before, but white voters did not necessarily become more Republican. The states where we found little evidence of white backlash were mainly those where the black population was small or highly concentrated in one or a few locales: Oregon, Minnesota, Colorado, and Connecticut. It is not a coincidence that these states also registered very little support for George Wallace's American Independent candidacy in 1968, or for Barry Goldwater four years earlier. Racially oriented platforms lacked salience at locations where few blacks lived. We did see white support for Democrats drop dramatically in Georgia, Texas, Florida, Illinois, and Michigan, all with larger black populations, who through civil rights protections and enforcement of antidiscrimination laws could make serious and substantial claims against the power and privilege of the white majority.

Related to the phenomenon of white countermobilization in response to black empowerment, in most states we found the blue-collar workforce to have moved toward greater Republican support between the 1950s and the end of the century. This shift may be in sync with greater black mobilization and activism within the Democratic party and the liberal positions Democrats have taken on civil rights and affirmative action (Cummings 1980, 1977). But there are some states, according to our estimates, where Democrats have not lost much ground among manufacturing workers. These include Texas and Georgia, where a sizable proportion of the blue-collar jobs filled by blacks and Latinos. In Colorado we found blue-collar employment associated with increased GOP voting only in higher-income counties with the lowest unemployment rates. Perhaps a distinction needs to be made between "new" manufacturing and "old" manufacturing in analyzing the politics of places (Piore and Sabel 1984). Those areas that have prospered with smaller, cleaner industry behave differently than those with the heavier, mass-production operations that have found themselves increasingly the victims of economic globalization and restructuring. Variations in union membership and in the militancy of unions may also help to explain the Democratic loyalties of manufacturing workers at some locations but their Republican inclinations at others.

Political Mobilization and Party Competition

Our survey of sectionalism and political behavior across twelve states between 1928 and the beginning of the new century has revealed two principal similarities: a widening gulf between urban and rural areas within states and the importance of increased black mobilization behind the Democratic party from the 1960s onward. In some places, the two phenomena are related because the black population is chiefly an urban one, and its mobilization has helped to distinguish urban from rural locations. Because of the large number of rural blacks still living in the black belt counties south of Atlanta, Georgia is perhaps the one stubborn exception to the rule that rural areas vote Republican. But even in Georgia, and presumably South Carolina, Alabama, and Mississippi, the black population has increasingly migrated off the farms and into the cities and now votes in much higher numbers than it did prior to 1960. The urban-rural gulf will eventually widen in these states too, but it may take more time.

We believe that sectional tensions within many states have increased in part because turnout among marginally interested voters has declined. To understand why sectionalism might be influenced by who happens to vote, we might consider the difference between low turnout and high turnout elections. High turnout elections are those in which most citizens vote, regardless of the intensity of their preferences or their political sophistication. Since turnout has dropped since mid-century, we might expect sectionalism to have increased with this electoral shrinkage. Lower turnout means that only the most committed and highly ideological voters are streaming to the polls, with those of less sophistication and interest dropping out of the electorate altogether. Elections early in the twenty-first century could be characterized as attracting a larger share of those who are most committed, most ideological, and most knowledgeable, but a smaller share of those on the low end of the commitment and knowledge scales. Naturally, this means that these later elections were more politically polarized (Bartels 2000). Lower turnout and greater partisan polarization often go hand in hand (Ansolabehere and Iyengar 1995). Of course, greater polarization does not necessarily make elections more sectional, unless the increasing residential mobility of the American electorate has separated Republican from Democratic turf. And this is exactly what has happened; since fewer Republicans and Democrats are found to be living near each other, we can see how a low turnout, highly polarized election could also be a more sectional one.

Candidates and Campaigns

There are a number of good reasons for the differences we found between substate regionalism in the 1930s and the early 2000s. Given seventy years of economic and demographic change, we should not expect that the forces causing the one to emerge also caused the other. Substate sectionalism will be contingent upon short-term factors, such as the familiarity of voters with an incumbent and the popularity of the incumbent and challenger. Presidential incumbency mainly works to diminish the degree of sectionalism in the majority of states because popular incumbents generate support across regions within states independently of the partisanship of those locales. This support is undoubtedly based on their job performance and name recognition among voters. Incumbency gives voters an additional cue, on top of party, on which to base their voting decision.

Comparing States by Behavioral Similarities

We are not committed believers in the concept of political culture, but many readers will still expect us to take the accumulated evidence and make some summary generalizations based on the political similarities we have found. Our analysis suggests that simple regional classifications of states (North, South, West, New England, Mid-Atlantic, etc.) probably do not capture electoral commonalities at the beginning of the new century and may be genuinely misleading.

We found that Texas and Colorado share similar traits, particularly in the size and growing importance of the Latino, mainly Mexican origin, population. Both of these states also exhibited substantial Democratic loyalty among their populations employed in manufacturing. California and New York are similar to one another mainly in their extent of population diversity, having large Democratic-leaning immigrant and black populations, more conservative and Republican elderly populations, along with significant pockets of youthful, liberal-leaning affluence. Minnesota and Oregon are similar for their prevailing liberal Democratic voting in a homogeneous ethnic setting of prosperous urban and fast-growing suburban areas, against a backdrop of a rich agricultural heritage and broad swaths of intense rural Republicanism.

Michigan and Illinois are highly similar, but they are joined in our estimation by a seemingly unlikely companion, Florida. The similarities between Michigan and Illinois are mostly obvious: both midwestern, both with large dominant cities and concentrated minority and poor populations, both adversely affected by globalization in traditional manufacturing. In both states, one can also find spectacularly affluent suburbs and a dispersed Republican rural and small town population. That Florida would appear with Illinois and Michigan is not quite so clear, but our defense of this categorization is that Florida too is a two-party competitive state, with a concentrated urban minority population, along with prosperous suburbs and centers of rural, conservative strain. Florida's manufacturing workers, like those of Illinois and Michigan, look increasingly less likely to vote Democratic in recent elections, while these states' farmers and white natives are among the most likely to favor the GOP. In our view, native Southerners are correct in characterizing Florida as a Northern state. While Florida is certainly not an old-line manufacturing state like Michigan or Illinois, and it has been the net recipient of out-migration from these sluggishly growing midwestern locations, it now stands closer to them than it does to its confederate neighbors.

Connecticut, Maryland, and Georgia stand alone and are neither significantly like each other nor especially close to any of the other states we have examined. In at least one surprising way, Connecticut is similar to Texas. Connecticut's population distribution, centered in a plurality of large cities, is similar to that of Texas, only on a much smaller scale. Georgia and Florida, as neighboring states, share some similarities—the principal one being the presence of large numbers of Republican-leaning interstate migrants, along with rural minority populations. Georgia also has these features in common with its Confederate colleague, Texas. Maryland is perhaps the most exceptional of the states, due, above all else, to the size of its government workforce. If forced to find a cognate for Maryland, we would choose New York, with its significant population of affluent, college-educated Democrats and a cross-state migrant population that is unusually Democratic.

Sectionalism, Political Geography, and the Study of American Politics

Our work has shown that it is premature to read the study of sectionalism and American electoral geography their last rites. The rise of two-party political competition in the South may make it less tenable to separate this region from the rest of the country, but political regionalism is alive and well at lower levels of aggregation, within states at the county, city, or precinct level. Population mobility, national media, the Internet, and improved transportation links may continue to make local political outcomes more similar to each other than they were in the past, but as that happens there will still be areas within states that are more and less resistant to these homogenizing forces.

The value of studying substate sections is that the way these regional rivalries change over time tells us something about how underlying social and economic forces are transforming states and regions. Sectionalism in California has been intensifying, as a simple north-south divide has been replaced by a more fractured regionalism with four main areas: north, south, coastal, and central. Observing this transformation on the California electoral map, we are led to probe for its causes. These causes will be found among a set of explanations that include population mobility, economic restructuring, shifting political values, and generational change. Understanding the development of these divisions at the beginning of the new millennium gives us insight into how people have altered the places where they live.

North-south differences were once prominent in Minnesota politics, but this simplistic division has disappeared with the depopulation of northern and western Minnesota and the increasing support of farmers for Republican presidential and gubernatorial candidates. By the 2000s, regionalism in Minnesota divided the northeast and southeast from a dealigned and realigned patchwork that was the rest of the state. Observing these changes in Minnesota's political geography leads us to explanations rooted in the decline of the agricultural economy and the migration from rural to metropolitan areas.

In Oregon, relatively low levels of regionalism have given way to intense geographic divisions separating rural eastern Oregon from the Willamette Valley and greater Portland metropolitan area. We find the force behind these changes in the migration and population growth in the two latter regions, coupled with the conversion of natives uncomfortable with the conservative drift of the Republican party nationally. The growth in Portland has actually helped create a sizable Democratic voting edge in the state, making it less politically competitive in presidential elections than in the past, and less competition has meant stalwart resistance as eastern Oregon stands stubbornly against the liberal tide rushing at it from the west.

The way political sections appear on maps is also very instructive for campaigns and candidates (Shaw 1999; Althaus et al. 2002). In many states, including Illinois, Texas, and Colorado, broad regional patterns have remained unaltered from the basic die cast at the time of the New Deal realignment. The study of short-term oscillations in sectionalism reveal interesting information about campaign politics and the appeal of candidates among certain traditional constituencies. Politicians spend millions of dollars in every presidential election cycle trying to understand the electoral behavior of states. They hire dozens of campaign staffers and recruit legions of volunteers to comb the geographic territory of states in search of friendly voters. Why do they bother to do this if state electorates are all the same? The answer is that states are not the same, and, more important, states are the units by which victory and defeat are measured on election day in the electoral college system. And yet for all the centrality of state politics to real live campaigning, we have surprisingly little political science research on states and regions as distinct electoral battlegrounds. Political science has preferred to separate voters from their context. But presidential candidates do not do that, in fact *cannot* do that, because they are competing to win the votes of a collection of smaller electorates, not the votes of a mythical national electorate that is represented in the usual poll.

When making comparisons across states, it is not only clear that states differ in their support for the two major parties, but that groups within those states differ in their support for the parties. Our comparisons have shown that the political polarization of groups varies across states and that cleavages between groups will be wider in some locations than in others (Wright et al. 2000), critical information when considering issue advertising and planning a voter mobilization strategy. We have shown that the geographic concentration of groups and partisans varies across states such that some are more sectional than others—valuable information to the campaigner who must target scarce campaign funds at voter-rich areas.

The study of political geography at some level of aggregation (county, city, state) will never replace polling and survey research as the primary instrument for studying political behavior and elections, nor should it. But polls also have their limitations. Conventional surveys are rarely able to show where people sharing specific political, economic, and social characteristics are concentrated. Polls are therefore very poor guides for those interested in activating and mobilizing important constituencies at particular locations. Students of politics frequently want to ask questions about the political consequences of social and economic changes in the places where they live and work. But typical polls cannot provide such detailed information about specific areas. Finally, polls will not be able to tell us much about how Texas politics in the 1930s compares with Texas in the 2010s because there were no polls of Texas voters in the 1930s. Placing modern times in historical context and studying political change over extended periods requires information that can take us back that far. The relevance of political geography for legislative redistricting and representation has long been recognized. But even when the malleability of geographic boundaries is not in question, the study of political geography can still help us to understand the social and economic interests that shape and define political life.

In 1982, Malcolm Jewell opined that political scientists "have given too little thought and devoted too little of our research resources to the field of state government and politics" (638). More than twenty years later, this is still true. We are convinced that it is the detail and complexity of states that researchers find intimidating. A generally pervasive lack of *local* knowledge among scholars puts state politics beyond their scope. Who could possibly match V. O. Key Jr.'s masterful work on the mid-century South, much less take on the other thirty-nine states and make sense of them? Then there is the age-old debate, not confined to the study of the American states, between analyzing states as individual cases or blocking them together to try to make broader generalizations (Stonecash 1991; Wright, Erikson, and McIver 1985; Nicholson-Crotty and Meier 2002). We have tried to do both in this book, as Key did. While there is no substitute for gathering detailed information on individual state electorates, that information is much more meaningful when discussed in a comparative framework (Wright et al. 2000). And there is still so much we do not know about state electorates and political institutions.

Where should the study of state politics go from here? If we can just test the impressive theories formulated from studies of national institutions and behavior on state institutions and behavior, there is much new knowledge to be generated. We might find that the theories that have held up so well under empirical tests carried out on data collected from national institutions and surveys hold up more or less well under local conditions. In this manner, the entire field of American politics stands to benefit should the desire to study the "E Pluribus" element of the federal equation be sparked in a new generation of scholars.

APPENDIX A

The Challenge of Ecological Inference

The estimates for Democratic support among the various demographic groups presented in chapters 3 through 14, as well as the voter transition models in those chapters, are based on the ecological inference maximum likelihood technique presented in Gary King's *A Solution to the Ecological Inference Problem* (1997). In this appendix, we can only provide an overview of the problem and an intuitive grasp of the method used to address it. For a more complete account, readers are advised to go directly to the King book and to related treatments such as *Cross Level Inference* by Achen and Shively (1995).

Part of the goal of this book has been to examine partisan and political change between 1928 and 2000. Ordinarily, the best tool for this purpose would be public opinion surveys for each election year and each state recording the relevant information about vote choice, political party preference, race, occupation, education, birthplace, migration, and so forth. From these data, one could then construct cross-tabulation tables of migration status and vote choice to examine aggregate quantities such as the ones we present—the percentage of cross-state migrant and native voters in Georgia who voted Democratic, for example:

Reading across the first row of table A1, then, we can clearly see that 66 percent of the state's native voters supported the Democratic candidate, compared with only 46 percent of nonnatives. The second row shows that the balance of the native population, 34 percent, supported the GOP candidate, compared with 54 percent of the nonnative population. The totals listed in the bottom row indicate the percentage of natives and migrants in the total population surveyed: 70 percent of the respondents were natives, 30 percent were cross-state migrants. Finally, the totals listed on the far right column indicate the percentage of all voters who voted Democratic and Republican—60 percent went Democratic, only 40 percent voted Republican (table AI). The most informative data in the table, however, are the comparisons across the rows where Democratic (or Republican) support can be contrasted by the migration status of the voters.

If we had comprehensive survey data for all states, we could compare the gap in Democratic and Republican support by migration and see if generalizations about political differences between natives and migrants hold up. The problem is that survey data with the appropriate questions are not available for a large number of states before 1982. Reliable national surveys date to the late 1940s, but national polls do not represent state electorates, so they cannot be substituted in place of state polls.

A second-best option is to rely upon aggregate data, by county or precinct, to estimate the political inclination of relevant demographic groups. We would collect demographic data on the percentage of each county consisting of migrants or natives, and election returns for the percentage of each county that voted Republican (or Democratic). We would not have the precise data about what percentage of natives and migrants voted Republican (or Democratic), but we could try to make an informed guess—an "ecological inference" based on the observed relationship between the aggregate quantities. Ecological inference, then, is simply the attempt to infer individual-level behavior from aggregate data such as that provided at the county or precinct level. Having only the aggregate quantities would be akin to having incomplete data in a crosstabulation table, as in table A2, where we have good summary data on the percentage of migrants and nonmigrants in each county (and in the state) and

TABLE A1.   Bivariate Crosstabulation of Presidential Vote by Migration Status: Georgia

	Natives of Georgia	Migrants	Totals
Voting Democratic	66.0%	46.0%	60.0%
	462	138	600
Voting Republican (or for others)	34.0%	54.0%	40.0%
	238	162	400
Totals	70.0%	30.0%	100.0%
	700	300	1000

equally adequate data on the percentage voting Democratic and Republican in each county (and in the state). What we lack that survey data usually provides is the valuable information in the interior cells of the table.

Making inferences based on the marginal totals in table A2 is challenging and fraught with potential error. For instance, we might observe across the state's counties that as the percentage of the migratory population goes up, the GOP's percentage of the vote increases—a positive association exists between the two variables when they are correlated. But this does not necessarily tell us that movers are voting Republican, much less the percentage of support they are awarding the GOP candidate, something statistician William S. Robinson pointed out in a famous article (1950). Migrant voters may not be turning out to vote at all, and/or nonmigrants in areas of migrant concentration may be especially likely to vote, casting Republican ballots, while the less numerous and less participatory migrant population is voting Democratic. Drawing faulty conclusions about individual-level behavior from the observation of aggregate quantities is called the ecological fallacy. In other words, it would be highly fallacious to conclude from the observed correlation that migrant voters were voting Republican if in fact they were voting Democratic, or not bothering to vote at all. Because we cannot rely on aggregate data to give us a precise picture of individual-level behavior, we have what has come to be known as the "ecological inference problem" (King 1997).

There is no deterministic solution to the ecological inference problem, but a number of scholars have developed methods for estimating the "true" values inside tables like A2. A statistician and sociologist at the University of Chicago, Leo Goodman (1953), came up with one method for estimating the interior cell quantities. We will not go into the details of his method here (see King 1997, chap. 4, or Achen

TABLE A2. Bivariate Crosstabulation of Presidential Vote by Migration Status: Georgia

	Natives of Georgia	Migrants	Totals
Voting Democratic	β_i^b	β_i^w	60.0%
Voting Republican (or for others)	$1-\beta_i^b$	$1-\beta_i^w$	40.0%
Totals	70.0%	30.0%	100.0%

and Shively 1995, chap. 2). Briefly, using OLS regression, Goodman's method regresses the percentage Democratic on the percentage who were natives and the resulting constant provides an estimate of the vote for Democrats among non-natives, while the sum of the constant and the slope coefficient estimates the percentage of migrants voting Democratic. Suffice it to say that Goodman's was an innovative breakthrough, but often led to implausible estimates of the quantities in the empty cells of table A2, such as that 112 percent of natives voted Democratic, or −13 percent of migrants voted Democratic—impossible results given that the percentage of any group voting Democratic or Republican cannot exceed 100 percent or drop below 0. Among other problems, Goodman's procedure required that we make many assumptions about the nature of data that did not correspond to reality (e.g., homoscedasticity—that all data points exhibited approximately equal variances).

The method proposed by King in *A Solution to the Ecological Inference Problem* does not require that aggregate data meet difficult standards, such as for the cell quantities in table A2 to be estimated with standard errors and confidence intervals that tell us precisely how accurate they are. It does not require that the data be homoscedastic (have the same error variance across observations). And while its estimates are not always highly precise (depending on the nature of the data in use), it does not generate implausible estimates that exceed 100 percent or drop below 0. A major improvement over Goodman's approach is that information from individual observations is used to generate upper and lower bounds within which the estimate of interest must vary (King 1997, chap. 5). The King method first uses the method of bounds to constrain the estimated quantities in the top row of table A2 to a narrower region than the [0,1] interval if possible (Duncan and Davis 1953; Achen and Shively 1995, 191–210). The insight here comes from realizing that the marginals in table A2 put maximum and minimum limits within which the interior cell quantities of the top row (β_i^b and β_i^w) can vary. Taking our example (table A1), .70 of the state's population are natives and .60 vote Democratic. This means that it is impossible that less than .10 of the state's population are Republican voting natives, since .70 are natives but only .60 voted Democratic. It is also impossible that more than .40 of the population are Republican voting natives, since only .40 voted Republican at all. Thus, while the potential GOP support by natives ranges between 0 and 100 percent, the aggregate proportions narrow the possible range to .10/.70 and .40/.70 or between .14 percent and .57 percent (Achen and Shively 1995, 191). Given that between .1 and .4 of the population are Republican voting natives, then between 0 and .3 of the population are Republican voting migrants, between .3 and .6 are Democratic voting natives, and between 0 and .3 are Democratic voting migrants.

This method does assume that the data follow a particular statistical distribution, described as "truncated bivariate normal"—essentially a normal distribution with its tails cut off at the deterministic bounds (King 1997, chap. 6). A tomography plot can be used to locate the most likely values of β_i^b and β_i^w. In such a plot (β_i^b by β_i^w), each line represents all possible values of migrant and nonmigrant partisanship for each county, given that county's migrant composition and party support. Inspection of these plots often reveals a mode on the plot where most of the lines intersect. Because the distribution is normal, the most likely values for β_i^b and β_i^w are nearest this mode: the peak of the three-dimensional normal bell shape (Schuessler 1999; Burden and Kimball 1998, 543).

Maximum likelihood estimation is used to estimate essential characteristics of the truncated bivariate normal distribution from the values of the independent (X_i) and dependent variables (T_i) provided in each data set. These characteristics include two means, two standard deviations, and the correlation between the variables, rho (ρ)—together King labels these six parameters by the Greek letter psi, Ψ. For each data set we work with, we first determine the bounds, then estimate psi. Based on this information, the method then uses simulations (or resampling) to arrive at point estimates, confidence intervals, and standard errors of the quantities of interest. The means of the distributions of β_i^b and β_i^w are used as point estimates and the standard errors (S_i^b and S_i^w) are based on the variation in the simulated values.

No method guarantees perfect estimates, completely faithful to reality. But compared to alternative methods, King's approach stands as a major improvement, particularly in the absence of additional complications in the data such as aggregation bias (extremely small values of the X_i or T_i variables from the data set we are using). However, we do have aggregation bias for most states in the data for the county-level immigrant population and the county-level farm population.

(We welcome the suggestions of those who may have ideas for generating more precise estimates of the political behavior of these populations.) Unlike older methods of ecological inference estimation (Goodman 1953), King's method does not require that the data meet rigid requirements of homoscedastic error variance, and it does not produce impossible results that exceed 100 percent or drop below 0.

In our results reported in appendixes B and C, we present the complete estimates for all of our ecological inference models. In these tables, additional output should be considered along with the "district-level" estimates we report in chapters 3 through 14, including the standard errors of our estimates (S_i^b and S_i^w) and particularly the deterministic bounds within which our estimates and standard errors lie. Readers should note that to economize on the amount of information to be presented and improve the quality of our estimates, we pooled sets of presidential elections, relying upon the U.S. decennial census for our demographic data and drawing our election returns from available data files at ICPSR and the *America Votes* series.

Having run hundreds of these models to generate our results, we found that as an empirical regularity, whenever the deterministic bounds were estimated to be less than 0 and 1, our point estimates were highly plausible based on other information we had available about the voting behavior of the groups of interest. Of course the narrower the bounds, the more accurate the estimate tended to be, but we found a major cut-point in accuracy to be between those estimates with 0,1 bounds and those with bounds narrower than 0,1, even if they were only slightly narrower, such as 0 and .95, or .10 and 1. Hence, in tables 3.2 through 14.2, and 3.3 through 14.3, we add asterisks to those point estimates where the bounds were less than 0 and 1. Those estimates with bounds of 0 and 1 are highly uncertain and should be interpreted tentatively—as a temporary estimate until additional work is done or additional information is made available in future research. Even these estimates are of interest, however, when compared to earlier or later estimates of the same quantities for the same state, as when we compare black and nonblack voting in the 1928–32 elections to black and nonblack voting in the 1968–72 elections. Occasionally in the text and notes we report the results of estimates that included a control variable (zb). In many cases, but not all, the addition of a control variable will change the estimates for the cell quantities in table A2. Generally, however, we stick to the two-variable model because the additional information ("priors" in eco-logical inference parlance) necessary to make optimal and consistent use of control variables was not readily available to us across the sev-enty-year time span of interest.

The software that generated our estimates, Ezi, was written by Gary King and Kenneth Benoit, and is available for download on Gary King's internet website: <http://gking.harvard.edu/>. Eager to beat back the frontiers of knowledge, we invite comments and criti-cisms about the way we have implemented the King model, and repli-cations of any of our results. All of our county-level election and de-mographic data are available from the University of Michigan's Inter University Consortium for Political and Social Research (ICPSR), and data files can be easily matched using appropriate county id codes for the cases found within each file. For more recent elections, we relied upon data contained in the *America Votes* series, which we usually had to key in by hand.

APPENDIX B

Complete Ecological Inference Estimates, by State

California

	Bb	Bw	Sb	Sw	Lowerb	Upperb	Lowerw	Upperw
1928–32								
black30	0.5528	0.4645	0.2555	0.0037	0.0000	1.0000	0.4580	0.4725
elderly30	0.3873	0.4714	0.2629	0.0182	0.0000	1.0000	0.4291	0.4981
foreign30	0.4932	0.4614	0.1967	0.0327	0.0000	1.0000	0.3770	0.5435
farm30	0.5635	0.4549	0.0639	0.0073	0.0387	0.9699	0.4087	0.5145
white30	0.4667	0.4598	0.0111	0.0882	0.3995	0.5240	0.0062	0.9917
1936–44								
black40	0.8234	0.5988	0.1825	0.0033	0.0000	1.0000	0.5955	0.6139
elderly40	0.5167	0.6104	0.1372	0.0121	0.0093	0.9964	0.5680	0.6554
foreign40	0.5692	0.6080	0.2126	0.0329	0.0000	1.0000	0.5414	0.6960
farm40	0.5671	0.6064	0.0431	0.0044	0.0386	1.0000	0.5626	0.6600
white40	0.6200	0.2385	0.0068	0.1441	0.5841	0.6312	0.0000	1.0000
1948–52								
black50	0.9917	0.4296	0.0031	0.0001	0.0000	1.0000	0.4293	0.4737
elderly50	0.1094	0.4853	0.1080	0.0100	0.0000	1.0000	0.4030	0.4955
foreign50	0.3770	0.4614	0.2021	0.0207	0.0000	1.0000	0.3975	0.5000
farm50	0.4020	0.4564	0.0790	0.0045	0.0000	0.9979	0.4227	0.4792
white50	0.4496	0.5099	0.0113	0.1609	0.4152	0.4853	0.0000	0.9999
mfg50	0.6566	0.4097	0.0978	0.0212	0.0000	1.0000	0.3351	0.5518
coll50	0.1236	0.4808	0.1371	0.0122	0.0000	1.0000	0.4048	0.4940
1956–64								
black60	0.8326	0.4893	0.1185	0.0072	0.0000	1.0000	0.4791	0.5462
elderly60	0.4427	0.5155	0.3077	0.0296	0.0000	1.0000	0.4619	0.5580
foreign60	0.5981	0.5500	0.2072	0.0193	0.0000	1.0000	0.4633	0.5566
farm60	0.5127	0.5090	0.1098	0.0024	0.0000	1.0000	0.4984	0.5202
white60	0.5075	0.5267	0.0084	0.0956	0.4658	0.5540	0.0000	0.9999
mfg60	0.6404	0.4711	0.0839	0.0243	0.0000	1.0000	0.3670	0.6564
coll60	0.4265	0.5180	0.2701	0.0291	0.0000	1.0000	0.4561	0.5640
bornst60	0.5912	0.4454	0.0580	0.0449	0.0713	0.9695	0.1523	0.8484
outst60	0.4383	0.5737	0.0699	0.0638	0.0612	0.9214	0.1331	0.9175

California—*Continued*

	Bb	Bw	Sb	Sw	Lowerb	Upperb	Lowerw	Upperw
1968–72								
black70	0.7435	0.4065	0.2565	0.0193	0.0000	1.0000	0.3872	0.4625
elderly70	0.2912	0.4436	0.1650	0.0164	0.0000	1.0000	0.3733	0.4725
foreign70	0.7261	0.4015	0.1547	0.0150	0.0000	1.0000	0.3750	0.4716
farm70	0.1903	0.4323	0.1317	0.0012	0.0000	1.0000	0.4248	0.4341
white70	0.3943	0.7196	0.0123	0.0995	0.3597	0.4831	0.0000	1.0000
mfg70	0.5790	0.3899	0.0872	0.0235	0.0000	0.9968	0.2773	0.5460
coll70	0.6882	0.3901	0.1089	0.0169	0.0000	1.0000	0.3417	0.4968
bornst70	0.4552	0.4109	0.0580	0.0443	0.0060	0.9302	0.0487	0.7539
outst70	0.2707	0.5770	0.0586	0.0586	0.0007	0.8520	0.0411	0.8259
1976–84								
black80	0.8791	0.3782	0.0894	0.0075	0.0000	1.0000	0.3681	0.4523
elderly80	0.5625	0.4078	0.2530	0.0162	0.0000	1.0000	0.3797	0.4440
foreign80	0.6407	0.3773	0.0983	0.0175	0.0000	1.0000	0.3133	0.4915
farm80	0.4854	0.4176	0.2831	0.0020	0.0000	1.0000	0.4131	0.4201
white80	0.3666	0.5875	0.0140	0.0640	0.2442	0.5401	0.0035	0.9993
mfg80	0.5088	0.3961	0.0951	0.0291	0.0000	0.9995	0.2841	0.5132
coll80	0.5271	0.3991	0.0726	0.0120	0.0000	1.0000	0.3212	0.4855
bornst80	0.3695	0.4596	0.0630	0.0526	0.0162	0.8637	0.0443	0.7519
outst80	0.3285	0.4751	0.0679	0.0444	0.0006	0.9007	0.1011	0.6895
Hispanic80	0.4386	0.4121	0.0824	0.0195	0.0003	0.9966	0.2797	0.5161
1988–92								
black90	0.8561	0.4359	0.1227	0.0098	0.0000	1.0000	0.4244	0.5046
white90	0.3960	0.6251	0.0250	0.0555	0.2273	0.6700	0.0209	1.0000
elderly90	0.2788	0.4839	0.0763	0.0090	0.0000	1.0000	0.4044	0.5221
foreign90	0.7050	0.4071	0.0934	0.0261	0.0000	1.0000	0.3185	0.5954
farm90	0.5629	0.4666	0.2943	0.0015	0.0000	1.0000	0.4644	0.4695
mfg90	0.6408	0.4325	0.1475	0.0294	0.0000	1.0000	0.3610	0.5601
coll90	0.8249	0.3596	0.0852	0.0256	0.0088	1.0000	0.3069	0.6049
bornst90	0.3970	0.5286	0.0610	0.0535	0.0353	0.8847	0.1009	0.8459
outst90	0.3009	0.5434	0.0621	0.0285	0.0028	0.9758	0.2370	0.6802
Hispanic90	0.4569	0.4707	0.1088	0.0379	0.0014	0.9960	0.2828	0.6294
1996–2000								
black00	0.9029	0.4950	0.0725	0.0058	0.0000	1.0000	0.4873	0.5668
white00	0.3643	0.8526	0.0224	0.0457	0.2920	0.7383	0.0902	1.0000
elderly00	0.3052	0.5505	0.1287	0.0149	0.0000	1.0000	0.4701	0.5858
foreign00	0.9938	0.3961	0.0025	0.0007	0.0084	1.0000	0.3597	0.5460
farm00	0.4813	0.5253	0.0930	0.0005	0.0000	1.0000	0.5225	0.5278
mfg00	0.5551	0.5199	0.3056	0.0520	0.0000	1.0000	0.4443	0.6143
coll00	0.6620	0.4845	0.2248	0.0501	0.0012	1.0000	0.4192	0.6418
bornst00	0.1828	0.8272	0.0316	0.0279	0.0727	0.9188	0.1774	0.9244
outst00	0.3692	0.5968	0.1027	0.0473	0.0059	0.9984	0.3069	0.7642
Hispanic00	0.6024	0.4909	0.0963	0.0425	0.0050	0.9936	0.3184	0.7323

Colorado

	Bb	Bw	Sb	Sw	Lowerb	Upperb	Lowerw	Upperw
1928–32								
black30	0.0058	0.4474	0.0024	0.0000	0.0000	1.0000	0.4360	0.4475
elderly30	0.4074	0.4446	0.2572	0.0163	0.0000	0.9972	0.4072	0.4705
foreign30	0.8229	0.4082	0.1607	0.0145	0.0000	1.0000	0.3922	0.4822
farm30	0.3871	0.4630	0.0365	0.0136	0.0705	0.8126	0.3046	0.5809
white30	0.4311	0.5876	0.0094	0.1210	0.3994	0.4766	0.1210	0.5876
1936–44								
black40	0.9956	0.5101	0.0016	0.0000	0.0000	1.0000	0.5100	0.5193
elderly40	0.4256	0.5220	0.3027	0.0252	0.0000	1.0000	0.4741	0.5574
foreign40	0.6395	0.5061	0.2508	0.0170	0.0000	1.0000	0.4816	0.5495
farm40	0.2984	0.5770	0.0237	0.0068	0.0224	0.9141	0.3991	0.6567
white40	0.5154	0.4589	0.0047	0.3012	0.5070	0.5225	0.0000	1.0000
1948–52								
black50	0.9947	0.4438	0.0029	0.0000	0.0000	1.0000	0.4437	0.4604
elderly50	0.2107	0.4759	0.1766	0.0168	0.0000	1.0000	0.4006	0.4960
foreign50	0.6191	0.5075	0.2621	0.0178	0.0000	1.0000	0.4816	0.5495
farm50	0.2921	0.4811	0.0430	0.0076	0.0032	0.9927	0.3694	0.5318
white50	0.4515	0.5222	0.0065	0.3309	0.4420	0.4618	0.0000	1.0000
mfg50	0.6836	0.4229	0.1569	0.0203	0.0000	1.0000	0.3820	0.5115
coll50	0.4238	0.4554	0.2608	0.0227	0.0000	1.0000	0.4052	0.4923
1956–64								
black60	0.6119	0.4836	0.3023	0.0070	0.0000	1.0000	0.4746	0.4978
elderly60	0.3148	0.5035	0.0652	0.0065	0.0000	1.0000	0.4356	0.5347
foreign60	0.9957	0.4685	0.0010	0.0000	0.0000	1.0000	0.4684	0.5037
farm60	0.2993	0.5012	0.0528	0.0041	0.0006	0.9829	0.4475	0.5247
white60	0.4856	0.5148	0.0026	0.0827	0.4705	0.5017	0.0000	1.0000
mfg60	0.5868	0.4687	0.1277	0.0226	0.0063	1.0000	0.3968	0.5715
coll60	0.3154	0.5061	0.1578	0.0179	0.0000	1.0000	0.4284	0.5418
bornst60	0.6436	0.3369	0.0526	0.0501	0.1097	0.8914	0.1010	0.8453
outst60	0.3197	0.6393	0.0439	0.0402	0.0749	0.8768	0.1288	0.8636
1968–72								
black70	0.9937	0.3576	0.0041	0.0001	0.0000	1.0000	0.3574	0.3883
elderly70	0.2702	0.3866	0.0748	0.0070	0.0000	1.0000	0.3187	0.4117
foreign70	0.8880	0.3623	0.1330	0.0037	0.0000	1.0000	0.3592	0.3872
farm70	0.1202	0.3875	0.0652	0.0026	0.0000	0.4664	0.3531	0.3924
white70	0.3657	0.6203	0.0120	0.2674	0.3487	0.3936	0.0000	1.0000
mfg70	0.4691	0.3611	0.1162	0.0196	0.0000	1.0000	0.2715	0.4402
coll70	0.4352	0.3663	0.1237	0.0219	0.0000	1.0000	0.2664	0.4433
bornst70	0.4965	0.2781	0.0495	0.0407	0.0248	0.8059	0.0234	0.6663
outst70	0.2637	0.4998	0.0465	0.0507	0.0103	0.6976	0.0269	0.7760
1976–84								
black80	0.9734	0.3390	0.0243	0.0009	0.0000	1.0000	0.3380	0.3750
elderly80	0.9565	0.3299	0.0443	0.0024	0.0002	1.0000	0.3275	0.3809
foreign80	0.9924	0.3370	0.0024	0.0001	0.0001	1.0000	0.3367	0.3757
farm80	0.1561	0.3659	0.0157	0.0003	0.0017	1.9876	0.3484	0.3692

Colorado—*Continued*

	Bb	Bw	Sb	Sw	Lowerb	Upperb	Lowerw	Upperw
1976–84								
white80	0.3425	0.5254	0.0116	0.0990	0.2880	0.4034	0.0037	0.9924
mfg80	0.7212	0.3057	0.1941	0.0301	0.0000	1.0000	0.2624	0.4178
coll80	0.1960	0.3960	0.0210	0.0041	0.0001	0.9993	0.2386	0.4313
bornst80	0.5626	0.2178	0.0377	0.0270	0.0275	0.8167	0.0358	0.6008
outst80	0.1778	0.5811	0.0288	0.0344	0.0149	0.6389	0.0386	0.7755
Hispanic80	0.7418	0.3110	0.0390	0.0052	0.0075	0.9940	0.2774	0.4088
1988–92								
black90	0.5850	0.4160	0.3044	0.0128	0.0000	1.0000	0.3987	0.4409
white90	0.3932	0.6460	0.0376	0.2812	0.3458	0.4797	0.0000	1.0000
elderly90	0.3609	0.4299	0.0788	0.0087	0.0000	1.0000	0.3591	0.4699
foreign90	0.6588	0.4124	0.2218	0.0100	0.0000	1.0000	0.3970	0.4422
farm90	0.0592	0.4281	0.0630	0.0009	0.0000	1.0000	0.4150	0.4289
mfg90	0.5235	0.4085	0.1696	0.0246	0.0000	1.0000	0.3394	0.4843
coll90	0.5014	0.3942	0.0948	0.0349	0.0003	0.9876	0.2153	0.5786
bornst90	0.5066	0.3591	0.0525	0.0402	0.0484	0.8857	0.0693	0.7095
outst90	0.3149	0.5418	0.0408	0.0448	0.0373	0.7404	0.0744	0.8468
Hispanic90	0.7756	0.3709	0.0412	0.0061	0.0078	0.9970	0.3382	0.4844
1996–2000								
black00	0.7022	0.4269	0.2585	0.0113	0.0000	1.0000	0.4139	0.4575
white00	0.3814	0.8426	0.0209	0.1484	0.3591	0.5003	0.0000	1.0000
elderly00	0.3186	0.4521	0.1109	0.0127	0.0000	1.0000	0.3741	0.4886
foreign00	0.9720	0.4146	0.0291	0.0013	0.0000	1.0000	0.4134	0.4580
farm00	0.0329	0.4400	0.0484	0.0007	0.0000	0.9974	0.4307	0.4445
mfg00	0.6092	0.4170	0.2074	0.0260	0.0000	1.0000	0.3680	0.4934
coll00	0.7498	0.3550	0.0842	0.0226	0.0002	0.9877	0.2886	0.5558
bornst00	0.4260	0.4478	0.0541	0.0407	0.0522	0.8985	0.0916	0.7296
outst00	0.4195	0.4596	0.0423	0.0472	0.0503	0.7606	0.0788	0.8716
Hispanic00	0.6876	0.3935	0.0438	0.0085	0.0085	0.9931	0.3383	0.5160

Connecticut

	Bb	Bw	Sb	Sw	Loweb	Upperb	Lowerw	Upperw
1928–32								
black30	0.9908	0.4176	0.0046	0.0001	0.0000	1.0000	0.4174	0.4373
elderly30	0.2743	0.4395	0.2459	0.0145	0.0000	1.0000	0.3950	0.4541
foreign30	0.8140	0.3033	0.2120	0.0690	0.0000	1.0000	0.2428	0.5684
farm30	0.3667	0.4307	0.2671	0.0082	0.0000	1.0000	0.4111	0.4420
white30	0.4261	0.5626	0.0057	0.2842	0.4172	0.4374	0.0000	1.0000
1936–44								
black40	0.6236	0.4958	0.2812	0.0061	0.0000	1.0000	0.4876	0.5094
elderly40	0.4180	0.5050	0.2701	0.0217	0.0000	1.0000	0.4581	0.5386
foreign40	0.9923	0.3760	0.0026	0.0006	0.0000	1.0000	0.3741	0.6222
farm40	0.2069	0.5087	0.1106	0.0039	0.0000	1.0000	0.4809	0.5160
white40	0.4983	0.5060	0.0026	0.1180	0.4873	0.5096	0.0000	1.0000

(continues)

Connecticut—*Continued*

	Bb	Bw	Sb	Sw	Loweb	Upperb	Lowerw	Upperw
1948–52								
black50	0.5134	0.4208	0.3076	0.0104	0.0000	1.0000	0.4044	0.4380
elderly50	0.0471	0.4610	0.0767	0.0076	0.0000	1.0000	0.3668	0.4657
foreign50	0.9942	0.3142	0.0013	0.0003	0.0000	1.0000	0.3131	0.5052
farm50	0.4034	0.4239	0.2705	0.0058	0.0000	1.0000	0.4112	0.4325
white50	0.4117	0.7728	0.0070	0.2019	0.4038	0.4384	0.0000	1.0000
mfg50	0.6576	0.2711	0.0481	0.0273	0.0302	0.9060	0.1089	0.6808
coll50	0.0043	0.4518	0.0011	0.0001	0.0000	1.0000	0.3853	0.4521
1956–64								
black60	0.4347	0.5021	0.3073	0.0168	0.0000	1.0000	0.4712	0.5259
elderly60	0.9958	0.4441	0.0007	0.0001	0.0000	1.0000	0.4436	0.5532
foreign60	0.8971	0.4458	0.0973	0.0129	0.0013	1.0000	0.4322	0.5644
farm60	N/A							
white60	0.4972	0.5232	0.0162	0.2938	0.4709	0.5260	0.0000	1.0000
mfg60	0.5749	0.4507	0.0320	0.0201	0.0699	0.9388	0.2258	0.7672
coll60	0.3933	0.5087	0.2937	0.0282	0.0000	1.0000	0.4505	0.5464
bornst60	0.5259	0.4589	0.0619	0.0899	0.2145	0.7863	0.0809	0.9109
outst60	0.3172	0.5737	0.1168	0.0484	0.0180	0.9657	0.3050	0.6977
1968–72								
black70	0.6933	0.4086	0.1568	0.0129	0.0000	1.0000	0.3834	0.4656
elderly70	0.9556	0.3722	0.0463	0.0051	0.0000	1.0000	0.3673	0.4777
foregin70	0.9935	0.3712	0.0020	0.0002	0.0000	1.0000	0.3707	0.4751
farm70	N/A							
white70	0.4065	0.7083	0.0145	0.1693	0.3816	0.4670	0.0000	1.0000
mfg70	0.3259	0.4835	0.1046	0.0534	0.0060	0.9753	0.1520	0.6468
coll70	0.3677	0.4397	0.2610	0.0371	0.0000	1.0000	0.3497	0.4920
bornst70	0.4070	0.4606	0.0197	0.0258	0.0763	0.7356	0.0305	0.8936
outst70	0.3961	0.4477	0.1147	0.0588	0.0139	0.9559	0.1611	0.6434
1976–84								
black80	0.8501	0.3851	0.0584	0.0044	0.0340	1.0000	0.3738	0.4465
elderly80	0.4949	0.3893	0.2555	0.0353	0.0000	1.0000	0.3195	0.4576
foreign80	0.6005	0.3811	0.2680	0.0283	0.0000	1.0000	0.3390	0.4445
farm80	N/A							
white80	0.3789	0.7697	0.0161	0.1466	0.3550	0.4533	0.0941	0.7866
mfg80	0.2109	0.4873	0.1050	0.0447	0.0000	0.9810	0.1557	0.5732
coll80	0.5471	0.3681	0.3470	0.0814	0.0000	1.0000	0.2619	0.4964
bornst80	0.3786	0.4344	0.0238	0.0327	0.0662	0.6759	0.0252	0.8643
outst80	0.3187	0.4423	0.0562	0.0271	0.0114	0.9342	0.1453	0.5906
Hispanic80	0.8994	0.3975	0.0648	0.0027	0.0000	1.0000	0.3933	0.4351
1988–92								
black90	0.9163	0.4841	0.0429	0.0039	0.1559	1.0000	0.4765	0.5531
white90	0.4626	0.9072	0.0123	0.0831	0.4489	0.5661	0.2091	1.0000
elderly90	0.6285	0.5043	0.1220	0.0177	0.0000	1.0000	0.4502	0.5957
foreign90	0.4881	0.5230	0.0640	0.0060	0.0000	1.0000	0.4755	0.5683
farm90	0.4991	0.5201	0.0552	0.0001	0.0000	1.0000	0.5193	0.5209

Connecticut—*Continued*

	Bb	Bw	Sb	Sw	Loweb	Upperb	Lowerw	Upperw
1988–92								
mfg90	0.4100	0.5464	0.0706	0.0169	0.0000	1.0000	0.4050	0.6447
coll90	0.3145	0.5958	0.0296	0.0109	0.0164	0.9520	0.3609	0.7056
bornst90	0.5419	0.4841	0.0159	0.0261	0.2717	0.7883	0.0797	0.9277
outst90	0.4219	0.5608	0.0335	0.0139	0.0475	0.9495	0.3416	0.7164
Hispanic90	0.6397	0.5121	0.1843	0.0122	0.0705	1.0000	0.4884	0.5497
1996–2000								
black00	0.9930	0.5636	0.0020	0.0002	0.2077	1.0000	0.5630	0.6355
white00	0.5532	0.7969	0.0321	0.1365	0.5054	0.6683	0.3076	1.0000
elderly00	0.6664	0.5885	0.1326	0.0221	0.0000	1.0000	0.5328	0.6996
foreign00	0.7935	0.5816	0.1700	0.0158	0.0087	1.0000	0.5624	0.6545
farm00	0.0180	0.6006	0.0013	0.0000	0.0000	1.0000	0.5990	0.6006
mfg00	0.6687	0.5831	0.0694	0.0166	0.0019	1.0000	0.5037	0.7429
coll00	0.3467	0.6928	0.0274	0.0101	0.0352	0.9731	0.4621	0.8076
bornst00	0.6448	0.5254	0.0152	0.0249	0.3832	0.8773	0.1439	0.9548
outst00	0.5361	0.6260	0.0564	0.0235	0.0766	0.9726	0.4446	0.8170
Hispanic00	0.9740	0.5667	0.0236	0.0021	0.1536	1.0000	0.5644	0.6388

Florida

	Bb	Bw	Sb	Sw	Lowerb	Upperb	Lowerw	Upperw
1928–32								
black30	0.8523	0.5282	0.0253	0.0106	0.2737	0.9900	0.4709	0.7692
elderly30	0.5003	0.6298	0.0263	0.0013	0.0190	1.0000	0.6044	0.6543
foreign30	0.7595	0.6179	0.0410	0.0017	0.1054	1.0000	0.6078	0.6453
farm30	0.7487	0.5947	0.0369	0.0085	0.2972	0.9638	0.5451	0.6988
white30	0.5256	0.8578	0.0093	0.0223	0.4703	0.7696	0.2744	0.9900
1936–44								
black40	0.9151	0.6845	0.0073	0.0027	0.2856	1.0000	0.6529	0.9185
elderly40	0.1388	0.7921	0.0635	0.0047	0.0008	1.0000	0.7282	0.8023
foreign40	0.1630	0.7719	0.0627	0.0027	0.0024	1.0000	0.7362	0.7788
farm40	0.9276	0.7129	0.0276	0.0052	0.4101	1.0000	0.6993	0.8105
white40	0.6880	0.9052	0.0294	0.0788	0.6526	0.9189	0.2861	1.0000
1948–52								
black50	0.4679	0.4843	0.0444	0.6123	0.0162	0.9958	0.3378	0.6097
elderly50	0.0166	0.5243	0.0244	0.0023	0.0000	1.0000	0.4321	0.5259
foreign50	0.1049	0.4744	0.1098	0.0083	0.0000	1.0000	0.4062	0.4824
farm50	0.8688	0.4451	0.0563	0.0052	0.0861	0.9983	0.4332	0.5170
white50	0.4891	0.4507	0.0089	0.0320	0.3373	0.6102	0.0161	0.9958
mfg50	0.7365	0.4511	0.2021	0.0235	0.0073	1.0000	0.4705	0.5357
coll50	0.0173	0.5114	0.0150	0.0010	0.0000	1.0000	0.4465	0.5126

(continues)

Florida—*Continued*

	Bb	Bw	Sb	Sw	Lowerb	Upperb	Lowerw	Upperw
1956–64								
black60	0.6633	0.4596	0.0650	0.0141	0.0109	0.9956	0.3878	0.6007
elderly60	0.3151	0.5185	0.0603	0.0076	0.0000	1.0000	0.4324	0.5581
foreign60	0.1086	0.5183	0.1123	0.0065	0.0000	1.0000	0.4665	0.5246
farm60	0.7411	0.4905	0.0756	0.0016	0.0181	0.9978	0.4850	0.5061
white60	0.4641	0.6408	0.0145	0.0661	0.3865	0.6018	0.0108	0.9956
mfg60	0.7007	0.4666	0.1308	0.0187	0.0012	1.0000	0.4238	0.5665
coll60	0.0330	0.5348	0.0271	0.0023	0.0000	1.0000	0.4533	0.5376
bornst60	0.6734	0.3884	0.0377	0.0228	0.1031	0.9409	0.2266	0.7334
outst60	0.3513	0.6859	0.0305	0.0401	0.1675	0.7850	0.1152	0.9279
1968–72								
black70	0.3708	0.2359	0.0635	0.0116	0.0000	0.9486	0.1302	0.3038
elderly70	0.3312	0.2442	0.0688	0.0117	0.0000	0.9180	0.1446	0.3004
foreign70	0.3794	0.3760	0.0533	0.0091	0.0000	0.9412	0.2806	0.4405
farm70	0.2004	0.2567	0.1457	0.0016	0.0000	0.9780	0.2483	0.2588
white70	0.2361	0.3663	0.0110	0.0581	0.1266	0.3053	0.0000	0.9462
mfg70	0.1699	0.2710	0.0721	0.0118	0.0000	0.9520	0.1432	0.2988
coll70	0.5310	0.2253	0.2324	0.0268	0.0000	0.9968	0.1716	0.2864
bornst70	0.2086	0.2786	0.0247	0.0112	0.0021	0.6728	0.0684	0.3722
outst70	0.2662	0.2442	0.0158	0.0247	0.0278	0.4207	0.0018	0.6132
1976–84								
black80	0.7985	0.3636	0.0516	0.0083	0.0079	0.9996	0.3314	0.4902
elderly80	0.4435	0.4215	0.2799	0.0305	0.0000	1.0000	0.3607	0.4699
foreign80	0.3299	0.4351	0.1689	0.0206	0.0000	1.0000	0.3533	0.4753
farm80	0.6100	0.4440	0.2810	0.0109	0.0000	1.0000	0.4249	0.4636
white80	0.3485	0.8176	0.0108	0.0568	0.3138	0.5031	0.0069	0.9996
mfg80	0.7770	0.3757	0.1504	0.0203	0.0000	1.0000	0.3457	0.4809
coll80	0.2270	0.4488	0.1809	0.0232	0.0000	1.0000	0.3498	0.4779
bornst80	0.6003	0.3436	0.0937	0.0425	0.0358	0.9318	0.1956	0.5994
outst80	0.2810	0.6202	0.0233	0.0321	0.1009	0.6870	0.0607	0.8684
Hispanic80	0.3823	0.4276	0.1570	0.0152	0.0000	1.0000	0.3678	0.4647
1988–92								
black90	0.5235	0.3396	0.0643	0.0101	0.0010	0.9954	0.2654	0.4219
white00	0.3360	0.5054	0.0163	0.0799	0.2361	0.4387	0.0009	0.9958
elderly90	0.4070	0.3552	0.1612	0.0361	0.0000	0.9841	0.2261	0.4463
foreign90	0.4724	0.3487	0.1582	0.0234	0.0000	0.9693	0.2753	0.4185
farm90	0.4050	0.3645	0.2599	0.0010	0.0000	1.0000	0.3623	0.3660
mfg90	0.2732	0.3754	0.1030	0.0121	0.0000	1.0000	0.2901	0.4074
coll90	0.3684	0.3638	0.0760	0.0171	0.0000	0.9988	0.2217	0.4468
bornst90	0.4014	0.3485	0.0260	0.0114	0.0045	0.9119	0.1245	0.5227
outst90	0.3267	0.4141	0.0189	0.0247	0.0499	0.6013	0.0556	0.7756
Hispanic90	0.4793	0.3488	0.2382	0.0330	0.0000	0.9184	0.2879	0.4152

Florida—*Continued*

	Bb	Bw	Sb	Sw	Lowerb	Upperb	Lowerw	Upperw
1996–2000								
black00	0.7395	0.4483	0.0554	0.0089	0.0055	1.0000	0.4064	0.5622
white00	0.4321	0.7566	0.0197	0.0937	0.3809	0.5905	0.0047	1.0000
elderly00	0.6078	0.4621	0.0850	0.0189	0.0000	1.0000	0.3751	0.5970
foreign00	0.7844	0.4456	0.0786	0.0114	0.0000	1.0000	0.4138	0.5575
farm00	0.5029	0.4892	0.1411	0.0005	0.0000	1.0000	0.4874	0.4911
mfg00	0.2906	0.5086	0.1721	0.0174	0.0000	1.0000	0.4370	0.5379
coll00	0.6798	0.4561	0.0957	0.0163	0.0000	1.0000	0.4017	0.5716
bornst00	0.4149	0.5219	0.0313	0.0137	0.9521	0.9521	0.2861	0.6980
outst00	0.4877	0.4912	0.0224	0.0292	0.7745	0.7745	0.1169	0.8956
Hispanic00	0.6213	0.4662	0.1014	0.0171	0.9743	0.9743	0.4066	0.5500

Georgia

	Bb	Bw	Sb	Sw	Lowerb	Upperb	Lowerw	Upperw
1928–32								
black30	0.8448	0.7119	0.0418	0.0244	0.5622	0.9854	0.7119	0.0244
elderly30	0.8630	0.7567	0.0942	0.0038	0.0780	1.0000	0.7512	0.7885
foreign30	0.6457	0.7614	0.2293	0.0011	0.0032	1.0000	0.7597	0.7645
farm30	0.7925	0.7309	0.0163	0.0154	0.6656	0.9309	0.6000	0.8509
white30	0.7007	0.8639	0.0155	0.0265	0.6299	0.8767	0.5622	0.9854
1936–44								
black40	0.9223	0.7857	0.0112	0.0060	0.6121	0.9995	0.7447	0.9508
elderly40	0.4333	0.8574	0.0597	0.0032	0.0331	1.0000	0.8241	0.8763
foreign40	0.8174	0.8332	0.0537	0.0002	0.0010	1.0000	0.8364	0.8325
farm40	0.8714	0.8035	0.0081	0.0063	0.1300	0.9895	0.7119	0.9131
white40	0.7826	0.9281	0.0068	0.0128	0.7446	0.9508	0.6123	0.9995
1948–52								
black50	0.6796	0.6428	0.0192	0.0086	0.2207	0.9693	0.5128	0.8487
elderly60	0.1880	0.6860	0.0759	0.0052	0.0005	1.0000	0.6306	0.6988
foreign50	0.5026	0.6549	0.2776	0.0013	0.0000	1.0000	0.6525	0.6574
farm50	0.8008	0.5973	0.0110	0.0043	0.3999	0.9738	0.5303	0.7528
white50	0.6392	0.6878	0.0088	0.0196	0.5134	0.8477	0.2213	0.9692
mfg50	0.6202	0.6637	0.0375	0.0106	0.1429	0.9970	0.5577	0.7981
coll50	0.1676	0.6754	0.1697	0.0077	0.0000	1.0000	0.6378	0.6830
1956–64								
black60	0.6204	0.5809	0.0306	0.0122	0.1830	0.9708	0.4415	0.7550
elderly60	0.4369	0.6045	0.1162	0.0092	0.0041	1.0000	0.5597	0.6390
foreign60	0.4314	0.5932	0.2843	0.0018	0.0000	1.0000	0.5895	0.5960
farm60	0.6433	0.5863	0.0221	0.0025	0.1486	0.9913	0.5462	0.6433
white60	0.5736	0.6386	0.0361	0.0904	0.4408	0.7556	0.1833	0.9708
mfg60	0.5107	0.6193	0.0474	0.0158	0.0911	0.9841	0.4619	0.7587
coll60	0.2738	0.6100	0.1070	0.0060	0.0005	1.0000	0.5693	0.6254
bornst60	0.6409	0.3811	0.0153	0.0663	0.5001	0.7177	0.0487	0.9909
outst60	0.3709	0.6413	0.0619	0.0138	0.0452	0.9922	0.5033	0.7136

(continues)

Georgia—*Continued*

	Bb	Bw	Sb	Sw	Lowerb	Upperb	Lowerw	Upperw
1968–72								
black70	0.4618	0.1823	0.0166	0.0058	0.0024	0.8035	0.0625	0.3433
elderly70	0.6907	0.2170	0.1361	0.0119	0.0000	0.9997	0.1901	0.2771
foreign70	0.3202	0.2544	0.1419	0.0010	0.0000	0.9744	0.2497	0.2568
farm70	0.0543	0.2625	0.0360	0.0014	0.0000	0.9346	0.2291	0.2645
white70	0.1811	0.4642	0.0066	0.0186	0.0670	0.3440	0.0023	0.8018
mfg70	0.1555	0.2916	0.0327	0.0121	0.0000	0.7072	0.0880	0.3490
coll70	0.5551	0.1950	0.0645	0.0129	0.0000	0.9491	0.1163	0.3058
bornst70	0.2142	0.1991	0.0112	0.0207	0.0291	0.2931	0.0532	0.5416
outst70	0.2219	0.2649	0.0260	0.0078	0.0030	0.8149	0.0862	0.3308
1976–84								
black80	0.7312	0.4800	0.0299	0.0109	0.1034	0.9977	0.3829	0.7086
elderly80	0.4801	0.5512	0.0257	0.0016	0.0000	1.0000	0.5189	0.5810
foreign80	0.4587	0.5485	0.2788	0.0048	0.0000	1.0000	0.5393	0.5564
farm80	0.9210	0.5386	0.0307	0.0007	0.0000	1.0000	0.5368	0.5594
white80	0.4874	0.6980	0.0130	0.0329	0.3730	0.7165	0.1183	0.9873
mfg80	0.5658	0.5415	0.0309	0.0092	0.0610	0.9866	0.4168	0.6910
coll80	0.1478	0.5926	0.1490	0.0170	0.0000	1.0000	0.4953	0.6094
bornst80	0.6213	0.3656	0.0174	0.0426	0.3783	0.7559	0.0369	0.9590
outst80	0.3501	0.6212	0.0504	0.0190	0.0266	0.9663	0.3892	0.7429
Hispanic80	0.4884	0.5477	0.0955	0.0011	0.0000	1.0000	0.5419	0.5532
1988–92								
black90	0.5548	0.3471	0.0257	0.0095	0.0188	0.9303	0.2085	0.5450
white90	0.3455	0.5442	0.0110	0.0270	0.1924	0.5588	0.0219	0.9193
elderly90	0.5150	0.3906	0.3632	0.0408	0.0000	1.0000	0.3361	0.4484
foreign90	0.4262	0.4025	0.2915	0.0080	0.0000	1.0000	0.3867	0.4142
farm90	0.5382	0.4014	0.3784	0.0047	0.0000	1.0000	0.3957	0.4082
mfg90	0.3979	0.4044	0.0609	0.0146	0.0004	0.9797	0.2651	0.4995
coll90	0.2212	0.4464	0.0544	0.0129	0.0000	0.9720	0.2678	0.4990
bornst90	0.4693	0.2829	0.0104	0.0189	0.1597	0.6202	0.0088	0.8454
outst90	0.2727	0.4668	0.0233	0.0114	0.0068	0.8753	0.1727	0.5965
Hispanic90	0.4088	0.4030	0.2745	0.0047	0.0000	1.0000	0.3929	0.4100
1996–2000								
black00	0.8323	0.3045	0.0132	0.0050	0.0891	0.9985	0.2420	0.5838
white00	0.2869	0.8344	0.0066	0.0158	0.2180	0.5926	0.1056	0.9985
elderly00	0.6832	0.4309	0.2399	0.0269	0.0000	1.0000	0.3953	0.5076
foreign00	0.3168	0.4525	0.0745	0.0021	0.0000	1.0000	0.4333	0.4610
farm00	0.6636	0.4460	0.2523	0.0031	0.0000	1.0000	0.4419	0.4542
mfg00	0.3821	0.4623	0.1617	0.0332	0.0004	0.9887	0.3378	0.5406
coll00	0.3199	0.4725	0.0543	0.0101	0.0000	1.0000	0.3464	0.5318
bornst00	0.5128	0.3341	0.0167	0.0297	0.2100	0.6692	0.0549	0.8747
outst00	0.3148	0.5152	0.0253	0.0126	0.0351	0.8907	0.2288	0.6543
Hispanic00	0.4956	0.4477	0.0496	0.0010	0.0000	1.0000	0.4372	0.4580

Illinois

	Bb	Bw	Sb	Sw	Lowerb	Upperb	Lowerw	Upperw
1928–32								
black30	0.3764	0.4932	0.1469	0.0066	0.0000	1.0000	0.4651	0.5102
elderly30	0.5120	0.4867	0.0764	0.0048	0.0296	0.9631	0.4582	0.5171
farm30	0.5170	0.4839	0.0368	0.0055	0.0502	0.9291	0.4222	0.5537
foreign30	0.4942	0.4870	0.2948	0.0560	0.0000	1.0000	0.3909	0.5809
white30	0.4887	0.4768	0.0075	0.1492	0.4675	0.5127	0.0000	1.0000
1936–44								
black40	0.5863	0.5313	0.0472	0.0050	0.0000	1.0000	0.5100	0.5614
elderly40	0.1973	0.5615	0.1754	0.0135	0.0000	1.0000	0.4997	0.5767
farm40	0.3883	0.5543	0.0206	0.0029	0.0179	0.9471	0.4763	0.6060
foreign40	0.5164	0.5364	0.1694	0.0237	0.0000	1.0000	0.4687	0.6088
white40	0.5295	0.6194	0.0081	0.1542	0.5094	0.5621	0.0000	1.0000
1948–52								
black50	0.7235	0.4526	0.1132	0.0091	0.0000	1.0000	0.4303	0.5107
elderly50	0.4731	0.4727	0.2588	0.0246	0.0000	1.0000	0.4227	0.5176
farm50	0.3457	0.4849	0.0378	0.0036	0.0015	0.9582	0.4260	0.5181
foreign50	0.4181	0.4781	0.2310	0.0228	0.0000	1.0000	0.4208	0.5193
white50	0.4483	0.7665	0.0104	0.1246	0.4289	0.5120	0.0000	1.0000
mfg50	0.5794	0.4269	0.0687	0.0295	0.0008	0.9887	0.2573	0.6752
coll50	0.1347	0.4939	0.0411	0.0026	0.0000	1.0000	0.4391	0.5023
1956–64								
black60	0.7965	0.4643	0.1080	0.0124	0.0001	1.0000	0.4409	0.5557
elderly60	0.8262	0.4633	0.1076	0.0115	0.0000	1.0000	0.4447	0.5519
farm60	0.3762	0.5057	0.0440	0.0026	0.0006	0.9949	0.4691	0.5279
foreign60	0.5344	0.4959	0.1338	0.0098	0.0000	1.0000	0.4619	0.5348
white60	0.4876	0.5900	0.0181	0.1525	0.4390	0.5576	0.0001	1.0000
mfg60	0.5363	0.4822	0.0502	0.0216	0.0031	0.9858	0.2885	0.7119
coll60	0.2152	0.5226	0.1489	0.0127	0.0000	1.0000	0.4557	0.5410
bornst60	0.4774	0.5510	0.0244	0.0608	0.2999	0.6970	0.0038	0.9933
outst60	0.5294	0.4898	0.0683	0.0191	0.0040	0.4974	0.3590	0.6337
1968–72								
black70	0.7119	0.3805	0.1173	0.0172	0.0000	1.0000	0.3382	0.4851
elderly70	0.5387	0.4103	0.1591	0.0174	0.0000	1.0000	0.3598	0.4692
farm70	0.2866	0.4284	0.0427	0.0017	0.0000	0.9927	0.4002	0.4398
foreign70	0.7200	0.4042	0.1206	0.0072	0.0000	1.0000	0.3884	0.4483
white70	0.3733	0.7378	0.0145	0.0917	0.3319	0.4897	0.0000	1.0000
mfg70	0.4261	0.4216	0.0617	0.0267	0.0000	0.9708	0.1864	0.6056
coll70	0.3801	0.4250	0.1415	0.0165	0.0000	1.0000	0.5560	0.4723
bornst70	0.3870	0.5005	0.0201	0.0433	0.1629	0.6190	0.0000	0.9839
outst70	0.5054	0.3934	0.0592	0.0212	0.0000	0.9932	0.2185	0.5746
1976–84								
black80	0.8392	0.3738	0.0640	0.0111	0.0000	1.0000	0.3458	0.5197
elderly80	0.4938	0.4306	0.3844	0.0280	0.0000	1.0000	0.3443	0.4660
farm80	0.2588	0.4478	0.0795	0.0022	0.0000	0.9986	0.4271	0.4551
foreign80	0.3842	0.4473	0.2146	0.0169	0.0000	1.0000	0.3989	0.4775

(continues)

Illinois—*Continued*

	Bb	Bw	Sb	Sw	Lowerb	Upperb	Lowerw	Upperw
1976–84								
mfg80	0.2047	0.5070	0.0554	0.0174	0.0000	1.0000	0.2589	0.5712
coll80	0.4087	0.4383	0.2817	0.0373	0.0000	1.0000	0.3601	0.4923
bornst80	0.4000	0.5375	0.0291	0.0645	0.2050	0.6422	0.0000	0.9701
outst80	0.5267	0.4164	0.0851	0.0266	0.0000	0.9917	0.2710	0.5811
Hispanic80	0.3508	0.4489	0.2398	0.0147	0.0000	1.0000	0.4092	0.4703
1988–92								
black90	0.8387	0.4278	0.0761	0.0132	0.0000	1.0000	0.3997	0.5757
white90	0.4160	0.7513	0.0155	0.0561	0.3472	0.6239	0.0000	1.0000
elderly90	0.5143	0.4853	0.1512	0.0130	0.0000	1.0000	0.4152	0.5589
foreign90	0.5238	0.4855	0.1056	0.0096	0.0000	1.0000	0.4455	0.5331
farm90	0.3012	0.4912	0.0817	0.0015	0.0000	1.0000	0.4792	0.4977
mfg90	0.1510	0.5702	0.0951	0.0230	0.0000	0.9980	0.3652	0.6067
coll90	0.5440	0.5547	0.1256	0.0245	0.0000	0.9821	0.3563	0.6198
bornst90	0.4592	0.5545	0.0253	0.0566	0.2642	0.7073	0.0000	0.9905
outst90	0.5303	0.4765	0.0582	0.0170	0.0000	0.9995	0.3397	0.6312
Hispanic90	0.5450	0.4838	0.1512	0.0130	0.0000	1.0000	0.4447	0.5307
1996–2000								
black00	0.9218	0.4876	0.0470	0.0083	0.0000	1.0000	0.4738	0.6508
white00	0.4493	0.9125	0.0126	0.0438	0.4241	0.6772	0.1219	1.0000
elderly00	0.4978	0.5612	0.1566	0.0234	0.0000	1.0000	0.4836	0.6354
foreign00	0.9737	0.5195	0.0296	0.0027	0.0000	1.0000	0.5172	0.6080
farm00	0.4645	0.5591	0.1592	0.0029	0.0000	1.0000	0.5492	0.5676
mfg00	0.3269	0.5994	0.1827	0.0376	0.0000	1.0000	0.4610	0.6666
coll00	0.5440	0.5547	0.1256	0.0245	0.0000	1.0000	0.4657	0.6608
bornst00	0.4830	0.7297	0.1095	0.0435	0.3595	0.7854	0.0477	0.9997
outst00	0.6627	0.5267	0.0653	0.0190	0.0001	0.9996	0.4284	0.7199
Hispanic00	0.8649	0.5205	0.0972	0.0101	0.0000	1.0000	0.5065	0.6104

Maryland

	Bb	Bw	Sb	Sw	Lowerb	Upperb	Lowerw	Upperw
1928–32								
black30	0.6493	0.5029	0.1298	0.0268	0.0027	0.9937	0.4319	0.6362
elderly30	0.6064	0.5234	0.2361	0.0142	0.0000	1.0000	0.4494	0.5600
foreign30	0.9503	0.5018	0.0498	0.0031	0.0000	1.0000	0.4988	0.5605
farm30	0.5191	0.5294	0.0772	0.0131	0.0482	0.9351	0.4589	0.6091
white30	0.5069	0.6304	0.0327	0.1596	0.4327	0.6354	0.0022	0.9934
1936–44								
black40	0.4829	0.6036	0.0648	0.0129	0.0000	0.9994	0.5010	0.6995
elderly40	0.2933	0.6048	0.2447	0.0179	0.0000	1.0000	0.5532	0.6262
foreign40	0.9429	0.5665	0.0584	0.0028	0.0000	1.0000	0.5638	0.6113
farm40	0.3715	0.6162	0.0436	0.0067	0.0207	0.9709	0.5239	0.6703
white40	0.6662	0.1698	0.0329	0.1647	0.5006	0.7001	0.0000	0.9994

Maryland—*Continued*

	Bb	Bw	Sb	Sw	Lowerb	Upperb	Lowerw	Upperw
1948–52								
black50	0.5641	0.4505	0.0807	0.0159	0.0000	1.0000	0.3645	0.5618
elderly50	0.5469	0.4634	0.1028	0.0077	0.0000	1.0000	0.4293	0.5045
foreign50	0.5134	0.4676	0.3191	0.0119	0.0000	1.0000	0.4494	0.4867
farm50	0.3500	0.4794	0.0579	0.0049	0.0000	0.9896	0.4250	0.5091
white50	0.4866	0.3818	0.0530	0.2671	0.3639	0.5623	0.0000	1.0000
mfg50	0.5205	0.4536	0.0981	0.0300	0.0000	1.0000	0.3072	0.6125
coll50	0.2447	0.4864	0.1614	0.0123	0.0000	1.0000	0.4287	0.5050
1956–64								
black60	0.6928	0.4992	0.0820	0.0165	0.0653	0.9999	0.4375	0.6254
elderly60	0.4419	0.5387	0.3205	0.0253	0.0000	1.0000	0.4947	0.5735
foreign60	0.4726	0.4032	0.3357	0.0110	0.0000	1.0000	0.3860	0.4186
farm60	0.3972	0.5366	0.1537	0.0057	0.0000	1.0000	0.5144	0.5512
white60	0.5019	0.6766	0.0187	0.0914	0.4357	0.6271	0.0660	0.9999
mfg60	0.3310	0.5920	0.1327	0.0399	0.0098	0.9908	0.3734	0.6886
coll60	0.7062	0.5135	0.2050	0.0213	0.0000	1.0000	0.4829	0.5870
bornst60	0.4834	0.6042	0.0338	0.0508	0.2792	0.7770	0.1630	0.9109
outst60	0.6096	0.4860	0.0484	0.0284	0.1384	0.9315	0.2973	0.7621
1968–72								
black70	0.6495	0.3524	0.0520	0.0113	0.0517	0.9932	0.2776	0.4825
elderly70	0.2943	0.4147	0.1180	0.0098	0.0000	1.0000	0.3563	0.4391
foreign70	0.9836	0.3865	0.0236	0.0008	0.0000	1.0000	0.3860	0.4188
farm70	0.1517	0.4096	0.1326	0.0021	0.0000	1.0000	0.3959	0.4120
white70	0.3495	0.6505	0.0134	0.0596	0.2712	0.4854	0.0559	0.9933
mfg70	0.3546	0.4180	0.0715	0.0175	0.0000	0.9824	0.2640	0.5049
coll70	0.7298	0.3427	0.0897	0.0145	0.0000	1.0000	0.3091	0.4712
bornst70	0.3642	0.4531	0.0319	0.0368	0.1228	0.6698	0.1009	0.7313
outst70	0.4510	0.3707	0.0420	0.0321	0.0726	0.7610	0.1340	0.6597
1976–84								
black80	0.8609	0.3880	0.0355	0.0103	0.2112	1.0000	0.3473	0.5782
elderly80	0.3361	0.5047	0.1527	0.0092	0.0000	1.0000	0.4646	0.5250
foreign80	0.6063	0.4896	0.3089	0.0150	0.0000	1.0000	0.4705	0.5191
farm80	0.3725	0.4964	0.2268	0.0024	0.0000	1.0000	0.4196	0.5004
white80	0.3934	0.7916	0.0115	0.0335	0.3276	0.5955	0.2026	0.9835
mfg80	0.2562	0.5334	0.1053	0.0163	0.0000	1.0000	0.4143	0.5744
coll80	0.5396	0.4874	0.1732	0.0300	0.0000	1.0000	0.4076	0.5810
bornst80	0.4326	0.5671	0.0327	0.0376	0.2080	0.7722	0.1759	0.8259
outst80	0.5988	0.4209	0.0477	0.0341	0.1263	0.8798	0.2198	0.7591
Hispanic80	0.8859	0.4891	0.1219	0.0019	0.0000	1.0000	0.4874	0.5027
1988–92								
black90	0.8815	0.3721	0.0352	0.0117	0.2926	1.0000	0.3328	0.5672
white00	0.3458	0.8733	0.0104	0.0254	0.2940	0.5834	0.2922	1.0000
elderly90	0.5473	0.4930	0.2559	0.0310	0.0000	1.0000	0.4381	0.5594
foreign90	0.9952	0.4641	0.0019	0.0001	0.0000	1.0000	0.4637	0.5339

(continues)

Maryland—*Continued*

	Bb	Bw	Sb	Sw	Lowerb	Upperb	Lowerw	Upperw
1988–92								
farm90	0.0071	0.5022	0.0020	0.0000	0.0000	1.0000	0.4954	0.5023
mfg90	0.5647	0.4911	0.2126	0.0255	0.0000	1.0000	0.4398	0.5577
coll90	0.6333	0.4509	0.2001	0.0713	0.0192	0.9958	0.3217	0.6699
bornst90	0.3381	0.6586	0.0251	0.0250	0.1900	0.7602	0.2391	0.8059
outst90	0.6014	0.4196	0.1411	0.1091	0.1647	0.8974	0.1908	0.7572
Hispanic90	0.8813	0.4886	0.1333	0.0036	0.0000	1.0000	0.4854	0.5123
1996–2000								
black00	0.9463	0.4383	0.0415	0.0140	0.3887	1.0000	0.4202	0.6259
white00	0.4530	0.8320	0.0706	0.1657	0.3815	0.6496	0.3704	1.0000
elderly00	0.4925	0.5754	0.3233	0.0405	0.0000	1.0000	0.5119	0.6371
foreign00	0.4854	0.5719	0.2023	0.0143	0.0000	1.0000	0.5356	0.6062
farm00	0.0057	0.5776	0.0022	0.0001	0.0000	1.0000	0.5708	0.5776
mfg00	0.3390	0.5894	0.3331	0.0340	0.0000	1.0000	0.5219	0.6240
coll00	0.5210	0.5764	0.3423	0.0775	0.0000	1.0000	0.4680	0.6944
bornst00	0.3901	0.7562	0.0346	0.0344	0.2410	0.8200	0.3288	0.9043
outst00	0.8002	0.3986	0.0454	0.0351	0.2594	0.9785	0.2608	0.8166
Hispanic00	0.6240	0.5643	0.2955	0.0096	0.0000	1.0000	0.5521	0.5846

Michigan

	Bb	Bw	Sb	Sw	Lowerb	Upperb	Lowerw	Upperw
1928–32								
black30	0.4752	0.4109	0.2667	0.0097	0.0000	1.0000	0.3919	0.4282
elderly30	0.4235	0.4126	0.2179	0.0121	0.0000	0.9992	0.3808	0.4361
foreign30	0.7624	0.3399	0.0514	0.0108	0.0000	0.9996	0.2900	0.5000
farm30	0.3734	0.4208	0.0416	0.0079	0.0235	0.7958	0.3402	0.4875
white30	0.4094	0.5046	0.0051	0.1230	0.3889	0.4303	0.0000	1.0000
1936–44								
black40	0.6585	0.5187	0.3003	0.0124	0.0000	1.0000	0.5037	0.5449
elderly40	0.2359	0.5427	0.1098	0.0074	0.0000	0.9479	0.4914	0.5586
foreign40	0.5443	0.5202	0.3531	0.0531	0.0000	1.0000	0.4517	0.6020
farm40	0.1877	0.5891	0.0172	0.0034	0.0062	0.8268	0.4636	0.6246
white40	0.5167	0.6779	0.0076	0.1761	0.5029	0.5459	0.0000	1.0000
1948–52								
black50	0.6782	0.4388	0.2596	0.0194	0.0000	1.0000	0.4147	0.4895
elderly50	0.0538	0.4868	0.0661	0.0052	0.0000	1.0000	0.4130	0.4909
foreign50	0.7927	0.4202	0.2221	0.0232	0.0000	1.0000	0.3985	0.5031
farm50	0.1009	0.4989	0.0326	0.0040	0.0000	0.8522	0.4069	0.5112
white50	0.4421	0.6299	0.0119	0.1557	0.4137	0.4903	0.0000	1.0000
mfg50	0.6837	0.3153	0.0533	0.0328	0.0205	0.9715	0.1385	0.7226
coll50	0.4051	0.4583	0.2273	0.0127	0.0000	1.0000	0.4250	0.4810

Michigan—*Continued*

	Bb	Bw	Sb	Sw	Lowerb	Upperb	Lowerw	Upperw
1956–64								
black60	0.5960	0.5297	0.3486	0.0352	0.0000	1.0000	0.4889	0.5899
elderly60	0.4170	0.5468	0.2753	0.0244	0.0000	1.0000	0.4951	0.5838
foreign60	0.7649	0.5196	0.1864	0.0135	0.0000	1.0000	0.5026	0.5757
farm60	0.1143	0.5614	0.0392	0.0023	0.0000	0.9768	0.5099	0.5682
white60	0.5278	0.6175	0.0117	0.1120	0.4879	0.5921	0.0000	1.0000
mfg60	0.5741	0.5157	0.0288	0.0156	0.0713	0.9804	0.2949	0.7888
coll60	0.4154	0.5451	0.1832	0.0134	0.0000	1.0000	0.5023	0.5755
bornst60	0.4850	0.6671	0.0334	0.0855	0.3570	0.7206	0.0649	0.9943
outst60	0.5977	0.5195	0.0312	0.0085	0.0114	0.9976	0.4108	0.6788
1968–72								
black70	0.8382	0.4017	0.1231	0.0154	0.0000	1.0000	0.3814	0.5068
elderly70	0.4156	0.4536	0.0898	0.0083	0.0000	1.0000	0.3994	0.4921
foreign70	0.7649	0.4229	0.0012	0.0001	0.0000	1.0000	0.4227	0.4730
farm70	0.1143	0.4600	0.1238	0.0040	0.0000	0.9971	0.4327	0.4649
white70	0.5278	0.7634	0.0307	0.2307	0.3772	0.5103	0.0000	1.0000
mfg70	0.5741	0.4767	0.0488	0.0272	0.0029	0.9515	0.1707	0.7000
coll70	0.4154	0.4394	0.1534	0.0162	0.0000	1.0000	0.3925	0.4987
bornst70	0.4850	0.6246	0.0215	0.0472	0.2074	0.6488	0.0135	0.9852
outst70	0.5977	0.4125	0.0636	0.0229	0.0000	0.9875	0.2571	0.6124
1976–84								
black80	0.8778	0.3689	0.0478	0.0071	0.0000	1.0000	0.3507	0.4993
elderly80	0.6476	0.4115	0.2613	0.0285	0.0000	1.0000	0.3730	0.4822
foreign80	0.9342	0.4111	0.0811	0.0038	0.0000	1.0000	0.4080	0.4522
farm80	0.0553	0.4421	0.0714	0.0014	0.0000	1.0000	0.4237	0.4432
white80	0.3573	0.8812	0.0078	0.0452	0.3367	0.5101	0.0000	1.0000
govemp80	0.7480	0.4206	0.1554	0.0070	0.0000	1.0000	0.4092	0.4544
mfg80	0.3105	0.4804	0.0596	0.0219	0.0000	0.9875	0.2314	0.5946
coll80	0.2629	0.4540	0.1329	0.0149	0.0000	1.0000	0.3716	0.4833
bornst80	0.3642	0.6176	0.0347	0.0899	0.2199	0.6025	0.0000	0.9915
outst80	0.5823	0.3898	0.0503	0.0153	0.0000	0.9939	0.2645	0.5671
Hispanic80	0.3515	0.4362	0.3580	0.0062	0.0000	1.0000	0.4250	0.4422
1988–92								
black90	0.9009	0.3802	0.0389	0.0063	0.0081	1.0000	0.3643	0.5243
white00	0.3769	0.8342	0.0124	0.0626	0.3440	0.5346	0.0396	1.0000
elderly90	0.7762	0.4088	0.1504	0.0203	0.0000	1.0000	0.3786	0.5138
foreign90	0.6126	0.4462	0.2462	0.0098	0.0000	1.0000	0.4308	0.4706
farm90	0.1701	0.4563	0.1449	0.0019	0.0000	1.0000	0.4454	0.4585
mfg90	0.2916	0.5052	0.0830	0.0251	0.0000	0.9903	0.3946	0.5094
coll90	0.3809	0.4677	0.0530	0.0112	0.0000	1.0000	0.3371	0.5481
bornst90	0.4132	0.5698	0.0182	0.0542	0.2706	0.6046	0.0000	0.9945
outst90	0.5780	0.4186	0.0567	0.0154	0.0000	0.9967	0.3052	0.5752
Hispanic90	0.4290	0.4531	0.2723	0.0060	0.0000	1.0000	0.4405	0.4626

(continues)

Michigan—*Continued*

	Bb	Bw	Sb	Sw	Lowerb	Upperb	Lowerw	Upperw
1996–2000								
black00	0.9565	0.4488	0.0320	0.0053	0.1505	1.0000	0.4416	0.5816
white00	0.4413	0.9059	0.0082	0.0398	0.4220	0.5954	0.1570	1.0000
elderly00	0.5451	0.5173	0.0987	0.0133	0.0000	1.0000	0.4559	0.5909
foreign00	0.9949	0.5064	0.0021	0.0001	0.0000	1.0000	0.5062	0.5460
farm00	0.4297	0.5263	0.3069	0.0040	0.0000	1.0000	0.5189	0.5320
mfg00	0.3641	0.5629	0.0830	0.0225	0.0000	0.9997	0.3911	0.6613
coll00	0.4581	0.5300	0.0776	0.0117	0.0000	1.0000	0.4481	0.5993
bornst00	0.4702	0.6887	0.0153	0.0454	0.3660	0.7014	0.0000	0.9989
outst00	0.6713	0.4855	0.0514	0.0139	0.0000	0.9992	0.3967	0.6673
Hispanic00	0.6425	0.5173	0.2047	0.0055	0.0000	1.0000	0.5077	0.5346

Minnesota

	Bb	Bw	Sb	Sw	Lowerb	Upperb	Lowerw	Upperw
1928–32								
black30	0.5140	0.5043	0.3630	0.0013	0.0000	1.0000	0.5025	0.5062
elderly30	0.0663	0.5341	0.0766	0.0052	0.0000	1.0000	0.4707	0.5386
foreign30	0.0056	0.5933	0.0022	0.0004	0.0000	0.9991	0.4161	0.5943
farm30	0.5552	0.4774	0.0240	0.0127	0.2033	0.8333	0.3301	0.6638
white30	0.5035	0.5848	0.0012	0.1216	0.4995	0.5092	0.0123	1.0000
1936–44								
black40	0.3674	0.5517	0.3977	0.0014	0.0000	1.0000	0.5496	0.5530
elderly40	0.0065	0.5950	0.0021	0.0002	0.0000	1.0000	0.5131	0.5955
foreign40	0.9563	0.5021	0.0418	0.0050	0.0004	1.0000	0.4969	0.6152
farm40	0.4816	0.5831	0.0294	0.0141	0.1528	0.8804	0.3917	0.7408
white40	0.5484	0.8785	0.0009	0.1127	0.5474	0.5557	0.0000	1.0000
1948–52								
black50	0.5293	0.5040	0.3051	0.0014	0.0000	1.0000	0.5018	0.5064
elderly50	0.0180	0.5526	0.0149	0.0015	0.0000	1.0000	0.4546	0.5544
foreign50	0.9870	0.4683	0.0099	0.0007	0.0000	1.0000	0.4673	0.5415
farm50	0.4080	0.5358	0.0349	0.0115	0.0586	0.8838	0.3787	0.6512
mfg50	0.7998	0.4512	0.0980	0.0177	0.0028	1.0000	0.4150	0.5953
white50	0.5035	0.5662	0.0017	0.1741	0.4993	0.5090	0.0000	1.0000
coll50	0.4457	0.5075	0.3001	0.0176	0.0000	1.0000	0.4750	0.5337
1956–64								
black60	0.5455	0.5344	0.2876	0.0019	0.0000	1.0000	0.5314	0.5379
coll60	0.4150	0.5441	0.2906	0.0234	0.0000	1.0000	0.4969	0.5775
elderly60	0.2598	0.5662	0.2319	0.0268	0.0000	1.0000	0.4806	0.5963
foreign60	0.9944	0.5142	0.0017	0.0001	0.0000	1.0000	0.5139	0.5580
farm60	0.4689	0.5481	0.0360	0.0075	0.0420	0.9686	0.4442	0.6368
mfg60	0.5248	0.5326	0.0549	0.0122	0.0007	1.0000	0.4308	0.6250
outst60	0.3847	0.5653	0.1258	0.0259	0.0001	1.0000	0.4386	0.6445
bornst60	0.5364	0.5274	0.0452	0.1671	0.4085	0.6789	0.0005	1.0000
white60	0.5343	0.5465	0.0015	0.1171	0.5286	0.5411	0.0000	1.0000

Minnesota—*Continued*

	Bb	Bw	Sb	Sw	Lowerb	Upperb	Lowerw	Upperw
1968–72								
black70	0.5265	0.4898	0.2940	0.0027	0.0000	1.0000	0.4854	0.4946
elderly70	0.2994	0.5131	0.1633	0.0197	0.0000	1.0000	0.4286	0.5492
foreign70	0.9578	0.4777	0.0518	0.0014	0.0000	1.0000	0.4766	0.5031
farm70	0.4424	0.4966	0.0350	0.0048	0.0035	0.9916	0.4221	0.5561
white70	0.4879	0.6106	0.0050	0.2719	0.4807	0.4991	0.0000	1.0000
mfg70	0.6169	0.4568	0.2153	0.0565	0.0023	1.0000	0.3562	0.6182
coll70	0.3754	0.5046	0.0855	0.0108	0.0000	1.0000	0.4259	0.5518
bornst70	0.4917	0.4854	0.0215	0.0614	0.3152	0.6587	0.0085	0.9898
outst70	0.4241	0.5096	0.0933	0.0276	0.0000	1.0000	0.3393	0.6351
1976–84								
black80	0.8778	0.4986	0.1401	0.0020	0.0000	1.0000	0.4970	0.5101
elderly80	0.3915	0.5119	0.0638	0.0048	0.0000	1.0000	0.4665	0.5410
foreign80	0.9900	0.4900	0.0040	0.0001	0.0000	1.0000	0.4897	0.5175
farm80	0.3101	0.5197	0.0428	0.0036	0.0000	0.9998	0.4614	0.5457
mfg80	0.4069	0.5258	0.0918	0.0212	0.0000	1.0000	0.3890	0.6197
white80	0.5007	0.5872	0.0080	0.2369	0.4867	0.5206	0.0000	1.0000
bornst80	0.4863	0.5549	0.0917	0.2733	0.3369	0.6725	0.0000	0.9999
outst80	0.4357	0.5232	0.2081	0.0604	0.0000	1.0000	0.3594	0.6497
coll80	0.4100	0.5169	0.1958	0.0275	0.0000	1.0000	0.4342	0.5744
Hispanic80	0.4348	0.5041	0.2947	0.0024	0.0000	1.0000	0.4946	0.5075
1988–92								
black90	0.9487	0.4662	0.0505	0.0011	0.0000	1.0000	0.4651	0.4873
white00	0.4649	0.6757	0.0087	0.1461	0.5049	0.5049	0.0000	1.0000
elderly90	0.4855	0.4754	0.0996	0.0142	1.0000	1.0000	0.4020	0.5448
foreign90	0.6818	0.4744	0.2594	0.0029	1.0000	1.0000	0.4268	0.4894
farm90	0.3718	0.4819	0.0782	0.0039	1.0000	1.0000	0.4506	0.5005
mfg90	0.3562	0.5032	0.0841	0.0185	0.9989	0.9989	0.3618	0.5816
coll90	0.5069	0.4683	0.0935	0.0260	1.0000	1.0000	0.3314	0.6091
bornst90	0.4790	0.4704	0.0236	0.0664	0.6462	0.6462	0.0003	0.9958
outst90	0.5079	0.4670	0.2306	0.0714	0.9960	0.9960	0.3158	0.6244
Hispanic90	0.5008	0.4764	0.3160	0.0039	1.0000	1.0000	0.4702	0.4826
1996–2000								
black00	0.5888	0.4916	0.2924	0.0069	0.0000	1.0000	0.4820	0.5055
white00	0.4814	0.6834	0.0074	0.1132	1.0000	0.5263	0.0000	1.0000
elderly00	0.5291	0.4889	0.0924	0.0129	0.0000	1.0000	0.4230	0.5630
foreign00	0.5291	0.4886	0.1505	0.0040	0.0000	1.0000	0.4824	0.5090
farm00	0.7643	0.5026	0.0534	0.0027	0.0000	1.0000	0.4706	0.5205
mfg00	0.3596	0.5226	0.0788	0.0151	0.0000	0.9980	0.3972	0.5883
coll00	0.3439	0.4440	0.1725	0.0382	0.0000	1.0000	0.3817	0.6033
bornst00	0.7189	0.5440	0.0243	0.0682	0.3175	0.6722	0.0000	0.9996
outst00	0.4786	0.4978	0.1058	0.0328	0.0000	0.9970	0.3405	0.6464
Hispanic00	0.6728	0.4911	0.2843	0.0043	0.0000	1.0000	0.4861	0.5014

New York

	Bb	Bw	Sb	Sw	Lowerb	Upperb	Lowerw	Upperw
1928–32								
black30	0.6498	0.5267	0.3029	0.0102	0.0000	1.0000	0.5148	0.5486
elderly30	0.2200	0.5481	0.1775	0.0099	0.0000	1.0000	0.5044	0.5604
foreign30	0.8998	0.4050	0.0681	0.0232	0.0339	1.0000	0.3708	0.6999
farm30	0.0691	0.5581	0.0242	0.0014	0.0000	0.9993	0.5064	0.5622
white30	0.5240	0.7171	0.0103	0.2867	0.5138	0.5497	0.0000	1.0000
1936–44								
black40	0.7991	0.4527	0.1763	0.0078	0.0000	1.0000	0.4438	0.4882
elderly40	0.1000	0.4945	0.1166	0.0086	0.0000	1.0000	0.4282	0.5108
foreign40	0.8234	0.3692	0.1392	0.0354	0.0006	1.0000	0.3205	0.5962
farm40	0.0312	0.4919	0.0148	0.0008	0.0000	0.9947	0.4406	0.4936
white40	0.4442	0.9671	0.0020	0.0439	0.4426	0.4892	0.0000	1.0000
1948–52								
black50	0.9933	0.3612	0.0030	0.0002	0.0000	1.0000	0.3607	0.4266
elderly50	0.1223	0.4260	0.1190	0.0104	0.0000	1.0000	0.3447	0.4374
foreign50	0.8323	0.3668	0.1591	0.0439	0.0060	1.0000	0.3205	0.5962
farm50	0.2100	0.4078	0.1385	0.0056	0.0000	0.9549	0.3776	0.4163
white50	0.3591	0.9950	0.0001	0.0017	0.3587	0.4280	0.0000	1.0000
mfg50	0.5491	0.3421	0.0475	0.0186	0.0000	0.9721	0.1768	0.5567
coll50	0.3902	0.4009	0.2831	0.0223	0.0000	1.0000	0.3528	0.4317
1956–64								
black60	0.5983	0.5276	0.2564	0.0405	0.0000	1.0000	0.4672	0.6221
elderly60	0.7403	0.4607	0.2307	0.0258	0.0000	1.0000	0.4317	0.5436
foreign60	0.6689	0.4605	0.2599	0.0410	0.0000	1.0000	0.4082	0.5661
farm60	0.2831	0.4960	0.1789	0.0033	0.0000	0.9955	0.4829	0.5012
white60	0.3591	0.4952	0.0001	0.0016	0.3587	0.4280	0.0000	1.0000
mfg60	0.5495	0.3419	0.0645	0.0252	0.0000	0.9721	0.1768	0.5567
coll60	0.9001	0.4491	0.0484	0.0047	0.0000	0.9998	0.4395	0.5361
bornst60	0.4165	0.7293	0.0251	0.0833	0.3362	0.6262	0.0324	0.9962
outst60	0.5711	0.4804	0.1847	0.0195	0.0000	0.9991	0.4354	0.5406
1968–72								
black70	0.9959	0.3442	0.0012	0.0002	0.0000	1.0000	0.3457	0.4789
elderly70	0.4339	0.4204	0.0881	0.0106	0.0000	1.0000	0.3522	0.4727
foreign70	0.8865	0.3609	0.0836	0.0110	0.0000	1.0000	0.3459	0.4773
farm70	0.1401	0.4248	0.1188	0.0013	0.0000	1.0000	0.4158	0.4263
white70	0.3464	0.9177	0.0127	0.0832	0.3339	0.4861	0.0000	1.0000
mfg70	0.3393	0.4484	0.0810	0.0260	0.0000	0.9806	0.2423	0.5575
coll70	0.6752	0.3881	0.1451	0.0193	0.0000	1.0000	0.3448	0.4781
bornst70	0.2106	0.8714	0.0073	0.0155	0.1510	0.6037	0.0350	0.9983
outst70	0.6099	0.3738	0.0553	0.0142	0.0000	0.9999	0.2740	0.5298
1976–84								
black80	0.9450	0.3985	0.0259	0.0041	0.0000	1.0000	0.3899	0.5486
elderly80	0.5740	0.4728	0.2755	0.0019	0.0000	1.0000	0.4698	0.4768
foreign80	0.9428	0.3996	0.0327	0.0052	0.0000	1.0000	0.3905	0.5480
farm80	0.1701	0.4756	0.1386	0.0010	0.0000	1.0000	0.4698	0.4768

New York—*Continued*

	Bb	Bw	Sb	Sw	Lowerb	Upperb	Lowerw	Upperw
1976–84								
white80	0.3781	0.8485	0.0062	0.0244	0.3410	0.5682	0.1007	0.9944
mfg80	0.2156	0.5356	0.0610	0.0147	0.0000	0.9976	0.3472	0.5875
coll80	0.7652	0.4290	0.1698	0.0258	0.0000	1.0000	0.3933	0.5456
bornst80	0.3167	0.8267	0.0111	0.0251	0.2398	0.6449	0.0873	0.9999
outst80	0.5377	0.4602	0.0440	0.0091	0.0000	1.0000	0.3648	0.5712
Hispanic80	0.9732	0.4212	0.0241	0.0025	0.0021	1.0000	0.4212	0.0025
1988–92								
black90	0.8695	0.4564	0.1378	0.0260	0.0831	1.0000	0.4317	0.6050
white00	0.3721	0.9577	0.0085	0.0247	0.3576	0.6107	0.2643	1.0000
elderly90	0.4495	0.5330	0.2892	0.0437	0.0000	1.0000	0.4498	0.6010
foreign90	0.9407	0.4431	0.0320	0.0060	0.0106	1.0000	0.4319	0.6184
farm90	0.2711	0.5232	0.1893	0.0001	0.0000	1.0000	0.5198	0.5244
mfg90	0.1954	0.5781	0.1069	0.0183	0.0000	1.0000	0.4400	0.6116
coll90	0.8566	0.4232	0.0900	0.0266	0.0647	1.0000	0.3808	0.6571
bornst90	0.3565	0.8666	0.0631	0.1313	0.2924	0.6798	0.1935	1.0000
outst90	0.4677	0.5328	0.0508	0.0101	0.0240	1.0000	0.4270	0.6211
Hispanic90	0.9497	0.4620	0.0459	0.0064	0.1009	1.0000	0.4550	0.5811
1996–2000								
black00	0.9618	0.5557	0.0287	0.0055	0.2484	1.0000	0.5484	0.6923
white00	0.5066	0.9374	0.0230	0.0636	0.4840	0.6884	0.4344	1.0000
elderly00	0.3526	0.6616	0.0728	0.0110	0.0000	1.0000	0.5635	0.7150
foreign00	0.9533	0.5593	0.0531	0.0100	0.2055	1.0000	0.5505	0.7003
farm00	0.3469	0.6231	0.2711	0.0012	0.0000	1.0000	0.6201	0.6247
mfg00	0.3156	0.6653	0.2499	0.0363	0.0000	1.0000	0.5659	0.7112
coll00	0.9243	0.5647	0.0980	0.0182	0.0313	1.0000	0.5507	0.7303
bornst00	0.4922	0.8917	0.0369	0.0768	0.4402	0.7640	0.3258	1.0000
outst00	0.7114	0.6040	0.1397	0.0278	0.0809	1.0000	0.5466	0.7294
Hispanic00	0.7769	0.5943	0.1439	0.0246	0.2533	1.0000	0.5561	0.6839

Oregon

	Bb	Bw	Sb	Sw	Lowerb	Upperb	Lowerw	Upperw
1928–32								
black30	0.9955	0.4605	0.0024	0.0000	0.0000	1.0000	0.4604	0.4628
elderly30	0.4966	0.4590	0.3177	0.0241	0.0000	1.0000	0.4208	0.4968
foreign30	0.4848	0.4588	0.2788	0.0347	0.0000	1.0000	0.9470	0.5192
farm30	0.4433	0.4673	0.0641	0.0194	0.0266	0.9122	0.3253	0.5934
white30	0.4597	0.5754	0.0047	0.2646	0.4521	0.4700	0.0000	1.0000
1936–44								
black40	0.5726	0.5640	0.3732	0.0006	0.0000	1.0000	0.5630	0.5653
elderly40	0.0080	0.6158	0.0041	0.0004	0.0000	1.0000	0.5234	0.6165
foreign40	0.9908	0.5255	0.0059	0.0005	0.0000	1.0000	0.5246	0.6149

(continues)

Oregon—*Continued*

	Bb	Bw	Sb	Sw	Lowerb	Upperb	Lowerw	Upperw
1936–44								
farm40	0.4534	0.5981	0.0495	0.0152	0.0297	0.9941	0.4314	0.7288
white40	0.5649	0.4961	0.0013	0.1037	0.5584	0.5713	0.0000	1.0000
1948–52								
black50	0.5011	0.4244	0.3190	0.0021	0.0000	1.0000	0.4191	0.4258
elderly50	0.5375	0.4120	0.2674	0.0256	0.0000	1.0000	0.3677	0.4635
foreign50	0.8187	0.3999	0.1283	0.0075	0.0000	1.0000	0.3894	0.4476
farm50	0.3407	0.4375	0.0664	0.0117	0.0000	0.9831	0.3242	0.4976
white50	0.4219	0.4697	0.0050	0.3083	0.4133	0.4294	0.0000	1.0000
govemp50	0.0443	0.4644	0.0528	0.0058	0.0000	0.9992	0.3599	0.4692
mfg50	0.5000	0.4020	0.0677	0.0184	0.0000	0.9921	0.2683	0.5379
coll50	0.0144	0.4519	0.0144	0.0008	0.0000	1.0000	0.3821	0.4529
1956–64								
black60	0.5283	0.5183	0.3043	0.0032	0.0000	1.0000	0.5133	0.5238
elderly60	0.3572	0.5371	0.0989	0.0115	0.0000	1.0000	0.4626	0.5784
foreign60	0.4104	0.5225	0.1511	0.0064	0.0000	1.0000	0.4977	0.5397
farm60	0.4168	0.5270	0.1045	0.0088	0.0008	0.9990	0.4777	0.5622
white60	0.5214	0.3680	0.0044	0.2196	0.5087	0.5288	0.0000	1.0000
govemp60	0.4950	0.5195	0.2823	0.0134	0.0000	1.0000	0.4956	0.5429
mfg60	0.6374	0.4845	0.0814	0.0232	0.0090	1.0000	0.3812	0.6635
coll60	0.2814	0.5419	0.0714	0.0071	0.0000	1.0000	0.4707	0.5697
bornst60	0.6705	0.3786	0.0697	0.0640	0.0948	0.9540	0.1180	0.9077
outst60	0.3562	0.6685	0.0694	0.0642	0.0871	0.9455	0.1230	0.9176
1968–72								
black70	0.8609	0.4222	0.1559	0.0020	0.0000	1.0000	0.4204	0.4332
elderly70	0.5753	0.4098	0.2423	0.0295	0.0000	1.0000	0.3581	0.4798
farm70	0.9181	0.4117	0.1047	0.0034	0.0000	1.0000	0.4091	0.4417
foreign70	0.3536	0.4315	0.2508	0.0129	0.0000	0.9942	0.3987	0.4497
white70	0.4287	0.3914	0.0062	0.2141	0.4110	0.4402	0.0000	1.0000
govemp70	0.3856	0.4366	0.2866	0.0601	0.0000	0.9968	0.3084	0.5174
mfg70	0.6489	0.3669	0.0702	0.0193	0.0000	0.9994	0.2705	0.5454
coll70	0.3716	0.4353	0.1539	0.0209	0.0000	1.0000	0.3501	0.4857
bornst70	0.4018	0.4494	0.0613	0.0512	0.0006	0.9065	0.0281	0.7843
outst70	0.3816	0.4764	0.0183	0.0193	0.0028	0.8244	0.0094	0.8758
1976–84								
black80	0.8508	0.4274	0.1487	0.0021	0.0000	1.0000	0.4253	0.4397
elderly80	0.5297	0.4266	0.2894	0.0205	0.0000	1.0000	0.3934	0.4641
farm80	0.8243	0.4173	0.2137	0.0088	0.0000	1.0000	0.4101	0.4513
foreign80	0.1664	0.4416	0.0903	0.0028	0.0000	1.0000	0.4161	0.4467
white80	0.4401	0.3148	0.0097	0.1750	0.4019	0.4576	0.0000	1.0000
govemp80	0.4585	0.4321	0.3404	0.0180	0.0000	1.0000	0.4036	0.4563
mfg80	0.7065	0.3741	0.1065	0.0232	0.0000	1.0000	0.3103	0.5277
coll80	0.5306	0.4197	0.2300	0.0346	0.0000	1.0000	0.3491	0.4996
bornst80	0.4164	0.4470	0.0804	0.0639	0.0021	0.9189	0.0475	0.7764
outst80	0.4404	0.4261	0.0710	0.0757	0.0202	0.8233	0.0167	0.8742
Hispanic80	0.0319	0.4438	0.0395	0.0010	0.0000	1.0000	0.4189	0.4446

Oregon—*Continued*

	Bb	Bw	Sb	Sw	Lowerb	Upperb	Lowerw	Upperw
1988–92								
black90	0.6464	0.4639	0.2829	0.0047	0.0000	1.0000	0.4580	0.4745
white00	0.4675	0.4815	0.0136	0.1747	0.4253	0.5032	0.0000	1.0000
elderly90	0.5694	0.4504	0.3548	0.0567	0.0000	1.0000	0.3817	0.5414
foreign90	0.6847	0.4566	0.3018	0.0156	0.0000	1.0000	0.4394	0.4909
farm90	0.4365	0.4676	0.3473	0.0086	0.0000	1.0000	0.4536	0.4784
mfg90	0.4903	0.4618	0.2646	0.0569	0.0000	1.0000	0.3521	0.5673
coll90	0.5655	0.4411	0.2829	0.0738	0.0000	1.0000	0.3278	0.5886
bornst90	0.3741	0.5477	0.1081	0.0943	0.0397	0.9188	0.0726	0.8394
outst90	0.4796	0.4548	0.1047	0.0987	0.0331	0.8820	0.0757	0.8755
Hispanic90	0.4577	0.4672	0.3157	0.0130	0.0000	1.0000	0.4448	0.4861
1996–2000								
black90	0.5357	0.4689	0.1670	0.0029	0.0000	1.0000	0.4604	0.4780
white00	0.4529	0.6648	0.0150	0.1744	0.4241	0.5102	0.0000	1.0000
elderly90	0.5132	0.4625	0.3999	0.0669	0.0000	1.0000	0.3810	0.5484
foreign90	0.4967	0.4683	0.2785	0.0144	0.0000	1.0000	0.4424	0.4940
farm90	0.1578	0.4788	0.1106	0.0027	0.0000	1.0000	0.4580	0.4828
mfg90	0.4435	0.4746	0.1996	0.0369	0.0000	1.0000	0.3718	0.5565
coll90	0.4659	0.4705	0.2490	0.0482	0.0000	1.0000	0.3670	0.5607
bornst90	0.5826	0.3738	0.0332	0.0290	0.0463	0.9215	0.0782	0.8416
outst90	0.3980	0.5399	0.0418	0.0394	0.0309	0.8885	0.0778	0.8858
Hispanic90	0.3472	0.4758	0.2014	0.0100	0.0000	0.9900	0.4434	0.4931

Texas

	Bb	Bw	Sb	Sw	Lowerb	Upperb	Lowerw	Upperw
1928–32								
black30	0.9470	0.6444	0.0167	0.0029	0.2924	0.9978	0.6357	0.7570
elderly30	0.6277	0.6914	0.0931	0.0039	0.0221	0.9995	0.6759	0.7166
foreign30	0.9931	0.6836	0.0010	0.0000	0.0121	1.0000	0.6835	0.7005
farm30	0.7093	0.6751	0.0150	0.0101	0.5158	0.9264	0.5290	0.8053
white30	0.6490	0.7995	0.0091	0.0254	0.5838	0.8075	0.3588	0.9807
1936–44								
black40	0.8711	0.7874	0.0201	0.0034	0.3190	0.9997	0.7658	0.8804
elderly40	0.3499	0.8253	0.1572	0.0090	0.0201	1.0000	0.7880	0.8442
foreign40	0.4333	0.8134	0.0666	0.0025	0.0454	1.0000	0.7919	0.8282
farm40	0.8485	0.7748	0.0084	0.0042	0.5946	0.9872	0.7049	0.9027
white40	0.7822	0.8662	0.0058	0.0342	0.7657	0.8808	0.3190	0.9997
1948–52								
black50	0.6065	0.5531	0.0498	0.0072	0.0166	0.9961	0.4965	0.6387
elderly50	0.2622	0.5810	0.0340	0.0024	0.0003	0.9996	0.5286	0.5996
foreign50	0.3191	0.5688	0.1079	0.0040	0.0047	1.0000	0.5435	0.5805
farm50	0.6370	0.5443	0.0259	0.0052	0.1451	0.9834	0.4745	0.6434

(continues)

Texas—*Continued*

	Bb	Bw	Sb	Sw	Lowerb	Upperb	Lowerw	Upperw
1948–52								
white50	0.5531	0.6052	0.0068	0.0457	0.4954	0.6401	0.0165	0.9960
mfg50	0.6111	0.5525	0.0810	0.0116	0.0050	1.0000	0.4967	0.6395
coll50	0.3003	0.5725	0.2195	0.0139	0.0000	1.0000	0.5320	0.5952
1956–64								
black60	0.6030	0.5171	0.0566	0.0080	0.0083	0.9974	0.4611	0.6015
elderly60	0.7413	0.5098	0.0702	0.0059	0.0002	0.9996	0.4880	0.5723
foreign60	0.6706	0.5232	0.0770	0.0025	0.0095	1.0000	0.5126	0.5445
farm60	0.7215	0.5127	0.0246	0.0019	0.0391	0.9951	0.4913	0.5660
white60	0.5169	0.6033	0.0081	0.0563	0.4603	0.6024	0.0084	0.9975
mfg60	0.4899	0.5346	0.0707	0.0127	0.0006	0.9999	0.4433	0.6222
coll60	0.3884	0.5442	0.0786	0.0091	0.0423	0.9908	0.4744	0.5837
bornst60	0.6165	0.2505	0.0139	0.0436	0.3781	0.6934	0.0100	0.9959
outst60	0.2505	0.6026	0.0464	0.0125	0.0055	0.9960	0.4014	0.6688
1968–72								
black70	0.4427	0.4141	0.0579	0.0084	0.0002	0.3331	0.4785	0.9989
elderly70	0.7226	0.3878	0.0531	0.0052	0.0000	0.9998	0.3606	0.4587
foreign70	0.9300	0.4039	0.0035	0.0001	0.0000	1.0000	0.4037	0.4277
farm70	0.6541	0.3644	0.0629	0.0142	0.0149	0.9980	0.2867	0.5086
white70	0.4144	0.4393	0.0096	0.0626	0.3282	0.4820	0.0002	0.9990
mfg70	0.3160	0.4400	0.0418	0.0092	0.0000	0.9970	0.2970	0.5093
coll70	0.5205	0.4048	0.1670	0.0207	0.0000	0.9996	0.3454	0.4639
bornst70	0.4916	0.2526	0.0108	0.0242	0.1893	0.5823	0.0500	0.9279
outst70	0.2111	0.5005	0.0246	0.0099	0.0489	0.9249	0.2146	0.5654
1976–84								
black80	0.7815	0.3845	0.0552	0.0075	0.0002	1.0000	0.3457	0.4909
elderly80	0.4916	0.4283	0.1768	0.0107	0.0000	1.0000	0.3976	0.4580
foreign80	0.4644	0.4300	0.0471	0.0030	0.0029	1.0000	0.3957	0.4595
farm80	0.4368	0.4320	0.0388	0.0007	0.0001	0.9983	0.4213	0.4403
white80	0.3654	0.6897	0.0158	0.0612	0.2852	0.5437	0.0004	0.9999
mfg80	0.6270	0.3925	0.0682	0.0138	0.0002	0.9983	0.3170	0.5198
coll80	0.0467	0.4833	0.0495	0.0063	0.1000	0.9996	0.3230	0.4888
bornst80	0.5295	0.2265	0.0115	0.0243	0.1847	0.6354	0.0032	0.9538
outst80	0.0988	0.5498	0.0417	0.0147	0.0007	0.9781	0.2392	0.5844
Hispanic80	0.5618	0.3977	0.0254	0.0067	0.1287	0.8975	0.3086	0.5125
1988–92								
black90	0.8067	0.3528	0.0345	0.0047	0.0000	1.0000	0.3267	0.4618
white90	0.3125	0.6930	0.0198	0.0602	0.2118	0.5398	0.0034	0.9980
elderly90	0.7099	0.3727	0.0536	0.0060	0.0000	1.0000	0.3402	0.4526
foreign90	0.3260	0.4147	0.0412	0.0041	0.0060	1.0000	0.3483	0.4463
farm90	0.2260	0.4089	0.1380	0.0016	0.0000	1.0000	0.4000	0.4115
mfg90	0.5383	0.3850	0.0898	0.0149	0.0000	1.0000	0.3084	0.4743
coll90	0.4609	0.4138	0.3975	0.0806	0.0000	0.9794	0.2609	0.5105
bornst90	0.5078	0.2214	0.0142	0.0260	0.1308	0.6243	0.0074	0.9139
outst90	0.0290	0.5415	0.0143	0.0051	0.0007	0.9620	0.2090	0.5516
Hispanic90	0.5345	0.3630	0.0405	0.0139	0.1284	0.8764	0.2457	0.5024

Texas—*Continued*

	Bb	Bw	Sb	Sw	Lowerb	Upperb	Lowerw	Upperw
1996–2000								
black00	0.7813	0.3722	0.0364	0.0050	0.0000	1.0000	0.3421	0.4798
white00	0.2871	0.8175	0.0154	0.0453	0.2256	0.5635	0.0051	1.0000
elderly00	0.4019	0.4239	0.0668	0.0074	0.0000	0.9981	0.3579	0.4685
foreign00	0.7929	0.3845	0.0822	0.0082	0.0083	1.0000	0.3638	0.4632
farm00	0.0200	0.4259	0.0155	0.0002	0.0000	1.0000	0.4147	0.4622
mfg00	0.7130	0.3805	0.0443	0.0063	0.0000	1.0000	0.3398	0.4815
coll00	0.4609	0.4138	0.3975	0.0806	0.0000	1.0000	0.3063	0.5073
bornst00	0.4828	0.3084	0.0159	0.0292	0.1343	0.6421	0.0159	0.9487
outst00	0.1538	0.5167	0.1061	0.0378	0.0000	0.9597	0.2295	0.5715
Hispanic00	0.5882	0.3495	0.0350	0.0152	0.1648	0.8949	0.2163	0.5333

APPENDIX C

Complete Voter Transition Results, by State

California

	Bb	Bw	Sb	Sw	Lowerb	Upperb	Lowerw	Upperw
Dem. 1928 → 1932	0.9204	0.4126	0.0740	0.0390	0.1000	1.0000	0.3700	0.8450
Dem. 1932 → 1936	0.9440	0.2832	0.0173	0.0246	0.4400	0.9970	0.2070	0.9985
Dem. 1936 → 1940	0.8527	0.0061	0.0015	0.0031	0.3664	0.8557	0.0000	0.9975
Rep. 1928 → 1932	0.5783	0.0096	0.0032	0.0057	0.0943	0.5838	0.0000	0.8532
Rep. 1932 → 1936	0.7707	0.0463	0.0289	0.0170	0.0000	0.8406	0.0051	0.5008
Rep. 1936 → 1940	0.9198	0.1937	0.0707	0.0326	0.0005	1.0000	0.1567	0.6181
Dem. 1960 → 1964	0.9181	0.2749	0.0526	0.0515	0.2041	1.0000	0.1948	0.9737
Dem. 1964 → 1968	0.5969	0.2407	0.1264	0.1843	0.1190	0.7620	0.0000	0.9372
Dem. 1968 → 1972	0.8090	0.1020	0.0564	0.0465	0.0282	0.9291	0.0029	0.7459
Rep. 1960 → 1964	0.5200	0.2912	0.2293	0.2310	0.0255	0.8090	0.0000	0.7894
Rep. 1964 → 1968	0.9569	0.1427	0.0540	0.0369	0.0331	1.0000	0.1133	0.7472
Rep. 1968 → 1972	0.9322	0.1956	0.0377	0.0339	0.1080	1.0000	0.1348	0.9362
Wallace 1968 → Dem. 1972	0.3047	0.4300	0.2470	0.0179	0.0000	1.0000	0.3796	0.4521
Wallce 1968 → Rep. 1972	0.5062	0.5470	0.3115	0.0226	0.0000	1.0000	0.5112	0.5837
Dem. 1964 → Wallace 1968	0.0665	0.0691	0.0315	0.0459	0.0000	0.1139	0.0000	0.1660
Rep. 1964 → Wallace 1968	0.0946	0.0491	0.0350	0.0239	0.0000	0.1664	0.0000	0.1137

Colorado

	Bb	Bw	Sb	Sw	Lowerb	Upperb	Lowerw	Upperw
Dem. 1928 → 1932	0.8448	0.3998	0.0506	0.0255	0.0541	1.0000	0.3237	0.7998
Dem. 1932 → 1936	0.8911	0.2441	0.0356	0.0436	0.2777	0.9830	0.1317	0.9442
Dem. 1936 → 1940	0.7315	0.1011	0.0510	0.0765	0.1746	0.7989	0.0000	0.9366
Rep. 1928 → 1932	0.5598	0.1339	0.0231	0.0438	0.1391	0.6305	0.0000	0.9299
Rep. 1932 → 1936	0.7619	0.1019	0.0464	0.0325	0.0000	0.8793	0.0195	0.6369
Rep. 1936 → 1940	0.8581	0.3075	0.0766	0.0458	0.0347	1.0000	0.2226	0.7998
Dem. 1960 → 1964	0.9091	0.3748	0.0469	0.0781	0.2096	1.0000	0.3010	0.4427
Dem. 1964 → 1968	0.6058	0.1240	0.0699	0.1113	0.1387	0.6837	0.0000	0.8676
Dem. 1968 → 1972	0.6786	0.1149	0.0970	0.0702	0.0034	0.8302	0.0051	0.6307
Rep. 1960 → 1964	0.5742	0.1460	0.0584	0.0706	0.0525	0.6949	0.0000	0.7769
Rep. 1964 → 1968	0.9082	0.2468	0.0804	0.0494	0.0287	1.0000	0.1904	0.7867
Rep. 1968 → 1972	0.9134	0.3277	0.0303	0.0301	0.2713	0.9989	0.2427	0.9657
Wallace 1968 → Dem. 1972	0.3150	0.3546	0.2385	0.0195	0.0000	1.0000	0.2986	0.3803
Wallace 1968 → Rep.1972	0.9110	0.5958	0.1211	0.0099	0.0000	1.0000	0.5885	0.6702
Dem. 1964 → Wallace 1968	0.0318	0.1452	0.0081	0.0129	0.000	0.1230	0.0000	0.1959
Rep. 1964 → Wallace 1968	0.9445	0.0332	0.0224	0.0137	0.0000	0.1986	0.0000	0.1219

Connecticut

	Bb	Bw	Sb	Sw	Lowerb	Upperb	Lowerw	Upperw
Dem. 1928 → 1932	0.9569	0.1121	0.0153	0.0126	0.1270	0.9990	0.0776	0.7932
Dem. 1932 → 1936	0.9586	0.2119	0.0094	0.0092	0.2736	0.9975	0.1741	0.8778
Dem. 1936 → 1940	0.8908	0.0086	0.0540	0.0119	0.2947	0.9254	0.0062	0.8772
Rep. 1928 → 1932	0.8937	0.0460	0.0104	0.0124	0.2049	0.9311	0.0013	0.8674
Rep. 1932 → 1936	0.7885	0.0409	0.0083	0.0085	0.1222	0.8259	0.0015	0.7264
Rep. 1936 → 1940	0.9462	0.1068	0.0098	0.0071	0.1222	0.9936	0.0725	0.7035
Dem. 1960 → 1964	0.9694	0.3497	0.0143	0.0156	0.4180	1.0000	0.3164	0.9512
Dem. 1964 → 1968	0.7237	0.0239	0.0094	0.0193	0.2832	0.7353	0.0000	0.9307
Dem. 1968 → 1972	0.7369	0.0769	0.0182	0.0178	0.0688	0.8075	0.0073	0.7310
Rep. 1960 → 1964	0.6452	0.0270	0.0121	0.0111	0.0488	0.6836	0.0000	0.5820
Rep. 1964 → 1968	0.9728	0.1874	0.0138	0.0067	0.0419	0.9999	0.1747	0.6396
Rep. 1968 → 1972	0.9214	0.3372	0.0192	0.0154	0.2180	0.9944	0.2788	0.8993
Wallace 1968 → Dem. 1972	0.3769	0.4051	0.2408	0.0156	0.0000	1.0000	0.3646	0.4295
Wallace 1968 → Rep. 1972	0.6129	0.5956	0.2834	0.0184	0.0000	1.0000	0.5705	0.6354
Dem. 1964 → Wallace 1968	0.0474	0.0888	0.0277	0.0570	0.0000	0.0905	0.0000	0.1864
Rep. 1964 → Wallace 1968	0.0972	0.0433	0.0568	0.0276	0.0000	0.1864	0.0000	0.0905

Florida

	Bb	Bw	Sb	Sw	Lowerb	Upperb	Lowerw	Upperw
Dem. 1928 → 1932	0.9290	0.6430	0.0800	0.0587	0.4746	1.0000	0.5887	0.9715
Dem. 1932 → 1936	0.9561	0.2082	0.0082	0.0262	0.7075	0.9841	0.1191	1.0000
Dem. 1936 → 1940	0.9442	0.1336	0.0083	0.0290	0.6961	0.9707	0.0408	1.0000
Rep. 1928 → 1932	0.3369	0.1215	0.0795	0.0952	0.0255	0.4299	0.0100	0.4926
Rep. 1932 → 1936	0.6972	0.0736	0.0644	0.0202	0.0000	0.8809	0.0159	0.2925
Rep. 1936 → 1940	0.8699	0.0548	0.0245	0.0070	0.0000	0.9592	0.0293	0.3039
Dem. 1960 → 1964	0.5773	0.4514	0.0406	0.0392	0.1439	0.9258	0.1149	0.8699
Dem. 1964 → 1968	0.5726	0.0409	0.0445	0.0469	0.0459	0.6113	0.0000	0.5962
Dem. 1968 → 1972	0.6006	0.1328	0.2180	0.0997	0.0000	0.8840	0.0034	0.4074
Rep. 1960 → 1964	0.5455	0.4259	0.0412	0.0427	0.1301	0.8851	0.0742	0.8561
Rep. 1964 → 1968	0.5900	0.1965	0.0091	0.0086	0.0418	0.7816	0.0148	0.7164
Rep. 1968 → 1972	0.6326	0.7713	0.1252	0.0794	0.3122	1.0000	0.5383	0.9744
Wallace 1968 → Dem. 1972	0.0997	0.3560	0.0214	0.0091	0.0000	0.6855	0.1071	0.3984
Wallace 1968 → Rep. 1972	0.9006	0.6397	0.0227	0.0096	0.3091	1.0000	0.5974	0.8910
Dem. 1964 → Wallace 1968	0.2505	0.3485	0.0573	0.0604	0.0155	0.5361	0.0414	0.6005
Rep. 1964 → Wallace 1968	0.3664	0.2336	0.0561	0.0532	0.0474	0.6005	0.0115	0.5361

Georgia

	Bb	Bw	Sb	Sw	Lowerb	Upperb	Lowerw	Upperw
Dem. 1928 → 1932	0.9859	0.8453	0.0038	0.0055	0.8819	1.0000	0.8249	0.9962
Dem. 1932 → 1936	0.9083	0.6121	0.0254	0.3293	0.8791	0.9486	0.0879	0.9911
Dem. 1936 → 1940	0.9466	0.1944	0.0035	0.0272	0.8446	0.9640	0.0577	0.9956
Rep. 1928 → 1932	0.2141	0.0174	0.0101	0.0032	0.0065	0.2664	0.0008	0.0835
Rep. 1932 → 1936	0.6960	0.0690	0.0523	0.0036	0.0098	0.9143	0.0538	0.1167
Rep. 1936 → 1940	0.4800	0.0098	0.0153	0.0019	0.0045	0.5554	0.0005	0.0684
Dem. 1960 → 1964	0.4596	0.4452	0.0380	0.0618	0.1737	0.7156	0.0286	0.9106
Dem. 1964 → 1968	0.3690	0.1871	0.0374	0.0311	0.0030	0.5900	0.0033	0.4917
Dem. 1968 → 1972	0.7848	0.0474	0.0258	0.0093	0.0006	0.9999	0.0057	0.3316
Rep. 1960 → 1964	0.5506	0.5426	0.0670	0.0411	0.0890	0.9715	0.2845	0.8258
Rep. 1964 → 1968	0.2330	0.3787	0.0660	0.0792	0.0122	0.5467	0.0002	0.6440
Rep. 1968 → 1972	0.7636	0.7465	0.0457	0.0193	0.2587	1.0000	0.6456	0.9621
Wallace 1968 → Dem. 1972	0.1520	0.3213	0.1722	0.1307	0.0000	0.4959	0.0610	0.4364
Wallace 1968 → Rep. 1972	0.9425	0.0182	0.6071	0.0138	0.5041	1.0000	0.5636	0.9390
Dem. 1964 → Wallace 1968	0.2635	0.5702	0.0464	0.0386	0.0506	0.7799	0.1405	0.7473
Rep. 1964 → Wallace 1968	0.5688	0.2653	0.0381	0.0458	0.1404	0.7974	0.0507	0.7798

Illinois

	Bb	Bw	Sb	Sw	Lowerb	Upperb	Lowerw	Upperw
Dem. 1928 → 1932	0.8956	0.2991	0.0746	0.0550	0.0621	1.0000	0.2221	0.9135
Dem. 1932 → 1936	0.8562	0.2370	0.0407	0.0501	0.2640	0.9687	0.0938	0.9673
Dem. 1936 → 1940	0.7715	0.1552	0.0867	0.1192	0.2087	0.8841	0.0004	0.9289
Rep. 1928 → 1932	0.7177	0.0290	0.0259	0.0340	0.0737	0.7398	0.0000	0.8746
Rep. 1932 → 1936	0.7394	0.1457	0.0356	0.0258	0.0291	0.9027	0.0276	0.6665
Rep. 1936 → 1940	0.9533	0.1764	0.0536	0.0350	0.0591	1.0000	0.1459	0.7603
Dem. 1960 → 1964	0.9366	0.2564	0.0558	0.0556	0.2575	1.0000	0.1914	0.9319
Dem. 1964 → 1968	0.7395	0.0085	0.0041	0.0060	0.1466	0.7452	0.0000	0.8801
Dem. 1968 → 1972	0.8706	0.0472	0.0271	0.0221	0.0000	0.9198	0.0035	0.7366
Rep. 1960 → 1964	0.8054	0.0067	0.0049	0.0048	0.0675	0.8122	0.0000	0.7400
Rep. 1964 → 1968	0.9728	0.1218	0.0118	0.0080	0.0654	1.0000	0.1070	0.7427
Rep. 1968 → 1972	0.9520	0.2623	0.0238	0.0210	0.1870	0.9997	0.2203	0.9366
Wallace 1968 → Dem. 1972	0.6924	0.3837	0.1789	0.0166	0.0000	1.0000	0.3552	0.4479
Wallace 1968 → Rep. 1972	0.2251	0.6188	0.1418	0.0131	0.0000	1.0000	0.5470	0.6396
Dem. 1964 → Wallace 1968	0.0761	0.0975	0.0582	0.0856	0.0000	0.1425	0.0000	0.2094
Rep. 1964 → Wallace 1968	0.1007	0.0740	0.0735	0.0500	0.0000	0.2094	0.0000	0.1425

Maryland

	Bb	Bw	Sb	Sw	Lowerb	Upperb	Lowerw	Upperw
Dem. 1928 → 1932	0.8546	0.4075	0.0349	0.0227	0.0482	1.0000	0.3130	0.9312
Dem. 1932 → 1936	0.7738	0.2718	0.0769	0.1077	0.2580	0.9455	0.0311	0.9944
Dem. 1936 → 1940	0.8345	0.2585	0.0766	0.0993	0.2735	0.9586	0.0976	0.9863
Rep. 1928 → 1932	0.3769	0.4274	0.1857	0.2766	0.0506	0.6638	0.0000	0.9135
Rep. 1932 → 1936	0.7749	0.1902	0.0185	0.0122	0.0039	0.9801	0.0550	0.6982
Rep. 1936 → 1940	0.7901	0.1393	0.0962	0.0704	0.0115	0.9253	0.0404	0.7087
Dem. 1960 → 1964	0.7313	0.5677	0.2307	0.2684	0.0686	0.9990	0.2563	0.9898
Dem. 1964 → 1968	0.6181	0.1170	0.0406	0.0773	0.2071	0.6795	0.0000	0.8998
Dem. 1968 → 1972	0.7969	0.0577	0.1385	0.0309	0.1017	0.8676	0.0009	0.6165
Rep. 1960 → 1964	0.5974	0.1268	0.0766	0.0658	0.0102	0.7437	0.0010	0.6314
Rep. 1964 → 1968	0.7637	0.2211	0.0423	0.0222	0.0070	0.9964	0.9890	0.6184
Rep. 1968 → 1972	0.9245	0.3742	0.0743	0.0512	0.2187	1.0000	0.3222	0.8604
Wallace 1968 → Dem. 1972	0.2407	0.4122	0.1562	0.0268	0.0000	0.9940	0.2829	0.4535
Wallace 1968 → Rep. 1972	0.7212	0.5776	0.1798	0.0309	0.0046	1.0000	0.5298	0.7007
Dem. 1964 → Wallace 1968	0.1021	0.2311	0.0495	0.0847	0.0000	0.2235	0.0000	0.4256
Rep. 1964 → Wallace 1968	0.2332	0.1010	0.0775	0.0407	0.0000	0.4256	0.0000	0.2235

Michigan

	Bb	Bw	Sb	Sw	Lowerb	Upperb	Lowerw	Upperw
Dem. 1928 → 1932	0.8445	0.3950	0.0403	0.0171	0.0061	1.0000	0.3292	0.7500
Dem. 1932 → 1936	0.7909	0.3232	0.0843	0.0946	0.2296	0.9744	0.1174	0.9530
Dem. 1936 → 1940	0.8784	0.0048	0.0140	0.0019	0.2259	0.8820	0.0000	0.8714
Rep. 1928 → 1932	0.5731	0.1325	0.0149	0.0340	0.1980	0.6312	0.0000	0.9879
Rep. 1932 → 1936	0.7009	0.1290	0.0468	0.0366	0.0185	0.8530	0.0101	0.6625
Rep. 1936 → 1940	0.9189	0.2280	0.0666	0.0408	0.1005	1.0000	0.1783	0.7295
Dem. 1960 → 1964	0.7515	0.5801	0.1721	0.1759	0.3866	1.0000	0.3261	0.9532
Dem. 1964 → 1968	0.7264	0.0063	0.0013	0.0026	0.2674	0.7295	0.0000	0.9247
Dem. 1968 → 1972	0.7450	0.1276	0.0177	0.0168	0.1163	0.8690	0.0102	0.7231
Rep. 1960 → 1964	0.6435	0.0296	0.0192	0.0185	0.0492	0.6471	0.0000	0.6085
Rep. 1964 → 1968	0.7199	0.2570	0.2261	0.1120	0.0227	1.0000	0.1183	0.6024
Rep. 1968 → 1972	0.9142	0.3008	0.0262	0.0182	0.1762	0.9998	0.2413	0.8145
Wallace 1968 → Dem. 1972	0.0098	0.4711	0.0075	0.0008	0.0000	0.0000	0.3690	0.4721
Wallace 1968 → Rep. 1972	0.9935	0.5071	0.0027	0.0003	0.0000	0.0000	0.5069	0.6095
Dem. 1964 → Wallace 1968	0.0644	0.1517	0.0117	0.0235	0.0000	0.1402	0.0000	0.2805
Rep. 1964 → Wallace 1968	0.1577	0.0616	0.0439	0.0218	0.0000	0.2821	0.0000	0.1397

Minnesota

	Bb	Bw	Sb	Sw	Lowerb	Upperb	Lowerw	Upperw
Dem. 1928 → 1932	0.8815	0.4079	0.0978	0.0673	0.1646	1.0000	0.3264	0.9014
Dem. 1932 → 1936	0.6980	0.4951	0.0440	0.0662	0.3637	0.9443	0.1242	0.9988
Dem. 1936 → 1940	0.6224	0.3349	0.0746	0.1203	0.2461	0.8301	0.0000	0.9412
Rep. 1928 → 1932	0.5855	0.0539	0.0328	0.0450	0.0435	0.6249	0.0000	0.7960
Rep. 1932 → 1936	0.6646	0.1112	0.0376	0.0212	0.0000	0.8326	0.0163	0.4869
Rep. 1936 → 1940	0.9931	0.2473	0.0041	0.0018	0.0261	1.0000	0.2442	0.6839
Dem. 1960 → 1964	0.9417	0.3250	0.0351	0.0360	0.3103	1.0000	0.2651	0.9726
Dem. 1964 → 1968	0.8083	0.0666	0.0400	0.0703	0.2943	0.8462	0.0000	0.9695
Dem. 1968 → 1972	0.5776	0.3768	0.0885	0.1035	0.1255	0.8918	0.0090	0.9059
Rep. 1960 → 1964	0.6857	0.0465	0.0257	0.0248	0.0265	0.7339	0.0000	0.6825
Rep. 1964 → 1968	0.5921	0.3159	0.2894	0.1630	0.0159	1.0000	0.0861	0.6405
Rep. 1968 → 1972	0.8979	0.2427	0.0305	0.0217	0.0759	0.9996	0.1705	0.8269
Wallace 1968 → Dem. 1972	0.5446	0.4824	0.2893	0.0131	0.0000	1.0000	0.4618	0.5070
Wallace 1968 → Rep. 1972	0.3909	0.5205	0.2847	0.0129	0.0000	1.0000	0.4930	0.5382
Dem. 1964 → Wallace 1968	0.0311	0.0648	0.0141	0.0248	0.0000	0.0180	0.0000	0.1194
Rep. 1964 → Wallace 1968	0.0741	0.0260	0.0395	0.0222	0.0000	0.1202	0.0000	0.0677

New York

	Bb	Bw	Sb	Sw	Lowerb	Upperb	Lowerw	Upperw
Dem. 1928 → 1932	0.9781	0.1404	0.0094	0.0094	0.3011	0.9999	0.1186	0.8205
Dem. 1932 → 1936	0.9129	0.0922	0.0291	0.0570	0.3149	0.9674	0.0226	0.8538
Dem. 1936 → 1940	0.7968	0.0388	0.0148	0.0182	0.1665	0.8278	0.0007	0.8152
Rep. 1928 → 1932	0.7008	0.1137	0.1739	0.1538	0.1442	0.8292	0.0001	0.6061
Rep. 1932 → 1936	0.8831	0.0462	0.0163	0.0104	0.1151	0.9377	0.0114	0.5357
Rep. 1936 → 1940	0.9287	0.1976	0.0171	0.0101	0.1630	0.9980	0.1565	0.6510
Dem. 1960 → 1964	0.8862	0.4231	0.0122	0.0111	0.2849	1.0000	0.3203	0.9663
Dem. 1964 → 1968	0.4540	0.1659	0.0266	0.0478	0.0507	0.5460	0.0000	0.8917
Dem. 1968 → 1972	0.7435	0.0416	0.0600	0.0325	0.0033	0.8204	0.0001	0.4420
Rep. 1960 → 1964	0.5157	0.1257	0.0340	0.0295	0.0013	0.6606	0.0000	0.5632
Rep. 1964 → 1968	0.9458	0.1950	0.0586	0.0260	0.0069	1.0000	0.1710	0.6107
Rep. 1968 → 1972	0.9504	0.1696	0.0201	0.0149	0.1491	1.0000	0.1329	0.7629
Wallace 1968 → Dem. 1972	0.4691	0.2782	0.3699	0.0200	0.0000	1.0000	0.2496	0.3036
Wallace 1968 → Rep. 1972	0.9560	0.1654	0.0153	0.0114	0.1491	1.0000	0.1329	0.7629
Dem. 1964 → Wallace 1968	0.0315	0.0867	0.0193	0.0347	0.0000	0.0796	0.0000	0.1433
Rep. 1964 → Wallace 1968	0.0847	0.0363	0.0299	0.0132	0.0000	0.1668	0.0000	0.0738

Oregon

	Bb	Bw	Sb	Sw	Lowerb	Upperb	Lowerw	Upperw
Dem. 1928 → 1932	0.9157	0.4093	0.0789	0.0409	0.0087	1.0000	0.3656	0.8793
Dem. 1932 → 1936	0.7287	0.5284	0.1525	0.2125	0.3933	0.9919	0.1616	0.9955
Dem. 1936 → 1940	0.7887	0.0834	0.0258	0.0469	0.2942	0.8345	0.0002	0.9817
Rep. 1928 → 1932	0.4143	0.2827	0.1198	0.2147	0.0542	0.5720	0.0000	0.9281
Rep. 1932 → 1936	0.6594	0.0845	0.1148	0.0666	0.0002	0.8048	0.0001	0.4669
Rep. 1936 → 1940	0.8931	0.2713	0.0725	0.0304	0.0051	1.0000	0.2765	0.6439
Dem. 1960 → 1964	0.8920	0.4084	0.0250	0.0224	0.2440	1.0000	0.3115	0.9896
Dem. 1964 → 1968	0.6013	0.1489	0.0690	0.1211	0.1492	0.6861	0.0000	0.9424
Dem. 1968 → 1972	0.8947	0.0569	0.0378	0.0294	0.0084	0.9557	0.0096	0.7451
Rep. 1960 → 1964	0.5914	0.1030	0.0227	0.0252	0.0096	0.6843	0.0000	0.7985
Rep. 1964 → 1968	0.4893	0.5054	0.3168	0.1781	0.0183	1.0000	0.2152	0.7672
Rep. 1968 → 1972	0.8924	0.1571	0.0082	0.0081	0.1201	0.9968	0.0537	0.9222
Wallace 1968 → Dem. 1972	0.2828	0.4324	0.2083	0.0138	0.0000	1.0000	0.3849	0.4511
Wallace 1968 → Rep. 1972	0.5315	0.5225	0.3145	0.0208	0.0000	1.0000	0.4914	0.5576
Dem. 1964 → Wallace 1968	0.0402	0.1006	0.0374	0.0657	0.0000	0.0975	0.0000	0.1711
Rep. 1964 → Wallace 1968	0.0490	0.0694	0.0308	0.0173	0.0000	0.1725	0.0000	0.0970

Texas

	Bb	Bw	Sb	Sw	Lowerb	Upperb	Lowerw	Upperw
Dem. 1928 → 1932	0.9560	0.8133	0.0075	0.0074	0.7672	0.9991	0.7708	0.9995
Dem. 1932 → 1936	0.9487	0.2983	0.0039	0.0296	0.8567	0.9711	0.1268	1.0000
Dem. 1936 → 1940	0.9017	0.1591	0.0040	0.0276	0.7811	0.9218	0.0206	0.9904
Rep. 1928 → 1932	0.1767	0.0429	0.0062	0.0063	0.0005	0.2182	0.0009	0.2212
Rep. 1932 → 1936	0.6996	0.0492	0.0453	0.0056	0.0000	0.8720	0.0279	0.1358
Rep. 1936 → 1940	0.7056	0.1177	0.1441	0.0198	0.0095	0.9761	0.0806	0.2135
Dem. 1960 → 1964	0.9308	0.3384	0.0390	0.0404	0.3248	0.9991	0.2626	0.9614
Dem. 1964 → 1968	0.6536	0.0095	0.0030	0.0053	0.1552	0.6590	0.0000	0.8555
Dem. 1968 → 1972	0.7102	0.0595	0.0321	0.0233	0.0150	0.7907	0.0012	0.5629
Rep. 1960 → 1964	0.6403	0.1005	0.0657	0.0611	0.0346	0.7491	0.0012	0.6639
Rep. 1964 → 1968	0.7574	0.1023	0.0257	0.0167	0.0077	0.8801	0.0224	0.5905
Rep. 1968 → 1972	0.9944	0.4448	0.0013	0.0009	0.2084	1.0000	0.4412	0.9567
Wallace 1968 → Dem. 1972	0.1749	0.3688	0.0497	0.0113	0.0000	0.9397	0.1946	0.4086
Wallace 1968 → Rep. 1972	0.8175	0.6761	0.0515	0.0117	0.0545	1.0000	0.5845	0.7998
Dem. 1964 → Wallace 1968	0.1089	0.3201	0.0227	0.0399	0.0041	0.2910	0.0000	0.5043
Rep. 1964 → Wallace 1968	0.3303	0.1038	0.0346	0.0195	0.0000	0.5067	0.0043	0.2901

Bibliography

Abbott, Carl. 1983. *Portland: Planning, Politics, and Growth in a Twentieth-Century City.* Lincoln: University of Nebraska Press.

Abbott, Carl, Stephen J. Leonard, and David McComb. 1982. *Colorado: History of the Centennial State.* Boulder: Colorado Associated University Press.

Abramson, Paul R. 1974. "Generational Change in American Electoral Behavior." *American Political Science Review* 68:93–105.

———. 1975. *Generational Change in American Politics.* Lexington, Mass.: D.C. Heath.

———. 1976. "Generational Change and the Decline of Party Identification in America, 1952–1974." *American Political Science Review* 70:469–78.

———. 1989a. "Generational Replacement, Ethnic Change, and Partisan Support in Israel." *Journal of Politics* 51:545–74.

———. 1989b. "Generations and Political Change in the United States." *Research in Political Sociology* 4:235–80.

Achen, Christopher H. 1992. "Social Psychology, Demographic Variables and Linear Regression: Breaking the Iron Triangle in Voting Research." *Political Behavior* 14, no. 3: 195–210.

Achen, Christopher H., and W. Phillips Shively. 1995. *Cross Level Inference.* Chicago: University of Chicago Press.

Agnew, John. 1987. *Place and Politics: The Geographical Mediation of State and Society.* London: Unwin Hyman.

———. 1988. "Beyond Core and Periphery: The Myth of Regional Political-Economic Restructuring and Sectionalism in Contemporary American Politics." *Political Geography Quarterly* 7, no. 1: 127–39.

———. 1996. "Mapping Politics: How Context Counts in Electoral Geography." *Political Geography* 15:129–46.

Ahlberg, Clark D., and Daniel P. Moynihan. 1960. "Changing Governors and Policies." *Public Administration Review* 20:195–204.

Alba, Richard D., Nancy A. Denton, Shu-yin Leung, and John R. Logan. 1993. "Neighborhood Change under Conditions of Mass Immigration:

The New York City Region, 1970–1990." *International Migration Review* 29:625–56.

Allen, Robert S. 1947. *Our Fair City.* New York: Vanguard.

Allsop, Dee, and Herbert F. Weisberg. 1988. "Measuring Change in Party Identification in an Election Campaign." *American Journal of Political Science* 32, no. 4: 996–1017.

Althaus, Scott L., Peter F. Nardulli, and Daron R. Shaw. 2002. "Candidate Appearances in Presidential Elections, 1972–2000." *Political Communication* 19, no. 1: 49–72.

Altman, Irwin, and Setha Low. 1992. *Place Attachment.* New York: Plenum Press.

Alvarez, R. Michael, and John Brehm. 1996. "Uncertainty and Ambivalence in the Ecology of Race." Prepared for the 1996 Annual Meetings of the American Political Science Association, San Francisco.

Alvarez, R. Michael, and Lisa Garcia Bedolla. 2001. "The Foundations of Latino Voter Partisanship: Evidence from the 2000 Election." Paper presented at the Annual Meeting of the 2001 Western Political Science Association Convention, Las Vegas, March 15–17.

America Votes. Various years. Washington, D.C.: Congressional Quarterly Press.

Andersen, Kristi. 1976. "Generation, Partisan Shift, and Realignment: A Glance Back at the New Deal." In Norman H. Nie, Sidney Verba, and John R. Petrocik, eds., *The Changing American Voter.* Cambridge: Harvard University Press.

———. 1979. *The Creation of a Democratic Majority, 1928–1936.* Chicago: University of Chicago Press.

Anderson, James E., Richard W. Murray, and Edward L. Farley. 1971. *Texas Politics: An Introduction.* New York: Harper and Row.

Anderson, Totton J. 1969. "California: Enigmatic Eldorado of National Politics." In Frank H. Jonas, ed., *Politics in the American West.* Salt Lake City: University of Utah Press.

Anselin, Luc. 1988. *Spatial Econometrics: Methods and Models.* Boston: Kluwer.

———. 1995. *SpaceStat Version 1.80 User's Guide.* Morgantown, W.Va.: Regional Research Institute. Copyright by the author.

Anselin, Luc, and Wendy K. Tam Cho. 2002. "Spatial Effects and Ecological Inference." *Political Analysis* 10, no. 3: 276–97.

Ansolabehere, Stephen, and Shanto Iyengar. 1995. *Going Negative: How Political Advertisements Shrink and Polarize the Electorate.* New York: Free Press.

Archer, J. Clark, and Fred M. Shelley. 1986. *American Electoral Mosaics.* Washington, D.C.: Association of American Geographers.

Archer, J. Clark, and Peter J. Taylor. 1981. *Section and Party: A Political Geography of American Presidential Elections from Andrew Jackson to Ronald Reagan*. Chichester, UK: Research Studies Press.

Atkeson, Lonna Rae, and Randell W. Partin. 1995. "Economic and ReferendumVoting: A Comparison of Gubernatorial and Senatorial Elections." *American Political Science Review* 89:99–107.

Axelrod, Robert. 1972. "Where the Votes Come From: An Analysis of Electoral Coalitions." *American Political Science Review* 66:11–20.

———. 1986. "Presidential Election Coalitions in 1984." *American Political Science Review* 80:281–84.

———. 1997. "The Dissemination of Culture: A Model with Local Convergence and Global Polarization." *Journal of Conflict Resolution* 41, no. 1: 203–26.

Ayers, Edward L., Patricia Nelson Limerick, Stephen Nissenbaum, and Peter S. Onuf. 1996. *All Over the Map: Rethinking American Regions*. Baltimore: Johns Hopkins University Press.

Baldassare, Mark. 2000. *California in the New Millennium: The Changing Social and Political Landscape*. Berkeley: University of California Press.

Balmer, Donald G. 1965. "The 1964 Election in Oregon." *Western Political Quarterly* 17 (June): 502–8.

Barbrook, Richard, and Andy Cameron. 1996. "The Californian Ideology." *Science as Culture* 6, no. 26, part 1: 44–72.

Barnett, James D. 1915. *The Operation of the Initiative, Referendum, and Recall in Oregon*. New York: Macmillan.

Bartels, Larry M. 2000. "Partisanship and Voting Behavior, 1952–1996." *American Journal of Political Science* 44, no. 1: 35–50.

Bartley, Numan V. 1990. *The Creation of Modern Georgia*. 2d ed. Athens: University of Georgia Press.

Bass, Jack, and Walter DeVries. 1976a. *The Transformation of Southern Politics: Social Change and Political Consequences since 1945*. New York: Basic Books.

———. 1976b. "Florida: Government in the Sunshine." In Jack Bass and Walter DeVries, *The Transformation of Southern Politics: Social Change and Political Consequences since 1945*. New York: Basic Books.

———. 1976c. "Georgia: The Politics of Consensus." In Jack Bass and Walter DeVries, *The Transformation of Southern Politics: Social Change and Political Consequences since 1945*. New York: Basic Books.

Baulch, Vivian M., and Patricia Zacharias. 1999. "The 1943 Detroit Race Riots." *Detroit News*. <http://www.detnews.com/history/riot/riot.html> (accessed September 2000).

Baybeck, Brady. 2001. "Race and Place: The Impact of Local Political Geography on Citizens." Paper presented at the Annual Meeting of the

American Political Science Association Convention, San Francisco, August 30–September 2.

Baybeck, Brady, and Robert Huckfeldt. 2002a. "Spatially Dispersed Ties Among Interdependent Citizens: Connecting Individuals and Aggregates." *Political Analysis* 10:261–75.

———. 2002b. "Urban Contexts, Spatially Dispersed Networks, and the Diffusion of Political Information." *Political Geography* 21:195–220.

Baybeck, Brady, and Scott D. McClurg. 2001. "What Do They Know and How Do They Know It? An Examination of Citizen Awareness of Context." Paper presented at the Annual Meeting of the Midwest Political Science Association Convention, Palmer House Hilton, Chicago, April 19–22.

Beck, Curt F. 1983. "Causes and Consequences of Declining Partisanship in Connecticut." In Josephine F. Milburn and William Doyle, eds., *New England Political Parties*. Cambridge, Mass.: Schenkman Publishing.

Beck, Paul Allen. 1977. "Partisan Dealignment in the Postwar South." *American Political Science Review* 71:477–96.

———. 1982. "Realignment Begins: The Republican Surge in Florida." *American Politics Quarterly* 10:421–38.

Beggs, John J., Wayne J. Villemez, and Ruth Arnold. 1997. "Black Population Concentration and Black-White Inequality: Expanding the Consideration of Place and Space Effects." *Social Forces* 76:65–91.

Benoit, Kenneth, and Gary King. 1998. "EZI: An Easy Program for Ecological Inference." Computer Program Instruction Manual. Harvard University Department of Government Manuscript. See <http://gking.harvard.edu/>.

Bensel, Richard Franklin. 1984. *Sectionalism and American Political Development, 1880–1980*. Madison: University of Wisconsin Press.

Berelson, Bernard R., Paul F. Lazarsfeld, and William N. McPhee. 1954. *Voting: A Study of Opinion Formation in a Presidential Election*. Chicago: University of Chicago Press.

Bernard, L. L. 1917. "A Theory of Rural Attitudes." *American Journal of Sociology* 22, no. 5: 630–49.

Bernard, William Charles. 1970. *Metro Denver: Mile High Government*. Rev. ed. Boulder: University of Colorado Press.

Bernd, Joseph L. 1972. "Georgia: Static and Dynamic." In William C. Havard, ed., *The Changing Politics of the South*. Baton Rouge: Louisiana State University Press.

Berthelot, Helen Washburn. 1995. *Win Some, Lose Some: G. Mennen Williams and the New Democrats*. Detroit: Wayne State University Press.

Black, Earl. 1998. "The Newest Southern Politics." *Journal of Politics* 60, no. 3: 591–612.

Black, Merle, and Earl Black. 1988. *Politics and Society in the South.* Cambridge: Harvard University Press.

———. 1992. *The Vital South.* Cambridge: Harvard University Press.

Blalock, Hubert M. 1956. "Economic Discrimination and Negro Increase." *American Sociological Review* 21:284–88.

Blegen, Theodore C. 1963. *Minnesota: A History of the State.* Minneapolis: University of Minnesota Press.

Books, John W., and Charles L. Prysby. 1991. *Political Behavior and the Local Context.* New York: Praeger.

Borjas, George J. 1999. *Heaven's Door: Immigration Policy and the American Economy.* Princeton: Princeton University Press.

Borjas, George J., Stephen G. Bronars, and Stephen J. Trejo. 1992. "Self-Selection and Internal Migration in the United States." *Journal of Urban Economics* 32:159–85.

Bowler, Shaun, Todd Donovan, and Joseph Snipp. 1993. "Local Sources of Information and Voter Choice in State Elections." *American Politics Quarterly* 21:473–89.

Brint, Steven. 1985. "The Political Attitudes of Professionals." *Annual Review of Sociology* 11:389–414.

Brooks, Clem, and Jeff Manza. 1997a. "The Social and Ideological Bases of Middle-Class Political Realignment in the United States, 1972 to 1992." *American Sociological Review* 62:191–208.

———. 1997b "Social Cleavages and Political Alignments: U.S. Presidential Elections, 1960–92." *American Sociological Review* 62:937–46.

———. 1997c. "Class Politics and Political Change in the United States, 1952–1992." *Social Forces* 76:379–408.

Brown, Robert D. 1995. "Party Cleavages and Welfare Effort in the American States." *American Political Science Review* 89:23–33.

Brown, Thad A. 1988. *Migration and Politics: The Impact of Population Mobility on American Voting Behavior.* Chapel Hill: University of North Carolina Press.

Browne, William P., and Kenneth VerBurg. 1995. *Michigan Politics and Government: Facing Change in a Complex State.* Lincoln: University of Nebraska Press.

Browning, Rufus P., Dale Rogers Marshall, and David H. Tabb, eds. 1990. *Racial Politics in American Cities.* New York: Longman.

Brundage, David. 1994. *The Making of Western Labor Radicalism.* Urbana: University of Illinois Press.

Bullock, Charles S., III. 1998. "Georgia: Election Rules and Partisan Conflict." In Charles S. Bullock III and Mark J. Rozell, eds., *The New Politics of the Old South.* Lanham, Md.: Rowman and Littlefield.

Bullock, Charles S., III, and Mark J. Rozell, eds. 1998. *The New Politics of the Old South*. Lanham, Md.: Rowman and Littlefield.

Burbank, Matthew J. 1995. "The Psychological Basis of Contextual Effects." *Political Geography* 14, no. 6/7: 621–35.

Burden, Barry C., and David C. Kimball. 1998. "A New Approach to the Study of Ticket-Splitting." *American Political Science Review* 92, no. 3: 533–44.

Burdette, Franklin L. 1983. "Modern Maryland Politics and Social Change." In Richard Walsh and William Lloyd Fox, eds., *Maryland: A History*. Annapolis, Md.: Hall of Records Commission, Department of General Services.

Burnham, Walter Dean. 1970. *Critical Elections and the Mainsprings of American Politics*. New York: Norton.

Burns, Nancy. 1994. *The Formation of American Local Governments: Private Values in Public Institutions*. New York: Oxford University Press.

Burton, Robert E. 1970. *Democrats of Oregon: The Pattern of Minority Politics, 1900–1956*. Eugene: University of Oregon Press.

Button, James W. 1989. *Blacks and Social Change: Impact of the Civil Rights Movement in Southern Communities*. Princeton: Princeton University Press.

Campbell, Angus. 1960. "Surge and Decline: A Study of Electoral Change." *Public Opinion Quarterly* 24:397–418.

Campbell, Angus, Philip E. Converse, Warren E. Miller, and Donald E. Stokes. 1960. *The American Voter*. New York: John Wiley and Sons.

Campbell, Angus, et al., eds. 1966. *Elections and the Political Order*. New York: John Wiley and Sons.

Campbell, Bruce A. 1977a. "Change in the Southern Electorate." *American Journal of Political Science* 21:37–64.

———. 1977b. "Patterns of Change in the Partisan Loyalties of Native Southerners, 1952–1972." *Journal of Politics* 39:730–61.

Campbell, Bruce A., and Richard J. Trilling, eds. 1980. *Realignment in American Politics: Toward a Theory*. Austin: University of Texas Press.

Campbell, James E. 1985. "Sources of the New Deal Realignment: The Contributions of Conversion and Mobilization to Partisan Change." *Western Political Quarterly* 38:357–76.

Canter, David. 1977. *The Psychology of Place*. New York: St. Martin's.

Caro, Robert A. 1975. *The Power Broker: Robert Moses and The Fall of New York*. New York: Vintage Books.

Carmines, Edward G., and Harold W. Stanley. 1992. "The Transformation of the New Deal Party System: Social Groups, Political Ideology, and Changing Partisanship among Northern Whites, 1972–1988." *Political Behavior* 14:213–37.

Carmines, Edward G., and James A. Stimson. 1981. "Issue Evolution, Population Replacement, and Normal Partisan Change." *American Political Science Review* 75:107–18.

Carsey, Thomas M. 1999. *Campaign Dynamics: The Race for Governor.* Ann Arbor: University of Michigan Press.

Carsey, Thomas M., and Gerald C. Wright. 1998. "State and National Factors in Gubernatorial and Senate Elections." *American Journal of Political Science* 42, no. 3: 994–1002.

Chapin, F. 1974. *Human Activity Patterns in the City: What People Do in Time and Space.* New York: John Wiley and Sons.

Chapman, Keith. 1979. *People, Pattern, and Process: An Introduction to Human Geography.* New York: John Wiley and Sons.

Cho, Wendy K. Tam. 1998. "If the Assumption Fits . . . : A Comment on the King Ecological Inference Solution." *Political Analysis* 7:143–63.

———. 2003. "Contagion Effects and Ethnic Contribution Networks." *American Journal of Political Science* 47, no. 2: 368–87.

Chubb, John E. 1978. "Systems Analysis and Partisan Realignment." *Social Science History* 2:144–71.

Clark, G. L., and J. Whiteman. 1983. "Why Poor People Do Not Move: Job Search Behavior and Disequilibrium amongst Local Labor Markets." *Environment and Planning* 15:85–104.

Clarke, Harold D., and Marianne C. Stewart. 1998. "The Dynamics of Party Identification in Federal Systems: The Canadian Case." *American Journal of Political Science* 42, no. 1: 97–113.

Clayton, Andrew R. L. 1992. "'Separate Interests' and the Nation-State: The Washington Administration and the Origins of Regionalism in the Trans-Appalachian West." *Journal of American History* 79, no. 1: 39–67.

Cliff, A., and J. Ord. 1981. *Spatial Processes, Models and Applications.* London: Pion.

Clubb, Jerome M., William H. Flanigan, and Nancy Zingale. 1990. *Partisan Realignment: Voters, Parties and Government in American History.* Boulder: Westview.

Colby, Peter W., and John K. White, eds. 1989. *New York State Today: Politics, Government, Public Policy.* 2d ed. Albany: State University of New York Press.

Conover, Pamela Johnston, and Stanley Feldman. 1981. "The Origins and Meaning of Liberal/Conservative Self-Identifications." *American Journal of Political Science* 25:617–45.

Converse, Philip E. 1966. "On the Possibility of Major Political Realignment in the South." In Angus Campbell et al., eds., *Elections and the Political Order.* New York: John Wiley and Sons.

Cross, Jennifer E. 2000. "Disruptions in Community Attachment: The Social-Psychological Impacts of Rapid Economic and Demographic Change."

Paper prepared for the 11th Annual Headwaters Conference, Western State College, Gunnison, Colorado, November 3–5.

Culver, John. 1991. "Population and Voter Demographics in California." *Comparative State Politics* 12, no. 5: 38–48.

Cummings, Scott. 1977. "Racial Prejudice and Political Orientations among Blue-Collar Workers." *Social Science Quarterly* 57:907–20.

———. 1980. "White Ethnics, Racial Prejudice, and Labor Market Segmentation." *American Journal of Sociology* 90:938–50.

Dahl, Robert. 1961. *Who Governs? Democracy and Power in An American City.* New Haven: Yale University Press.

———. 1967. "The City in the Future of Democracy." *American Political Science Review* 61:953–70.

Dahl, Robert A., and Edward R. Tufte. 1973. *Size and Democracy.* Palo Alto, Calif.: Stanford University Press.

Dauer, Manning J. 1972. "Florida: The Different State." In William C. Havard, ed., *The Changing Politics of the South.* Baton Rouge: Louisiana State University Press.

Davidson, Chandler. 1990. *Race and Class in Texas Politics.* Princeton: Princeton University Press.

Davis, Sandra K. 1995. "Water Politics in Colorado: Change, or Business as Usual?" In Richard Lowitt, ed., *Politics in the Postwar American West.* Norman: University of Oklahoma Press.

Day, Frederick A., and Alice L. Jones. 1994. "A Portrait of Modern Texas Politics: The Regional Geography of the 1990 Governor's Race." *Social Science Journal* 31:99–110.

DeBow, Ken, and John C. Syer. 1997. *Power and Politics in California.* 5th ed. Boston: Allyn and Bacon.

deHaven-Smith, Lance. 1995. *The Florida Voter.* Tallahassee: Florida Institute of Government.

de la Garza, Rodolfo G., Louis DeSipio, F. Chris Garcia, John Garcia, and Angelo Falcon. 1992. *Latino Voices: Mexican, Puerto Rican, and Cuban Perspectives on American Politics.* Boulder: Westview.

de la Garza, Rodolfo G., and Louis DeSipio, eds. 1996. *Ethnic Ironies: Latino Politics in the 1992 Elections.* Boulder: Westview.

DiMaggio, Paul, John Evans, and Bethany Bryson. 1996. "Have Americans' Social Attitudes Become More Polarized?" *American Journal of Sociology* 102, no. 3: 690–755.

Dogan, Mattei, and Stein Rokkan. 1969. *Quantitative Ecological Analysis in the Social Sciences.* Cambridge: MIT Press.

Duncan, Otis Dudley, and Beverly Davis. 1953. "An Alternative to Ecological Correlation." *American Sociological Review* 18:665–66.

Dye, Thomas R. 1966. *Politics, Economics and the Public: Policy Outcomes in the American States.* Chicago: Rand McNally.

Dyer, James, Arnold Vedlitz, and David B. Hill. 1988. "New Voters, Switchers, and Political Party Realignment in Texas." *Western Political Quarterly* 41:155–67.

Earle, Carville. 1992. *Geographical Inquiry and American Historical Problems.* Stanford: Stanford University Press.

Earle, Carville, Kent Mathewson, and Martin S. Kenzer, eds. 1996. *Concepts in Human Geography.* Lanham, Md.: Rowman and Littlefield.

Elazar, Daniel J. 1984. *American Federalism: A View from the States.* 3d ed. New York: Harper and Row.

———. 1994. *The American Mosaic: The Impact of Space, Time and Culture on American Politics.* Boulder: Westview.

Elazar, Daniel J., Virginia Gray, and Wyman Spano. 1999. *Minnesota Politics and Government.* Lincoln: University of Nebraska Press.

Eldersveld, Samuel J., et al. 1957. *Political Affiliations in Metropolitan Detroit.* Michigan Governmental Studies Report No. 34. Ann Arbor: University of Michigan Press.

Erikson, Robert S. 1986. "Voter Conversion and the New Deal Realignment: A Response to Campbell." *Western Political Quarterly* 39:729–32.

Erikson, Robert S., Thomas D. Lancaster, and David W. Romero. 1989. "Group Components of the Presidential Vote, 1952–1984." *Journal of Politics* 51:337–46.

Erikson, Robert S., and Kent L. Tedin. 1981. "The 1928–1936 Partisan Realignment: The Case for the Conversion Hypothesis." *American Political Science Review* 75:951–62.

Erikson, Robert S., Gerald C. Wright, and John P. McIver. 1993. *Statehouse Democracy: Public Opinion and Policy in the American States.* Cambridge, Mass.: Cambridge University Press.

Federal Election Commission. 2001. "Congressional Financial Activity Soars for 2000." Federal Election Commission Press Release (January 9): <http://www.fec.gov/press/hselong3000.htm>.

Federal Writers' Project of the Works Progress Administration. 1938. *Minnesota: A State Guide.* New York: Viking.

———. 1940. *Oregon: End of the Trail.* Portland: Binfords and Mort.

Fenton, John H. 1966. *Midwest Politics.* New York: Holt, Rinehart and Winston.

Ferejohn, John A., and James H. Kuklinski, eds. 1990. *Information and Democratic Processes.* Urbana: University of Illinois Press.

Fiorina, Morris P. 1981. *Retrospective Voting in American National Elections.* New Haven: Yale University Press.

Fleischmann, Arnold, and Carol Pierannunzi. 1997. *Politics in Georgia.* Athens: University of Georgia Press.

Fleming, Roscoe. 1947. "Denver: Civic Schizophrenic." In Robert S. Allen, ed., *Our Fair City.* New York: Vanguard.

Fotheringham, A. S., and D. W. S. Wong. 1991. "The Modifiable Areal Unit Problem in Multivariate Statistical Analysis." *Environment and Planning* 23:1025–45.

Frank, Michael W., Peter F. Nardulli, and Paul M. Green. 1991. "Representation, Elections, and Geo-Political Cleavages: The Political Manifestations of Regionalism in Twentieth-Century Illinois." In Peter F. Nardulli, ed., *Diversity, Conflict, and State Politics: Regionalism in Illinois.* Urbana: University of Illinois Press.

Frendreis, John P. 1989. "Migration as a Source of Changing Party Strength." *Social Science Quarterly* 70:211–20.

Frey, William H. 1995. "Immigration and Internal Migration 'Flight': A California Case Study." *Population and Environment* 16:353–75.

Gabriel, Paul, and Susanne Schmitz. 1995. "Favorable Self-Selection and the Internal Migration of Young White Males in the United States." *Journal of Human Resources* 30:460–69.

Galderisi, Peter F., Michael S. Lyons, Randy T. Simmons, and John G. Francis, eds. 1987. *The Politics of Realignment: Party Change in the Mountain West.* Boulder: Westview.

Gamm, Gerald. 1999. *Urban Exodus: Why the Jews Left Boston and the Catholics Stayed.* Cambridge: Harvard University Press.

Garcia, Maria Cristina. 1996. *Havana USA: Cuban Exiles and Cuban Americans in South Florida, 1959–1994.* Berkeley: University of California Press.

Garling, Tommy, and Reginald Golledge, eds. 1993. *Behavior and Environment: Psychological and Geographical Approaches.* Amsterdam: Elsevier Science Publishers.

Gastil, Raymond D. 1973. "The Pacific Northwest as a Cultural Region." *Pacific Northwest Quarterly* 64, no. 1: 147–56.

———. 1975. *Cultural Regions of the United States.* Seattle: University of Washington Press.

Gibson, James L. 1987. "The Role of Party Organizations in the Mountain West, 1960–1980." In Peter F. Galderisi, Michael S. Lyons, Randy T. Simmons, and John G. Francis, eds., *The Politics of Realignment: Party Change in the Mountain West.* Boulder: Westview.

Gieske, Millard L. 1979. *Minnesota Farmer-Laborism: The Third Party Alternative.* Minneapolis: University of Minnesota Press.

Giles, Michael W. 1977. "Percent Black and Racial Hostility: An Old Assumption Reexamined." *Social Science Quarterly* 58:412–17.

Giles, Michael W., and Arthur Evans. 1985. "External Threat, Perceived Threat, and Group Identity." *Social Science Quarterly* 66:50–66.

Giles, Michael W., and Kaenan Hertz. 1994. "Racial Threat and Partisan Identification." *American Political Science Review* 88:317–26.

Gimpel, James G. 1996. *National Elections and the Autonomy of American State Party Systems.* Pittsburgh: University of Pittsburgh Press.

———. 1999. *Separate Destinations: Migration, Immigration, and the Politics of Places.* Ann Arbor: University of Michigan Press.

Gimpel, James G., and Jason E. Schuknecht. 2000. "The Content of Urban-Rural Conflict in American Presidential Elections." Paper presented at the Annual Meeting of the American Political Science Association, Washington, D.C., August 31–September 3.

———. 2001. "Interstate Migration and Electoral Politics." *Journal of Politics* 62, no. 1: 207–31.

———. 2002. "Reconsidering Regionalism in American Politics." *State Politics and Policy Quarterly* 2, no. 4: 325–52.

Glaser, James M. 1994. "Back to the Black Belt: Racial Environment and White Racial Attitudes in the South." *Journal of Politics* 56:21–41.

Glenn, Norval D., and J. L. Simmons. 1967. "Are Regional Cultural Differences Diminishing?" *Public Opinion Quarterly* 31, no. 1: 176–93.

Gomez, Rudolf. 1969. "Colorado: The Colorful State." In Frank H. Jonas, ed., *Politics in the American West.* Salt Lake City: University of Utah Press.

Goodenough, Richard. 1992. "The Nature and Implications of Recent Population Growth in California." *Geography* 77, no. 335, part 2: 123–33.

Goodman, Leo. 1953. "Ecological Regressions and the Behavior of Individuals." *American Sociological Review* 18:663–66.

Gosnell, Harold F., and Norman N. Gill. 1935. "An Analysis of the 1932 Presidential Vote in Chicago." *American Political Science Review* 29:967–84.

Gove, Samuel K., and James D. Nowlan. 1996. *Illinois Politics and Government: The Expanding Metropolitan Frontier.* Lincoln: University of Nebraska Press.

Gray, Virginia, and David Lowery. 1996. *The Population Ecology of Interest Representation: Lobbying Communities in the American States.* Ann Arbor: University of Michigan Press.

Green, Donald Philip, and Eric Schickler. 1993. "Multiple-Measure Assessment of Party Identification." *Public Opinion Quarterly* 57, no. 4: 503–35.

Gregory, James N. 1989. *American Exodus: The Dustbowl Migration and the Okie Culture in California.* New York: Oxford University Press.

Grenier, Guillermo J., and Alex Stepick, eds. 1992. *Miami Now! Immigration, Ethnicity and Social Change.* Gainesville: University Press of Florida.

Grimshaw, William J. 1992. *Bitter Fruit: Black Politics and the Chicago Machine, 1931–1991.* Chicago: University of Chicago Press.

Groat, Linda, ed. 1995. *Giving Places Meaning.* New York: Harcourt Brace.

Hadley, Charles D., and Susan E. Howell. 1980. "Partisan Conversion in the Northeast: An Analysis of Split Ticket Voting, 1952–1976." *American Politics Quarterly* 8:128–35.

Hahn, Harlan. 1971. *Urban-Rural Conflict: The Politics of Change.* Beverly Hills, Calif.: Sage.

Haining, Robert. 1990. *Spatial Data Analysis in the Social and Environmental Sciences.* New York: Cambridge University Press.

Hamilton, Alexander, James Madison, and John Jay. 1961. *The Federalist Papers.* New York: Penguin.

Hanson, Russell L. 1992. "The Political Acculturation of Migrants in the American States." *Western Political Quarterly* 45, no. 2: 355–83.

Hanson, Susan, and Perry Hanson. 1993. "The Geography of Everyday Life." In Tommy Garling and Reginald Golledge, eds., *Behavior and Environment: Psychological and Geographical Approaches.* Amsterdam: Elsevier Science Publishers.

Hauser, Robert M. 1974. "Contextual Analysis Revisited." *Sociological Methods and Research* 2:365–75.

Havard, William C., ed. 1972. *The Changing Politics of the South.* Baton Rouge: Louisiana State University Press.

Haynes, John Earl. 1984. *Dubious Alliance: The Making of Minnesota's DFL Party.* Minneapolis: University of Minnesota Press.

Hermalin, Albert, and Reynolds Farley. 1973. "The Potential for Residential Segregation in Cities and Suburbs: Implications for the Busing Controversy." *American Sociological Review* 38:595–610.

Hero, Rodney. 1987. "The Election of Hispanics in City Government: An Examination of the Election of Federico Pena as Mayor of Denver." *Western Political Quarterly* 40:93–105.

———. 1989. "Multiracial Coalitions in City Elections Involving Minority Candidates: Some Evidence for Denver." *Urban Affairs Quarterly* 25: 342–51.

———. 1996. "An Essential Vote: Latinos and the 1992 Elections in Colorado." In Rodolfo O. de la Garza and Louis DeSipio, eds., *Ethnic Ironies: Latino Politics in the 1992 Elections.* Boulder: Westview.

———. 1998. *Faces of Inequality: Social Diversity in American Politics.* New York: Oxford University Press.

Herrnson, Paul S. 2000. *Congressional Elections: Campaigning at Home and in Washington.* 3d ed. Washington, D.C.: CQ Press.

Hesseltine, William B. 1960. "Sectionalism and Regionalism in American History." *Journal of Southern History* 26, no. 1: 25–34.

Hill, Richard. 1978. "At the Crossroads: The Political Economy of Postwar Detroit." *Urbanism Past and Present* (summer): 1–21.

Holmes, Thomas J. 1998. "The Effect of State Policies on the Location of Manufacturing: Evidence from State Borders." *Journal of Political Economy* 106, no. 4: 667–705.

Hout, Michael, Clem Brooks, and Jeff Manza. 1995. "The Democratic Class

Struggle in the United States, 1948–1992." *American Sociological Review* 60:805–28.

Huckfeldt, Robert. 1979. "Political Participation and the Neighborhood Social Context." *American Journal of Political Science* 23, no. 3: 579–92.

———. 1984. "Political Loyalties and Social Class Ties: The Mechanisms of Contextual Influence." *American Journal of Political Science* 28, no. 2: 399–417.

———. 1986. *Politics in Context: Assimilation and Conflict in Urban Neighborhoods.* New York: Agathon.

Huckfeldt, Robert, Paul Allen Beck, Russell J. Dalton, and Jeffrey Levine. 1995. "Political Environments, Cohesive Social Groups and the Communication of Public Opinion." *American Journal of Political Science* 39, no. 4: 1025–54.

Huckfeldt, Robert, Eric Plutzer, and John Sprague. 1993. "Alternative Contexts of Political Behavior: Churches, Neighborhoods, and Individuals." *Journal of Politics* 55:365–81.

Huckfeldt, Robert, and John Sprague. 1987. "Networks in Context: The Social Flow of Political Information." *American Political Science Review* 81:1197–1216.

———. 1990. "Social Order and Political Chaos: The Structural Setting of Political Information." In John A. Ferejohn and James H. Kuklinski, eds., *Information and Democratic Processes.* Urbana: University of Illinois Press.

———. 1995. *Citizens, Politics, and Social Communication: Information and Influence in an Election Campaign.* New York: Cambridge University Press.

Huckshorn, Robert J., ed. 1998. *Government and Politics in Florida.* 2d ed. Gainesville: University Press of Florida.

Hummasti, Paul George. 1979. *Finnish Radicals in Astoria, Oregon, 1904–1940: A Study in Immigrant Socialism.* New York: Arno Press.

Hundley, Norris, Jr. 1975. *Water and the West: The Colorado River Compact and the Politics of Water in the American West.* Berkeley: University of California Press.

Hunt, Alan. 1993. *Explorations in Law and Society: Toward a Constitutive Theory of Law.* New York: Routledge.

Ignatiev, Noel. 1995. *How the Irish Became White.* New York: Routledge.

Irwin, Galen A., and Duane A. Meeter. 1969. "Building Voter Transition Models from Aggregate Data." *Midwest Journal of Political Science* 13:545–66.

Jackson, Bryan O., and Michael B. Preston. 1991. *Racial and Ethnic Politics in California.* Berkeley, Calif.: Institute of Governmental Studies Press.

Jackson, Robert A., and Thomas M. Carsey. 1999. "Presidential Voting across the American States." *American Politics Quarterly* 27:379–402.

James, Franklin J. 1995. "Research Plan for Studying Minority Neighborhoods in Denver." Paper prepared for the Rockefeller Institute of Government, State University of New York.

Janick, Herbert F., Jr. 1975. *A Diverse People: Connecticut 1914 to the Present.* Chester, Conn.: Pequot.

Jennings, Edward T. 1979. "Competition, Constituencies, and Welfare Policies in American States." *American Political Science Review* 73:414–29.

Jennings, M. Kent, and Richard G. Niemi. 1981. *Generations and Politics: A Panel Study of Young Adults and Their Parents.* Princeton: Princeton University Press.

Jensen, Richard J. 1978. *Illinois.* New York: Norton.

Jewell, Malcolm E. 1982. "The Neglected World of State Politics." *Journal of Politics* 4:638–57.

Jewell, Malcolm E., and David M. Olson. 1988. *Political Parties and Elections in American States.* 3d ed. Chicago: Dorsey.

Johnson, Charles A. 1976. "Political Culture in the American States: Elazar's Formulation Examined." *American Journal of Political Science* 20, no. 3: 491–509.

Johnson, Martin, W. Phillips Shively, and Robert M. Stein. 2001. "Contextual Explanations of Presidential Vote Choice." Paper presented at the Annual Meeting of the Midwest Political Science Association, Palmer House Hilton, April 19–22, Chicago.

———. 2002. "Contextual Data and the Study of Elections and Voting Behavior: Connecting Individuals to Environments." *Electoral Studies* 21, no. 2: 219–33.

Johnston, R. J. 1982. "The Changing Geography of Voting in the United States, 1946–1980." *Transactions, Institute of British Geographers* 7: 187–204.

———. 1986. "Places and Votes: The Role of Location in the Creation of Political Attitudes." *Urban Geography* 7, no. 2: 103–17.

———. 1987. "The Rural Milieu and Voting in Britain." *Journal of Rural Studies* 3, no. 2: 95–103.

———. 1992. *A Question of Place: Exploring the Practice of Human Geography.* Cambridge, Mass.: Blackwell.

Johnston, R. J., F. M. Shelley, and P. J. Taylor, eds. 1990. *Developments in Electoral Geography.* London: Routledge.

Jones, Eugene W., Joe E. Ericson, Lyle C. Brown, and Robert S. Trotter Jr. 1971. *Practicing Texas Politics.* Boston: Houghton Mifflin.

Jones, Eugene W., Joe E. Ericson, Lyle C. Brown, Robert S. Trotter Jr., and Joyce A. Langenegger. 1998. *Practicing Texas Politics.* 10th ed. Boston: Houghton Mifflin.

Jones, Mack H. 1978. "Black Political Empowerment in Atlanta: Myth and

Reality." *Annals of the American Academy of Political and Social Science* 439:90–117.

Kaufmann, Karen Malmuth. 1998. "Voting in American Cities: The Group Interest Theory of Local Voting Behavior." Ph.D. dissertation. University of California, Los Angeles.

Keen, Lisa, and Suzanne B. Goldberg. 1998. *Strangers to the Law: Gay People on Trial*. Ann Arbor: University of Michigan Press.

Kelley, Jonathan, and Ian McAllister. 1985. "Social Context and Electoral Behavior in Britain." *American Journal of Political Science* 29, no. 3: 564–86.

Ketcham, Ralph, ed. 1986. *The Antifederalist Papers and the Constitutional Convention Debates*. New York: Mentor.

Key, V. O., Jr. 1949. *Southern Politics in State and Nation*. New York: Alfred A. Knopf.

———. 1955. "A Theory of Critical Elections." *Journal of Politics* 17, no. 1: 3–18.

———. 1956. *American State Politics: An Introduction*. New York: Alfred A. Knopf.

———. 1959. "Secular Realignment and the Party System." *Journal of Politics*. 21, no. 2: 198–210.

———. 1964. *Politics, Parties and Pressure Groups*. 5th ed. New York: Thomas Y. Crowell.

King, Gary. 1996. "Why Context Should Not Count." *Political Geography* 15:159–64.

———. 1997. *A Solution to the Ecological Inference Problem*. Princeton: Princeton University Press.

Kitchin, Robert M. 1993. "Bringing Psychology and Geography Closer." *Journal of Environmental Psychology* 13:183–86.

Kitchin, Robert M., Mark Blades, and Reginald G. Golledge. 1997. "Relations between Psychology and Geography." *Environment and Behavior* 29:554–73.

Kling, Rob, Spencer Olin, and Mark Poster, eds. 1991. *Postsuburban California: The Transformation of Postwar Orange County, California*. Berkeley: University of California Press.

Kollmorgen, Walter. 1936. "Political Regionalism in the United States—Fact or Myth." *Social Forces* 15, no. 1: 111–22.

Kousser, J. Morgan. 1995. "Reapportionment Wars: Party, Race, and Redistricting in California, 1971–1992." Social Science Working Paper No. 930. California Institute of Technology.

Kuklinski, James H., Michael D. Cobb, and Martin Gilens. 1997. "Racial Attitudes and the 'New South.'" *Journal of Politics* 59, no. 2: 329–43.

Lacy, Dean, and Quin Monson. 2002. "The Origins and Impact of Support for

Third Party Candidates: A Case Study of the 1998 Minnesota Guberna-torial Election." *Political Research Quarterly.* 55, no. 2: 409–37.

Ladd, Everett Carll, Jr., and Charles D. Hadley. 1975. *Transformations of the American Party System: Political Coalitions from the New Deal to the 1970s.* New York: Norton.

Lamare, James W., J. L. Polinard, and Robert D. Wrinkle. 1998. "Texas: Lone Star (Wars) State." In Charles S. Bullock III and Mark J. Rozell, eds., *The New Politics of the Old South.* Lanham, Md.: Rowman and Littlefield.

Lamis, Alexander P. 1984a. *The Two-Party South.* New York: Oxford University Press.

———. 1984b. "Florida: Recast by Rapid Growth." In Alexander P. Lamis, *The Two-Party South.* New York: Oxford University Press.

———. 1984c. "Georgia: Triumph of a 'Night-and-Day' Alliance." In Alexander P. Lamis, *The Two-Party South.* New York: Oxford University Press.

———. 1984d. "Texas: A World unto Itself." In Alexander P. Lamis, *The Two-Party South.* New York: Oxford University Press.

———, ed. 1999. *Southern Politics in the 1990s.* Baton Rouge: Louisiana State University Press.

LaPalombara, Joseph G. 1950. *The Initiative and Referendum in Oregon, 1938–1948.* Corvallis: Oregon State College Press.

———. 1955. *Guide to Michigan Politics.* New York: Citizenship Clearing House, Law Center of New York University.

Layman, Geoffrey. 1997. "Religion and Political Behavior in the United States: The Impact of Beliefs, Affiliations and Commitment from 1980 to 1994." *Public Opinion Quarterly* 61, no. 3: 288–316.

Layman, Geoffrey C., and Edward G. Carmines. 1997. "Cultural Conflict in American Politics: Religious Traditionalism, Postmaterialism and U.S. Po-litical Behavior." *Journal of Politics* 59:751–77.

Leamann, Nicholas. 1991. *The Promised Land.* New York: Alfred A. Knopf.

Lewis, Thomas R., and John E. Harmon. 1986. *Connecticut: A Geography.* Boulder: Westview.

Lewis-Beck, Michael S., and Tom W. Rice. 1983. "Localism in Presidential Elections: The Home State Advantage." *American Journal of Political Science* 26, no. 3: 548–56.

Lipset, Seymour Martin. 1981. *Political Man: The Social Bases of Politics.* Baltimore: Johns Hopkins University Press.

Lloyd, Robert, and Theodore Steinke. 1986. "The Identification of Regional Boundaries on Cognitive Maps." *Professional Geographer* 38, no. 2: 149–59.

Lockard, Duane. 1959. *New England State Politics.* Princeton: Princeton University Press.

Locke, Herbert. 1969. *The Detroit Riot of 1967.* Detroit: Wayne State University Press.

Lovrich, Nicholas P., Jr., and Otwin Marenin. 1976. "A Comparison of Black and Mexican American Voters in Denver: Assertive versus Acquiescent Political Orientations and Voting Behavior in an Urban Electorate." *Western Political Quarterly* 29:284–94.

Lowitt, Richard, ed. 1995. *Politics in the Postwar American West.* Norman: University of Oklahoma Press.

Lubenow, Gerald C. 1995. *California Votes—The 1994 Governor's Race: An Inside Look at the Candidates and Their Campaigns by the People Who Managed Them.* Berkeley, Calif.: Institute of Governmental Studies Press.

Luebke, Paul. 1990. *Tar Heel Politics: Myths and Realities.* Chapel Hill: University of North Carolina Press.

Lunch, William O. 1987. *The Nationalization of American Politics.* Berkeley: University of California Press.

MacColl, E. Kimbark. 1979. *The Growth of a City: Power and Politics in Portland, Oregon, 1915 to 1950.* Portland: Georgian Press.

MacDonald, Stuart Elaine, and George Rabinowitz. 1987. "The Dynamics of Structural Realignment." *American Political Science Review* 81:775–96.

MacKuen, Michael, and Courtney Brown. 1987. "Political Context and Attitude Change." *American Political Science Review* 81, no. 2: 471–90.

MacMahon, Arthur W., ed. 1955. *Federalism: Mature and Emergent.* Garden City, N.J.: Doubleday.

Maisel, Louis, and Joseph Cooper, eds. 1978. *Political Parties: Development and Decay.* Beverly Hills, Calif.: Sage.

Manza, Jeff, Michael Hout, and Clem Brooks. 1997. "Class Voting in Capitalist Democracies since World War II: Dealignment, Realignment or Trendless Fluctuation?" *Annual Review of Sociology* 21:137–63.

Marchant-Shapiro, Theresa, and Kelly D. Patterson. 1995. "Partisan Change in the Mountain West." *Political Behavior* 17:359–78.

Markus, Gregory B., and Philip E. Converse. 1979. "A Dynamic Simultaneous Equation Model of Electoral Choice." *American Political Science Review* 73:1055–70.

Martin, Boyd A. 1949. "The 1948 Elections in the Eleven Western States." *Western Political Quarterly* 1:89–91.

Martinez, Michael D., and Michael M. Gant. 1990. "Partisan Issue Preferences and Partisan Change." *Political Behavior* 12:243–64.

Mason, Robert, G. David Faulkenberry, and Alexander Seidler. 1975. *The Quality of Life as Oregonians See It.* Corvallis: Oregon State University Press.

Mason, Thomas L. 1994. *Governing Oregon: An Inside Look at Politics in One American State.* Dubuque: Kendall/Hunt.

Massey, Douglas S., and Nancy A. Denton. 1993. *American Apartheid: Segre-*

gation and the Making of the Underclass. Cambridge: Harvard University Press.

Maxwell, William Earl, and Ernest Crain. 1998. *Texas Politics Today.* 8th ed. Belmont, Calif.: West/Wadsworth.

Mayer, George H. 1951. *The Political Career of Floyd B. Olson.* Minneapolis: University of Minnesota Press.

Mayhew, David R. 1966. *Party Loyalty among Congressmen.* Cambridge: Harvard University Press.

———. 1986. *Placing Parties in American Politics.* Princeton: Princeton University Press.

———. 2002. *Electorial Realignments: A Critique of An American Genre.* New York: Yale University Press.

McCleskey, Clifton. 1963. *The Government and Politics of Texas.* Boston: Little, Brown.

McCormick, Richard L. 1974. "Ethno-Cultural Interpretations of Nineteenth-Century American Voting Behavior." *Political Science Quarterly* 89: 351–77.

McCormick, Richard P. 1959. "Suffrage Classes and Party Alignments: A Study in Voter Behavior." *Mississippi Valley Historical Review* 46:397–410.

McGrath, Dennis J., and Dane Smith. 1995. *Professor Wellstone Goes to Washington.* Minneapolis: University of Minnesota Press.

McKee, Clyde D., Jr. 1983. "Connecticut: A Political System in Transition." In Josephine Milburn and William Doyle, eds., *New England Political Parties.* Cambridge, Mass: Schenkman Publishing.

McKee, Clyde D., Jr., and Paul Petterson. 1997. "Connecticut: Party Politics as a Steady Habit." In Jerome M. Mileur, ed., *Parties and Politics in the New England States.* Amherst, Mass.: Polity.

McMichael, Lawrence G., and Richard J. Trilling. 1980. "The Structure and Meaning of Critical Realignment: The Case of Pennsylvania, 1928–1932." In Bruce A. Campbell and Richard J. Trilling, eds., *Realignment in American Politics: Toward a Theory.* Austin: University of Texas Press.

McVeigh, Rory. 1995. "Social Structure, Political Institutions, and Mobilization Potential." *Social Forces* 74, no. 2: 461–85.

Mebane, Walter R., Jr., ed. 1999. *Political Analysis: An Annual Publication of the Methodology Section of the American Political Science Association.* Vol. 7, 1998. Ann Arbor: University of Michigan Press.

Milburn, Josephine F., and William Doyle, eds. 1983. *New England Political Parties.* Cambridge, Mass.: Schenkman Publishing.

Mileur, Jerome M., ed. 1997. *Parties and Politics in the New England States.* Amherst, Mass.: Polity.

Miller, Penny M., and Malcolm E. Jewell. 1990. *Political Parties and Primaries in Kentucky.* Lexington: University Press of Kentucky.

Miller, Warren E., and J. Merrill Shanks. 1996. *The New American Voter.* Cambridge: Harvard University Press.

Moakley, Maureen, ed. 1992. *Party Realignment and State Politics.* Columbus: Ohio State University Press.

Mondak, Jeffrey, Diana Mutz, and Robert Huckfeldt. 1996. "Persuasion in Context: The Multilevel Structure of Economic Evaluations." In Diana Mutz, Paul M. Sniderman, and Richard A. Brody, eds., *Political Persuasion and Attitude Change.* Ann Arbor: University of Michigan Press.

Monmonier, Mark. 1996. *How to Lie with Maps.* Chicago: University of Chicago Press.

Moran, P. 1948. "The Interpretation of Statistical Maps." *Journal of the Royal Statistical Society* B. 10: 243–51.

Morgan, Dan. 1992. *Rising in the West.* New York: Vintage Books.

Moreno, Dario, and Nicol Rae. 1992. "Ethnicity and Partnership: The Eighteenth Congressional District in Miami." In Guillermo Grenier and Alex Stepick, eds., *Miami Now! Immigration, Ethnicity and Social Change.* Gainesville: University Press of Florida.

Munger, Frank, ed. 1966. *American State Politics: Readings for Comparative Analysis.* New York: Crowell.

Muñoz, Carlos, Jr., and Charles Henry. 1990. "Coalition Politics in San Antonio and Denver: The Cisneros and Peña Mayoral Campaigns." In Rufus P. Browning, Dale Rogers Marshall, and David H. Tabb, eds., *Racial Politics in American Cities.* New York: Longman.

Murauskas, G. Tomas, J. Clark Archer, and Fred M. Shelley. 1988. "Metropolitan, Nonmetropolitan, and Sectional Variations in Voting Behavior in Recent Presidential Elections." *Western Political Quarterly* 41:63–84.

Murdock, Steve H., Nazrul Hoque, Martha Michael, Steve White, and Beverly Pecotte. 1997. *The Texas Challenge: Population Change and the Future of Texas.* College Station: Texas A&M University Press.

Murray, Richard, and Arnold Vedlitz. 1978. "Racial Voting Patterns in the South: An Analysis of Major Elections from 1960 to 1977 in Five Cities." *Annals of the American Academy of Political and Social Science* 439:29–39.

Mutz, Diana. 2002. "Cross-cutting Social Networks: Testing Democratic Theory in Practice." *American Political Science Review.* 96:111–28.

Mutz, Diana C., and Jeffrey J. Mondak. 2002. "The Workplace as a Context for Crosscutting Political Discourse." Columbus: Ohio State University, unpublished manuscript.

Nardulli, Peter F., ed. 1989. *Diversity, Conflict, and State Politics: Regionalism in Illinois.* Urbana: University of Illinois Press.

———. 1994. "A Normal Vote Approach to Electoral Change: Presidential Elections, 1828–1984." *Political Behavior* 16:467–503.

————. 1995. "The Concept of Critical Realignment, Electoral Behavior and Political Change." *American Political Science Review* 89:10–22.

————. 1997. "The Concept of a Critical Realignment, Electoral Behavior and Political Change." *American Political Science Review* 89:10–22.

Nardulli, Peter F., and David Darmofal. 1998. "The Dynamics of Critical Realignments: Conceptions of Democratic Citizens and Enduring Partisan Change." Prepared for the 1998 Annual Meetings of the American Political Science Association, Boston.

Nicholson-Crotty, Sean, and Kenneth J. Meier. 2002. "Size Doesn't Matter: In Defense of Single-State Studies." *State Politics and Policy Quarterly* 2, no. 4: 319–31.

Nie, Norman H., Sidney Verba, and John R. Petrocik, eds. 1976. *The Changing American Voter.* Cambridge: Harvard University Press.

Niemi, Richard G., and Herbert F. Weisberg, eds. 1984. *Controversies in Voting Behavior.* Washington, D.C.: CQ Press.

Niemi, Richard G., Stephen Wright, and Lynda W. Powell. 1987. "Multiple Party Identifiers and the Measurement of Party Identification." *Journal of Politics* 49, no. 4: 1093–2003.

Nimmo, Dan, and William Oden. 1971. *The Texas Political System.* Englewood Cliffs, N.J.: Prentice-Hall.

Noelle-Neumann, Elisabeth. 1993. *The Spiral of Silence: Our Social Skin.* Chicago: University of Chicago Press.

Oliver, J. Eric. 2000. "City Size and Civic Involvement in Metropolitan America." *American Political Science Review* 94, no. 2: 361–74.

Olzak, Susan. 1992. *The Dynamics of Ethnic Competition and Conflict.* Stanford: Stanford University Press.

O'Reilly, Kathleen, and Gerald R. Webster. 1998. "A Sociodemographic and Partisan Analysis of Voting in Three Anti-Gay Rights Referenda in Oregon." *Professional Geographer* 50, no. 4: 498–515.

Orfield, Myron. 1997. *Metropolitics.* Washington, D.C.: Brookings Institution.

Orleans, P. 1973. "Differential Cognition of Urban Residents: Effects of Social Scale on Mapping." In R. Downs and D. Stea, eds., *Image and Environment: Cognitive Mapping and Spatial Behavior.* Chicago: Aldine.

Ormrod, Richard K., and David B. Cole. 1996. "Tolerance and Rejection: The Vote on Colorado's Amendment Two." *Professional Geographer* 48, no. 1: 14–27.

Orser, W. Edward. 1994. *Blockbusting in Baltimore: The Edmondson Village Story.* Lexington: University Press of Kentucky.

Ortquist, Richard T. 1982. *Depression Politics in Michigan, 1929–1933.* New York: Garland Publishing.

Page, Benjamin I., and Calvin Jones. 1979. "Reciprocal Effects of Policy Preferences, Party Loyalties and the Vote." *American Political Science Review* 73:1071–89.

Page, Benjamin I., and Robert Y. Shapiro. 1992. *The Rational Public: Fifty Years of Trends in Americans' Policy Preferences.* Chicago: University of Chicago Press.

Palmquist, Bradley, and D. Stephen Voss. 1996. "Racial Polarization and Turnout in Louisiana: New Insights from Aggregate Data Analysis." Presented at the Annual Meeting of the Midwest Political Science Association, Chicago, April 18–20.

Parker, Suzanne L. 1988. "Shifting Party Tides in Florida: Where Have All the Democrats Gone?" In *The South's New Politics: Realignment and Dealignment,* ed. Robert H. Swansbrough and David M. Brodsky. Columbia: University of South Carolina Press.

Patterson, James T. 1969. "The New Deal in the West." *Pacific Historical Review* 38:317–27.

Patterson, Samuel C. 1968. "The Political Cultures of the American States." *Journal of Politics* 30, no. 1: 187–209.

Peirce, Neal R. 1972a. "Colorado: Life beside Shining Mountains." In Neal R. Peirce, *The Mountain States of America: People, Politics, and Power in the Eight Rocky Mountain States.* New York: Norton.

———. 1972b. "Oregon: 'For God's Sake, Don't Move Here.'" In Neal R. Peirce, *The Pacific States of America: People, Politics, and Power in the Five Pacific Basin States.* New York: Norton.

———. 1972c. *The Megastates of America: People, Politics, and Power in the Ten Great States.* New York: W. W. Norton.

———. 1973. "Minnesota: The Successful Society." In Neal R. Peirce, *The Great Plains States of America: People, Politics, and Power in the Nine Great Plains States.* New York: Norton.

———. 1974. "Georgia: Empire State of the South." In Neal R. Peirce, *The Deep South States of America: People, Politics, and Power in the Seven Deep South States.* New York: Norton.

———. 1976. "Connecticut: State of Steady Habits." In Neal R. Peirce, *The New England States: People, Politics, and Power in the Six New England States.* New York: Norton.

Perkins, Jerry, and Randall Guynes. 1976. "Partisanship in National and State Politics." *Public Opinion Quarterly* 40:376–78.

Peterson, Paul. 1981. *City Limits.* Chicago: University of Chicago Press.

Petrocik, John R. 1981. *Party Coalitions: Realignments and the Decline of the New Deal Party System.* Chicago: University of Chicago Press.

———. 1987. "Realignment: New Party Coalitions and the Nationalization of the South." *Journal of Politics* 49:347–75.

———. 1996. "Issue Ownership in Presidential Elections, with a 1980 Case Study." *American Journal of Political Science* 40, no. 3: 825–50.

Phillips, Kevin P. 1970. *The Emerging Republican Majority.* Garden City, N.Y.: Anchor Books.

Pinderhughes, Dianne M. 1987. *Race and Ethnicity in Chicago Politics: A Reexamination of Pluralist Theory.* Urbana: University of Illinois Press.

Piore, Michael J., and Charles F. Sabel. 1984. *The Second Industrial Divide.* New York: Basic Books.

Pollock, James K., and Samuel J. Eldersveld. 1942. *Michigan Politics in Transition.* Governmental Studies Report No. 10. Ann Arbor: University of Michigan Press.

Pomeroy, Earl. 1967. "What Remains of the West?" *Utah Historical Quarterly* 35:37–55.

Preston, Michael B., Bruce E. Cain, and Sandra Bass. 1998. *Racial and Ethnic Politics in California.* Vol. 2. Berkeley, Calif.: Institute of Governmental Studies Press.

Price, Hugh D. 1955. "The Negro and Florida Politics, 1944–1954." *Journal of Politics* 17:199–220.

Proshansky, Harold M., Abbe K. Fabian, and Robert Kaminoff. 1995. "Place Identity: Physical World Socialization of the Self." In Linda Groat, ed., *Giving Places Meaning.* New York: Harcourt Brace.

Prysby, Charles L. 1989. "Attitudes of Southern Democratic Party Activists toward Jesse Jackson: The Effects of Local Context." *Journal of Politics* 51, no. 2: 305–18.

Putnam, Robert D. 1966. "Political Attitudes and the Local Community." *American Political Science Review* 60, no. 3: 640–54.

Rabinowitz, George, Paul Henry Gurian, and Stuart Elaine McDonald. 1984. "The Structure of Presidential Elections and the Process of Realignment, 1944 to 1980." *American Journal of Political Science* 27:611–35.

Rabinowitz, George, and Stuart Elaine McDonald. 1986. "The Power of the States in U.S. Presidential Elections." *American Political Science Review* 80:65–87.

Rae, Nicol C. 1992. "The Democrats' 'Southern Problem' in Presidential Politics." *Presidential Studies Quarterly* 22:135–51.

Ranney, Austin. 1960. *Illinois Politics.* New York: New York University Press.

Rey, Roberto. 1996. "Leverage Without Influence: Illinois Latino Politics in 1992." In Rodolfo de la Garza and Louis DeSipio, eds., *Ethnic Ironies: Latino Politics in the 1992 Elections.* Boulder: Westview.

Reynolds, David R. 1990. "Whither Electoral Geography? A Critique." In R. J. Johnston, F. M. Shelley, and P. J. Taylor, eds., *Developments in Electoral Geography,* 22–38. London: Routledge.

Rice, Tom W., and Alisa A. Macht. 1987. "Friends and Neighbors Voting in Statewide General Elections." *American Journal of Political Science* 31, no. 2: 448–52.

Rich, Wilbur C. 1989. *Coleman Young and Detroit Politics: From Social Activist to Power Broker.* Detroit: Wayne State University Press.

Robinson, William S. 1950. "Ecological Correlation and the Behavior of Individuals." *American Sociological Review* 15:351–57.

Rogers, E. M., and J. K. Larsen. 1984. *Silicon Valley Fever.* New York: Basic Books.

Rogers, Rod, and Wayne Horman. 2000. "Labor in the Headwaters Region, Past and Present." Paper prepared for the 11th Annual Headwaters Conference, Western State College, Gunnison, Colorado, November 3–5.

Rohse, Mitch. 1987. *Land-Use Planning in Oregon.* Corvallis: Oregon State University Press.

Rosenstone, Stephen J. 1982. "Economic Adversity and Voter Turnout." *American Journal of Political Science* 26:25–46.

Rosenstone, Stephen J., and John Mark Hansen. 1993. *Mobilization, Participation, and Democracy in America.* Needham Heights, Mass.: Allyn and Bacon.

Rosenstone, Stephen J., and Raymond E. Wolfinger. 1978. "The Effects of Registration Laws on Voter Turnout." *American Political Science Review* 72:22–45.

Rosenthal, Alan, and Maureen Moakley, eds. 1984. *The Political Life of the American States.* Westport, Conn.: Praeger.

Rusk, David. 1995. *Cities Without Suburbs.* Washington, D.C.: Woodrow Wilson Center Press.

Santos, Robert. 1996. "The Origins of the Portuguese." *Californians* 13: 32–48.

Savitch, H. V., and John Clayton Thomas, eds. 1991. *Big City Politics in Transition.* Newbury Park, Calif.: Sage.

Scarrow, Howard A. 1983. *Parties, Elections, and Representation in the State of New York.* New York: New York University Press.

Schantz, Harvey L. 1992. "The Erosion of Sectionalism in Presidential Elections." *Polity* 24, no. 3: 355–77.

Schlesinger, Arthur M. 1957. *The Age of Roosevelt.* Vol. 2, *The Coming of the New Deal.* Boston: Houghton Mifflin.

Schreiber, E. M. 1971. "Where the Ducks Are: Southern Strategy versus Fourth Party." *Public Opinion Quarterly* 35:157–69.

Schuessler, Alexander A. 1999. "Ecological Inference." *Proceedings of the National Academy of Sciences* 96, no. 19: 10578–81.

Schuknecht, Jason E. 2001. "The Federal Leviathan and Subnational Political Landscapes." Ph.D. Diss. Dept. of Government, University of Maryland, College Park.

Schumacher, Waldo. 1949. "The 1948 Elections in Oregon." *Western Political Quarterly* 2:121–23.

Scicchitano, Michael J., and Richard K. Scher. 1998. "Florida: Political Change, 1950–1996." In Charles S. Bullock III and Mark J. Rozell, eds., *The New Politics of the Old South.* Lanham, Md.: Rowman and Littlefield.

Sears, David O. 1994. "Urban Rioting in Los Angeles: A Comparison of 1965 with 1992." In Mark Baldassare, ed., *The Los Angeles Riots: Lessons for the Urban Future.* Boulder: Westview.

Sears, David O., and Nicholas A. Valentino. 1997. "Politics Matters: Political Events as Catalysts for Preadult Socialization." *American Political Science Review* 91:45–65.

Seligman, Lester G. 1959. "A Prefatory Study of Leadership Selection in Oregon." *Western Political Quarterly* 1:153–67.

Shafer, Byron E., ed. 1991. *The End of Realignment? Interpreting American Electoral Eras.* Madison: University of Wisconsin Press.

Shaw, Daron R. 1999. "The Effect of TV Ads and Candidate Appearances on Statewide Presidential Votes, 1988–96." *American Political Science Review* 93, no. 2: 345–62.

Shelley, Fred M., and J. Clark Archer. 1989. "Sectionalism and Presidential Politics: Voting Patterns in Illinois, Indiana, and Ohio." *Journal of Interdisciplinary History* 20:227–55.

Shelley, Fred M., J. Clark Archer, Fiona M. Davidson, and Stanley D. Brunn. 1996. *Political Geography of the United States.* New York: Guilford Press.

Silbey, Joel A., Alan G. Bogue, and William H. Flanigan, eds. 1978. *The History of American Electoral Behavior.* Princeton: Princeton University Press.

Simmons, Thomas H. 1984. "Colorado." In Alan Rosenthal and Maureen Moakley, eds., *The Political Life of the American States,* chap. 3. Westport, Conn.: Praeger.

Skerry, Peter N. 1993. *Mexican Americans: The Ambivalent Minority.* New York: Free Press.

Smith, Eric R. A. N., and Peverill Squire. 1987. "Direct Election of the President and the Power of States." *Western Political Quarterly* 40:29–44.

Sniderman, Paul M., Richard A. Brody, and Philip E. Tetlock. 1991. *Reasoning and Choice: Explorations in Political Psychology.* New York: Cambridge University Press.

Sommers, Lawrence M., ed. 1984. *Michigan: A Geography.* Boulder: Westview.

Soukup, James R., Clifton McCleskey, and Harry Holloway. 1964. *Party and Factional Division in Texas.* Austin: University of Texas Press.

Southwell, Priscilla, and Justin Burchett. 2000. "Does Changing the Rules Change the Players? The Effect of All-Mail Elections on the Composition of the Electorate." *Social Science Quarterly* 81, no. 3: 837–45.

Spencer, Christopher, and Mark Blades. 1986. "Pattern and Process: A Review Essay on the Relationship between Behavioural Geography and Environmental Psychology." *Progress in Human Geography* 10:230–48.

Spooner, Denise S. 1997. "A New Perspective on the Dream: Midwestern Images of Southern California in the Post–World War II Decades." *California History* 86:45–58.

Sprague, John. 2001. Personal electronic mail communication to James G. Gimpel, June 14.

Squire, Peverill, Raymond E. Wolfinger, and David P. Glass. 1987. "Residential Mobility and Voter Turnout." *American Political Science Review* 81: 45–65.

Stanley, Harold W. 1988. "Southern Partisan Changes: Dealignment, Realignment, or Both?" *Journal of Politics* 50:64–88.

Stanley, Harold W., William T. Bianco, and Richard G. Niemi. 1986. "Partisanship and Group Support over Time: A Multivariate Analysis." *American Political Science Review* 80:969–78.

Stanley, Harold W., and Richard G. Niemi. 1991. "Partisanship and Group Support, 1952–1988." *American Politics Quarterly* 19:189–210.

Steel, Brent S., and Nicholas P. Lovrich. 1998. "Determinants of Public Support for Tax and Expenditure Initiatives: An Oregon and Washington Case Study." *Social Science Journal* 35, no. 2: 213–29.

Stegmaier, Harry I., Jr., David M. Dean, Gordon E. Kershaw, and John B. Wiseman. 1976. *Allegany County: A History.* Parsons, W.Va.: McClain Printing.

Stein, Robert M., Stephanie Shirley Post, and Allison L. Rinden. 1997a. "Attitude Accessibility and Anglo-American Opinions on Immigration Policy." Prepared for the 1997 Annual Meeting of the Midwest Political Science Association, Chicago.

———. 1997b. "The Effect of Contact and Context on White Attitudes toward Immigrants and Immigration Policy." Prepared for the 1997 Annual Meetings of the American Political Science Association, Washington, D.C.

Stokes, Donald E. 1966. "Some Dynamic Elements of Contests for the Presidency." *American Political Science Review* 60:19–28.

Stokes, Donald E., Angus Campbell, and Warren E. Miller. 1958. "Components of Electoral Decision." *American Political Science Review* 52, no. 2: 367–87.

Stokes, Donald E., and Warren E. Miller. 1966. "Party Government and the Saliency of Congress." In Angus Campbell, Philip E. Converse, Warren E. Miller, and Donald E. Stokes, eds., *Elections and the Political Order.* New York: John Wiley and Sons.

Stonecash, Jeffrey M. 1989. "Political Cleavage in Gubernatorial and Legislative Elections: Party Competition in New York, 1970–1982." *Western Political Quarterly* 42, no. 1: 69–81.

———. 1991. "Observations from New York: The Limits of 50-State Studies and the Case for Case Studies." *Comparative State Politics* 12, no. 4: 1–9.

Storing, Herbert J. 1981. *What the Anti-Federalists Were For.* Chicago: University of Chicago Press.

Sundquist, James L. 1983. *Dynamics of the Party System.* Washington, D.C.: Brookings Institution.

Swarthout, John M. 1954. "The 1954 Election in Oregon." *Western Political Quarterly* 7, no. 3: 620–24.

———. 1957. "The 1956 Election in Oregon." *Western Political Quarterly* 10, no. 1: 142–50.

———. 1959. "The 1958 Election in Oregon." *Western Political Quarterly* 12, no. 1: 328–44.

Swarthout, John M., and Kenneth R. Gervais. 1969. "Oregon: Political Experiment Station." In Frank H. Jonas, ed., *Politics in the American West.* Salt Lake City: University of Utah Press.

Sykes, Patricia. 1993. "Party Constraints on Leaders in Pursuit of Change." *Studies in American Political Development* 7:151–76.

Tajnai, Carolyn E. 1995. "Fred Terman: The Father of Silicon Valley," manuscript available at <www.internetvalley.com/archives/mirrors/terman.html>.

Tatalovich, Raymond. 1975. "'Friends and Neighbors' Voting: Mississippi, 1943–73." *Journal of Politics* 37, no. 3: 807–14.

Taub, Richard P., D. Garth Taylor, and Jan D. Dunham. 1984. *Paths of Neighborhood Change: Race and Crime in Urban America.* Chicago: University of Chicago Press.

Teaford, Jon C. 1997. *Post-suburbia: Government and Politics in the Edge Cities.* Baltimore: Johns Hopkins University Press.

Thomas, G. Scott. 1994. *The Rating Guide to Life in America's Fifty States.* Amherst, N.Y.: Prometheus Books.

Tiebout, Charles. 1956. "A Pure Theory of Local Expenditures." *Journal of Political Economy* 64, no. 3: 416–24.

Timpone, Richard J. 1995. "Mass Mobilization or Government Intervention? The Growth of Black Registration in the South." *Journal of Politics* 57, no. 2: 425–42.

———. 1998. "Structure, Behavior, and Voter Turnout in the United States." *American Political Science Review* 92:145–58.

Tolleson-Rinehart, Sue, and Jeanie R. Stanley. 1994. *Claytie and the Lady: Ann Richards, Gender and Politics in Texas.* Austin: University of Texas Press.

Tompkins, Mark E. 1988. "Have Gubernatorial Elections Become More Distinctive Contests?" *Journal of Politics* 50:192–205.

Truman, David B. 1955. "Federalism and the Party System." In Arthur W. MacMahon, ed., *Federalism: Mature and Emergent.* Garden City, N.J.: Doubleday.

Turner, Frederick Jackson. 1911. "Social Forces in American History." *American Historical Review* 16, no. 2: 217–33.

———. 1920. *The Frontier in American History.* New York: Henry Holt.

———. 1932. *The Significance of Sections in American History.* New York: Henry Holt.

Ulack, R., and K. Raitz. 1981. "Appalachia: A Comparison of the Cognitive and Appalachian Regional Commission Regions." *Southeastern Geographer* 21, no. 1: 40–53.

U.S. News and World Report. 1958. Vol. 45, no. 22 (Nov. 28), 84.

Valelly, Richard M. 1989. *Radicalism in the States: The Minnesota Farmer-Labor Party and the American Political Economy.* Chicago: University of Chicago Press.

Vance, Rupert B. 1960. "The Sociological Implications of Southern Regionalism." *Journal of Southern History* 26, no. 1: 44–56.

Wade, Larry L. 1989. "The Influence of Sections and Periods on Economic Voting in American Presidential Elections, 1829–1984." *Political Geography Quarterly* 8, no. 3: 271–88.

Walsh, Richard, and William Lloyd Fox, eds. 1983. *Maryland: A History.* Annapolis, Md.: Hall of Records Commission, Department of General Services.

Weakliem, David. 1997. "Race Versus Class? Racial Composition and Class Voting, 1936–1992." *Social Forces* 75:939–56.

Webster, Gerald R. 1987. "Size of Place and Voting in Presidential Elections in the Interior West." *Geographical Perspectives* 59, no. 1: 78–92.

———. 1989. "Partisanship in American Presidential, Senatorial, and Gubernatorial Elections in Ten Western States." *Political Geography Quarterly* 8:161–79.

Weed, Clyde P. 1989. "What Happened to the Republicans in the 1930s: Minority Party Dynamics during Political Realignment." *Polity* 22:5–23.

Weinstein, Bernard L., and Harold T. Gross. 1988. "The Rise and Fall of Sun, Rust, and Frost Belts." *Economic Development Quarterly* 2:9–18.

Weisberg, Herbert F. 1980. "A Multidimensional Conceptualization of Party Identification." *Political Behavior* 2:33–60.

Weisberg, Herbert F., and Jerrold G. Rusk. 1970. "Dimensions of Candidate Evaluation." *American Political Science Review* 64:1167–85.

Weiss, Michael J. 2000. *The Clustered Masses.* Boston: Little, Brown.

White, John Kenneth. 1983. *The Fractured Electorate: Political Parties and Social Change in Southern New England.* Hanover, N.H.: University Press of New England.

Whiteside, Henry O. 1997. *Menace in the West: Colorado and the American Experience with Drugs, 1873–1963.* Denver: Colorado Historical Society.

Whitson, Carter, and Dennis Judd. 1991. "Denver: Boosterism versus Growth." In H. V. Savitch and John Clayton Thomas, eds., *Big City Politics in Transition.* Newbury Park, Calif.: Sage.

Wickens, James F. 1969. "The New Deal in Colorado." *Pacific Historical Review* 38:275–91.

Willis, John T. 1984. *Presidential Elections in Maryland.* Mt. Airy, Md.: Lomond Publications.

Wilson, William Julius. 1987. *The Truly Disadvantaged: The Inner City, the Underclass and Public Policy.* Chicago: University of Chicago Press.

Winters, Richard. 1976. "Party Control and Policy Change." *American Journal of Political Science* 20:597–636.

Wirt, Frederick M. 1989. "The Changing Social Bases of Regionalism: Peoples, Cultures and Politics in Illinois." In Peter F. Nardulli, ed., *Diversity, Conflict and State Politics: Regionalism in Illinois.* Urbana: University of Illinois Press.

Wirt, Frederick M., Benjamin Walter, Francine F. Rabinovitz, and Deborah R. Hensler. 1972. *On the City's Rim: Politics and Policy in Suburbia.* Lexington, Mass.: Lexington Books.

Wolfinger, Raymond. 1965. "The Development and Persistence of Ethnic Voting." *American Political Science Review* 59:896–908.

Wolfinger, Raymond, and Robert B. Arseneau. 1978. "Partisan Change in the South, 1952–1976." In Louis Maisel and Joseph Cooper, eds., *Political Parties: Development and Decay.* Beverly Hills, Calif.: Sage.

Wolfinger, Raymond, and Fred I. Greenstein. 1967. "Comparing Political Regions: The Case of California." *American Political Science Review* 63, no. 1: 74–85.

Wolfinger, Raymond, and Michael G. Hagen. 1985. "Republican Prospects: Southern Comfort." *Public Opinion* 8, no. 5: 8–13.

Wolfinger, Raymond, and Steven J. Rosenstone. 1980. *Who Votes?* New Haven: Yale University Press.

Woodell, Marshall E. 1936. *Grange Influence on Direct Legislation in Oregon, 1902–1934.* Master's thesis. Eugene: University of Oregon Press.

Wright, Gavin. 1986. *Old South, New South: Revolutions in the Southern Economy Since the Civil War.* New York: Basic Books.

Wright, Gerald C., Robert S. Erikson, and John P. McIver. 1985. "Measuring State Partisanship and Ideology with Survey Data." *Journal of Politics* 47:469–89.

Wright, Gerald C., John P. McIver, Robert S. Erikson, and David B. Holian. 2000. "Stability and Change in State Electorate, Carter through Clinton." Paper presented at the annual meeting of the Midwest Political Science Association, Chicago, April 17–19.

Wrinkle, Robert D. 1971. *Politics in the Urban Southwest.* Albuquerque: University of New Mexico, Division of Government Research.

Zaller, John. 1992. *The Nature and Origins of Mass Opinion.* New York: Cambridge University Press.

Zuckerman, Alan. 1975. "Political Cleavage: A Conceptual and Theoretical Analysis." *British Journal of Political Science* 5:231–48.

Name Index

Achen, Christopher H., 393
Agnew, Spiro, 247, 256
Andersen, Kristi, 348

Bates, Katherine Lee, 141
Benoit, Kenneth, 399
Bradley, Tom, 62
Bush, George H. W., 124, 148, 222, 232, 303
Bush, George W.
  Colorado votes for, 148, 153
  elderly rural Texans vote for, 133n. 2
  election of 2000 and, 30, 43, 54, 79, 83
  Georgia votes for, 197
  Texas votes for, 125
  on vote recounts in Florida, 96

Castro, Fidel, 87, 108
Clinton, Bill, 47–48
  California votes for, 54, 82, 83
  Connecticut votes for, 222, 223
  Florida votes for, 90, 104
  Georgia votes for, 197, 209
  Illinois votes for, 361, 366
  Maryland votes for, 257, 261, 262
  Michigan votes for, 303, 309, 317
  Minnesota votes for, 171, 177, 185
  New York votes for, 327, 338, 340
  Oregon votes for, 287

Coleman, Norm, 184
Converse, Philip, 206–7

Dewey, Thomas, 258, 324
Disney, Walt, 89
Dole, Bob, 83, 133n. 2, 148, 197–98, 303
Dukakis, Michael, 82, 104, 209, 309, 327

Eisenhower, Dwight D., 144, 171, 220, 255, 275
Eldersveld, Samuel J., 297

Fenton, John H., 4–5, 315, 376
Fiorina, Morris, 47
Ford, Gerald R., 300

Gingrich, Newt, 189
Giuliani, Rudolph, 327
Glendening, Parris, 247, 251
Goldwater, Barry
  California votes for, 68, 82, 336
  Colorado votes for, 154, 156
  Connecticut votes for, 230, 232
  Florida votes for, 92, 102, 104
  Georgia votes for, 194, 196–97, 203–4
  Illinois votes for, 362–63
  Maryland votes for, 260–61
  Michigan votes for, 312

Subject Index

Page numbers in italics indicate tables, figures, or maps.

aerospace industry: in Florida, 88, 89; in Texas, 115

African Americans: in Atlanta suburbs, 190–91, 206; in Baltimore, 240, 247; in California, 63; California's political realignment and, 83; in Chicago, 347, 352–53; Chicago's 1930s political realignment and, 348–49; in Connecticut, 219, 220, 221–22, 235–36, 237; context for voting, 375; decline in Savannah, Ga., 192; in Denver, Colo., 138; on Eastern Shore of Maryland, 246; in East St. Louis, Ill., 350; in East Texas, 111–12; in Georgia's black belt counties, 193, 208–9, 213, 213n. 2; Georgia's Democratic Party and, 197; in Grand Rapids, Mich., 301; in Houston, Tex. area, 115; ideologically based sectionalism and, 371; in Illinois, 346, 366; in Maryland, 243–44, 248, 254, 258, 261–62, 263; in Maryland suburbs, 240–41, 242; in Michigan, 295, 299–300, 302–3; migration to Michigan auto industry, 309; migration to New York City suburbs, 333–34; in Minnesota,

185–86; mobilization in Colorado of, 158–59, 160; mobilization in Florida of, 105–6, 107; mobilization in Georgia of, 211–12; mobilization in Illinois of, 365; mobilization in Michigan of, 316–17; mobilization in Oregon of, 289; mobilization of, party competition and, 385; in New York, 339–40; in New York City suburbs, 321; in Oregon, 281–82; political changes after civil rights movement and, 29; in Portland, Ore., 269–70; racially based sectionalism and, 374–75; in Rockford, Ill., 352; in San Antonio, Tex., 115; segregation in Georgia and, 195–96; similarities and differences across states, 54; in Texas Panhandle, 111; voting in Georgia, 197; voting preferences of, 375; in Washington, D.C., 241–42; white political conversion and mobilization of, 384

age: presidential vote prediction and, *37;* voting in 1988–96 elections and, *38,* 40–41, *56–57;* voting in 2000 elections and, *59–60*

Democratic percentage estimates of presidential vote, by groups, 1928–2000, 77; ecological inference estimates for, *400–401;* estimated percentage of Republican voters in 1928 who voted Republican again in 1932, *379;* estimated percentage of Republican voters in 1960 who voted Republican again in 1964, *380;* generational replacement in, 78–79, 84; immigrant-based sectionalism and, 373–74; Los Angeles, 62–63; migration from dust bowl states to, 382; mobilization targets in, 70–74, *71;* new voter mobilization in, 82–83; New York's similarities with, 387; northern, 66; Orange Co., 65; partisanship during 2000 elections in, 47–48; party dominance areas, 1988–2000, *73;* political change in, 66–67, 77–78; political conversion in, 74, 79–80, *81,* 82, 84; political realignment in, 83–85; political regions of, 60–70, *64,* 388; polling data in, 74; population mobility and, 61–62, 74, 76–78; precinct returns in, 74–75; progressives and cross-filing in, 67; San Diego, 63–65; voter transition results, *422*
campaign politics: electoral college votes and, 47; substate sectionalism and, 386, 389–90; targeted, 368
campaign spending, voter mobilization geography and, 370
Campbell's Soup, in Minnesota, 164
candidates: political boundaries and, 10; substate sectionalism and, 386
Cape Canaveral, 89

Caribbean, immigrants to Florida from, 90
Catholics, in Maryland, 242. *See also* religiously based sectionalism
census data, California county-level, 75
Central America, immigrants from, 90, 98, 107, 110
Chicago, Ill.: African Americans in, 346; Democratic dominance during and after New Deal, 347–48; Democratic dominance in, 352–53; Hispanics in, 345–46; New York City vs., 343–44
Chicago, Ill. suburbs, 344, 346
civil rights movement: effects in Connecticut, 230, 232; effects in Florida, 105–6; effects in Georgia, 203–4; effects in Maryland, 246, 247; effects in Michigan, 300, 316–17; effects in New York, 336, 340; effects in Oregon, 281–82; ideologically based sectionalism and, 371; political changes for African Americans after, 29
Clarkston, Wash., and Lewiston, Idaho, 7
Coca-Cola, 189
cognitive boundaries, 8, 12
Colorado, 134–61; African American mobilization in, 384; changing electoral foundations in, 149–50; Democratic percentage estimates of presidential vote, by groups, 1928–2000, *151;* Denver, 137–39; eastern mountains, 140, 142–43; eastern plains, 140; ecological inference estimates for, *402–3;* economically based sectionalism in, 373; economy in, 139–40; estimated percentage of Republican voters in 1928 who

Levittown, N.Y., 321
Lewiston, Idaho, and Clarkston, Wash., 7
liberal ideology, economic vs. social, 55
liberal states, voting patterns in, 36–37
local electorates, 150; dual partisanship in southern Illinois, 360; in Oregon, 290
local laws and customs, political regionalism and, 23
Lockheed-Martin, in Denver, Colo., 140
Long Island, N.Y., 325
Los Angeles, Calif., 62–63; immigrant-based sectionalism and, 373–74; as mobilization target, 72
lumber production. *See* timber industry

mail-in ballots, 266
Mall of America, Minn., 166
manufacturing workers: African Americans in Illinois as, 346; agriculture in Michigan vs., 298–99, 314–15; in Baltimore, Md., 246–47, 254; in Baltimore suburbs, 240; in California, 82; in Chicago's collar counties, 352; in Colorado, 139, 146, 156–57, 160; in Connecticut, 216, 232–34; as context for voting, 375, 376, 377; in Florida, 104–5; in Georgia, 194, 204, 206; in Illinois, 349, 350–51, 363, 365, 366; in Maryland, 243, 247, 261; in Michigan, 292, 297, 308–9, 310, 311, 383; migration within Michigan of, 309; in Minnesota, 184–85; "new" vs. "old" industry and, 384–85; in New York, 338; in north Michigan, 296; in Oregon, 270, 285–86; political

conversion of, 384–85; in Texas, 112. *See also* United Auto Workers
Maryland, 238–64; average Democratic percentage of presidential vote, 1928–36, 244, *245, 248;* Baltimore, 239–40, 264n. 1; Baltimore suburbs, 239, 240, 247, 249, 254–55; changing electoral foundations in, 252–53; Democratic percentage estimates of presidential vote, by groups, 1928–2000, *257;* Eastern Shore, 239, 246, 249–50, 252; ecological inference estimates for, *410–12;* economically based sectionalism in, 373; estimated percentage of Republican voters in 1928 who voted Republican again in 1932, *379;* estimated percentage of Republican voters in 1960 who voted Republican again in 1964, *380;* generational replacement in, 256–57; images of, 238–39; migrants to, 180; mobilization targets in, 250–52; new voter mobilization in, 261–62; New York's similarities with, 388; party dominance areas, 1988–2000, *252;* political conversion in, 257–58, *259,* 260–61; political regions of, 239–50, *241;* population mobility and, 254–56, 383; rural western, 239, 243–45, 248–49, 252; sectionalism in, 262–63; southern, 239, 242–43; voter transition results, *425;* Washington suburbs, 239, 240–41, 245–46
Mayo Clinic, Rochester, Minn., 167
media, sectionalism and, 388
Mexican Americans: in Denver, Colo., 139; mobilization in Texas of, 118, 122–23
Mexico, immigrants to Texas from, 110